A GUIDE BOOK OF
GOLD EAGLE COINS

Complete Source for History, Grading, and Values

Q. David Bowers

Foreword by
Douglas Winter

Whitman
Publishing, LLC
PUBLISHING SINCE 1934
Whitman.com

A GUIDE BOOK OF
GOLD EAGLE COINS

© 2017 Whitman Publishing, LLC
1974 Chandalar Drive, Suite D, Pelham, AL 35124

THE OFFICIAL RED BOOK is a trademark of Whitman Publishing, LLC.

Correspondence concerning this book may be directed to
Whitman Publishing, Attn: Gold Eagle Coins, at the address above.

ISBN: 0794845304
Printed in China

Disclaimer: Expert opinion should be sought in any significant numismatic purchase. This book is presented as a guide only. No warranty or representation of any kind is made concerning the completeness of the information presented. The author, a professional numismatist, regularly buys, sells, and holds certain of the items discussed in this book.

Caveat: The value estimates given are subject to variation and differences of opinion. Before making decisions to buy or sell, consult the latest information. Past performance of the rare-coin market or any coin or series within that market is not necessarily an indication of future performance, as the future is unknown. Such factors as changing demand, popularity, grading interpretations, strength of the overall coin market, and economic conditions will continue to be influences.

Other books in the Bowers Series include: *A Guide Book of Morgan Silver Dollars; A Guide Book of Double Eagle Gold Coins; A Guide Book of United States Type Coins; A Guide Book of Modern United States Proof Coin Sets; A Guide Book of Shield and Liberty Head Nickels; A Guide Book of Flying Eagle and Indian Head Cents; A Guide Book of Washington and State Quarters; A Guide Book of Buffalo and Jefferson Nickels; A Guide Book of Lincoln Cents; A Guide Book of United States Commemorative Coins; A Guide Book of United States Tokens and Medals; A Guide Book of Gold Dollars; A Guide Book of Peace Dollars; A Guide Book of the Official Red Book of United States Coins; A Guide Book of Franklin and Kennedy Half Dollars; A Guide Book of Civil War Tokens; A Guide Book of Hard Times Tokens; A Guide Book of Mercury Dimes, Standing Liberty Quarters, and Liberty Walking Half Dollars; A Guide Book of Half Cents and Large Cents; A Guide Book of Barber Silver Coins; A Guide Book of Liberty Seated Silver Coins; A Guide Book of Modern United States Dollar Coins;* and *A Guide Book of the United States Mint.*

Whitman Publishing is a leader in the antiques and collectibles field.
For a complete catalog of numismatic reference books, supplies, and
storage products, visit Whitman Publishing online at www.Whitman.com.

If you enjoy Gold Eagle coins, join the American Numismatic Association.
Visit www.Whitman.com/ANA for membership information.

CONTENTS

FOREWORD

The year was 1985. I had been invited to La Jolla to visit with an up and coming doctor at Scripps Clinic. After getting acquainted and exchanging pleasantries I was asked a pointed question: "What's the best value in the United States gold coin market?"

I pondered this semi-unexpected question for about ten seconds and replied, "That's easy. Liberty Head eagles."

The completely unexpected result of this answer was a commission for me to put together a complete set of pre-1900 Liberty tens in the best value grades. My client would buy any coin which made sense to me and that I recommended.

I was off to the races!

The first show I attended with this want list was in June in Long Beach. I had taken a Red Book and the David W. Akers 1980 book on eagles and, after a good deal of study, created a "List of 50"—the dates and mintmarks I felt represented the best value. Naively, I expected to find five or six at the show—easy enough I thought!—and was actually a little nervous about being able to pay for all the coins I was going to buy, especially if I found some of the rarities. In three days of looking at the coins on display and in boxes at the various dealer tables I found exactly one coin on my list: a perfect EF 1871-CC eagle which, if I recall correctly, I paid $1,500 for.

For five years, every show I went to included a hunt of the List of 50. I think I found close to half of them before I got the dreaded call: my client was beginning his own practice and he needed to sell his growing collection in order to finance some needed medical machinery. Sadly, we consigned his eagles to an auction and I would have to wait a few more years before I would again handle many on the List of 50.

Cut to 2008. Now better known, I was approached by a very prominent professional numismatist and tasked with a challenge: to assist in assembling a world-class set of Liberty Head eagles. After I said yes, I asked the obvious question, "Why are you choosing this series as your focus?"

His response, he said, was based on his own careful study, "Because they are the best value in the United States gold market."

He returned to me the very same answer I gave my client in La Jolla two decades earlier!

I have had long-standing love affair with the ten-dollar gold denomination.

First comes the Capped Bust Right, Small Eagle–type, issued from 1795 to 1797. In my opinion, the 1795 eagle is one of the all-time classic "trophy" coins; a classic issue which isn't really rare from a classic supply sense, especially in grades such as Extremely Fine and About Uncirculated, but which has been in constant demand since the earliest days of American gold coin collecting.

This type is followed by the Capped Bust Right, Heraldic Eagle–type, made from 1797 to 1804, including the two rare 1798 varieties and the magically dated 1804. Even after owning dozens of these big, beautiful coins, I still get a thrill buying one today, especially one dated in the 1790s.

After a long hiatus comes the Liberty Head design which is generally divided by the No Motto (1838–1866) and With Motto (1866–1907) types.

The No Motto issues were made at the Philadelphia (1838–1865), New Orleans (1841–1860) and San Francisco (1854–1866) mints. Many of these issues have tiny original mintages and even tinier survival rates. The collector who demands perfect, frosty MS-65 and finer No Motto Liberty Head eagles is in for a rude surprise—they are essentially non-existent and a host of dates are either unknown or excessively rare in MS-60, let alone in higher grades.

The With Motto issues were made at Philadelphia (1866–1907), Carson City (1870–1893), San Francisco (1866–1907), New Orleans (1879–1906), and Denver (1906–1907). More of the With Motto dates exist in relatively higher grades due to hundreds of thousands of coins being shipped to overseas banks to pay trade debts. But there are some real rarities, including the unheralded 1875 business strike (mintage 100!), an issue which is so rare that most collectors and dealers have never seen one, let alone owned one.

Next comes the glorious Saint-Gaudens Indian Head design struck from 1907 to 1933. In my humble opinion, this is the apex of United States coinage design. When you have seen a pristine Gem rich with mint frost and delicately toned in rose and green-gold hues—well, it doesn't get much better than that!

Dave Bowers is uniquely qualified to write this much-needed guide to U.S. eagles and I, for one, will be an avid user of this book. I hope you will become as big a fan of this remarkable denomination as Dave and I are.

Doug Winter
Portland, Oregon

PREFACE

Q. David Bowers has been studying U.S. gold coins for more than 60 years, and writing about them almost as long. He has examined more than 5,000 numismatic catalogs, read countless periodicals, and studied all the available books on gold coins. On top of this old-fashioned "book learning," he has personally examined hundreds of thousands of gold coins and cataloged some of the most famous coin collections ever sold.

Dave's studying began even before he laid hands on his first gold coin. He has told me that when he was a young numismatist (he got started as a coin dealer in his early teens, in the 1950s), gold pieces weren't seen very often. Even among the "grown-ups" in his hobby club, such coins were rarely brought in for show-and-tell, or to trade. It wouldn't be until the early 1970s that President Franklin Roosevelt's Depression-era restrictions on gold ownership would be lifted. Then, Congress and the Treasury Department spent 10 years of trial and error developing a very successful gold-bullion program. Since the 1986 debut of the U.S. Mint's American Eagle coinage, Americans find it easier than ever to buy, sell, and trade gold bullion. On the *numismatic* side (apart from bullion coins), today many factors make classic pre-1934 American gold coins easy to study and collect:

- The *Guide Book of United States Coins* (the perennial "Red Book") gave numismatics a huge boost starting in the late 1940s, making the hobby popular and accessible;
- world economic conditions brought an influx of U.S. gold coins back from Europe starting in the 1950s;
- the invention of modern professional third-party coin certification in the 1980s brought seemingly scientific stability to the art of grading, and gave birth to a robust sight-unseen market; and
- the communications boom provided by modern technology has made the available pool of gold coins broader and deeper for any collector with an Internet connection.

Looking back to the 1950s, when Dave Bowers started in the hobby, books about gold coins were even rarer than the coins themselves. In 1964 researcher Walter Breen wrote a 24-page monograph on gold dollars. In 1975 numismatist David W. Akers, after spending more than 20 years researching gold coins (dollars in particular), published *United States Gold Coins: An Analysis of Auction Records, Gold Dollars*. Over the next seven years Akers compiled volumes covering every U.S. gold coin series. Breen, too, had continued to write monographs on other gold coins (up to the $10 denomination, published in 1967), and included gold coins in his two encyclopedias published in 1977 and 1988.

In the meantime, other researchers slowly added to the hobby community's knowledge of U.S. gold coins. Articles were published in *Numismatic Scrapbook Magazine*, *Numismatic News*, *Coin World*, *The Numismatist*, *Coins Magazine*, and other periodicals. Cornelius Vermeule explored the aesthetics of U.S. coinage, including gold, in *Numismatic Art in America* (1971). *Coin World* published its *Almanac* in several editions starting in 1975, providing much technical information and data. Kenneth Bressett and others codified the grading of U.S. coins, including gold, in the *Official American Numismatic Association Grading Standards for United States Coins* (first edition, 1978). Later, Richard Doty, curator of the Smithsonian Institution's National Numismatic Collection, wrote his wonderful *America's Money, America's Story*, and Roger W. Burdette dug into the National Archives and other primary sources to build his award-winning *Renaissance of American Coinage* books. The gold coins of individual mints were covered by Rusty Goe (Carson City), Douglas Winter (Carson City, Charlotte, Dahlonega, and New Orleans), and other specialists.

In the midst of this activity, Q. David Bowers emerged as the preeminent author on U.S. gold coinage—a position he holds to this day.

Bowers's *History of United States Coinage, As Illustrated by the Garrett Collection*, published in 1979, included his analysis of the nation's gold coins. In 1982 he published *United States Gold Coins: An Illustrated History*. His numismatic history of collecting U.S. gold coins was released as part of the proceedings of the 1989 Coinage of the Americas Conference. Various of his other books of the 1990s and early 2000s, plus hundreds of articles and columns before and since, have shared stories and insight on U.S. gold coins.

In 2003 Bowers joined forces with Whitman Publishing, longtime publisher of the Red Book and other hobby books, signing on as the company's numismatic director. This collaboration has led to a modern renaissance in American book-publishing in the field of numismatics. Since then Whitman has published an average of one new book either entirely or substantially about gold coins per year, ranging from popular softcovers to (also popular) 650-page encyclopedias. The first came out in 2004: Bowers's *Guide Book of Double Eagle Gold Coins* was the first book to cover the entire spectrum of the $20 denomination since David Akers's 1982 volume on the subject. The most recent is my own *American Gold and Silver: U.S. Mint Collector and Investor Coins and Medals, Bicentennial to Date*, published in 2016.

As Whitman's numismatic director, Dave Bowers has advised on all of these books, while keeping up his own research and writing.

The famous and influential Mr. Akers, who broke new ground publishing his numismatic research in the 1970s and 1980s, has said, "If one had a library consisting only of books and auction catalogs that Dave Bowers has written, the field of U.S. numismatics would be quite thoroughly and satisfactorily covered. Such a claim could not be made about any other person, past or present."

The *Guide Book of Gold Eagle Coins*—the 24th volume in the Bowers Series, and the 18th of those volumes written by Bowers himself—adds to and solidifies that distinction.

Dennis Tucker
Publisher, Whitman Publishing, LLC

INTRODUCTION

Research for this book began in the 1950s, although I did not know it at the time. As a young teenager I studied and read all I could about rare coins. By 1954 I had a good working library and was keeping notes of interesting things I learned.

Fast forward to adulthood, a highly successful rare coin business, and other activities and pleasures. One of my greatest satisfactions continues to be research followed by writing on subjects from esoteric to popular.

The present book on $10 gold eagles includes the basic information you expect to find in a Whitman *Official Red Book*. Beyond that you can take many side excursions to explore mints and minting of days gone by, to acquaint yourself with great collectors and collections of the past, and to tap into many anecdotes, trivia, and other items that, I hope, will add to any $10 gold coin in your collection.

You will learn why a political movement that started in the West in the 1870s is directly responsible for countless hundreds of thousands of About Uncirculated and Mint State eagles being available to collectors today—one of the most remarkable unintended consequences in numismatics. You will also learn a lot about the market and the factors that influence change.

In summary, by the time you read the last page I believe you will be as familiar with eagles as is someone who has spent years in rare coins.

Enjoy!

Q. David Bowers
Wolfeboro, New Hampshire

1

Overview of $10 Gold Coins

The eagle, or $10 gold piece, was intended to be the foundational gold coin in the American monetary system as outlined in the Mint Act of April 2, 1792. This was to be the largest denomination and was the standard against which fractional coins were measured, the $2.50 quarter eagle and $5 half eagle being proportionate divisions as to their weight. The name was derived from the national bird pictured on the reverse of the first coins, but it was not a clear choice. In his earlier report, "On the Establishment of a Mint," Treasury Secretary Alexander Hamilton stated, "The eagle is not a very expressive or apt appellation for the largest gold piece, but nothing better occurs." According to legend, the suggestion was made that a goose would be ideal for the largest coin, and smaller denominations could be called goslings.

Benjamin Franklin in a letter to Mrs. Bache, expressed this:

> For my own part, I wish the bald eagle had not been chosen as the representative of our country; he is a bird of bad moral character; he does not get his living honestly.
>
> You may have seen him perched on some dead tree, where, too lazy to fish for himself, he watches the labor of the fishing hawk; and when that diligent bird has at length taken a fish, and is bearing it to his nest for the support of his mate and

$10 gold eagle from the first year of coinage. This type with the Small Eagle reverse was minted from 1795 to 1797.

young ones, the bald eagle pursues him and takes it from him. With all this injustice he is never in good case, but, like those among men who live by sharping and robbing, he is generally poor, and often very lousy. Besides, he is a rank coward; the little king-bird, not bigger than a sparrow, attacks him boldly, and drives him out of the district.

He is, therefore, by no means a proper emblem for the brave and honest Cincinnati of America, who have driven all the king-birds from our country.

I am, on this account, not displeased that the figure is not known as a bald eagle, but looks more like a turkey. For, in truth, the turkey is, in comparison, a much more respectable bird, and withal a true original native of America. Eagles have been found in all countries, but the turkey was peculiar to ours; the first of the species seen in Europe being brought to France by the Jesuits from Canada, and served up at the wedding-table of Charles IX.

The eagle name persevered, and the bird was used on all $10 gold coins from the first coin issued in 1795 to the last in 1933.

Although copper half cents and cents were coined as early as 1793, and silver coinage (half dollars and dollars, more specifically) followed in 1794, it was not until 1795 that gold coins made their debut. There was a delay in production until the chief coiner and assayer were able to post high bonds—originally set at $10,000 each, now somewhat reduced—a task required of them before striking precious metals.

From the first year of coinage to the last, eagles were made in six major design types, more if star positions are noted among the earlier issues and the portrait variations of 1838 and 1839 are included. No coins of the denomination were struck from 1805 to 1837 inclusive. Thus, certain Capped Bust and Classic Head issues found in the $2.50 and $5 series have no counterparts among eagles.

Coinage was at the Philadelphia Mint for the early years, 1795 to 1804. After a hiatus since 1804, eagles were again coined in 1838. From that time until the debut of the double eagle in 1850, the $10 was the largest gold coin of the realm.

For Liberty Head coins issued between 1838 and 1907, certain pieces were struck at the New Orleans, San Francisco, and Carson City mints. Beginning in 1906, the Denver Mint also produced coins. The Charlotte and Dahlonega mints, although their output was limited to gold issues, never coined pieces above the $5 denomination.

EARLY $10 ISSUES

In their own time, eagles of the 1795–1804 era were seldom seen in everyday circulation, as the face value was equivalent to a week or more of wages for the typical person. Instead, these pieces were the coins of choice for large transactions and international commerce.

Government accounts indicate that most were exported and melted, thus being of little value to the intended purpose of establishing a circulating federal coinage. Accordingly, production of this denomination was stopped in 1804 and depositors who furnished bullion to the Mint were given $5 half eagles as the largest denomination. In time half eagles were also exported, showing that the problem wasn't with the denomination of the coin, but with the value of what they were made of. The situation was not remedied until the Act of June 28, 1834, which reduced the authorized weight of gold coins, making them unprofitable to melt down, and permitting them to circulate at face value in the United States. Under this legislation, eagles were not produced until 1838. Thus, the entire span of years from 1805 through 1837 does not include any $10 coins.

The first eagle variety of 1795 continued through early 1797, depicting Miss Liberty with a conical cap, facing right, with stars to each side, LIBERTY above, and the date below. The reverse illustrated an eagle perched on a palm leaf, holding aloft a wreath, a classical motif said to have been taken from an ancient cameo. Production of this design was very small, amounting to just 5,583 in 1795; 4,146 in 1796; and an estimated 3,615 in 1797.

During this time the Spanish-American gold doubloon (or "eight escudos piece"), valued at about $16, was the mainstay of commerce, along with its fractional coin parts. These kept good company with the Spanish-American silver eight-real coins and their fractional parts. It was many years until the passage of the Act of February 21, 1857, when Congress felt that enough federal coins had been produced and legislation was passed to eventually discontinue the legal-tender status of certain foreign silver and gold issues. Likely, a well-to-do citizen in New York City in 1797 with $1,000 of current coins on hand would have few if any U.S. silver or gold pieces— they would all be foreign—but might have a few copper cents plus various state copper coins and tokens.

Gold doubloons valued at about $16 were issued by Spain and various Spanish possessions in the New World. The illustrated coin was struck by the Popayan Mint in Columbia in 1816. It was in circulation in the United States and was recovered from the wreck of the SS *New York* steamship lost in 1846 en route from Galveston to New Orleans.

In 1797 the Heraldic Eagle reverse was combined with the preceding obverse, a type continued through and including 1804, after which coinage lapsed until 1838.

The Heraldic Eagle reverse was introduced part way through 1797 and continued to 1804, after which no eagles were struck until 1838.

Liberty Head Eagles

In 1838 Christian Gobrecht's Liberty Head (or Coronet Head) made its appearance. This was the first depiction of a design that would be modified slightly and eventually used on copper half cents and cents as well as gold $2.50 and $5 coins. Miss Liberty faces to the left, wearing a tiara (or coronet) inscribed LIBERTY, with stars surrounding the frame and the date below. The reverse depicts a perched eagle holding an olive branch and three arrows. Inscriptions surround the image.

The new Liberty Head eagles were produced in quantity and served well in large transactions, including in domestic commerce. Many of these coins, like their predecessors, were also exported and melted. In 1850 the advent of the new $20 denomination reduced the call for gold eagles, and mintages tended to be low for the next several decades.

In 1866 the motto IN GOD WE TRUST was added above the eagle, creating a new type that was produced continuously through 1907.

The Liberty Head design by Christian Gobrecht was minted continuously from 1838 to 1907.

Branch mints issued eagles at various times, commencing with New Orleans (1841), San Francisco (1854), Carson City (1870), and Denver (1906). From early 1862 through December 17, 1878, gold coins were not used in commerce in the United States, but were hoarded. Their melt-down value was greater than their face value in terms of federal paper money, such as Legal Tender Notes. In anticipation of gold coins once again returning to circulation and being used widely, large quantities of eagles were made in 1879, 1880, 1881, and 1882. Unfortunately, citizens continued to use paper money and eagles were not wanted, except for areas in the West. For large international transactions the double eagle remained the coin of choice, causing the mintages of eagles to generally decline, except for a few years.

The motto IN GOD WE TRUST was added to the reverse of the Liberty Head eagle in 1866.

The Saint-Gaudens Coinage

From 1905 to 1907 President Theodore Roosevelt was in continuous correspondence with Augustus Saint-Gaudens, America's best-known sculptor, in relation to the complete change of American coin designs from the cent to the double eagle. Roosevelt felt the artistry of current coinage was severely lacking. Saint-Gaudens set to work, but he was in declining health, and prior to his death from cancer on August 3, 1907, he had only completed basic models for the $10 and $20 values. An assistant, Henry Hering, finessed the models and made them suitable for coinage production.

Later, artistic coinage of various denominations was continued by other sculptors, including Bela Lyon Pratt for the 1908 $2.50 and $5; Victor D. Brenner for the Lincoln cent of 1909; James Earle Fraser for the Indian Head or Buffalo nickel of 1913; Adolph Weinman for the "Mercury" dime and Liberty Walking half dollar of 1916; and Hermon MacNeil for the quarter of 1916.

In autumn 1907 the Indian Head design by Augustus Saint-Gaudens made its debut. The obverse featured a female head, possibly modeled by Hettie Anderson, facing left, wearing a feathered Indian war bonnet as typically used by a *male* chief. Thirteen stars were placed along the top border, and the date below. For the first time in this denomination there were no denticles (tooth-like projections) around the rim of the coin. The reverse of the new $10 piece depicted an eagle standing and facing to the viewer's left, a motif taken from an inaugural medal privately created for President Theodore Roosevelt by Augustus Saint-Gaudens. The edge (as viewed edge-on) had 46 raised stars—one for each state in the Union, a number increased to 48 in 1912 when Arizona and New Mexico became states.

Two rare varieties of Indian Head eagles were made with periods or pellets before and after the words in the reverse inscriptions, creating the "With Periods" issues. One had a regular (sometimes called "rounded") rim. Although several tens of thousands were minted, nearly all were melted, with the result that only about 30 to 40 are known today. The second With-Periods variety was made with a wire rim, to the extent of about 500 coins, most of which survive today. The With-Periods eagles were distributed through the Treasury Department to friends, certain coin dealers, and others, but were not publicized or generally available to anyone without "connections." Later issues of 1907 and subsequent years lacked periods on the reverse and were made in quantity and were available to all.

In the summer of 1908 the motto IN GOD WE TRUST, absent from the 1907 and early 1908 Indian Head coins, was added, constituting the final type. Indian Head eagles were produced fairly regularly from 1907 through 1916, then occasionally from 1920 through 1933. In that year the production of $10 gold coins for commerce ceased forever.

Today these coins are well remembered and collected in the realm of numismatics.

The Indian Head design was introduced in 1907 and minted intermittently until 1933.

The motto IN GOD WE TRUST was added to the reverse of the Indian Head eagle in 1908.

2
Mints and Minting

From 1795 to 1804, 1838 to 1915, and again in 1926, 1932, and 1933, gold eagles were struck each year at the Philadelphia Mint. In addition, for certain years they were made at the branch mints at New Orleans, San Francisco, Carson City, and Denver. While the history of these mints is well known, brief sketches of each are appropriate here.[1]

A steam-powered coining press and attendant at the Philadelphia Mint, with visitors watching the operation. (*Harper's Weekly*, September 3, 1893)

THE PHILADELPHIA MINT

The Philadelphia Mint was the epicenter of activity for the eagle—where the first coins were designed and struck, where later motifs were designed, and where Proofs were made for collectors, among other aspects. There have been four Philadelphia Mint buildings over the years, and the first three coined eagles.

The first was constructed in 1792 and remained in operation for four decades. Operations took place in several buildings under conditions that would be viewed as primitive today. During the era that eagles were struck there, from 1795 to 1804, horses provided the power to operate the mill to roll out strips for planchets. Steam was not introduced for this procedure until 1816. The presses were hand-operated by men who swung a weighted lever arm to actuate a die traveling downward to meet its mate, with a metal planchet in between. By the late 1820s the facilities were cramped and outmoded, point moot to the present study as no eagles had been coined since 1804.

On July 4, 1829, the cornerstone was laid for the second Philadelphia Mint. The new building was ready for occupancy in January 1833, with assaying, refining, planchet preparation, and coinage equipment in place, along with related offices for supervisors and for the director, and a special section for the engraving department.

Built in the Greek Revival style extremely popular in America at the time, the second Mint was used through 1901. During that time the Mint saw many evolutions and changes, including the production of new designs, the introduction of steam-powered coinage presses in 1836, the beginning of the Mint Cabinet in 1838, and more. In 1838 eagles were struck at the second Philadelphia Mint for the first time, the first coinage of the denomination since production at the first Mint ended in 1804.

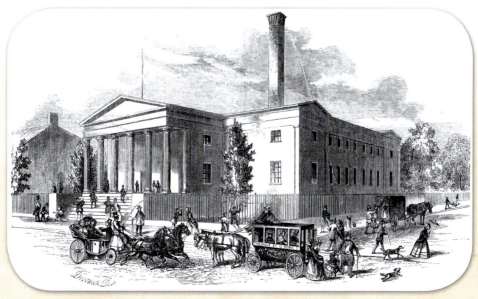

The second Philadelphia Mint was in operation from 1833 to 1901.
(Gleason's Pictorial Drawing Room Companion, **August 17, 1852)**

Within the engraving department and in related shops, large models were made of the obverse and reverse of coin designs (first in wax or plaster, then by casting into harder material), then were mechanically reduced on a Janvier transfer lathe, hub dies were created, and through various processes the working dies were used for actual coinage.

Eagle dies destined for the branch mints were made in Philadelphia, at first for New Orleans in 1841, then San Francisco in 1854, Carson City in 1870, and, finally, Denver in 1906. Dies for each coming year were often shipped in advance, with obverses dated 1855, for example, being dispatched to New Orleans and San Francisco late in 1854 so they would be on hand and ready for use in January if called for at that time. Mintage was done at the request of depositors of gold bullion, who specified the denomination desired.

In the early years the director of the Mint had his office in Philadelphia. From there he supervised the branch mints, with the advice and consent (but not often close oversight) from the secretary of the Treasury in Washington. He also directed affairs within the Philadelphia Mint and had the final say on most decisions. Those in charge of the branches were referred to as "superintendents."

In 1873 the office of director of the Mint was moved to the Treasury Department in Washington, D.C., and Philadelphia was placed under control of a superintendent, an arrangement that was continued for many years. Today the title is "plant manager."

While coinage laws were made by Congress, signed by the president, and facilitated by the Treasury Department, it was the director of the Mint who made nearly all of the operating decisions.

The Assay Commission met early each year at the Philadelphia Mint to review the silver and gold coinage from the previous year. From each production run at the various mints samples were taken and set aside. These were sealed in boxes and placed before the commissioners, who then selected a small number at random and had them tested

**The third Philadelphia Mint in the early 1900s. It
opened in 1901 and remained in operation until 1967.**

on the spot, for weight and fineness. Proceedings of the various Assay Commission ceremonies were usually given in the *Annual Report of the Director of the Mint.* Many of these are available today on the Newman Numismatic Portal Web site (nnp.wustl.edu).

Over a period of time in the second half of the 19th century, many innovations were introduced at the second Philadelphia Mint. Relevant to eagles were automatic devices used for weighing planchets and counting coins. In 1891 the first electric motors were used to drive the presses and most of the machinery. In time, steam power became obsolete.

By the 1890s the tremendous coinage of silver dollars, double eagles, and other denominations, plus lack of storage vault

Part of the coining room at the Philadelphia Mint in the early 1900s.

space and other situations, rendered the Mint obsolescent. In particular, the building was essentially a depot for millions of unwanted Morgan silver dollars that were struck despite not being needed, under terms of the 1878 boondoggle known as the Bland-Allison Act. Storage in the building was filled to overflowing, and an extra steel vault had to be put in the Mint yard to house incoming silver ingots.

Plans were made to build a new facility, the third Philadelphia Mint, and in October 1901 it was occupied for the first time. The new premises were used through the end of the eagles series in 1933 and beyond, and were home to many scenarios of interest to numismatists and historians. The first new Proof $10 dies made in the new building in 1902 were apparently by an amateur and featured polished portraits rather than the frosted or cameo style.

In 1933 the last eagles were minted at the third Mint, with most being relegated to storage vaults in the same building—although it seems that every now and then a Mint employee would tiptoe in and out and, perhaps (wink), trade a worn old one for a sparkling new 1933. Only a handful are recorded as having been paid out officially.

The third Mint remained in use until 1969, when it was relinquished in favor of the newly constructed fourth Mint on Independence Square.

THE NEW ORLEANS MINT

The New Orleans Mint, opened in 1838, became important in the annals of eagles. From 1841 to 1860, and then for scattered years in the late 1800s and 1900s, the Mint struck pieces which are highly prized today.

The new mint was ready for coinage in 1838—over a year behind schedule—and at a cost far beyond anticipation—$182,000 for the building and about $118,000 for the equipment, furnishing, and grounds. In that year silver half dimes and dimes were coined of the Liberty Seated design without obverse stars, the first production being a silvery stream of ten-cent pieces on May 8. The 1838-O half dollar, a rarity of legendary status, was struck the following year using an 1838 obverse.

Most trade in and out of New Orleans was done by ship, usually through steamboats operating far to the north and calling on various river ports, St. Louis being the most important. To the south commerce took place with steamer connections to many destinations, among the most important being Havana, Charleston, and, when the Gold Rush was in effect, to the port of Aspinwall in Panama. For the early years of its existence, most production was in silver half dimes, dimes, quarters, and half dollars, although an 1851-O silver three piece was made as well (the only instance of such). Gold coins of denominations from the dollar to the double eagle were made, the $20 being by far the most important in terms of the amount of metal converted to coins.

In 1849, gold, generally referred to as "treasure" in newspaper accounts, began arriving in quantity in the East, and in this year and in 1850 many ingots, privately minted gold coins, and "gold dust" (nuggets and flakes) went to the New Orleans Mint. Eagles continued to be minted, and in 1850 double eagles were struck there for the first time. In the same year the capital of the state, which had been in New Orleans, was moved north to Baton Rouge.

In 1851 the Mint achieved its record year with over $10,122,000 in coins produced, mostly in the form of double eagles. Frenetic coining activity continued through 1852.

Treasury records of California gold converted to coins at the New Orleans Mint (all denominations from $1 to $20) show these figures for the first several years, with a comparison to the Philadelphia Mint during the same era:[2]

The New Orleans Mint. $10 gold coins were minted there from 1841 to 1860, and intermittently from 1879 to 1906. (*Ballou's Pictorial*, September 11, 1858)

1850: New Orleans Mint: $4,575,567. Philadelphia Mint: $31,667,505.

1851: New Orleans Mint: $8,769,682. Philadelphia Mint: $46,939,367.

1852: New Orleans Mint: $3,777,784. Philadelphia Mint: $49,663,623.

1853: New Orleans Mint: $2,006,673. Philadelphia Mint: $52,732,227.

These amounts reflect what numismatists know well: New Orleans gold coins are far more elusive today than are those of the Philadelphia Mint.

In San Francisco in 1853 the United States Assay Office of Gold began the large-volume production of $10 and $20 coins of on an obverse design with an eagle perched on a rock. This reduced the shipping of bullion from that city to far off New Orleans or Philadelphia for coinage.

Coinage matters went from bad to worse for New Orleans in 1854 when the San Francisco Mint opened for business and began making gold coins. The New Orleans Mint had always had its share of physical problems. It was built on what once had been river bed, now dry but still not necessarily stable soil close to the Mississippi River levee. The foundation settled in places, causing uneven floors and buckling of some walls.

The structure was in such poor repair by 1854 that the Senate (in a resolution on May 31, 1854) requested the secretary of the Treasury to determine whether it was better to remedy the defects in the original structure or whether it was "a wise economy [to] render it expedient to erect a new building." Further: "The foundation was defective, causing the walls to spread, same being of insufficient strength to support the arches below the floors. To correct this and other problems the estimated sum of $25,000 was required."

The repairs commenced in 1855 and continued to September 30, 1858, by which time $588,812.70 had been spent! The entire process had been conducted in confusion and disarray, and government reports reflect much waste, inefficiency, and poor planning. For a period of several months in 1857 a large section of the building interior, already restored and rebuilt, was exposed to torrential rains as the roof had not been covered, due to late arrival of materials. In 1857 the New Orleans Mint was closed for coinage for the earlier part of the year, to permit repairs to be made and fireproofing elements to be installed. However, during this time deposits of precious metals continued to be received. Coinage recommenced in July.

In early 1861 the Confederate States of America was formed. Troops of the State of Louisiana and of the Confederacy occupied the Mint. Production of eagles had ended in 1860 with a production of 11,100 pieces. The Mint closed in early 1861 after coining half dollars and double eagles, some under federal auspices and others under the secessionists.

In 1870, Secretary of the Treasury George S. Boutwell reported that an inspector had visited the idle mint at New Orleans with the view of determining if the machinery should be moved elsewhere, such as to the city of New York (which had lobbied for a mint for many years) or the new facility at Carson City.[3] Most equipment was either too old, too heavy, or in unsatisfactory condition, except for the four coining presses, the largest of which was capable of coining silver dollars and double eagles as well as any smaller coins. Nothing was done, and the equipment continued to deteriorate.

The requirement under the Bland-Allison Act of 1878 for the mints to coin millions of silver dollars each year strained the capacity of the operating facilities. The

45th Congress provided that the long-idle New Orleans Mint, in disrepair and with much of its contents damaged or now missing, should be refurbished and reopened. In 1879 all was set, and coinage of silver dollars commenced. Eagles and double eagles were also struck, but of the small quantity of just 1,500 and 2,325, respectively.

It was anticipated that a more substantial production of gold coins would take place, but the Treasury Department decided to "enable the Philadelphia Mint to employ as much of its force as possible in the coinage of gold," and therefore directed additional silver sent to New Orleans.[4] After that time eagles were coined in scattered years through 1906.

THE SAN FRANCISCO MINT

On January 24, 1848, in California John Marshall discovered a gleaming nugget of gold in the tail race of the mill he and others were constructing on the American River for John Sutter, merchant and rancher of Sacramento. By summer the "rush" was on, towns and farms were abandoned, and able-bodied men rushed to the foothills of the Sierras, where, with good luck, $20 to $50 or more per day could be found in stream beds. Some occasional strikes were for far more, and tales spread of some adventurers making several hundred dollars for a day's work panning.

San Francisco, with its fine harbor, became the epicenter of Gold Rush commerce, as thousands of fortune hunters arrived by sea from ports all over the world, while others came over land via different trails. Commerce thrived in the city in 1849, by then a rag-tag mixture of wooden buildings, tents, and other hastily improvised structures among a few solid ones. Although gold in the form of dust and nuggets was common, coins were scarce. To fill the need, various private minters issued coins, mostly of $5 and $10 values. The roster of private minters included Norris, Gregg & Norris; Moffat & Co.; Wright & Co. (Miners Bank); and Pacific Co., all active that year, plus J.S. Ormsby in Sacramento. In time, other companies joined the business, with Kellogg & Co. and Wass, Molitor & Co. being among the most prominent.

In 1851 the facilities of Moffat were used by Augustus Humbert, United States Assayer of Gold, to strike octagonal $50 gold "slugs" and, eventually, other varieties and denominations. Soon, these other coins were struck under the title of the United States Assay Office of Gold, directed by Humbert, which produced an extensive coinage in 1852 and 1853, with the Treasury Department contracting with Moffat to conduct the works. In the meantime, on July 3, 1852, Congress passed an act authorizing an official mint. After some consideration of alternate solutions, the government bought the Moffat building and equipment from its owners, the partnership of Curtis, Perry & Ward, in 1854. The building, 60-feet square and three-stories high, was extended 20 feet to the west and the exterior was covered with cement, giving it an adobe appearance.

The first San Francisco Mint was a rather sorry affair—housed in cramped, poorly lighted premises smaller than even the tiny branch mints in Charlotte and Dahlonega, and far smaller than the impressive branch in New Orleans. All was set for its opening in March 1854. In the same year the New York City Assay Office was housed in a large Greek Revival structure on Wall Street, formerly a branch of the Bank of the United

States that was bought for $530,000, without equipment. No coinage was to occur there, but its refining facilities for incoming shipments of California gold would take the pressure off of the strained facilities at the Philadelphia Mint.

At the new Mint 70 people were hired as staff (including more than a dozen ladies to weigh and adjust the planchets for gold coins), equipment arrived by ship (via Cape Horn) and was set in place, and other matters were tended to by many experienced in coinage matters through prior service as assayers and minters in private capacities.

The first dies shipped from the Philadelphia Mint arrived on March 15, 1854, along with some additional equipment. The first gold deposit was taken in on April 3, 1854, and on April 15 the first coins were struck—double eagles of the federal design, but with an S mintmark below the eagle's tail. The first delivery of new product to the coiner occurred on April 19 and consisted of $2.50, $5, $10, and $20 denominations.[5] Gold dollars were first delivered later in the month. No coins of the other denomination then in use, the $3 gold, were struck until 1855. Two rarities would emerge from this lineup: the 1854-S quarter eagle, of which only 246 were struck, and the 1854-S half eagle, with a mintage of 268. The reason that over a dozen of the quarter eagles survive, but only three of the half eagles, is not known—perhaps simply a matter of chance.

Depositors of gold bullion preferred to receive their returns in high-denomination coins, such as $10 and $20, as they were easier to store and keep track of. At the time, paper currency was illegal in California under state law, and the double eagle reigned supreme as the coin of choice in many transactions and of necessity in large ones.

The first San Francisco Mint operated from 1854 to 1874. (*Hutchins' California Magazine,* October 1856)

On May 1, 1855, the *Alta California* reported that about $1.5 million was the largest coinage per *month* from the San Francisco Mint, whereas Kellogg & Co. for many weeks made from $60,000 to $80,000 worth of coins per *day*, mostly in the form of double eagles, which loosely copied the design of the federal product. In this year, private minters shut down their presses. The business of assaying and refining continued afterward in grand fashion, and by 1857, as reflected by gold ingots found in the wreck of the SS *Central America*, Kellogg & Humbert was the leading assay firm, while Henry Hentsch, Blake & Co.; Justh & Hunter; and Harris, Marchand & Co. were also important in the business.

Production of gold coins continued apace in coming years, although in time the yield from the California gold fields, which had reached its peak in 1853, went to lower levels. Whereas early miners worked with pans or with pick and shovel, by the 1860s mining was a corporate affair—with companies using huge monitor hoses to wash away entire hillsides in the quest for precious metal, and sinking shafts to obtain ore underground, for processing in large stamping mills.

In 1870 the cornerstone was laid for a new San Francisco Mint building, an action long overdue. Built of impressive size and filled with modern equipment, the facility was intended to coin the continuing but lessened stream of California gold, plus vast quantities of silver and gold from the Comstock Lode and elsewhere. Located at the corner of Fifth and Mission streets it was the largest mint in the world. The facility opened for business in 1874, and remained in use throughout the gold coin–issuing era.

In 1901 a record 2,178,740 eagles were struck at the second San Francisco Mint— the highest figure in the entire history of the denomination. Ever since the San Francisco Mint opened in 1854, depositors had a strong preference for double eagles—as a given amount of gold was easier to mint, count, and store. Eagles were made in quantity, but in far lower numbers.

The second San Francisco Mint as it appeared in the early 1900s.

During the San Francisco earthquake and fire in April 1906 the Mint was the only building in its area left standing. It served as a provisional headquarters for banking and communications. Until the World War I era, gold coins were common in local and regional circulation. During the war, all gold coins disappeared, only to reappear in the early 1920s, by which time paper money had become a popular substitute. It is likely that the 1920-S eagles, of which 126,500 were struck, were stored at the Mint, with only a few being paid out or exported. Later, this variety would be recognized as an incredible rarity. The next and last San Francisco mintage of eagles was 96,000 in 1930, nearly all of which were melted. This too is a notable rarity today.

Later in the 1930s, a new building was constructed, and in 1937 it was opened. The old one stands to this day and is affectionately known as the Granite Lady, at the corner of 5th and Mint streets, near Mission Street.

Canvas bags filled with $10 gold coins in storage at the San Francisco Mint in 1930. These included most of the 1930-S coinage and much of the 1920-S production.

THE CARSON CITY MINT

The Comstock Lode was discovered in Nevada in 1858, at a site 15 miles away from Carson, a trading post named after the western explorer, Christopher "Kit" Carson. As silver (primarily) and gold ore was extracted and processed, Virginia City, situated on top of the lode, expanded and became the center of mining and refining activity. Carson City was not as important in that commerce, but by 1860 it was a bustling community that was the capital of the Nevada Territory and the terminus of the Virginia & Truckee Railroad.

Almost exclusively, historical accounts of the Nevada Territory emphasize silver and say little or nothing about gold—bullion from this source consisted on the average of 21 parts of silver to 1 part of gold.[6] The market value yield of both metals from that source were about the same.

In early times ore, later refined metal, was shipped from Virginia City by wagon to Carson City, then by train to San Francisco and the mint there. To save shipping expense and to facilitate regional commerce, citizens of Nevada petitioned the government to establish a mint. On March 3, 1863, President Abraham Lincoln signed the appropriate legislation for a mint to be established in the state. No location was specified, but Abraham Curry, a principal in the extensive Gould & Curry mine and works in Virginia City, was instrumental in having Carson City selected, and, in time, the contract for construction was awarded to him.

The building cost, estimated at $150,000, escalated to $426,000 by the time it was completed. An early account told of its specifications and use:

> Granite from the prison stone quarry. Pict style of architecture. Portico, Ionic. Hall, 12 feet in width; main hall 12x40; on the right of the entrance.
>
> Paying teller's office, 13x16 feet. Coining room, 19x19. Spiral staircase conducts above. Whitening room 10x14.5, with a vault in solid masonry 5x6. Annealing furnace and rolling room, 17x24. Gold and silver melting room 10x24. Melters' and refiners' office, 12x19 feet. Deposit melting room 14.5x19. Deposit weighing room, 19x19, with a strong vault 6.5x10.5 feet. Treasurer's office, 13x16, with a vault five feet square. Engine room, 16.5x53 feet. Beside which there is a cabinet, adjusting room, ladies' dressing room, humid assay room, assayer's office, assayer's room, watchman's room, two store-rooms, attic, and basement.
>
> As a preventive against fire the floors are double, with an inch of mortar between. The foundations are seven feet below the basement floor and laid in concrete. Building two and a half stories high. The machinery for the Mint arrived November 22, 1868. The Mint has a front of 90 feet on Carson Street. November 1, 1869.[7]

On the afternoon of November 1, 1869, the machinery was set in motion and coinage tests were performed. The nature of the pieces minted is not known. Abe Curry was superintendent, but no dies or bullion were on hand. When dies did arrive from Philadelphia they were in an unhardened state, and needed to be heat-treated, then cleaned and finished. This procedure took place in the shop of the Carson City Mint.

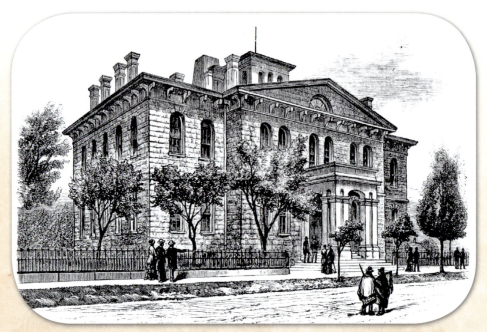

The Carson City Mint. (*Frank Leslie's Illustrated Newspaper*, February 23, 1878)

Opening ceremonies were staged on January 6, 1870, and on the 8th the first deposit was made. On February 10, Liberty Seated dollars were struck, followed in time by other coinage, including quarters, half dollars, half eagles, eagles, and double eagles. The first dime coinage with the CC mintmark took place in 1871. In 1873 a new denomination, the trade dollar, made its debut.

In the *Annual Report of the Director of the Mint*, for the fiscal year ended June 30, 1870, Director James Pollock included this:

> The deposits at this Branch during the year, were, gold, $124,154.44; gold coined, $110,576.05; silver deposits and purchases, $28,262.16; silver coined, $19,793. Total deposits and purchases, $152,416 60; total coinage, $132,369.05; total number of pieces, 38,566. The report is very encouraging, and it is earnestly desired that the present anticipations of its officers may be fully realized in the future prosperity of this branch.

As mintmarked coins were of little interest to anyone, the *American Journal of Numismatics*, the hobby magazine of record at the time, paid scant editorial notice to the 1870-CC coinage or any other from this or other branch mints.

The 1870-CC eagles, as well as those minted for the next several years, were probably used mostly in local and regional commerce, as there was no particular need to send them elsewhere. Such coins were made only at the request of depositors of gold bullion who asked for eagles in exchange. In the meantime the production of this denomination at the San Francisco Mint filled the needs of California and the export trade.

Curry was not a popular figure as superintendent of the Mint, and it is likely that his competitors in the mining and refining industry deliberately took much of their business elsewhere. The San Francisco Mint became the leading producer of silver and gold coins from Comstock Lode metal, never mind that the Carson City Mint was just 15 miles away, almost next door!

Curry exited in September 1870 in the midst of an unsuccessful bid for election as lieutenant governor on the Republican ticket. One of his followers in the mint office was H.F. Rice, who earlier served as a Wells Fargo express agent. Rice was also intensely disliked, probably another reason that metal flowed to San Francisco. His term lasted until May 1873, when he resigned amidst a storm of controversy concerning charges that gold coins were underweight. The charges were enthusiastically supported by the numerous adversaries of the mint, but were never completely substantiated by evidence.

Shenanigans concerning freight rates worked against Carson City, as evidenced by the *Annual Report of the Director of the Mint*, 1879:

> Notwithstanding the fact that the Mint at Carson City is located but a short distance from the productive mines of the Comstock Lode, higher prices were demanded for bullion deliverable at Carson than at San Francisco, and, in addition, the rates charged by the express company for transportation of silver dollars [and other coins] were higher at Carson than for San Francisco."[8]

The Carson City Mint continued in operation until 1885, after which its refining and assaying activities continued, but the presses were idle. The facility continued to be beset with problems, as reflected by this comment and overview in the *Annual Report of the Director of the Mint,* 1887:

> It will be shown that the mint at Carson has at no period of its history received considerable deposits from the mines of the Comstock Lode, their product having continued to be sent to San Francisco for coinage, the same as before the establishment of that mint.
>
> It will appear, indeed, that very important considerations, now affected by the cost of transportation of bullion, specie, and currency to and from Carson, are most unfavorable to the operations of coinage at the mint, and even to the minor operations of an assay office now carried on that institution.
>
> The Mint at Carson was opened for business January 8, 1870. Carson is on the line of the Virginia and Truckee Railroad, 34 miles from Reno, on the Central Pacific Railroad, and 300 from San Francisco, and some 14 miles from Virginia City—the location of the great mines of the Comstock Lode. Its population as given by census for 1880 was then 4,229.
>
> Substantially the whole product of these mines, instead of being transported south this short distance to Carson for parting and refining and coinage has always been shipped directly to San Francisco for parting and refining, for coinage of all gold, and for as much of the silver as required.
>
> Notwithstanding the fact that the mint at Carson City is located but a short distance from the productive mines of the Comstock Lode, higher prices were demanded for bullion deliverable at Carson than at San Francisco, and, in addition, the rates charged by the express company for transportation of silver dollars were higher from Carson than from San Francisco.
>
> The cost per piece of coinage at the mint at Carson when mainly occupied with double eagles and silver dollars was 7.28 cents in 1884 and 9.13 cents in 1885, against 1.55 in 1884 and 1.49 in 1885 at the mint at New Orleans—the two mints being occupied with about the same class of coinage.[9]

As noted above, coinage costs were high in Carson City, and various reports stated that from the advantage of the Treasury Department it was better to have the work done at the other three mints, Philadelphia, New Orleans, and San Francisco.

Again, the *Annual Report of the Director of the Mint,* in this case for the fiscal year ended June 30, 1890, tells of events:

> The mint at Carson was reopened for coinage on July 1, 1889, but, owing to the dilapidated condition in which the building and machinery was found, after four years of idleness, repairs and betterment of the building and overhauling and repairing the machinery were necessary, and consequently the coinage of gold and silver was not commenced until October 1, 1889.
>
> The coiner received from the superintendent 192,722.350 standard ounces of gold. There were coined in his department and delivered to the superintendent 92,460 double eagles of the value of $1,849,200, being 51.5% of good coin produced from ingots operated on. He had a gold wastage of 6.689 standard ounces.

The *Annual Report of the Director of the Mint,* 1893, told of the end of coinage at the Carson City Mint:

By direction of the secretary of the Treasury coinage operations at the mint at Carson City were suspended on June 1, 1893, and the force employed in the coiner's department dispensed with. A corresponding reduction was also made in other departments of the mint.

The mint at Carson City being of limited capacity, and the amount of gold deposited and silver purchased there being small as compared with the amount of gold deposited and silver purchased at the San Francisco Mint, which possesses a large coinage capacity, the expenses for coinage were much greater at Carson than at San Francisco.

The gold deposited at the mint at Carson City can be transported to the mint at San Francisco and converted into coin without any additional appropriation either for labor or contingent expenses. The heavy outlay for coinage at the former and the accumulation of an amount of gold coin at a point where it is not required for use may be thus avoided.

The facility remained in service as an assay office afterward, then ceased business in 1900. In the late 1800s many Carson City double eagles and a lesser number of eagles in commerce were included in bags of gold exported to Central America, South America, and Spain during the eve of the Free Silver Movement.

Today the substantial structure serves as home of the Nevada State Museum. Among its exhibits are a coining press and CC coins of various silver and gold issues.

Government records show the gold coinage of 1870 to 1893 as follows:

$5 half eagles: 709,617 coins with face value of $3,548,085.

$10 eagles: 299,778 coins with face value of $2,997,780.

$20 double eagles: 864,178 coins with face value of $17,283,560.

Double eagles overwhelmed the two smaller denominations, a logical decision as depositors of bullion wanted their returns in coins that were easy to store and count.

THE DENVER MINT

In the days of "Pikes Peak or Bust" signs on the sides of covered wagons, thousands of fortune seekers made their way to what would become Denver, in the Territory of Colorado. Although that particular peak was not visible from Denver and was about 75 miles to the south, the name stuck. In 1860 the banking house of Clark, Gruber & Co. set up a private mint, which turned out a stream of $10 and $20 gold coins depicting a fanciful view of Pikes Peak on one side and an eagle on the other. In 1861 the coinage was expanded to include $2.50 and $5 coins as well, and the obverse was changed to feature a Liberty Head, a copy of the federal coinage.

On April 21, 1862, Congress passed an act to purchase the Clark-Gruber facility for $25,000, after which it was known as the Denver Mint. It was anticipated that gold coins would be made there, and for the fiscal year 1863 $75,000 was budgeted for expenses.

Reality proved to be different, and in ensuing decades the Denver Mint operated and was listed in annual reports, but not a single coin was struck there. Instead, the facility served as an assay office, refinery, and storage depot.

In the 1890s the Cripple Creek Gold District began to yield a bonanza, and soon it was evident that large amounts of freshly mined gold would be available for coining. Lassitude turned to action, and the idea of a real mint (with coining presses and related equipment) began to develop in a serious manner.

A bill in Congress approved on March 2, 1895, allowed for the acquisition of a new site and the construction of a building to be used for coinage. Budgeted for the site, construction, and interior finishing was $100,000, which soon proved to be inadequate when on April 22, 1896, a fine piece of real estate was purchased for $60,261.71. Additional appropriations totaled up to $800,228.01 by the time that the new building was occupied in 1904.[10]

At 10:59 a.m. on Thursday, February 1, 1906, Superintendent F.M. Downer gave a signal, and as part of a public ceremony the first official Denver Mint coins were struck. On hand was a crowd who heard commentaries and watched the machinery in motion.[11]

In time, the Denver Mint, unlike those at Carson City and New Orleans which only struck silver and gold coins, produced denominations from the bronze cent upward. Eagles of the Liberty Head design were struck in 1906 and 1907, and those of the Saint-Gaudens Indian Head style from 1908 to 1911 and again in 1914. The coinage of 2,236,640 for 1910-D set a Denver Mint record for the $10 denomination.

Today the Liberty Head issues are very collectible in Mint State, with most being well struck and quite attractive; some have partially prooflike surfaces. Saint-Gaudens eagles are readily available except for the key 1911-D of which only 30,100 were coined.

Today, the same Denver Mint building is still used and is a vital part of coin production. The facility is somewhat larger, having undergone expansion in 1937.

The Denver Mint in the early 1900s. The State Capitol can be seen in the distance.

3

Proofs for Collectors

Proof Coinage and Styles

Proof coins are but a footnote in the chronicles of the $10 eagle. So few were struck that not more than 100 exist of *any* date today, and for many early years the number known can be counted on the fingers of one hand. And yet, Proofs played an important part in the 19th century to collectors who wanted an eagle of each date. As noted, mintmarks were of no interest until the late 1800s, and even then they were not pursued by many.

By the time Liberty Head eagles were introduced in 1838, following a lapse of the denomination since 1804, Proofs were being struck regularly at the Philadelphia Mint. From that time through the 1840s, interested numismatists could obtain them in sets or singly. Most popular were copper half cents and cents. Gold coins played to a very small audience, as is evidenced by the fact that today for some years Proof eagles range from only one to several. Each year Proofs were placed in the Mint Cabinet. Most of these still exist and are on display with the National Numismatic Collection at the Smithsonian Institution.

Gold coins were sold individually in the early days, often at face value as an accommodation to interested collectors. On occasion full sets of Proofs were fitted into morocco leather cases, such as for presentation to dignitaries. The Mint did not keep track of Proof production until the year 1859. For some years in the early 1850s no Proof eagles are known to have been made.

On the morning of Thursday, June 13, 1860, the Japanese ambassador and a contingent of princes and other dignitaries visited the Philadelphia as part of their trip to America. On the next day they returned and were given an address and reception by Director James Ross Snowden, who presented a cased Proof set, including gold, to the contingent.

Liberty Head Proofs

Proofs are characterized by wide rims, sharper details (usually) than circulation strikes, *full*, unequivocal deep-mirror Proof surfaces in *all* areas of the obverse and reverse fields, and full Proof surface within most or all of the vertical shield stripes on the reverse. These were struck one at a time on a medal press in the medal department of the Mint.

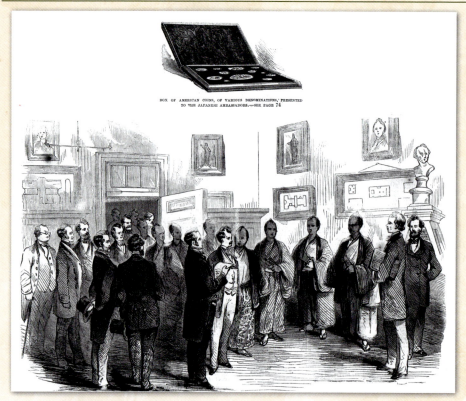

BOX OF AMERICAN COINS, OF VARIOUS DENOMINATIONS, PRESENTED
TO THE JAPANESE AMBASSADORS.—SEE PAGE 74

The Japanese delegation and entourage visited the Mint in June 1860 and
were given a cased Proof set. (*Frank Leslie's Illustrated Newspaper*, June 23, 1860)

The typical mirror Proof Liberty Head eagle from 1838 into the early 1900s was struck from dies that had the fields or flat surfaces highly polished. The lettering, date, portrait, and eagle were not touched and had a frosted surface, giving what is called cameo or deep-cameo contrast. That changed after the opening of the third Philadelphia Mint in 1901. Proof dies for gold coins were made with the portrait polished, eliminating the traditional contrast. A few years later this process faded, and certain later Liberty Head gold coins have cameo contrast, but not equal to the appearance of 19th-century coins.

The numismatic record for Proofs as given in auction catalogs must be taken with a generous grain of salt. In the 19th century extending into the 20th, many circulation strikes with reflective surfaces were called Proof or "almost Proof." In the 20th century such leading dealers as B. Max Mehl and Thomas L. Elder often mused in print whether a coin was a Proof. They weren't sure.

Today that has changed, starting in a significant way with the advent of certified, encapsulated grading

A Proof 1890 eagle with
frosted portrait giving a cameo
contrast with the mirror field.

(beginning with the Professional Coin Grading Service—known as PCGS—in 1986, followed by the Numismatic Guaranty Corporation of America—known as NGC—in 1987, and other services). This is true for mirror Proof eagles of the Liberty Head type.

Large-denomination Proof gold coins were little esteemed in their time, and on the resale market a $10 coin often sold for little premium. Often a gold Proof set offered at auction from the 1860s onward would bring little more than face value. This continued well into the 20th century. Accordingly, many if not most were spent. Those that did survive seem to have acquired nicks and other marks, no doubt including marks caused by careless handling by Mint personnel before the pieces were sold. An affidavit by a prominent rare coin dealer stated the following (excerpt):

> Harlan P. Smith, being duly sworn, says that he resides in the City of New York and that he called on the U.S. Mint in Philadelphia in June 1886 and went to the Coin and Medal Clerk and requested to be furnished with a Proof gold dollar of the current year.

A Proof 1904 eagle with the portrait polished in the die, removing cameo contrast.

**The medal room at the Philadelphia Mint in 1903.
Proofs were struck there, using a hydraulic press.**

> The clerk opened a small writing desk and took out a round paper box which contained numerous gold Proofs. He scraped them over with his fingers and rubbed them together, upon which the proceeding deponent looked with utter astonishment as it defaced the coins with pin marks and scratches.[1]

Because of such actions, and the general lack of appreciation for Proof gold coins of higher denominations, even the most important "name" collections, if they had a Proof at all of a given date, were apt to include one grading by today's standards as Proof-62 or Proof-63, rarely Proof-64, and still less often any higher grade. Beyond mishandling at the Mint, some Proofs were incompletely struck at the center due to improper spacing of the dies in the press.

The appreciation of existing Proof gold coins changed in the late 1930s when collecting high-denomination gold coins became popular. By the 1940s and 1950s they were showcased in auctions. Today, any nice Proof merits an illustration and detailed description in a catalog or other presentation.

Sand Blast and Satin Finish Proofs

In the early 1900s, several other types of Proof formats were made, including Matte Proofs (Lincoln cents from 1909 to 1916), Sand Blast Proofs (gold coins of 1908 and 1911 to 1915), and Satin Proofs (gold coins of 1909 and 1910). Sometimes the last have been called Roman Finish Proofs for reasons unexplained, but the tradition lingers in some listings. Sometimes various Sand Blast and Satin Finish coins are called Matte Proof. That is incorrect, as Matte Proofs, such as Lincoln cents and Buffalo nickels, were made from *dies* that were lightly sandblasted.

Sand Blast Proof gold coins were made by carefully striking coins on a medal press, slowly as to bring up the details. After striking they are put into a cabinet and given a special surface by sandblasting—the directing of a fine stream of sand particles in a high-speed air stream. Coins of the Sand Blast Proof style have surfaces that are minutely grainy, not frosty or lustrous. As the sand blasting was done coin-by-coin it varied, and several Proofs of the same year if viewed side-by-side can have slightly different characteristics. The edges of the coins—as viewed edge-on—are mirrorlike. Generally, the borders of such coins, where the rim meets the field, are squared off. As the difference between a circulation strike and a coin that has been doctored by dipping in acid or blasting with sand outside of the Mint can be difficult to discern, I strongly recommend that you buy coins that have been certified by one of the leading services.

A Sand Blast Proof 1908, With Motto, eagle.

The introduction of Sand Blast Proofs caused a great ruckus. Collectors wanted and strongly preferred coins with mirrored fields. Starting in 1909, Satin Finish Proofs were made in response to complaints about the 1908 coins, such as this barb in *The Numismatist:*

> The types of the gold coins now being issued at the United States Mint do not permit the making of bright finish or brilliant Proof specimens. The face of the die touches almost every part of the planchet, dulling the surface of even a polished blank. Proof coins of the present gold series, so far as issued, have a very dull appearance, the finish being what is known as "sandblast," and are far less pleasing to the eye than the coinage for circulation, which is brighter and of lighter color.[2]

Matte Proof cents and nickels and Sand Blast and Satin Finish gold Proofs were intended to make the coins more beautiful by highlighting the design. Certain of these processes had been used at the Paris Mint earlier, and at the Philadelphia Mint beginning in the 1890s for use on certain medals. Mint personnel considered them to be artistic, but hardly anyone else agreed.

A Satin Finish Proof 1909 eagle.

At its annual convention held in September 1910, the American Numismatic Association passed a resolution against the making of coins of either non-mirror format— Sand Blast or Satin Finish. Edgar H. Adams, America's foremost numismatic scholar of the era, prepared the wording, which stated that current Proofs are "scarcely distinguishable from those issued for general circulation," while with the old-style mirror Proofs, "a most artistic effect is produced, throwing the design to the eye in a most attractive way, and provides the collector with a superior coin for cabinet purposes and at the same time one which cannot possibly be confused with the coin struck for circulation."

Of the Sand Blast Proofs and Satin Finish Proofs that did find homes in cabinets, many, perhaps even most, were later spent. Because of this, such Proofs are scarcer today than their mintage figures would suggest. As complaints were frequent, and even the popularity of silver Proofs (which remained of the mirror Proof style) declined, the Mint terminated the production of silver and gold Proofs after 1915 and the Matte Proof cent and nickel after 1916.

A Sand Blast Proof 1915 eagle, the final year of Proof coinage.

Curiously, surviving Sand Blast and Satin Finish Proofs of the later Saint-Gaudens coinages are usually in high grades, with few marks.

Sand Blast and Satin Finish Proofs remained in the numismatic doghouse for many years. There was hardly any market for them until the 1960s. When the Numismatic Gallery (Abe Kosoff and Abner Kreisberg) obtained them as part of collections they had few customers. Fortunately, a Beverly Hills collector liked them and purchased a large quantity of mainly $10 and $20 pieces (he did not like the $2.50 and $5).[3] Years later when there was a market for them, Abner Kreisberg fed them to my company a few dozen at a time and we found homes for each. The values were very modest in comparison to what happened in the marketplace in later years. Today, these Proofs are very popular and attract a lot of attention when offered.

COLLECTING PROOF EAGLES

The first known Proofs in the Liberty Head eagle series are thought to have been four examples sent from the Philadelphia Mint to the secretary of the Treasury on December 6, 1838. These may have been to secure the Treasury Department's approval of the new design. The first delivery of circulation strikes from the coiner took place on December 26, 1838, with a quantity of 6,700 pieces, followed by 500 more on December 31.

The Mint Cabinet was authorized by Congress in July 1838, with a stipend of $1,000 to start with, plus $300 to be sent each year to maintain the collection. William E. DuBois and Jacob R. Eckfeldt were the co-curators. They performed admirably, this activity being in addition to their other duties at the Mint. Regarding contemporary coinage they sought to obtain one example of each denomination each year for the Cabinet. The denominations varied over a period of time. A Proof set of 1838 would have included a copper cent, silver half dime, dime, quarter, half dollar, and gold $2.50, $5, and $10.

William E. DuBois was a numismatist and readily traded and sold coins to collectors, including Proofs as an accommodation for face value. Nearly all such activity was with copper and silver coins as well as patterns. There was hardly any interest in eagles, the high face value being a deterrent. In the 1830s and 1840s $10 was more than the weekly wage of most employed Americans.

William H. Woodin and an Early Proof

Today only three Proof eagles are known from the first year of the Liberty Head design. In Thomas L. Elder's March 1911 sale of the William H. Woodin Collection this was offered:

> Lot 1201: 1838. Splendid, brilliant Proof. New small head of Liberty to left. Reverse: Small eagle standing with open wings. Edge milled. Almost unique in this preservation, and in such condition should bring $1,000.

It proved to be a great bargain and sold for just $200 to Lyman H. Low bidding for Chicago collector Virgil M. Brand (Brand journal item 57063).[4] This represented a nice profit for Woodin, who had attended the 1890 sale of the Lorin G. Parmelee Collection held by the New York Coin and Stamp Company. He had hoped to buy the 1839 Proof as well, but the competition was too strong. In the May 1911 issue of *The Numismatist*, Woodin told of the Parmelee sale:

I bought my 1838 Proof eagle at this sale, paying $45 for it. I bid the 1839 Proof up to about this figure, but Henry Chapman overbid me and took it. It seems foolish now to have let it go, but in those days $45 to $50 was a big price for an eagle. The 1798 five dollar gold piece, Small Eagle reverse, only brought $50.

William H. Woodin, a Renaissance Man of his era, was a highly successful industrialist, composer of music, and knowledgeable in many fields. He became interested in collecting coins in 1888 when he met J. Colvin Randall, the well-known Philadelphia dealer, who gave him this advice:

United States gold coins are the cheapest things in the world today. Collectors pay hundreds of dollars for specimens of other issues and won't pay twenty dollars for a half eagle or quarter eagle of which only four or five are known. You pick up United States gold and ten years from now you will find them bringing the highest prices of all the issues.[5]

Woodin became a careful student of gold, specializing in half eagles. He planned to write a definitive book on die varieties, but never did. Later, certain of his information was used by Edgar H. Adams and was published by Wayte Raymond. In 1933 President Franklin D. Roosevelt named Woodin to be his first secretary of the Treasury. In ill health from throat cancer, he took a leave of absence before year end, and in 1934 he passed away.

4
Circulation and Distribution of $10 Gold Coins

Coins of the Early Era

The distribution of $10 gold coins in America took many unexpected turns, all of which combined to make many varieties of these and double eagles—the other large-denomination gold coins—in plentiful supply today.

Gold eagles of the 1795 to 1804 years were intended to be the mainstay of American commerce, the largest coin of the realm, a coin intended to compete with the Spanish eight *escudo* or doubloon coin. The dies were made by engraver Robert Scot and staff assistants. Scot had been appointed in 1793 and remained in that post until his death in 1823.

Though the Mint Act of April 2, 1792, authorized the striking of gold and silver coins, no silver coins were made until 1794, and no gold until 1795, as the coiner and assayer were required to personally post bonds of $10,000 each. After this requirement was fulfilled by sureties, coinage of precious metals commenced. The first gold coins were $5 pieces delivered in late July 1795, followed by eagles in the autumn. The first $2.50 coins were produced in 1796.

While many eagles saw service stateside in business, it is likely that most were exported and valued as bullion. At their destinations, primarily in Europe, they were melted and converted into other coins, such as British guineas.

Silver and more silver. Too much silver. What to do with it all? This is why *gold* eagles and double eagles exist in large quantities today—an unusual twist in history. Shown are miners and a pile of silver ingots in Black Hawk, Colorado.

This was standard practice for foreign countries, as gold coins from various places and eras had different weights and purity. By melting them and refining the gold to a given country's standard, the value of treasury gold could be audited and evaluated easily.

To stem the flight of eagles to distant places the Treasury Department terminated the denomination in 1804. How puzzling this must have seemed to those who framed the Mint Act of April 2, 1792, authorizing the $10 gold coin to be produced in quantiles as a pillar of commerce.

The discontinuation of the eagle proved to be entirely ineffective, as the $5 gold half eagle became the largest American coin and was exported in quantity. Beginning in 1820 the rising price of gold on the international market made it necessary to deposit more than $5 at the Mint to obtain a half eagle. This was no problem, as nearly all were used in the export trade and valued for their bullion content. A $5 coin costing $5.03 to produce was accordingly valued at more than $5 at its destination.

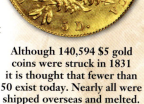

From that time, continuing to early 1834, the vast majority of $5 gold coins were exported and melted. In the process, great numismatic rarities were created. Who could have anticipated that from 1820 through the first part of 1834 there would be absolutely no federal gold coins in circulation? Another amazing twist in the story of the $10 gold eagle!

The Coinage Act of June 28, 1834, reduced the gold content of coins, effective August 1 of that year. After that time the current denominations—the $2.50 quarter eagle and the $5 half eagle—circulated in commerce at face value. From then until the Civil War, gold coins were familiar in domestic commerce.

Although 140,594 $5 gold coins were struck in 1831 it is thought that fewer than 50 exist today. Nearly all were shipped overseas and melted.

Eagles in the Mid-1800s

Coinage of eagles was resumed in 1838, the first mintage since 1804. The Liberty Head (or Coronet) design was created by Christian Gobrecht, who had been hired by the Mint in the late summer of 1835 with the title of second engraver, working with engraver William Kneass. Not long afterward, Kneass was incapacitated by a stroke, after which Gobrecht created models and dies for new designs. The Liberty Head was continued as the standard design for the eagle until 1907, the only major change being the addition of the motto IN GOD WE TRUST in 1866.

As detailed in chapter 2, in 1835 branch mints were authorized for Charlotte, North Carolina; Dahlonega,

Christian Gobrecht, designer and engraver of the Liberty Head eagle, was on the Mint staff from 1835 to 1844.

Georgia; and New Orleans, Louisiana. The equipment at the Charlotte and Dahlonega mints could not coin any denomination with a diameter larger than a $5 coin. At the New Orleans Mint production of eagles commenced in 1841 with the 1841-O issue.

During the 1840s eagles were made in quantity and mostly saw stateside service, although some were exported. The Gold Rush began on January 24, 1848, with the discovery of an abundance of gold in California at Sutter's Mill on the American River. By 1849 unprecedented quantities of gold had been produced. Congress authorized two new denominations—the gold dollar and the $20 double eagle—in 1849. Double eagles were first struck for commerce in 1850. These displaced the eagle as the largest coin of the realm.

By the time that production of all gold coins for circulation ended in 1933, over 75% of the gold used in coinage in the United States was in the form of double eagles. It was more efficient to coin a given amount of gold into $20 coins than into two $10 coins, four $5 coins, eight $2.50 coins, or twenty gold dollars. Because of this the average mintage quantities for $10 gold coins were often a fraction of that for double eagles. This created many issues that became numismatic rarities. The San Francisco Mint opened in 1854 and produced gold coins of the denominations then in use—$1, $2.50, $5, $10, and $20. Silver-coinage production began there in 1855. No copper coins were made until 1908.

Not that they directly affected coinage at the time, but the two great social causes of the mid-1800s were temperance and slavery. The publication in 1852 of Harriet Beecher Stowe's novel, *Uncle Tom's Cabin*, became the best-selling fiction book in American history. Within a short time millions of Northerners took a stance against slavery, and the abolition movement became the most powerful element in American politics.

The North became divided against the South, and much business in Congress was slowed or disrupted. James Buchanan, who served as president for four years beginning March 4, 1857, is viewed by historians as perhaps the most ineffective in American history. He tried to please both the North and the South and pleased neither side.

In November 1860 Abraham Lincoln, running in a field of four contenders, was elected president. Abolition was his credo, to the dismay and frustration of the South. In December, South Carolina seceded from the Union. By early 1861 seven states had seceded and formed the Confederate States of America.

At the outset the Confederate government sought to be an independent country and to have normal trade relations with the North. In fact, in early 1861 Confederate bonds and the first issue of paper money were printed in New York City by the American Bank Note Company and the National Bank Note Company.

THE CIVIL WAR BEGINS

The idea of peace between the two sides did not last long. The North did not recognize the existence of the Confederate States of America. In the South the secessionists resented the Union forts, especially in South Carolina. Abraham Lincoln was inaugurated president on March 4, 1961.

A $1,000 Confederate States of America bill printed in New York City in early 1861 by the National Bank Note Company. At the time the CSA envisioned that as a separate country it would develop normal trading relations with the United States of America.

In April 1861 Fort Sumter was shelled and reduced to ruins. The Union troops were permitted to leave under a white flag of truce. The war had begun. In the North it was the "War of the Rebellion" or the War of 1861. In the South it was considered to be the "War of Northern Aggression."

Lincoln and Congress viewed the war as an easy win—the industrialized North against the agricultural South. Lincoln called for volunteers to enlist in the Army for 90 days. Surely, the conflict would be over by then. Festive parties and parades were held as soldiers boarded trains in New York and elsewhere, headed south. Nothing much happened save some skirmishes and encounters.

In the third week of July the Yankees met the Rebels (as both sides were called) in Manassas, Virginia, not far from the nation's capital in Washington, D.C. Heralded in the newspapers, the Battle of Bull Run promised to be great entertainment, prompting

The remains of Fort Sumter with a Confederate flag flying in the breeze.

At the Battle of Bull Run in July 1861 the Confederate troops had a decisive win over the Union forces, the first major battle of the Civil War.

many citizens to go to the battlefield and watch. Reality proved to be different from expectation. Surprise! The Rebels took the day, and the Yankee troops broke apart and scattered in retreat.

Other battles took place after Bull Run, with neither side being dominant. By December many observers, especially in England, favored the South and bought Confederate bonds.

LATER IN THE 19TH CENTURY

Citizens became worried and began hoarding gold coins. By the end of December, banks stopped paying them out. After that point they were available only by paying a premium in paper money or silver coins to an exchange broker or bank. The Treasury, running low on funds, issued Legal Tender Notes in the spring, with denominations eventually including $1, $2, $5, $10, $20, $50, $100, $500, and $1,000. These were not redeemable at par for gold or silver, but could only be exchanged for other Legal Tender Notes, such as one $100 bill for five $20s.

Concerns deepened, and by late spring all silver coins were gone from commerce in the East and Midwest. In the second week of July, copper-nickel cents disappeared into the hands of hoarders as well. On July 17, 1862, the Treasury made ordinary postage stamps legal tender for some obligations. For the first time since the Philadelphia Mint opened in the 1790s, there were no federal coins in circulation. Commerce took place in paper money, privately issued scrip and tokens, encased postage stamps, and in late summer, Postage Currency notes with stamp designs.

There was, of course, an exception—paper money was not used on the West Coast. The California Constitution of 1850 forbid transactions in paper and mandated the use of coins. As a result federal coins circulated there during the Civil War, and any Legal Tender Notes brought into the area, as by the government to pay soldiers, San Francisco Mint employees, and other federal workers, traded at a deep discount in relation to gold and silver.

The Civil War ended in April 1865, and it was thought that silver and gold coins would soon return to circulation. That did not happen, as the Treasury was still in

A series of 1869 Legal Tender Notes. Such bills, first issued
in 1862, were not redeemable at par in silver or gold coins.

uncertain condition. Hoarders held on to their gold tightly. It was not until years later on December 17, 1878, that gold coins traded at par with paper money.

In the meantime, in 1870 the Carson City Mint opened for business in Nevada. Production of gold and silver coins for circulation was limited to the West Coast, as was expected.

This scenario had an effect on numismatics. Eagles and other gold coins struck at the Philadelphia Mint were made only in reduced quantities, to the order of depositors of gold. Such coins were mainly used for export, as at one point it took over $250 in Legal Tender Notes to buy $100 face value in gold. Today, San Francisco and Carson City gold coins of these are often worn, sometimes extensively so, due to their circulation. Surviving Philadelphia Mint gold coins of 1861 to 1878 tend to show relatively little wear.

THE "SILVER QUESTION"

In the 1860s all was well with the silver-mining industry. In Nevada, Virginia City sat atop the Comstock Lode and refined huge quantities of ore into silver and gold.[1] The Carson City Mint opened 14 miles away in 1870 as a convenience for coinage.

During the 1860s and into the 1870s, more mines opened in Nevada, Utah, and Colorado. Leadville, Colorado, high in the Rocky Mountains, became an especially productive and important center for silver production. In the meantime, several European countries changed their coinage standards to use less silver. In the United States silver coins were not in circulation in the East or Midwest and would not be until parity with Legal Tender Notes was achieved in April 1876. Trade dollars of silver were made beginning in 1873 and used up some of the newly produced silver metal. Supply far exceeded demand, and the price of silver fell. The outlook became grim in the Western mining areas.

What to do?

For several years Western politicians and mining interests had been agitating for government support of the price of silver metal. This became known as the "Silver Question," also known as the Free Silver Movement. Advocates were known as Silverites, sometimes as Free Silverites or Greenbackers. Their credo was that if silver could replace gold as the precious metal of choice, prosperity would resume. In the Prairie States many others joined the movement. If debts could be paid in silver instead of gold, many financial obligations would be eased.

Congressman Richard P. Bland of Missouri and Senator William Allison of Iowa were among the strongest advocates. There was puzzlement, however; by 1877, there were so many silver coins in circulation and in vaults that there was no need to produce any more.

In November 1877 an earlier proposal by Bland for the free and unlimited coinage of silver was reintroduced into the House of Representatives and was carried by a vote of 163 to 34, with 93 congressmen absent or abstaining. The sentiment for the bill was hardly that strong, but many felt that voting against it would impair their reelection chances as the Free Silver movement by that time was viewed by many as the key to ending the economic slump. The reaction of the Senate was unknown. Most senators were against it, but practicality intervened and it was thought that with a revision, passage would be a certainty.

The end result was the Bland-Allison Act. It was passed by both houses of Congress, but was vetoed by President Rutherford B. Hayes. His veto message was presented on February 28, 1878, and was promptly overridden by a 196 to 73 vote in the House and 46 to 19 in the Senate. The act became law.

The 1878 legislation mandated that Uncle Sam buy between two and four million dollars in silver bullion each month at the current market price and coin it into standard silver dollars of 412.5 grains weight, the same as the Liberty Seated dollars last minted in 1873. In an illogical move, the highly successful trade dollar minted since 1873 was discontinued. Trade dollars, however, had been made to the order of bullion depositors seeking export coins. The quantities were far lower than for the new Bland-Allison dollars.

The new silver dollars were made legal tender without limit. Over 50 million of the newly authorized silver dollars alone were coined in their first two years of production in 1878 and 1879. The Silverites' dreams had come true!

New dollars were first struck on March 11, 1878, using obverse and reverse designs made by George T. Morgan in 1877 for a pattern half dollar. At first numismatists and others called them Bland dollars. Generations later the designation was changed to Morgan dollars, the term we use today.

There was a problem, however; a newly minted Morgan dollar contained only 89 cents' worth of metal while a gold dollar had nearly a dollars' worth of gold. Another problem was that silver dollars had never been popular in the East or Midwest. What to do with all of them? The Bland-Allison Act also provided for the creation of Silver Certificates of Deposit (later simply called Silver Certificates) whereby, for example, 20 silver dollars could be stored in a Treasury vault and a $20 bill be issued in place of them, exchangeable at will.

As it turned out the Treasury bought the minimum acceptable amount of 24 million ounces in silver each year. The number of dollars coined depended on the market price of the metal. There was so much available on the international market that the price of silver continued to decline. By 1879 a Morgan dollar contained only 87 cents' worth.

Bankers' Magazine printed this in its June issue of that year:

A silver dollar of the new Morgan design, 1878-CC, from the Carson City Mint.

> A vault for storing silver is now being constructed in the Sub-Treasury, in New York City. The vault will be 47 feet in length, 24 in breadth, and 12 feet high, and will hold $40,000,000 in silver when it is finished. The cost of the iron and steel work employed in its construction will be about $20,000, including the doors and their levers. The floor of the vault will be made of iron and steel two inches thick, and under this floor will be four feet of concrete. An elevator will be used to move the silver received and taken out.

The Free Silver Movement expanded in the 1880s. Magazines and newspapers were filled with articles extolling the advantages of silver.

What if America replaced gold coins with silver dollars in the payment of gold-backed bonds and other obligations? Worry spread. In Europe this brought about a dramatic change in the outlook of banks and national treasuries.

Beginning in about 1878, a demand for American gold coins arose and was mostly filled by double eagles, but also, to a much lesser extent, by eagles and half eagles. Untold millions of coins were sent to Europe. Many were melted, especially in England (for conversion to gold sovereigns), but millions were kept intact in vaults in Switzerland, France, and elsewhere. Similarly, many were shipped to Central America and South America.

Although facts are elusive, later repatriations suggest that high-grade EF and AU Carson City eagles were sent from the Port of San Francisco to South America. From the same port went many S-Mint coins to the same continent and also to Spain. Most exported Philadelphia coins went to Europe.

A Treasury vault with thousands of bags containing 1,000 silver dollars each.

Silver by the ton. Piles of ingots at the American Smelter in Leadville, Colorado. (*Harper's Weekly*, July 29, 1893)

The large *Silver is King* exhibit at the World's Columbian Exposition in Chicago in 1893. Silver-mining interests spared no political or commercial expense in their effort to have silver dollars take the place of gold coins as standards of financial value.

THE GOLD COIN CRISIS

In the United States the slump in silver continued, and matters worsened in the early 1890s. During the previous decade many towns and cities had expanded in the Prairie States, financed by selling bond that yielded 9 percent or so to Eastern investors. Bonds issued in the East yielded 5 percent to 6 percent. The Prairie State bonds had a magnetic attraction. The boom ended. By 1890 and 1891 many municipalities in the Midwest were in default of their obligations. Problems continued, resulting in the Financial Panic of 1893. Thousands of businesses and many banks failed.

By 1894 it took only 49 cents worth of the metal to coin a new silver dollar! The Silver Question and the Free Silver movement dominated political discussions. The economic depression continued, more banks and businesses failed, and for Uncle Sam to buy more silver and to print quantities of paper money to create inflation seemed to be the answer for many. Books and pamphlets on the subject found a ready audience.

To help stem the drain of double eagles to Europe 1,368,940 coins were struck at the Philadelphia Mint in 1894 and 1,048,560 in San Francisco. Considering all denominations, the production of gold coins totaled $79,546,160 for the year. By January 1895, Treasury officials and congressmen had endured two years of worrying about the nation's gold reserves.

In the meantime, gold coins by the millions, mostly in the form of double eagles, continued to be exported. By August 1894 the gold reserve was only $52,200,000, a crisis

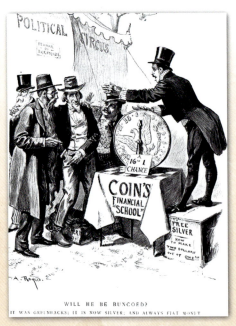

In this cartoon "Coin's Financial School" with the "Political Circus" told onlookers "How to make two dollars out of one." This was a parody on a popular book. By this time a silver dollar had less than 50 cents worth of silver content!

"A Perilous Situation": Adopting a silver standard was "Wild-eyed finance" per this cartoon and provide for "repudiation of debts." It was hoped that debts payable in gold, as most large commercial and international obligations were, could be paid in silver dollars really worth less than half of face value.

averted by issuing $50,000,000 in interest bearing gold bonds. This resulted in an influx of coins to the point at which the reserves were about $61,000,000 in October of that year. In November another $50,000,000 in such bonds was issued, increasing the reserve to $105,424,000. This did nothing to staunch the drain, and by year's end the reserve was down to $86,000,000.

J. Pierpont Morgan.

The crisis deepened, with no end in sight. On February 1, 1895, President Grover Cleveland and Secretary of the Treasury John J. Carlisle met with financier J. Pierpont Morgan to attempt to solve the problem. By February 9 only $41,393,212 was held by the Treasury for the redemption of its obligations payable in gold. Arrangements were quickly made, and J.P. Morgan & Co. and August Belmont & Co. of New York, in cooperation with N.M. Rothschild & Sons of London, organized an offering of securities aimed at foreign investors who held gold. The 30-year bonds, at least half of which were required to be sold in Europe, yielded 4 percent interest. They sold out in 22 minutes! The Bond Syndicate, as it was known, also promised to use its influence to prevent further "runs" on the Treasury, as in the fifth provision:

> *Fifth*—In consideration of the purchase of such coin the parties of the second part and their associates hereunder assume and will bear all the expense and inevitable loss of bringing gold from Europe hereunder; and. As far as lies in their power, will exert all financial influence and will make all legitimate efforts to protect the treasury of the United States against the withdrawals of gold pending the complete performance of this contract. In witness whereof the parties hereto have hereunto set their hands in five parts this 8th day of February. 1895.

Counting quantities of gold coins at the Philadelphia Mint in the early 1890s. Most eagles and double eagles of this era were counted, bagged, and exported. Decades later beginning in the late 1940s millions were repatriated from foreign vaults where they had been stored.

By March 30 the Treasury reserves had been built back up to $90,000,000, with more gold yet to arrive. The crisis was over. It became popular to say that J.P. Morgan saved the country from bankruptcy.

INTO THE 20TH CENTURY

The economy gradually improved in the late 1890s. Vast new gold strikes in and near Cripple Creek, Colorado, in the early 1890s plus the Klondike Gold Rush a few years later resulted in record high coinages, mainly of double eagles—the most efficient way to convert a given amount of bullion into coins. The production of gold eagles ramped up as well, but to a lesser extent. Coins of the early 1900s were made in especially large quantities.

With the exception of in the Rocky Mountain States and on the West Coast, gold coins were not often seen in everyday commerce. Their place was taken by paper money, including by Gold Certificates that could be exchanged for gold coins if desired.

In 1914 the World War began in Europe. By 1917 this had tightened the movement of gold coins, including in America, and with the exception of about 5,000 commemorative McKinley gold dollars in 1917, there were no gold coins minted until 1920. In many areas banks stopped paying them out.

In the meantime, millions of American gold coins from the 1870s onward remained in foreign vaults, augmented by continuing exports of newly minted coins. Gold offered security, while foreign currencies were often of uncertain value or, in the instance of the German states, in complete disarray.

Most American gold coins were stored in cloth bags. Those in Treasury vaults in America were counted at regular intervals, including during changes of administration. They were dumped out on tables, sorted into piles, and then put back in bags.

The City of Cripple Creek Gold Mining Company was a private venture with, per the illustration at the upper left of the certificate, a shaft near the center of town—an artist's conception of an improbable location.

The same thing was done with the hundreds of millions of silver dollars in government hands. In foreign treasuries gold coins were similarly counted. The result was that nearly all sustained extensive bagmarks.

THE 1920S ONWARD

The World War ended in 1918. In America prosperity continued for a short time, then in 1921 a financial recession set in. Conditions improved, and by 1924 prosperity and inflation were the order of the day. Business expanded, skyscrapers were built, luxury automobiles became popular, and the "Roaring Twenties" era was enjoyed by many Americans.

Over expansion, speculation in securities, and other excesses resulted in storm clouds gathering on the economic horizon in 1929 and the stock market crash in October. The Great Depression set in. Although President Herbert Hoover said that "prosperity is just around the corner," that did not happen. The crisis deepened and thousands of banks experienced losses or failed.

In the presidential contest of 1932 Franklin D. Roosevelt on the Democratic ticket promised a "New Deal" for Americans if elected. Hoover, running for a second term, was trounced.

Roosevelt was inaugurated on March 4, 1933. For his secretary of the Treasury he selected industrialist William H. Woodin, who, incidentally, was a dedicated numismatist. In the early 1900s he formed a great collection of gold coins and patterns and hoped to write a book on the varieties of $5 half eagles. His plans changed, and in 1911 Thomas L. Elder, prominent New York City rare-coin dealer and auctioneer, sold his gold coins. Woodin's interest in patterns continued, and with Edgar H. Adams he wrote the standard reference on the subject, published by the American Numismatic Society in 1913.

On March 6, 1933, Roosevelt issued an order closing all banks. The "Bank Holiday," as it was called, permitted federal auditors to examine each institution. Those that passed muster with assets and financial strength were allowed to reopen. Others were closed down or forced to be merged into stronger banks.

Not long afterward, Roosevelt prohibited the Treasury from paying out gold coins. By that time eagles and double eagles with the 1933 date had been produced. Production of double eagles continued into April, for reasons unclear today.

Citizens who were not numismatists were commanded to turn in their gold coins, effective at 3:10 p.m. Eastern time on January 31, 1934. Elsewhere in the world, those owning American gold held on to them more tightly than ever!

Bags of gold coins turned into the Empire Trust Company, New York City, in 1933.

Roosevelt raised the price of gold from $20 per ounce to $35 per ounce, in effect stealing hundreds of millions of dollars from loyal citizens who had turned in their gold.

A gold eagle contains 0.4856265 troy ounce of pure gold, which at $35 per ounce equals $16.997 melt value, rounded off to $17.

Were any 1933 $10 and $20 coins officially released? Later research has indicated that only five 1933 eagles were paid out and no double eagles.[2] No matter, many 1933 eagles and dozens of double eagles were acquired by numismatists. In 1944 Stack's offered a 1933 $20 for sale in the Flanagan Collection. The writer of a coin column for the *New York Times* set about writing a story about it and learned from the Treasury Department that no twenties had been officially released. However, in 1944 an export permit was granted to King Farouk of Egypt (see Appendix E) to obtain one for his collection.

As to how these 1933 $10 and $20 coins left the Philadelphia Mint has been a matter of debate, acrimonious at times. It would seem logical that Treasury Secretary Woodin would have readily allowed any other numismatist to exchange another gold coin of equal value. In any event, in the mid- and late 1930s, when stored coins were scheduled for melting, many Mint employees exchanged common gold for 1933 $10 and $20 coins and sold them to dealers. Abe Kosoff, interviewed by the author, remembered a steady stream of Mint people taking the train to New York City with coins of various scarce dates (1932-dated double eagles by the hundreds were another favorite) and selling them to dealers. This was done openly—a win-win situation. The Mint lost nothing as the coins were to be melted. Numismatists gained coins for their collections.

THE ERA OF REPATRIATION

Interest in coin collecting expanded greatly during the 1930s, even though it was the era of the Depression. New books, holders, and folders increased interest. Then came World War II. Cash was common and consumer goods were scarce. A lot of money flowed into the coin market (see the next chapter). Gold coins were very popular.

James Kelly at his desk in Dayton, Ohio. He was the first American coin dealer to repatriate American gold coins in quantity.

Beginning in about 1949 Dayton coin dealer James F. Kelly arranged with California dealer Paul Wittlin to go to Europe to buy coins. The coin business on the Continent was active again. In Switzerland, especially in Zurich, numismatic interest had never slowed. Wittlin found that Swiss banks had millions of U.S. gold coins on hand from years earlier.

All of this was a result of the Free Silver Movement of decades earlier. If foreign banks had not kept millions of American gold coins, the supply available to collectors today would consist of coins that citizens did not turn into the government in the 1930s—perhaps 10 percent or less of the quantity that numismatists now enjoy!

This treasure hunt expanded in later years as many others became involved. The result was that many gold coins, including eagles, formerly considered to be rare became plentiful or even common.

Wait, there's more!

The gates opened wide in the late 1900s and early 2000s. Certain eagles that had ranged from scarce to rare to extremely rare in grades of MS-63 to MS-65 in some instances were repatriated by the multiple thousands. This is continuing as we go to press. As is usual, few details are released. Changing numbers on NGC and PCGS population reports will tell part of the story—only part as many coins that are not in high Mint State grades will not be submitted and many more are sold to investors who do not have their coins certified.

Accordingly, some of the prices of yesteryear when these varieties were rare cannot be compared to modern auction prices of coins now plentiful.

Details are given under the listings for individual varieties.

5
Eagles on the Numismatic Scene

IN THE EARLY YEARS

With their face value of $10, eagles were expensive to collect. In the early 1800s when numismatics was becoming a hobby, few sought gold coins. Eagles of the early mintage years from 1795 to 1804 were acquired for the Mint Cabinet after it began in June 1838, but in the private sector the perhaps 100 to 200 enthusiasts ignored American gold. Instead, emphasis was on ancient Greek and Roman coins and in the American series— colonials such as Pine Tree shillings and related early issues.

Large copper cents seem to have been the only federal coins systematically collected, and not by many people. Robert Gilmor Jr., the scion of a wealthy Baltimore family, may have been the only numismatist who collected early eagles by date at that time.

In 1857 the discontinuation of the copper half cent and cent generated a wave of nostalgia, and in the next several years thousands of people became interested in collecting coins. In the eagle series the 1795 to 1804 issues appeared in auctions and had attracted many bidders. A number of specialists endeavored to get one of each date and type, the last including the different star arrangements of 1798. There was no knowledge of or interest in the leaf count on the palm branch on the reverse of the 1795 coins.

There were no useful texts to assist the few collectors interested in gold coins at the time. The first to give eagles extensive coverage was the *American Numismatical Manual*, by Dr. Montroville W. Dickeson, published in 1859. It was followed in 1860 and 1865 by other editions,

The last of the large copper cents, the end of a series that started in 1793.

slightly retitled *American Numismatic Manual*. Dickeson did not acknowledge branch mints or mintmarks, and for eagles gave the mintages of only Philadelphia coins. Elsewhere in the book he incorrectly stated that a C mintmark on a coin meant that it had been struck in California.

Gold coins were arranged by date first and denomination (from $20 down to $1) second. Dickeson gave his opinion of the availability of each coin, such as "Plenty" for a common issue.

Proof eagles had been struck since 1838, and one of each date was placed in the Mint Cabinet. Some others were sold in cased sets. There is no record of anyone systematically acquiring Proof $10 coins by date, and it may be the case that in 1857 the only Proof made was for the Mint Cabinet. Later, Proofs were made in small numbers throughout the 1860s and 1870s and were usually collected as part of sets, such as 20 Proofs of each gold denomination struck in 1877. Sometime these sets were disassembled and the gold dollars extracted, as this was the one federal gold denomination that multiple people collected by date at that time.

Gold-colored plate illustrating gold coins in the *American Numismatic Manual*, 1860 edition.

EAGLE.	
1856.	The designs unaltered, with one type and three varieties, and the amount coined was 60,490. Plenty.

Dickeson's entry for the 1856 eagle.

Coinage of eagles at the branch mints began with the 1841-O in New Orleans, followed by the 1854-S in San Francisco, and the 1870-CC in Carson City. There is no record of even the slightest numismatic interest in such coins! Not even the curators of the Mint Cabinet desired to acquire specimens, although they could have had them for face value easily enough.

Because of this, most early branch mint eagles, even those made in large quantities, range from very rare to unknown in true Mint State. By the early 1890s the only two numismatists known to have collected

The Mint Cabinet at the Philadelphia Mint as it appeared in the late 1800s. For most years since its establishment in 1838, full Proof sets were added to the display. Included were Proof eagles that today range from unique to rare.

branch-mint eagles were Thomas Cleneay, an old-time specialist in Cincinnati (his other collections including Civil War tokens were also memorable), and John H. Clapp, an oil man in Pennsylvania who sorted through gold coins in banks in and near Bradford in that state.

The Appeal of Mintmarks

The inattention to mintmarks on coins changed, and dramatically, with the entry of Augustus Goodyear Heaton, a highly accomplished numismatist, artist, poet, author, and architect. During the early era of the American Numismatic Association he was one of its most important members and served a term as president. Over a long period of years numerous letters, poems, articles, and other contributions from his pen regularly reached print in *The Numismatist*. Heaton moved around a bit, and while his home base was Washington, D.C., he summered in the mountains of Virginia near Luray. In 1897 he was in Perry, out in Oklahoma Territory, where he was sketching Native Americans and their way of life. In 1908 he did certain of his work at Studio 45 in Carnegie Hall, New York City.

Augustus G. Heaton, the father of collecting coins by mintmarks. A professional artist, Heaton also served at one time as president of the American Numismatic Association.

In 1892 he was the designer of the 50¢ commemorative stamp, "The Recall of Columbus," for the 1893 World's Columbian Exposition, a motif copied from his painting of the same name hanging in the Senate wing of the U.S. Capitol building. In May 1893 *The Numismatist* offered Heaton's advertisement for a publication that would restructure the very being of American numismatics, *Mint Marks: A Treatise on the Coinage of the United States Branch Mints.*

Heaton suggested or at least hoped that:

> Every alert collector of United States coins from 1838 to the present day will require it. It has full descriptive lists of the branch mint dates of every denomination, and of many hitherto unknown varieties, indications of scarcity and value, comparisons with Philadelphia issues, historic suggestions and other material of great interest to numismatists. It is the only guide book to a new field now eagerly invaded. Several prominent collectors who have seen the manuscript commend it highly, and leading coin dealers have welcomed the treatise as a timely and much needed work.

Heaton in *Mint Marks* listed 17 "causes of attractiveness," a list as sensible to read today as it was when published well over a century ago:

Causes of Attractiveness

1st. Mint Marks in their progressive issue at New Orleans, Dahlonega, Charlotte, San Francisco, and Carson City show the direction of our country's growth and its development of mineral wealth.

2nd. Mint Marks in their amount of issue in varied years at different points offer the monetary pulse of our country to the student of finance.

3rd. The denominations of any one Branch Mint, in their irregular coinage and their relation to each other at certain periods, indicate curiously the particular needs of the given section of the land.

4th. A knowledge of the Branch Mint coinage is indispensable to an understanding of the greater or lesser coinage of the Philadelphia Mint and its consequent numismatic value.

5th. A knowledge of the coinage of the different Branch Mints gives to many usually considered common dates great rarity if certain Mint Marks are upon them.

6th. Mint-Mark study gives nicety of taste and makes a mixed set of pieces unendurable.

7th. Several dies were used at Branch Mints which never served in the Philadelphia coinage, and their impressions should no longer be collected as mere varieties.

8th. The very irregularity of dates in some denominations of Branch Mint issues is a pleasant exercise of memory and numismatic knowledge.

9th. This irregularity in date, and in the distribution of coinage, gives a collection in most cases but two or three, and rarely three or more contemporaneous pieces, and thus occasions no great expense.

10th. As the Branch Mints are so far apart their issues have the character of those of different nations, and tend to promote correspondence and exchange, both to secure common dates in fine condition and the rarities of each.

11th. The United States coinage has a unique interest in this production at places far apart of pieces of the same value and design with distinguishing letters upon them.

12th. As Mint Marks only occur in silver and gold coins they can be found oftener than coins of the baser metals in fine condition, and neither augment or involve a collection of the minor pieces.

13th. As Mint Marks have not heretofore been sought, or studied as they deserve, many varieties yet await in circulation the good fortune of collectors who cannot buy freely [at premium prices from dealers] of coins more in demand, and who, in having access to large sums of money [large quantities of coins in circulation], may draw there from prizes impossible to seekers after older dates.

14th. The various sizes of the mint marks O, S, D, C, and CC, ranging from the capital letters of average book type to infinitesimal spots on the coin, as well as the varied location of these letters, defy any accusation of monotony, and are far more distinguishable than the characteristics of many classified varieties of old cents and "colonials."

15th. Mint Marks include noble enough game for the most advanced coin hunter, as their rarities are among the highest in value of United States coinage, and their varieties permit the gathering in some issues of as many as six different modern pieces of the same date.

16th. The face value of all the silver Mint Marks to 1893, being less than one hundred and fifty dollars, they are within the means of any collector, as, aside from the economy of those found in circulation, the premiums for rarities are yet below those on many coins of far inferior intrinsic worth.

17th. As the new Mint at Philadelphia [which was eventually opened in 1901] will have a capacity equal to all existing United States Mints, it is probable that others will be greatly restricted or even abolished in no long time, and that Mint Marks will not only cease as an annual expense, but be a treasure in time to those who have the foresight to collect them now.

It seems that Heaton was not aware of even a single numismatist who collected large denomination gold coins—$5, $10, and $20—by mintmark varieties. The collection of Cincinnati numismatist Thomas Cleneay, laden with mintmarked gold coins, had been sold by the Chapman brothers in 1890, but Heaton seems to have been unaware of that. John M. Clapp was rapidly collecting high-denomination gold by mintmarks, but his collection was not publicized and Heaton would not have been aware of this activity.

Additional Heaton commentary reflects the potential awaiting any collector of mintmarked gold in 1893 (excerpts):

Eagles With Mint Marks

Certain gold coins have a uniformly larger issue of dates at some one branch mint than at all others, and if collectors or numismatic associations in New Orleans, San Francisco. Carson City, Charlotte, or their vicinity, who have access to bank deposits should begin to collect sets of mintage in their sections as well as chance scarce pieces of others, and should establish correspondence and exchange, one might soon hear of far advanced gold mint mark collectors which would be an honor to the enterprising numismatists possessing them.

The Eagle or $10 Piece: This was coined in New Orleans from 1841 to 1861 and also from 1879 to 1883 and also in 1888. The date 1883 is a high prize. 1879 is very

The O mintmark on the reverse of an 1879-O eagle. $10 gold coins were first struck at the New Orleans Mint in 1841.

The S mintmark on the reverse of an eagle on the reverse of an 1876-S eagle. $10 gold coins were first minted in San Francisco in 1854.

The S mintmark on a 1914-S Indian Head eagle.

The CC mintmark on the reverse of an 1892-CC eagle, the first of a series that began in Carson City in 1870 and ended in 1893.

The Denver Mint opened in 1906 and struck Liberty Head $10 gold coins in that year and in 1907. The striking of Indian Head eagles began in 1908.

The D mintmark on a 1914-D Indian Head eagle.

rare, 1859 and 1851 are rare and 1857 scarce. With these gained one might be sure of the rest at leisure.

No eagles were coined at Charlotte or Dahlonega—a great saving of time and money to the collector.

The coinage at San Francisco is from 1854 to the present, except 1875. There are no very small issues, but pieces of 1864 must be very scarce and 1860, 1876, 1859, 1870, 1855, and 1867 follow in moderating importance.

In Carson City eagles were coined from 1870 to 1884 continuously. 1879 is rare, 1878, 1877, 1873, and 1876 are more or less scarce, and chances favor the finding of the other dates where CC issues are much seen.

The total value of eagle mint marks to 1893 number 80, or a face value of $800.

The rarest branch mint eagles are, New Orleans 1883, 1879, 1859, 1841; San Francisco 1864; Carson City 1879.[1]

INTEREST IN COLLECTING EAGLES EXPANDS

Ever so slowly, interest in collecting eagles expanded. By the turn of the century several dozen or so numismatists acquired them by *date* by ordering Proofs as they were issued each year. Interest in mintmarks remained at a low level. John M. Clapp, after his death in 1906, was succeeded by his son John H. Clapp, who continued ordering directly from the branch mints. Waldo Newcomer, a prominent Baltimore banker collected by mintmarks as well, usually from pieces found in bank stocks.

In the 1910s and 1920s perhaps several dozen or more numismatists continued to collect eagles by date, but probably fewer than a dozen sought mintmarks. That changed after 1933 when Franklin D. Roosevelt called in gold coins held by citizens. Numismatists could legally collect them. This inspired at least several dozen to form collections of eagles, including mintmarks. Louis E. Eliasberg of Baltimore and Floyd Starr of Philadelphia were prominent among them. Still, premiums on branch mint coins as well as Proofs remained low.

The first edition of *The Standard Catalogue of United States Coins* was published in 1934 (see Appendix B) and listed eagles by date and mint and gave prices. Mintage figures were given in the back of the book in the form of total dollar value of the amount coined, necessitating the reader to mathematically calculate the number of individual coins. This reference, published in 18 editions through 1958, was indeed the standard reference until the *Guide Book of United States Coins* appeared in 1947 and through later editions replaced the *Standard Catalogue* for most collectors and dealers.

Widespread interest in eagles of the Liberty Head and Indian Head types changed in the 1940s when catalogs issued by B. Max Mehl, Stack's, and the Numismatic Gallery showcased scarce varieties, including mintmarks, when they were consigned. This activity spurred more interest. By the late 1940s eagles of all kinds played to a wide audience. As strange as it may seem today, the main objective of most collectors was simply to get a "nice" coin. This was also true of other series. In 1949 in *Early American Cents*, Dr. William H. Sheldon's combined grading and market price system had it that a MS-60 copper cent was worth three times the price of a VF-20 coin.

B. Max Mehl's description of an eagle in the February 1944 Belden E. Roach Collection reflects the situation at the time—collectors did not attach a great premium to a Mint State coin in comparison to a worn one. The quoted listing for Very Fine is from the *Standard Catalogue of United States Coins:*

> Lot 311: $10 gold eagle. 1798 over 97. With thirteen stars, nine on left and four on right of bust. Magnificent Uncirculated specimen with brilliant Proof surface, almost equal to a perfect brilliant Proof. Extremely rare in any condition, but of excessive rarity so choice. Listed at $300 in only Very Fine. This one worth at least double that amount.

The coin sold for $315. Imagine that!

INTO THE MODERN MARKET

A page from B. Max Mehl's sale of the William Forrester Dunham Collection, June 1941.

The year 1949 was probably the turning point that launched the market we know today. Dr. Sheldon's book prompted collectors of large cents to study their coins carefully. An MS-65 coin was worth more than an MS-60, AU-50, EF-40, or some other lower level. In time this attention spread to other series. New Netherlands Coin Co., for one, began giving numerical grades to series other than large cents. Also in 1949 B. Max Mehl sold the Dr. Charles W. Green collection. Attention was primarily paid to double eagles, especially rare mintmarks in the Saint-Gaudens series, but eagles had their share of attention as well. Green had studied the market appearances of branch-mint gold. For eagles he paid little attention to grade, and for the vast majority of his dates and mintmarks he had circulated coins, even for 20th-century issues. Amon Carter of Fort Worth, Texas, built a great collection of gold, including eagles. For that series he had magnificent coins for the 1795 to 1804 years, but for later years including into the 20th century, most of his coins were circulated. Exceptions were many nice Philadelphia Mint Proofs starting with a remarkable 1858.

Interest in the mintage history of eagles and other coins took a giant step forward in 1950 when at the suggestion of John J. Ford Jr., Wayte Raymond hired Walter Breen to do research in the National Archives in Washington, D.C. Although this repository held Mint correspondence dating back to the 1790s, it had never been examined in depth before. Breen, a polymath with a degree from the Johns Hopkins University, had deep knowledge in many fields, including music, literature, and philosophy.

In the Archives he discovered much information about the making of dies, the distribution of coins, various interactions between Mint officials, and more. He made extensive use of this in later years, including as the main cataloger for the New Netherlands Coin Company in New York City starting in 1952. In 1967 Hewitt Brothers, publisher of *The Numismatic Scrapbook Magazine*, issued his monograph, *United States Eagles.* This was and remains a valuable source for the numbers of dies made and certain dates of distribution.

In 1988 Doubleday and First CoinVestors published *Walter Breen's Complete Encyclopedia of U.S. and Colonial Coins.* This was an instant success. As an example, Bowers and Merena Galleries sold over 10,000 copies in the first year of its availability.

In the meantime, Breen had been viewed as *the* authority on coinage matters, a status gained from many articles in *The Numismatist* and in *The Numismatic Scrapbook Magazine*, descriptions in New Netherlands catalogs, and programs and seminars at conventions of the American Numismatic Association and elsewhere.

There was trouble in paradise, so to speak. In time it was found by other scholars that a number of Breen's "facts" were guesswork. Some were pure fantasy, such as his scenario of the "Midnight Minters" in Philadelphia who after hours used old dies to make restrikes of rarities. Another Breen story related that Philadelphia pharmacist Robert Coulton Davis, a collector of pattern coins in the 1880s, secretly supplied laudanum to Mint officials in exchange for rarities (reality was that at the time anyone could buy opiates at drug stores; there were no restrictions). Breen also ran into trouble in his personal life and was convicted and jailed in 1992 for sex crimes against minors. In 1993 he died in prison.

Particularly where he quoted Mint and other correspondence verbatim, his work had lasting value. The problem with his numismatic writing and research was that he added a lot of guesses. Today, probably 20 percent of his work is unreliable, but the challenge is to determine what is and what is not!

Into the second half of the 20th century, more attention began to be paid to grade. Into the 1950s the auction catalogs of leading firms called out when a particularly attractive Mint State or Proof was offered. Premiums for quality coins advanced dramatically, continuing into the 1960s and 1970s. In 1975 Paramount International Coin Corporation published a study by David W. Akers on the gold dollars from 1849 to 1889 that appeared in catalogs he studied. In 1980 his book on $10 coins appeared with emphasis placed on a combination of rarity and grade. It became evident to many readers who were not familiar with past sales that certain eagles had hundreds of auction appearances, but very few in Mint State.

Mint State coins continued to be emphasized, now often with numbers attached. In the late 1970s the American Numismatic Association published *The Official*

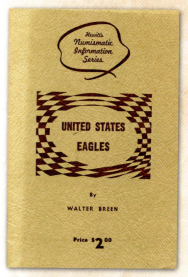

"Important Announcement" about Walter Breen.

United States Eagles, **published in 1967, included much information about dies and distribution.**

ANA Grading Standards for United States Coins. Adjectives such as Choice and Gem were also used. Prices went up, up, and up some more. The American Numismatic Association Certification Service (ANACS) in Colorado Springs began to grade coins for a fee. Submitted coins were returned with a certificate to which a photograph was attached, with separate numerical grades given for the obverse and reverse, such as MS-63/65. On many coins—Morgan silver dollars and Liberty Head eagles are some examples—the high relief of Miss Liberty on the obverse often gathered more scraps, scuffs, nicks, and marks than did the reverse in lower relief and of a more complex, shallow design.

In 1986 David Hall, Gordon Wrubel, John Dannreuther, Steve Cyrkin, Bruce Amspacher, and Silvano DiGenova formed the Professional Coin Grading Service (PCGS) which gave a single grade, averaging the obverse and reverse, and sealed the coins in a hard plastic holder, soon nicknamed a "slab." In 1987 John Albanese, who had been a grader at PCGS, and other dealers formed the Numismatic Guaranty Corporation of America (NGC). Year by year interest in acquiring high-grade coins, especially in Mint State, increased. No longer were there small separations between the prices of Extremely Fine coins and those of Mint State. Prices of Proofs went off the charts.

The reaction of the marketplace to third-party graders (TPG) was mixed. Some dealers felt that these upstart companies could not evaluate a coin as well as they could. Also, as grading was and is a matter of opinion, who was to say that the opinion of PCGS or NGC was more or less correct than that of a long-time dealer or auctioneer? In the early years both PCGS and NGC had reference collections. In 1990 each advertised that their interpretation of grading standards was fixed and would never change.

At the 1991 ANA Convention the ANA and the Professional Numismatists Guild (PNG) held a grading seminar. On hand was Phoebe Morse, director of the Northeast office of the Federal Trade Commission (which had been investigating exploitative coin advertising and sales) and Barry Cutler, an FTC attorney. On stage was Cutler and a group of professional graders who worked for the TPG services. He had a 1908 double eagle in a holder, with the grade masked. Professional opinions as to the grade ranged from AU-58 to MS-64.

It was reinforced that grading is, indeed, a matter of opinion, and that opinions can vary widely. If it were even slightly scientific, standards could be published that would not change and that anyone using them could understand. A 1926 eagle sent to a collector in Wildwood Crest, New Jersey, who had a copy of the definitive standard would grade it as MS-63. The same coin, if sent to an auction house in New York City, or to a dealer in Austin, Texas, or to a museum curator at the Smithsonian Institution would also be graded as MS-63. Also, 10 years from now it would still be MS-63.

Not making matters any easier is the expansion of grading numbers. In early times the ANA Grading Standards in the Mint State range had MS-60, 63, 65, 67, and 70, or five different levels. That was later expanded to cover all grades from 60 to 70, or 11 different numbers. In the second decade of the 21st century PCGS and NGC added + marks to all grades from 60 to 69 (MS-70+ would not have made sense, as a coin cannot be better than perfect). Today there are 21 grading numbers. There is no definition of these at all, nor can anyone consistently apply them.

As if that were not enough, in modern times there has been gradeflation. Probably, most gold coins graded as AU-58 in 1990 are now graded at Mint State levels. Further, the exact same coin submitted to the same third-party grading service can receive a different grade.

Lost in this milieu is the absence of a certified coin to say anything about whether a coin is sharply struck or weakly struck (with a few exceptions) or whether a coin is beautiful as can be or is as ugly as sin. The Certified Acceptance Corporation for a fee will review a PCGS or NGC coin and affix a CAC sticker if it is considered to be a "nice" example of the grade assigned, but with no comment about gradeflation. As CAC stickers are an innovation of the second decade of the 21st century and as the vast majority of auction offerings did not include them, they are not included here. The complete original catalog descriptions can be found on the Internet and often include stars, + signs, CAC tags, and other modifications.

Population reports give the number of coins certified in a given grade. If the same coin is sent in five different times, it appears as five coins in the report. Eagles graded above MS-65 were rarities in the early 1990s. Today, there are many such pieces listed. This has often been very disturbing to buyers. If someone bought the only known MS-66 coin at a high price years ago, but today there are 10 or more listed as 66 and perhaps 1 or 2 higher, a financial loss is often sustained. The over 200 listings of eagle dates and mintmarks in the chapters ahead give dramatic evidence of how the aspect of rarity changes. There are *many* coins that were great rarities the 1980s in such grades as MS–63 or 64 that are *very common* in those grades today. Countless eagles have been repatriated from foreign governments and other holdings and filtered into the market without publicity or information concerning hoards. Gradeflation has vastly increased the number of coins certified in grades from MS–60 to 62—coins that were AU a few decades ago. It is an easy exercise to go on the Internet and examine coins certified in these grades as most show *wear*.

The preceding analysis is the author's view on coin grading. Information that grading is not scientific or precise is of practically no interest or consequence to the majority of buyers in the marketplace. For these people the one and only factor to consider is the numerical grade marked on the holder, which has resulted in coins in high certified grades being in exceptionally strong demand.

Reality is different: knowledge and study, such as is endeavored to be included in this book, is the *only* key to market success.

Market velocity, a little-studied aspect of the market, has resulted in many if not most

**A page from Stack's sale
of the James A. Stack Sr.
Collection in October 1994.**

high-grade and rare coins coming on the marketplace staying only for a short time with the buyers. Unlike the situation of decades ago when an eagle would land in a collection and stay there for a long time, today it is common for the same coin to be sold several times within a decade. This yields more opportunities than ever before. If your bid for a certain coin does not win today, stay tuned for a reappearance next year or the year after.

The market has changed dramatically over the years. The availability of eagles has changed due to the repatriation of vast quantities of coins from overseas hoards. Grading interpretations continue to evolve. Many gold coins marked with high grades were rarities a few generations ago but are common today, as noted previously in the chapter.

Due to the Internet, market velocity, and other considerations, eagles are *easier to collect* than ever before! If you stay away from the highest-graded coins, there are countless eagles that are good buys in terms of rarity. As the next chapter emphasizes, if you buy slowly and carefully and cherrypick for quality, your collection can be every bit as nice, or nicer, as the finer specialized collections of eagles formed generations ago. Opportunities abound!

6
Collecting $10 Gold Coins

How to Build a Fine Collection

Many scarce and rare issues are found within the series of gold eagles. Mint State coins are generally rare prior to the late 1800s. This chapter gives you my view of the coin market from the inside, based on a lifetime of experience, and suggestions for being a smart buyer.

By proceeding slowly and carefully, a quality type set or specialized collection can be built. The secret that isn't secret is that certified and other listed grades do not necessarily reflect the best quality. There are many MS-63 coins that are more attractive and more desirable than some graded MS–64 or 65. Use numbers as *part* of what you do, not the final answer.

Places to Buy Eagles

The places to buy eagles are about the same as for other types of coins, but presented here are a few of the most popular.

Dealer advertisements, catalogs, and price lists often feature eagles, each with a grade and asking price. An advantage is that most dealers offer a money-back guarantee of satisfaction.

Placing your "want list" with a favorite dealer is also a great way to build a nice collection, although this was more popular years ago than it is today due to the ease of finding information on the Internet. You can state your requirements as to grade, budget, and your emphasis (high quality or low price—rarely can you have both in a single coin) and the dealer will act as your eyes and select pieces for you. If you are a busy professional or executive, this is a good way to acquire quality coins, assuming that you choose a dealer who acts in your best interests. The dealer you choose should be deeply and intimately familiar with eagles from 1795 onward, their characteristics and their rarity.

Auctions offer many eagles and can be a very important place to buy, especially for rarities. It is a good idea to study the catalog carefully and on the Internet take a very close look at the images. Today you can often bid in real time on the Internet.

Beyond auctions held by leading firms, the Internet offers many buying opportunities, but there can be traps for the unwary. I recommend that you purchase only coins that have been certified by a leading TPG service, such as PCGS or NGC, that guarantee authenticity.

Coin conventions are fun to attend and have the advantage that you can do a lot of window shopping. Also, you can make the acquaintance of people you've known only through the mail, and thus gain an impression of their personalities. Many dealers are willing to "talk coins" if they have the time. If a dealer is busy making a sale (remember, dealers have expenses to cover), ask if it would be convenient to come back another time. If a dealer is interested only in your checkbook, my advice is to keep walking!

The number of professional numismatists and firms and their diversity contribute to the richness of numismatics. There are many fine individuals and companies that are ready to help you with your purchase interests.

Sources of Information

There are dozens of printed publications relating to coins with occasional content about eagles, including newspapers, magazines, and club bulletins. Most popular of all are the weekly newspapers, *Coin World* (including a special issue at the beginning of each month with an extensive listing of prices) and *Numismatic News* (with its "Marketplace" and Numismaster Web site). Both have been around for a long time, and both have tens of thousands of readers. Each is a good source for information and carries many dealer advertisements. *CoinWeek* online and the Web sites maintained by NGC and PCGS have much information to share, including populations of certified coins and market prices.

It is important to remember that these publications do *not* guarantee the quality or value delivered by their advertisers, any more than the *New York Times* guarantees that a used car advertised in its classifieds or that a condo featured in the Real Estate section will be as described, or that a franchise with a quarter-page advertisement will be your key to fortune. There is much hyperbole.

The *Certified Coin Dealer Newsletter* and the *Coin Dealer Newsletter* are published weekly. Both are issued by the same company and are widely used as market guides. "Bid" prices are given for many coins, but there is a *caveat*. A "bid" price for Coin X at $10,000 may be what someone will pay if *he needs it*. Often such bidder, when queried, will state that he doesn't need one right now, or bought one yesterday, etc. For this reason, if you check lists of auction prices realized you will often see some pieces selling for below "bid." Moreover, most "bid" prices are for average quality examples. Choice pieces, or well-struck coins of a variety that often comes weakly struck, can be worth more, sometimes much more. Ugly coins can be worth less.

The bibliography at the end of this text lists many books, including some that specialize in eagles. If you make eagles a specialty, add one of each to your library. There is no better way to gain knowledge.

MARKET VALUES MAY VARY

Just as "bid" prices can have lots of wiggle room, so can listed market prices. Standard references including monthly or weekly listings as well as the annual *Guide Book of United*

States Coins by necessity list a single price for a given coin and grade. Accordingly, eagle 18xx in MS-63 grade may be listed at $2,350. In actuality, transactions may take place at that price, or slightly higher, or slightly lower, or *much higher or much lower.*

If you have the slightest doubt about this go on the Internet and pick an eagle variety that comes on the market regularly. See what coins in the same grade certified by the same service have brought in the past year. You will find *wide* variances. This is another secret that for advanced buyers is not a secret at all, but is not widely known in the general collecting community. For you it provides the opportunity to shop around for the best price, assuming that an eagle is of the quality you are seeking.

Over a period of years, market trends and cycles cause changes in prices.

GENERAL DETERMINANTS OF VALUE
Grade and the ANA Grading System

The grade assigned to a coin, reflecting the amount of contact or wear a coin has received, is an important element in determining a coin's value. A pristine coin, in "new" condition, in recent times has been called Mint State, although the term was used as early as the 19th century.

Mint State coins are graded from MS-60, the lowest level, up to a theoretical MS-70, or absolute perfection. Intermediate steps are designated MS-61, MS-62, and so on, with the MS-63 having the adjectival equivalent of "choice," and MS-65 or better, "gem." While numbers give the appearance of being precise, they are simply shorthand for someone's opinion.

Decades ago, most grading was purely adjectival, as Good, Very Good, Fine, Very Fine, Extremely Fine, About Uncirculated, and Uncirculated. In the chapters to follow you will see many listings from 100 to 150 years ago with "fine," "very fine," and similar adjectives. These meant "nice" and "very nice," not the adjectival use of these descriptions today. Today Very Fine (always capitalized) means a coin graded from VF-20 to VF-35.

Unfortunately, a newcomer to the hobby might not know that a "Good" coin might not be *good* at all to collect, or that a Very Fine coin was *very fine* to own, or that it was better than an About Good one. Today, the attaching of numbers such as VF-20 (Very Fine-20), EF-40, and so on make grading easier to understand. A "65" coin is better than a "58" one, and both are better than "40."

In case you wonder why the scale does not go to up to 100 for perfection, the system lies in a rather hokey (opinion here) market formula for large copper cents of the 1793 to 1814 years, delineated by Dr. William H. Sheldon in *Early American Cents* (1949). At that time the market for cents was far different from what it is now, and an MS-60 coin was worth just twice as much as a VF-30 one. By assigning a *Basal Value* (another Sheldon concept) to a cent, say a Basal Value of $2, then you could calculate that a VF-20 coin was worth $2 x 20 or $40, an EF-40 coin was worth $2 x 40 or $80, and so on. Today, there is a huge difference between VF-30 and MS-60, and the system is invalid. In fact, it lasted only a few years before it was recognized as being useless, though the concept of using numbers lived on, and today we have them. We cannot, however, calculate that a 60 coin is worth twice the price of a 30 coin, etc.

There are exceptions to most numismatic rules, and for a common 1901-S $10 coin an AU-58 will not have much price difference between that level and, say, MS-62.

The American Numismatic Association decided to get into the grading game and set up a Grading Committee. In 1977 they published *The Official ANA Grading Standard for United States Coins*, largely supervised by dealer Abe Kosoff, and compiled by Kenneth E. Bressett, of Whitman Publishing, editor of the *Guide Book of United States Coins*. I had the opportunity to write the general introductory material. At first, the ANA Grading system mirrored the Sheldon system, more or less, but in successive editions intermediate grades were added, such as MS-60, MS-63, MS-65, MS-67, and MS-70, then the full range of Mint State possibilities.

Years ago the ANA Standards were widely used, including by third-party grading services. Starting in a large way in the 1990s and continuing to today, the interpretations of these services often diverged widely from the ANA text. And, as mentioned earlier, now with services adding + marks starting in the second decade of the present century, there are 21 grades from MS-60 to MS-70. Today more than ever I suggest using grading labels only as a beginning as you contemplate a purchase. Very often a coin that is in a lower grade and less expensive is far nicer than one bearing a high-grade designation. Today the grading interpretations are "wild and wooly," and anything goes. Really not much different than from before the ANA and related standards were published.

Sharpness of Strike

While most eagles are fairly well struck, there are variables, as noted under the descriptions of the various dates and mintmarks given in subsequent chapters.

Among early eagles from 1795 to 1804 check the rims, the details on Liberty's portrait, and the details at the center on the reverse. Many have adjustment marks caused at the Mint by filing metal from a planchet that was slightly overweight. Light adjustment marks may be okay if they are not prominent (such as on the obverse portrait). Coins with heavy adjustment marks should be avoided.

For Liberty Head eagles from 1838 to 1907 check the centers of the stars. Ideally, each star should be well defined. Often, all stars 1 to 12 are sharp and 13 is weak at the center. Check the high points of the portrait, particularly hair to the left of the ear. Look at the reverse as well, but reverses are generally quite sharp. Check the rims on both sides for light spots. Sharpness is not always possible for some varieties, so if, say, 10 or 20 photographs reveal that a certain date or mintmark does not exist with needle-sharpness, accept that and stop seeking sharpness.

Indian Head eagles from 1907 to 1933 are generally well struck, but check the center of the portrait and the feathers on the highest part of the eagle, and inspect the rims on both sides.

Surface Characteristics

Planchet quality can vary for eagles, even on Proofs especially made for collectors. These are the characteristics to be avoided:

Copper spots: On many eagles, but most often on issues from the 1890s through the 1920s, the copper alloy (up to 10 percent in the composition) was not completely mixed with the gold. Bits of copper on the surface of a coin toned over a period of time, yielding brown or orange spots or freckles. These are even found on some Proofs. Perhaps with the popularity of scientific conservation of coins, there may be some way to remove these spots, but in the meantime I suggest that you avoid them.

Carbon spots: On a few eagles there are black dots, inclusions, or streaks—the result of "carbon" or other impurities in the alloy. Take care to avoid such coins.

Roughness and fissures: Every now and then some eagles, especially those of 1795 to 1804, are found with rough spots or even little crevices or low spots on the surface. Later eagles are usually on good planchets, but check for areas in which metal has flaked off.

Lint marks: This general term refers to foreign matter on the surface of a die, a thread or hair, a small piece of dirt, that on the struck coin leaves a depression. Sometimes this feature is seen on Proofs in the Liberty Head series. While a minor lint mark or two may be acceptable on an early Proof rarity, such as one in the 1860s, I would avoid them on later issues.

Some warm orangish-gold toning is perfectly fine and, in fact, is desirable for early issues. Note that the toning should be even, not in patches or blotches. Many eagles, especially worn ones from overseas hoards, can have black dirt or stains, or sometimes reddish stains. It is best to avoid such pieces. Simple dirt can be removed harmlessly by a jeweler who uses an ultrasonic bath.

When struck, a typical eagle was usually highly lustrous. The appearance of the luster varied widely, from deep and frosty to prooflike to finely "grainy." With today's gradeflation, richly lustrous surfaces are often absent in grades below MS-63. Prooflike coins with some aspects of mirror surface are a conundrum; mirror surfaces highlight nicks and scratches and can be unattractive unless in a high grade. In general an MS-63 coin with prooflike surfaces is not as attractive or desirable as is an MS-63 with frosty luster.

Whatever the style of luster, on a choice Mint State coin, it should be largely intact with no "bright" areas of scrapes or marks. Select a coin with good eye appeal.

Marks, Nicks, and Abrasions

After a coin was struck in a press it was mechanically ejected into a rectangular box. In time, other eagles were heaped on it. Afterward the coins were taken to another location, spread out, and reviewed by women who picked out any error coins, such as misstruck or clipped pieces. The acceptable ones were tossed in a box or container with others.

Next they were counted by heaping them in a pile on a table, and putting them into stacks of 20 coins each. Then they were put into a canvas "duck" bag in quantities that varied. At other times wooden barrels would be employed.

At their destination, either within the mint or at a distance, the bags were tossed into a vault where the eagles remained, often with dozens or hundreds of other canvas bags on top. At regular intervals, the coins would be taken out and counted, sometimes again run through mechanical devices putting more marks on them, sometimes by hand. This was necessary for accounting and inventory purposes, often at the end of the Treasury Department's fiscal year (which ended on June 30), and other times when there was a change in political administration. As mentioned earlier, eagles stored in foreign banks and other vaults were often inventoried and counted in the same manner.

Beginning in 1870 national gold bank notes were issued of different denominations from $5 up by California institutions that redeemed them in gold coins on demand. At the time other federal paper bills, such as Legal Tender Notes and National Bank Notes, were not used in that state. These national gold bank notes were backed by gold coins held in reserve in vaults, again bagged and often mishandled. In the 1880s gold certificates were first issued and were also backed by gold coins in storage, to which the coin notes of 1890 were added (redeemable in either gold or silver coins, at the choice of the owner).

Depots for the storage of vast quantities of double eagles in particular, but also eagles, as backing for these specific types of currency included vaults in the Treasury Building in Washington and in the Philadelphia, Denver (after 1906), and San Francisco mints. Elsewhere, eagles were stored at Sub-Treasury and Assay Office facilities operated by the government, the most important of which was on Wall Street in New York City.

Most national banks (first chartered in 1863) kept at least some eagles on hand, and those in the West were apt to have larger quantities in their vaults.

Marks, dings, scuffs, scrapes, and abrasions go with the territory in the eagle series, but can vary widely from issue to issue. For some varieties, especially Mint State coins repatriated from overseas hoards, a pristine coin may elude your grasp, and the best you can do is find one with fewer bagmarks than usual. Often the population reports for certified NGC and PCGS coins will show a variety to be very common in grades MS–60 to 63 but to range from scarce to rare MS-65 and above.

Prooflike eagles, similar to prooflike Morgan dollars, have good news and bad news. The good news is that a *high-grade* prooflike can be very beautiful, especially if it has cameo-frosted designs and letters. The bad news is that in grades such as MS-60 to MS-62 the mirror surface emphasizes even the smallest bagmarks, creating ugly coins.

When selecting an eagle, you will find bagmarks and nicks on just about all, until you reach the MS-65 grade, and even then there may be some (more today than when grading was conservative circa 1990). The trick is to be sure they are small, scattered, and not distracting. Coins with deep marks or gouges should be avoided—and there are plenty of these around. There are no rules and no two coins are alike.

Sometimes coins with edge knocks are gently filed or smoothed to remove the marks. This is worth checking for and seems to occur mostly on coins of the 1795 to 1804 years.

RARITY AS A DETERMINANT OF VALUE
Common or "Bullion" Issues

The value of common or "bullion" coins depends on the market price of gold, not on numismatic considerations. Examples among $10 gold coins include worn common varieties from the 1890s through 1932 that are also available in Mint State. When a Mint State specimen is readily available for a modest price increment not a collector on earth will want an EF. Common-date coins in AU or even very low Mint State are often traded for their bullion value plus a percentage.

Accordingly, years ago when gold bullion was $35 per troy ounce and $10 gold coins had a melt-down value of $17, common eagles sold at $18 to $20 (as reflected by many price citations given in later chapters). Gold rose in value and so did the price of common issues. When gold was $300 per ounce, common eagles in worn grades sold for $160 to $175. When gold was at $1,200 per ounce, common-date eagles in worn grades could be bought for in and around $700. When gold was over $1,800 per ounce, common eagles such as 1901-S, were much higher in market price. The gold market peaked at $1,828 in 2011. As a general rule, eagles of common dates and mintmarks from the 1880s to 1932, in grades below MS-64, rise and fall with bullion prices. Thus, any market analysis must reflect this.

A factor dynamically affecting demand by non-numismatic investors for common-date $10 and $20 coins has been the rise in exchange-traded funds (ETFs) that allow an investor to "own" bullion (not coin) gold in common storage areas. Such gold can be bought and sold by pushing a few keys or making a telephone call. An element of faith is required that the gold in reserve actually exists should all ETF holders wanted to redeem all at once. No such problem seems to be real, but some people worry. Holding physical gold privately remains appealing to many people.

To reiterate, bullion prices affect choice examples of common dates. For example, an MS-63 1901-S, 1926, or 1932 will rise and fall with the price of gold, but at a premium above the melt-down price. On the other hand, whether gold is $250 per ounce or $1,800 does not affect the price of a rare 1870-CC in VF-20 grade, or a Proof 1861, and who cares what the melt value is of an 1804 eagle?

"Condition Rarity"

As noted before, the concept of *condition rarity* has become very important in the numismatic market in recent decades. A condition rarity usually refers to a date or mintmark that is common in lower grades, but which emerges as an incredible rarity if MS-65 or some other high grade.

The easiest way to figure out condition rarity is to review the certified populations. If an eagle is as common as can be in, say, MS-64 or MS-65, but only a few have been certified as MS-67, be careful. With gradeflation and resubmissions, a decade from now there may be many more MS-67 coins and a few graded MS-68. To own a "trophy" coin that is the finest graded can be a comfort and satisfaction. In my opinion, a "trophy" eagle from the San Francisco Mint in the 1860s is apt to have more long-lasting value (but still be wary of gradeflation) than a "trophy" eagle of a common variety of the early 1900s.

In a discussion with Mark Borckardt he made this suggestion:

> A good buying strategy is to consider the grade level where a given coin becomes a condition rarity, and then seek out a nice quality example at the grade level immediately below the conditio n rarity. For example, as you say, at the time of this writing PCGS has certified 111 MS-63 examples of the 1883 eagle, and exactly 3 MS-64 examples, with none finer. Seek out a nice quality example at the MS-63 grade level for this issue.

DEMAND AS A DETERMINANT OF VALUE

Investor Demand

Investors in all kinds of coins, including gold, tend to come and go. In the early 1970s you couldn't throw a *Guide Book* without hitting two or three investors, mostly new to the market, checkbook in hand, salivating at the prospect of buying a dozen eagles or double eagles. By 1976 they all disappeared—not a single one to be seen! Then in the late 1970s, when there was a great run-up in the price of gold bullion, investors once again beat down the doors of coin dealers. In the early 1980s most disappeared once again. They returned in force later in that decade, creating a market peak in 1988 and 1989, after which they went back into hiding.

Often, investors will decide to become *numismatists* and then they stay, but if investment is their sole purpose, they travel in swarms and buy in cycles. The way to tell if investors are prevalent is to watch for advertisements in non-numismatic media. If all of a sudden people on the street corner are talking about buying gold coins, then there is a lot of investor demand.

Investor demand fluctuates, and sometimes widely. Accordingly, if you are a "gold bug," go with the flow. However, numismatists are often a bit wary when gold is "hot."

Numismatic Demand

Numismatic demand is usually solid and stable. If 15 well-financed numismatists are aspiring to build complete sets of Carson City eagles from 1870 to 1893 and only three of them have a rare 1870-CC then it stands to reason that the 1870-CC has a rather solid market. On the other hand if there are 15 collectors desiring an MS-65 coin of which a few dozen are known, there will be lots of bidding action for a while, after which the price may fall. New collectors are essential. If there are no fresh faces in the market, there will be less auction action and prices will be lower.

Years ago specialists in eagles tended to stay active for many years and hold their coins for a long time. Today the market velocity has changed, as noted, and collections tend to be held for a shorter time. The velocity is ever faster when a buyer who is a numismatist but not a specialist buys a "trophy coin," say a gem 1907 Indian Head eagle with wire rim, or even a rare 1933. The novelty often tires and such a coin is often back on the market within a year or two.

Such a buyer misses the thrill of the hunt. By way of analogy, a fisherman spends a day standing in a mountain stream, fly rod in hand, trying to outguess his prey, sometimes with success and sometimes not—a combination of art, skill, enthusiasm, and patience. If the same fisherman went to a market and bought a wrapped trout there would be no excitement at all. Similarly, if anyone could play the violin by picking it up and becoming skilled in one hour, few would pursue the art. Instead, the quest for virtuosity can become a lifetime ambition. In England in the 1790s there was a book titled *The Virtuoso's Companion.* A dedicated collector was indeed a virtuoso in numismatics.

Numismatic demand for eagles is usually quite broad. It takes a dedicated specialist to desire and to pay thousands of dollars for a VF, EF, or AU San Francisco eagle of the 1860s, but there are usually players on hand. For varieties that are in high grades and *obvious,* the number of potential buyers is usually very extensive. A good example is the key 1911-D Indian Head eagle. A coin in MS–63 or 64 will attract many bidders when offered at auction.

There are hundreds of thousands of active numismatists today, and of these there are thousands who buy eagles. Upon study and contemplation the series has much to attract educated collectors.

How to Be a Smart Buyer
Step By Step

There are enough gold eagles in the marketplace that with very little effort you could easily acquire a type set or even a running start on a set of dates and mintmarks within a short time. Quality, however, will be a mixed bag under such a buying plan.

My advice is to be a connoisseur. Buy only certified coins, such as from PCGS or NGC, the two leading services. Coins are marked with grades. These numbers say nothing about whether a coin is weakly struck or is ugly or beautiful. Sometimes a Certified Acceptance Corporation (CAC) sticker is applied to a holder to indicate that within a given grade this is a "nice" coin. Still there may be some problems, although CAC-stickered coins are usually very nice.

Eye appeal is not only important—it is absolutely essential. A certified Mint State eagle can be dull, dipped to be overly bright, can be weakly struck in some areas, or have other problems. Such should be avoided. For Mint State coins look for pieces that have rich frosty mint luster and are brilliant or with light iridescent toning.

Price is important. For most eagles there are many buying opportunities. Once you find one that suits your requirements, pay a fair market price for it. If it is a common issue, spend a few weeks or a few months until you land on one that is inexpensive within the context of the variety.

Again, take your time. All the coins that meet your particular requirements are in the marketplace, but finding them may take weeks or months. Study each coin carefully before making a purchase. The thrill of the chase is part of the fun of numismatics.

If the eagle is not a great rarity, and you muse, "It is nice, except for that scratch," you may want to continue looking. Except for great rarities, most varieties of eagles are readily available in the marketplace. You will have many opportunities to be selective, to cherrypick.

If a coin meets your strict requirements for quality and value, when time comes to sell, buyers will gather around. You will say "I like it!" and others will as well—an ideal situation!

Ideas for Sets of Eagles

Most often eagles are collected by types, but basic varieties as listed in the *Guide Book of United States Coins* offer a challenge for anyone with an appropriate budget.

Type Set of 3 Basic Designs

Collecting one of each of the three basic obverse types is an ideal way to start if you are not familiar with the gold series. This set will never become obsolete and can be blended into a larger type set or collection if you decide to go further.

Capped Bust to Right, 1795–1804: The most available and least expensive date is 1799. Examples are readily available in grades from Extremely Fine through lower Mint State categories.

Liberty Head, 1838–1907: Made continuously at the Philadelphia Mint and for many years at branch mints as well. Eagles of the early 1900s are readily available in About Uncirculated and Mint State grades.

Indian Head, 1907–1933: Readily available in About Uncirculated and Mint State grades.

Standard Type Set of 6 Designs

This set of six basic obverse and reverse design combinations is the plan followed by most collectors. While the two early types are elusive, the later ones can be obtained with ease. This makes a very nice display. The six numbered types are the designations often used.

Type I: Capped Bust to Right, Small Eagle Reverse, 1795–1797: This is the earliest of the types. Each of the dates is somewhat scarce. Grades range from Extremely Fine to Mint State.

Type II: Capped Bust to Right, Large or Heraldic Eagle Reverse, 1797–1804: Coins of this type are somewhat scarce. The most available date is 1799. Grades range from Extremely Fine to Mint State.

Type III: Liberty Head, No Motto, 1838–1866: This is a very challenging type. True Mint State coins are few and far between. Most great collections in the past have had coins ranging from VF to EF to AU.

Type IV: Liberty Head, With Motto, 1866–1907: Motto IN GOD WE TRUST added to the reverse above the eagle. There are many common coins within this type. Those from the turn of the 20th century are easily available in Mint State.

Type V: Indian Head, No Motto, 1907 and 1908: This is the famed design created by Augustus Saint-Gaudens. It is readily available in About Uncirculated and Mint State grades. The 1907 coins with periods on the reverse are a rare sub-type and are sometimes included as a separate coin in a type set by those who can afford to do so.

Type VI: Indian Head, With Motto, 1908–1933: Motto IN GOD WE TRUST added to the reverse beginning in August 1908. High-grade coins are readily available.

Specialized Collections

Collecting by dates, mintmarks, and major varieties has been popular for a long time. In the forefront are sets of Indian Head eagles from 1907 to 1933.

Early Eagles, 1795–1804: A set by *Guide Book* varieties includes two rare varieties of 1798, 8 Over 7, each with a different star count. The others are somewhat scarce, and in true Mint State most are rare.

Liberty Head Eagles, 1838–1907: Among all U.S. gold coins of this era, the rarest, by far, are the eagles of the earlier years of this type, from 1838 into the 1870s. No one has ever come close to acquiring a set in Mint State. Most great collections have had the earlier issues in VF and EF, punctuated by the occasional AU. From the 1880s onward these are more available in high grades, and from the late 1890s to 1907 most can be found in Mint State. The San Francisco eagles from 1854 through the 1870s are found in lower average condition than Philadelphia coins, and the same can be said for Carson City eagles of the 1870s and 1880s.

Carson City Eagles, 1870–1884 and 1890–1893: Forming a set of Carson City eagles has been a specialty for several collectors, usually in conjunction with other Carson City denominations in silver and gold.

Indian Head Eagles, 1907–1933: Collecting this series is a very popular pursuit. Among regular dates and mintmarks the 1920-S is a rarity, especially in high grades. The 1930-S is rare as well. The 1933, which is nearly always found in attractive Mint State, is another key. Among earlier issues the 1911-D is scarce in all grades and rare in Mint State. There are two varieties of 1907 with periods on the reverse—Wire Rim and Rolled Rim. These are nearly always found in Mint State and are rare, the Rolled Rim being particularly so.

7

Using This Book to Understand the Market

The information given under the individual listings in each catalog incorporates the essentials to understanding the market. Each date and mintmark eagle issued from 1795 to 1933 is given a separate analysis, as are several major varieties. The title photographs are of actual coins of that variety, obverse and reverse (not composites).

The market value of an eagle is determined by many factors. Before making significant purchases it is advisable to learn as much as you can and to consult other sources for opinions as to grade, rarity, desirability, and market value. Often, a trustworthy professional numismatist can be of great assistance.

In the field of eagles after the 1860s the traditional estimates of rarity have changed greatly and continue to change. In 1980 Paramount International Coin Corporation published *United States Gold Coins: An Analysis of Auction Records, Volume V, Eagles, 1795–1933* by David W. Akers. The author had surveyed 369 catalogs mainly from the 1940s onward and compiled information as to the frequency of appearance of each date and mintmark in various grades. For many early Liberty Head eagles there were few if any known in Mint State and many of the later coins of this type from the 1880s through the early 1900s ranged from scarce to rare.

Availability changed dramatically toward the end of the 20th century and into the 21st when vast quantities of coins stored overseas were repatriated. Beginning in the late 1870s quantities of new as well as circulated coins were shipped to foreign banks, governments, and merchants as a result of the Free Silver Movement. These modern imports rearranged the rarity landscape nearly completely. Many coins that were rarities or even unknown in Mint State now were available by the hundreds or even the thousands! This has made former rarities very affordable today.

Many common eagles in lower grades are priced in the market depending on the bullion value of gold. If gold is $1,800 per ounce and drops to $1,250, an AU or lower-range Mint State coin of a common variety, say 1901-S, falls in price sharply. The numismatic demand has not changed. Such coins remained as desirable as ever for inclusion in type sets or sets by date and mintmark.

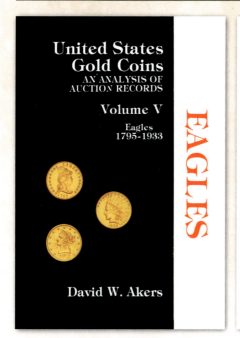

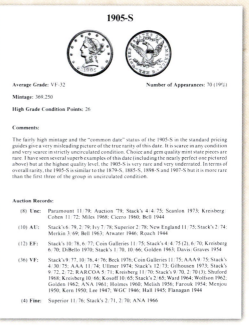

The cover of *United States Gold Coins: An Analysis of Auction Records, Volume V, Eagles, 1795–1933* by David W. Akers. Published in 1980, this book was widely used for years afterward.

The Akers study of the 1905-S eagle, a rarity in Mint State in 1980. Today such coins are plentiful due to repatriations from foreign holdings.

As these words are being written, very large quantities of eagles and double eagles continue to be repatriated. For the latest population report figures check the PCGS and NGC Web sites.

CIRCULATION STRIKES
Circulation-Strike Mintage

This figure is the quantity minted to be used in general circulation in commerce. For eagles from 1795 to 1804, the figures are largely guesswork and estimates, earlier by Walter Breen, sharply refined by Harry W. Bass Jr. and John Dannreuther. Breen believed that any given delivery of eagles from the coiner to the treasurer consisted of a single die pair or linked group of die pairs. The individual listings point out some unusual situations. For example, eagles of 1804 with a mintage of 3,757 for that calendar year used a reverse die also used to coin eagles dated 1803. This is based on examination of the reverse die that revealed that coins dated 1803 with this die were of a *later* die state. Estimated mintages are moot in any event, as the number of surviving coins is more important.

For eagles dated 1838 and onward, figures from the *Annual Report of the Director of the Mint* are used. Exceptions are the 1866-S eagles without and with motto. The date when the old reverse style was discontinued and the new one used in its place was not given in the *Annual Report*. Accordingly, for these two coins mintage figures are estimates. Roger W. Burdette Jr. finessed mintage figures for the With Periods eagles of 1907 as earlier published numbers varied.

Estimated Population (Mint State)

This reflects *modern grading interpretations.* Countless coins that were graded AU–50 to 58 years ago are now certified as MS–60 to 62, sometimes even higher. If this book had been compiled and published in, say, 1980, the number range would be much smaller, although the coins are the same now—but with elevated grades. Taking the listings at face value, many eagles that were great rarities or even unknown in Mint State now exist with several or more certified in that state.

Much more important than the expansion of populations in high grades is the repatriation of eagles brought back from foreign lands, as noted previously.

This number is based on auction appearances, research, and study of certified populations as published by PCGS and NGC, plus an element of guesswork. Many certified coins, especially those that are valuable, have been resubmitted many times. Accordingly, 10 listings or events in a population report may represent just two or three different coins.

Both PCGS and NGC have Registry Sets—competitions in which thousands of participants strive to have the greatest number of points possible. Each service gives instructions on how these numbers are compiled. As a general rule, for the PCGS Registry a coin that is the finest of its kind or is tied for the finest wins many points. Ditto for the NGC competition. Such coins can be exceedingly expensive. An eagle that is as common as can be in MS-65 grade can be inexpensive and very desirable to the traditional specialist. If just a few are known in, say, MS-67 grade, the price for a Registry Set player can be many multiples of the MS-65 valuation. High valuations for ultra-grade eagles can be risky as two dangers are present: (1) More coins will be certified from repatriations and other sources, and (2) Coins will graduate a point or more in certified grade.

The *velocity* of coin movement in the market has gone from very slow in early times to a rapid pace today. It is not unusual for the same coin to appear in a half dozen different auctions during a span of a decade or two, often with different grades each time.

In modern times PCGS and NGC have added + marks to certain Mint State listings. Such listings with + marks, such as MS-64+, are incorporated into the regular listings, such as MS-64. As it is, population reports suggest that coins with + marks are of great rarity, whereas it is a reality that many earlier coins, if regraded now, would also have plus marks. Probably more than 90 percent of eagles certified by PCGS and NGC were done before + marks were invented as additions.

More about population reports: These reports are among the most misunderstood elements in the marketplace today. These are the number of the *highest-graded* Mint State coins known to collectors today. For most listings we show the top two, three, or four grade categories.

Emphasis is placed on the more valuable coins. Coins that are not valuable usually exist in huge quantities, but population reports show them to be rare. An example is furnished by the population of NGC-certified 1894 eagles:

AU-50 (1), AU-53 (11), AU-55 (26), AU-58 (200), MS-60 (1,760), MS-61 (13,041), MS-62 (15,881), MS-63 (6,169), MS-64 (436), MS-65 (16).

To the uninitiated it would seem that an AU-50 coin is a fantastic rarity. In reality it is a common coin for which certification would not add value. Its market value is mostly dependent on its melt or bullion value. Certification adds nothing. On the other hand, at the high end of the range we see that MS-64 coins are plentiful and that MS-65 coins are somewhat rare. The owner of an MS-64 coin might want to send it one, two, or more times to see if it could be upgraded to MS-65. If this could happen, the certification fee would be worth it.

We see that only 16 have been certified as MS-65, and not a single coin finer. This 1894 NGC MS-65 is "top of the pop," as they say, or top of the population list. What a coup it would be if one of these could be certified as MS-66! As of early 2017 when these figures were compiled, we have no way of knowing how many of the 16 certification *events* represent different coins. Are there 5 different coins? Or 10? Or 12?

To reiterate: beyond this, there is a danger present. Anyone paying a deservedly strong price for an MS-65 is in real danger of one or more being certified as MS-66 or 67 in the future for reasons given above.

The operative advice here is: *be careful!*

Estimated Population (Circulated Grades)

This is the author's estimate or educated (hopefully!) guess of the number of coins in numismatic hands in grades below MS-60. Under this heading there is often an explanation as to why these coins exist in the quantities they do, such as: "EF and AU are the usually seen grades as many were repatriated from overseas holdings. AU coins tend to be heavily bagmarked."

Key to Collecting

Here I have compiled suggestions and observations of numismatic interest, mostly quick takes, some of which invite further exploration beyond the scope of this book.

Market News and Commentary

This section gives information from past auctions, citations showing how elements of rarity and publicity have changed over the years, and other transitions that have taken place. These are *not* the latest listings nor the highest grades and prices. For that information consult the Web sites of the auction companies.

Among auction citations, emphasis has been placed on early listings as these often include comments and theories from an era in which factual information was lacking. In modern times auction listings have often been recitations of population reports published by PCGS and NGC, not much on numismatic history. For expanded information many auction catalogs are available for free on the Newman Numismatic Portal Web site.

Eagles and double eagles—the two largest regular-gold denominations—are unusual in that their market values are often tied more to the value of gold bullion than to pure numismatic demand. A gold eagle contains about a half ounce of pure gold plus

10 percent alloy. For the vast majority of $10 gold coins of the Liberty Head (1838–1907) and Indian Head (1907–1933) years there are far more coins available than there are specialists who collect them. For many issues from the late 1800s onward there are thousands of Mint State coins that can be purchased. The number of collectors assembling Liberty Head eagles by date and mintmark is probably fewer than 100, and those collecting the more popular Indian Head eagles, perhaps 1,000 to 2,000.

Most collectors acquire whatever their budget permits, and often this does not include the expensive rarities. Thus, a fine collection of Liberty Head eagles may lack some Philadelphia Mint dates in the 1860s and 1870s and may not have the rare 1870-CC and some of the other Carson City issues. Most collectors assembling Indian Head eagles omit the With-Periods coins of 1907, the 1920-S, 1930-S, and 1933. This is not particularly unusual. A fine collection of Liberty Seated dollars may lack the 1851, 1852, and 1873-CC, and no more than a handful of collectors can ever own an 1870-S dollar as fewer than a dozen are known to exist.

HISTORIC DEALERS OF PAST AND PRESENT

Significant dealers of the past and present are often mentioned under each coin listing. The following sketches of some of the more well-known groups may be of interest for historical and numismatic context.

In the 19th century many important sales were conducted by W. Elliot Woodward of Roxbury, Massachusetts. Woodward, a polymath, was a pharmacist by trade, and studied numismatics intently. His library comprised thousands of volumes. His first auction was held in 1860. Within a few years he was considered to be the most erudite of the coin dealers. The *American Journal of Numismatics* called him "the lion of the day."

His main competitor was Edward Cogan, who came from England to America in 1855 and set up as an art dealer in Philadelphia. He enjoyed coins, and in the autumn of 1858 had a small mail-bid sale ("letter offering") of large cents that realized a few hundred dollars. Not long afterward, Cogan made a specialty of numismatics, and later moved to New York City where he conducted auctions into the early 1880s. He was a prideful, boastful man who liked to refer to himself as the "father of the rare coin business" in America, based on his 1858 sale. In actuality, by that time a number of others had been in professional numismatics, including John Allan in New York City since the early 1820s.

Toward the end of the 19th century the Chapman brothers were the most prominent dealers who conducted auctions. Samuel Hudson Chapman, born in 1857, and his brother Henry Chapman Jr., born in 1859, went to work in the Philadelphia coin shop of Captain John W. Haseltine when they were teenagers. In 1878 they hung out their own shingle as numismatists and antiquarians, referred to in the trade as the Chapman brothers, although they never used that designation. Their partnership went from one success to another, and in the 1880s they succeeded Woodward as the leading American auction firm. In the summer of 1906 the Chapmans dissolved their partnership. In later years they each conducted their own businesses with great success.

B. Max Mehl was the most famous and perhaps the most successful professional numismatist of the early 1900s. He handled more "name" collections than any other dealer of his time. All of his auctions were conducted by mail bidding, with no in-person gallery representation. He was more of a promoter than a numismatic student. Abe Kosoff likened him to the P.T. Barnum of numismatics. Mehl was personable, kind, and did much to promote numismatics. He really had two businesses in one: his mail-bid sales (never with a public attendance) and a regular coin business on one hand, and on the other the seller of the *Star Rare Coin Encyclopedia* to the general public—suggesting that if they found a rare coin in pocket change, they could sell it to Mehl and help pay Junior's way to college. This was misleading in a way, but it did bring a lot of coins out of hiding. The author knew and met with Mehl in the 1950s, though he passed away in 1957. His numismatic estate was handled by Abe Kosoff.

Concerning Kosoff, he was born in New York and planned to be an accountant, but went into the coin business part time. In 1937 he dove in full time and adopted the Numismatic Gallery trade name. At the end of that decade he had a coin boutique in a New York City jewelry store. Enthusiastic and aggressive from the outset, he handled many coins, including large quantities of gold coins that Mint and Treasury officials rescued from destruction by substituting common varieties. Included were many rarities. This was a win-win situation for numismatics and for the government employees involved; many rare coins were saved from destruction by melting, the government sustained not the slightest loss, collectors gained 1933 $10 and $20 gold coins and other pieces that would have been destroyed otherwise, and the government employees made money on the side in an era in which the Depression was still ongoing. In 1944 he took in Abner Kreisberg as a partner. In the late 1940s the firm relocated to Beverly Hills, California. From the 1940s into the very early 1950s the Numismatic Gallery and Stack's were America's leading auctioneers. The Numismatic Gallery split up in the spring of 1954. Abe Kosoff pursued his own business and conducted sales, such as the Melish auction, and Abner Kreisberg set up Coin Gallery in the Numismatic Gallery store on North Beverly Drive in Beverly Hills. Later, he took Jerry Cohen of Tucson, Arizona, as a partner.

In the meantime the Stack siblings, Joseph, Morton, and their sister Shirley, set up business in New York City in 1933, in the depth of the Depression. By dint of hard work and good business sense their trade grew by leaps and bounds. Their first auction was held in 1935. In time they had a virtual stranglehold on handling many "name" collections. In 1939 when the World's Fair was conducted in New York City the ANA had its annual convention there, and Stack's was the official auctioneer—the first of many ANA sales conducted by the firm.

In later years the business was conducted by their sons—Harvey, Ben, and Norman. For a while Ben split off and operated the Imperial Coin Company in Las Vegas, later returning to New York City. Harvey was the main figure in the gallery at 123 West 57th Street, and Norman was the primary cataloger. A large staff of experts worked at Stack's and its Coin Galleries subsidiary. Dr. Vladimir Clain-Stefanelli, one of the professionals, was appointed curator of the National Numismatic Collection in 1956. Over the years Stack's was the most important dealership in relation to that collection. The Josiah K. Lilly Collection of gold coins, formed exclusively by Stack's, was donated by the Lilly estate to the Smithsonian and was the source of nearly all of the mintmarked eagles in the National Numismatic Collection.

Bowers and Merena Galleries, founded in Wolfeboro, New Hampshire, by the author and partner Raymond N. Merena was the favorite of many and was the leading worldwide auctioneer of rare coins in its time, from 1992 to 2000. Many name collections were handled, including those of Emery May Holden Norweb, Virgil M. Brand (selections therefrom), Louis E. Eliasberg, Harry W. Bass Jr., and Walter Childs—this being a short list. American Numismatic Rarities was established in Wolfeboro in 2003 by Christine Karstedt, who built a staff (including the author) that resulted in almost overnight success. By 2006, when the firm was merged into Stack's, ANR had become the world's second-largest rare-coin auctioneer. Today it is an element of Stack's Bowers Galleries.

Heritage Auctions, billing itself as the world's largest collectibles auctioneer, handles comics, posters, art, jewelry, and other items in addition to rare coins. The coin part began with the businesses of Steve Ivy and Jim Halperin (and his New England Rare Coin Galleries). Both are entrepreneurs who have grown their business to great prominence, now with offices in a number of different cities around the world. In the early 2000s Heritage was the nation's highest-volume numismatic auction company. The firm branched into other areas including art, fashions, books, posters, and other collectibles. The Heritage Web site is a rich resource for coin auction information.

Ira and Larry Goldberg, cousins, grew up in the family business, Superior Galleries, in Los Angeles. In the early years stamps were a specialty, adding coins in a large way in the 1960s and 1970s, during which time, continuing to the turn of the 20th century, many "name" collections were handled. Superior was dissolved following business difficulties, and Ira and Larry formed Ira & Larry Goldberg Auctioneers in Beverly Hills, having enjoyed a fine trade ever since.

Regency Auctions (Laura Sperber), Spink America, Bonhams, and other firms have also sold many coins.

PROOFS
Proof Mintage

This figure is estimated for early issues through the 1850s and is taken from the *Mint Report* for later dates.

Estimated Population (Proofs)

This number is an estimate of the number of Proofs known to exist today. The National Numismatic Collection in the Smithsonian Institution has many Proofs from 1838 into the 1850s and a full run of all dates after that time. The American Numismatic Society has gold Proof sets from the 1860s into the early 1900s, as does the Joseph Mitchelson Collection preserved by the Connecticut State Library. These are included in the estimates. For most Proofs a significant number of any given mintage has been lost by having been spent when they had little resale value.

Proof Commentary

Comments relating to dies, striking, market appearances, or other factors.

MARKET VALUES

Average market values as of press time have been provided by Whitman Publishing using information from over 100 different professionals and others who have contributed to *A Guide Book of United States Coins* and to the *Guide Book of United States Coins: Deluxe Expanded Edition.*

These are suggested typical market values for an *average quality* specimen of the grade indicated. As gradeflation or liberalized interpretation has been practiced by the third-party services in recent decades, a coin certified, for example, as MS-65 might be of the same quality as one certified as MS-63 or MS-64 in 1990, when certified grades were viewed by many as conservative. Many of yesteryear's About Uncirculated coins are today's Mint State. For that reason it is not possible to use historic *Guide Book* or other prices to formulate accurate market trends or performance.

The prices are intended to reflect what an informed buyer will pay to an established and reputable seller, at the time this book goes to press. Market prices can and do vary among sellers and buyers at any given time. As a study of auction prices reveals, it is often the case that in a given year multiple examples of a particular variety in a given grade and certified by the same service can vary widely. It is wise to check multiple sources before making purchases.

8

Early $10 Gold Coins, 1795–1804

CAPPED BUST TO RIGHT, SMALL EAGLE REVERSE (1795–1797)

Designer: *Robert Scot.* **Weight:** *17.50 grams.*
Composition: *.9167 gold, .0833 silver and copper.*
Diameter: *Approximately 33 mm.* **Edge:** *Reeded.* **Mint:** *Philadelphia.*

Inaugural Design

The first gold eagles were struck in September 1795, soon after the initial coinage of half eagles, which began in July. The motif is attributed to Chief Engraver Robert Scot. The obverse illustrates Miss Liberty facing right, wearing a cloth cap, also known in the *Guide Book* as the "Capped Bust to Right" style. The star count for 1795-dated coins is 15, arranged 10 along the border behind the head and 5 at the right-side border in front of the head, and is popularly known as "5 stars facing" or "10x5 stars." Coins dated 1796 and 1797 had different obverse star counts.

The reverse depicts an eagle perched on a palm branch holding a wreath aloft in its beak, the "Small Eagle reverse" as it is known. The inscription UNITED STATES OF AMERICA surrounds the border. There are two widely publicized varieties of the reverse on 1795 eagles: 13 leaves in branch (or 12, depending upon the method of counting), this being the usual variety; and the rare variety with only 9 leaves in the branch. 1796- and 1797-dated pieces have 11 leaves in the branch. Little notice of the leaf count in the branch was given in catalogs until recent decades. Thus, unless specific coins auctioned years ago were illustrated in the catalogs—which was not often the case—we have no way of attributing them today unless there is a pedigree chain linking them to modern times.

Both obverse and reverse of the 1795 eagle are the same general design as the 1795 half eagle.

The total mintage of the 1795 to 1797 $10 gold coins with the Small Eagle reverse is probably fewer than 14,000 coins, although the exact figure may never be known, as in the early years the Mint did not keep strict accounting of calendar year mintage vis-à-vis the dates actually appearing on the coins.

Collecting Commentary

It is evident that most $10 coins dated 1795 to 1797 with the Small Eagle reverse were used in domestic commerce, although many were probably exported. As these coins circulated, they acquired wear, with the result that grades such as VF are often seen today.

Most collectors who seek early eagles desire one of each date and major type as listed in *A Guide Book of United States Coins*. Collecting by die varieties has been done only by Harry W. Bass Jr., to the best of my knowledge. In the 18th century J. Colvin Randall studied die varieties and made a listing of those seen, but no copy is known to exist today. Scattered references to Randall numbers can be found in the auction catalogs of W. Elliot Woodward. In July 1934 a study by Edgar H. Adams, "Early United States Gold Coins: Eagles," was published in *The Coin Collector's Journal*.

In 1967 Walter H. Breen, America's most publicized numismatic scholar from the 1950s through the late 1970s, created a monograph, *United States Eagles*, with die combinations. This was not widely distributed in its time and remains obscure today. This was rendered obsolete in 1988 by the die varieties listed in *Walter Breen's Complete Encyclopedia of U.S. and Colonial Coins*.

In 1999 Anthony J. Taraszka published *United States Ten Dollar Gold Eagles, 1795–1804* with Taraszka numbers and letters for various dies. This was a *tour de force* in research and was widely acclaimed and used.

The *Harry W. Bass Jr. Museum Sylloge* by the author and Mark Borckardt, 1991, is an essential text and incorporates years of research by Harry Bass.

The latest study and the most widely used today is *Early U.S. Gold Coin Varieties: A Study of Die States, 1795–1834*, by John W. Dannreuther and Harry W. Bass Jr. (posthumously). BD numbers refer to such listings. Bass, in his lifetime, was a consummate scholar of gold varieties. His extensive notes on early issues were compiled in book form by Dannreuther and published by Whitman in 2006.

Here is a synopsis of the varieties for each year:

1795: 5 varieties coined from three obverse and three reverse dies. The most famous combination is BD-3 (Taraszka-3) with 9 leaves in the palm branch. This reverse die was used only in 1795 and, apparently, for only a short time.

The most often encountered $10 coin of this type is the 1795 with 13 leaves on the reverse, which exists in 4 die combinations (BD and Taraszka–1, 2, 4, and 5). The 1795 with 9 leaves (BD and Taraszka-3) accounts for only a tiny fraction of the survivors of that year.

1796: 1 variety coined from a single die pair, BD-1 (Taraszka-1). The reverse die used to coin the 1796 was also used to make the 1797 Small Eagle reverse gold eagle.

The eagles of 1796 are of the same general design, but have 16 stars, reflective of the addition of the sixteenth state to the Union, Tennessee, on June 1, 1796. The stars are arranged 8 left and 8 right ("8 stars facing"). As a class, the eagles of 1796 are considerably scarcer than those dated 1795.

1797: 1 variety coined with the Type I Small Eagle reverse (Taraszka-1). A 1797 obverse was combined with the reverse found on 1796-dated $10 coins.

The eagles of 1797 are the scarcest of all within this type. The star count remained at 16, but in this year the arrangement was 12 left and 4 right ("4 stars facing"). Of the 1797 $10 gold coins, two reverse varieties exist—the presently discussed Small Eagle type, which is considerably the rarer, and the 1797 Heraldic Eagle type with stars arranged 10 left and 6 right, discussed later under Type II $10 Gold.

Small Eagle Varieties, 1795–1797

EAGLES OF 1795

1795: BD-1, Taraszka-1, Breen 1-A. *Obverse:* The Y in LIBERTY is crowded between the T and star 11; *definitive.* *Reverse:* The tip of the broad leaf appears to touch the left curve of the U in UNITED; *definitive.* This is the most plentiful 1795 variety with a population estimate greater than the other four varieties combined, according to John Dannreuther in the BD reference, and it was the *first-struck* 1795 variety, making it the quintessential type coin to represent the design.

1795: BD-2, Taraszka-2, Breen 2-A. *Obverse:* The upper-right tip of the 5 in 1795 is covered by drapery; *definitive.* *Reverse:* The tip of the broad leaf appears to touch the left curve of the U in UNITED; *definitive.*

1795: BD-3; Taraskza-3, Breen 4-C. *Obverse:* The upper-right tip of the 5 in 1795 is covered by drapery; *definitive.* *Reverse:* There are *9 leaves* in palm branch; *definitive.*

1795: BD-4, Taraszka-4, Breen 3-B. *Obverse:* The ray of star 10 almost touches the cap; *definitive.* *Reverse:* The tip of the broad leaf is distant from the left curve of the U in UNITED; *definitive.*

1795: BD-5, Taraszka-5, Breen 4-B. *Obverse:* The upper-right tip of the 5 in 1795 is covered by drapery; *definitive.* *Reverse:* The tip of the broad leaf is distant from the left curve of the U in UNITED; *definitive.*

EAGLE OF 1796

1796: BD-1, Taraszka-6, Breen 1-A. *Obverse:* There was only one obverse die for this year; *definitive.* *Reverse:* There was also only one reverse die for this year; *definitive.*

EAGLE OF 1797 (SMALL EAGLE REVERSE)

1797: BD-1, Taraszka-7, Breen 1-A. *Obverse:* The stars are arranged 12 to the left and 4 to the right; *definitive.* *Reverse:* There was only one Small Eagle reverse die for this year; *definitive.*

Grading Standards

MS-60 to 70 (Mint State). *Obverse:* At MS-60, some abrasion and contact marks are evident, most noticeably on the hair to the left of Miss Liberty's forehead and on the higher-relief areas of the cap. Luster is present, but may be dull or lifeless, and interrupted in patches. At MS-63, contact marks

1795, 13 Leaves; BD-5. Graded MS-63.

are few, and abrasion is very light. An MS-65 coin has hardly any abrasion, and contact marks are so minute as to require magnification. Luster should be full and rich. On prooflike coins in any Mint State grade, abrasion and surface marks are much more noticeable. Coins above MS-65 exist more in theory than in reality for this type—but they do exist, and are defined by having fewer marks as perfection is approached. *Reverse:* Comments apply as for the obverse, except that abrasion and contact marks are most noticeable on the breast and head of the eagle. The field area is mainly protected by the eagle, branch, and lettering.

AU-50, 53, 55, 58 (About Uncirculated). *Obverse:* Light wear is seen on the cheek, the hair immediately to the left of the face, and the cap, more so at AU-50 than at AU–53 or 55. An AU-58 coin has minimal traces of wear. An AU-50 coin has luster in protected areas among the stars and letters, with little

1796. Graded AU-58.

in the open fields or on the portrait. At AU-58, most luster is present in the fields, but is worn away on the highest parts of the motifs. *Reverse:* Comments as preceding, except that the eagle shows light wear on the breast and head in particular, but also at the tip of the wing on the left and elsewhere. Luster ranges from perhaps 40% remaining in protected areas (at AU-50) to nearly full mint bloom (at AU-58).

Illustrated coin: This example shows light wear overall, with hints of original luster in protected areas.

EF-40, 45 (Extremely Fine).
Obverse: Wear is evident all over the portrait, with some loss of detail in the hair to the left of Miss Liberty's face. Excellent detail remains in low-relief areas of the hair, such as the front curl and at the back of her head. The stars show wear, as do the date and letters. Luster, if present

1795, 9 Leaves; BD-3. Graded EF-45.

at all, is minimal and in protected areas. *Reverse:* Wear is greater than on an About Uncirculated coin. The breast, neck, and legs of the eagle lack nearly all feather detail. More wear is seen on the edges of the wing. Some traces of luster may be seen, more so at EF-45 than at EF-40.

VF-20, 30 (Very Fine).
Obverse: The higher-relief areas of hair are well worn at VF-20, less so at VF-30. The stars are flat at their centers. *Reverse:* Wear is greater, the eagle is flat in most areas, and about 40% to 60% of the wing feathers can be seen.

1795, 13 Leaves; BD-2. Graded VF-30.

The Capped Bust to Right eagle coin with Small Eagle reverse is seldom collected in grades lower than VF-20.

1795, 13 Leaves Below Eagle

Circulation-Strike Mintage: 5,583 (all varieties)

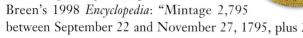

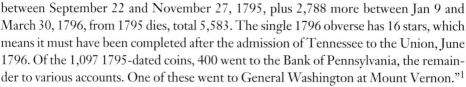

Notes regarding mintages: From Walter Breen's 1998 *Encyclopedia*: "Mintage 2,795 between September 22 and November 27, 1795, plus 2,788 more between Jan 9 and March 30, 1796, from 1795 dies, total 5,583. The single 1796 obverse has 16 stars, which means it must have been completed after the admission of Tennessee to the Union, June 1796. Of the 1,097 1795-dated coins, 400 went to the Bank of Pennsylvania, the remainder to various accounts. One of these went to General Washington at Mount Vernon."[1]

At the time the Mint paid little attention as to whether dies were used later than the calendar years dated. If dies had not yet been hardened, as for two of 1798, they might be overdated, in that instance 1798, 8 Over 7.

Estimated population (Mint State): *60–80.* Quite a few pieces were saved as souvenirs or otherwise, with the result that in Mint State the 1795 with 13 leaves is seen more often than all other Mint State Type I eagles combined. Still, with the great demand for this date as the first year of the design, and the often long retention of specimens in cabinets, it usually takes intensive searching to locate a choice example. Grades range from MS-60 up to the choice level. Any coin finer is an ultra rarity.

Estimated population (circulated grades): *500–650.* VF, EF, and AU are typical grades, with most being in the latter two categories. The 1795 with 13 leaves is rare enough to be highly acclaimed whenever one is offered, but available enough that the advanced numismatist will have no trouble obtaining an example.

Submissions certified at highest grades (as of March 2017): *PCGS:* MS-62 (20), MS-63 (15), MS-64 (2), MS-65 (5), MS-66 (1). *NGC:* MS-62 (18), MS-63 (11), MS-64 (4), MS-65 (3).

Die data: The obverse has stars arranged 10 to the left and 5 to the right. The reverse has 13 (or 12, depending upon how they are counted) leaves in the palm branch.

Characteristics of striking and die notes: Many if not most high-grade specimens have prooflike surfaces, though a few are lustrous and frosty.

Key to collecting: Beginning with this listing, the first in the eagle series, biographical and related notes are given concerning certain numismatists. These will serve as a background to the many later offerings by the same people and companies.

As to the 1795 eagle with 13 leaves, this coin has always been very popular and is usually the first choice when selecting an example for a type set to illustrate the 1795 to 1797 Small Eagle reverse. Most coins grade Extremely Fine or About Uncirculated.

MARKET NEWS AND COMMENTARY

When coin collecting became widely popular in America starting in the late 1850s early gold coins of the 1795 to 1804 years were sought by numismatists who could afford them. Accordingly, auction listings from this time on are numerous.

The number of leaves in the reverse branch was not published until the early 1930s, and even then the leaf count was hardly noticed. Most had 13 leaves, but a few had just 9. Among early auction descriptions the leaf count was not mentioned and is not known today, except in rare instances in which they were illustrated.

The following comments are selected from hundreds of listings. As the 1795 was the first year of the design, the Chapman brothers, Mehl, and others typically prefaced their listings with descriptions of the type, mostly edited from the following descriptions. Descriptions in catalogs from the late 1900s onward sometimes ran over 100 words, mostly salesmanship, similarly edited from the following.

In his sale of the John F. McCoy Collection, May 1864, W. Elliot Woodward offered lot 1930: "1795. Splendid Uncirculated, scarce." This coin realized $28, a very strong price for the cradle days of collecting U.S. gold coins. The McCoy Collection offered a date run of early $10 gold coins from 1795 to 1804, including two reverse varieties of 1797. Woodward's October 1864 sale of the Levick, Emery, Ilsley, and Abbey Collections had lot 1614: "1795 Very Fine; Uncirculated, scarce." The term "very fine" meant "very nice" to Woodward and his contemporaries. This coin brought in $21.50. "Nearly Proof," another term of the time, was used by the same cataloger in his March 1863 sale of the Bache, Bertsch, Lightbody, Lilliendahl, Vinton, and Watson Collections, lot 2734: "1795 Splendid, Uncirculated, nearly Proof; scarce." This sold for $20.

How the following coin would be rated today is hard to determine from Edward Cogan's description in December 1878 of a coin in the James E. Root Collection, lot 1526: "1795 Eagle. A little circulated, but good and desirable." It sold for $15.25.

Woodward, in his sale of June 1885, offered coins from the collection of J. Colvin Randall, this being the earliest such detailed listing found, lot 841: "1795 No. 1; reverse, small standing eagle holding an olive wreath, a leaf in the olive branch turns down, but does not touch U in UNITED; splendid, nearly Proof, very rare." This coin sold for $16. Next is lot 842: "1795 No. 2; small eagle reverse, in the olive branch the turned up leaf touches the U; Very Fine indeed, almost Proof surface, rare." This sold for $16. From lot 843: "1795 No. 3; small stars; reverse, small eagle with wings widely spread; nearly Proof, rare." It was sold for $15.50. Finally, lot 844: "1795 No. 4; small stars; reverse, eagle with olive wreath; very rare variety." This sold for $14. Randall created variety numbers for early gold coins that were used in a few catalogs of the era. No copy of the original study or expanded listing has been found. Earlier, Randall created descriptions for die varieties of silver coins, but these silver listings were plagiarized by John W. Haseltine and published under the heading of "Type Table" in 1881, without credit to Randall.

Reading early auction listings can be very enjoyable. The Numismatic Bibliomania Society invites those interested in out-of-print publications to join. The Newman Numismatic Portal, a Web site in the process of being developed, offers many auction catalogs.

In the early 1900s descriptions of die varieties of the 1795 eagle were usually not given, unless there were two or more coins in the same sale. In the latter instances S. Hudson Chapman and Thomas L. Elder were in the forefront. Chapman's catalog of the David S. Wilson sale, March 1907, included:

> Lot 1: 1795 Bust of Liberty right, draped, with cap; above, LIBERTY, beneath, 1795; 10 stars behind and 5 before head. Reverse, UNITED STATES OF AMER-ICA. Eagle standing on palm branch bears wreath of laurel. Die in which top of 5 joins bust, and star distant from cap. Reverse: Small flake out of die between F-A, Eagle's wing clear of R. Uncirculated. Mint luster. Sold for $32. Lot 2: 1795 Same obverse die. *Reverse:* Eagle's wing touches R and leaf of laurel touches U. Extremely Fine. Sold for $31. Lot 3: 1795 Star touches cap, but 5 clear of bust. Reverse, same die as first. Very Fine. [Sold for $33]

In April 1956, in the Thomas G. Melish Collection, Abe Kosoff offered lot 2345:

> 1795. A superb Uncirculated gem. One of the finest specimens I have seen. Catalogs for $300 but this beauty is far superior to one I saw recently which had an asking price of $500.

This sold for $460. The so-called "Melish Collection" was mainly the consignment of R.E. Naftzger Jr. of California, who wanted to remain anonymous. Some of these coins were from the estate of Thomas G. Melish, a Cincinnati industrialist who at one time controlled the pricing and distribution of 1936 Cincinnati commemorative half dollars and, later, was president of the ANA.

In modern times, the finest of all 1795 eagles is generally conceded to be the one offered in Part 3 of the Garrett Collection (Bowers and Ruddy Galleries, October 1980), lot 1655:

> 1795 Choice Brilliant Uncirculated, prooflike. A virtually flawless piece. The finest coin by far we have ever seen of this issue. Well centered, exceedingly well struck, without adjustment marks, and a gem in every respect. One of the most important coins in the Garrett Collection. Ex George Stenz Collection; Ed Frossard's sale of the Stenz Collection of Modern Coins, Medals and Tokens, February 1880, lot 636; T. Harrison Garrett Collection; T. Harrison Garrett to Robert and John Work Garrett, by descent, 1888; Robert Garrett interest to John Work Garrett, 1919; transfer completed 1921; John Work Garrett to The Johns Hopkins University, by gift, 1942.

T. Harrison Garrett, a scion in the family that controlled the Baltimore & Ohio Railroad, began his interest in coins in 1864 while a student at Princeton. In the 1870s and 1880s he spent much of his life studying and enjoying rare coins in Evergreen House, his mansion on North Charles Street in Baltimore (today owned and conserved by Johns Hopkins University). After his death in a boating accident on Chesapeake Bay in 1888, his coins passed to his son Robert, then to another son, Ambassador John Work Garrett, as noted in the provenance listing.

This coin sold for $130,000 to D. Brent Pogue and his father Mack Pogue. The Pogue Collection, Part II, sale by Stack's Bowers Galleries and Sotheby's, September 2015, included the same coin, lot 2092, now attributed as 1795 BD-4 and graded as MS-66 by PCGS. The description was done by John Kraljevich of the firm. It sold for $2,585,000, the highest price for any eagle sold at auction.

Brent Pogue discovered the appeal of rare coins as a young teenager in 1974. By study and connoisseurship, backed by a family that was prominent in real estate development, Brent spent nearly 40 years forming a collection that emphasized federal coins from 1792 to about 1840. Nearly every one of the coins was among the finest of its kind, and many were the absolute finest. Included was the finest set of 1795 to 1804 eagles by Guide Book varieties ever assembled, not to overlook treasures in other series (two 1804 Class I silver dollars, the only 1822 $5 in private hands, and more). Working through the author in company with Christine Karstedt, the Pogue family consigned the collection to Stack's Bowers Galleries in 2014. This set the stage for two books about the collection (with a third in progress) and a memorable series of D. Brent Pogue Collection sales conducted in cooperation with Sotheby's. The first four were held at Sotheby's international headquarters in New York City, and sale five was conducted in March 2016 at the Evergreen House in Baltimore, the ancestral home of the Garrett family. The sales set a world record for the value of a single collection sold at auction.

The July 2003 Bowers and Merena Galleries' ANA sale included lot 4039: "1795 MS-65 PCGS." It sold for $506,000.

From the May 2008 Stack's auction of the Minot Collection, lot 4291: "1795 13 Leaves Below Eagle. MS-63 PCGS." It sold for $402,500. In July 2008 at Stack's auction of the Samuel Berngard and SS *New York* Collections, lot 2564 was offered: "1795 13 Leaves MS-64 PCGS." It sold for $546,250.

The list of 1795 eagles in lower grades or that sold for lower prices is a long one and can be found by consulting sites on the Internet.

F-12	VF-20	EF-40	AU-50	AU-55	MS-60	MS-62	MS-63
$25,000	$35,000	$45,000	$55,000	$67,500	$100,000	$150,000	$300,000

1795, 9 Leaves Below Eagle

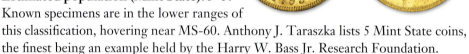

**Circulation-Strike Mintage: *210–500*
(Bass-Dannreuther estimate)**

Estimated population (Mint State): *3–5*.
Known specimens are in the lower ranges of this classification, hovering near MS-60. Anthony J. Taraszka lists 5 Mint State coins, the finest being an example held by the Harry W. Bass Jr. Research Foundation.

Estimated population (circulated grades): *20–25+*. As this variety is not well known and has been publicized only in recent decades, more may exist. Certification service data is unreliable, as 1795 $10 gold coins have been mostly listed by date, rather than by variety. The Bass-Dannreuther study suggests 20 to 22 known totally (all grades).

Submissions certified at highest grades (as of March 2017): *PCGS*: MS-60 (1), MS-61 (3), MS-63 (3). ***NGC*:** MS-61 (1), MS-63 (1).

Die data: The obverse has stars arranged 10 to the left and 5 to the right. The reverse has 9 leaves in the palm branch below the eagle instead of the 13 usually seen. The 1795 with 9 Leaves reverse was first described by Edgar H. Adams in the May 1934 issue of *The Coin Collector's Journal*, page 32: "End of stem does not touch or come very close to 'A.' End of one leaf touches center of 'U.' Nine distinct leaves in branch. There is a die defect at the end of the second leaf. Clapp." Walter Breen found that the John H. Clapp Collection did not contain an example, and the coin referred to was probably the one described by Howard R. Newcomb.

Characteristics of striking and die notes: The die seems to have failed at an early time, as all known examples show die failure, most visible at the top of the first T in STATES, the first A in AMERICA, and below the right side of the palm branch.

Key to collecting: This variety is listed in the *Guide Book of United States Coins*, thus creating a strong demand for it. Most buyers have been $10 gold specialists.

MARKET NEWS AND COMMENTARY

The market history of this coin is rather curious. First publicized as an extreme rarity in the early 1960s it caught the attention of Michael Brownlee, of Dallas, Texas, who had as his clients several avid collectors of gold coins and who often acquired duplicates. He found that collectively they owned several of this variety. In time more were discovered.

The New Netherlands' sale of the Cicero Collection on December 1960 included the first detailed auction listing of the variety, lot 61:

1795. Adams 5; Not in Clapp; Newcomer 439. Rarity 8. Eagle standing on branch with nine leaves (regular has thirteen). Extremely Fine, weak in centers and with many adjustment marks; some chips out of planchet (as made) on both sides. The first one we have seen, and only the second we have heard of. Of extreme desirability as a type coin; potentially a $2,000 item! Probably included with the 911 delivered November 27, 1795 the last coinage of the year. The other four varieties have 13 leaves in branch; the 1796-7 have 11. The other specimen known to us is the Newcomer coin, illustrated by Adams in the 1934 Coin Collector's Journal, and it has dropped out of sight. It was VF and cost Newcomer $100, which was then at least double the ordinary price. To account for the rarity of this variety is difficult. Probably the reverse die breaks—at next to right leaf on branch, and the first T in STATES—advanced rapidly, rendering the die useless. At least fifty times rarer than the regular type of this year, which is now at least a $600 coin EF; therefore our estimate is not unreasonable.

This coin sold for $725 after opening at $600. In modern times, the identical specimen was later offered by RARCOA in August 1990, there as lot 956, including this comment:

The coin offered here is the above-named Cicero specimen, sold by New Netherlands, and for accuracy in description, we note that the coin is About Uncirculated from a standpoint of actual wear, but was struck on an imperfect planchet with numerous minor defects on both sides, the most noticeable on the obverse by the 8th star, behind Miss Liberty's head. The fields are prooflike and reflective on both obverse and reverse. Truly a coin for the connoisseur of great rarities.

This time it sold for $23,100.

The October 2001 sale by Stack's and Sotheby's of the Dallas Bank (Jeff Browning) Collection included lot 376: "1795 9 Leaves. Extremely Fine." It sold for $26,450. Browning, a Texas oil man, bought many of his gold coins from R.E. ("Ted") Naftzger Jr., a long-time California collector.

In the FUN sale of January 2007 Heritage included lot 3606: "1795 9 Leaves. AU-55 PCGS." It sold for $149,500. The June 2008 Stack's auction of the Huskey Collection included lot 2054: "1795 $10 9 Leaves. AU-58, NGC." It sold for $207,000. The August 2011 Stack's Bowers Galleries Rarities Auction included lot 7705: "1795 BD-3. 9 Leaves. AU-58 NGC." It sold for $218,500.

The D. Brent Pogue Collection, Part II, by Stack's Bowers Galleries and Sotheby's, September 2015, included lot 2091 (excerpted):

1795 BD-3. 9 Leaves. Mint State-63+ PCGS. Finest in private hands. This is the single finest example certified by PCGS, potentially surpassed by only the Harry Bass Core Collection coin on display at the American Numismatic Association Museum. From Superior Galleries' session of Auction '89, July 1989, lot 908, via RARCOA. [Sold for $1,057,500]

F-12	VF-20	EF-40	AU-50	AU-55	MS-60	MS-62	MS-63
$40,000	$55,000	$77,500	$120,000	$165,000	$250,000	$350,000	$500,000

1796

Circulation-Strike Mintage: *3,500–4,146* (Bass-Dannreuther estimate)

Notes regarding mintages: From Walter Breen's *Encyclopedia*, 1988: "First production run was 2,332 pieces, June 2; total dated 1796, 4,146 pieces, the other two deliveries being 960 on June 21 and 854 on December 22 during the emergency following the yellow fever epidemic."

Robert Hilt, who also studied the series, suggested a mintage of 3,615 from March 25, 1796, to May 2, 1797. Estimating what specific dies were used for certain deliveries is mainly guesswork and usually does not allow for the seemingly realistic fact that a delivery could have been from more than one die pair. As also noted elsewhere, Hilt, Harry Bass, and Walter Breen studied the same delivery figures for early eagles and came up with different theories. In actuality, Mint records tell delivery dates from the coiner to the treasurer, but do not say what obverse and reverse dies were used. It is not correct, in my opinion, to state that all coins delivered on a certain date were from the same die pair.

Estimated population (Mint State): *10–14.* Such pieces are usually very attractive, of rich yellow gold, and are highly prooflike, so much so that some have been called "Proof" in the past. Most probably, all 1796 $10 coins were made with prooflike surfaces in the regular course of business.

Estimated population (circulated grades): *140–180.* Scarce by any evaluation, the 1796, the second year of the type, is seen far less often than the 1795. EF and AU are typical grades. As is the case with all early $10 dates, some exist with jewelry mountings or evidence of polishing; such coins are described in various auction listings (throughout the present text, few such citations are given).

Submissions certified at highest grades (as of March 2017): *PCGS:* MS-60 (1), MS-61 (3), MS-63 (3). *NGC:* MS-60 (1), MS-61 (1), MS-63 (2).

Die data: The obverse has stars arranged 8 to the left and 8 to the right. Dr. Montroville W. Dickeson, *American Numismatical Manual* (1859) observed:

> The designs the same as the preceding [year] with the addition of another star, emblematic of the admission of Tennessee into the Union. The system of the adornment of our coinage was commenced, not only upon the gold, but the silver and copper, but afterwards abandoned. We think the adding of such a symbol, upon the admission of a state, as an expressive and beautiful idea; and we cannot but regret that it was not continued. Of this emission there was one type and two varieties. They are extremely rare.

Today, only one die variety is recognized.

Characteristics of striking and die notes: High-grade specimens usually have prooflike surfaces. Late states show an obverse die crack.

Key to collecting: This is a very popular issue and is generally collected for the design type or as part of a set of *Guide Book*–listed varieties. Most grade EF or AU.

MARKET NEWS AND COMMENTARY

Among the earliest offerings is one in the February 1859 sale of the Henry Bogert Collection by Augustus B. Sage, lot 1209: "1796 Eagle. *Extremely Fine*." It sold for $12.50 to John Curtis, pioneer New York City rare coin dealer. Sage, a numismatic *wunderkind*, is best remembered today as the teenage founder of the American Numismatic Society in March 1858 at a meeting at his home at 121 Essex Street, New York City. From 1857 through early 1860 he was one of the most prominent figures in professional numismatics.

W. Elliot Woodward included this in his May 1864 sale of the John F. McCoy Collection, lot 1931: "1796 Uncirculated, almost Proof, extremely rare." It sold for $35.50, a strong price for the era. This later reappeared in Woodward's sale of the Heman Ely Collection in January 1884. Woodward, in his March 1883 sale of the A. Dohrmann Collection, offered lot 489: "1796 Very fine, rare." It sold for $17.50. In October 1980 it was offered in the Garrett Collection, lot 1656: "1796 AU-50. Well centered, well struck, and without adjustment marks. Light even wear on obverse and reverse covers what originally virtually a full Proof surface. An extraordinary striking. Obtained by T. Harrison Garrett from the Dohrmann Collection." It sold for $40,000 in the modern era in a vastly expanded market. It is interesting to see the changing grade descriptions. In 1882 "Very Fine" meant "very nice" or a "very choice" specimen. Dohrmann also had a magnificent collection of gold ore, nuggets, and related minerals, much of which is preserved today at the Harvard Mineralogical Museum.

The October 1996 Spink America sale of selections from the Byron Reed Collection included lot 151:

> 1796 Some tiny marks and planchet porosity, Uncirculated, much sharper at the centers than usual, sharp feather details on the reverse eagle, golden toning in the protected areas, from a mintage of 4,146 coins, of which perhaps just three or four dozen are now accounted for in all grades.

The coin sold for $66,000. In September 2005 the American Numismatic Rarities sale of the C.L. Lee Collection included the same coin as lot 1301: "1796 MS-62 PCGS. Ex the Byron Reed Collection sold by Spinks in 1996." This time around it sold for $115,000. Byron Reed, a pioneer land developer in Omaha, built one of the finest coin collections of his time. After his death in 1890 it passed to the Omaha City Library. To raise money, coins were sold in 1996. The remainder of the collection is now with the Durham Western Heritage Museum in Omaha. The highlight is an 1804 silver dollar.

In March 2004 the American Numismatic Rarities Whitman Expo sale included lot 1490: "1796 MS-62 NGC." It sold for $108,100. The Whitman Coin & Collectibles Expos have been held for many years in the Baltimore Convention Center, three times a year, usually March, June, and November. These are among the top five shows of the year, following the World's Fair of Money (ANA Summer Convention) and the Florida United Numismatists (FUN show).

In the ANA Convention sale in August 2006 Heritage included lot 5540: "1796 AU-58 NGC." It sold for $103,500. The June 2008 Stack's auction of the Huskey Collection included lot 2092: "1796 MS-63 NGC." It sold for $322,000. In the January 2014 Pre-Long Beach sale Ira and Larry Goldberg offered lot 1824: "1796 AU-58 NGC." It sold for $92,062.50. At the Long Beach sale of April 2015 Heritage included lot 5376: "1796 MS-61 PCGS." It sold for $103,500.

The D. Brent Pogue Collection, Part II, by Stack's Bowers Galleries and Sotheby's, September 2015, included lot 2093, which included this as part of the description:

> 1796 BD-1. Mint State-62+ PCGS. Ex Bowers and Ruddy's sale of the Dr. William A. Bartlett Collection, November 1979, lot 2788; Paramount's session of Auction '80, August 1980, lot 950.

The Pogue coin sold for $411,250.

F-12	VF-20	EF-40	AU-50	AU-55	MS-60	MS-62	MS-63
$32,500	$42,500	$55,000	$60,000	$75,000	$125,000	$225,000	$350,000

1797, Small Eagle Reverse

Circulation-Strike Mintage: *1,250–3,615* (Bass-Dannreuther estimate)

Estimated population (Mint State): *4–6.* Although Mint State coins are listed in various auction catalogs, in the modern era very few have been seen or graded at this level. It must be presumed that in Mint State the 1797 Small Eagle is incredibly rare, and if there is such a thing as a gem, it would be even more so. In his historical survey completed in 1980, David W. Akers found as many Mint State 1797 Small Eagle $10 coins as he did of 1796, but today this ratio cannot be verified.

Estimated population (circulated grades): *60–80.* This is the rarest of the $10 dates with the Small Eagle reverse. Most are in the grades of EF and AU, the latter category including examples that years ago were called Uncirculated. These are rare by any evaluation. The offering of an example at auction nearly always furnishes the occasion for expanded commentary.

Submissions certified at highest grades (as of March 2017): *PCGS:* MS-60 (1), MS-61 (2). ***NGC:*** MS-60 (1), MS-61 (4), MS-62 (3), MS-63 (1).

Die data: The obverse has stars arranged 12 to the left and 4 to the right. A unique feature of this variety not seen elsewhere in early American coinage is the relationship of star 1 and the date; star 1 has two points solidly joined to the digit 1 in the date.[2] These are struck from the same reverse die used to coin 1796 eagles.

Dr. Montroville W. Dickeson noted in his *American Numismatical Manual* (1859):

> Of this emission we have met with but one type and three varieties. They are more numerous than any of the previous issues of this denomination, but cannot be said

to be easily obtained. It has been stated that there was an issue of this year with 15 stars on the obverse; we can only say that in our extensive researches we have not been fortunate enough to meet with it, and hence we cannot accede to the correctness of this statement.

Today, all known 1797 eagles have 16 obverse stars. Dickeson does not mention the Heraldic Eagle reverse.

Characteristics of striking and die notes: According to David W. Akers, "Most, if not all, 1797 eagles of this type have a die break in the field below the last (16th) star." Most descriptions of this and other 1797 eagle varieties in catalogs over the years, especially those of earlier days, overlook die cracks. Only in modern times is it possible to learn of die cracks and their progression via auction listings. Although Walter Breen stated that this crack occurred during the die hardening process, it seems likely that it happened during use, as the crack occurs in various progressions."

Key to collecting: This is the last of the Small Eagle reverse varieties. It has always been popular as a representative of the 1795 to 1797 type and also as a *Guide Book*–listed variety. Most are in higher grades such as EF and AU.

MARKET NEWS AND COMMENTARY

From W. Elliot Woodward's sale of the John F. McCoy Collection, May 1864, lot 1932: "1797 With small eagle reverse, four stars facing. This splendid piece is in almost Proof condition and one of the rarest of American gold coins." It sold for $51, the highest price of any $10 coin in the McCoy sale. The buyer was Heman Ely, who was in the process of building an outstanding collection. Elyria, Ohio, was named after his family. The Ely Collection was sold in January 1884 by Woodward, lot 795: "1797 Four stars facing, and small eagle reverse; Very Fine indeed, and one of the rarest pieces in the gold series. Bought in the McCoy Sale, No. 1932, for $51. Should now command at least twice that amount." It sold for $30.50 to Ed Frossard, a dealer who snapped up a bargain. Frossard, who came to America from France, was one of the most scholarly in the professional numismatic community of the late 1800s.

In Woodward's March 1865 sale of the Bache, Bertsch, Lightbody, Lilliendahl, Vinton, and Watson Collections, a "splendid condition" coin was offered, lot 2736: "1797 Small eagle; reverse, four stars facing; in splendid condition and of the highest rarity." It sold for $38 to J. Osborn Emery (whose name appears on the title page of Woodward's December 1865 and March 1880 sales). In this era, indeed for decades afterward, grading and descriptions in all numismatic sales were so erratic and inconsistent that buyers needed to attend sales to examine the coins in person. Collectors usually bid through dealers acting as agents.

In 1867 Woodward bought the gold coin collection of Joseph J. Mickley en bloc and sold the entire group to William Sumner Appleton of Salem, Massachusetts. In 1882 Appleton, having extracted what he wanted, sold or consigned the coins to John C. Schayer, a Boston collector and dealer of whom little has ever been written in numismatic circles. In January 1883 Woodward reacquired many of the Mickley gold coins. Generations later in October 1980, in a different market, Bowers and Ruddy Galleries offered this in the Garrett Collection, Part III, lot 1657:

1797 Small Eagle. AU-50, nearly full prooflike surface. Obtained by T. Harrison Garrett from W. Elliot Woodward on January 18, 1883. Earlier in the collection of William Sumner Appleton and, before that, in the celebrated cabinet of Joseph J. Mickley.

The coin sold for $39,000. Mickley was one of the most prominent collectors in Philadelphia. It is said that he started his interest in 1816 when he was frustrated that he could not find a cent of his birth year, 1799. A repairer of musical instruments by trade, Mickley became one of the most knowledgeable numismatists of the mid-1800s. William Sumner Appleton was one of the most prominent American numismatists in the mid- and late 1800s.

William H. Strobridge, an auction cataloger who was highly regarded in his era, offered this coin in his November 1875 sale of the Colonel James H. Taylor Collection, lot 387: "Eagle. Reverse, small eagle; nearly Proof; splendid. Rare." It sold for $18. The "Almost Proof" term, which has no equivalent today, was in common use in the 19th century. Presumably, it referred to high-grade coins with a prooflike surface.

An especially nice example was offered by B. Max Mehl in his February 1944 sale of the Belden E. Roach Collection, lot 309:

1797 the extremely rare variety with small eagle on reverse. Eleven stars to left and four to right of bust. Beautiful Uncirculated specimen with brilliant semi-proof surface, almost equal to a brilliant Proof. Listed at $175 in only Very Fine. This gem coin is worth at least double that amount.

It sold for $290. This reflects the truism that in this era and for generations earlier, Mint State coins did not bring multiples of circulated examples.

In January 1946 the Numismatic Gallery sale of "The World's Greatest Collection" (F.C.C. Boyd) included lot 629: "1797 Small Eagle. A superb example, Uncirculated." It sold for $275. The descriptions in this sale, even for rarities, often consisted of just one or two sentences. The collection, far from being the world's greatest (but the name stuck), was a fine holding formed by F.C.C. Boyd, a New Jersey businessman, earlier a coin dealer and later specializing in colonial and early American issues.[3]

In the William Cutler Atwater Collection sale, held by B. Max Mehl in June 1946, this was included, lot 1406:

1797. Practically Uncirculated with mint luster; just the slightest touch of cabinet friction. Perfectly centered and well struck; the reverse is really a semi-proof. Very rare and valuable. One of the real rare early eagles. Now catalogs at $225, but has an auction record for a higher amount made two years ago.

It sold for $377.50. This coin was mentioned by Mehl a few years later in his Golden Jubilee sale of May 1950, lot 483:

1797 The rarest type of this scarce date. This is a beautiful Uncirculated specimen with semi-proof surface. Sharp and well centered with broad milled borders. Superior to the specimen in the Atwater Sale which brought $377.50.

The coin sold in 1950 brought $300. In 1948 the coin market entered a slump and remained there for several years.

In January 1984 Stack's sale of the Amon G. Carter Jr. Family Collection included lot 730:

1797 Small Eagle. With the ever-present die crack from the rim below the last star in the field. Brilliant Uncirculated and wholly prooflike. Light planchet adjustment marks.

The 1984 coin sold for $30,250. This coin was later in Stack's Americana sale of January 2000, lot 1859, with a very long description that included this:

> 1797 Small Eagle. Taraszka 7:5-D, Breen 1-A. With there being less than a handful of Mint State survivors of this extremely rare issue, this marvelous coin is certainly a candidate for finest known! Ex Amon G. Carter, Jr. Family Collection (Stack's, January 1984, lot 730).

On this occasion the realization was $135,200. By this time there were many more players in the marketplace and the pricing structure bore little resemblance to what it had been a generation or two earlier.

In August 2006 the American Numismatic Rarities sale of the Old West and Franklinton Collections included lot 1527: "1797 Small Eagle. MS-62 NGC. At one time owned by Harry W. Bass Jr. Later in a Heritage Sale." This coin sold for $276,000.

The D. Brent Pogue Collection, Part II, by Stack's Bowers Galleries and Sotheby's, September 2015, included lot 2094: "1797 BD-1. Small Eagle. Mint State-61 PCGS. Ex Goliad Corporation (Mike Brownlee with backing by Harry W. Bass Jr.), by sale, September 1978." Sold for $440,625.

In the ANA Convention sale of August 2016 Heritage included lot 4306: "1797 Small Eagle, BD-1. MS-61 PCGS." Sold for $258,500. This convention and those several years earlier were held at the Convention Center in Rosemont, Illinois. Stack's Bowers Galleries also had official sales at the same events, working with Heritage in scheduling.

F-12	VF-20	EF-40	AU-50	AU-55	MS-60	MS-62	MS-63
$37,500	$55,000	$75,000	$115,000	$130,000	$215,000	$325,000	$450,000

Capped Bust to Right, Heraldic Eagle Reverse (1797–1804)

Designer: *Robert Scot.* **Weight:** *17.50 grams.*
Composition: *.9167 gold, .0833 silver and copper.*
Diameter: *Approximately 33 mm.* **Edge:** *Reeded.* **Mint:** *Philadelphia.*

New Reverse Design

Beginning with coins dated 1797, the Heraldic Eagle reverse was mated to the obverse style used earlier. In keeping with the new reverse style used on silver and other gold denominations of the era, the reverse depicts an eagle with a shield on its breast, holding in its talons a bundle of arrows and an olive branch, and in its beak a ribbon inscribed E PLURIBUS UNUM. A galaxy of stars and an arc of clouds is above. The inscription UNITED STATES OF AMERICA surrounds the border. There is no mark of denomination or value.

The obverse remained the same as the preceding, except that the star configuration varies on certain issues.

No eagles were struck after 1804, as it was felt that because of rising bullion prices the pieces would be melted or exported as soon as they were produced. The 1804 with plain 4 in date and "beaded" border is a restrike made in the mid-1830s for inclusion in presentation specimen sets, including those given by Edmund Roberts to the Sultan of Muscat in 1835 and the King of Siam in 1836.

It is generally thought that about 120,000 coins were struck of the 1797 to 1804 type with Heraldic Eagle reverse, but the exact figure will never be known due to the Mint's practice of using earlier-dated dies in later times. Mintage figures concerning dated coins are estimates (often delineated by deliveries in Breen's *Encyclopedia*, 1988), but facts are scarce.

Collecting Considerations

If you are forming a type set you will find that issues of 1799, 1800, 1801, or 1803 will be the most likely candidates with the 1799 being the most available. Examples are typically found in Very Fine to AU condition. Uncirculated pieces are rare, and such coins have frosty surfaces. The 1804 usually has problems ranging from strike to surface damage. Beyond that, it is the rarest date of the early 1800s.

The most famous varieties are the two of 1798, 8 Over 7, variously described from rare to incredibly rare—and, by any evaluation, very hard to find—but enough exist that the patient (and well-financed) specialist will have no trouble acquiring one.

Grading of Type II eagles is apt to be erratic, and one person's or a grading service's AU-58 from the conservative era of 1990 may be Mint State today, even up to MS–62 or 63. Eagles of 1804 are nearly always irregular in appearance from buckled or imperfect dies. 1804-dated eagles in particular are subject to widely differing grading interpretations.

There are *many* early $10 coins that have traces of use as jewelry in the form of irregular reeding (usually at the top of the obverse), burnishing, polishing, etc. It is likely that at least 10 percent of survivors fit this category. Such coins are not likely to be certified by the leading services unless such traces are not noticed (which is sometimes the case).

The well-known rarities within this type are the two styles of 1798, 8 Over 7, with stars 9x4 and with stars 7x6, the latter being especially difficult to locate. The 1804 original is regarded as scarce, but quite a few have crossed the auction block during the last century. The 1804 restrike was made in the 1830s for inclusion in diplomatic presentation sets (rather than being made as a delicacy for the numismatic market).

Die varieties of this type form a collecting challenge for the specialist with a generous checking account balance. The beauty of acquiring varieties is that, within a given year, there is little market premium for a rare die combination.

Small Eagle Varieties, 1797–1804

Die identifications are cross-referenced to the same texts used for the Type I $10 coins. The following is a listing of the die varieties known, the star arrangement on the obverse, and other information, contributed by Mark Borckardt. There were 15 different obverse dies and 16 different reverse dies used to coin 1797 to 1804 eagles in combination with Heraldic Eagle reverses. Interestingly, despite careful study by Harry W. Bass Jr. in particular, no new dies or combinations have been found in recent decades. There exists the remote possibility that certain dies used to strike half dollars with the Heraldic Eagle reverse, 1801 to 1807, might be found to have been used as well on eagles, as the dies are of identical size and design.[4] In the series of dimes and $2.50 gold coins, certain Heraldic Eagle dies were used for both denominations.

The following die varieties are listed by Bass-Dannreuther, Taraszka, and Breen numbers.

EAGLES OF 1797 (HERALDIC EAGLE REVERSE)

1797: BD-2, Taraszka-8, Breen 2-B. *Obverse:* Stars are arranged 10 to the left, 6 to the right; *definitive*. This is the only obverse die of this year and type. *Reverse:* The three leftmost stars are aligned and star 3 touches the left center of cloud 4; *definitive*.

1797: BD-3, Taraszka-11, Breen 2-D. *Obverse:* Stars are arranged 10 to the left, 6 to the right; *definitive*. This is the only obverse die of this year and type. *Reverse:* The three leftmost stars form a triangle; *definitive*.

1797: BD-4, Taraszka-12, Breen 2-C. *Obverse:* Stars are arranged 10 to the left, 6 to the right; *definitive*. This is the only obverse die of this year and type. *Reverse:* The three leftmost stars are aligned and star 3 is distant from the left side of cloud 4; *definitive*.

EAGLES OF 1798, 8 OVER 7

1798, 8 Over 7: BD-1, Taraszka-9, Breen 1-A. The star count reverted to 13 for the number of original colonies and would remain at 13. *Obverse:* Stars are arranged 9 to the left, 4 to the right; *definitive*. *Reverse:* There is only one reverse die for this year; *definitive*.

1798, 8 Over 7: BD-2, Taraszka-10, Breen 2-A. *Obverse:* Stars are arranged 7 to the left, 6 to the right; *definitive*. *Reverse:* There is only one reverse die for this year; *definitive*.

EAGLES OF 1799

1799: BD-1, Taraszka-13, Breen unlisted ("6-A"). *Obverse:* Small Stars obverse. The ray of star 9 joins the upper serif of the Y in LIBERTY. The ray of star 13 is extremely close to the drapery; *definitive*. *Reverse:* The leaf joins the center of the base of the I in AMERICA. Star 4 has one ray close to the fifth cloud; *definitive*.

1799: BD-2, Taraszka-14, Breen 2-A. *Obverse:* Small Stars obverse. The ray of star 9 is closer to base of the Y in LIBERTY than another ray is to the upper serif; *definitive*. *Reverse:* The leaf joins the center of the base of the I in AMERICA. Star 4 has one ray close to the fifth cloud; *definitive*.

1799: BD-3, Taraszka-15, Breen 1-A. *Obverse:* Small Stars obverse. The ray of star 9 is farther from the base of the Y in LIBERTY than another ray is to the upper serif; *definitive*. *Reverse:* The leaf joins the center of the base of the I in AMERICA. Star 4 has one ray close to the fifth cloud; *definitive*.

1799: BD-4, Taraszka-16, Breen 3-A. *Obverse:* Small Stars obverse. The ray of star 9 joins the upper serif of the Y in LIBERTY. Star 13 is distant from the drapery, and the 1 in 1799 nearly touches the lowest curl; *definitive*. *Reverse:* The leaf joins the center of the base of the I in AMERICA. Star 4 has one ray close to the fifth cloud; *definitive*.

1799: BD-5, Taraszka-17, Breen 3-B. *Obverse:* Small Stars obverse. The ray of star 9 joins the upper serif of the Y in LIBERTY. Star 13 is distant from the drapery, and the 1 in 1799 nearly touches the lowest curl; *definitive*. *Reverse:* The leaf joins the center of the base of the I in AMERICA. Star 4 has two rays touching the fifth cloud; *definitive*.

1799: BD-6, Taraszka-18, Breen 4-E. *Obverse:* Small Stars obverse. The ray of star 9 joins the upper serif of the Y in LIBERTY. Star 13 is distant from the drapery, and the 1 in 1799 nearly touches the lowest curl; *definitive*. *Reverse:* The leaf joins the lower-right serif of the I in AMERICA. Star 13 is well above the scroll; *definitive*.

1799: BD-7, Taraszka-19, Breen 2-E/B. *Obverse:* Small Stars obverse. The ray of star 9 joins the upper serif of the Y in LIBERTY, and the 1 in 1799 is far below and right of the lowest curl; *definitive*. *Reverse:* The leaf joins the lower-right serif of the I in AMERICA. Star 13 is well above the scroll; *definitive*.

1799: BD-8, Taraszka-20, Breen 4-D. *Obverse:* Small Stars obverse. The ray of star 9 joins the upper serif of the Y in LIBERTY, and the 1 in 1799 is far below and right of the lowest curl; *definitive*. *Reverse:* The leaf joins the lower-right serif of the I in AMERICA. Star 13 touches the scroll; *definitive*.

1799: BD-9, Taraszka-21, Breen 5-F. *Obverse:* Large Stars obverse. Stars 8 and 13 are each misaligned (rotated clockwise); *definitive*. *Reverse:* The leaf point is midway between the I and C in AMERICA; *definitive with the large stars obverse*.

1799: BD-10, Taraszka-22, Breen 5-G. *Obverse:* Large Stars obverse. Stars 8 and 13 are each misaligned (rotated clockwise); *definitive*. *Reverse:* The leaf point joins the lower-right serif of the I in AMERICA; *definitive with the large stars obverse*.

EAGLE OF 1800

1800: BD-1, Taraszka-23, Breen 1-A. *Obverse:* There is only one obverse die for this year; *definitive*. *Reverse:* There is only one reverse die for this year; *definitive*.

EAGLES OF 1801

1801: BD-1, Taraszka-24, Breen 1-A. *Obverse:* Star 1 is closer to the lowest curl than star 8 is to the cap; *definitive*. *Reverse:* The leaf joins the lower-right serif of the I in AMERICA; *definitive for 1801*.

1801: BD-2, Taraszka-25, Breen 2-B. *Obverse:* Star 1 is farther from the lowest curl than star 8 is to the cap; *definitive*. *Reverse:* The leaf is separated from the lower-right serif of the I in AMERICA; *definitive for 1801*.

EAGLES OF 1803

1803: BD-1, Taraszka-26, Breen 1-A. ***Obverse:*** There is only one obverse die for this year; *definitive*. ***Reverse:*** Small reverse stars. The ray of the lowest-left star points to the right edge of the B in PLURIBUS. The tip of the third outside arrowhead extends past the right upright of the N in UNITED; *definitive with small reverse stars.*

1803: BD-2, Taraszka-27, Breen 1-B. ***Obverse:*** There is only one obverse die for this year; *definitive*. ***Reverse:*** Small reverse stars. The ray of the lowest-left star points to the right edge of the B in PLURIBUS. The tip of the third outside arrowhead is below the center of the N in UNITED; *definitive with small reverse stars.*

1803: BD-3, Taraszka-28, Breen 1-C. ***Obverse:*** There is only one obverse die for this year; *definitive*. ***Reverse:*** Small reverse stars. The ray of the lowest-left star points to the left upright of the second U in PLURIBUS. The tip of the second outside arrowhead is below the left upright of the N in UNITED; *definitive with small reverse stars.*

1803: BD-4, Taraszka-29, Breen 1-D. ***Obverse:*** There is only one obverse die for this year; *definitive*. ***Reverse:*** Small reverse stars. The ray of the lowest-left star points to the left upright of the second U in PLURIBUS. The tip of the third outside arrowhead is below the right upright of the N in UNITED; *definitive with small reverse stars.*

1803: BD-5, Taraszka-30, Breen 1-E. ***Obverse:*** There is only one obverse die for this year; *definitive*. ***Reverse:*** Large reverse stars with *small* stray 14th star punched into the rightmost cloud. The tip of the third outside arrowhead is below the center of the N in UNITED; *definitive with large reverse stars.*

1803: BD-6, Taraszka-32, Breen 1-F. ***Obverse:*** There is only one obverse die for this year; *definitive*. ***Reverse:*** Large reverse stars. The tip of the third outside arrowhead is below the right upright of the N in UNITED; *definitive with large reverse stars.*

EAGLES OF 1804

1804, Original: BD-1, Taraszka-31, Breen 1-A. ***Obverse:*** There is a crosslet 4 in 1804; *definitive*. ***Reverse:*** The third outside arrowhead is below the right upright of the N in UNITED; *definitive for 1804.*

1804, Restrike: BD-2, Taraszka-33, Breen 2-B. ***Obverse:*** There is a plain 4 in 1804; *definitive*. ***Reverse:*** The third outside arrowhead is below the center of the N in UNITED; *definitive for 1804.*

Grading Standards

MS-60 to 70 (Mint State). *Obverse:* At MS-60, some abrasion and contact marks are evident, most noticeably on the hair to the left of Miss Liberty's forehead and on the higher-relief areas of the cap. Luster is present, but

1799, Large Stars; BD-10. Graded MS-65.

may be dull or lifeless, and interrupted in patches. At MS-63, contact marks are few, and abrasion is very light. An MS-65 coin has even less abrasion (most observable in the right field), and contact marks are so minute as to require magnification. Luster should be full and rich. Coins graded above MS-65 are more theoretical than actual for this type—but they do exist, and are defined by having fewer marks as perfection is approached. Large-size eagles are usually graded with slightly less strictness than the lower gold denominations of this type. *Reverse:* Comments apply as for the obverse, except that abrasion and contact marks are most noticeable on the upper part of the eagle and the clouds. The field area is complex, without much open space, given the stars above the eagle, the arrows and olive branch, and other features. Accordingly, marks are not as noticeable as on the obverse.

AU-50, 53, 55, 58 (About Uncirculated). *Obverse:* Light wear is seen on the cheek, the hair immediately to the left of the face, and the cap, more so at AU-50 than at AU–53 or 55. An AU-58 coin has minimal traces of wear. An AU-50 coin has luster in protected areas among the stars and letters, with

1799, Small Stars; BD-7. Graded AU-50.

little in the open fields or on the portrait. At AU-58, most luster is present in the fields, but is worn away on the highest parts of the motifs. *Reverse:* Comments as preceding, except that the eagle's neck, the tips and top of the wings, the clouds, and the tail now show noticeable wear, as do other features. Luster ranges from perhaps 40% remaining in protected areas (at AU-50) to nearly full mint bloom (at AU-58). Often the reverse of this type retains much more luster than the obverse.

EF-40, 45 (Extremely Fine). *Obverse:* Wear is evident all over the portrait, with some loss of detail in the hair to the left of Miss Liberty's face. Excellent detail remains in low-relief areas of the hair, such as the front curl and at the back of her head. The stars show wear as do the date and letters. Luster, if present

1801; BD-2. Graded EF-45.

at all, is minimal and in protected areas. *Reverse:* Wear is greater than on the preceding. The neck lacks some feather detail on its highest points. Feathers have lost some detail near the edges of the wings, and some areas of the horizontal lines in the shield may be blended together. Some traces of luster may be seen, more so at EF-45 than at EF-40. Overall, the reverse appears to be in a slightly higher grade than the obverse.

VF-20, 30 (Very Fine).
Obverse: The higher-relief areas of hair are well worn at VF-20, less so at VF-30.
Reverse: Wear is greater, including on the shield and wing feathers. The star centers are flat. Other areas have lost detail as well. E PLURIBUS UNUM may be faint in areas, but is usually sharp.

1799, Small Stars; BD-7. Graded VF-30.

The Capped Bust to Right eagle coin with Heraldic Eagle reverse is seldom collected in grades lower than VF-20.

PF-60 to 70 (Proof).
Obverse and Reverse: PF–60 to 62 coins have extensive hairlines and may have nicks and contact marks. At PF-63, hairlines are prominent, but the mirror surface is very reflective. PF-64 coins have fewer hairlines. At PF-65, hairlines should be minimal and mostly seen only under magnification. There should be no nicks or marks.

1804, Plain 4; BD-2. Proof.

1797, Heraldic Eagle Reverse

Circulation-Strike Mintage: 10,940

Estimated population (Mint State):
50–65. These are much more available than the 1797 with the earlier "Small Eagle" style reverse, but are still quite rare on an absolute basis. Often the reverse will grade a point or two (or three) higher than the obverse, a nuance lost in the "one number signifies all" method used by commercial grading services. Among Mint State pieces, assigned single-number grades are mostly MS-60 to MS-62.

Estimated population (circulated grades): *250–325.*

Submissions certified at highest grades (as of March 2017): *PCGS:* MS-61 (2), MS-62 (3). *NGC:* MS-62 (12), MS-63 (3), MS-64 (1).

Die data: The obverse stars are arranged 10 to the left and 6 to the right. There are three die varieties with one obverse mated to three different reverses.

Key to collecting: These are in the context of American numismatics, but are available enough so that several examples come on the market each year. VF, EF, and AU are typical grades. Again, the reverse usually grades higher than the obverse. Some pieces appear to have an AU obverse and a Mint State reverse.

MARKET NEWS AND COMMENTARY

The February 1859 sale of the Henry Bogert Collection by Augustus B. Sage offered this, lot 1209: "1797 Eagle. *Extremely Fine.*" It sold for $12.75 to John Curtis. No indication was given as to the style of the eagle on the reverse and likely it was of the Heraldic Eagle style. Curtis, a friend of Sage, had set up in the coin trade several years earlier and was one of America's first rare coin dealers.

W. Elliot Woodward's sale of the J. Colvin Randall Collection, June 1885, was unprecedented in its selection of several varieties, lot 846: "1797 No. 1; reverse, large eagle; obverse with 16 large stars; proof, rare." It sold for $13.50. Lot 847: "1797 No. 2; small stars; reverse, large eagle; Very fine indeed, scarce." It sold for $14. Lot 849: "1797 No. 4; 6 stars facing; reverse, large eagle; obverse, Very Fine; reverse proof." It sold for $13.75. The term *Proof*, capitalized today but not often in the 19th century, was often used to describe coins with partially mirrorlike surfaces.

Auction Sale No. 1, held by the Guttag Brothers in October 1927, included lot 415: "1797. Three stars to left of eagle's head form triangle. Extremely Fine." This comment concerning star arrangement is unusual for the period (but years later was finessed by Walter Breen). Julius and Henry Guttag were securities brokers, well financed, that were prominent in their side business of professional numismatics. They miscalculated in 1929, acquired a large building, but went down with the market crash. Years later Julius, who lived in New Rochelle, New York, dealt in numismatics on a casual basis. He befriended Abe Kosoff and consigned coins to the latter's first several auctions starting in 1940.

B. Max Mehl's sale of the Samuel H. McVitty Collection, March 1938, included lot 397: "1797 Variety with large eagle on reverse. Magnificent brilliant Uncirculated specimen, the reverse of which is a perfect brilliant Proof. The nearest to a Proof I have ever seen of this coin, and as such, of extreme rarity." It sold for $43.50.

In April 1949 B. Max Mehl's sale of the Dr. Charles W. Green Collection included lot 499:

> 1797 Obverse with 6 stars to right and 10 to left of bust. Reverse Heraldic Eagle. Beautiful brilliant semi-Proof; the reverse is equal to a perfect brilliant Proof. Originally purchased by Dr. Green as a brilliant Proof. Very slight hardly noticeable cabinet friction shows in obverse field. Truly a gem. Catalogs $100 in only Very Fine.

The coin sold for $106. This is one of countless examples of the era that reflect that Mint State coins often sold for prices little if anything above high-grade circulated examples.

Into modern times, in November 2000 the Bowers and Merena Galleries' sale of the Harry W. Bass Jr. Collection, Part IV, included lot 577:

> 1797 Breen-2C, Taraszka-12. Rarity-4. Heraldic Eagle. MS-61 PCGS. In his excellent study of early eagles, Anthony Taraszka determined that this variety was struck after all other 1797 eagles and also after 1798/7 eagles! From Quality Sales

Corporation's sale of the John A. Beck Collection, January 1975, Lot 486, an 11-piece set of early eagles from 1795 to 1804, including 1797 small and large eagle issues, and both varieties of 1798/7. In addition to the set, this sale offered 41 other early eagles, a most impressive selection. [Sold for $20,700]

In the Long Beach sale of April 2015 Heritage included lot 3321: "1797 Large Eagle, BD-4. MS-62 NGC." It sold for $82,200. Also, lot 5381: "1797 Large Eagle, BD-2. MS-63 PCGS." It sold for $164,500.

The D. Brent Pogue Collection, Part II, by Stack's Bowers Galleries and Sotheby's, September 2015, included lot 2095:

> 1797 BD-4. Heraldic Eagle. Mint State-63 PCGS. Since the sale of the Bass coin 15 years ago, only two PCGS MS-62s and a single PCGS MS-63 have come to market. This one has reposed peacefully in the Pogue Collection for nearly 35 years, during which time there has not been a single opportunity to upgrade it. Ex RARCOA's session of Auction '81, July 1981, lot 456.

This coin sold for $152,750. The Pogue early eagles are all cited in sharply abbreviated form in the present text as the set of *Guide Book* varieties is the finest ever assembled.

F-12	VF-20	EF-40	AU-50	AU-55	MS-60	MS-62	MS-63	MS-64
$12,500	$15,000	$20,000	$27,500	$37,500	$52,500	$85,000	$125,000	$200,000

1798, 8 Over 7, 9 Stars Left, 4 Right

Circulation-Strike Mintage: *1,200–1,600* (Bass-Dannreuther estimate)

Notes regarding mintages: The *Guide Book* has this mintage listed as 900.

Estimated population (Mint State): *4–6.* These are exceedingly rare in Mint State, and for all practical purposes are unavailable.

Estimated population (circulated grades): *100–120.* Very rare. Typical grades are VF, EF, and AU, with EF being the grade usually seen. Estimates as to the number known of this variety vary widely, with Walter Breen (*Encyclopedia*, 1988) suggesting 18 to 20 including 6 Mint State and 3 mutilated. In his cataloging of the Long Beach Connoisseur Collection (1999) Mark Borckardt, a later and more careful student, suggested that about 100 to 120 may be known in various grades.

Submissions certified at highest grades (as of March 2017): *PCGS:* MS-61 (2), MS-62 (2). *NGC:* MS-61 (5), MS-62 (2), MS-63 (1).

Die data: The obverse is struck with an overdate, and stars are arranged 9 to the left and 4 to the right; *definitive.*

Key to collecting: The lead article in the November 1883 issue of *Steigerwalt's Coin Journal* (Charles Steigerwalt, Lancaster, Pennsylvania), "Early Gold," by "an Old Collector," included this:

It has generally been thought that of the 1798 eagles, the variety with four stars facing was by far the rarer of the two; but from my own observation, and by reference to past sales, I think there is no difference in their degree of rarity.

This and its companion variety of the year have always been famous and highly prized rarities. Most grade EF or AU, but an example in any lower grade is eagerly competed for as well.

Market News and Commentary

Edward Cogan's October 1875 sale of the Colonel Mendes I. Cohen Collection included lot 107: "1798 Large Eagle, Struck over 1797. Extremely Fine and equally rare." It sold for $16. Cogan, whose marketing of himself was great, did not have extensive knowledge in comparison to Woodward, Strobridge, and some other dealers. Here Cogan seems to have thought that the 1798 eagle was struck over one dated 1797. Mendes I. Cohen, who was from a banking family in Baltimore, collected in many different series, ranging from antiques of ancient times onward. His collection, including a great run of full gold Proof sets, was skimpily cataloged by Cogan and did not attract much attention.

Woodward, in his June 1885 sale of the J. Colvin Randall Collection, offered lot 851: "1798 No. 2; die altered from 1797; 13 stars, 4 of which are facing; splendid Proof, one of the rarest of the eagles." It sold for $35.

Henry Chapman's June 1912 sale of the George H. Earle Jr. Collection included lot 2292:

> 1798 Over 1797. Four stars before bust and 9 behind it. Die cracked from edge through L to near the ear. Extremely Fine – Uncirculated were it not for slight abrasion in the fields. Semi-proof surface and probably the finest known example of this extremely rare coin.

B. Max Mehl's description of a coin in the February 1944 Belden E. Roach Collection reflects the situation at the time—collectors did not attach a great premium to a Mint State coin in comparison to a worn one. The quoted listing for Very Fine is from the *Standard Catalogue of United States Coins*, lot 311:

> 1798 Over 97. Type as last, but with thirteen stars, nine on left and four on right of bust. Magnificent Uncirculated specimen with brilliant Proof surface, almost equal to a perfect brilliant Proof. Extremely rare in any condition, but of excessive rarity so choice. Listed at $300 in only Very Fine. This one worth at least double that amount. [Sold for $315]

It was déjà vu for Mehl—a bad guess as to value—in his June 1946 William Cutler Atwater Collection sale, as there was no particular extra premium for a higher-graded coin, lot 1408:

> 1798 Over 97. Type with four stars to right of bust and nine stars to left. Practically Uncirculated with semi-proof surface; the reverse is almost equal to a Proof; just the slightest cabinet friction. A magnificent specimen of this extremely rare coin. Catalogues at $350 in only Very Fine. Has a record of over $400 made two years ago. Should bring more today.

The coin sold for $325. This is hard to understand today in the 21st century. Such listings contribute a lot to the appreciation of coins and of changes over the years.

Frank J. Katen, in his Milford [Connecticut] Coin & Stamp Company sale for the ANA Convention, August 1948, took a swipe at an unnamed competitor's grading. Lot 1321: "1798 over 97, 9 stars left, 4 stars before bust. This coin was sold in a famous name sale as Uncirculated. It is, however, Extremely Fine and worth $500."

Katen got into deep trouble a few years later when he criticized the spending habits and other actions of certain Board of Governors members and was summarily booted out of the ANA (long afterward, the ANA Board of Governors apologized). Years later Katen moved from Milford to Washington, D.C., where he and his wife Laurese bought and sold out-of-print numismatic literature. His main activity was public relations with politicos. The "power wall" in his home had many pictures of Frank with various luminaries.

Grading was a problem in 1955 and still is a problem, now with a different twist (how to give numbers to *tiny* differences in grades). This description by Norman Stack for a coin in the Farish-Baldenhofer Collection sale, November 1955, told of a wide difference in opinion, lot 1441: "1798 Over 97. 4 stars facing. Although this coin was purchased as Uncirculated we cannot call it better than Very Fine, choice. Still a great rarity and in great demand." It sold for $275. It also points out the flaws in studying historical catalogs for information about the availability of coins in certain grades. Such listings quoted in the present text need to be taken with the classic grain of salt.

In the Garrett Collection, Part III, sale, October 1980, Bowers and Ruddy Galleries included lot 1659:

> 1798/7 Overdate. Nine stars left, four stars right. Choice Brilliant Uncirculated, MS-65, but with a myriad of tiny parallel adjustment marks, and some minor handling One of the most important pieces in the present offering. Obtained by T. Harrison Garrett from Harold P. Newlin on October 31, 1884.

The above coin brought $52,500. The auction also included lot 1660:

> 1798/7 Overdate. Seven stars left, six stars right. Choice AU-55 with virtually full prooflike surface on the obverse Obtained by T. Harrison Garrett from Harold P. Newlin on October 31, 1884. As correspondence reprinted in the *History of United States Coinage as Illustrated by the Garrett Collection* indicates, Newlin was a connoisseur. He befriended Garrett and for some curious reason sold Garrett the finest pieces from his cabinet, reserving duplicates in lesser grade for his own use.

It sold for $120,000. The coin market was in a slump in autumn 1980, but excitement for the Garrett coins, many of which had been off the market since the 1870s and 1880s, carried the day. Even with the slump, elsewhere in the market prices were still above what they had been a few years earlier.

In May 2000 the Bowers and Merena Galleries' sale of the Harry W. Bass Jr. Collection, Part III, included lot 561:

> 1798/7 Breen-6836, B-1A, T-9. Overdate, 9x4 Stars. MS-61 PCGS. Similar in quality to an example in our August 1999 Rarities Sale, the present coin is the only Mint State piece of this variety certified by PCGS. In his day, Walter Breen estimated that

only 18 to 20 examples were known, but we suggest that the availability is considerably more, perhaps as many as 100 to 120. However, of that number, the present piece stands high in the lineup for quality. Interestingly, this die marriage and another variety of 1798 overdate with stars arranged seven left and six right were both struck after the first 1797 Heraldic Eagle variety pieces. PCGS Population: 1; none finer. Purchased from RARCOA, February 1, 1975. [Sold for $75,900]

In the Long Beach sale of April 2014 Heritage included lot 5761: "1798/7 9x4 Stars. BD-1. MS-62 PCGS." It sold for $176,500. Heritage sales at this popular venue have been a tradition for many years. In the FUN sale of January 2015 Heritage included lot 4324: "1798/7 9x4 Stars. BD-1. MS-61 PCGS." It sold for $117,500.

The D. Brent Pogue Collection, Part II, by Stack's Bowers Galleries and Sotheby's, September 2015, included lot 2096 cataloged as: "1798/7 BD-1. Stars 9x4. Mint State-62+ PCGS." This came from the 1982 sale of the Eliasberg Collection. In 2015 it sold for $258,500.

F-12	VF-20	EF-40	AU-50	AU-55	MS-60	MS-62	MS-63
$22,500	$30,000	$40,000	$55,000	$70,000	$125,000	$215,000	$300,000

1798, 8 Over 7, 7 Stars Left, 6 Right

Circulation-Strike Mintage: *300–842* **(Bass-Dannreuther estimate)**

Estimated population (Mint State): *4–5.* The finest pieces are currently graded in the low Mint State range. It could be that some of these were called AU earlier (see Breen comment directly below).

Estimated population (circulated grades): *20–25.* With regard to the number known, Walter Breen in his 1988 *Encyclopedia* estimated 13, with the highest being "borderline Uncirculated." In his 1980 study, David W. Akers located 23 auction appearances (including duplicate appearances of certain coins) and noted that there are "several Uncirculated examples known." Mark Borckardt, in cataloging the Long Beach Connoisseur Collection (1999), suggested that about 20 to 25 are known.

As a *major* variety listed in *A Guide Book of United States Coins* the 1798, 8 Over 7, with 7x6 stars is the most elusive of the Type II design, handily outdistancing everything else, with its closest competitor being the 1798, 8 Over 7, with stars arranged 9x4. It is also rarer than any major variety of the earlier type with the exception of the 1795, 9 Leaves, that has a nearly identical population estimate.

Submissions certified at highest grades (as of March 2017): *PCGS:* MS-61 (2), MS-62 (1). *NGC:* MS-60 (1).

Die data: This is the only Heraldic Reverse $10 gold obverse die in which the word LIBERTY extends completely over the cap (the 1796 Small Eagle Reverse $20 gold obverse has the word extending over the cap but not as far as here). Stars arranged are arranged 7 to the left and 6 to the right; *definitive*.

In his *American Numismatical Manual* (1859), Dr. Montroville W. Dickeson noted:

> The designs the same as the preceding, except that the number of stars is reduced from 16 to 13 on the obverse—7 on the left, and 6 at the right of the effigy. Of this issue there was one type and three varieties. They are quite scarce.

Key to collecting: This famous and expensive rarity is a classic as noted. Across the different gold denominations it is one of the rarest early issues listed in the *Guide Book of United States Coins.*

MARKET NEWS AND COMMENTARY

W. Elliot Woodward, in his sale of the J. Colvin Randall Collection, June 1885, included lot 850: "1798 No. 1 over 1797; large stars, 6 facing; reverse, large eagle; about Proof; extremely rare." It sold for $47. Woodward's sale of September of the same year included more Randall coins. It is not clear if the following is another 1798, 8 Over 7, or a reoffering of the June coin, lot 983: "1798 over 1797 No. 1, Large stars, six facing; splendid, nearly Proof, extremely rare. Brought in the Randall Sale $47." It sold for $31.

Thomas L. Elder in his sale of the William H. Woodin Collection, March 1911, offered this, lot 1189: "1798, over 1797 Six stars before bust, 7 behind it. Beautiful, sharp impression with broad even milling. A gem. The finest known of this rare variety. Uncirculated, mint luster, with a Proof surface." It sold for $410.

B. Max Mehl, in the May 1922 sale of the James Ten Eyck Collection, included lot 262:

> 1798 Over '97. The exceedingly rare variety with six stars to right of Liberty and seven to left. Strictly Fine. Exceedingly rare. The first that I have ever offered either at auction or at private sale. I believe this variety to be at least twenty times as rare as Lot 261 (the other variety of the year). Last record, made in 1912, for an Uncirculated specimen was $400. [Sold for $225]

Mehl forgot to take his memory pills, for in his sale of the Belden E. Roach Collection, February 1944, this description was given of lot 312:

> 1798 Over '97. The excessively rare variety with seven stars to left and six stars to right of bust. Uncirculated with full mint luster, brilliant; the field on obverse is not as brilliant as that of reverse. The rarest $10 gold piece in the entire series. I do not recall of ever having offered a specimen in my sales in the past forty-three years. Listed in the 1942 catalog at $600 in only Very Fine condition. Considering the great rarity and the choice condition of this specimen. It is certainly worthy of membership in the $1,000 class of coins.

That coin sold for $750. He had even more memory problems in his June 1946 William Cutler Atwater Collection catalog, lot 1409:

> 1798 Over '97. The excessively rare variety with six stars to right and seven stars to left. Strictly Very Fine with considerable mint luster. The only evidence of circulation is slight cabinet friction on highest portions. Nicely struck and perfectly centered with broad milled borders. Free from any nicks or dents. By far the rarest of all

early U.S. $10 gold pieces. In my sale of the great Dunham Collection, in 1941, which was then the first specimen I offered in some forty years, and the coin was then catalogued at $600, it brought $750. I have not had a specimen either at auction or at private sale since then. Another specimen offered at auction about two years ago, brought $1,125. I doubt if more than six specimens are known and I believe that its present record of $1,125 is still in its 'infancy.' Not even in the large sale held recently where the collection was described as "The World's Greatest." [Sold for $715]

In April 1949 B. Max Mehl's sale of the Dr. Charles W. Green Collection included lot 501:

> 1798 Over '97. The excessively rare variety with 6 stars to the right and 7 to the left of bust. Extremely Fine; slight evidence of circulation, mainly on the obverse. Excessively rare and valuable. Record over $1,100. Dr. Green purchased this coin as Uncirculated in 1944 and paid $1,000 for it. Originally said to have come from the Colonel Green Collection. [Sold for $785]

Colonel E.H.R. Green began collecting coins in the early 1900s along with many other things, ranging from the original sheet of 100 1918 24-cent airmail stamps with the inverted airplane to an old whaling boat, not to overlook having his own radio station and living in a large mansion. After his death in 1936 his estate was widely dispersed, including through B.G. Johnson of St. Louis and Stack's in New York City.[5]

Into an era in which prices were much different, but there was still a lot of room to grow, the January 1986 Stack's sale of the James Walter Carter and Margaret Woolfolk Carter Collections included lot 179 as described by Norman Stack:

> 1798/7 Overdate. Obverse stars 7 left, 6 right. The legendary rarity of the series. From the King of Egypt's Collection [actually duplicates] sold by B. Max Mehl in 1948. It was described as follows:
>
> > "1798 Over '97 $10. The excessively rare variety with six stars to right and seven stars to left of bust. The most perfect and most beautiful specimen of this rarity that has ever been handled by me. Strictly Uncirculated with Proof surface. The field on obverse shows just the barest touch of cabinet friction. It is unusually sharply struck with every star filled and broad milled borders, especially on obverse, with slightly raised edge. It was sold to His Majesty as 'unique in this condition.'
> >
> > "This is a dangerous statement to make. I can say, however, that it is as beautiful a specimen of this rare eagle as I know of. It is so perfectly struck that it shows a light die break from border through E of LIBERTY, and another light die break from border through left portion of first star at top of left to Liberty cap. The price of cost marked on the original envelope in which this coin came to me from His Majesty is marked close to $2,000. I hardly think the coin is worth that much, but it is certainly worth well into the four figure mark. The coin has a record of over $1,100 for not nearly so choice a specimen."
>
> We fully agree with Mr. Mehl as to his condition and rarity. Further research indicates that this is the only Mint State specimen offered since the Pierce Sale (this coin) in 1965. The Uncirculated. Baldenhofer specimen, also sold by us, was sold in 1955. An opportunity which should not be taken lightly. Ex Grant Pierce & Sons Collections (Stack's), lot 1436, May 1965. [Sold for $68,750]

In the Long Beach sale of April 2015 Heritage included lot 3321: "1798/7 7x6 Stars. BD-2. AU-58 PCGS." It sold for $329,000. By this time there was a great passion for collecting early gold coins, especially by *Guide Book* varieties, but not excluding die combinations of certain dates. Harry W. Bass Jr. was the most careful and most dedicated student of American gold in the history of American numismatics.

The D. Brent Pogue Collection, Part II, by Stack's Bowers Galleries and Sotheby's, September 2015, included lot 2097, here excerpted:

> 1798/7 BD-2. Stars 7x6. Mint State-61 PCGS. The magnificent Garrett coin, with a provenance extending 130 years into the past, reappears here for the first time in three and a half decades. Ex Harold P. Newlin Collection; Harold P. Newlin, by sale, October 31, 1884; T. Harrison Garrett Collection; T. Harrison Garrett to Robert and John Work Garrett, by descent, 1888; Robert Garrett interest to John Work Garrett, 1919; transfer completed 1921; John Work Garrett to The Johns Hopkins University, by gift, 1942; Bowers and Ruddy's sale of the Garrett Collection, Part III, October 1980, lot 1660.

The Garrett-Pogue coin sold for $705,000.

F-12	VF-20	EF-40	AU-50	AU-55	MS-60	MS-62
$40,000	$55,000	$87,500	$165,000	$195,000	$325,000	$450,000

1799

Circulation-Strike Mintage: 37,449 (all varieties)

Estimated population (Mint State): 225–350. These are plentiful in Mint State in the context of the early eagle series. Most coins of this year are Small Stars, by a slight margin; however, among *Mint State* coins there are more of the Large Stars.

1799, Small Stars on Obverse

Estimated population (circulated grades): 900–1,200. The most plentiful early eagle, with the only contender (and that by a distance) being the 1801 (which in *Mint State* is actually more available than the 1799). Typical grades are VF, EF, and

1799, Large Stars on Obverse

AU. Many dozens of specimens have been used for jewelry or are otherwise impaired.

Submissions certified at highest grades (as of March 2017): *PCGS:* MS-64 (36), MS-65 (7), MS-66 (1). ***NGC:*** MS-64 (36), MS-65 (6).

Die data: Ten die varieties are known. Most obverses have small stars, but one obverse die has large stars and is combined with two reverses. Per Dr. Montroville W. Dickeson, *American Numismatical Manual* (1859):

The designs the same, with the exception of the arrangement of the stars on the obverse—8 on the left and 5 on the right of the effigy. There were of this issue one type and three varieties. One variety has 14 stars on the reverse, evidently an error.[6] This emission is more plenty than any of the same denomination for previous years, and yet they may be considered scarce.

Key to collecting: This is the most plentiful date among early eagles and is a good candidate for inclusion in a type set. Most grade EF to AU into lower Mint State ranges.

MARKET NEWS AND COMMENTARY

W. Elliot Woodward's June 1885 sale of the J. Colvin Randall Collection used Randall's variety designations (such being lost today): lot 852: "1799 No. 1; close date, the last 9 nearly touches the bust; reverse, large eagle; Very Fine." It sold for $13. Lot 853: "1799 No. 2; wider date, large stars; Very Fine." It sold for $12. Lot 854: "1799 No. 3; in date 1 and 7 close together, small stars; reverse, stars different from the others; Very Fine indeed; reverse, Proof." It sold for $13. Lot 855: "1799 No. 4; obverse from die of No. 2; reverse, variety in eagle and stars; Extremely Fine." It sold for $12. Lot 856: "1799 No. 5; open date, small stars, break in die extends from the border near to center; reverse, like No. 3; nearly Proof." It sold for $12. The Randall study on early gold die varieties has been lost and is known only by scattered mentions of it, especially by Woodward, the most scholarly cataloger of the era.

The offering of multiple coins in the December 1890 Chapman brothers' sale of the Thomas Cleneay Collection, seemingly of lower-grade pieces, drew a collective yawn from bidders, as evidenced by the prices: lot 463: "1799 8 stars behind and 5 before bust. Extremely Fine." It sold for $12. Lot 464: "1799 Same. Extremely Fine." It sold for $12. Lot 465: "1799 Same. Extremely Fine." It sold for $11.50. Lot 466: "1799 Same. Very Fine." It sold for $11. Lot 467: "1799 Same. Very Fine." It sold for $11. Lot 468: "1799 Same. Very Fine and Fine. 2 pieces." It sold for $11 per piece. Cleneay, of Cincinnati, had been a collector for many years and enjoyed many series. He was a pioneer in the Civil War–token series and had the local shops of William Lanphear and John Stanton strike special numismatic delicacies such as rare die combinations to his order.

A very nice example of this early eagle was offered by B. Max Mehl in his June 1941 William Forrester Dunham Collection sale, lot 2201:

> 1799 Variety with the small stars on the obverse. Struck in light yellow gold. Magnificent Uncirculated specimen with full brilliant mint luster. The reverse is almost equal to a Proof; sharp and perfect in every respect. This is not a rare date, but I consider it extremely rare in this remarkable condition. Have never seen its equal. [Sold for $37.60]

In January 1946 the Numismatic Gallery sale of "The World's Greatest Collection" (F.C.C. Boyd) included lot 634: "1799 Large obverse stars. Uncirculated. Choice." It sold for $90. In July 2004 the Oliver Jung Collection sale by American Numismatic Rarities included lot 99: "1799 Large Stars on obverse. MS-65 PCGS. From the 'World's Greatest Collection,' 1946." This time the same coin sold for $230,000. The D. Brent

Pogue Collection, Part II, by Stack's Bowers Galleries and Sotheby's, September 2015, included lot 2099, excerpted:

> 1799 BD-10. Large Obverse Stars. Mint State-65+ PCGS. A treasure and a gem, this eagle ranks among the very finest examples of the entire type. Ex F.C.C. Boyd Collection; Numismatic Gallery's (Abe Kosoff and Abner Kreisberg) sale of the World's Greatest Collection of U.S. Gold Coins (F.C.C. Boyd), January 1946, lot 634; American Numismatic Rarities' sale of the Oliver Jung Collection, July 2004, lot 99.

The coin brought $352,500. This is a poster example of a gem coin increasing dramatically in value!

In April 1949 B. Max Mehl's sale of the Dr. Charles W. Green Collection included lot 502:

> 1799 Variety with large stars. Beautiful brilliant Uncirculated specimen. Probably the least rare of our early eagles, but I consider it quite rare when so perfect. A similar specimen sold for $150 at private sale. [Sold for $165]

In modern times, the August 2002 ANA Convention sale by Superior Galleries included lot 2057: "1799 Small Stars on obverse. MS-61 (ANACS)." It sold for $9,200; also the same variety and grade, lot 2058, but by PCGS, a coin that sold for $16,100.

High-level Mint State 1799 eagles are not landmark rarities, but when they have been sold in recent years they have brought very strong prices, as indicated by the following samples.

The August 2006 Bowers and Merena Galleries' ANA sale included lot 4300: "1799 Large Stars Obverse MS-65, PCGS." It sold for $241,500. The August 2011 Stack's Bowers Galleries' Rarities sale included lot 7713: "1799 BD-10. Large Obverse Stars. MS-64 PCGS." It sold for $207,000. The August 2012 Stack's Bowers Galleries sale at the Philadelphia ANA World's Fair of Money offered lot 11732: "1799 BD-10. Large Obverse Stars. MS-64 PCGS." It sold for $172,500. In the Long Beach sale of April 2015 Heritage included lot 5386: "1799 BD-9. MS-65 PCGS." It sold for $376,000. In the Long Beach sale of September 2015 Heritage included lot 4191: "1799 BD-7. MS-63 PCGS." It sold for $70,500. The D. Brent Pogue Collection, Part II, by Stack's Bowers Galleries and Sotheby's, September 2015, included lot 2098: "1799 BD-7. Small Obverse Stars. Mint State-64+ (PCGS)." It sold for $258,500. In the March 2016 Rarities Auction Stack's Bowers Galleries offered lot 13198: "1799 BD-10. MS-66 PCGS." It sold for $493,500.

SMALL STARS ON OBVERSE

F-12	VF-20	EF-40	AU-50	AU-55	MS-60	MS-62	MS-63	MS-64
$8,750	$12,500	$16,000	$20,000	$23,500	$32,500	$42,500	$67,500	$135,000

LARGE STARS ON OBVERSE

F-12	VF-20	EF-40	AU-50	AU-55	MS-60	MS-62	MS-63	MS-64
$8,750	$12,500	$16,000	$20,000	$23,500	$32,500	$42,500	$67,500	$115,000

1800

Circulation-Strike Mintage: 5,999–12,500 (Bass-Dannreuther estimate)

Notes regarding mintages: It is likely that this mintage figure does not represent all 1800-dated eagles struck, and that additional pieces of this date were made in 1801.

Estimated population (Mint State): *65–80.* Although the 1800 is scarce in circulated grades, in Mint State a number of really beautiful specimens have come on the market over the years. In absolute terms a Mint State 1800 is rare, but it is not among the rarest dates in this regard.

From Walter Breen's 1988 *Encyclopedia*: "I have seen two and have heard of several others that qualify as possible presentation pieces; occasion unknown, but if these were actually included among presentation coins, the ceremony must have taken place very late in the year. Most of the mintage of eagles in 1800 consisted of coins dated 1799."

Estimated population (circulated grades): *200–300.* The 1800 is quite scarce in circulated grades. In 1980 David W. Akers commented: "This is an underrated date when compared to the 1795, 1797 Heraldic Eagle, 1799, 1801 and 1803. It is considerably more rare than those five dates and is not much more common than the 1796 and 1804."

John Beck, a wealthy Pittsburgh collector, had a large number of these when he died in 1925. In the 1970s they came on the market through Quality Sales Corporation (Abner Kreisberg and Jerry Cohen).

Submissions certified at highest grades (as of March 2017): *PCGS:* MS-62 (20), MS-63 (11), MS-64 (3), MS-65 (1). *NGC:* MS-62 (16), MS-63 (8), MS-64 (3).

Die data: Only one die combination this year has been noted in modern times. The reverse die of that particular combination was later used to strike 1801-dated eagles. There was only one die this year; *definitive.* The O in OF and the 0 in 1800 are similar. In the Mint's early days the letter O from the letter-punch font was sometimes interchangeable with the zero from a font of numbers.

Dr. Montroville W. Dickeson noted: "One type and two varieties. They are scarce." *American Numismatical Manual* (1859).

MARKET NEWS AND COMMENTARY

A sale held in the auction room of Bangs, Merwin & Co. in June 1859 featured the John K. Curtis Collection with this, lot 62: "Proof eagle or $10 piece. 1800."[7] It sold for $10.50. W. Elliot Woodward's December 1885 sale of the W. Matthews, J. Colvin Randall, and J.N.T. Levick Collections raises a mystery for modern students of the series, lot 1003: "1800 Very Fine indeed, nearly Proof, scarce." It sold for $10.50. Lot 1004: "1800 Obv. Different; Fine, scarce." It sold for $10.50. Woodward notes two *obverse die varieties* of this year.

Into the modern era with hundreds of thousands of people interested in American coins, many of whom were specialists. Although early gold was rare and expensive, there were still many who sought fine examples. Heritage's June 2000 Long Beach sale gives information regarding the certified population at that time, lot 7599: "1800 MS-63 PCGS. B. 1-A, the only known dies, R.4. Population: 5 in 63, only 2 finer." It sold for $44,850. In the Long Beach sale of April 2015 Heritage included lot 5391: "1800 BD-1. MS-64 PCGS." It sold for $282,000. The D. Brent Pogue Collection, Part II, by Stack's Bowers Galleries and Sotheby's, September 2015, included lot 2101: "1800 BD-1. Mint State-63+ PCGS." It sold for $99,875.

F-12	VF-20	EF-40	AU-50	AU-55	MS-60	MS-62	MS-63	MS-64
$9,000	$13,000	$16,500	$21,500	$24,500	$35,000	$52,500	$85,000	$160,000

1801

Circulation-Strike Mintage: 44,344.

Estimated population (Mint State): 225–300. While most are around MS-60, a number of choice and gem specimens exist.

Estimated population (circulated grades): 600–800. The second most available Type II eagle (the 1799 being first). Typical grades are VF, EF, and, less often, AU.

Submissions certified at highest grades (as of March 2017): *PCGS:* MS-63 (37), MS-64 (36), MS-65 (3). *NGC:* MS-63 (40), MS-64 (25), MS-65 (2).

Die data: There are two die varieties this year. Dr. Montroville W. Dickeson noted: "One type and two varieties. They may be considered as scarce." *American Numismatical Manual* (1859).

Key to collecting: This is another early eagle date that is readily available in grades from EF through low Mint State.

MARKET NEWS AND COMMENTARY

The May 1893 offering of the H. Graser, M.D., Collection by the New York Coin & Stamp Co. included a rather curious grade for lot 119: "1801 Stars sharp but 2; Proof surface; Very Fine or Uncirculated; rare in this condition." It sold for $13.75.

Thomas L. Elder, in his March 1911 sale of the William H. Woodin Collection, included this, lot 1195: "1801 Large stars on obverse. On reverse, star touches top of eagle's beak. Looks to be a Proof, but fields may have been polished." This coin sold for $18.50. This is a significant entry which reveals that at this stage of his career, Elder could not distinguish between a polished coin and a Proof. This is an observation, not a criticism, and simply illustrates that various coins called "Proof" by Elder (and similar situations existed with others) might not have been Proofs. Later generations of scholars have needed to take early descriptions of grades with a very large grain of salt. In the same sale Elder seems to have been certain with the grade of lot 1196: "1801 Stars on obverse slightly smaller. On reverse, star does not quite touch top of eagle's beak. Gem Proof piece with mint luster. Finest 1801 I have ever offered." This sold for $39.

An unusual listing by B. Max Mehl appeared in his June 1942 Colonel J.A. Porter Collection sale, lot 1210:

> 1801 Extremely Fine, but the coin has apparently been lacquered and looks just like a perfect brilliant Proof. I presume the lacquer can easily be removed, but the coin is so attractive, that I thought best to offer it as is. It was purchased by the former owner as a Proof coin at a very high price.

The coin sold for $26.25. One would think that even the most uninformed beginner could tell if a coin had been lacquered. If so, it could have been dipped in inert acetone to remove it.

Into the modern market, the August 2002 ANA Convention sale by Superior Galleries included lot 2063: "1801 MS-63 NGC." It sold for $18,400; also lot 2064: "1801 MS-61 PCGS," which sold for $15,525. In March 2004 the American Numismatic Rarities Whitman Expo sale included lot 1492: "1801 MS-63 PCGS." It sold for $35,630. In the ANA Convention sale of August 2014 Heritage included lot 5662: "1801 BD-2. MS-63 PCGS." It sold for $45,534. Also lot 5223, same variety and grade, but NGC graded, sold for $48,762.50.

The D. Brent Pogue Collection, Part II, by Stack's Bowers Galleries and Sotheby's, September 2015, included lot 2102: "1801 BD-2 R Mint State-65 PCGS. Tied for finest. Ex Larry Hanks April 2008." It sold for $217,375. Also lot 2013: "1801 BD-2. Mint State-64+ PCGS. Ex Henry Chapman's sale of the Matthew A. Stickney Collection, June 1907, lot 622; David Akers, by sale, July 1990." It sold for $188,000.

F-12	VF-20	EF-40	AU-50	AU-55	MS-60	MS-62	MS-63	MS-64
$8,750	$11,000	$15,000	$18,500	$21,000	$30,000	$40,000	$65,000	$125,000

1803

Circulation-Strike Mintage: 15,017 (all varieties)

Estimated population (Mint State): 100–140. The 1803 is one of the more available early eagles. Grades range from MS-60, continuing upward well into the choice category. There are Small Stars and Large Stars reverses, with the first being seen about twice as often as the last.

1803, Small Stars on Reverse

Estimated population (circulated grades): 400–550. EF (primarily) and AU are grades usually seen.

Submissions certified at highest grades (as of March 2017): PCGS: MS-63 (16), MS-64 (10), MS-65 (2). **NGC:** MS-63 (25), MS-64 (6).

1803, Large Stars on Reverse

Die data: There are six die varieties this year, all of which use the same obverse. One unusual reverse die has a tiny fourteenth star on the last cloud to the right, a feature first noticed by Harry W. Bass Jr. Dr. Montroville W. Dickeson noted: "One type and three varieties. They are considered as rare." *American Numismatical Manual* (1859).

Key to collecting: This is another popular date. The number of die varieties is a record for early eagles. Most coins grade from EF through lower Mint State.

MARKET NEWS AND COMMENTARY

Scott & Company on March 1882 offered these 1803 eagles from the John W. Scott Collection: lot 77: "1803 Rev. large stars; very rare, fine." It sold for $11.25. Lot 78: "1803 Reverse, small stars; Very good." It sold for $11. The designations of Fine and Very Good probably were the equivalent of "very nice" and "nice," or similar, and were not adjectival grades.

Bowers and Ruddy Galleries used split grading, popular at the time as it was much more descriptive than single-number grading, in the Eliasberg Collection sale in October 1982: lot 657: "1803 Choice Brilliant Uncirculated, MS-65 obverse, Choice Brilliant Uncirculated, MS-65 to Gem Brilliant Uncirculated reverse, MS-67." It sold for $27,500. Lot 658: "1803 AU-55 obverse, Select Brilliant Uncirculated, MS-63 reverse." It sold for $14,200. By that time there were many people seeking early gold coins.

Into what is still today's market, in August 2006 the American Numismatic Rarities sale of the Old West and Franklinton Collections included lot 1538: "1803. Large Stars on reverse. MS-66 NGC." It sold for $333,500. The same sale included an 1803 with Large Stars reverse, AU-53 (NGC), at $34,500, and an 1803 with Small Stars reverse, MS-63 (NGC), that sold for $69,000.

The June 2008 Stack's sale of the Huskey Collection included lot 2101: "1803 Small Stars Reverse. MS-64 NGC." It sold for $138,000. In the FUN sale of January 2014 Heritage included lot 5485: "1803 BD-5, Extra Star. MS-64 NGC." It sold for $99,875. In the June 2014 Pre-Long Beach sale Ira and Larry Goldberg offered lot 1887: "1803 Large Stars on Reverse. MS-60 NGC." It sold for $35,837.50. The D. Brent Pogue Collection, Part II, by Stack's Bowers Galleries and Sotheby's, September 2015, included lot 2104: "1803 BD-5. Large Reverse Stars, Extra Star. Mint State-65 PCGS. Finest Certified by PCGS." The coin went to a new home for $235,000.

SMALL STARS ON REVERSE

F-12	VF-20	EF-40	AU-50	AU-55	MS-60	MS-62	MS-63	MS-64
$9,500	$12,000	$16,000	$21,500	$23,500	$37,500	$50,000	$65,000	$135,000

LARGE STARS ON REVERSE

F-12	VF-20	EF-40	AU-50	AU-55	MS-60	MS-62	MS-63	MS-64
$9,500	$12,000	$16,000	$21,500	$23,500	$37,500	$50,000	$65,000	$135,000

1804, Crosslet 4, Original

Circulation-Strike Mintage: 3,757 (some dated 1803)

Notes regarding mintages: The mintage of 1804-dated eagles is unknown. Presumably no 1804 eagles were struck *before* 1804, and thus the maximum number is fixed at 3,757. However, a reverse die state of the 1803 with Large Reverse Stars (BD-6) exists showing a *later* die state; thus, some of the 3,757 mintage must include 1803-dated coins. This is a poster example of delivery times not matching the dates on the coins (also see note under 1796).

Estimated population (Mint State): *12–16.*

Estimated population (circulated grades): *90–125.* The 1804 is very elusive as a date, being multiples rarer than the highly acclaimed 1795. Most examples are VF to AU, with EF or AU being representative of many "name" collection offerings. Often, surfaces are irregular for reasons unknown today. Quite a few 1804 eagles have been cleaned, polished, or used as jewelry.

Submissions certified at highest grades (as of March 2017): *PCGS:* MS-61 (6), MS-62 (1), MS-63 (1), MS-64 (1). *NGC:* MS-61 (11), MS-62 (5), MS-63 (5), MS-64 (1).

Die data: There is a crosslet 4 in the date. Large stars are used on the reverse. Only one die pair was used to coin original $10 coins of this date. The reverse die was also used *later* to coin certain *1803* eagles (1803 Taraszka-32, Breen 1-F).

In his *American Numismatical Manual* (1859), Dr. Montroville W. Dickeson noted:

> One type and two varieties. They are indeed rare. This was the last of the emission of the old-fashioned eagle, whose diameter is so remarkable, contrasted with the same denomination since coined at our Mint. We look upon it with somewhat of a feeling of reverence, it being the pioneer of that description of currency in our country, and characterized by an appearance that partakes much of the times when our forefathers had the same quaint resemblance, but not the less allied to those solid and substantial qualities so essential in laying the foundations of a government, which for enlightened and perfect workmanship, has ever seen been the model and admiration of the thinking portion of the human family."

Characteristics of striking and die notes: These are usually lightly struck at the obverse center. Later strikings have bulged and somewhat irregular fields due to die use.

Key to collecting: The lead article from *Steigerwalt's Coin Journal* (November 1883), "Early Gold, by 'An Old Collector,'" included this comment about collecting preferences:

> Of late, however, interest in early gold has been to some extent resurrected, and new collectors have come into the field. Just why this has not always been the most popular branch of numismatics is a mystery, and why a collector will pay $200 for an Uncirculated 1804 cent, and will hesitate to give $15 for an Uncirculated 1804 eagle is 'one of those things that no fellow can find out.[8]

The 1804 has always been the key date among early 1800s eagles. More than any other, this year is difficult to find with excellent eye appeal.

MARKET NEWS AND COMMENTARY

Edward Cogan's sale of miscellaneous coins in June 1871 included lot 76: "1804 The most beautiful piece I remember to have seen. A Proof impression, but slight scratches on the obverse. Very rare in this condition." It sold for $35.

In April 1897 the Chapman brothers sale of the M.A. Brown Collection included lot 114:

> 1804 Extremely Fine. Slight abrasion in field of obverse; otherwise Uncirculated. Sharp impression, the profile perfect, and the finest specimen of this date we remember to have seen. Extremely rare. [Sold for $46]

The Belden E. Roach Collection, February 1944, by B. Max Mehl, included lot 318:

> 1804 Last year of the large early eagles. Beautiful Uncirculated specimen, sharp and bold impression. A very slight planchet mark on left wing. A magnificent specimen of this rarity. Perfectly centered and well struck. Very rare and valuable. Listed in 1942 at $125 in only Very Fine. This gem coin worth a great deal more.

The lot sold for $162.50, one of many examples of a Mint State coin selling for little more than a circulated example.

Into the modern era of numismatics: The Eliasberg Collection sale of October 1982 by Bowers and Ruddy Galleries included lot 659:

> 1804 Crosslet 4. Breen 1-A, A-1, C-1. With Crosslet 4 in date. A rare issue in all grades. Select Brilliant Uncirculated, MS-63 obverse; Choice Brilliant Uncirculated, MS-65 to Gem Brilliant Uncirculated, MS-67 reverse. Believed to be from Hans M.F. Schulman, 1944. [Sold for $35,200] (For more on Schulman see Appendix E.)

In his description in Paramount's Auction in July 1985 David W. Akers used the short-lived, but very informative split grading system, lot 1450:

> 1804 Choice Uncirculated (63/63+). Rich gold and copper toning. Fully prooflike obverse and semi-prooflike reverse. Well struck for the issue but still displaying the weak facial features on Miss Liberty and some softness on the eagle's wing and clouds. The reverse is uniformly choice and virtually gem quality. [Sold for $11,550]

The John J. Pittman Collection, Part II, cataloged by David Akers and sold in October 1998, included lot 1909:

> 1804, Choice Uncirculated. Very sharply struck and perfectly centered. There are die scratches near the denticles below and to the right of the date which shows signs of double punching on the 8 (upper left loop) and 0 (inside right curve). The only other example of comparable quality that I have seen is the Mack Pogue coin which has been conservatively graded MS-63 by NGC. Ex New Netherlands, 1948. [Sold for $82,500]

In June 2005 the American Numismatic Rarities Cardinal Collection sale included lot 1016: "1804 MS-63 NGC. From the John J. Pittman Collection sold by David W. Akers." It sold for $110,400.

In July 2009, in the "Treasures from the SS *New York*" sale, Stack's offered lot 1472: "1804 Crosslet 4. MS-63 NGC." It sold for $128,800. In the Long Beach sale of April 2015 Heritage included lot 5396: "1804 BD-1. MS-63 PCGS." It sold for $176,250.

The D. Brent Pogue Collection, Part II, by Stack's Bowers Galleries and Sotheby's, September 2015, included lot 2105: "1804 BD-1. Crosslet 4. Mint State-63+ PCGS." This coin had a long provenance back to Elder's sale of the Woodin collection in 1911. In 2015 it sold for $440,625.

F-12	VF-20	EF-40	AU-50	AU-55	MS-60	MS-62	MS-63
$20,000	$25,000	$37,500	$50,000	$65,000	$85,000	$100,000	$175,000

1804, Plain 4, Proof, Restrike

Proof mintage: At least 4.

Proof notes: Proofs were not struck in 1804, but were first made in 1834 in connection with presentation sets of U.S. coins intended as diplomatic gifts. These sets contained 1834-dated Proofs of the half cent, cent, half dime, dime, quarter dollar, half dollar, $2.50 (two types), and $5. Added to these were an 1804-dated silver dollar and an 1804-dated eagle. Traditionally, it was believed the 1804 coins were made from dies created in the 1830s, with some differences in style from dies of the 1804 era. Recent research indicates the dies for the eagle were actually prepared much earlier, but were never used before 1834. We know the obverse was never used, as the 180 was already in the die, but the 4 was added from the 1834 half dollar punch set. The reverse probably was never used, but since it was a *half dollar* reverse, it is possible it was briefly used on the 1805, 5 Over 6, to which it is easily dated because of broken serifs on several letters. It is theoretically possible that a related half dollar might be discovered someday. As there were no originals of the dollar or eagle, the correct numismatic term for them is *novodels*.

Proof restrikes were also made in *silver*, probably as patterns. Two varieties are known, listed as Judd-34 and Judd-34A. For many years the gold impression has been listed as a *pattern*, which it is not. The same incorrect pattern attribution has been given to original 1836 Gobrecht dollars (Judd-60) and a few other coins. This tradition dates from earlier times, beginning with Wayte Raymond's *Standard Catalogue of United States Coins*, 1944 edition. Conversely, there are many patterns that are popularly considered to be or are listed in the *Guide Book* among regular coins, such as 1856 Flying Eagle cents, silver transitional patterns of 1859, and $4 gold Stellas.

Estimated population (Proofs): *3–4.* Three are confirmed. Two are choice specimens, one is impaired.

Restrikes: Proof restrikes have a plain 4 in the date, struck in a close collar with old-style denticles and no raised rim. The edge has 200 reeds—far more than the 126 to 142 encountered on eagles actually struck during the years from 1795 to 1804 (original eagles of 1804 have 126 reeds).

An overview and summary of the 1804 Restrike has been created for the present text and is given under the heading below.

Overview of the 1804 Restrike Eagle
by David Stone

In the course of study for an article I wrote with John Dale Beety for *Coin World* in November 2014, much new information about the 1804 Proof eagle came to light. Remarkably, Bill Nyberg and Bryce Brown identified the reverse die as an unused half dollar die from 1806 in two articles they published in the June 2007 edition of the *John Reich Journal*.

Similarly, after the Bass-Dannreuther series reference on early gold coins was published, John Dannreuther discovered the punch used for the bust on the obverse was the same one used on eagle dies before 1804. Using computer overlays, he noted the perceived differences between the earlier coins and the Proofs struck in 1834 (such as the die line in Liberty's hair) were actually features on the original die that were effaced by die polishing and reworking in 1834. He believes the silver patterns (Judd-34 and Judd-34A) were actually a series of die trials, noting the die line and a lot of die rust are present on the earliest die state of these coins, but become weaker on each later striking, as the dies were polished in between, until they disappear on the Plain 4 Proof gold coins. From this (and other evidence, including the style of the punches) he deduced the obverse die was actually created before 1804, with the final digit in the date left off until it was used in 1834.

The four diplomatic Proof sets were struck on two separate occasions. Two were struck in late 1834 and the other two were struck just before Edmund Roberts left on his mission to the Far East aboard the USS *Peacock* in April 1835. I believe the subsidiary silver coins and lower-denomination gold coins in the later two sets were probably dated 1835, but I can't prove that for certain. John Dale and I noted that Bob Simpson's 1804-dated eagle and the King of Siam specimen both have a very weak center on star 3, as if the recessed impression in the die was partially filled when the coins were struck. Both coins show a die crack from Liberty's front hair curl to the left base of the R in LIBERTY. The Harry W. Bass Jr. coin does not show the crack and has a pretty sharp star 3, despite being slightly worn. From this, we concluded the King of Siam and Simpson coins were probably struck at the same time, while the Bass coin was one of the two struck in 1835, after more polishing to remove the crack and clearing the obstruction from star 3. Accordingly, we believe the Simpson coin must be the Sultan of Muscat specimen.[9]

Registry of Proof 1804 Restrike Eagles
by David Stone

1. Sultan of Muscat specimen. Philadelphia Mint in 1834, part of the Sultan of Muscat diplomatic presentation Proof set; Sayyid Sa'id-bin-Sultan, Sultan of Muscat; unknown intermediaries; Colonel E.H.R. Green; Green estate, Chase Manhattan National Bank, executors; purchased by Stack's in 1943; purchased privately by Clifford T. Weihman; Farish-Baldenhofer Collection (Stack's, 11/1955), lot 1459; Rare and Important U.S. Gold Coins (Stack's, 10/1988), lot 119; private collector via Dean Albanese in 2003 for $1 million; private collector via Dean Albanese in 2005

for $2.74 million; private collector in October 2007 via Dean Albanese for $5 million; Legend Numismatics in 2010, with the assistance of John Albanese; Simpson Collection. The David W. Akers plate coin. Note: Some researchers have suggested this coin was owned by Baltimore collector Waldo Newcomer and, possibly, William Woodin before it passed to Colonel Green. This seems unlikely, as there is no record of the coin in the Newcomer inventory. Proof-65 Ultra Cameo NGC, later crossed over to be PCGS Proof-65 Ultra Cameo.

2. King of Siam specimen. Philadelphia Mint in 1834, part of the King of Siam diplomatic presentation Proof set; King Ph'ra Nang Klao (Rama III) of Siam in April 1836; King Mongkut (Rama IV), his half-brother; King Chulalongkorn (Rama V) his son in 1868; unknown intermediaries, possibly Mrs. Anna Leonowens, of *The King and I* musical fame; possibly Leonowens' descendants; David Spink in 1962 (creating much controversy when he informed the staff of his company, which had multiple owners, that his transaction was his personally); Lester Merkin, acting as an agent for Spink in 1979; purchased by Elvin I. Unterman; Lester Merkin, acting as an agent for Unterman in 1987; King of Siam Sale (Bowers and Merena, 10/1987), lot 2209, reserve not met; purchased by a private collector via Stack's on October 18, 1987; purchased by the Rarities Group (Martin Paul) and Continental Rarity Coin Fund I (Greg Holloway) in 1989; Boy's Town Sale (Superior, 5/1990), lot 3364; Iraj Sayeh and Terry Brand; the January-February Auction (Superior, 1/1993), lot 1196; Dwight Manley (Spectrum Numismatics); Western Collection, exhibited at the Mandalay Bay Casino in Las Vegas; West Coast business executive in 2001, via Spectrum Numismatics and Mike's Coin Chest of Torrance, California; Steve Contursi purchased the set, via Ira and Larry Goldberg, for $8.5 million on November 1, 2005. Private California collection. Proof 64 PCGS.

3. Undelivered presentation specimen. Philadelphia Mint in 1835, part of the diplomatic presentation Proof set for either the Emperor of Japan or the Emperor of Cochin China; never delivered by Special Agent Edmund Roberts, who died before the cased set could be presented; returned to the State Department; unknown intermediaries; Dr. Benjamin Betts, illustrated in the August 1869 issue of the *American Journal of Numismatics*; Public Auction Sale (Edward Cogan, 6/1871), lot 76, realized $35; Isaac F. Wood; Isaac F. Wood Collection (Cogan, 5/1873), lot 1334; Lorin G. Parmelee; Parmelee Collection (New York Coin & Stamp Co. 6/1890), lot 814; Charles Steigerwalt; Steigerwalt's List No. 50, November 1894; William H. Woodin; Woodin Collection (Thomas Elder, 3/1911), lot 1200; John H. Clapp; Clapp estate; Louis E. Eliasberg in 1942 via Stack's; Eliasberg estate; United States Gold Coin Collection (Bowers and Ruddy, 10/1982), lot 660; Harry W. Bass Jr.; Harry W. Bass Foundation. Proof-58 PCGS.

4. Undelivered presentation specimen (untraced today). Philadelphia Mint in 1835, part of the diplomatic presentation Proof set for either the Emperor of Japan or the Emperor of Cochin China; never delivered by Special Agent Edmund Roberts, who died before the cased set could be presented; returned to the State Department; not traced since. Carl Carlson believed this coin was offered in lot 639 of Thomas Elder's sale of 2/7/1913, but the description of that lot indicates that coin was a high-grade circulation strike example. Similarly, Walter Breen cited an

example in Virgil Brand's collection, but several researchers have found no mention of this issue in the Virgil Brand journals at the ANS. Breen also indicates the Brand coin was handled by coin dealer Charles E. Green in the 1940s, but he might have been handling the Colonel Green specimen on consignment, as it came on the market in the early 1940s. Breen also cites an example in Stack's H.R. Lee Sale in 1947, but that coin is also a circulation strike.[10] Several sources indicate the fourth 1804 Proof eagle may be in a private collection today, but we have not been able to reliably trace any appearance of this piece since the 1830s.

PF-63	PF-64	PF-65
$4,000,000	$4,500,000	$5,000,000

VF-20	EF-40	AU-50	AU-55	AU-58	MS-60	MS-63	MS-65
$20,000	$25,000	$37,500	$50,000	$65,000	$85,000	$100,000	$175,000

PF-63	PF-64	PF-65
$4,000,000	$4,500,000	$5,000,000

9

Liberty Head $10 Gold Coins, 1838–1907

LIBERTY HEAD, No MOTTO (1838–1866)

Designer: *Christian Gobrecht.* **Weight:** *16.718 grams.* **Composition:**
.900 gold, .100 copper (net weight: .48375 oz. pure gold). **Diameter:** *27 mm.*
Edge: *Reeded.* **Mints:** *Philadelphia, New Orleans, and San Francisco.*

The Liberty Head Design

Eagles of this design were made continuously at the Philadelphia Mint from 1838 to 1907, and at other mints at separate intervals. The weight was specified at 258 grains consisting of 90 percent gold, equal to 0.48375 ounce of pure gold.

Secretary of the Treasury Levi Woodbury contacted Mint Director Robert Maskell Patterson in July 1838, instructing him to once again strike eagles for circulation, the denomination having been in suspension since 1838.

On the 30th of the month, Patterson replied:[1]

> I have the honor to acknowledge the receipt of your letter of the 27th inst. and am
> pleased to receive your instruction relative to the coinage of eagles. I have ordered
> immediate measure to be taken for the preparation of the dies. We shall spare no
> pains to make our chief coin worthy of the mint. You are probably aware that the
> last coinage of eagles was made in 1804.

Christian Gobrecht, *de facto* the main mint engraver while engraver William Kneass was incapacitated by his stroke, prepared the new designs. In this era he experimented with several different portraits of Miss Liberty for the various denominations, such efforts taking the form of different varieties of copper cents (particularly in 1839), pattern half dollars, and elsewhere.

This general design was later used elsewhere on U.S. circulating coinage, including on half cents dated 1840 to 1857, large copper cents dated 1839 to 1857, $5 gold dated 1839 to 1908, and $10 gold dated 1838 to 1907, and may have been inspired by the head of Venus in Benjamin West's painting, *Omnia Vincit Amor*, though Gobrecht commented that it was "a female head resembling everybody and nobody."[2]

The obverse of the new type depicts a female head facing left, her hair in a bun secured by a string of beads, wearing a coronet inscribed LIBERTY. Stars surround, and the date is below. The reverse shows an eagle with a shield on its breast perched on an olive branch holding three arrows. The inscription UNITED STATES OF AMERICA, TEN D. surrounds the perimeter.

The new design was ready December 6, 1838, on which day Director Patterson sent four examples to Woodbury. In *Description of Ancient and Modern Coins, in the Cabinet Collection at the Mint of the United States* (1860), Mint Director James Ross Snowden described the new $10 design:

> The next change of type took place very near the end of the year 1838. The pattern then adopted for the gold coins has been continued down to the present time. It is as follows: *Obverse:* A bust of Liberty; the shoulders undraped. The hair is looped up in a roll behind, and entwined with beads; a couple of stray curls hang loosely upon the neck. The front of the head is embellished with a tiara, inscribed with the word "LIBERTY." Around the edge are thirteen stars, and beneath, the date "1838." There was no noticeable change in the type of the reverse.
>
> This pattern [design] first made its appearance on the twenty-sixth of December, and consisted of 6,700 eagles, and on the thirty-first of December the Chief Coiner returned to the Treasurer 500 eagles, making 7,200 eagles of the new type issued in this year. This pattern was adopted on the half eagle of 1839, and on the quarter eagle of 1840.

The Liberty head used on $10 gold coins in 1838 and early 1839 is slightly differently styled than that used beginning in October 1839, continuing to the end of the series. The most prominent difference can be noted in the shape of the neck truncation and the relation of star 6 to the coronet point and star 13 to the tip of the neck.

The modified portrait continued in service through the end of the Liberty Head series in 1907. In 1848 there was a minor modification to the back of Miss Liberty's hair; a new master die was made, and there are minute differences in certain star positions vis-à-vis border denticles.[3] In 1859 there was a minor revision of the reverse hub, most evident on the new version by the eagle having shorter and more delicate claws. This modification was used thereafter on Philadelphia Mint coins, but not those of the branch mints.

The addition of the motto IN GOD WE TRUST to the reverse in 1866 constituted a new type, discussed in more detail later in the chapter.

For the Without Motto type, mintages were continuous at the Philadelphia Mint from 1838 to 1865 and at the San Francisco Mint from 1854 to 1866. In addition, pieces were produced at the New Orleans Mint intermittently between 1841 and 1906.

Circulation strikes were strictly utilitarian and saw long, hard use in commerce until late December 1861, when payment of gold coins was suspended in the East and Midwest. On the West Coast, circulation of gold coins continued. The circulation-strike mintage for the 1838 to 1866-S, No Motto, type totals slightly over 5,250,000 coins.

Prior to the advent of the double eagle in 1850, many eagles were used in international commerce. An article in the *American Journal of Numismatics*, October 1873, stated that in 1870 the German Empire acquired from the Bank of England some 193,194 ounces of American eagle gold coins, and melted them into bullion.[4] This would have been equivalent to 364,769 freshly minted, unworn coins. As the Bank of England evaluated its foreign gold coins by weight, not by count, allowing for slight wear, the quantity was probably in the range of 360,000 pieces. It is likely that most such pieces were dated prior to 1850 (before the era of the $20). It is further likely that many other eagles were held in other foreign banks and later reduced to bullion.

In later times when the Free Silver Movement dominated politics quantities of eagles were shipped overseas, but the amounts were small in comparison to double eagles. This exportation started in a large way in 1879 and involved quantities of coins taken from bank and exchange house stocks as well as newly minted coins. Existing stocks included many high-grade coins that numismatists would later classify as AU or low-level Mint State.

After the fall of the "Iron Curtain" in the late 1980s, many eagles were found in eastern European banks—but, again, in smaller numbers than the $20 pieces. Among these were circulated $10 gold coins of the 1838 to 1866-S, No Motto, type, typically VF to EF in grade, occasionally slightly finer (such as low-level AU), and nearly always with extensive bagmarks. (See chapter 4 for more information on that.) The flood of repatriations began in the late 1900s and included millions of eagles, mostly AU and Mint State, that vastly changed the availability of high-grade coins. Many varieties from the 1870s onward considered by David W. Akers in 1980 to be great rarities became common in later years. The auction citations given reflect many such changes.

Die Varieties in Profusion

The advanced specialist will find eagles of this type to offer many interesting and curious die variations. Such varieties include the two portrait styles found among 1839 eagles (head of 1838 and head of 1840), variations in date logotype placement, and variations in mintmarks. Within most (but not all) years the same size date was used for all dies, except for 1842 (Large and Small Date), 1850 (Large and Small Date), and 1854-O (Large and Small Date).

Date numerals for eagles of 1838 and 1839 were entered into the working dies by hand. For the dates between 1840 and 1866, a four-digit logotype was used. In some instances—1847 is an example—the different depths to which the logotype was punched into the working die created interesting differences in spacing. By examining dozens of specimens of this date, and a few other dates for which the author had questions, it has been concluded that a four-digit logotype was used.[5]

The $10 dies of 1840, 1841, and some of 1842 are all Small Date, with the numerals small and with the 4 plain (without a crosslet at the right side of the crossbar). All other dates of the 1840s use a crosslet 4.

Among eagles dated 1846, those of the Philadelphia Mint are Small Date and those of New Orleans are Large Date. For 1856 logotypes, two four-digit punches were made, one with a "regular" 6 and the other with a "fallen" 6; the reason we know that these were each four-digit logotypes is that each was used on multiple working dies.

There are many dates with repunchings varying from slight to dramatic. Dies of 1843 to 1849 are particularly fertile hunting grounds for such peculiarities and are probably the result of an incompetent, inebriated, or otherwise clumsy employee of the die department (certainly not James B. Longacre, the chief engraver, who was not at the Mint when the situation began).[6] The year 1849 is one that offers fascinating examples of die-punching naiveté, including the Large Date over Small Date variety.

Minor changes to the obverse hub were made in 1848 and to the reverse in 1859. Other differences are noted in the descriptions of the individual dates.

Grading Standards

MS-60 to 70 (Mint State). *Obverse:* At MS-60, some abrasion and contact marks are evident, most noticeably on the hair to the right of Miss Liberty's forehead and on the jaw. Luster is present, but may be dull or lifeless, and interrupted in patches. At MS-63, contact marks are few, and abrasion

1880. Graded MS-63.

is very light. An MS-65 coin has hardly any abrasion, and contact marks are so minute as to require magnification. Luster should be full and rich. For most dates, coins graded above MS-65 exist more in theory than in actuality—but they do exist, and are defined by having fewer marks as perfection is approached. *Reverse:* Comments apply as for the obverse, except that abrasion and contact marks are most noticeable on the eagle's neck and to the lower left of the shield.

AU-50, 53, 55, 58 (About Uncirculated). *Obverse:* Light wear is seen on the face, the hair to the right of the face, and the highest area of the hair bun, more so at AU-50 than at AU–53 or 55. An AU-58 coin has minimal traces of wear. An AU-50 coin has luster in protected

1839, Large Letters, 9 Over 8. Graded AU-53.

areas among the stars and letters, with little in the open fields or on the portrait. At AU-58 most luster is present in the fields, but is worn away on the highest parts of the motifs. *Reverse:* Comments as preceding, except that the eagle shows wear in all of the higher areas, as well as the leaves and arrowheads.

Luster ranges from perhaps 40% remaining in protected areas (at AU-50) to nearly full mint bloom (at AU-58). Often the reverse of this type retains more luster than the obverse.

EF-40, 45 (Extremely Fine).

Obverse: Wear is evident on all high areas of the portrait, including the hair to the right of the forehead, the tip of the coronet, and the hair bun. The stars show light wear at their centers. Luster, if present at all, is minimal and in protected areas such as between the star points.

1868. Graded EF-40.

Reverse: Wear is greater than on an About Uncirculated coin. On the $10 coins (in contrast to the $2.50 and $5 of the same design), most of the details on the eagle are sharp. There is flatness on the leaves and arrowheads. Some traces of luster may be seen, more so at EF-45 than at EF-40.

VF-20, 30 (Very Fine).

Obverse: The higher-relief areas of hair are worn flat at VF-20, less so at VF-30. The hair to the right of the coronet is merged into heavy strands. The stars are flat at their centers.

Reverse: The eagle is worn further, with most neck feathers gone and with the feathers in the

1838. Graded VF-25.

wing having flat tips. The branch leaves have little or no detail. The vertical shield stripes, being deeply recessed, remain bold.

The Liberty Head eagle is seldom collected in grades lower than VF-20.

PF-60 to 70 (Proof).

Obverse and Reverse: PF–60 to 62 coins have extensive hairlines and may have nicks and contact marks. At PF-63, hairlines are prominent, but the mirror surface is very reflective. PF-64 coins have fewer hairlines. At PF-65, hairlines should be minimal and mostly seen only

1862. Graded PF-65.

under magnification. There should be no nicks or marks. PF-66 and higher coins should have no marks or hairlines visible to the unaided eye.

1838

Circulation-Strike Mintage: 7,200
Proof Mintage: *4–6*

Notes regarding mintages: The first examples intended for circulation were delivered on December 26, 1838, some 6,700 pieces, followed by 500 more on December 31.

Estimated population (Mint State): *8–11.* Most are at low levels, and some may have been called AU in the past. Concerning the tremendous demand for the 1838 eagle as the first year of its type, a true Mint State coin is by any evaluation a fantastic numismatic landmark. After the publication of my *American Coin Treasures and Hoards* book in 1997, a leading dealer (who wished to remain anonymous) stated that he had purchased and sold three choice Mint State 1838 eagles from the wreck of the SS *Lexington* lost in Long Island Sound in 1840. Prior to this I estimated the population of Mint State coins to be 3 to 5.

In his 1980 study of $10 gold coins appearing in several hundred auction sales David W. Akers only found six appearances of Uncirculated 1838 eagles, two coins of which had rubbing or friction. The study did not take account of multiple sales of the same coin. Gradeflation became rampant leading into the new millennia, and many coins of various issues that were designated as AU, including by the certification services, graduated to become encapsulated as Mint State. As to how many Mint State 1838 eagles exist by old-time conservative standards, the answer is very few as previously suggested.

Estimated population (circulated grades): *55–80.* Scarce in any grade, and very rare at the AU level. Very Fine is the preservation typically encountered. In fantastic demand for type set purposes.

Estimated population (Proofs): *3.*

Submissions certified at highest grades (as of March 2017): *PCGS:* AU-55 (1), AU-58 (2), MS-61 (2), MS-63 (2). *NGC:* AU-55 (9), AU-58 (11), MS-62 (1), MS-63 (1). As this is a prime rarity, submission numbers probably include repetitions of the same coins.

Die data: Dr. Montroville W. Dickeson noted in his 1859 *American Numismatical Manual:*

> *Obverse:* A female head—Goddess of Liberty—facing to the left, the hair done up behind, and bound by a fillet, upon which is inscribed the word LIBERTY, curls falling down on the neck. Around the edge of the field, 13 stars. In the exergue, 1838. *Reverse:* The eagle proportionally reduced in size, otherwise the same in design as on the half eagle of 1834. Legend, UNITED STATES OF AMERICA. Exergue, TEN D. Of this issue there was one type and two varieties, and the number coined was 7,200. Rare.

The date was entered into the obverse working die by four individual numeral punches. The 1 is bolder (it was entered more deeply into the die) than the other three figures. The first 8 is slightly double punched at the center and upper left. The top of the 3 is slightly low and a loop without a ball. There are "script" style 8's with a heavy crossbar from upper left to lower right, covering the curve in the other direction from upper right to lower left. The second 8 in 1838 was overpunched with a 9 the next year, and 1839, 9 Over 8, eagles were coined from it.

Characteristics of striking and die notes: These are usually very well struck with excellent detail on the obverse and reverse. They were considered perfect dies, with no cracks, relapping, etc.

Key to collecting: A few early "Uncirculated" citations excepted (and it is not known if these would merit the Uncirculated or Mint State designation today), nearly all of the "name" collections offered over the years have had VF and EF pieces. Such grades remain highly desirable today. This coin is showcased in the Smithsonian's National Numismatic Collection.

MARKET NEWS AND COMMENTARY

The news of a new gold eagle appearing in circulation spread quickly, igniting much interest in the new Liberty Head design. From *Niles' National Register*, January 19, 1839:

> THE GOLD EAGLE: This beautiful coin, after a long absence, has reappeared in our country. The Mint at Philadelphia is striking them, and a quantity has arrived here [in Washington, D.C.]. It is not only a noble coin, but in its improved appearance, a fine specimen of art. As yet, only the Mint in Philadelphia has issued this coin, but the branch mints will soon follow, as it is found that Philadelphia is an exceedingly difficult place to diffuse the coins from. It is found that they diffuse much better from other points, and therefore the coinage of the branches will be sedulously attended to. It is now 35 years since an eagle has been coined at our Mint.

W. Elliot Woodward's March 1865 sale of the Bache, Bertsch, Lightbody, Lilliendahl, Vinton, and Watson Collections included lot 2743: "1838. Uncirculated." It sold for $21 to Clemmy. The identity of "Clemmy" is not known today. The unreliability of grading in early listings is demonstrated by B. Max Mehl in the February 1921 sale of the Dr. G.F.E. Wilharm Collection, lot 335: "1838 Brilliant Uncirculated with Proof surface. Dr. Wilharm purchased this coin as a Proof at $50. While I hardly think the coin as a Proof but it is by far the finest I ever saw." It sold for $40. This coin was later in the October 1982 sale of the Louis E. Eliasberg Collection, where the present author listed it as lot 661: "1838 Choice AU-55 obverse; Brilliant Uncirculated, MS-60 reverse. Much original mint luster." It sold for $30,800.

Back to the 1940s when Mint State eagles sold for only a modest advance over circulated coins, examples include:

The December 1944 sale of the J.F. Bell Collection by Stack's included lot 601: "1838 The first year of issue of reduced size. Brilliant Uncirculated." It sold for $90. In May 1945 Stack's sale of the George H. Hall Collection included lot 2103: "1838 Brilliant Uncirculated with slight scratch in field. Very scarce." It sold for $85. Barney Bluestone, who operated his Salt City Coin Company business in Syracuse, New York, offered this in an undated circa 1947 fixed price list, inventory no. 551: "1838 Unc. $42.50." Bluestone conducted auctions from the 1930s onward, and later retired to Florida. He mainly stayed at home and was not a familiar figure at conventions.

In April 1949 B. Max Mehl's sale of the Dr. Charles W. Green Collection included lot 507: "1838 About Uncirculated with semi-proof surface. Dr. Green purchased this as a Proof. It is, however, a beautiful coin and rare so choice. Catalogs $75 in Very Fine. Cost $100." It sold for $77.50. The Green Collection, of mixed quality, came on the market early in a period during several years of a slump in the coin market. The high-grade gold coins, particularly double eagles of the 1920s, considered to be great rarities at the time, created a lot of excitement. This sale was the linchpin of the modern market for collecting rare 20th-century gold coins.

Mehl's May 1950 Golden Jubilee sale included lot 494: "1838. Uncirculated with almost full mint lustre. The reverse has considerable Proof surface. The obverse shows just a slight touch of cabinet friction, probably from having been handled with other coins. But it is a beautiful specimen of this rare eagle. Catalogs $75 in only Very Fine. Much superior to the Atwater specimen." It sold for $137.50. Mehl had sold the Atwater Collection in 1946.

Forward to the modern era, the Bowers and Merena Galleries' sale of the Eliasberg Gold Collection in October 1982 included lot 661: "1838 Liberty Head $10 MS-62." It sold for $30,800. Stack's March 1995 sale of the James A. Stack Sr. collection included lot 564: "1839/8 Liberty Head $10 Type of 1838, BU, no certification." It sold for $28,600. There were not many Mint State coins to be had, but AU coins appeared on occasion, such as in the May 1992 sale of the H.C. ("Heck") Dodson Collection, where Mid-American Rare Coin Auctions included lot 294: "1838 AU-50." It sold for $4,400. Similarly, the October 1996 Spink America sale of selections from the Byron Reed Collection included lot 155: "1838 surface marks, Almost Uncirculated, much luster in the recessed design areas." It sold for $5,720.

In April 2003, in the Central States sale, Heritage included lot 7095: "1838 MS-63 PCGS. A few of the obverse stars lack complete centers, but the strike is sharp otherwise." It sold for $63,250. In January 2007, in the sale of the Freedom Collection, Heritage included lot 3638: "1838 MS-63 NGC. Tied for finest known." It sold for $115,000.

> The D. Brent Pogue Collection, Part IV, sold by Stack's Bowers Galleries and Sotheby's in May 2016, included lot 4063: 1838 Liberty Head eagle. Mint State-63 PCGS. 1838 eagles are rare in all Mint State grades, and PCGS has assigned a grade over Mint State-60 on only four occasions. This is one of the top two, tied at MS-63 with a coin that has not sold publicly since 2002. Aside from this coin's last sale, nearly a decade ago, another certified Mint State example has not sold at auction since that time. From Heritage's FUN Sale of January 2007, lot 3638, via Richard Burdick. [Sold for $105,750]

PROOF MARKET NEWS AND COMMENTARY

Proofs were struck from the same die pair as circulation pieces. The Proof illustrated in *Walter Breen's Complete Encyclopedia of U.S. and Colonial Coins* seems to have a light bottom bun on the portrait, but illustrations of other Proofs show a full bun.

VF-20	EF-40	AU-50	AU-55	AU-58	MS-60	MS-63
$4,500	$10,000	$20,000	$30,000	$65,000	$80,000	$125,000

1839, Large Letters

Circulation-Strike Mintage: 25,801
Proof Mintage: *4–6*

Notes regarding mintages: Deliveries from the coiner took place from March 30 to June 29, 1839.

Estimated population (Mint State): *5–8.* These are quite rare in Mint State, and are mostly found in lower ranges, such as MS-60 or a notch or two higher. More generous figures given in population report totals probably represent a combination of resubmissions and of grading optimism. *True* Mint State coins are very rare.

Several Mint State coins are said to have been recovered from a sunken ship, possibly the SS *Lexington* (author's conjecture), in the 1990s, but no information has been learned.

Estimated population (circulated grades): *125–200.* Very scarce.

Estimated population (Proofs): *3.* The Mint Cabinet has a specimen; another is the J.S. Jenks coin, later in the Eliasberg Collection; and a third was located by Marc Emory in Europe in 1982.

Submissions certified at highest grades (as of March 2017): *PCGS:* MS-63 (1), MS-64 (1), MS-65 (1). *NGC:* MS-62 (2), MS-63 (1), MS-64 (1).

Die data: The obverse style is of the so-called "First Head" which for 1838 and early 1839 was differently positioned than on later issues, with the portrait of Miss Liberty tilted forward and the front of the neck truncation above the 18 of the date, and the right side of the truncation above and slightly to the right of star 13. Apparently this configuration was considered to be clumsy or less than artistic, and after being used for a short time, it was changed by October 1839.

The obverse has the "script" style 8, with a heavy crossbar from the upper left to the lower right, covering the curve in the other direction from upper right to lower left. Digit 3 is low, and with the top as a loop without the ball. All Large Letter style $10 coins of this year were made with the die which has been overdated by punching a 9 over the 8. These are also referred to as "Type of 1838," or "1839, 9 Over 8."

Strangely enough, the letters on the reverse, called *Large* in literature, are actually the same as those used in 1838 and are fairly small and delicate, being only slightly larger in size from those used on the "Small Letters" variety of the same year. Due to their being so similar in size, I believe this nomenclature should be discarded.

Characteristics of striking and die notes: Early die states have traces of the under-digit 8, later fading so as to appear as a perfect date. The overdate feature, faint at best and requiring a degree of interpretation, was not mentioned widely in catalogs until the late 1900s; most simply called this issue an 1839 eagle.

A very late reverse state shows a bisecting crack from the border through the second T in STATES, to the eagle's head, to the upper left corner of the shield, claws, and through the center of the E in TEN to the border. Another crack is seen from the border, touching the top of the O in OF, through the F, eagle's wing, and to the field below the AM in AMERICA. Still another crack begins above the A and continues through MERIC. Another crack extends from the border at the left, through the U in UNITED, crossing the earliest-mentioned crack, and ending below the arrow feather.[7]

Key to collecting: Typical grades are VF and EF, although there are enough AU coins around that the specialist can locate one without undue difficulty. Some high-grade AU coins of yesterday may be today's low-end Mint State pieces.

MARKET NEWS AND COMMENTARY
Certain listings that do not describe the portrait or letter size may be of the later Head of 1839 style with "Small Letters" reverse (better called the Type of '40, in my opinion). The two types were not generally differentiated until the mid-1900s. Early listings of Uncirculated coins were few and far between. Starting in the 1940s, offerings were made on occasion. In recent decades there have been quite a few—caused in part by multiple offerings of the same coin and by AU coins being reclassified as Mint State.

Stack's sale of the J.F. Bell Collection, December 1944, included lot 602: "1839 Large letters. Brilliant Uncirculated." It sold for $105. B. Max Mehl's June 1946 sale of the William Cutler Atwater Collection included lot 1417: "1839 Large letters on reverse. Uncirculated with even frosty mint surface. Quite rare so choice. Record over $100." It sold for $85.

Later, the January 1984 Stack's sale of the Amon G. Carter Jr. Family Collection included lot 741: "1839 type of 1838. The 9 is slightly recut giving the illusion of an overdate. Brilliant Uncirculated. A fully frosty example of this rarity." It sold for $12,100. In the March 1995 sale of the James A. Stack Sr. Collection Stack's offered lot 564: "1839/8 Type of 1838. Brilliant Uncirculated." It sold for $28,600.

Into modern times, Heritage Auctions offered this in the January 2001 FUN sale, lot 30056: "1839 type of 1838. Large letters. MS-66 PCGS. The finest known!" It sold for $402,500.

PROOF MARKET NEWS AND COMMENTARY
In December 1921 Henry Chapman, in his sale of the John Story Jenks Collection, offered lot 5735: "1839 Brilliant Proof; a magnificent specimen and excessively rare. From the Parmelee collection. Mr. Jenks' natal year!" It sold for $105. In October 1982 it reappeared in the Eliasberg Collection auction as lot 662: "Proof-65." It sold for $121,000. In September 1999 Larry and Ira Goldberg offered it as part of the Bradly Bloch Collection, lot 1817: "1839 Large Letters (Type of 1838). Eliasberg. A superb specimen of this two-year type coin. NGC Proof-67." It sold for $690,000. This coin reappeared in the January 2007 FUN sale by Heritage as lot 3657: "1839/8 Type of 1838 Proof-67 NGC. An American numismatic classic. Ex Eliasberg Collection." It sold for $1,610,000.

VF-20	EF-40	AU-50	AU-55	AU-58	MS-60	MS-63	MS-65
$1,500	$3,750	$6,500	$10,500	$15,000	$32,500	$85,000	$350,000

1839, Small Letters

Circulation-Strike Mintage: 12,447

Notes regarding mintages: This revised Liberty Head portrait by Christian Gobrecht made its debut in October 1839, with deliveries taking place from October 30 to December 31.

Estimated population (Mint State): *3.* They are exceedingly rare.

Estimated population (circulated grades): *50–80.* These are very rare, but are not widely appreciated as such.

Submissions certified at highest grades (as of March 2017): *PCGS:* AU-55 (1), AU-58 (2), MS-62 (1). ***NGC:*** AU-55 (19), AU-58 (24), MS-64 (1).

Die data: The date numerals were entered into the working die with four separate single-digit punches. At least two obverse dies were made (distinguishing points include the position of the 1 in relation to the denticles below and the alignment of the numerals).

The new portrait received no notice by numismatists until into the 20th century. In *Mehl's Numismatic Monthly,* December 1910, the variety was described as a "pattern," but even then, most collectors and dealers paid little attention. It was not until the 1940s that significant listings occurred. Until then, all 1839 half eagles were simply categorized by date.

About the newly recognized distinction, from *Mehl's Numismatic Monthly,* December 1910, "Newly Discovered Variety 1839 Eagle":

> I recently picked up an 1839 eagle, the type of which is new to me, at least the common type of 1839 Eagle is an exact copy of 1838, with date under and in front of bust; hair combed down over ear, except the point of lobe; large stars and large letters. But the one under consideration is decidedly different. The letters and stars are smaller, the head is upright with date exactly under the neck and very compact; the hair is combed back exposing the ear; the profile is finer in expression. I have seen a large number of 1839 eagles, but this is the first one of this type; it is an exact copy of 1840, and I shall designate it as "1839 type of 1840." I have had much pleasure in collecting mint marked coins, as well as seeking decided varieties of the Philadelphia Mint.

The letters on the reverse, called *Small* in literature, actually only *slightly* smaller than those used in 1838 and on the reverse of the 1839 with Head of 1838; I believe the Small Letters nomenclature should be discarded as on an absolute basis, both reverse styles are small—it is just that the present reverse is slightly smaller than the other.

Key to collecting: The typical specimen is VF or EF. AU coins are very elusive.

MARKET NEWS AND COMMENTARY

In April 1949 B. Max Mehl's sale of the Dr. Charles W. Green Collection included lot 508: "1839 Small letters in legend on reverse. Just About Uncirculated with an even frosty mint surface, bold impression, raised borders. A beautiful specimen of this rare variety. Not even in the Atwater Sale. Catalogs $75 in only Very Fine. This is far superior." It sold for $105.

In March 1988 the Bowers and Merena Galleries' sale of the Norweb Collection, Part II, included lot 2146: "1839 Type of '40, Small Letters. VF-30. Some luster is still seen in protected areas. From New Netherlands Coin Company, March 1955." It sold for $2,530.

This description by David Akers in the October 1998 catalog of the John J. Pittman Collection, Part II, gives an excellent overview of the variety, lot 1912:

> 1839, Type of 1840. Choice Uncirculated. Small letters on the reverse. This is another of the truly great coins in the Pittman Collection, acquired from the Farouk sale in 1954 as part of Lot 188. The 1839 Type of 1840 issue is one of the greatest rarities among all Liberty Head eagles, especially in high grade. It is also far more rare than the 1839 type of 1838 or even the 1838, both of which have traditionally been more highly prized due to their type coin status. Of the relatively few examples of this issue that are known (probably no more than 40-50 pieces total, if that many), almost all are well circulated and typically grade only Very Fine or Extremely Fine. In AU condition, the 1839 Type of 1840 eagle is very rare and Mint State examples are exceedingly rare with only the following three specimens known. 1. John Jay Pittman, the specimen offered here; Farouk: 188; William H. Woodin: 1202. 2. Charles Jay: 316. 3. 1976 ANA sale (Stack's): 3057. I have seen several other examples called Uncirculated in the past, but I did not consider any of them strictly Uncirculated." [Sold for $143,000]

In the June 2010 Whitman Expo sale, Stack's Bowers Galleries offered lot 3733: "1839 type of 1840. MS-62 NGC. Population 7, 10 finer only one of which is in Mint State." It sold for $9,995.

VF-20	EF-40	AU-50	AU-55	AU-58	MS-60	MS-63
$1,500	$3,750	$8,500	$20,000	$25,000	$42,500	$135,000

1840

Circulation-Strike Mintage: 47,338
Proof Mintage: 1–2

Estimated population (Mint State):
5–7. Data is inconclusive. In any event, they are exceedingly rare. In 1980 David W. Akers remarked that he had never seen a Mint State coin, but later one came his way and was cataloged by him as part of Auction '85. Shortly thereafter, Superior offered a remarkable Mint State coin. In modern times some have been certified as Mint State that earlier would have been called About Uncirculated.

Estimated population (circulated grades): *200–300.* They are very scarce in proportion to the original mintage.

Estimated population (Proofs): *1.* The Mint Cabinet specimen presently in the Smithsonian Institution.

Submissions certified at highest grades (as of March 2017): *PCGS:* MS-61 (3), MS-62 (1). ***NGC:*** MS-61 (3), MS-62 (1).

Die data: Beginning this year, a four-digit logotype was used to produce most (but not all) $10 dies in the Liberty Head series. All of the dates from 1840 to 1907 are in a straight line, the style also used for other gold issues of the era. This logotype was also used on dies for copper cents.

Key to collecting: As is the case with all $10 gold of this design, most were used extensively in commerce, then melted. No circulation strike 1840 $10 coins are known to have been saved for numismatic purposes except one to illustrate the date in the Mint Cabinet. As a result nearly all coins in numismatic hands show evidence of having been used in commerce.

MARKET NEWS AND COMMENTARY

William H. Strobridge, in his June 1873 offering of Selections from the Cabinets of L.G. Parmelee and G.F. Seavey, included lot 808: "1840. Fine." It sold for $12.25. Early listings of circulation-strike Liberty Head $10 coins are few and far between, as most numismatists terminated their collections with the 1804 $10. Moreover, an 1840 eagle such as this could be obtained for face value at a bank, this being true into the early 1930s. Early listings for Uncirculated coins are practically non-existent. Years later in the March 1911 sale of the William H. Woodin Collection by Thomas L. Elder, an 1840 in Fine grade sold for $11—still hardly worth listing.

The Belden E. Roach Collection, sold by B. Max Mehl in February 1944, offered a high-grade coin with lot 321: "1840 About Uncirculated with frosty mint surface. Very scarce." It sold for $37.50.

B. Max Mehl's Golden Jubilee sale included lot 496: "1840 Extremely Fine; just a shade from Uncirculated; some mint luster. A very scarce date especially so choice. Better than the specimens in both the Atwater and the Dr. Green Collections. This is one of the best specimens of this date eagle that has been offered in many years." It sold for $40.

Into modern times, in the May 1992 sale of the H.C. ("Heck") Dodson Collection, Mid-American Rare Coin Auctions included lot 298: "1840 Uncirculated." It sold for $12,650. In May 1993 the Bowers and Merena Galleries' sale of the Stetson University Collection included lot 2002: "1840 EF-45. Much mint brilliance; a scattering of tiny marks." It sold for $2,530.

In September 1994 the sale by Bowers and Merena Galleries of the Richard and Jean Salisbury and Ted K. Woods Collections included lot 1387: "1840 AU-58 PCGS. This is the only AU-58 specimen certified by PCGS, with none graded higher." It sold for $8,250.

Stack's March 1996 sale of the W.R. Walling Collection included lot 894: "1840 Liberty Head $10, MS-61 NGC." It sold for $7,700. The October 1996 Spink America sale of selections from the Byron Reed Collection included lot 156: "1840 light circulation marks, Almost Uncirculated; much luster remains." It sold for $4,180.

In November 2000 the Harry W. Bass Jr. Collection, Part IV, included lot 586: "1840 MS-61 PCGS. Lustrous yellow gold with sharply struck details. A supremely important coin in this series, tied with one other MS-61 as the only Mint State specimens of the year certified by PCGS. An opportunity not likely to be repeated in the near future. PCGS Population: 2; none finer." It sold for $7,705. In the September 2016 Twelve Oaks Collection, Heritage included lot 14134: "1840 MS-61 PCGS. Ex Harry W. Bass Jr. Collection Part IV, lot 586." It sold for $35,250.

In August 2006 the American Numismatic Rarities sale of the Old West and Franklinton Collections included lot 1542: "1840 MS-61 PCGS." It sold for $19,550. In August 2011, in the ANA World's Fair of Money sale, Heritage included lot 7606: "1840 MS-61 PCGS." It sold for $12,650.

The December 2016 Regency Auction XIX included lot 464: "1840 AU-58 PCGS." It sold for $8,106.25.

VF-20	EF-40	AU-50	AU-55	AU-58	MS-60
$1,000	$1,100	$1,550	$2,750	$6,000	$10,000

1841

Circulation-Strike Mintage: 63,131
Proof Mintage: *4–6*

Notes regarding mintages: Coinage was accomplished on multiple occasions from March through December.

Estimated population (Mint State): *6–9,* by conservative grading. Here we go again! Some coins now certified as low Mint State do show circulation and used to be called About Uncirculated. In his 1980 study of hundreds of auction catalogs David Akers found only three listings for Uncirculated coins.

Estimated population (circulated grades): *300–450.* VF is the typical grade seen, although occasional EF examples appear. AU coins with luster are quite rare, although a few have appeared on the auction block.

Estimated population (Proofs): *3* . One in the Mint Collection, since 1923 on loan to the Smithsonian Institution.

Submissions certified at highest grades (as of March 2017): *PCGS:* MS-61 (2), MS-62 (2), MS-63 (1). *NGC:* MS-61 (6), MS-62 (2).

Die data: The date logotype was also used on dies for copper cents. In May 2005 in the Harry W. Bass Jr. Collection Part III under lot 572, an AU-55 coin:

> The date was punched from a four-digit logotype. The first three numerals, 184, are identical in position and alignment to those seen on the preceding date, 1840. It may be that the following scenario occurred: In 1840 the four-digit logotype was made by punching the individual numerals 1, 8, 4, and 0 into a soft steel matrix, hardening it, and creating a four-digit logotype for the eagle coinage. Subsequently, the 0 was ground off of the four-digit logotype, and the three-digit logotype, 184, was used in 1841 by impressing in a new blank of soft steel, creating 184, to which a single 1 was added. Then the process was repeated, the matrix was hardened, and the four-digit logotype 1841 was created. This would neatly explain the identical position of the first three letters. To answer the inquiry as to whether simply a three-digit logotype was used on the working dies, with the digit 1 added separately, we need but point to the fact that all 1841 dies, including those of the New Orleans Mint, are of the same alignment, spacing, etc. indicating use of a four-digit logotype.

Key to collecting: The 1841 eagle is not a rarity in a relative sense, for most other Liberty Head coins of the era are more elusive. However, considering millions of Americans collect coins, a population in the low hundreds designates a rarity. By way of comparisons—and such have been minimized in the present text—in any worn grade, an 1841 $10 is rarer than a Proof 1895 silver dollar, the latter being the rarest of all Morgan dollars (880 minted, perhaps 600 to 700 survive today).

MARKET NEWS AND COMMENTARY

In January 1884 W. Elliot Woodward's sale of the Honorable Heman Ely Collection included this, a typical listing cited here as an example, lot 804: "1841 Very Fine, scarce." It sold for $10.50 to Major Charles P. Nichols.

In March 1988 the Bowers and Merena Galleries' sale of the Norweb Collection, Part II, included lot 2148: "1841 MS-60. Lustrous and frosty surfaces. Some contact marks keep this from a higher grade, but still it is head and shoulders above nearly every other coin offered in recent years. Purchased by Albert F. Holden from Elmer Sears on October 1, 1909." It sold for $8,250.

Stack's sale in March 1991 of the James A. Stack Collection included lot 567: "1841 Liberty Head $10, Brilliant Uncirculated." It sold for $11,000. In their May 1992 sale of the H.C. ("Heck") Dodson Collection, Mid-American Rare Coin Auctions description of lot 300 told of the number of certified pieces as of that time: "1841 Uncirculated (61). Over the years, only a handful of Mint State examples have appeared; often, they are duplications of the same coin (as in the case of the Dunham-Alto specimen). The only Mint State piece graded by NGC is MS-60; PCGS has graded a lone MS-62!" It sold for $9,900.

The year 1992 was early in the third-party grading (TPG) game, and many coins had not been sent into the services yet. Later submissions plus resubmissions plus gradeflation greatly expanded the population reports.

In May 2000 the Bowers and Merena Galleries' sale of the Harry W. Bass Jr. Collection, Part III, included lot 571:

> 1841 AU-55. Breen-6854. A lustrous yellow gold specimen with a whisper of olive iridescence. Typically found in VF or occasionally EF; lustrous AU or finer specimens can be considered rare. Date logotype small, continuing the style of 1840. The following notes by the editor (QDB) are tentative in nature, as investigations are still progressing. We would be pleased to correspond with anyone making parallel inquiries. The date was punched from a four-digit logotype. The first three numerals, 184, are identical in position and alignment to those seen on the preceding date, 1840. It may be that the following scenario occurred: In 1840 the four-digit logotype was made by punching the individual numerals 1, 8, 4, and 0 into a soft steel matrix, hardening it, and creating a four-digit logotype for the eagle coinage. Subsequently, the 0 was ground off of the four-digit logotype, and the three-digit logotype, 184, was used in 1841 by impressing in a new blank of soft steel, creating 184, to which a single 1 was added. Then the process was repeated, the matrix was hardened, and the four-digit logotype 1841 was created. This would neatly explain the identical position of the first three letters. To answer the inquiry as to whether simply a three-digit logotype was used on the working dies, with the digit 1 added separately, we need but

point to the fact that all 1841 dies, including those of the New Orleans Mint, are of the same alignment, spacing, etc. indicating use of a four-digit logotype. Reverse with die crack from rim at 10:00, along the length of the eagle's wing, across the shield, then terminating in the field above the top arrowhead. From Lester Merkin's sale of March 1969, Lot 394. [Sold for $1,610]

In its Long Beach sale of October 1995, Heritage included lot 6266: "1841 MS-62 PCGS. In Mint State the 1841 is very rare with only three pieces certified by the two leading grading services, this being the finest of the three." It sold for $18,700.

PROOF MARKET NEWS AND COMMENTARY

Superior Galleries, in their sale of October 1990, offered this commentary with lot 2135:

1841. NGC Proof-61. The only Proof 1841 graded. And probably the only one to be had. Breen lists two 1841 Proof eagles in his Proofs encyclopedia: "Centered date, rev. of 1840. (1) Smithsonian Institution, ex Mint coll. (2) A somewhat questionable Proof is in ANS, from J.P. Morgan, presumably ex R.C.W. Brock. This is from polished dies and is very sharp but the quality of the later Proofs." Well, here is a third example; a coin whose quality is definitely "the quality of the later Proofs." [Sold for $25,300]

VF-20	EF-40	AU-50	AU-55	AU-58	MS-60
$1,000	$1,050	$1,250	$2,500	$4,500	$8,500

1841-O

Circulation-Strike Mintage: 2,500

Notes regarding mintages: This is the smallest mintage quantity for any $10 coin of the era.

Estimated population (Mint State): *None.*

Estimated population (circulated grades): *50–80.* Scarce, as the low mintage suggests. Some small effort was made to find these pieces in bank holdings in the early 1900s, by which time such coins were worn down to about Very Fine, thus neatly providing the reason why most coins known today are in this grade. A few others have turned up in overseas holdings after World War II. From all sources, past and in recent decades, the population has amounted to the estimate given.

Submissions certified at highest grades (as of March 2017): *PCGS:* AU-50 (6), AU-53 (2), AU-55 (5), AU-58 (1). *NGC:* AU-50 (8), AU-53 (5), AU-55 (1), AU-58 (1).

Die data: For this coinage—the first eagle to be made at a branch mint—a pair of dies was shipped from Philadelphia to New Orleans on January 1, 1841. The four-digit date logotype was also used on dies for copper cents. Also see comments under the 1841 Philadelphia eagle previously listed. The O mintmark is small, heavy, and with a narrow vertical interior opening.

Characteristics of striking and die notes: Fairly well struck, save for some trivial lightness on the eagle to the left of the shield.

Key to collecting: By 1980, David W. Akers in his study of the $10 series had not been able to locate any offering of a coin even as high as in the AU range, with EF being the limit. Since that time, a scattered few have been certified as AU, perhaps including some that had been called EF earlier. EF and AU coins have brought very strong prices at auction with many bidders in competition.

MARKET NEWS AND COMMENTARY

No record before 1893 has been found of anyone collecting branch-mint eagles other than John M. Clapp and Thomas Cleneay. For circulated coins Clapp usually obtained them for face value through his local bank in Bradford, Pennsylvania. As the auction citations reveal, the 1841-O was not seriously collected until the present century.

In April 1907 the David S. Wilson Collection, sold by S. Hudson Chapman, offered lot 17: "1841-O Fine. Rare." It sold for $31. By this time several collectors were forming sets. In June 1934 J.C. Morgenthau & Co.'s sale of coins from the Waldo C. Newcomer Collection included lot 111: "1841-O Very Fine and exceedingly rare." It sold for $50, a very strong price for the time. Newcomer was one of the few numismatists of the early 1900s who collected Liberty Head eagles from branch mints.

J.C. Morgenthau & Co. was a quiet enterprise—a division of Scott Stamp & Coin. It was supervised by Wayte Raymond. Cataloging was minimal—and even for great rarities little was said. The descriptions were done by Raymond and by James G. Macallister of Philadelphia, who came to New York City by train on occasion. Julius C. Morgenthau, born in Germany on August 2, 1858, came to America with his family. He ran an auction house that sold stamps, prints, etc., starting in the profession in 1895 at which time he was in Chicago. He is not known to have had any numismatic knowledge or special interest in the field. In 1915 he was president of the Philatelic Collectors Club. He died in New York City, his long-time home, in May 1929 at the age of 79. His brother Henry served as ambassador to Turkey and in 1934 would become Franklin D. Roosevelt's secretary of the Treasury, succeeding William H. Woodin.

In February 1944, in the Belden E. Roach Collection, B. Max Mehl offered lot 396: "1841-O First year of issue. Extremely Fine with mint luster. Minute nick on edge below date. Record over $50." It sold for $40. Seemingly, most people desiring an 1841-O had obtained one. The market had not advanced. In the December 1944 sale of the J.F. Bell Collection, Stack's included lot 686: "1841-O First year of issue. Extremely Fine." It sold for $45.

In October 1982, in a different market with many more players, the Louis E. Eliasberg Collection of U.S. Gold Coins, sold by Bowers and Ruddy Galleries, offered lot 665: "1841-O AU-50. Much original mint lustre still remaining. From the John H. Clapp Collection, 1942. Earlier from Elmer S. Sears, October 1920." It sold for $4,400.

In March 2004 the American Numismatic Rarities Whitman Expo sale included lot 1498: "1841-O AU-50 NGC." It sold for $11,500. In July 2005 the American Numismatic Rarities sale of the William H. LaBelle Sr. Collection included lot 297: "1841-O AU-55 PCGS. From the Reed Hawn Collection sold in 1993 by Stack's where it realized $19,800." It sold for $28,750. In February 2009, in its sale of the Grand Lake Collection, Heritage included lot 2862: "1841-O AU-55 PCGS." It sold for $25,300.

The Stack's Bowers Galleries' sale at the August 2012 Philadelphia ANA World's Fair of Money Auction included lot 11739: "1841-O Liberty Head $10, EF-45 PCGS." It sold for $16,100.

In its Long Beach sale of September 2016, Heritage included lot 14135: "1841-O AU-50 NGC." It sold for $21,150. The Stack's Bowers Galleries' November 2016 Baltimore Auction included lot 2150: "1841-O Liberty Head $10, AU-55 PCGS." It sold for $61,688.

VF-20	EF-40	AU-50	AU-55	AU-58
$7,000	$15,000	$22,500	$35,000	$45,000

1842, Small Date

Circulation-Strike Mintage: 18,623
Proof Mintage: 2

Notes regarding mintages: Deliveries of eagles were as follows (without regard to date size): *January 31: 2,792; February 28: 5,674; March 31: 4,388; April 30: 5,769; June 30: 10,477; July 30: 9,199; August 31: 3,407; September 30: 6,603; October 31: 5,500; November 30: 10,000;* and *December 31: 9,408.*

Estimated population (Mint State): *1–2.* These are exceedingly rare at this grade level, and for all practical purposes, unobtainable.

Estimated population (circulated grades): *75–125.* VF and EF grades are usual.

Estimated population (Proofs): *2.* One in the Mint Collection, since 1923 on loan to the Smithsonian Institution.

Submissions certified at highest grades (as of March 2017): *PCGS:* MS-61 (2), MS-62 (1), MS-63 (1). *NGC:* MS-60 (1), MS-61 (3).

Die data: This logotype with small digits was also used on dies for copper cents.

Characteristics of striking and die notes: These coins are usually well struck.

Key to collecting: Data is inconclusive as to quantities surviving. In 1980 David W. Akers suggested that in terms of auction appearances, both Small Date and Large Date were about equal. However, this may be due to there being enough pieces to supply most specialists, never mind that one is scarcer than the others. Certification service data shows the Small Date to be significantly the rarer of the two.

MARKET NEWS AND COMMENTARY

In February 1944, in the Belden E. Roach Collection, B. Max Mehl offered lot 324: "1842 Small date. Practically Uncirculated with bright mint luster." It sold for $32.50.

Years later in October 1982, in the Louis E. Eliasberg Collection of U.S. Gold Coins, Bowers and Ruddy Galleries offered lot 666: "1842 Small Date. AU-50. From the John H. Clapp Collection, 1942. Earlier from Elmer S. Sears, July 1909." It sold for $1,650.

Stack's sale in May 2001 of the Samuel Berngard and SS *New York* Collections included lot 2071: "1842 Liberty Head $10 Small Date, MS-61 NGC." It sold for $16,100. In May 1992 Bowers and Merena Galleries included this in its sale of the Somerset Collection, lot 1524: "1842 Large Date. MS-61 PCGS. Brilliant and lustrous. One of the finest examples of this issue we have ever handled." It sold for $14,850.

In October 1999, in the Harry W. Bass Jr. Collection, Part II, Bowers and Merena Galleries offered lot 1324: "1842 Small Date. MS-62 PCGS. Purchased from Numismatic Enterprises (Steve Kosoff and Mike Kliman), November 1971, Lot 412." It sold for $18,400.

VF-20	EF-40	AU-50	AU-55	AU-58	MS-60	MS-63
$1,000	$1,050	$1,750	$3,000	$7,500	$13,500	$40,000

1842, Large Date

Circulation-Strike Mintage: 62,884

Notes regarding mintages: Walter Breen has estimated that of the mintage of 81,507 for the 1842 eagle, 18,623 were of the Small Date variety and that 62,884 were of the Large Date variety. Breen suggests that the Large Date eagles were made from May through December.

Estimated population (Mint State): *20–30.* This number is largely buoyed by MS–60 and 61 coins that began appearing at sales in the late 1900s and early 2000s. Probably, many if not most of these were upgraded from AU.

Estimated population (circulated grades): *250–400.* VF is the grade usually found. EF pieces are scarcer, and at the AU level the 1842, Large Date, is rare.

Submissions certified at highest grades (as of March 2017): *PCGS:* MS-63 (2), MS-64 (1), MS-65 (1). *NGC:* MS-60 (1), MS-61 (1).

Die data: This Large Date logotype was also used on 1842 copper cents and silver half dollars.

Characteristics of striking and die notes: Usually well struck.

Key to collecting: VF is the grade usually found. EF pieces are scarcer, and at the AU level the 1842, Large Date, is rare. Most of the eagles of this era can be easily collected in grades of VF or EF, or, if budget permits, AU. The prices of lower grades are influenced by movements in the gold bullion market. The numismatic market has remained strong and steady, but bullion values fluctuate.

MARKET NEWS AND COMMENTARY

B. Max Mehl, in his March 1945 sale of the William A. Knapp Collection, included lot 1048: "1842 Large date. Uncirculated, brilliant mint luster. Rare so choice. Lists at $40 in only Very Fine. This one worth at least double." The prediction proved correct, and the coin sold for $125. It was unusual in 1945 for a Mint State coin to sell for multiples of the VF listing in the *Standard Catalogue*.

Norman Stack cataloged the May 1965 Grant Pierce & Sons Collection that included lot 1447: "1842 Large Date. Brilliant Uncirculated. Full frosty mint luster. It catalogs at $110 but we seriously doubt if a truly Uncirculated coin such as this could be purchased for double that price." It sold for $130.

RARCOA's Central States sale in May 1992 included this highlight, lot 877: "1842 Large Date Choice Brilliant Uncirculated (PCGS MS-63). Actually a discovery piece in this quality, no other Mint State 1842 Eagle has been graded by either service. The opportunity of a lifetime for some lucky collector." It sold for $26,500. After this time a number of MS–60 and 61 coins were offered at auction.

Into modern times, in November 2000, in the Harry W. Bass Jr. Collection, Part IV, Bowers and Merena Galleries offered lot 593: "1842 Large Date. MS-64 PCGS. PCGS Population: 2, none finer. From Heritage's sale of October 16, 1995, Lot 6239." It sold for $23,000.

Heritage's FUN sale of January 2001 included lot 8270:

> 1842 Large Date MS-63 PCGS. Deep green-gold undertones and softer orange-gold patina confirms the originality of this exquisite example. Both sides have predominantly frosty mint luster, but modest brightness is noted in the fields at select angles. The surfaces are equally free of sizable abrasions and bothersome striking incompleteness. Population: 1 in 63, with only 2 finer (10/00). From the Bob Bisanz U.S. Type Set. [Sold for $12,650]

Heritage's Long Beach sale in September 2008 included lot 3841: "1842 Large Date. MS-64 NGC." It sold for $74,750. The same firm's June 2016 sale included lot 53537: "1842 Large Date. AU-58 PCGS." It sold for $4,230.

VF-20	EF-40	AU-50	AU-55	AU-58	MS-60	MS-63	MS-65
$1,000	$1,050	$1,650	$2,500	$5,000	$15,000	$35,000	$125,000

1842-O

Circulation-Strike Mintage: 27,400

Notes regarding mintages: Eagles of this type are believed to have been struck very late in the year, as the dies were not sent from Philadelphia until October 22, 1842. Presumably, this indicates that at the time the prevailing style for the denomination was the Large Date. Thus, by inference the *Philadelphia Mint* Large Date eagles were struck later than the Small Date pieces.

Estimated population (Mint State): 5–8. A couple are highly prooflike and may have been specimen strikings. David W. Akers in 1980 stated that he had never seen a *choice* example. This comment refers to his personal inspections, which were necessarily only a tiny percentage of the coins in the marketplace.

Estimated population (circulated grades): *200–300.*

Submissions certified at highest grades (as of March 2017): *PCGS:* MS-60 (1), MS-61 (1), MS-63 (1). *NGC:* MS-60 (2), MS-61 (1).

Die data: One pair of dies for the 1842-O coinage was shipped late in the year, on October 22, 1842. However, two reverse die varieties are known: one quite similar to, but differing slightly from the reverse of 1841-O, and the other from a new reverse (the one shipped October 22, 1842). Apparently, one or more additional die shipments were not recorded.

Characteristics of striking and die notes: Usually fairly well struck. At least one coin has the appearance of a prooflike specimen striking.

Key to collecting: The 1842-O is readily available in grades of VF and, less often, EF. These are quite elusive at the AU level. Although all eagles of this era are rarities on an absolute basis, with a population as estimated above there are enough to supply a far lesser number of specialists seeking them. If even 100 new entrants decided to become specialists, the market would see an incredible rise in prices! So, perhaps don't tell anyone while you are building your collection!

MARKET NEWS AND COMMENTARY

The lack of high premiums being paid for worn coins vis-à-vis Uncirculated coins was demonstrated endless times in this era, such as in the November 1939 William B. Hale Collection sold by Stack's, lot 1702: "1842-O Beautiful Uncirculated specimen; struck in light yellow gold. Very scarce. Listed at $40 in Very Fine condition." It sold for $25.

In the May 1992 sale of the H.C. ("Heck") Dodson Collection, Mid-American Rare Coin Auctions included lot 305: "1842-O MS-61." It sold for $5,170. Stack's sale in September 1996 of the Devries & Melzer Collections included lot 1614: "1842-O Liberty Head $10, Brilliant Uncirculated." It sold for $26,400.

In its Long Beach sale of February 2008 Heritage included lot 2611:

> 1842-O AU-55 NGC. The 1842-O is midway in rarity between the nearly uncollectible 1841-O and the relatively plentiful 1843-O. The 1842-O is scarce in all grades. Most certified examples are in EF and AU, and NGC has certified only three pieces as Mint State, one each between MS-60 and MS-62. [Sold for $4,600]

Stack's sale in August 2010 of the Johnson-Blue Collection included lot 1094: "1842-O Liberty Head $10, MS-61 PCGS." It sold for $74,750. In its FUN Convention sale of January 2017 Heritage included lot 6897: "1842-O AU-53 PCGS." It sold for $4,465.

VF-20	EF-40	AU-50	AU-55	AU-58	MS-60	MS-63
$1,150	$1,250	$3,000	$7,500	$13,500	$25,000	$75,000

1843

Circulation-Strike Mintage: 75,462
Proof Mintage: 6–8

Notes regarding mintages: Deliveries took place once a month from January through October. Record deposits of gold from domestic mines resulted in all-time high gold coinage figures at all four mints this year, although only the Philadelphia and New Orleans mints struck coins of the $10 denomination.

Estimated population (Mint State): *1–2.*

Estimated population (circulated grades): *500–750.*

Estimated population (Proofs): *5.* One is in the National Numismatic Collection.

Submissions certified at highest grades (as of March 2017): *PCGS:* AU-55 (5), AU-58 (1), MS-61 (1). *NGC:* AU-55 (42), AU-58 (26), MS-60 (4), MS-61 (1).

Die data: Repunched date varieties exist, including "Triple Date" (Breen-6861).

Characteristics of striking and die notes: Usually well struck.

Key to collecting: VF is the order of the day, EF next often seen, and rarely AU.

MARKET NEWS AND COMMENTARY

In early times circulated examples had little premium value and thus were not candidates for listing in auction catalogs. When they were, typically they did not sell for much, as this in W. Elliot Woodward's January 1884 sale of the Honorable Heman Ely Collection, lot 805: "1843 Very Fine." It sold for $10.50 to Major Charles P. Nichols.

Matters were not much different in March 1911 in Thomas L. Elder's sale of the William H. Woodin Collection, lot 1208: "1843. Nearly Fine." It sold for $11. It was not until modern times that AU and Mint State coins were offered in sales, a few at first, many later—from repatriations.

Now, to the 21st century, the Stack's sale in July 2008 of the Samuel Berngard and SS *New York* Collections included lot 2076: "1843 MS-60 NGC." It sold for $19,550. In the Long Beach sale of September 2016 Heritage included lot 14136: "1843 AU-58 PCGS." It sold for $14,687.50.

PROOF MARKET NEWS AND COMMENTARY

In March 1911, in his sale of the William H. Woodin Collection, Thomas L. Elder offered lot 1207: "1843 Brilliant Proof. Almost unique. A great rarity." It sold for $100. In January 1946 the Numismatic Gallery sale of "The World's Greatest Collection" (F.C.C. Boyd) included lot 648: "1843 A superb brilliant Proof. It is not likely that there were even ten Proofs struck of this date." It sold for $310.

VF-20	EF-40	AU-50	AU-55	AU-58	MS-60
$950	$1,050	$1,750	$3,000	$5,000	$12,500

1843-O

Circulation-Strike Mintage: 175,162

Notes regarding mintages: Record deposits of gold from domestic mines resulted in all-time high gold coinage figures at all four mints this year, although  only the Philadelphia and New Orleans mints struck coins of the $10 denomination.

Estimated population (Mint State): *8–12.* A formidable rarity, a once-in-a-generation availability grade. Although David W. Akers (1980) reported 7 auction appearances, he never examined a coin which he considered to be Mint State.

Estimated population (circulated grades): *800–1,200.*

Submissions certified at highest grades (as of March 2017): *PCGS:* MS-60 (1), MS-61 (4), MS-62 (2). *NGC:* MS-60 (2), MS-61 (4), MS-62 (3), MS-64 (1). When the highest populations hover around lower MS grades, chances are good that some were graded AU in earlier times.

Die data: A total of four obverse dies and five reverse dies were sent for this coinage, yielding variations in logotype and mintmark placement and appearance.

Characteristics of striking and die notes: Usually seen well struck.

Key to collecting: The most available Liberty Head $10 coin dated up to this point. VF and EF are usual grades. Mint State 1843-O eagles, while not common, appeared in various sales in the 1930s onward, with more coming on the market in recent times due to repatriations. Mint State coins are mostly in lower levels as shown above.

MARKET NEWS AND COMMENTARY

In December 1890, in their sale of the Thomas Cleneay Collection, the Chapman brothers offered lot 490: "1843-O Extremely Fine. Mint luster." It sold for $12. This was among the earliest auction appearances, as circulated examples were not worth much more than face value.

Into modern times, the Harry W. Bass Jr. Collection, Part IV, by Bowers and Merena Galleries, sold in November 2000, included lot 600: "1843-O MS-61 PCGS. PCGS Population: 2, 1 finer (MS-62). Purchased from Stanley Kesselman, February 23, 1971. Earlier from Stack's sale of the Pierce Collection, May 1965, Lot 1451." It sold for $8,625.

In August 1999, in the ANA World's Fair of Money sale, Heritage included lot 8081: "1843-O MS-62 PCGS. Very well struck except on the curl above the ear of Liberty which is weak." It sold for $17,135.

In the August 2006 ANA World's Fair of Money sale Bowers and Merena Galleries offered lot 4313: "1843-O MS-64 NGC." It sold for $58,650. In the Long Beach sale of September 2016 Heritage included lot 14126: "1843-O AU-53 PCGS." It sold for $10,575.

VF-20	EF-40	AU-50	AU-55	AU-58	MS-60
$1,050	$1,100	$1,800	$3,250	$5,500	$12,500

1844

Circulation-Strike Mintage: 6,361
Proof Mintage: *6–8*

Notes regarding mintages: Two deliveries were made: 4,600 on November 20, 1844, and 1,761 on December 31, the last settling accounts for the year.

Estimated population (Mint State): *2–3.* Incredibly rare.

Estimated population (circulated grades): *60–80.* The 1844 has not been well recognized for its rarity, with the more available 1858 hogging the limelight.

Estimated population (Proofs): *3–4.* One is in the National Numismatic Collection. Another that was in the F.C.C. Boyd collection went to Jacob Shapiro, later to John J. Pittman. Yet another was in a cased Proof set of 1844 once owned by Dr. J. Hewitt Judd.

Submissions certified at highest grades (as of March 2017): *PCGS:* AU-55 (3), AU-58 (1). ***NGC:*** AU-55 (6), AU-58 (6), MS-61 (1), MS-63 (1).

Die data: Crosslet 4 in denomination, the only gold denomination of this year to use this style.

Characteristics of striking and die notes: Usually well struck.

Key to collecting: The typical specimen is just VF or so, with AU examples of the date considered quite rare.

Market News and Commentary
In the December 1944 sale of the J.F. Bell Collection Stack's included lot 609: "1844 Uncirculated choice. Very scarce." It sold for $77.50. The same firm's May 1945 George H. Hall Collection had a similar coin as lot 2112: "1844 Brilliant Uncirculated." It sold for $65.

Into modern times with thousands more bidders and buyers: In its Long Beach sale of September 2016 Heritage included lot 14138: "1844 MS-61 NGC. NGC and PCGS combined list 69 submissions of the 1844 eagle (7/16), including possible resubmissions, and PCGS accurately estimates that only 50 to 75 examples are known in all grades." It sold for $30,550.

Proof Market News and Commentary
In January 1946 the Numismatic Gallery sale of "The World's Greatest Collection" (Boyd) included lot 649: "1844 Gem brilliant Proof." It sold for $310. This was in the era in which most specialists in eagles desired one to illustrate the date. Those seeking high-grade coins found the occasional Proof to be a good acquisition as most dates were not available in high Mint State grades. In numismatic literature no specific studies were made of gold Proof coins until Walter Breen published on the subject beginning in the early 1950s.

Heritage's sale of April 2015 included lot 5405: "81444 Proof-63 Cameo. NGC." It sold for $423,000.

VF-20	EF-40	AU-50	AU-55	AU-58	MS-60	MS-63
$1,200	$2,500	$4,750	$7,500	$15,000	$18,500	$50,000

1844-O

Circulation-Strike Mintage: 118,700
Proof Mintage: *1*

Estimated population (Mint State): ***12–16.*** Mostly in low grades and, presumably, many upgraded from AU years ago.

Estimated population (circulated grades): *800–1,100.*

Estimated population (Proofs): *1.*

Submissions certified at highest grades (as of March 2017): *PCGS:* MS-61 (3), MS-63 (1). *NGC:* MS-60 (9), MS-61 (5), MS-62 (3), MS-63 (2).

Die data: There were six pairs of dies made for this coinage.

Characteristics of striking and die notes: Usually well struck.

Key to collecting: One of the more available eagles of the era. VF and EF are usual grades. Mint State coins are rare, but so are specialists seeking them, with the result that with persistence and a good bank balance a nice example can be obtained.

Market News and Commentary

In January 1884 W. Elliot Woodward's sale of the Honorable Heman Ely Collection included lot 806: "1844-O Very Fine, scarce." It sold for $10 (face value). There were many later listings of worn coins, none of which attracted attention until the late 1900s.

The June 1941 sale of the William Forrester Dunham Collection by B. Max Mehl included lot 2213: "1844-O Brilliant Uncirculated with Proof surface; slight cabinet friction on obverse. Scarce so choice." It sold for $21.50. Mehl's description of a coin in the March 1945 A. Knapp Collection sale is oxymoronic: lot 1050: "1844-O New Orleans Mint. Uncirculated, just the slightest touch of circulation. Mint luster. Rare so choice." It sold for $34.

The October 1996 Spink America sale of selections from the Byron Reed Collection included lot 157: "1844-O Mint State, very nice overall, although not quite choice, still certainly among the finest known of the date." It sold for $21,900. Stack's sale in July 2008 of the Samuel Berngard and SS *New York* Collections included lot 2080: "1844-O MS-63 NGC." It sold for $11,500.

Proof Market News and Commentary

A pair of Proof 1844-O gold coins, a half eagle and an eagle, were owned by George Seavey, Lorin G. Parmelee, William H. Woodin (sold for $50 in Elder's 1911 sale), and Virgil Brand. Years later they were sold into the John Murrell Collection in Texas, and in the 1990s were offered on the market through dealer Michael G. Brownlee. The coins must have been struck for some special occasion, now unknown, and kept carefully after that time.

From *Numismatic News*, October 17, 2008, "Gold piece goes home":

The 1844-O Proof eagle, a one-of-a-kind gold coin struck at the New Orleans Mint, has returned "home" with the help of New Orleans coin dealer, Paul Hollis.

This unique gold piece apparently was specially struck as a presentation piece, and over the decades it's been in the famous coin collections of a former U.S. Treasury secretary and an early 20th century Chicago beer baron.

VF-20	EF-40	AU-50	AU-55	AU-58	MS-60
$1,050	$1,100	$1,850	$3,250	$8,500	$15,000

1845

Circulation-Strike Mintage: 26,153
Proof Mintage: *6–8*

Estimated population (Mint State): *3–5*. Exceedingly rare and for all purposes unobtainable.

Estimated population (circulated grades): *175–250*. These coins were used intensely in commerce.

Estimated population (Proofs): *4–5*. In *relative* terms one of the larger quantities for a Proof of the decade, but in absolute terms an awesome rarity.

Submissions certified at highest grades (as of March 2017): *PCGS:* MS-62 (1). *NGC:* MS-60 (1), MS-61 (1), MS-62 (1).

Die data: 1845 four-digit date logotype with 84 very close, 18 medium separation, and 45 widest apart. The base of the 4 is lower than the bases of 18; the base of the 5 lower still. The top interior of the 8 is smaller than the bottom interior. There is the crosslet 4 with heavy upright, the upright 5, and the flag is thick with the tip ending over the right curve of the bottom. These were used on all dies for both mints this year.

Characteristics of striking and die notes (circulation strikes): Usually well struck.

Characteristics of striking and die notes (Proofs): There is a tiny thorn from the denticle, diagonally up to the right to near the tip of the lower right serif of the 1 in 1845. The 84 is connected and each digit is partially filled. Horizontal shield stripes with many light vertical lines extend upward from the vertical lines below.

Key to collecting: As is true of all other eagles of this era, VF and EF are par for grades usually seen, with VF predominating. Mint State coins are rarities deluxe.

MARKET NEWS AND COMMENTARY

The January 1986 Stack's sale of the James Walter Carter and Margaret Woolfolk Carter Collections included lot 199: "1845 About Uncirculated, lustrous about the devices. The reverse, as is always the case, is nicer than the obverse. Rare and underrated." It sold for $1,100.

The Bowers and Merena Galleries' July 2008 Baltimore Rarities sale included lot 1159: "1845 MS-61 NGC." It sold for $14,490. In August 2011, in the ANA World's Fair of Money sale, Heritage included lot 2607: "1845 MS-61 NGC. NGC and PCGS combined have certified just four pieces as Mint State." It sold for $16,100.

PROOF MARKET NEWS AND COMMENTARY

In January 1990 the Superior Galleries' sale of the S. Chalkley and Austin Ryer Collections included lot 4778: "1845 Proof-63 PCGS." It sold for $74,250.

VF-20	EF-40	AU-50	AU-55	AU-58	MS-60
$950	$1,050	$2,000	$2,500	$6,000	$12,500

1845-O

Circulation-Strike Mintage: 47,500

Estimated population (Mint State): *10–15.* These are usually seen at lower levels. Includes coins that have graduated from being AU.

Estimated population (circulated grades): *300–450.*

Submissions certified at highest grades (as of March 2017): *PCGS:* MS-61 (2), MS-62 (1), MS-64 (1). *NGC:* MS-60 (3), MS-61 (6), MS-62 (3).

Die data: Five pairs of new dies were sent to New Orleans for this coinage. In addition, at least one serviceable reverse die was on hand from earlier times.

1845 four-digit date logotype with the 84 very close, the 18 medium separation, and the 45 widest apart. The base of the 4 is lower than the bases of the 18; the base of the 5 is lower still. The top interior of the 8 is smaller than the bottom interior. There is the crosslet 4 with the heavy upright, the upright 5, and the flag is thick with the tip ending over the right curve of the bottom. Used on all dies for both mints this year.

Varieties exist with from two to all four numerals repunched, furnishing many opportunities over the years for interesting descriptions.

During this era there were many such variations among dies of different denominations. Some have attributed this to newly installed (1844) Chief Engraver James B. Longacre, who was an accomplished engraver of metal printing plates, but who was relatively unfamiliar with die sinking. Regardless, the entry of a four-digit logotype into a working die should not have tested Longacre's ability, and it is reasonable that an assistant did the date punching.

The present author discredits "1845-O, 5 Over 4," listed as Breen-6871 for a "Texas private collection," that being the Bass coin, which is *not* an overdate.

Characteristics of striking and die notes: Generally well struck, but as multiple pairs of dies and production runs were involved, no single statement fits all coins.

Key to collecting: VF is the grade usually seen, followed in availability by EF. At the AU level the 1845-O is decidedly scarce and an attractive Mint State coin is a rarity.

Market News and Commentary

In December 1890, in their sale of the Thomas Cleneay Collection, the Chapman brothers offered lot 492: "1845-O Same condition [Extremely Fine] and mint as last." It sold for $10. This same coin was offered in May 1922 by B. Max Mehl in the James Ten Eyck Collection as lot 275: "1845. New Orleans Mint. Brilliant Uncirculated, with Proof surface, nearly equal to a Proof. From the famous Cleneay collection. The finest specimen I have ever seen, and as such very rare and valuable." It sold for $23. The author cataloged this specimen for the Eliasberg Collection sale in 1982 as lot 674: "1845-O Select Brilliant Uncirculated, MS-63. Frosty and lustrous." It sold for $28,600. Not many circulation-strike Liberty Head eagles have a provenance dating back to the 1890s.

Fast forward to years later, in January 1990 the Superior Galleries' sale of the S. Chalkley and Austin Ryer Collections included lot 4779: "1845-O. Mint State-63." It sold for $2,750. The June 2001 Stack's sale of the Lemus Collection of U.S. Gold Coins included lot 428: "1845-O Brilliant Uncirculated. A very important branch mint rarity." It sold for $10,350. In the August 2010 ANA sale Stack's Bowers Galleries offered lot 1718: "1845-O MS-60 NGC." It sold for $11,500.

VF-20	EF-40	AU-50	AU-55	AU-58	MS-60	MS-63
$1,050	$1,150	$2,750	$5,000	$8,000	$15,000	$50,000

1846

Circulation-Strike Mintage: 20,095
Proof Mintage: *6–8*

Estimated population (Mint State):
5–7. None were seen decades ago by the writer or David W. Akers. Unknown until recent times.

Estimated population (circulated grades): *125–175.*

Estimated population (Proofs): *5.* Two in private hands, the Eliasberg and Pittman specimens. One each in the Smithsonian Institution and the American Numismatic Society collections. The fifth example, Proof-55 (NGC), was sold by Heritage in June 2015 for $76,375, and again in January 2017 for $51,700.

Submissions certified at highest grades (as of March 2017): *PCGS:* MS-62 (1). *NGC:* MS-60 (1), MS-61 (2), MS-62 (1).

Die data: From the notes of Harry W. Bass Jr.:

> 1846 four-digit *Small Date* logotype composed of Small Date logotype composed of small, somewhat squat digits. 18 slightly closer than either 84 or 46, bases of digits about on the same level, top interior of 8 slightly smaller than bottom interior, 6 small and squat, with top close to curve below it and about as wide as the curve. This logotype appeared on the Philadelphia Mint eagles of the year, as well as the Small Date variety of the year's copper cents. The Small Date and Medium Date varieties exist among 1846 Philadelphia eagles—but have not been widely recognized. However, when examples are held side by side the difference is quite noticeable. (The New Orleans $10 used the *Medium Date* logotype). Also used on the 1846 Small Date copper cent.

Key to collecting: Typically found in VF or occasionally EF, with AU examples rare and underrated. Unknown in Mint State until the late 1900s.

MARKET NEWS AND COMMENTARY

The typical listing of the past was for a coin in VF or EF grade. AU coins were few and far between.

In November 1939 the William B. Hale Collection sold by B. Max Mehl included lot 1655: "1846 Practically Uncirculated; light nick on obverse; considerable mint luster. Very scarce, especially so choice." It sold for $26. In October 1999, in the Harry W. Bass Jr. Collection, Part II, Bowers and Merena Galleries offered lot 1357: "1846 AU-50 PCGS. PCGS Population: 5; 2 finer (AU-55 finest)." It sold for $5,290. This was before large-scale importations of eagles that caused great adjustments in TPG population reports.

In its Long Beach sale of September 2008 Heritage included lot 3853: "1846 MS-62 NGC." It sold for $51,750.

VF-20	EF-40	AU-50	AU-55	AU-58	MS-60
$1,050	$1,250	$3,500	$6,500	$10,000	$20,000

1846-O

Circulation-Strike Mintage: 81,780 (all varieties)

Estimated population (Mint State): 4–6.

Estimated population (circulated grades): 500–700. This number includes some that have been classified as "1846-O, 6 Over 5" earlier.

Submissions certified at highest grades (as of March 2017): *PCGS:* MS-60 (1), MS-61 (1), MS-64 (1). *NGC:* MS-62 (1); MS-63 (1).

Die data: One pair of dies for the 1846-O coinage was sent to New Orleans from Philadelphia on December 12, 1845; one pair was sent on January 24, 1846; two pairs in May; and two obverse dies on September 11. Adding to these were five serviceable reverse dies left over from the preceding year.

The 1846 four-digit *Medium Date* logotype composed of taller digits than on the Small Date. The base of the 1 is high; the 84 is close; the top interior of the 8 is significantly smaller than the bottom interior; the 4 has the thick upright and leans slightly right; the 6 is tall, with significant opening above the curve, and with the top of the 6 extending to above the curve at the right, but not as wide. Also used on certain 50¢ dies. The logotype punch itself has evidences of repunching, a highly unusual situation. It must have been the case that—follow closely here—the logotype punch was made as follows: The numerals 1, 8, 4, and 6 were punched individually into a soft steel block or matrix using four hardened steel punches. During this process, double punching was done on the 6, thus creating the "artifact" mentioned. The matrix was tempered or hardened, after which it could be used to make four-digit logotype punches. Individual logotype punches—one or more—were multiplied by pressing a soft steel logotype punch into the matrix, then hardening each one for use in die making. What these two coins of two denominations reveal is that a logotype punch can in itself have double-punched features. It is conventional wisdom that most date doubling is caused by impressing a perfect logotype punch into a *die* twice. In the present case, one impression of the curiously doubled *punch* did the trick. This *doubled logotype punch* was also used in the *half dollar* series.[8] Neither the 1846-O $10 nor the 50¢ of 1846-O is an overdate.

Thus, the so-called "1846/5-O overdate" is simply a repunched date; there are two different repunchings that have been called overdates in the past, but neither qualifies.

Characteristics of striking and die notes: Typically with some lightness at the eagle near the lower left of the shield. Often partially prooflike.

Key to collecting: This issue is readily available and similar to certain other eagles of the era, includes varieties with interesting date repunchings. Mint State coins were virtually unheard of until a few were found among repatriated eagles.

MARKET NEWS AND COMMENTARY

One particular coin has a long pedigree chain: In December 1890, in their sale of the Thomas Cleneay Collection, the Chapman brothers offered lot 493: "1846-O Uncirculated. Only faintest hair marks. Proof surface." It sold for $11.50. The identical coin later appeared in B. Max Mehl's May 1922 sale of the James Ten Eyck Collection as lot 276: "1846 New Orleans Mint. While this coin was undoubtedly struck as Uncirculated but it can be classed as a Proof. It is brilliant and sharp. In original box from Cleneay collection. Extremely rare and valuable so choice." It sold for $23.

Jump to October 1982 and a vastly expanded market with many more players, to the Louis E. Eliasberg Collection of U.S. Gold Coins, sold by Bowers and Ruddy Galleries, which included lot 676: "1846-O Choice Brilliant Uncirculated, MS-65, prooflike. From the John H. Clapp Collection, 1942. Earlier from the James Ten Eyck Collection (B. Max Mehl, May 1922). Previously from the Thomas Cleneay Collection (Chapman brothers, December 1890)." It sold for $36,800. Harry W. Bass Jr. was the buyer. In November 2000, in the Harry W. Bass Jr. Collection, Part IV, Bowers and Merena Galleries offered lot 616:

> 1846/5-O So-called "Overdate." MS-64 PCGS. An amazing specimen of the so-called "1846/5-O overdate," lately thought to be the result of a doubled date logo-type punch. This variety was unknown to Breen in Uncirculated. Indeed, this coin seems to be head and shoulders above any other offering of this issue we've seen from any die pair. A breathtaking beauty. PCGS Population: 1, none finer. No others certified Mint State by any certification service. Breen 6875. [Sold for $48,300]

VF-20	EF-40	AU-50	AU-55	AU-58	MS-60
$1,050	$1,200	$3,200	$6,000	$8,500	$13,500

1847

Circulation-Strike Mintage: 862,258
Proof Mintage: *1–2*

Notes regarding mintages: The high coinage of $10 pieces at Philadelphia this year—exceeding by *multiples* any earlier production—was mostly from a record amount of foreign gold coins, particularly British sovereigns, deposited there for recoinage, amounting to $13,171,679 in gold bullion value.

Estimated population (Mint State): *40–50.*

Estimated population (circulated grades): *3,500–4,500.*

Estimated population (Proofs): *1.* Held in the Mint Collection in the Smithsonian Institution.

Submissions certified at highest grades (as of March 2017): *PCGS:* MS-62 (19), MS-63 (3), MS-64 (1). *NGC:* MS-60 (17), MS-61 (33), MS-62 (11), MS-63 (2), MS-64 (1).

Die data: Dates on 1847 eagles exist in many variations of spacing and alignment, indicating that individual number punches or, in some instances, pairs were used. Variations include depth of numerals punched into the die (one Philadelphia Mint die has the 1 and 7 very deep into the die, the 84 shallow), the 1 and 8, 8 and 4, and 4 and 7 closely or widely spaced, thick or medium upper left serif to 1, etc. *In addition* to the preceding, at least one four-digit logotype was used to create multiple dies from both mints. This has the figures of the same strength, the 18 farthest apart, 84 closer, 47 closer yet, with the top of the crosslet of the 4 even with and close to the right of the bottom of the serif on the 7.

Characteristics of striking and die notes: Usually fairly well struck. Lightness, when seen, is apt to be on the eagle to the left of the shield.

Key to collecting: VF and EF are the usually seen grades, but dozens of AU coins exist. The 1847 is with the 1849 one of the two most available Mint State eagles of the 1840s—a span of years in which any Mint State coin is a rarity and earlier-dated coins are especially so. The 1847 and 1849 are oases—resting points for the weary searcher—who without too much effort can acquire a coin in the MS-60 to MS-62 range. Among the extant pieces are a few in the choice category, these being harder to find.

MARKET NEWS AND COMMENTARY

As the 1847 eagle is a common issue, little numismatic attention has ever been paid to it, except for examples in high grades. Until well into the 20th century most collectors forming sets by date and mint were content to acquire a worn coin with nice appearance. As examples, some of the finest cabinets sold early in the century included these grades. Exceptions were relatively few.

The "1934 Baltimore Find" included 13 pieces of this variety in various grades.

The Belden E. Roach coin was described by Mehl in February 1944, lot 328: "1847 Brilliant Uncirculated with Proof surface; unusually bold impression. Rare so choice." It sold for $36. The buyer was Floyd T. Starr, a Pennsylvania numismatist who began collecting gold coins by dates in the 1930s when collectors were allowed to own them, but typical American citizens were not. When Stack's sold the Starr Collection in October 1992 it was offered as lot 1244: "1847 Choice Brilliant Uncirculated. A lustrous and attractive example of this early Coronet type date. Lightly hairlined above date." It sold for $4,125.

In April 1949 B. Max Mehl's sale of the Dr. Charles W. Green Collection included lot 518: "1847 Uncirculated with frosty mint luster. Just the slightest evidence of being handled with other coins. Very scarce so choice." It sold for $42.50.

The Louis E. Eliasberg Collection (Bowers and Ruddy Galleries, October 1982) had an exceptional coin in lot 678: "1847 Choice Brilliant Uncirculated, MS-65." It sold for

$15,400. In July 2004 the American Numismatic Rarities sale of the Oliver Jung Collection included lot 101: "1847 MS-64. From the Eliasberg Collection." It sold for $30,100.

David W. Akers' offering of Part II of the John J. Pittman Collection, October 1998, included lot 1922: "1847, Uncirculated. Purchased from Ralph E. Elser, 11/5/49, for $30. Elser was a county sheriff in Lima, Ohio, who had obtained a number of gold coins, including this one, from Michael F. Higgy of Columbus, Ohio, in 1942." It sold for $20,900.

Most of Higgy's coins were purchased by Abe Kosoff and sold at auction by him in the next year, 1943. This event took place when cash was common and consumer goods to spend them on were scarce. Kosoff was fond of referring to the Higgy sale as the jumping-off spot for a great advance in coin market prices.

On August 4, 1967, Abe Kosoff sold Harry W. Bass Jr. a group of 27 mixed 1847 and 1847-O (mostly the latter) eagles, each "seawater Uncirculated," with etched surfaces showing no signs of actual wear, these probably part of a larger find, but no documentation is known to exist. These must have come from a wreck lost in 1847, but no further information is known.

Stack's Bowers Galleries' March 2004 Adelphi Collection sale included lot 906: "1847 62+." It sold for $21,850. Regency Auction XX January 2017 included lot 279: "1847 MS-62." It sold for $13,512.50. In its sale of April 2017 Heritage included lot 16714: "1847 MS-61 NGC." It sold for $3,290.

VF-20	EF-40	AU-50	AU-55	AU-58	MS-60	MS-63
$850	$950	$1,000	$1,050	$1,450	$3,500	$21,500

1847-O

Circulation-Strike Mintage: 571,500

Notes regarding mintages: The record-high coinage of $10 pieces at New Orleans this year was mostly from a large amount of foreign gold coins deposited there for recoinage, amounting to $6,220,700 in gold bullion value. However, even more foreign gold coins were deposited at the Philadelphia Mint.

Estimated population (Mint State): *20–30.* Mostly MS-60 to MS-63, but a few higher-graded pieces exist.

Estimated population (circulated grades): *3,000–4,000.*

Submissions certified at highest grades (as of March 2017): *PCGS:* MS-62 (1), MS-63 (3), MS-64 (3). *NGC:* MS-60 (4), MS-61 (16), MS-62 (3), MS-63 (1).

Die data: See listing for 1847 Philadelphia coin.

Characteristics of striking and die notes: Typically with lightness of strike at the high areas of the portrait on the obverse and the lower center of the reverse. As multiple die pairs were employed on different production runs, sharpness varies.

Key to collecting: One of the more available issues of this era. VF and EF are typical grades encountered.

Market News and Commentary

In February 1944, in the Belden E. Roach Collection, B. Max Mehl offered lot 402: "1847-O Uncirculated with frosty mint surface. Not a rarity, but quite rare so choice." It sold for $32.25.

In June 1946, in the William Cutler Atwater Collection, B. Max Mehl offered lot 1521: "1847-O Uncirculated with full frosty mint luster. Not a rarity, but certainly very scarce so choice. Only a Very Fine specimen recently brought $35. This specimen is worth at least double." It sold for $36. This reflects the rather low premium placed on Mint State (otherwise) common gold coins in this era.

In August 1980 Superior Galleries' Auction '80 offered lot 422: "1847-O. Mint State-65." It sold for $17,500. For the same coin in July 1984 David W. Akers hinted that the Superior grade was okay, sort of, lot 943: "1847-O MS-63+. A gorgeous borderline gem with an above average strike, superb mint luster and beautiful light gold and copper toning. Some light bagmarks on both obverse and reverse but the coin is sufficiently choice to be called a full "gem MS-65" by most catalogers. Ex Auction '80, lot 422." It sold for $17,500. Back in the hands of Superior Galleries in July 1986 for Auction '86, it was offered as lot 1419: "1847-O. MS-65. By today's stricter standards, this pristine Brilliant Uncirculated specimen would more accurately be graded MS-64, due to some trivial light contact marks. From our session of Auction '80, lot 422." It sold for $6,380.

In January 1990 the Superior Galleries' sale of the S. Chalkley and Austin Ryer Collections included lot 4782: "1847-O MS-63 NGC." It sold for $27,700.

In August 1999, in the ANA World's Fair of Money sale, Heritage included lot 8089:

> 1847-O MS-60 PCGS. The 1847-O is the most common No Motto eagle from New Orleans in high grade. There are as many as two dozen known in mint condition with most in the MS 60 to 61 range. The finest that we are aware of is the piece sold as lot 6260 in our Warren Miller Sale of 10/95. It realized $28,600 and was graded MS 64 by PCGS. [Sold for $5,980]

In May 2000 the Bowers and Merena Galleries' sale of the Harry W. Bass Jr. Collection, Part III, included lot 605: "1847-O MS-63 PCGS. PCGS Population: 1; 2 finer (MS-64 Purchased from Julian Leidman, October 28, 1971." It sold for $14,950. In November 2000 the Bowers and Merena Galleries' sale of the Harry W. Bass Jr. Collection, Part IV, included lot 626: "1847-O Repunched 18. MS-64 (PCGS Purchased from Stanley Kesselman on April 30, 1968." It sold for $21,850.

VF-20	EF-40	AU-50	AU-55	AU-58	MS-60	MS-63
$950	$1,050	$1,150	$1,350	$2,500	$6,000	$25,000

1848

Circulation-Strike Mintage: 145,484
Proof Mintage: 3–5

Estimated population (Mint State): 20–25. Very scarce. Usually in lower grades, MS-60 to MS-62.

Estimated population (circulated grades): *800–1,200.*

Estimated population (Proofs): *2.* One is in the National Numismatic Collection in the Smithsonian Institution the other was in the Woodin, W.G.C., Pittman, and other collections. In the Woodin catalog of 1911, the cataloger Thomas L. Elder, referred to this Proof as unique. Apparently, he had never visited or asked about the Mint Collection.

Submissions certified at highest grades (as of March 2017): *PCGS:* MS-62 (1), MS-63 (6), MS-64 (2). *NGC:* MS-60 (6), MS-61 (13), MS-62 (2), MS-63 (4), MS-64 (1), MS-65 (1).

Die data: Some examples were struck from highly polished dies closely resembling Proof format (but without mirror surface among the vertical shield stripes). A coin of this nature (and also with a hollow ring above the second pair of vertical shield stripes) was offered in the Bowers and Merena Galleries sale of March 2003; a related with-ring piece, but with "lustrous" surface appeared in Christie's sale of the Byron Reed Collection (1996).

A minor change was made to the obverse hub this year, continuing to later years, noticeable at the back of the hair and also in the relationship of a ray of star 10 to the denticles.[9]

Key to collecting: VF and EF grades are those usually seen, but AU specimens appear on the market with some frequency. Mint State coins are few and far between. Patience is required to find a nice one.

MARKET NEWS AND COMMENTARY

Thomas L. Elder, New York City's leading dealer at the time, offered a number of notable 1848 eagles, including these to follow. In January 1936, as part of the Charles W. Sloane and Frank Lenz Collections, was lot 2605: "1848 . Brilliant Mint State Uncirculated gem. Very rare, small coinage." It is probably from the Baltimore Find. It sold for $27.50. In the Wilson S. Harrison Collection, September 1936, included was lot 362: "1848. Bright Uncirculated. Rare." It sold for $19.25.

In February 1944, in the Belden E. Roach Collection, B. Max Mehl offered lot 329: "1848 Brilliant Uncirculated; the reverse almost equal to a Proof. Rare so choice. Listed at $35 in only Very Fine." It sold for $35.

Now, into the late 1900s and beyond, the January 1984 Stack's sale of the Amon G. Carter Jr. Family Collection included lot 749: "1848 Brilliant Uncirculated. Full frosty surface. This underrated coin with full 'cartwheel' effect is unquestionably one of the finest known." It sold for $4,180.

Stack's October 1994 James A. Stack sale included lot 1297: "1848 Choice Brilliant Uncirculated." It sold for $33,000. In November 2000 the Bowers and Merena Galleries' sale of the Harry W. Bass Jr. Collection, Part IV, included the same coin as lot 630: "1848 MS-63 PCGS. From Stack's sale of the James A. Stack Collection, October 1994, lot 1297." It sold for $19,550. The Bass Collection nearly always generated a large profit over cost. Exceptions were very rare, as here.

Stack's Bowers Galleries' October 2014 Rarities sale included lot 10045: "1848 MS-64 PCGS." It sold for $64,625.

VF-20	EF-40	AU-50	AU-55	AU-58	MS-60	MS-63
$850	$950	$1,000	$1,050	$1,600	$4,500	$22,500

1848-O

Circulation-Strike Mintage: 35,850

Estimated population (Mint State):
10–14. Very rare.

**Estimated population (circulated
grades):** *250–325.*

Submissions certified at highest grades (as of March 2017): *PCGS:* MS-63 (1), MS-64 (3), MS-66 (1). *NGC:* MS-60 (1), MS-61 (4), MS-64 (1), MS-65 (1).

Die data: A minor change was made to the obverse hub this year, continuing to later years, noticeable at the back of the hair and also in the relationship of a ray of star 10 to the denticles.[10]

Certain eagles of 1848-O, 1849-O, 1851-O, 1852-O, and 1853-O exist with a hollow circular ring at the top of the second vertical shield stripe on the reverse.

Characteristics of striking and die notes: Lightly struck at the centers.

Key to collecting: VF and EF are typical grades encountered. AU and Mint State coins are collectible but scarce. Most are from repatriations made in recent decades.

MARKET NEWS AND COMMENTARY

Such coins were produced in an era in which not even the Mint Cabinet desired to save mintmarked varieties. Nearly all New Orleans gold coins went into circulation and were used intensely.

In December 1890, in their sale of the Thomas Cleneay Collection, the Chapman brothers offered lot 499: "1848-O Very Fine." It sold for $10 (face value). Again, this was representative of the low value of circulated coins at the time.

The May 1965 Stack's sale of the Pierce & Sons Collection offered lot 1459: "1848-O Brilliant Uncirculated. Full frosty mint luster. Some minuscule handling marks in the field. Easily worth $150." It sold for $105. The Pierces were lumber dealers in Ottumwa, Iowa, and over long period of years assembled high-grade collections in different specialties.

Stack's, in October 1994, offered this in their sale of the James A. Stack Sr. Collection, lot 1298: "1848-O Gem Brilliant Uncirculated. In his years of research, David Akers reported seeing only two Mint State examples of this date." It sold for $154,000. The Akers study of 1980 was done prior to the extensive repatriation of many high-grade Liberty Head eagles.

In its sale of the Ashland City Collection in May 2000 Heritage included lot 7243: "1848-O MS-61 NGC." It sold for $8,625. The March 2005 American Numismatic Rarities Richard C. Jewell Collection sale included lot 759: "1848-O MS-61 NGC. Ex Ashland City Collection." It sold for $11,500.

In November 2000 the Bowers and Merena Galleries' sale of the Harry W. Bass Jr. Collection, Part IV, included lot 631: "1848-O MS-64 PCGS. Weakly struck, as are most of this issue, but very appealing. Purchased from Dan Messer on August 16, " It sold for $36,800.

In its sale of April 2016 Heritage included lot 4796: "1848-O MS-61 PCGS." It sold for $15,275. In the November 2016 Whitman Expo sale Stack's Bowers Galleries offered lot 2152: "1848-O MS-61 PCGS." It sold for $23,500.

VF-20	EF-40	AU-50	AU-55	AU-58	MS-60	MS-63	MS-65
$1,000	$1,500	$3,000	$6,000	$8,500	$15,000	$35,000	$85,000

1849

Circulation strike mintage: 653,618

Estimated population (Mint State): 50–65. The certification services have listed *dozens* in the Mint State category, while in 1980 David W. Akers reported that he had only seen one in his career, and in 1988 in his *Encyclopedia* Walter Breen called such pieces "extremely rare." Such coins were seldom seen by collectors of the 19th and 20th centuries, until about 1980. Today within the context of eagles of this era they are common due to a combination of repatriated coins and AU coins graduating to become Mint State!

Estimated population (circulated grades): 3,000–4,000.

Submissions certified at highest grades (as of March 2017): PCGS: MS-62 (13), MS-63 (9), MS-64 (2). **NGC:** MS-60 (12), MS-61 (21), MS-62 (11), MS-63 (7), MS-64 (4).

Die data: The 1849 four-digit date logotype is fairly widely spaced; the 84 is closer spaced than the 18, with the 49 being the farthest apart; the bases of the 49 are low; the upright of the 4 leans slightly right; the 9 has the lower right side curved inward (as on certain other denominations of this date), the bottom outline is somewhat flat, the knob distant from the upper curve. Numerals have a delicate "open," rather than heavy, appearance. Used on all dies for both mints.

The large mintage of 653,618 employed many different dies and combinations. Breen (*Encyclopedia*, 1988) mentions knowledge of at least eight varieties and delineates four of them. The varieties listed are particularly significant.

Breen's 6888, "1849/8," does not seem to be an overdate; Harry Bass discredited it, and the present author agrees. However, it is very significant. It seems that a *smaller* 1849 four-digit logotype, intended for a smaller denomination, was entered into the die, then overpunched with the regular 1849 $10 logotype. The under-logotype begins under the 1, then as it is not as wide as the correctly sized logotype, the other three figures are seen to the left of the final 849 digits. This error is somewhat similar in concept to the 1876 half dollar with the date punched over a small logotype intended for a 20¢ piece. This variety turns up with regularity.

The 1849, High Date over Low Date, a.k.a. the Double Date, is the result of a four-digit logotype first punched too low, partially effaced, and then overpunched in the correct position.

Characteristics of striking and die notes: Usually somewhat lightly struck at the centers. However, sharpness varies due to multiple die combinations and striking sequences.

Key to collecting: VF is the usually encountered grades, but enough EF coins and occasional AU examples are on the market that the specialist will have no trouble finding one. The same can be said for Mint State coins from modern repatriations. As noted previously, in 1980 when David W. Akers did his study Mint State examples were incredibly rare.

MARKET NEWS AND COMMENTARY

The "1934 Baltimore Find" included 10 pieces of this date in various grades.

In May 1936, in the Linton L. Fraser Collection, Thomas L. Elder offered lot 881: "1849 Uncirculated, with luster." It sold for $20. This was probably from the Baltimore Find. Before this discovery Mint State coins were considered to be rare.

In January 1946 the Numismatic Gallery sale of "The World's Greatest Collection" (F.C.C. Boyd) included lot 654: "1849 Uncirculated." It sold for $45. In October 1947 in the H.R. Lee Collection (Eliasberg duplicates) Stack's offered this lot 1505: "1849 Brilliant Uncirculated yellow gold, with semi-proof surface." It sold for $35.

In October 1982 the Louis E. Eliasberg Collection of U.S. Gold Coins, sold by Bowers and Ruddy Galleries, included lot 682: "1849 Brilliant Uncirculated, MS-60 obverse; Choice Brilliant Uncirculated, MS-65 reverse." It sold for $11,550.

In October 1994 this was offered in Stack's sale of the James A. Stack Sr. Collection, lot 1299: "1849 Very Choice Brilliant Uncirculated. This remarkable coin shows deep-mirror prooflike surfaces of unusual gleaming depth. No example of this date appeared in the Garrett collection. This dramatic coin may be the only such prooflike piece available to today's collectors." It sold for $20,350.

In November 2000 the Bowers and Merena Galleries' sale of the Harry W. Bass Jr. Collection, Part IV, included lot 633: "1849 MS-63 PCGS. PCGS Population: 6, 3 finer (MS-64). From Abner Kreisberg's sale of September 1971, lot 1119." It sold for $8,625.

In August 2013, in the ANA World's Fair of Money sale, Heritage included lot 5877: "1849 MS-64 NGC. Mint State coins are scarce and most commonly seen in MS-60 to MS-62. The issue is elusive at the Select level and infrequently seen any finer. NGC and PCGS combined have graded six near-Gems and none finer." It sold for $32,900.

VF-20	EF-40	AU-50	AU-55	AU-58	MS-60	MS-63
$850	$950	$1,000	$1,050	$1,750	$3,750	$13,500

1849-O

Circulation-Strike Mintage: 23,900

Estimated population (Mint State): **5–7.** This and other eagles are reported on modern interpretations; if this text had been written in, say, 1980, the estimated populations of Mint State coins would have been much less across the board.

Estimated population (circulated grades): *150–200.*

Submissions certified at highest grades (as of March 2017): *PCGS:* MS-60 (1), MS-61 (1). *NGC:* MS-60 (1), MS-61 (1).

Die data: Six obverse dies were prepared for this coinage, to be used with as many as 12 serviceable reverses on hand from earlier times. However, the mintage was restricted and most were not used. See preceding listing for logotype information.

Certain eagles of 1848-O, 1849-O, 1851-O, 1852-O, and 1853-O exist with a hollow circular ring at the top of the second vertical shield stripe on the reverse. Presumably, the ring is from the center of a compass or is an artifact from a lathe chuck.

Key to collecting: VF is the grade usually seen. Echoing the sentiment of David W. Akers (1980), Douglas Winter (1992) called this the "second rarest New Orleans eagle to be struck during the 1840s," adding: "It is, in my opinion, the single most under-rated eagle from this mint and is among the most difficult dates of this entire type to locate in higher grades." A lot of water has passed under the numismatic bridge since 1980 and 1992, but both books still contain a wealth of useful information and are essential to a working library.

MARKET NEWS AND COMMENTARY

In April 1937 the George M. Agurs Collection, sold by B. Max Mehl, offered lot 315: "1849-O Usually bold impression; struck from light yellow gold. Pin-point nick on cheek; otherwise About Uncirculated. Rare." It sold for $31.

Many years later in November 2000 in the Harry W. Bass Jr. Collection, Part IV, Bowers and Merena Galleries offered lot 637: "1849-O MS-61 PCGS." It sold for $21,850. At the time it was the only Mint State coin certified.

VF-20	EF-40	AU-50	AU-55	AU-58	MS-60
$1,500	$3,500	$5,500	$7,000	$11,000	$25,000

1850, Large Date

Circulation-Strike Mintage:
Large part of 291,451
Proof Mintage: None verified

Notes regarding mintages: A Proof *may have been* included in a set produced for the Congressional Committee on the Library (cf. a letter by Mint Director Robert Maskell Patterson, September 26, 1850, which mentions coins were sent; Walter Breen has assumed these were Proofs). This piece is not traced today. No example was retained for the Mint Cabinet.

Estimated population (Mint State): *15–22.* Mostly in lower Mint State levels. Rare.

Estimated population (circulated grades): *1,500–2,000.*

Submissions certified at highest grades (as of March 2017): *PCGS:* MS-62 (4), MS-63 (1), MS-64 (1). *NGC:* MS-60 (7), MS-61 (7), MS-62 (4), MS-63 (4).

Die data: The 1850 logotype in numerals is only *slightly* larger than the Small Date. The 18 is close, the 85 is wider, and the 50 is still wider. The upright of the 5 slants very slightly to the right; a slightly smaller space (than seen on the Small Date) is seen between the bottom of the flag and the top of the curve below; the upright is slightly slanted to the right; the ball is close to upright; the 0 is better positioned than on the *Small Date* Philadelphia Mint $10, but still with the base slightly low and slanting very slightly right. Used on all most but not all 1850 Philadelphia Mint and all 1850-O $10 dies.

Beginning with this year, date repunchings and blunders became fewer than during the years from 1843 to 1849.

Certain eagles of 1848-O, 1849-O, 1851-O, 1852-O, and 1853-O exist with a hollow circular ring at the top of the second vertical shield stripe on the reverse; in addition, one 1850 Philadelphia Mint eagle die has a break in the horizontal line directly above the second vertical stripe at this point, indicating that a ring might have been removed. Presumably, the ring is from the center of a compass or is an artifact from a lathe chuck.

Characteristics of striking and die notes: Usually well struck.

Key to collecting: VF and EF are typical grades. The 1850 Philadelphia issue is one of the more plentiful eagles of this era. Mint State coins are nearly all from modern repatriations.

Market News and Commentary

Most historical listings did not mention the date size. Later listings were erratic.

In January 1946 the Numismatic Gallery sale of "The World's Greatest Collection" (F.C.C. Boyd) included lot 655: "1850 Uncirculated." It sold for $40. In April 1949 B. Max Mehl's sale of the Dr. Charles W. Green Collection included lot 522: "1850 Brilliant Uncirculated. Slightly larger date. Just why there are two different sizes in the date of this particular eagle I have never been able to discover. Very scarce, especially so choice. Valued at $75." It sold for $31. In October 1982 at the Louis E. Eliasberg Collection of U.S. Gold Coins sale Bowers and Ruddy Galleries offered lot 685: "1850 Large date. Punches as used on the dies for the cent. Brilliant Uncirculated, MS-60. From the John H. Clapp Collection, 1942. Earlier from the Warren Loan & Trust Co. July 1891." It sold for $4,400.

Stack's June 1999 Globus Collection sale included lot 1158: "1850 Large Date, Brilliant Uncirculated." It sold for $12,070. In November 2000 the Bowers and Merena Galleries' sale of the Harry W. Bass Jr. Collection, Part IV, included lot 639: "1850 Large Date. MS-62 PCGS. PCGS Population: 4, 3 finer (MS-63). From Stack's sale of the Bartle Collection, October 1984, lot 1120." It sold for $9,200.

VF-20	EF-40	AU-50	AU-55	AU-58	MS-60	MS-63
$850	$950	$1,000	$1,050	$1,750	$4,000	$20,000

1850, Small Date

Circulation-Strike Mintage:
Small part of 291,451

Estimated population (Mint State):
8–12. As not all 1850 $10 coins have been classified as to date logotype, the data is inconsistent. By any reckoning a Mint State coin is a rarity.

Estimated population (circulated grades): *400–650.* Typically VF or EF.

Submissions certified at highest grades (as of March 2017): *PCGS:* MS-60 (1), MS-61 (3), MS-63 (1). *NGC:* MS-60 (3), MS-61 (4).

Die data: This 1850 four-digit date logotype widely spaced numerals, seemingly *too widely* spaced, and the 1 and the 8 are closer than other figures. The upright of the 5 slants very slightly to the right. There is a *large* space between the bottom of the flag and the top of the curve below the upright is slightly slanted to the right. The ball is not close to the upright. The 85 and the 50 are each about the same width apart. The 0 *seems to be* distant from the 5—the base is low, it is tilted slightly to the right, and there is a large open center. On impressions in which the four-digit logotype is punched lightly into the die, the distance of the 0 seems more pronounced. Used on all $5 dies of all mints and on one 1850 Philadelphia Mint $10 die (called *Small Date* on the $10 die; no designation on the $5 dies).

Characteristics of striking and die notes: Usually well struck.

Key to collecting: The 1850, Small Date, is much scarcer than the Large Date variety, but enough are around that the specialist will find one easily.

MARKET NEWS AND COMMENTARY

In March 1911, in his sale of the William H. Woodin Collection, Thomas L. Elder offered lot 1215: "1850. Small date. Very Good." It sold for $10.50. Nearly all early listings were for circulated coins.

In November 1939 the William B. Hale Collection, sold by B. Max Mehl, included lot 1660: "1850 Small date. Just about Uncirculated. Extremely rare variety. I do not recall of ever having handled another one." It sold for $36.

Heritage, in its August 1996 ANA Convention sale, offered lot 8422: "1850 Small Date MS-61 PCGS. This is the coin Warren Miller considered his primary 1850 Small Date. This is the only Mint State example thus far certified of this scarce date type, and it is most likely also the finest known." It sold for $8,250.

VF-20	EF-40	AU-50	AU-55	AU-58	MS-60	MS-63
$950	$1,100	$2,250	$3,000	$4,500	$8,000	$30,000

1850-O

Circulation-Strike Mintage: 57,500

Estimated population (Mint State): *6–9.* Exceedingly rare.

Estimated population (circulated grades): *300–400.*

Submissions certified at highest grades (as of March 2017): *PCGS:* MS-60 (1), MS-65 (1), MS-66 (1). *NGC:* MS-60 (3).

Die data: Eight obverse dies were made for this coinage, plus two new reverses. In addition, serviceable reverse dies were on hand from earlier times.

The 1850 logotype in numerals is only *slightly* larger than the Small Date from Philadelphia. The 18 is close, the 85 is wider, and the 50 is wider still. The upright of the 5 slants very slightly to the right. There is a slightly smaller space between the bottom of the flag and the top of the curve below. The upright is slightly slanted to the right. The ball is close to the upright. The 0 is better positioned than on the *Small Date* Philadelphia Mint $10, but still with base slightly low and slanting very slightly to the right. It is used on most but not all 1850 Philadelphia Mint coins, and all 1850-O $10 dies.

Although no 1850-O has been seen with this feature, it may be worth watching for, as eagles of 1848-O, 1849-O, 1851-O, 1852-O, and 1853-O exist with a hollow circular ring at the top of the second vertical shield stripe on the reverse. Presumably, the ring is from the center of a compass or is an artifact from a lathe chuck.

Key to collecting: VF and EF are the grades usually seen. AU and Mint State coins are available but are scarce.

MARKET NEWS AND COMMENTARY

B. Max Mehl, in his sale of the James Ten Eyck Collection, May 1922, included lot 280: "1850. New Orleans Mint. A gem from the Cleneay collection. Yellow gold, unusual bold impression, with fine bright frosty mint surface. A magnificent coin and of great rarity so choice. In original box from the Cleneay sale." It sold for $19.

In October 1982, in the Louis E. Eliasberg Collection of U.S. Gold Coins, Bowers and Ruddy Galleries offered lot 686: "1850-O Choice Brilliant Uncirculated, MS-65." It sold for $37,400. Later, in July 1986, in Auction '86, Superior presented it as lot 1421: "1850-O MS-65. Gem brilliant Uncirculated specimen of this scarce issue. Boldly struck with satiny mint surfaces and full golden orange mint bloom color. The Eliasberg specimen, lot 686. The finest known specimen of this date." It sold for $26,700.

Heritage, in its August 2014 ANA World of Money sale, offered lot 4013: "1850-O AU-58+ PCGS." It sold for $18,100.

VF-20	EF-40	AU-50	AU-55	AU-58	MS-60
$1,350	$2,000	$3,500	$5,500	$8,500	$20,000

1851

Circulation-Strike Mintage: 176,328

Estimated population (Mint State): *15–22.* Most are at lower Mint State levels. Very rare.

Estimated population (circulated grades): *1,200–1,500.*

Submissions certified at highest grades (as of March 2017): *PCGS:* MS-62 (2), MS-63 (2), MS-64 (1). *NGC:* MS-60 (8), MS-61 (10), MS-62 (4), MS-63 (1).

Die data: There were five obverse dies and eight reverse dies made for this coinage, but probably not all were used.

The 1851 four-digit date logotype numerals are about evenly spaced. The 5, basically of the upright (not italic) style, is tilted to the right, with the result that the top surface of the flag is oriented downward to the right, rather than horizontal; this gives the illusion of an italic 5. The ball is close to upright and may touch on deep impressions. The base of the second 1 is slightly lower than the bases of other numerals. This logotype was used on all dies of both mints.

This item in the personal diary of James B. Longacre indicates that, presumably, five different sizes of date logotypes for the 1851 coinage were prepared by an outside engraver, W. Dougherty, who had done other work for the Mint:[11] "Saturday, August 31, 1850: Certified W. Dougherty's bill to mint U.S. for 5 date punches for 1851, $4 each, $20."

Key to collecting: VF and EF are the grades usually seen—a comment applicable to all eagles of this era. Enough Mint State coins are available to supply the needs of the relatively few specialists in Liberty Head eagles by date and mint.

MARKET NEWS AND COMMENTARY

In December 1890, in their sale of the Thomas Cleneay Collection, the Chapman brothers offered lot 504: "1851 Extremely Fine. Mint luster." It sold for $10.50. Such a coin could have been found easily enough in circulation. In March 1907 the David S. Wilson Collection, sold by S. Hudson Chapman, offered lot 26: "1851 Fine." It sold for $11. The July 1937 sale of the Walter P. Innes Jr. Collection conducted by J.C. Morgenthau & Co. included lot 59: "1851 Very Good." It sold for $16.25.

In May 1939, sale 399, Rare U.S. Gold Coins by J.C. Morgenthau & Co. included lot 338: "1851 Very Fine." It sold for $17. In November 1939 the William B. Hale Collection, sold by B. Max Mehl, included lot 1661: "1851 Very Fine." It sold for $20. In the December 1944 sale of the J.F. Bell Collection Stack's included lot 616: "1851 Extremely Fine." It sold for $30.

In March 1948 the Memorable Collection (consigned by Jacob Shapiro) was sold by Numismatic Gallery and included lot 553: "1851. Uncirculated. Brought $75. In W.G.C." It sold for $60. In April 1956, in his sale of the Thomas G. Melish Collection, Abe Kosoff offered lot 2413: "1851. High date. About Uncirculated." It sold for $34.

The October 1996 Spink America sale of selections from the Byron Reed Collection included lot 159: "1851 some scuffs, choice Mint State, lustrous surfaces with warm olive tones, an important coin, both Akers and Breen concurred that this date was extremely rare Uncirculated." It sold for $4,400.

In the August 2016 ANA World's Fair of Money sale Stack's Bowers Galleries offered lot 3315: "1851 EF-40 PCGS." It sold for $998.75.

In the February 2017 Pre-Long Beach sale Ira and Larry Goldberg offered lot 1309: "1851 AU-53 from the SS *Republic*. AU-53 NGC." It sold for $2,291.

VF-20	EF-40	AU-50	AU-55	AU-58	MS-60	MS-63
$850	$1,000	$1,050	$1,250	$1,750	$4,000	$26,000

1851-O

Circulation strike mintage: 263,000

Estimated population (Mint State):
12–18. Most grades are at lower levels,
MS-60 and MS-61. The possibility of
multiple resubmissions clouds the data.

Estimated population (circulated grades): *1,500–1,800.*

Submissions certified at highest grades (as of March 2017): *PCGS:* MS-61 (9),
MS-62 (1), MS-64 (2). *NGC:* MS-60 (11), MS-61 (6), MS-62 (2), MS-64 (1).

Die data: There were seven obverse and five reverse dies sent to New Orleans for this
coinage, with additional serviceable reverses being on hand from earlier times.

The 1851 four-digit date logotype is described in the previous listing.

Certain eagles of 1848-O, 1849-O, 1851-O, 1852-O, and 1853-O
exist with a hollow circular ring at the top of the second vertical
shield stripe on the reverse. Presumably, the ring is from the center
of a compass or is an artifact from a lathe chuck. The 1851-O with
the ring feature is Breen-6898 and is plentiful; indeed, it is seen
more often than any other die variation of the 1851-O. There
are at least two 1851-O reverse dies with the ring feature, one
having a complete ring and the other with the upper third of the
ring obscured by the lowest horizontal shield stripe.

Detail showing the
curious hollow ring
seen on the reverse of
certain New Orleans,
this on an 1851-O die.

Characteristics of striking and die notes: Some lightness at the centers is usual.
Striking varies due to multiple die pairs and striking periods.

Key to collecting: VF and EF are the grades usually seen.

MARKET NEWS AND COMMENTARY

In December 1890, in their sale of the Thomas Cleneay Collection, the Chapman
brothers offered lot 505: "1851-O Uncirculated. Mint luster." It sold for $12.50. In
March 1911, in his sale of the William H. Woodin Collection, Thomas L. Elder
offered lot 1270: "1851-O Leaf close to I in United. Fine." It sold for $10. Also lot
1271: "1851-O Leaf farther from I. Fine." It sold for $10.

In November 1939 the William B. Hale Collection, sold by B. Max Mehl, included
lot 1710: "1851-O Struck in light yellow gold. Brilliant Uncirculated. A gem, and as
such, rare and valuable." It sold for $26. In the December 1944 sale of the J.F. Bell
Collection Stack's included lot 696: "1851-O Uncirculated." It sold for $38.

In October 1982 the Louis E. Eliasberg Collection of U.S. Gold Coins sale by
Bowers and Ruddy Galleries offered lot 688: "1851-O Choice Brilliant Uncirculated,
MS-65. Only three Uncirculated pieces have been offered at auction during the past
60 years. From the John H. Clapp Collection, 1942. Earlier from Elmer S. Sears,
November 1920." It sold for $24,200.

In November 2000 the Bowers and Merena Galleries' sale of the Harry W. Bass Jr.
Collection, Part IV, included lot 645:

1851-O MS-64 PCGS. It is interesting to note that in the 1890 Chapman brothers sale of the Cleneay Collection, nearly a complete collection of eagles by date and mint hit the auction block, most Liberty eagles sold for precisely their face value even in the highest grades, while an Uncirculated 1851-O eagle sold for $12.50! From our sale of the Louis E. Eliasberg Sr. Collection, October 1982, lot 688. [Sold for $29,900]

In the May 1992 sale of the H.C. ("Heck") Dodson Collection, Mid-American Rare Coin Auctions included lot 326: "1851-O MS-61." It sold for $9,350. In August 1999, in the ANA World's Fair of Money sale, Heritage included lot 8097: "1851-O MS-60 NGC. The reverse shows a hollow ring on the shield. It has been claimed that examples of this issue also exist with a normal shield. If this is true, these coins are very rare as the owner of the Acadiana collection searched for such a coin for many years but was unable to locate one." It sold for $5,865.

Stack's January 2007 Americana sale included lot 5236: "1851-O MS-60." It sold for $8,050. Heritage, in its October 2016 Long Beach sale, offered lot 3323: "1851-O MS-62 PCGS." It sold for $29,375.

VF-20	EF-40	AU-50	AU-55	AU-58	MS-60	MS-63
$1,000	$1,200	$1,750	$2,750	$3,750	$6,500	$27,500

1852

Circulation-Strike Mintage: 263,106

Estimated population (Mint State): *35–50.* Mostly in grades MS–60 to 62.

Estimated population (circulated grades): *1,800–2,200.*

Submissions certified at highest grades (as of March 2017): *PCGS:* MS-61 (14), MS-62 (6), MS-66 (1). *NGC:* MS-60 (10), MS-61 (20), MS-62 (5).

Die data: There were 8 obverse dies and 12 reverse dies made for this coinage.

The 1852 four-digit logotype "1852-A" with the 18 and the 85 about the same closeness; the 5 and the 2 are slightly wider in separation; the numerals with bases are about on the same level. It is an italic or slanting 5; the top of flag is horizontal (compared to the different 5 in the 1851 logotype); the ball is very close to upright and is touching on deep impressions. It is a fancy 2 with the curved base and curled top with small knob. Used on most (but not all dies) for both mints.

The 1852 four-digit logotype "1852-B," is as the preceding, but with the 5 and 2 significantly wider apart (most noticeable at the top of the digits). Die use not studied; seen on one Philadelphia Mint coin; may exist on New Orleans dies as well.

Characteristics of striking and die notes: Usually with light striking at obverse and reverse centers.

Key to collecting: VF and EF were the usually seen grades in the early days. By now in this text you already know that! Modern repatriations have made many AU and Mint State coins available.

MARKET NEWS AND COMMENTARY

In March 1907 the David S. Wilson Collection, sold by S. Hudson Chapman, offered lot 27: "1852 Fine." It sold for $16. In November 1939 the William B. Hale Collection sold by B. Max Mehl included lot 1662: "1852 Sharp, nearly Uncirculated, with raised borders on obverse. Scarce." It sold for $21.

In the December 1944 sale of the J.F. Bell Collection Stack's included lot 617: "1852 Brilliant Uncirculated gem. Scarce." It sold for $60. In January 1946 the F.C.C. Boyd sale included lot 657: "1852 Uncirculated." It sold for $42.50.

In a vastly expanded market in October 1982 the Louis E. Eliasberg Collection of U.S. Gold Coins sale by Bowers and Ruddy Galleries offered lot 689: "1852 Choice AU-55 obverse; Brilliant Uncirculated, MS-60 reverse. From the John H. Clapp Collection, 1942. Earlier from Elmer S. Sears, November 1920." It sold for $5,500.

This previous coin had improved when examined by a certification service, as on November 2000 in the Harry W. Bass Jr. Collection, Part IV, sold by Bowers and Merena Galleries as lot 648. It was described as: "1852 MS-61 PCGS." The price was $4,485, a rare instance of an Eliasberg coin not increasing in value.

In January 2008, in the FUN sale, Heritage included lot 3261: "1852 MS-66 PCGS. The terminal grade for this date would have been MS-62 except for an incredible PCGS MS-66 coin (one of the three finest No Motto eagles of any date; this remarkable coin was sold as a PCGS MS-65 in January 2005 for $130,410!" This time it crossed the block for $253,000. This is a poster example of the market effect of condition rarity.

VF-20	EF-40	AU-50	AU-55	AU-58	MS-60
$850	$1,000	$1,050	$1,250	$1,500	$5,000

1852-O

Circulation-Strike Mintage: 18,000

Estimated population (Mint State): 4–6. Exceedingly rare. Absent in this grade from the "name" collections of early years.

Estimated population (circulated grades): *100–140.*

Submissions certified at highest grades (as of March 2017): *PCGS:* AU-55 (17), AU-58 (3), MS-60 (1). *NGC:* AU-55 (24), AU-58 (8), MS-60 (1), MS-61 (1).

Die data: There were six obverse dies sent to New Orleans for this coinage. There were enough usable reverses on hand that no new ones were needed. See logotype information under the previous listing.

Certain eagles of 1848-O, 1849-O, 1851-O, 1852-O, and 1853-O exist with a hollow circular ring at the top of the second vertical shield stripe on the reverse. It may be the case that *all* 1852-O eagles have this "ring" feature.

Characteristics of striking and die notes: Typically with some lightness of striking at the centers, but sharper than 1852 (Philadelphia Mint).

Key to collecting: VF and EF were the usually seen grades until modern times. Today a specialty can easily obtain an AU coin.

Market News and Commentary

In December 1890, in their sale of the Thomas Cleneay Collection, the Chapman brothers offered lot 506: "1852-O Very Fine." It sold for $10.50. In February 1944, in the Belden E. Roach Collection, B. Max Mehl offered lot 406: "1852-O Practically Uncirculated. Rare. Listed at $35 in only Very Fine condition. This one worth much more." It sold for $30.

In April 1956, in his sale of the Thomas G. Melish Collection, Abe Kosoff offered lot 2417: "1852-O. Mint mark centered over EN. Very Fine, scarce." It sold for $38. Also lot 2418: "1852-O. Mint mark is farther right. Very Fine." It sold for $31. It is not known if both of these different dies had the "ring" feature atop the second vertical shield stripe. R.E. Naftzger Jr., who owned most of the coins in the "Melish Collection," is one of only two dedicated specialists who collected Liberty Head eagles by minute die differences, the other being Harry W. Bass Jr.

The October 1996 Spink America sale of selections from the Byron Reed Collection included lot 160: "1852-O variety with hollow ring above second vertical stripe on the reverse shield (Breen, Encyclopedia, 6902), some small marks, Mint State or thereabouts with reflective fields and strong luster." It sold for $30,800.

The above coin was offered in the Stack's Bowers Galleries' November 2016 Whitman Baltimore Expo sale as lot 2153: "1852-O MS-60 (PCGS)." It sold for $111,625.

VF-20	EF-40	AU-50	AU-55	AU-58	MS-60
$1,500	$2,500	$6,000	$8,500	$20,000	$35,000

1853

Circulation-Strike Mintage: 201,253

Estimated population (Mint State): 45–55. Although in absolute terms any eagle of which only 45 to 55 Mint State coins are known is rare, in relative terms it is one of the more available issues of its era. Walter Breen comments: "The few Uncirculateds known are mostly from a hoard found in North Carolina before 1973."[12] Today this is irrelevant due to many repatriated coins from overseas.

Estimated population (circulated grades): 1,400–1,700. This includes some that have been classified as "1853, 3 Over 2."

Submissions certified at highest grades (as of March 2017): PCGS: MS-62 (4), MS-63 (2), MS-64 (4). **NGC:** MS-62 (7), MS-63 (2), MS-64 (1).

Die data: The 1853 four-digit date logotype with numerals shows the 18 as closest, the 85 slightly wider, the 53 wider still (but differences minor), and with the bottoms of digits on the same level. The slanting or italic 5 is used, the top of the flag is horizontal, and the ball is close to the upright and touches on some deep impressions. The 3 leans slightly right. Used on all dies for both mints.

Characteristics of striking and die notes: In the writer's opinion, no overdate exists. One obverse die, Breen-6905, has been called an "1853, 3 Over 2, overdate," but a detailed examination of several high-grade examples show this: Two lines are within the bottom of the final digit (3) and are said by Breen to represent an underdigit (2). A comparison of the final digit on the *1852* eagle logotype shows that the lower part of the 2 contains an element, right above the base, that is somewhat similar to the artifact seen within the 3 of the 1853, 3 Over 2, but the angle does not seem correct. Thus, it would seem that some imagination is needed to call this an overdate.[13] *Many* auction listings describe this as an overdate, especially but not entirely in the era before modern study when just about everything Breen said or wrote was accepted as fact.

Key to collecting: The 1853 is one of the more plentiful eagles of this era.

MARKET NEWS AND COMMENTARY

In December 1890, in their sale of the Thomas Cleneay Collection, the Chapman brothers offered lot 507: "1853 Very Fine." It sold for $10 (face value). In November 1939 the William B. Hale Collection, sold by B. Max Mehl, included lot 1663: "1853 Uncirculated, with mint luster. Not a rare date, but very scarce so choice." It sold for $21. In the December 1944 sale of the J.F. Bell Collection Stack's included lot 618: "1853 Brilliant Uncirculated." It sold for $52.50.

Many years later in the sale of December 2009 Heritage included lot 1753:

> 1853 MS-64 PCGS. The issue is one of the more available No Motto eagles in circulated grades, and lower Mint State examples are not too difficult to locate. The situation changes dramatically at the Choice Uncirculated level, where only four specimens have been certified by NGC and PCGS combined (10/09). [Sold for $27,600]

In October 2014 the Stack's Bowers Galleries' Rarities sale included lot 10047: "1853 MS-64 PCGS. Purchased from us through Joel Rettew Jr., May 1992." It sold for $34,075. Heritage, in its January 2016 FUN sale, offered lot 5617: "1853/2 MS-61 PCGS." It sold for $15,275.

VF-20	EF-40	AU-50	AU-55	AU-58	MS-60	MS-63
$850	$900	$1,050	$1,150	$1,500	$4,000	$17,000

1853-O

Circulation-Strike Mintage: 51,000

Estimated population (Mint State): 7–11. Exceedingly rare. The specimen in Lester Merkin's March 1969 sale may be the finest and was earlier called a "Proof."

Estimated population (circulated grades): *200–300.*

Submissions certified at highest grades (as of March 2017): *PCGS:* MS-60 (1), MS-61 (2). *NGC:* MS-60 (2), MS-61 (5).

Die data: The 1853 four-digit date logotype was used on all dies for both mints. There were six new obverse dies sent to New Orleans for the 1853-O coinage. Sufficient usable reverses were still on hand.

Certain eagles of 1848-O, 1849-O, 1851-O, 1852-O, and 1853-O exist with a hollow circular ring at the top of the second vertical shield stripe on the reverse. For the 1853-O, at least two different reverse dies have the "ring" feature.

Key to collecting: VF and EF are the usually seen grades.

MARKET NEWS AND COMMENTARY

In March 1907 the David S. Wilson Collection, sold by S. Hudson Chapman, offered lot 28: "1853-O Very Fine." It sold for $17. In November 1939 the William B. Hale Collection, sold by B. Max Mehl, included lot 1711: "1853-O. O over EN. Brilliant Uncirculated. The reverse is almost equal to a brilliant Proof. Remarkable condition for this date and mint." It sold for $22.

In March 1968 Lester Merkin's sale offered lot 421:

> 1853-O Brilliant gem Uncirculated, prooflike impression, struck from brilliantly burnished die; revere has broad borders and a knife-rim, both side show unusual sharpness. If not a true Proof, this is a presentation piece of some kind. Only two other Mint State example ever claimed for this date: G.H. Hall 2131 (1945) and "Memorable" 621 (1948), and neither of these was described as prooflike.14 A most extraordinary coin. [Sold for $32]

The above coin was sold later, in July 1979, in RARCOA's section of Auction '79, as 1303: "1853-O Unique Branch Mint Proof. From a Lester Merkin auction (3/69: #421) where it was called a Presentation Piece." It sold for $17,500. Twenty years later in October 1999 it appeared in the Harry W. Bass Jr. Collection, Part II, sold by Bowers and Merena Galleries, as lot 1422: "1853-O MS-61 PCGS. Prooflike obverse. A splendid coin that is quite special in overall appearance, a memorable example. PCGS Population: 1; none finer. From RARCOA's, Auction '79, lot 1303. Formerly from Lester Merkin's sale of March 1969, lot 421." At the Bass sale it sold for $18,400.

In its sale of November 2014 Heritage included lot 4016: "1853-O MS-61 NGC. Census: 5 in 61, 0 finer (9/14)." It sold for $16,450.

VF-20	EF-40	AU-50	AU-55	AU-58	MS-60
$1,000	$1,350	$1,850	$3,000	$6,500	$15,000

1854

Circulation-Strike Mintage: 54,250

Proof Mintage: Unknown, but very small

Notes regarding mintages: Deliveries were made on March 21 (24,012), April 29 (12,552), July 25 (9,234), and September 20 (8,452).

Estimated population (Mint State): *20–30.* Rare. Grades range from MS-60 up to MS-64 or so.

Estimated population (circulated grades): *350–450.*

Estimated population (Proofs): *1.* A single Proof is said to have been struck for inclusion in a Proof set sent to the city of Bremen, Germany. Its whereabouts are unknown today.

Submissions certified at highest grades (as of March 2017): *PCGS:* MS-61 (5), MS-62 (3), MS-64 (2). *NGC:* MS-60 (5), MS-61 (5), MS-62 (1), MS-63 (1), MS-64 (2).

Die data: These have the "medium"-size date numerals, sometimes called "small," but they are hardly such. The 18 is close, the 85 is wider, and the 54 closest. There is a slanting or italic 5, and the ball is distant from the upright. Used on all Philadelphia Mint dies, some New Orleans dies, and all San Francisco dies.

Key to collecting: VF and EF were the usually seen grades in great collections sold at auction. Mint State coins, once quite rare, are now collectible due to coins coming back from overseas holdings.

MARKET NEWS AND COMMENTARY

In March 1865 the Dr. James R. Chilton Collection, held by Bangs, Merwin & Co., included lot 1265: "1854 Good and scarce. Dickeson, page 172." It sold for $18.15 In May 1939, sale 399, Rare U.S. Gold Coins by J.C. Morgenthau & Co. included lot 343: "1854 Very Fine." It sold for $20.50; also "1854 Extremely Fine." It sold for $50. In May 1945 Stack's sale of the George H. Hall Collection included lot 2132: "1854 Brilliant Uncirculated." It sold for $40.

In the August 2016 ANA World's Fair of Money sale Stack's Bowers Galleries offered lot 3321: "1854 MS-62 PCGS." It sold for $15,275.

VF-20	EF-40	AU-50	AU-55	AU-58	MS-60	MS-63
$900	$1,050	$1,250	$1,650	$2,750	$6,500	$27,500

1854-O, Small Date

Circulation-Strike Mintage:
Part of 52,500

Estimated population (Mint State): *3–4.*

Estimated population (circulated grades): *150–225.*

Submissions certified at highest grades (as of March 2017): *PCGS:* AU-55 (14), AU-58 (9), MS-60 (1). *NGC:* AU-55 (41), AU-58 (23), MS-61 (1).

Die data: There were eight or more obverse dies shipped to New Orleans in anticipation of this coinage, though Mint records are incomplete.

The "medium" size date numerals are sometimes called "small," but they are hardly such. The 18 is close, the 85 is wider, and the 54 is closest. There is a slanting or italic 5 and the ball is distant from the upright. Used on all Philadelphia Mint dies, some New Orleans dies, and all San Francisco dies.

Large and Small (Medium) Date varieties exist for 1854 New Orleans eagles only.

Key to collecting: The Small (Medium) Date and Large Date varieties of 1854-O seem to be of about equal availability. The Small Date would be better called the Medium Date. Harry W. Bass Jr. found *more* of the Large Date than of the Small Date—opposite to conventional wisdom of the late 1900s. VF and EF were the usual grades seen in notable auctions of generations ago. Today AU coins are plentiful.

MARKET NEWS AND COMMENTARY

The citations below include 1854-O eagles not attributed to date size; some Large Date pieces may be included.

In December 1890, in their sale of the Thomas Cleneay Collection, the Chapman brothers offered lot 508: "1854-O Extremely Fine." It sold for $10.50. In May 1939, sale 399, Rare U.S. Gold Coins by J.C. Morgenthau & Co. included lot 344: "1854-O Very Fine." It sold for $17. The June 1941 sale of the William Forrester Dunham Collection by B. Max Mehl included lot 2223: "1854-O Struck in light yellow gold. Very Fine; bold impression." It sold for $18.

In the December 1944 sale of the J.F. Bell Collection Stack's included lot 699: "1854-O Uncirculated. Choice." It sold for $40. In May 1945 Stack's sale of the George H. Hall Collection included lot 2134: "1854-O Brilliant Uncirculated." It sold for $30.

In the May 1992 sale of the H.C. ("Heck") Dodson Collection, Mid-American Rare Coin Auctions included lot 336: "1854-O Small Date. MS-60." It sold for $7,425. What a difference a Mint State coin made in the market by this time!

VF-20	EF-40	AU-50	AU-55	AU-58	MS-60
$1,150	$1,350	$2,000	$3,250	$4,750	$10,500

1854-O, Large Date

Circulation-Strike Mintage: Part of 52,500

Estimated population (Mint State):
15–22. Very rare.

Estimated population (circulated grades):
150–225. VF and EF are usual grades, but AU coins are available on a regular basis.

Submissions certified at highest grades (as of March 2017): *PCGS:* MS-60 (1), MS-61 (1), MS-63 (1). *NGC:* MS-60 (3), MS-61 (10), MS-63 (1).

Die data: These have the large-size date numerals, sometimes called "huge" (with justification). The 18 is wide and the 85 and 54 are each closer and about the same. There is the slanting or italic 5 and the ball close to upright. Used on at least *three* New

Orleans Mint dies, a rather curious situation as the date has not been observed on even a single Philadelphia Mint die.

Large and Small (Medium) Date varieties exist for 1854 New Orleans eagles only.

Key to collecting: VF and EF were the usual grades in collections formed generations ago, but today AU coins are available on a regular basis.

MARKET NEWS AND COMMENTARY

In June 1942 the Colonel J.A. Porter Collection, cataloged by B. Max Mehl, included lot 1212: "1854-O New Orleans Mint. Unusually large date. Extremely Fine, bold; just a shade from Uncirculated." It sold for $16.50. This was a very early listing mentioning the Large Date. In February 1944, in the Belden E. Roach Collection, B. Max Mehl offered lot 408: "1854-O Huge date. Just a shade from Uncirculated. Considerable luster." It sold for $24.25.

In June 1946, in the William Cutler Atwater Collection, B. Max Mehl offered lot 1529:

> 1854-O. Unusually large date. The preceding coin is with the usual size date, which is not small, but the date on this specimen is at least 50% larger [than on the preceding lot]. The top of figure 1 and 4 almost touch bust. I do not recall ever having seen this variety before and it is undoubtedly rare. Not listed in the *Standard Catalogue*.

Mehl had a memory lapse, not at all unusual for him.

In April 1956, in his sale of the Thomas G. Melish Collection, Abe Kosoff offered lot 2423: "1854-O. Large date. Very Fine, scarce." It sold for $37.50.

In June 1957 New Netherlands' 49th Sale, Eliasberg duplicates included lot 253:

> 1854-O. Large date, as on the silver dollars. This date is quite unforgettable once seen, as it fills up practically the entire space below the bust. Extremely Fine; beautifully struck and preserved. The only other one we have seen in recent years is the VF Melish coin, which went as a "sleeper" at $37.50, while we were out of the room. The discovery example sold of the 1854-O eagle with Large Date appeared as lot 1529 in the W.C. Atwater collection, sold in 1946. It realized $42, in spite of the fact that friend B. Max Mehl was so exuberant (and justifiably so) in describing the piece, that he neglected (in 56 words) to mention anything about condition. [Sold for $47]

The above is a great example of Walter Breen's hokum in cataloging. It is highly unlikely that Breen ever saw the Melish coin. He hardly ever examined auction lots of other companies. Moreover, Breen was not a bidder at the sale anyway. The Atwater coin was *not* the discovery coin. The Melish coin in VF grade at $37.50 could not been much of a sleeper if the significantly finer EF coin sold a year later by New Netherlands brought $47. That said, when the New Netherlands catalogs arrived in the mail they always furnished an evening of enjoyable and entertaining reading. No others were even close in prolixity.

In the FUN sale of January 2008 Heritage included lot 9219: "1854-O Large Date. MS-61 NGC. Population: 3 in 61, 1 finer (12/04)." It sold for $11,500. In August 2013 the Stack's Bowers Galleries' ANA World's Fair of Money sale included lot 4510: "1854-O Large Date, MS-60 PCGS." It sold for $10,869.

VF-20	EF-40	AU-50	AU-55	AU-58	MS-60
$1,150	$1,350	$2,000	$3,250	$5,500	$10,500

1854-S

Circulation-Strike Mintage: 123,826

Notes regarding mintages: Deliveries from the coiner to the treasurer were as follows: *April 3:* 260 coins (This was on the day that the San Francisco Mint opened for coinage business.); *May:* 1,764; *June:* 46,002; *July:* 57,800; *September:* 23,000.

Estimated population (Mint State): *15–22.*

Estimated population (circulated grades): *700–900.*

Submissions certified as highest grades (as of March 2017): *PCGS:* MS-61 (3), MS-62 (1). *NGC:* MS-61 (2), MS-62 (1).

Die data: Six (or 11; accounts vary) pairs of dies were shipped from the Philadelphia Mint to San Francisco for use on the 1854-S $10 coinage.

These coins use "medium"-size date numerals, sometimes called "small," but they are hardly such. The 18 is close, the 85 is wider, and the 54 is closest. There is a slanting or italic 5 and the ball is distant from the upright. Used on all Philadelphia Mint dies, some New Orleans dies, and all San Francisco dies.

All known specimens have a medium S (1.3 mm) mintmark.

Characteristics of striking and die notes: Usually fairly well struck.

Key to collecting: VF and EF are typical grades. Mint State coins, once great rarities, are now collectible. In grades up through AU the 1854-S is of the more available Liberty Head eagles of the era and is the most often seen San Francisco $10 of the No Motto type. Ever popular as the first San Francisco Mint eagle.

MARKET NEWS AND COMMENTARY

In December 1890, in their sale of the Thomas Cleneay Collection, the Chapman brothers offered lot 509: "1854-S Very Fine." It sold for $10.75. In March 1907 the David S. Wilson Collection, sold by S. Hudson Chapman, offered lot 29: "1854-S First year. Fine." It sold for $15. In March 1911, in his sale of the William H. Woodin Collection, Thomas L. Elder offered lot 1294: "1854-S. Large date. Fine." It sold for $10. Also lot 1295: "1854-S Smaller, thicker date. Very Good." It sold for $10.

The January 1986 Stack's sale of the James Walter Carter and Margaret Woolfolk Carter Collections included lot 221: "1854-S Brilliant Uncirculated, frosty mint bloom, with the normal bag abrasions." It sold for $2,420.

In October 1999 Stack's offered the Dombrowski and Orwen Collections with lot 1055: "1854-S Gem Brilliant Uncirculated. An 1854-S 20 Proof exists [in the National Numismatic Collection] and it is certainly possible that an eagle of that year would have been struck for presentation." It sold for $21,275.

In the FUN sale of January 2007 Heritage included lot 3645:

> 1854-S MS-63 NGC. This is the finest Mint State piece at NGC by two full points, and the only specimen that NGC has encapsulated with the SS *Central America* pedigree. The other Mint State piece at NGC is an MS-61, ex: SS *Republic*. PCGS

has graded six Mint State coins, two each in MS-62, MS-63, and MS-64, none with the SSCA pedigree. [Sold for $13,800]

VF-20	EF-40	AU-50	AU-55	AU-58	MS-60
$1,000	$1,200	$1,650	$3,000	$5,500	$12,500

1855

Circulation-Strike Mintage: 121,701
Proof Mintage: None confirmed

Notes regarding mintages: All were delivered between January 24 and June 30.

Estimated population (Mint State): *25–35.*
Grades are mostly toward MS-60, although choice examples come on the market occasionally.

Estimated population (circulated grades): *700–900.*

Submissions certified at highest grades (as of March 2017): *PCGS:* MS-62 (6), MS-63 (2), MS-64 (3). *NGC:* MS-62 (9), MS-63 (2), MS-65 (1).

Characteristics of striking and die notes: Usually fairly well struck, but as multiple die pairs were used at different times, no one rule fits all. Some are lightly struck, especially around the obverse border.

Key to collecting: VF and EF were the usual grades seen years ago, this being a standard rule for eagles of this era. Mint State coins, once considered to be great rarities, are collectible today.

MARKET NEWS AND COMMENTARY

In December 1935, sale 356, Ludger Gravel and Byron Carney Collections by J.C. Morgenthau & Co. included lot 265: "1855 Uncirculated, mint luster." It sold for $25. In March 1988 the Norweb Collection, Part II, sale by Bowers and Merena Galleries included the same coin as lot 2170: "1855 MS-60 to 63. There is some friction in the left obverse field, where the piece was rubbed, otherwise the coin would be a candidate for an overall MS-63 status, or close to it. A sharp and lustrous example of a coin which in this grade is decidedly elusive. From J.C. Morgenthau & Co. on December 10, 1935." It sold for $3,080.

In June 1936, sale 366, U.S. and Foreign Gold Coins, also held by J.C. Morgenthau & Co., included lot 39: "1855 Uncirculated." It sold for $22.50. In February 1944, in the Belden E. Roach Collection, B. Max Mehl offered lot 334: "1855 Uncirculated, frosty mint surface. Just about as perfect as the day it was minted. Rare so choice. Listed at $45." It sold for $45.

Fast forward to the new market. In the May 1992 sale of the H.C. ("Heck") Dodson Collection, Mid-American Rare Coin Auctions included lot 340: "1855 MS-63." It sold for $10,175. In October 1994 Stack's sale of the James A. Stack Sr. Collection, Part II, included lot 1312: "1855 Brilliant Uncirculated." It sold for $44,000. In the April 2005 sale of "Treasures of the SS *Republic*" Bowers and Merena Galleries offered lot 2002: "1855 MS-62 NGC." It sold for $12,650.

The Bowers and Merena Galleries sale of the Harry W. Bass Jr. Collection, Part III, in May 2000 included lot 629: "1855 MS-64. From Paramount's sale of August 1969, lot 2097." It sold for $6,900. In the Long Beach sale of February 2001, Heritage included lot 7012: "1855 MS-63 PCGS. Population: 1 in 63, 1 finer (5/00)." It sold for $8,625. Stack's October 2006 71st Anniversary sale included lot 2241: "1855 Brilliant Uncirculated." It sold for $10,350.

VF-20	EF-40	AU-50	AU-55	AU-58	MS-60	MS-63
$900	$1,100	$1,350	$1,500	$2,000	$4,750	$17,500

1855-O

Circulation-Strike Mintage: 18,000

Notes regarding mintages: Mintage sharply reduced from the preceding year. By this time the San Francisco Mint was in full operation (having opened in spring 1854), and California gold that might otherwise have been struck in New Orleans was sent to the San Francisco facility.

Estimated population (Mint State): *3–5*. Exceedingly rare.

Estimated population (circulated grades): *100–130*.

Submissions certified at highest grades (as of March 2017): *PCGS:* AU-55 (3), AU-58 (2), MS-61 (2). *NGC:* AU-55 (20), AU-58 (13).

Die data: Four obverse dies were sent to New Orleans. Sufficient reverses were on hand from earlier years.

Characteristics of striking and die notes: Usually seen with some evidence of light striking at the centers. Nearly always with partial to extensive prooflike fields.

Key to collecting: The 1855-O is quite scarce in all grades. Otherwise the usual comments about rarity then and availability now in higher grades.

MARKET NEWS AND COMMENTARY

In December 1890, in their sale of the Thomas Cleneay Collection, the Chapman brothers offered lot 510: "1855-O Very Fine." It sold for $10.50. May 1939, sale 399, Rare U.S. Gold Coins by J.C. Morgenthau & Co. included lot 346: "1855-O Very Fine." It sold for $21.50.

In November 1939 the William B. Hale Collection, sold by B. Max Mehl, included lot 1713: "1855-O. O high. Extremely Fine, with mint luster. Rare. Listed up to $50." It sold for $24.75.

The January 1986 Stack's sale of the James Walter Carter and Margaret Woolfolk Carter Collections included lot 223: "1855-O Brilliant Uncirculated. Prooflike surface, with some friction in the field, but really a stunning example. Ex R. L. Miles Jr. Collection (Stack's), lot 647, October 1968; Scanlon Collection (Stack's), lot 2475 October 1973." It sold for $5,280.

In the ANA World's Fair of Money sale of August 1999 Heritage included lot 8206:

1855-O MS-61 NGC. Easily the finest 1855-O eagle we have seen and quite possibly the finest known. There are currently two MS 61 1855-O eagles listed in the PCGS Population Report. We have never seen the other and are not certain if this listing does not represent a resubmission of the Acadiana collection specimen. If this is the case, then the presently offered coin is unique in Mint State. [Sold for $23,000]

VF-20	EF-40	AU-50	AU-55	AU-58	MS-60
$1,150	$2,500	$6,000	$9,000	$12,500	$25,000

1855-S

Circulation-Strike Mintage: 9,000

Notes regarding mintages: All were delivered in the third quarter of the year.

Estimated population (Mint State): *None.*

Estimated population (circulated grades): *80–10.*

Submissions certified at highest grades (as of March 2017): *PCGS:* AU-50 (7), AU-53 (9), AU-55 (2). *NGC:* AU-50 (2), AU-53 (11), AU-55 (5), AU-58 (3).

Die data: Six obverse dies were sent to San Francisco on November 2, 1854, for this coinage, according to one account. Another account states that 10 obverses and 5 reverses were shipped, the additional dies being sent after November 2, 1854. Most remained unused.

Reverses with medium S (1.3 mm) mintmark were on hand from 1854.

Key to collecting: A key issue in the series. When seen, the 1855-S is apt to be VF or, less often, EF. AU coins are slightly scarce. Some are from the SS *Central America* treasure.

MARKET NEWS AND COMMENTARY

In March 1907 the David S. Wilson Collection, sold by S. Hudson Chapman, offered lot 30: "1855-S Fine. Scarce." It sold for $16. In February 1944, in the Belden E. Roach Collection, B. Max Mehl offered lot 426: "1855-S Extremely Fine. Rare. Listed at $40 in VF." It sold for $32.50.

In December 2000, in its Gold Rush / SS *Central America* auction (guest cataloged by Q. David Bowers), Christie's had lot 69: "1855-S AU-53 PCGS." It sold for $4,370. Heritage, in its February 2017 sale, had lot 2993: "1855-S AU-53 NGC." It sold for $6,462.50.

VF-20	EF-40	AU-50	AU-55	AU-58
$2,250	$3,500	$6,500	$9,500	$20,000

1856

Circulation-Strike Mintage: 60,490
Proof Mintage: None confirmed

Notes regarding mintages: Deliveries were scheduled as follows: February 29 (31,195), May 31 (8,400), June 6 (5,938), and June 16 (14,957).

Estimated population (Mint State): *35–50.*

Estimated population (circulated grades): *400–550.*

Submissions certified at highest grades (as of March 2017): *PCGS:* MS-62 (8), MS-63 (1), MS-64 (1). *NGC:* MS-62 (2), MS-63 (2), MS-64 (2).

Die data: Five pairs of dies were produced for this issue. One die has a stray top of the 1 in 1856 protruding from the denticles below the knob of the 5.[16]

Key to collecting: EF is about par for a typical coin encountered in the marketplace, although Mint State coins have appeared now and then over a long period of years. Leading collections often contained them. Today, AU coins are easy to find. Enough Mint State coins are around to supply specialists.

MARKET NEWS AND COMMENTARY

In December 1890, in their sale of the Thomas Cleneay Collection, the Chapman brothers offered lot 511: "1856 Uncirculated. Mint luster." It sold for $12.75. In March 1907 the David S. Wilson Collection, sold by S. Hudson Chapman, offered lot 31: "1856 Uncirculated. Mint luster. Rare state." It sold for $18.

In April 1937 the George M. Agurs Collection, sold by B. Max Mehl, offered lot 320: "1856 Uncirculated, with bright mint luster; only slightest cabinet friction; with considerable Proof surface. Very scarce." It sold for $26.

The June 1941 sale of the William Forrester Dunham Collection by B. Max Mehl included lot 2225: "1856 Uncirculated; sharp, with full mint luster. Very scarce so choice." It sold for $18. The same specimen was offered by Stack's in October 1947 in the H.R. Lee Collection (Eliasberg duplicates) as lot 1512: "1856 Brilliant Uncirculated gem with semi-proof surface. From the Dunham Collection." It sold for $37.50.

Jumping again into later times, in the May 1992 sale of the H.C. ("Heck") Dodson Collection, Mid-American Rare Coin Auctions included lot 344: "1856 MS-63." It sold for $18.700. By this time condition rarity led the marketplace, as it has ever since. Still, high-grade coins were on the scarce side. In the May 1993 Bowers and Merena Galleries' sale of the Stetson University Collection, lot 2035 included: "1856 AU-58." It sold for $6,875. Stack's March 1990 James A. Stack Sr. sale included lot 1181: "1856 Brilliant Uncirculated." It sold for $18,700.

Reflective of repatriations, in December 2004 the American Numismatic Rarities Classics sale included lot 518: "1856 AU-58." It sold for $1,323. The price bounced around, and in the August 2016 ANA World's Fair of Money sale Stack's Bowers Galleries included lot 3327: "1856 AU-58 (PCGS)." It went to a successful bidder for $2,585.

VF-20	EF-40	AU-50	AU-55	AU-58	MS-60	MS-63
$900	$1,000	$1,150	$1,250	$1,500	$4,000	$15,000

1856-O

Circulation-Strike Mintage: 14,500

Estimated population (Mint State): *3–5.*

Estimated population (circulated grades): *90–115.*

Submissions certified at highest grades (as of March 2017): *PCGS:* AU-55 (4), AU-58 (7), MS-60 (1). *NGC:* AU-55 (25), AU-58 (21), MS-60 (4).

Die data: Four obverse dies and two reverse dies were sent to New Orleans for this coinage.

Characteristics of striking and die notes: Sometimes lightly struck on the obverse stars, particularly at the left.

Key to collecting: VF is the grade usually seen. The 1856-O is elusive at any level. In his lifetime, Harry W. Bass Jr. acquired seven specimens, the highest of which was graded EF-45. Since that time repatriations have altered the register of available grades.

MARKET NEWS AND COMMENTARY

In March 1907 the David S. Wilson Collection, sold by S. Hudson Chapman, offered lot 32: "1856-O Very Fine." It sold for $15. The December 1944 sale of the J.F. Bell Collection by Stack's included lot 701: "1856-O Extremely Fine with auction records as high as $82.50. Very scarce." It sold for $72.50. In June 1946, in the William Cutler Atwater Collection, B. Max Mehl offered lot 1531: "1856-O About Uncirculated with considerable mint luster. Rare so choice. Record up to $80." It sold for $35.

In April 1960 New Netherlands' 54th sale, Jonathan Glogower Consignment, Etc. included this lot 697:

> 1856-O. Thin, weak mintmark. Close to Extremely Fine, bright; somewhat bag marked. Despite all contrary listings, we have been unable to locate in any sale in the past fourteen years a record of even one specimen that will rate a full. Extremely Fine, let alone any higher grade. This makes ridiculous the *Guide Book* price of $67.50 Uncirculated, and understandable the 1954 record of $70 for the VF Graves coin!

This coin sold for $77.50. What about Mehl's Atwater coin described as AU with considerable mint luster? Walter Breen mainly relied on his usually excellent memory. His knowledge of auction appearances was based on viewing only a small percentage of sales. As an example, he seems to have studied only a handful of auction catalogs issued by Thomas L. Elder, none by M.H. Bolender, none by Barney Bluestone, and none of a number of others. In 1960 only a few people studied old auction catalogs and periodicals, so the Breen comments were hardly ever challenged. Today, unfounded statements would be challenged by many scholars. All of this is fascinating to contemplate.

Many years later in October 1998 in the John J. Pittman Collection sale, Part II, David Akers offered lot 1940:

> 1856-O Very Fine to Extremely Fine. Very similar in overall rarity to the 1852-O and 1855-O; most known specimens are well circulated like this one and the 1856-O is seldom seen above the Extremely Fine grade level. Purchased from Stack's for $125, date of purchase unknown. [Sold for $3,080]

Although Akers did not do much if any studying of numismatics and tradition in auctions held before 1940, he carefully analyzed most catalogs issued since that time.

As a result, what he wrote was hardly ever, perhaps never, challenged. His books on gold coins were essential to every library at the time. They are still valuable and interesting today, a window on the market in which many coins that are easily found today were rarities at that time.

In November 2000, in the Harry W. Bass Jr. Collection, Part IV, Bowers and Merena Galleries offered lot 663: "1856-O AU-58 PCGS. PCGS Population: 6, none finer." It sold for $6,325.

In the November 2016 Whitman Expo sale Stack's Bowers Galleries offered lot 2154: "1856-O MS-60 NGC." It sold for $47,000. In the FUN sale of January 2017 Heritage included lot 5812:

> 1856-O MS-62 PCGS. PCGS has certified precisely two pieces in MS-62 including this piece, and the other example we handled 15 years ago in our Exclusively Internet Auction #21043, lot 3407, where it realized $10,000. From the photo, we believe the present coin represents the second MS-62 PCGS example. [Sold for $32,250]

VF-20	EF-40	AU-50	AU-55	AU-58	MS-60
$1,350	$2,500	$4,500	$7,000	$9,500	$16,500

1856-S

Circulation-Strike Mintage: 68,000

Notes regarding mintages: Deliveries from the coiner were made as follows: January (10,000), September (55,500), and December (2,500).

Estimated population (Mint State): *20–30.* Mostly from the wreck of the SS *Central America.* Prior to then, probably 4 to 6 were known.

Estimated population (circulated grades): *400–450.*

Submissions certified at highest grades (as of March 2017): *PCGS:* MS-61 (3), MS-62 (3), MS-63 (1). *NGC:* MS-61 (4).

Die data: Nine 1856-dated obverse dies and two reverse dies were shipped to San Francisco in December 1855. Also, leftover reverses were on hand. Medium S (1.3 mm) mintmark is the norm. Large S (1.7 mm) mintmark variety is very rare; one variety with large S has the mintmark tilted right.

Key to collecting: VF and EF are the grades usually encountered. AU examples are rare. Mint State coins are scarce, but enough are around to supply specialists. Most of these are from stocks shipped out of San Francisco to Europe starting in the late 1870s. Across all grades this is the second most available (1854 is *the* most available) San Francisco $10 of the No Motto type.

Market News and Commentary

In December 1890, in their sale of the Thomas Cleneay Collection, the Chapman brothers offered lot 512: "1856-S Very Fine." It sold for $10 (face value). In March

1907 the David S. Wilson Collection, sold by S. Hudson Chapman, offered lot 33: "1856-S Extremely Fine." It sold for $17.

Years later in October 1999, in the Harry W. Bass Jr. Collection, Part II, Bowers and Merena Galleries offered lot 1450: "1856-S Medium Mintmark. AU-50. Partly proof-like. From Stack's sale of the Miles Collection, October 1968, lot 651." It sold for $1,495. Also lot 1451: "1856-S Medium Mintmark. EF-45. Purchased from Stanley Kesselman, February 7, 1972." It sold for $920. Also lot 1452: "1856-S Medium Mintmark. EF-40. From Superior Galleries' sale of March 15, 1973." It sold for $747.50, Also lot 1453: "1856-S Large Mintmark. EF-45. Obverse from deeply dished, notably basined die, sufficiently so that a separate listing would be merited in a technical catalog prepared for the specialist (if same is ever done). From Paramount's sale of February 1973, lot 1107." It sold for $517.50.

In December 2000, in its Gold Rush / SS *Central America* auction (guest cataloged by Q. David Bowers), Christie's offered lot 73: "1856-S MS-63 PCGS." It sold for $19,550. In May 2005 the American Numismatic Rarities sale of the J.B. Worthington Collection included lot 378: "1856-S MS-62 PCGS. From the SS *Central America* treasure." It sold for $19,550. In its Long Beach sale of September 2010 Heritage included lot 26380: "1856-S MS-61 NGC." It sold for $9,200.

VF-20	EF-40	AU-50	AU-55	AU-58	MS-60	MS-63
$900	$1,000	$1,500	$2,500	$4,000	$9,000	$25,000

1857

Circulation-Strike Mintage: 16,606
Proof Mintage: *2–3*

Notes regarding mintages: Of the mintage, 2,916 were delivered in the first half of the year and the remaining 13,690 in the second half.

Estimated population (Mint State): 6–9. Extremely rare. Known examples are in lower grades, some probably having graduated from AU.

Estimated population (circulated grades): *130–150.*

Estimated population (Proofs): 2. The Eliasberg specimen, ex James Ten Eyck Collection. Now at the Smithsonian Institution.

Submissions certified at highest grades (as of March 2017): *PCGS:* MS-60 (1), MS-62 (1). *NGC:* MS-60 (3), MS-61 (4), MS-62 (1).

Characteristics of striking and die notes: Some lightness is usual at the centers, but generally well struck.

Key to collecting: VF and EF are typical grades encountered. Scarce in all grades. AU coins are somewhat scarce. Mint State coins, once super-rare, are now available on scattered occasions.

MARKET NEWS AND COMMENTARY

In May 1939, sale 399, Rare U.S. Gold Coins by J.C. Morgenthau & Co. included lot 350: "1857 Fine." It sold for $17. In October 1962, in the Samuel W. Wolfson Collection, Stack's offered lot 669: "1857 Almost Extremely Fine. Scarce." It sold for $150.

The January 1986 Stack's sale of the James Walter Carter and Margaret Woolfolk Carter Collections included lot 228: "1857 About Uncirculated, frosty mint bloom." It sold for $150. Then came a market increase. In October 1994 Stack's sale of the James A. Stack Sr. Collection, Part II, included lot 1319: "1857-O Brilliant Uncirculated." It sold for $26,400. This sale was the high-water mark for many federal coins.

In January 1999, in the Rarities sale, Bowers and Merena Galleries included lot 1457:

> 1857 MS-61 PCGS. One of the most amazing coins in this sale, hidden for decades in a bank vault, and not available to any modern researchers including David Akers, Walter Breen, or ourselves, this piece has come to light in the Pennsylvania Cabinet. [Sold for $13,800]

This coin was from the estate of one of America's most prominent numismatists. Like many dedicated collectors, he spent most of his adult life in rare coins, moving from one specialty to another, once a series had neared completion. He formed definitive collections in large and small copper cents, patterns, commemoratives, and Proof coins.

Heritage, in its September 2016 Long Beach sale, offered lot 14145: "1857 MS-60 NGC." It sold for $16,687.50.

VF-20	EF-40	AU-50	AU-55	AU-58	MS-60
$900	$1,000	$1,650	$3,500	$5,500	$12,000

1857-O

Circulation-Strike Mintage: 5,500

Estimated population (Mint State): *0–1.* None reported in modern times. The Bell Collection coin (1944) was listed as Mint State.

Estimated population (circulated grades): *45–55.*

Submissions certified at highest grades (as of March 2017): *PCGS:* AU-50 (11), AU-53 (10), AU-55 (4), AU-58 (5). *NGC:* AU-50 (9), AU-53 (12), AU-55 (12), AU-58 (12).

Die data: At least two logotype positional varieties are known, and at least two different reverse mintmark positional varieties are known.

Characteristics of striking and die notes: Usually fairly well struck.

Key to collecting: Very scarce in all grades. Typically VF or EF, but AU coins are in sufficient supply that specialists can find an example easily.

MARKET NEWS AND COMMENTARY

In May 1915, in his sale of the B.W. Smith Collection, B. Max Mehl offered lot 77: "1857-O Very Fine. Rare. Only 5500 coined." It sold for $15. In June 1934 J.C. Morgenthau & Co.'s sale of coins from the Waldo C. Newcomer Collection included lot 112: "1857-O Extremely Fine and very rare." It sold for $35.

In the December 1944 sale of the J.F. Bell Collection Stack's included lot 702: "1857-O Only 5500 minted. Brilliant Uncirculated. Rare." It sold for $77.50.

Two generations later in November 2000, in the Harry W. Bass Jr. Collection, Part IV, Bowers and Merena Galleries offered lot 668: "1857-O AU-55 PCGS. PCGS Population: 5, 1 finer (AU-58). From Stack's offering of the Bartle Collection, October 1984, lot 1182." It sold for $5,060. In July 2005 the American Numismatic Rarities sale of the William H. LaBelle Sr. Collection included lot 306: "1857-O AU-58 PCGS. From Heritage's sale of the Galveston Collection." It sold for $19,550.

VF-20	EF-40	AU-50	AU-55	AU-58
$2,000	$3,500	$6,000	$9,500	$25,000

1857-S

Circulation-Strike Mintage: 26,000

Notes regarding mintages: The coiner delivered 10,000 in the first half of the year and the balance of 16,000 in the second half.

Estimated population (Mint State): *10–14.* None were known in numismatic hands prior to the SS *Central America* treasure discovery.

Estimated population (circulated grades): *150–180.*

Submissions certified at highest grades (as of March 2017): *PCGS:* MS-62 (2), MS-63 (2), MS-64 (2). **NGC:** MS-63 (1).

Die data: Obverse dies are known with the date centered between the bust and the denticles and with the date low. These have the medium S (1.2 mm) mintmark.

Key to collecting: VF and EF grades are the norm plus some lightly circulated pieces recovered from the SS *Central America.* That was not always the case. David W. Akers in his 1980 study stated, "Low-grade specimens are the norm for this date yet the 1857-S is sufficiently rare that even VF and EF examples are seldom seen." Today, Mint State coins are seen on rare occasions. Earlier, they were virtually unknown.

MARKET NEWS AND COMMENTARY

In February 1944, in the Belden E. Roach Collection, B. Max Mehl offered lot 428: "1857-S Just a shade from Uncirculated with mint luster." It sold for $23.25. The January 1986 Stack's sale of the James Walter Carter and Margaret Woolfolk Carter Collections included lot 230: "1857-S About Uncirculated. A prooflike example." It sold for $1,265.

In December 2000, in its Gold Rush / SS *Central America* auction (guest cataloged by Q. David Bowers), Christie's offered lot 74: "1857-S MS-64 PCGS." It sold for $40,250. In the FUN sale of January 2007 Heritage included lot 3645: "1857-S MS-63 (NGC)." This is the finest Mint State piece at NGC by two full points, and the only specimen that NGC has encapsulated with the SS *Central America* pedigree. The other Mint State piece at NGC is an MS-61, ex: SS *Republic*. PCGS has graded six Mint State coins, two each in MS-62, MS-63, and MS-64, none with the SSCA pedigree. It sold for $27,600.

VF-20	EF-40	AU-50	AU-55	AU-58	MS-60	MS-63
$1,000	$1,250	$2,500	$4,500	$6,000	$11,000	$25,000

1858

Circulation-Strike Mintage: 2,521
Proof Mintage: 4–6

Estimated population (Mint State): *4–6.* Exceedingly rare in Mint State. Any given example has the possibility today of being resubmitted to grading services, then resubmitted again—inflating the numbers. In 1976 a repatriated coin described as Gem Uncirculated was advertised at $85,000.

Estimated population (circulated grades): *35–50.* Very scarce and very famous, although there are a number of other Liberty Head $10 coins which are rarer, but are little known (examples being San Francisco issues of the early 1860s). Nearly all were repatriated from overseas sources in the late 1900s.

Estimated population (Proofs): *4.* One each in the Smithsonian Institution and the American Numismatic Society. Two are in private hands.

Submissions certified at highest grades (as of March 2017): *PCGS:* MS-65 (1). *NGC:* MS-60 (2), MS-61 (1).

Die data: The 1858 four-digit date logotype was used with the 18 closest, the 85 wider, and the 58 widest in spacing.[17] The top interior of the 8's are slightly smaller than bottom interior; the upright of the 5 slants slightly to the right; and the second 8 is slightly low and leans slightly right. Used on all dies for all mints.

Characteristics of striking and die notes (circulation strikes): Usually well struck. Obverse die lapped, and with certain curls behind the neck detached or nearly so, these being particularly evident at the top of the neck.

Characteristics of striking and die notes (Proofs): In *United States Eagles, 1795–1933* (1967) Walter Breen described the Proof die: "Normal die, not lapped; curls behind neck normally joined to neckline and to each other. Date a light to right of center, the right side of 8 nearly in line with right corner of truncation."

Key to collecting: It would seem that with all of the history surrounding this issue that if you can afford a nice VF or EF coin, go for it!

Market News and Commentary

Circulation strikes of the 1858 have been in demand for many years, although in the 19th century numismatists who collected only by date, as nearly all did, could be satisfied easily enough with an 1858-O or 1858-S. In the late 1900s many were repatriated from overseas. Today a circulated 1858 is easily enough found. As the 1858 was once considered to be among the very rarest American gold coins, expanded citations are given in view of the change of status.

In April 1937 the George M. Agurs Collection, sold by B. Max Mehl, offered lot 1770: "1858 Can easily be classed as fine. Excessively rare. Seldom offered. Only 2521 coined." It sold for $135. It was indeed rare at the time, but specialists in eagles were rare as well!

In June 1946, in the William Cutler Atwater Collection, B. Max Mehl offered lot 1436:

> 1858. While this great rarity was purchased by Mr. Atwater as Uncirculated, and while I feel it justifies that description, the coin shows slight handling or cabinet friction on obverse field, but the highest portions of the obverse and reverse hardly show the slightest wear. I consider this $10 gold piece by far the rarest of the series, in other words, the rarest U.S. $10 gold piece! From carefully compiled records which I have maintained of all the U.S. gold rarities for a period of more than forty years, I realized many years ago that here was a coin—(the 1858 $10)—which few collectors recognized its truly great rarity and notwithstanding the fact that this coin was not bringing the price of other gold eagles of much less rarity. And now, after careful research and comparison with other rarities of this series, I find that my theory of its rarity is well founded. I find that certainly no more than probably six specimens are known. In fact I know of can find records of only four specimens including the one in the U.S. Mint Collection. Going as far back as the Cleneay and Parmelee Sales in 1890, more than a half century ago, I find that these great collections, as well as later collections of equal greatness, such as the Stickney, Ten Eyck, and others, which were almost complete in all of the United States series of gold, did not possess a specimen of this coin Of all of the 221 different dates, mints and varieties of the U.S. $10 gold pieces, minted by the United States from 1795 to 1933, the 1858 Philadelphia Mint $10 gold piece is by far the rarest. It may be of interest to note here that a specimen sold at auction in January of this year brought $3,750. And the purchaser just recently informed me that he was offered $500 profit for it.

The Melish coin sold for $3,675. This coin later appeared in the October 1982 Eliasberg U.S. Gold Coin Collection (Bowers and Ruddy Galleries) as lot 705: "1858 AU-50." It sold for $7,150. In May 1993 the Bowers and Merena Galleries' sale of the Stetson University Collection included it as lot 691: "1858 AU-53 PCGS. From the Eliasberg Collection, offered by us in 1982." It sold for $19,250.

Amazement swept the numismatic scene when this coin appeared. David W. Akers in August 1980 described this coin in Auction '80, lot 954:

> 1858, Superb Gem Uncirculated 67. Most of the relatively few known specimens (perhaps 25-30 in all grades) are well worn with VF being typical. Until this one-of-a-kind specimen was "discovered" in 1972, there had not even been a rumor of a

Mint State 1858 Eagle. As a final note on this coin, we would like to mention that it has been consigned to Auction '80 by the F.W. Bohren Trust Fund. The Fund purchased it from Paul Nugget of Manfra, Tordella & Brookes, a New York numismatic firm. MTB had acquired it in 1972 and prior to that time, the coin had reportedly resided in the same leather pouch since it was struck in 1858! [Sold for $115,000]

The same coin, now with a much more modest grade was given by Superior Galleries in July 1989, in Auction '89, lot 916: "1858 MS-64 Premium Quality. Formerly lot 954 in Paramount's session of Auction '80."

In the Bowers and Merena Galleries' April 2004 sale of the Robert Lindesmith Collection it was offered as lot 2443:

1858 MS-64 PCGS. This is one of the most exciting gold coin rarities we have ever offered—quite a statement coming from us, considering all that we have seen, handled, and done. From Paramount's Auction '80 sale, August 1980, Lot 954; later in Superior Galleries' Auction '89 sale, July 1989, Lot 916. [Sold for $154,000]

In its Long Beach sale of May 2006 Heritage included the identical coin as lot 2343:

1858 MS-64 PCGS. When this coin surfaced more than 30 years ago it was universally considered the finest 1858 in existence. Today it is still regarded as such, unrivalled in quality by any other coin of this date (the NGC MS-64 is this same coin). Only three other Mint State pieces have been graded by NGC and PCGS combined. [Sold for $276,000]

The same company in its January 1914 FUN Convention sale offered lot 5935: "1858 MS-60 NGC." It sold for $21,150.

VF-20	EF-40	AU-50	AU-55	AU-58	MS-60
$6,000	$7,500	$12,500	$17,500	$25,000	$40,000

1858-O

Circulation-Strike Mintage: 20,000

Estimated population (Mint State): *10–14.* MS-60 or thereabouts. Very scarce. See John Dannreuther's hoard note.

Estimated population (circulated grades): *120–140.*

Submissions certified at highest grades (as of March 2017): *PCGS:* MS-61 (2), MS-62 (3), MS-63 (1). *NGC:* MS-61 (2), MS-62 (3). MS-63 (1).

Die data: Top interior of the 8's are slightly smaller than the bottom interior; the upright of the 5 slants slightly to the right; and the second 8 is slightly low and leans slightly right. Used on all dies for all mints.

Characteristics of striking and die notes: With some evidence of light striking at highest central areas and stars.

Key to collecting: VF and EF were the typical grades in the marketplace years ago, punctuated by occasional higher grade. Today AU coins are occasionally seen. Mint State coins are mostly in the lower levels and are nearly all from modern repatriations.

Market News and Commentary

In December 1890, in their sale of the Thomas Cleneay Collection, the Chapman brothers offered lot 513: "1858-O Uncirculated. Faintest hair marks." It sold for $11.50. In March 1911, in his sale of the William H. Woodin Collection, Thomas L. Elder offered lot 1278: "1858-O About Uncirculated; scarce." It sold for $10.50.

In April 1937 the George M. Agurs Collection, sold by B. Max Mehl, offered lot 321: "1858-O Practically Uncirculated, with almost full mint luster." It sold for $24. In June 1946, in the William Cutler Atwater Collection, B. Max Mehl offered lot 1340: "1858-O Nearly Uncirculated; light hair-line on obverse; considerable mint luster. Bold impression. Very scarce. Record over $100." It sold for $105.

In April 1956, in his sale of the Thomas G. Melish Collection, Kosoff offered lot 2439: "1858-O. Uncirculated, scarce in this condition." It sold for $55. In October 1982 the Louis E. Eliasberg Collection of U.S. Gold Coins Bowers and Ruddy Galleries offered lot 706: "1858-O Brilliant Uncirculated, MS-60. An incredible rarity in this condition. From the John H. Clapp Collection, 1942. Earlier from Elmer S. Sears, October 1920." It sold for $4,950. This coin was later resold several times.

In November 2000, in the Harry W. Bass Jr. Collection, Part IV, Bowers and Merena Galleries offered lot 671: "1858-O MS-62 PCGS. PCGS Population: 3, none finer. Purchased from the Goliad Corporation on December 13, 1985." It sold for $13,225. To this, John Dannreuther added this comment: "This, and four other Mint State 1858-O eagles were from the Jackson, Tennessee, hoard, which was from an 1859 robbery. I sold this coin to Mike Brownlee at a Dallas show in 1986 and the other four to Kevin Lipton at the same event."[18]

VF-20	EF-40	AU-50	AU-55	AU-58	MS-60	MS-63
$1,250	$1,500	$2,750	$3,750	$5,500	$9,000	$32,500

1858-S

Circulation-Strike Mintage: 11,800

Notes regarding mintages: Eight hundred coins were delivered in the first quarter of the year and 11,000 in the second quarter. Minting of various denominations was mainly done in response to the specific requests of depositors, although some coins were struck for the "bullion fund" at the Mint, so that payment of popular denominations (mainly the $20, but some smaller values as well) could be made without the depositor having to wait until his specific deposit was assayed, refined, and coined. Quite possibly the low-mintage eagles of this era were mainly used for the bullion fund.

Estimated population (Mint State): *None.*

Estimated population (circulated grades): *100–130.*

Submissions certified at highest grades (as of March 2017): *PCGS:* AU-50 (5), AU-53 (5), AU-55 (1). *NGC:* AU-50 (4), AU-53 (9), AU-55 (13), AU-58 (12).

Die data: Four 1858-dated obverse dies were shipped to the San Francisco Mint in October 1857. Sufficient reverses were on hand that no new ones were needed.

The 1858 four-digit date logotype shows the 18 is closest, the 85 wider, and the 58 is the widest in spacing.[19] The top interior of the 8's are slightly smaller than the bottom interior; the upright of the 5 slants slightly to the right; and the second 8 is slightly low and leans slightly right. Used on all dies for all mints.

The medium S (1.3 mm) mintmark on examples seen.

Characteristics of striking and die notes: Usually fairly well struck, save for some lightness at the highest hair curls on the center of the obverse.

Key to collecting: The 1858-S is scarce in all grades. AU coins are nearly all from modern repatriations.

Market News and Commentary

In December 1908 Henry Chapman offered the David M. Kuntz Collection with lot 77: "1859 San Francisco Mint. Good." It sold for $11.50. In June 1946, in the William Cutler Atwater Collection, B. Max Mehl offered lot 1556: "1858-S. About Uncirculated with mint luster. Scarce, especially so choice. Record of $75 for a specimen not so choice." It sold for $47.50.

In a later era in June 2000, in the Harry W. Bass Jr. Collection, Part III, Bowers and Merena Galleries included lot 642: "1858-S AU-55 PCGS. This date is unknown in Mint State! A curious bunch of horizontal die lines runs below the eagle, giving it a "perched" appearance. Purchased from Stanley Kesselman, September 5, 1967." It sold for $10,350.

VF-20	EF-40	AU-50	AU-55	AU-58
$1,800	$3,000	$5,000	$12,000	$22,500

1859

Circulation-Strike Mintage: 16,013
Proof Mintage: 80

Estimated population (Mint State):
9–12. MS-60 to MS-63.

Estimated population (circulated grades):
130–160.

Estimated population (Proofs): *8–12.* At least three are in museums: one each in the Smithsonian Institution and American Numismatic Society and one in the British Museum.[20] Citations for the 1859 are fairly numerous, but there is a strong possibility that some represent reofferings of the same specimens. At any given time, an offering of a Proof 1859 eagle on the market would be a very notable event.

Submissions certified at highest grades (as of March 2017): *PCGS:* MS-61 (2), MS-63 (2). *NGC:* MS-61 (3), MS-62 (3), MS-63 (1).

Characteristics of striking and die notes (circulation strikes): Some lightness is usual at the centers.

Characteristics of striking and die notes (Proofs): Apparently, the Proof dies were relapped and used to make circulation strikes (see Bass Collection II comments).

Key to collecting: VF and EF are the grades usually found in old-time collections, but there are exceptions. Today, higher-grade coins are available in sufficient numbers to supply specialists.

Market News and Commentary

In the December 1944 sale of the J.F. Bell Collection Stack's included lot 623: "1859 Brilliant Uncirculated. Very scarce." It sold for $62.50.

In December 1970 Stack's Alto Collection sale included lot 345: "1859 Brilliant Uncirculated, fully lustrous, though mostly proof-like. Some bag abrasions in the field, but still one of the best in existence. Rare!" It sold for $340.

The Alto coin was offered again in October 1999 in the Harry W. Bass Jr. Collection, Part II, as lot 1468:

> 1859 MS-61 PCGS. Considered by Harry Bass to be a Proof, which it probably is, as, per Harry Bass's notes, the die markers are correct. Rich golden surfaces with some abrasions. PCGS Population: 2; 1 finer (MS-62). Date widely spaced and delicate in appearance. Low on the die, about twice as close to the dentils as to the neck truncation above. Full Proof surface on obverse and reverse, including within the shield stripes. Harry Bass' notes reveal that at first he questioned this being a Proof, calling it "doubtful," but later compared it to a Proof, and changed his mind. From Stack's sale of the Alto Collection, December 1970, lot 345. [Sold for $12,650]

In the FUN sale of January 2014 Heritage included lot 5488: "1859 MS-62 NGC. NGC and PCGS have seen a total of only 10 Uncirculated pieces, the finest a single MS-63." It sold for $39,656.25. The Stack's Bowers Galleries' July 2015 Baltimore U.S. Coin Auction included lot 6052: "1859 MS-62 PCGS." It sold for $58,750.

Proof Market News and Commentary

In December 1890, in their sale of the Thomas Cleneay Collection, the Chapman brothers offered lot 407, a complete gold Proof set of the year 1859 ($1, $2.50, $3, $5, $10, $20). Realized for the set, $9.50 above face value. This commenced a run of gold Proof sets, (including duplicates of 1861, 1869, and 1870) that stretched unbroken through 1888.

B. Max Mehl, in his sale of the James Ten Eyck Collection, May 1922, included lot 289: "1859. Perfect brilliant Proof, sharp. Extremely rare." It sold for $34.

It was not until years later that Proof Liberty Head eagles sold for strong premiums. In October 1982 the Ten Eyck coin was sold with the Louis E. Eliasberg Collection through Bowers and Ruddy Galleries as lot 708: "1859 Choice Brilliant Proof-65. An exceedingly rare issue. From the John H. Clapp Collection, Earlier from the James Ten Eyck Collection." It sold for $41,800.

VF-20	EF-40	AU-50	AU-55	AU-58	MS-60	MS-63	PF-63	PF-64	PF-65
$1,000	$1,250	$1,500	$2,250	$4,000	$9,000	$40,000	$75,000	$150,000	$225,000

1859-O

Circulation-Strike Mintage: 2,300

Estimated population (Mint State): *1*.

Estimated population (circulated grades): *45–65*.

Submissions certified at highest grades (as of March 2017): *PCGS:* AU-55 (6), AU-58 (1). *NGC:* AU-55 (4), AU-58 (3), MS-62 (1).

Die data: Three obverse dies were sent to New Orleans for this issue, but it seems that only one was used. Sufficient usable reverse dies were on hand from earlier times.

Although the reverse motif was slightly modified in 1859 (most evident on the new version by the eagle having shorter and more delicate claws), the New Orleans and San Francisco mints used reverse dies remaining from earlier years, and thus all are of the earlier style.

Characteristics of striking and die notes: Slight lightness of striking at the centers and obverse stars.

Key to collecting: Walter Breen in his 1988 *Encyclopedia* stated this: "Fewer than 12 survive. Usually in low grades; prohibitively rare EF." In 1992 in *New Orleans Mint Gold Coins, 1839–1909,* Douglas Winter estimated the total population as only 30 to 35 coins, noting that the finest known to him was AU-50. All bets were off and the room was up for grabs when high-grade eagles and double eagles were repatriated in quantity at the end of the 20th century. Today, AU, once rarely seen, is a very collectible grade for many Liberty Head eagles of this era.

MARKET NEWS AND COMMENTARY

In March 1911, in his sale of the William H. Woodin Collection, Thomas L. Elder offered lot 1279: "1859-O Edge nick. Fine. Very rare. Coinage 2,800." It sold for $10. In May 1915, in his sale of the B.W. Smith Collection, B. Max Mehl offered lot 79: "1859-O Fine. Very rare. Only 2200 coined." It sold for $16.50. In June 1957 New Netherlands' 49th sale, Eliasberg duplicates, included lot 258: "1859-O. Strictly Very Fine. Sharp and with unimportant signs of handling. About equal to the Melish coin at a far too low $47.50. The Davis-Graves specimen, in our eyes only Fine (although called VF), sold for $90 over three years ago." It sold for $92.50.

In October 1982, in the Louis E. Eliasberg Collection of U.S. Gold Coins, Bowers and Ruddy Galleries offered lot 709: "1859-O Choice Extremely Fine-45. Very scarce date: only 2,300 were minted. From the John H. Clapp Collection, 1942. Earlier from J.C. Mitchelson, June 1908." It sold for $3,080. Mitchelson, of Tariffville, Connecticut, was a wholesale tobacco dealer. He formed a magnificent collection that today is owned by the Connecticut State Library. In his time he often traded in coins, buying coins for clients as he traveled around the country. The same made an encore appearance in August 2006 in the American Numismatic Rarities sale of the Old West and Franklinton Collections as lot 1545: "1859-O AU-55 PCGS. From the Eliasberg Collection" It sold for $52,900.

The June 2000 Stack's U.S. Coins sale included lot 1337:

> 1859-O Choice About Uncirculated, nearly fully Mint State. Lovely, rich medium yellow gold. The devices are brightly reflective and the fields are fully semi-prooflike. A definite candidate for Finest Known honors. The 1859-O has the honor of being the rarest "O" Mint eagle of any date. The presently offered specimen has been described by those who have been privileged to see it as a "moose" and a "monster."[21] No one who has seen it has walked away without shaking his head in wonder that a coin of this rarity could survive so nice. Breen suggested that only 12 different specimens survive. Extremely rare: only 2,300 were struck. [Sold for $19,550]

The August 2002 ANA Convention sale by Superior Galleries included lot 2085: "1859-O AU-55." It sold for $5,463. Regency Auction XII, June 2015, included lot 425: "1859-O AU-55 PCGS." It sold for $42,200.

VF-20	EF-40	AU-50	AU-55	AU-58
$5,000	$10,000	$25,000	$35,000	$55,000

1859-S

Circulation-Strike Mintage: 7,000

Estimated population (Mint State): *None.*

Estimated population (circulated grades): *50–75.*

Submissions certified at highest grades (as of March 2017): *PCGS:* AU-50 (5), AU-53 (5), AU-55 (1). *NGC:* AU-50 (4), AU-53 (5), AU-55 (4), AU-58 (1), MS-60 (1).

Die data: Although the reverse motif was slightly modified in 1859 (most evident on the new version by the eagle having shorter and more delicate claws), the New Orleans and San Francisco mints used reverse dies remaining from earlier years, and thus all are of the earlier style.

Six obverse dies were shipped to the San Francisco Mint, but most remained unused. The large S (1.7 mm) mintmark is seen on all.

Characteristics of striking and die notes: Some light striking at centers.

Key to collecting: In older offerings the typical grade encountered was VF, with an occasional EF. In recent times a number of AU coins have been certified, some of which may have been called EF years ago. One of the foremost key issues of the series, although not widely recognized by popular modern writers, for high-grade coins are virtually non-existent—and high grade often supersedes rarity in the current market (many buyers would rather have a very high-grade Mint State common coin than an exceedingly rare AU coin).

MARKET NEWS AND COMMENTARY

In May 1939, sale 399, Rare U.S. Gold Coins by J.C. Morgenthau & Co. included lot 352: "1859-S Very Good." It sold for $16.50.

In a later era in October 1999, in the Harry W. Bass Jr. Collection, Part II, Bowers and Merena Galleries offered lot 1472: "1859-S AU-53 PCGS. From Stack's sale of the Miles Collection, October 1968, lot 660." It sold for $13,650. Heritage, in its September 2016 Long Beach sale, offered lot 14146: "1859-S AU-53 NGC." Sold for $22,325 The same company in its FUN Convention sale offered lot 5936: "1859-S AU-50 NGC." It sold for $12,337.50.

VF-20	EF-40	AU-50	AU-55	AU-58	MS-60
$3,000	$7,500	$20,000	$20,000	$27,500	$50,000

1860

Circulation-Strike Mintage: 15,055
Proof Mintage: 50

Estimated population (Mint State): *15–20.*

Estimated population (circulated grades): *120–140.*

Estimated population (Proofs): *8–12.* Very rare.

Submissions certified at highest grades (as of March 2017): *PCGS:* MS-61 (4), MS-62 (2), MS-64 (3). *NGC:* MS-60 (7), MS-61 (5).

Characteristics of striking and die notes: Usually fairly well struck.

Key to collecting: EF and AU are the grades usually seen for Philadelphia eagles of this era. Mint State coins, as here, are rarities.

The rarity of $10 gold coins in EF and AU grades of the dates before 1870 can be appreciated by perusing auction catalogs. We know from experience, having looked through *thousands* keeping meticulous notes of observations—this being done with the help of a team of about a half-dozen research assistants who helped in the late 1900s. Even most of the "name" collections were apt to lack certain $10 pieces completely, or to have them in grades such as VF. Never in the history of numismatics has a complete run been assembled in AU grade, never mind Mint State (at which level certain issues are nonexistent). Modern repatriations have vastly increased the number of AU and lower-range Mint State coins available. However, the overall supply is rather small. If a contingent of dedicated enthusiasts all of a sudden decided to specialize in Coronet Head eagles, prices would multiply!

Market News and Commentary

In May 1939, sale 399, Rare U.S. Gold Coins by J.C. Morgenthau & Co. included lot 353: "1860 Very Fine." It sold for $16.50. The June 1941 sale of the William Forrester Dunham Collection by B. Max Mehl included lot 2229: "1860 Extremely Fine, with considerable luster; just a shade from Uncirculated. Scarce." It sold for $21.

In April 1949 B. Max Mehl's sale of the Dr. Charles W. Green Collection included lot 532: "1860 Brilliant Uncirculated. A magnificent specimen. Catalogs $50 and certainly worth it." It sold for $42.

In October 1982 in the Louis E. Eliasberg Collection of U.S. Gold Coins Bowers and Ruddy Galleries offered lot 711: "1860 Select Brilliant Uncirculated, MS-63 obverse; Choice Brilliant Uncirculated, MS-65 to Gem Brilliant Uncirculated, MS-67 reverse. Exceedingly rare. From the John H. Clapp Collection, 1942. Earlier from the James Ten Eyck Collection (B. Max Mehl, May 1922)." It sold for $24,200.

In October 1999 in the Harry W. Bass Jr. Collection Part II Bowers and Merena Galleries offered lot 1474: "1860 MS-64 PCGS. From Superior Galleries' Auction '85, lot 959." It sold for $39,100. In November 2000 in the Harry W. Bass Jr. Collection Part IV Bowers and Merena Galleries offered another as lot 676: "1860 MS-64 PCGS. From Abe Kosoff's sale of August 1968 at the ANA Convention, lot 1015." It sold for $29,900.

The Stack's Bowers Galleries March 2013 Whitman Baltimore Expo Auction included lot 2178: "1860 MS-64 PCGS." It sold for $70,500.

PROOF MARKET NEWS AND COMMENTARY

Many columns could be devoted to listings of Proof eagles, but as they are so rare as not to be widely collected, only scattered citations are given in the present text. In October 1980 in the Garrett Collection Part III Sale Bowers and Ruddy Galleries offered lot 1668:

> 1860 Choice Brilliant Proof. Obtained by T. Harrison Garrett from W. Elliot Woodward on September 5, 1883. Earlier in the collection of W. Foster Ely of Elyria, Ohio. As correspondence reprinted in *The History of Untied States Coinage as Illustrated by the Garrett Collection* indicates gold Proofs of this genre were rare a century ago. Today, of course, they are even rarer. [Sold for $39.000]

Stack's January 2009 Orlando sale included lot 1118: "1860 Proof-64 PCGS." It sold for $83,375. Kagin's March 2017 ANA Auction included lot 1427: "1860 Proof-65 PCGS. PCGS Population: 1; none finer." It sold for $258,500.

VF-20	EF-40	AU-50	AU-55	AU-58	MS-60	MS-63	PF-63	PF-64	PF-65
$900	$1,100	$1,750	$2,700	$3,000	$7,500	$25,000	$50,000	$80,000	$140,000

1860-O

Circulation-Strike Mintage: 11,100

Estimated population (Mint State): *12–18.* In 1980 David W. Akers reported that he had seen two "very choice Uncirculated" specimens. Superior reported a newly discovered Mint State coin in 1984.

Estimated population (circulated grades): *70–85.*

Submissions certified at highest grades (as of March 2017): *PCGS:* MS-61 (3), MS-62 (2), MS-63 (1). *NGC:* MS-61 (1), MS-62 (2), MS-63 (1).

Die data: Although the reverse motif was slightly modified in 1859 (most evident on the new version by the eagle having shorter and more delicate claws), the New Orleans and San Francisco mints used reverse dies remaining from earlier years, and thus all are of the earlier style.

Characteristics of striking and die notes: Usually fairly well struck.

Key to collecting: VF and EF are typical grades seen among coins that were preserved stateside. AU and Mint State coins are nearly all from modern repatriations. Suggestion: Consider collecting one each of the New Orleans Liberty Head eagles.

Market News and Commentary

The June 1941 sale of the William Forrester Dunham Collection by B. Max Mehl included lot 2230: "Struck in yellow gold. Beautiful Uncirculated; a few minute marks result of having been handled with other coins. A beautiful specimen, and as such, quite rare." It sold for $22.

In February 1944, in the Belden E. Roach Collection, B. Max Mehl offered lot 414: "1860-O Just a shade from Uncirculated with semi-proof surface. Very scarce." It sold for $21.75.

In the vastly different numismatic scenario of November 2000, in the Harry W. Bass Jr. Collection, Part IV, Bowers and Merena Galleries offered lot 678:

> 1860-O MS-62 (PCGS This is the only Mint State 1860-O $10 certified by PCGS. PCGS Population: 1, none finer. Thin crack from left rim to wing tip. This reverse was previously used on 1858-O issues, as noted by Breen, though the shield now shows significant central die rust. From Stack's sale of the Gaston DiBello Collection, May 1970, Lot 1070. [Sold for $25,300]

In March 2004 the American Numismatic Rarities Whitman Expo sale included lot 1526: "1860-O MS-60 NGC." It sold for $11,500. Heritage, in its September 2016 Long Beach sale, offered lot 14148: "1860-O MS-61 NGC." It sold for $28,200.

VF-20	EF-40	AU-50	AU-55	AU-58	MS-60
$1,200	$1,500	$2,500	$5,000	$6,500	$15,000

1860-S

Circulation-Strike Mintage: 5,000

Estimated population (Mint State): *3–4.* The only early citation located is the Bell Collection coin (1944), presently untraced.

Estimated population (circulated grades): *35–45.*

Submissions certified at highest grades (as of March 2017): *PCGS:* AU-55 (5), AU-58 (1), MS-60 (1). *NGC:* AU-55 (2), AU-58 (5), MS-61 (1), MS-62 (1).

Die data: Four obverse dies were sent to San Francisco for this issue, but not all were used. The large S (1.7 mm) mintmark is used.

Although the reverse motif was slightly modified in 1859 (most evident on the new version by the eagle having shorter and more delicate claws), the New Orleans and San Francisco mints used reverse dies remaining from earlier years, and thus all are of the earlier style.

Key to collecting: When seen the typical specimen is apt to be VF, although a few EF coins are known as are still fewer AU examples, although high-grade coins were in a number of older sales. The 1860-S is a major rarity in Mint State.

MARKET NEWS AND COMMENTARY

In the December 1944 sale of the J.F. Bell Collection Stack's included lot 746: "1860-S Uncirculated. Rare." It sold for $102.50.

In March 1988 the Bowers and Merena Galleries' sale of the Norweb Collection, Part II, included lot 2183:

> 1860-S AU-50. A coin which ranks among the top dozen finest known. In fact, the only finer one found by David Akers was the Bell Collection sale coin sold over 40 years ago in 1944! From Spink & Son, Ltd. London in 1958. [Sold for $5,060]

In its sale of April 2014 Heritage included lot 5772:

> 1860-S AU-58 NGC. Ex SS *Republic*. The population reports confirm the rarity of this San Francisco eagle, with PCGS reporting no Mint State examples, and just one piece in AU-58 condition. NGC lists one piece in MS-62, another in MS-61, and five AU-58 examples (3/14). The top NGC listings may include other SS *Republic* survivors, because four examples of this rare date were recovered from the wreck. [Sold for $28,850]

In the May 2016 Rarities Auction Stack's Bowers Galleries offered lot 105: "1860-S AU-55 PCGS." It sold for $25,850.

VF-20	EF-40	AU-50	AU-55	AU-58	MS-60
$3,000	$5,500	$13,000	$30,000	$45,000	$60,000

1861

Circulation-Strike Mintage: 113,164
Proof Mintage: 69

Notes regarding mintages: The Proof figure was taken from a delivery notice located by R.W. Julian in the Mint records in the National Archives. However, it is highly unlikely that many were ever distributed, the sales probably not exceeding 15 to 20 coins. Presumably, the others were melted.

Estimated population (Mint State): *55–70.* Typically MS–60 to 63, very rarely higher.

Estimated population (circulated grades): *800–1,000.*

Estimated population (Proofs): *8–10.* Exceedingly rare. Specimens are in the Smithsonian Institution and the American Numismatic Society.

Submissions certified at highest grades (as of March 2017): *PCGS:* MS-63 (3), MS-64 (1), MS-66 (1). *NGC:* MS-63 (4), MS-64 (1).

Die data: Harry Bass in his notes observes that there was a very minute adjustment made to the portrait of Miss Liberty this year, the circulation strikes being slightly different from the Proofs of the this year. The differences are not obvious except under close study.

Key to collecting: EF and AU are the grades usually seen for Philadelphia eagles of this era. Pieces were probably hoarded during this first year of the Civil War. Thus, the average grade encountered is higher. Some of the last are also from modern repatriations.

MARKET NEWS AND COMMENTARY

In June 1907 the Chapman brothers sale of the Major W.B. Wetmore Collection included lot 39: "1861 Uncirculated. Mint luster." It sold for $11. In March 1911, in his sale of the William H. Woodin Collection, Thomas L. Elder offered lot 1225: "1861. Uncirculated, mint luster." It sold for $11.50.

In May 1993 the Bowers and Merena Galleries' sale of the Stetson University Collection included lot 2047 in an era in which the market had advanced sharply: "1861 MS-62." It sold for $16,500. In November 2000, in the Harry W. Bass Jr. Collection, Part IV, Bowers and Merena Galleries offered lot 679: "1861 MS-66 (PCGS). This coin has few equals among the type, as PCGS has certified only one other specimen (an 1848-O) at this lofty grade. From Stack's sale of the DiBello Collection, May 1970, lot 1072." It sold for $50,900.

The Stack's Bowers Galleries' March 2013 Whitman Baltimore Expo Auction included lot 4261: "1861 MS-62 NGC." It sold for $8,225.

PROOF MARKET NEWS AND COMMENTARY

In October 1875 Edward Cogan's sale of the Colonel Mendes I. Cohen Collection included lot 248, a complete gold Proof set of the year 1861 ($1, $2.50, $3, $5, $10, $20). A total of $58 was realized for the set. The Cohen Collection was one of the greatest ever, but it did not seem to attract wide attention when sold.

In January 1984 Stack's sale of the Amon G. Carter Jr. Family Collection included lot 762: "1861 Brilliant Proof. Like the 1860, most were destroyed or melted. Consider the fact that, including the Eliasberg sale last year, there were only four appearances at auction in a half century!" It sold for $28,600.

VF-20	EF-40	AU-50	AU-55	AU-58	MS-60	MS-63	PF-63	PF-64	PF-65
$925	$1,050	$1,100	$2,500	$4,000	$6,500	$20,000	$45,000	$70,000	$125,000

1861-S

Circulation-Strike Mintage: 15,500

Estimated population (Mint State): *1.*

Estimated population (circulated grades): *70–90.*

Submissions certified at highest grades (as of March 2017): *PCGS:* AU-55 (6), AU-58 (3). *NGC:* AU-55 (16), AU-58 (13), MS-61 (1).

Die data: Three obverse dies were sent to the Philadelphia Mint. There was still a supply of usable reverses on hand. The large S (1.7 mm) mintmark is seen on those studied. Although the reverse motif was slightly modified in 1859 (most evident on the new version by the eagle having shorter and more delicate claws), the San Francisco Mint used reverse dies remaining from earlier years, and thus all are of the earlier style.

Characteristics of striking and die notes: Sometimes seen weakly struck.

Key to collecting: Most known examples are VF or EF, the former being slightly more available. AU coins, once rarities, are collectible from modern imports.

Market News and Commentary

In February 1944, in the Belden E. Roach Collection, B. Max Mehl offered lot 430: "1861-S Large S. Extremely Fine, with frosty mint surface. Very scarce. Listed at $40 and worth it." It sold for $37.50. In the December 1944 sale of the J.F. Bell Collection Stack's included lot 747: "1861-S Extremely Fine. Very scarce." It sold for $82.50. In June 1946, in the William Cutler Atwater Collection, B. Max Mehl offered lot 1559: "1861-S About Uncirculated with frosty mint surface. Very scarce so choice. Limited coinage. Record of $82.50 for a similar specimen." It sold for $35.

New Netherlands Coin Co.'s 46th sale, the Dr. Clarence W. Peake Collection, June 1955, included lot 145: "1861-S. While marked 'Extremely Fine,' this very scarce item is closer to Very Fine. Just 15,500 struck. Record of $82.50 for an About Uncirculated example, according to B.M. Mehl." It sold for $45.

The October 2001 sale by Stack's and Sotheby's of the Dallas Bank (Jeff Browning) Collection included lot 441: "1861-S About Uncirculated." It sold for $4,025. In the August 2016 ANA World's Fair of Money sale Stack's Bowers Galleries offered lot 3341: "1861-S AU-55 PCGS." It sold for $14,100.

VF-20	EF-40	AU-50	AU-55	AU-58	MS-60
$4,000	$7,500	$11,000	$16,000	$22,500	$47,500

1862

Circulation-Strike Mintage: 10,960
Proof Mintage: 35

Notes regarding mintages: Deliveries were made as follows: March 25 (980), September 15 (2,410), and November 13 (7,570). No eagles or other gold coins minted at Philadelphia from 1862 through autumn 1878 were paid out at par; such pieces were stored by the Treasury and were available only by paying a premium.

The Proof mintage this year was only 35 pieces, all delivered on February 16, but probably fewer than half that number actually found buyers. The 1 in 1862 is about centered between the bust and denticles. The base of the 1 is higher from the denticles than is the base of the 2.

Estimated population (Mint State): *7–10.* In his 1980 study of the series David W. Akers reported seeing an average quality Mint State coin. Otherwise, the sheet is blank for the *early* sales studied.

Estimated population (circulated grades): *70–90.*

Estimated population (Proofs): *10–12.* Very rare. Although the auction record spread over more than a century shows multiple pieces appearing on the market, likely many citations represent duplicate appearances of the same single coin. Of the extant pieces, some are impaired and at least two are comfortably ensconced in institutions (the Smithsonian and the American Numismatic Society).

Submissions certified at highest grades (as of March 2017): *PCGS:* MS-61 (2). *NGC:* MS-61 (2), MS-62 (2), MS-63 (1), MS-64 (1).

Key to collecting: One of the key issues of the era. EF and AU are the grades usually seen for Philadelphia eagles of this era. Mint State coins are somewhat scarce and are mostly from modern repatriations.

MARKET NEWS AND COMMENTARY

In March 1883 Dr. George W. Massamore's sale included lot 511: "1862 Very Fine, rare." It sold for $11. Massamore was a Baltimore dentist who also dealt in coins.

The June 1941 sale of the William Forrester Dunham Collection by B. Max Mehl included lot 2232: "1862 Extremely Fine, with considerable luster on reverse." It sold for $21.25. In February 1944, in the Belden E. Roach Collection, B. Max Mehl offered lot 339: "1862 Extremely Fine with considerable mint luster. Very lightly nicked on obverse, hardly noticeable. Rare. Very limited coinage." It sold for $26. In October 1947, in the H.R. Lee Collection (Eliasberg duplicates), Stack's offered lot 1517: "1862 Extremely Fine, with mint luster, small coinage." It sold for $32. In April 1956 Abe Kosoff's sale of the Thomas G. Melish and Clinton W. Hester Collections included lot 2450: "1862 About Extremely Fine." It sold for $25.

In April 1960 New Netherlands' 54th sale, Jonathan Glogower Consignment, Etc., included this lot 698:

> 1862. Very Fine or better, somewhat lustrous; tiny obv. rim nick. Records for non-Proofs of this date are few and far between (understandably, as only 10,995 were minted) and they are almost never of specimens above VF, the only exception we can locate being Peake's EF, but then that was a former Proof. Under the circumstances, the $35 called for by both references is too, too conservative. [Sold for $72.50]

This was typical New Netherlands misinformation disguised as scholarship and widely believed at the time, except for those who cared to peruse earlier catalogs. Quite a few coins finer than EF has been offered earlier!

In the vastly expanded market of November 2000, in the Harry W. Bass Jr. Collection, Part IV, Bowers and Merena Galleries offered lot 681: "1862 MS-62 PCGS. PCGS Population: 1; none finer. Early die state. Purchased from Stanley Kesselman on February 17, 1971." It sold for $12,650. Where is this coin in the PCGS data base?

In the April 2005 sale of "Treasures of the SS *Republic*" Bowers and Merena Galleries offered lot 2004: "1862 MS-64 NGC." It sold for $41,975.

PROOF MARKET NEWS AND COMMENTARY

In the December 1944 sale of the J.F. Bell Collection Stack's included lot 626: "1862 Perfect Brilliant Proof. Gem." It sold for $145. In January 1946 the Numismatic Gallery sale of "The World's Greatest Collection" (F.C.C. Boyd) included lot 667: "1862 Brilliant Proof." It sold for $140.

In January 1984 Stack's sale of the Amon G. Carter Jr. Family Collection included lot 763: "1862 Brilliant Proof. Of those struck, only about 10 specimens are extant. Although there are 16 records of auction, one of the coins has appeared five times and certainly others are repeat offerings." It sold for $26,400.

Stack's Bowers Galleries' March 2012 Baltimore Expo Auction included lot 4335: "1862 Proof-65 NGC." It sold for $109,250. Heritage in its January 2016 FUN Convention sale offered lot 5626: "1862 Proof-64 Cameo NGC." It sold for $82,250.

VF-20	EF-40	AU-50	AU-55	AU-58	MS-60	MS-63	PF-63	PF-64	PF-65
$1,000	$2,250	$5,000	$8,500	$11,000	$18,500	$37,500	$42,500	$70,000	$125,000

1862-S

Circulation-Strike Mintage: 12,500

Notes regarding mintages: These eagles circulated at par in the West at a time when gold coins were not seen in circulation in the East or Midwest (until mid-December of 1878).

Estimated population (Mint State): *1–2.*

Estimated population (circulated grades): *80–110.*

Submissions certified at highest grades (as of March 2017): *PCGS:* AU-50 (6), AU-53 (3), AU-55 (6), AU-58 (1), MS-61 (1). *NGC:* AU-50 (7), AU-53 (6), AU-55 (9), AU-58 (2).

Die data: Six obverse dies were shipped to the San Francisco Mint, but were mostly unused. The supply of reverse dies on hand remained sufficient.

The large S (1.7 mm) mintmark is seen on all 1862-S eagles. Although the reverse motif was slightly modified in 1859 (most evident on the new version by the eagle having shorter and more delicate claws), the San Francisco Mint used reverse dies remaining from earlier years, and thus all are of the earlier style.

Key to collecting: The 1862-S eagle, earlier a rarity typically seen in VF and EF grades is now scarce but quite collectible at the AU level.

MARKET NEWS AND COMMENTARY

In May 1915, in his sale of the B.W. Smith Collection, B. Max Mehl offered lot 87: "1862-S Large S. Very Fine. Rare." It sold for $11.50. In the December 1944 sale of the J.F. Bell Collection Stack's included lot 748: "1862-S Extremely Fine. Scarce." It sold for $50. In October 1962, in the Samuel W. Wolfson Collection, Stack's offered lot 684: "1862-S Extremely Fine. Very scarce. Worth $150." It sold for $125.

In March 1988 the Norweb Collection, Part II, sale by Bowers and Merena Galleries included lot 2186: "1862-S EF-45." It sold for $5,410. By this time there was a greatly expanded interest in collecting Liberty Head eagles by date and mint. In May 1992, in their sale of the H.C. ("Heck") Dodson Collection, Mid-American Rare Coin Auctions included lot 362: "1862-S EF-45." It sold for $4,510.

In June 2000, in the Harry W. Bass Jr. Collection, Part III, Bowers and Merena Galleries included lot 653: "1862-S AU-55 PCGS. Purchased from Stanley Kesselman, May 21, 1968." It sold for $8,050. In its sale of April 2011 Heritage included lot 5427: "1862-S MS-61 NGC. This specimen is the finest certified 1862-S Liberty eagle at either of the leading grading services by a full three points (3/11)." It sold for $103,500.

Heritage, in its September 2016 Long Beach sale, offered lot 16149: "1862-S AU-55 NGC." It sold for $12,925.

VF-20	EF-40	AU-50	AU-55	AU-58	MS-60
$2,750	$4,000	$7,000	$12,500	$20,000	$40,000

1863

Circulation-Strike Mintage: 1,218
Proof Mintage: *Less than 30*

Estimated population (Proofs): *9–12.* Very rare.

Notes regarding mintages: At this time, continuing until after December 17, 1878, gold coins did not circulate in the East or Midwest.

It is said that 30 Proofs were delivered on March 27. It is not known if all were sold. This is per conventional wisdom, however it is likely that 30 was the mintage figure for $2.50, $3, and $5 Proofs of this year, but not for the other denominations.[22]

Estimated population (Mint State): *1–2.*

Estimated population (circulated grades): *30–40.* Exceedingly rare, one of the most elusive circulation-strike issues in the Liberty Head eagle series. One thing is certain: over a long period of years there have been more Proof offerings than there have been of EF and AU examples.

Submissions certified at highest grades (as of March 2017): *PCGS:* AU-55 (2), AU-58 (1), MS-63 (1). *NGC:* AU-55 (4), AU-58 (1), MS-60 (1), MS-62 (1), MS-63 (1).

Die data: The same 1863 obverse die was used to strike circulation coins as well as Proofs. Some curlicue raised die finish lines are seen on the portrait in front of the ear.

Key to collecting: EF and AU are the grades usually seen for Philadelphia eagles of this era. Mint State coins are rare prizes and are usually from finds in overseas vaults.

MARKET NEWS AND COMMENTARY

In April 1949 B. Max Mehl's sale of the Dr. Charles W. Green Collection included lot 534: "1863 Extremely Fine, nearly Uncirculated with considerable mint luster." It sold for $41.50.

In May 1992, in their sale of the H.C. ("Heck") Dodson Collection, Mid-American Rare Coin Auctions included lot 363: "1863 EF-45." It sold for $7,700. In November 2000, in the Harry W. Bass Jr. Collection, Part IV, Bowers and Merena Galleries offered lot 683:

1863 MS-63 PCGS. Population: 1; none finer. One MS-63 is noted in the NGC Census report as well. We believe the MS-63 noted in that report is in fact this coin, as it was described as an NGC MS-63 in the Mid-American Rare Coin Galleries' sale from which Harry Bass purchased it in 1991. Obverse die same as the Proof issues. Raised die rust pimple on bottom of bust over left side of 8. From Mid-American Rare Coin Auctions sale of August 1991, Lot 755. Incredible Mint State 1863-S $10. [Sold for $52,900]

In the August 2016 ANA World's Fair of Money sale Stack's Bowers Galleries offered lot 3344: "1863 EF-45 PCGS." It sold for $35,250. The next coin was lot 3345: "1863-S EF-40 PCGS." It sold for $11,162.50. In September of the same year Heritage sold an EF-45 (PCGS) coin for $42,300. Price variations have always been a part of numismatics, and advanced collectors take advantage of them and often seek out better values at slightly lower grades. The preceding lots are examples of a wide variation between two coins in nearly the same grade. At the EF level there is not much difference between 40 and 45. In contrast, at the MS level there is a huge difference between 60 and 65. Such are the complexities of grading numbers!

PROOF MARKET NEWS AND COMMENTARY

In March 1911, in his sale of the William H. Woodin Collection, Thomas L. Elder offered lot 1227: "1863. Excessively rare, probably not over a dozen struck in Proof condition. Entire coinage only 1,248 pieces!" It sold for $25.

Heritage's ANA Convention sale of August 2011 included lot 7620: "1863 Proof- 65 Deep Cameo. PCGS." It sold for $299.000.

VF-20	EF-40	AU-50	AU-55	AU-58	MS-60	PF-63	PF-64	PF-65
$9,000	$16,000	$30,000	$40,000	$55,000	$75,000	$42,500	$70,000	$125,000

1863-S

Circulation strike mintage: 10,000

Notes regarding mintages: These eagles circulated at par in the West at a time when gold coins were not seen in circulation in the East or Midwest (until after December 17, 1878).

Estimated population (Mint State): *3–4.* Exceedingly rare.

Estimated population (circulated grades): *55–70.*

Submissions certified at highest grades (as of March 2017): *PCGS:* AU-55 (2), AU-58 (1), MS-60 (1), MS-61 (1). *NGC:* AU-55 (3), AU-58 (4), MS-61 (1).

Die data: Four 1863 obverse dies were shipped to San Francisco in November 1862, with four more sent later. At least two obverse dies are known to have been used.

These all have the medium S mintmark. Although the reverse motif was slightly modified in 1859 (most evident on the new version by the eagle having shorter and more delicate claws), the San Francisco Mint used reverse dies remaining from earlier years, and thus all are of the earlier style.

Key to collecting: The usually seen specimen is VF, less usual, EF. AU coins are exceedingly rare, and until the 1980s seem to have been unknown in this grade. Mint State coins are even rarer.

Market News and Commentary

The June 1941 sale of the William Forrester Dunham Collection by B. Max Mehl included lot 2233: "1863-S Bold impression. Extremely Fine." It sold for $21.50. In October 1982 the Louis E. Eliasberg Collection of U.S. Gold Coins sale by Bowers and Ruddy Galleries offered lot 719: "1863-S Choice Extremely Fine-45. Believed to be from the William Forrester Dunham Collection (B. Max Mehl, June 1941)." It sold for $1,430.

In July 1984, in Auction '84, Superior Galleries included lot 412: "1863-S. MS-60. A needle sharp strike with full frosty mint lustre throughout. This beauty, a heretofore unknown specimen, was discovered in a group of United States gold coins found in Central America. A unique opportunity to own the finest." It sold for $9,900.

In March 1988 the Norweb Collection, Part II, sale by Bowers and Merena Galleries included lot 2188:

> 1863-S AU-58. The finest we have ever seen, and possibly either the finest known or tied for this honor. The only comparable example we can trace is a piece described as MS-60 in 1984, sold as part of Auction '84. How this coin would grade today, with stricter interpretations in effect, is not known From New Netherlands Coin Company, 1960. [Sold for $7,700]

In February 2014, in its Long Beach sale, Heritage included the Norweb coin as lot 4176: "1863-S AU-53 PCGS. Finest known. Only one other piece, a PCGS MS 60, is close. Ex Norweb II (Bowers and Merena, (3/88), lot 2188." It sold for $32,900.

VF-20	EF-40	AU-50	AU-55	AU-58	MS-60
$5,500	$13,000	$25,000	$32,500	$37,500	$45,000

1864

Circulation-Strike Mintage: 3,530
Proof Mintage: 50

Notes regarding mintages: Deliveries were made as follows: February 25 (160) and March 14 (3,370). At this time, continuing until after December 17, 1878, gold coins did not circulate in the East or Midwest.

The mintage figure of 50 Proof pieces represents specimens delivered on February 11, and no doubt produced in advance for possible sale. However, buyers did not materialize, and probably no more than 20 were ever sold.

Estimated population (Mint State): *8–12.* In notes for this book compiled years ago in the early 1980s I said this: "Virtually unobtainable. Known specimens are in low Mint State ranges. Proofs *abound* in comparison to Mint State coins—and Proofs are *rare.*"

Estimated population (circulated grades): *25–32.*

Estimated population (Proofs): *12–15.* Very rare, but among Proofs of this decade, one of the more available issues. Still, a period of years may elapse between offerings.

Submissions certified at highest grades (as of March 2017): *PCGS:* MS-60 (1), MS-61 (1). *NGC:* MS-61 (3), MS-63 (1).

Characteristics of striking and die notes (Proofs): The date is placed very high, and nearly twice as close to the neck truncation as to the denticles. Deeply impressed into the die. With large "open" 4 as used on certain other denominations, providing a rather ungainly appearance, but one that is common to all pieces of this denomination. Unlike the Proof of the preceding year, the head of Miss Liberty on the present coin is very carefully finished, with scarcely a notable marker in sight, though she has two raised stripes on her earlobe.

Key to collecting: EF and AU are the grades usually seen for Philadelphia eagles of this era. Mint State coins are rarities and are mostly from modern repatriations.

MARKET NEWS AND COMMENTARY

In February 1944, in the Belden E. Roach Collection, B. Max Mehl offered lot 341: "1864 Practically Uncirculated with considerable mint luster. Very rare. Limited coinage. Listed at $60." It sold for $37.50. In March 1945 the William A. Knapp Collection, sold by B. Max Mehl, included lot 1057: "1864 Very Fine with some mint luster. Lists at $40 and certainly worth it." It sold for $41.

The January 1986 Stack's sale of the James Walter Carter and Margaret Woolfolk Carter Collections included lot 244: "1864 About Uncirculated, lustrous, light circulation marks." It sold for $2,200. In March 1988 the Bowers and Merena Galleries' sale of the Norweb Collection, Part II, included lot 2189: "1864 AU-58. The coin is definitely among the top half dozen finest specimens known. From J.C. Morgenthau on October 14, 1937." It sold for $5,500.

From Stack's sale of the DiBello Collection, May 1970, lot 1076 sold for $6,900. In its March 2005 sale Heritage included lot 11514: "1864 MS-61 NGC." It sold for $10,766.

PROOF MARKET NEWS AND COMMENTARY

Ordering Proofs was not an easy matter during this era. The Philadelphia Mint would not accept federal greenback notes at par for its own coins, and thus gold could only be purchased at a steep premium (the government kept separate books on gold coins sold at premiums, and later published a list, or else accepted payment in other gold coins, plus a proofing charge). To obtain other gold coins, a numismatist had to go to a bullion or exchange broker and at that location buy them at a sharp premium in greenbacks. The procedure was anything but simple.

Proofs appeared in many auctions over the years, the same coins passing to different owners. It was not until the 1950s that they attracted a lot of attention and they became very expensive—justifiably so based on their rarity.

In December 1890, in their sale of the Thomas Cleneay Collection, the Chapman brothers offered lot 516: "1864 Brilliant Proof. Extremely rare." It sold for $13.50. By this time the 1864 was recognized as being incredibly rarer, but collectors desiring such pieces were few and far between. In the December 1944 sale of the J.F. Bell Collection Stack's included lot 628: "1864 Perfect Brilliant Proof Gem. Rare." It sold for $185. In January 1946 the Numismatic Gallery sale of "The World's Greatest Collection" (F.C.C. Boyd) included lot 669: "1864 Brilliant Proof." It sold for $150.

In the March 1995 sale of the James A. Stack Sr. Collection, Stack's offered lot 584: "1864 Choice Proof." It sold for $39,600. Stack's July 2008 sale of the Samuel Berngard and SS *New York* Collections included lot 2570: "1864 Proof-64 PCGS." It sold for $115,000. Heritage, in its 2017 FUN Convention sale, sold lot 5956: "1864 Proof-63+ Deep Cameo. PCGS." for $99,875.

VF-20	EF-40	AU-50	AU-55	AU-58	MS-60	PF-63	PF-64	PF-65
$5,000	$10,000	$20,000	$27,500	$32,500	$42,500	$42,500	$75,000	$125,000

1864-S

Circulation-Strike Mintage: 2,500

Notes regarding mintages: These eagles circulated at par in the West at a time when gold coins were not seen in circulation in the East or Midwest (until after mid-December of this year).

Estimated population (Mint State): *None.*

Estimated population (circulated grades): *18–25.*

Submissions certified at highest grades (as of March 2017): *PCGS:* AU-50 (4), AU-55 (2). *NGC:* AU-53 (1), AU-55 (1).

Die data: Three obverse dies dated 1864 were shipped to San Francisco in November 1863, but only one seems to have been used.

The medium S mintmark is seen on all of these. Although the reverse motif was slightly modified in 1859 (most evident on the new version by the eagle having shorter and more delicate claws), the San Francisco Mint used reverse dies remaining from earlier years, and thus all are of the earlier style.

Key to collecting: A great rarity, one of the most elusive of all eagles of this era, and eclipsing the famous 1858. VF is the grade usually seen, and *usually* is not very often. By any serious reckoning, the 1864-S eagle should be famous as one of America's premier gold rarities. Indeed, the 1864-S eagle is a rarity of *legendary* proportions, although this fact is hidden from all who do not delve into specialized references.

David W. Akers commented in 1980:

> In my 369 catalog survey, the 1864-S tied for first in the entire series in rarity according to average grade and was second in rarity according to frequency of appearance. Thus it is obvious that from the standpoint of both overall rarity and condition rarity, the 1864-S is one of the rarest dates in the series, more rare than such famous dates as 1798/7, 7x6 Stars and 1858 and only a little less rare than the 1875. Most of the relatively few known 1864-S eagles grade from VG to VF. Only two or three are known in EF and I am unaware of any 1864-S that grades AU or better.

Walter Breen commented in 1988: "Possibly 10 to 12 known. Usually seen in low grades, unknown above EF."

Very few have been certified as AU in the past decade, pieces unknown to either Akers or Breen. These are from modern repatriations.

The actual population is very difficult to determine, as only a few that have appeared at auction have been tagged with pedigrees, and the value of the 1864-S is such that it is an ideal candidate for resubmission to grading services. In his 1980 study of 369 auction catalogs David W. Akers found only 16 coins offered, these including duplicate listings of the same coins that passed from one collection to another.

MARKET NEWS AND COMMENTARY

In May 1939, sale 399, Rare U.S. Gold Coins by J.C. Morgenthau & Co. included lot 359: "1864-S Very Fine." It sold for $25. In the December 1944 sale of the J.F. Bell Collection Stack's included lot 750: "1864-S Only 2,500 coins minted. Very Fine and rare." It sold for $155. In June 1946, in the William Cutler Atwater Collection, B. Max Mehl offered lot 1562: "1864-S Rare. Fine to Very Fine. Record over $150." It sold for $48.50.

In October 1962, in the Samuel W. Wolfson Collection, Stack's offered lot 688: "1864-S Very Fine and very scarce. We have been trying to find this particular coin for some time, but to no avail. Very much under-rated and, as a result, undervalued in the *Guide Book*." It sold for $560.

Wolfson, a Florida operator of a chain of theatres, began his interest in coins by visiting Stack's at 123 West 57th Street in New York City. Soon he was on his way to building one of America's finest rare coin collections.

In May 1992, in their sale of the H.C. ("Heck") Dodson Collection, Mid-American Rare Coin Auctions included lot 367: "1864-S AU-50." It sold for $15,400.

In October 1998, in the John J. Pittman Collection sale, Part II, David Akers offered lot 1945: "1864-S, Very Fine. JJP purchased this coin from Numismatic Gallery's Menjou sale, 6/15/50, lot 1675, for $55." It sold for $11,000.

In June 2000, in the Harry W. Bass Jr. Collection, Part III, Bowers and Merena Galleries included lot 656: "1864-S AU-55 PCGS. PCGS Population: 2; none finer. From Paramount's sale of August 1969, lot 2116." It sold for $36,800. In its March 2014 Long Beach sale Heritage offered lot 30366: "1864-S AU-53 NGC. It is one of just two pieces graded AU-53 at NGC, where only one other 1864-S is graded even higher, at AU-55." It sold for $146,875.

VF-20	EF-40	AU-50	AU-55
$35,000	$75,000	$100,000	$150,000

1865

Circulation-Strike Mintage: 3,980
Proof Mintage: 25

Notes regarding mintages: Deliveries of circulation-strike coins were made on January 27 (650) and March 14 (3,330). At

this time, continuing until after December 17, 1878, gold coins did not circulate in the East or Midwest. The Proofs were delivered on March 8.

Estimated population (Mint State): *3–5.* Exceedingly rare.

Estimated population (circulated grades): *55–70.*

Estimated population (Proofs): *7–9.*

Submissions certified at highest grades (as of March 2017): *PCGS:* AU-55 (6), AU-58 (1), MS-63 (1). *NGC:* MS-60 (4).

Die data: The 1865 four-digit logotype for the eagle showed the 18 close, the 86 widest, and the final 5 about as close as the 18. The base of the 5 is usually on the same level as the base of the other numerals, except for the 1865-S, 865 Over Inverted 186, for which the final 6 is low. The inverted date is of the three-digit logotype only. Three-digit logotype used on all dies for both mints.

Key to collecting: Another significant rarity in the eagle series, although this characteristic is not widely known. EF and AU are typical grades encountered.

MARKET NEWS AND COMMENTARY

In May 1939, sale 399, Rare U.S. Gold Coins by J.C. Morgenthau & Co. included lot 360: "1865 Very Fine and rare." It sold for $35. The December 1944 sale of the J.F. Bell Collection held by Stack's included lot 629: "1865 Extremely Fine" It sold for $80. The January 1986 Stack's sale of the James Walter Carter and Margaret Woolfolk Carter Collections had lot 246: "1865 Extremely Fine and choice, prooflike surface in the protected areas." It sold for $1,870. In May 1992, in their sale of the H.C. ("Heck") Dodson Collection, Mid-American Rare Coin Auctions included lot 368: "1865 EF-45." It sold for $4,620.

In October 1999, in the Harry W. Bass Jr. Collection, Part II, Bowers and Merena Galleries offered lot 1498: "1865 AU-55 PCGS. PCGS Population: 3; 2 finer (MS-63 finest). From Stack's sale of the Shapero Collection, October 1971, Lot 1106." It sold for $7,475. In October 2001 the George Mouhtouris Collection offered by Ira and Larry Goldberg included lot 2178: "1865 AU-58." It sold for $6,900. In the March 2016 Rarities Auction Stack's Bowers Galleries offered lot 13202: "1865 AU-50 PCGS." It sold for $15,275. In the August 2016 ANA Stack's Bowers Galleries offered lot 3346: "1865 AU-58 PCGS." It sold for $28,200.

PROOF MARKET NEWS AND COMMENTARY

In February 1944, in the Belden E. Roach Collection, B. Max Mehl offered lot 342: "1865 Perfect brilliant Proof. Extremely rare and valuable. Probably not more than a dozen Proofs known." It sold for $127.50. In October 1962, in the Samuel W. Wolfson Collection, Stack's offered lot 689: "1865 Brilliant Proof. Extremely rare. Missing in many of the great collections offered in the past." It sold for $1,300.

In October 1980, in the Garrett Collection, Part III, sale Bowers and Ruddy Galleries offered lot 1669: "1865 Choice Brilliant Proof. Provenance not known, but probably obtained by T. Harrison Garrett during the 19th-century possibly from the [Heman] Ely Collection." It sold for $37,000.

Stack's Bowers Galleries' August 2013 Chicago ANA World's Fair of Money auction included lot 4512: "1865 Proof-66+ PCGS." It sold for $528,750.

VF-20	EF-40	AU-50	AU-55	AU-58	MS-60	MS-63	PF-63	PF-64	PF-65
$5,000	$9,000	$15,000	$20,000	$27,500	$47,500	$90,000	$42,500	$80,000	$135,000

1865-S

Circulation-Strike Mintage:
Part of 16,700

Notes regarding mintages: These eagles circulated at par in the West at a time when gold coins were not seen in circulation in the East or Midwest (until after December 17, 1878).

Estimated population (Mint State): *2.*

Estimated population (circulated grades): *35–50.*

Submissions certified at highest grades (as of March 2017): *PCGS:* AU-50 (4), AU-53 (1). *NGC:* AU-50 (5), AU-53 (8), AU-55 (5), AU-58 (3), MS-60 (1), MS-62 (1). For NGC these numbers most assuredly include Inverted Date coins. For rare issues such as this it is very difficult to say whether by conservative grading they would merit low Mint State numbers. Many eagles that were exceedingly rare decades ago now have from several to many certified in grades from MS–60 to 62.

Die data: Six 1865-dated obverses were shipped to San Francisco in November 1864. Obverse varieties are known with perfect date (slightly scarcer) and 1865-S, 865 Over Inverted 186.

These all have the large S (1.7 mm) mintmark. Although the reverse motif was slightly modified in 1859 (most evident on the new version by the eagle having shorter and more delicate claws), the San Francisco Mint used reverse dies remaining from earlier years, and thus all are of the earlier style.

Key to collecting: VF and EF are the grades usually seen, to which can be added fewer AU coins.

MARKET NEWS AND COMMENTARY

The June 1941 sale of the William Forrester Dunham Collection by B. Max Mehl included lot 2235: "1865-S Unusual edge on left; raised and almost like a wire edge. Very Fine." It sold for $18.50.

In February 1944, in the Belden E. Roach Collection, B. Max Mehl offered lot 432, the start of a trail of auction appearances: "1865-S Large S. Struck with raised border on left obverse and reverse. Quite curious. Very scarce." It sold for $25. In October 1982 the Louis E. Eliasberg Collection of U.S. Gold Coins sale by Bowers and Ruddy Galleries offered lot 723: "1865-S Extremely Fine-40. One of the finest known examples. Believed to be from the Belden Roach Collection (B. Max Mehl, February 1944)." It sold for $1,650. In October 1999, in the Harry W. Bass Jr. Collection, Part II, Bowers and Merena Galleries offered lot 1499: "1865-S AU-50 PCGS. PCGS Population: 2; none finer From our sale of the Louis E. Eliasberg Sr. Collection, October 1982, lot 723, there called EF-40." It sold for $9,775.

Years later in the January 2017 FUN sale, Heritage offered lot 5939: "1865-S AU-55 NGC. The Smithsonian lacks a Normal Date 1865-S eagle, and there are only 25 to 35 pieces known in private hands, almost all in circulated condition. This piece grades finer than any coin reported by PCGS." It sold for $28,200.

VF-20	EF-40	AU-50	AU-55	AU-58	MS-60
$8,000	$12,500	$17,500	$30,000	$37,500	$65,000

1865-S, 865 Over Inverted 186

Circulation-Strike Mintage: Part of 16,700

Notes regarding mintages: These eagles circulated at par in the West at a time when gold coins were not seen in circulation in the East or Midwest (until after December 17, 1878).

Estimated population (Mint State): _1._ The only known coin in this grade is a specimen recovered from the wreck of the SS _Brother Jonathan_, sunk on July 30, 1865.

Estimated population (circulated grades): 75–90.

Submissions certified at highest grades (as of March 2017): *PCGS:* AU-50 (3), AU-53 (5), AU-55 (2). *NGC:* See comments for the 1865-S.

Die data: Six 1865-dated obverses were shipped to San Francisco in November 1864. Obverse varieties are known with perfect date (slightly scarcer) and 1865-S, 865 Over Inverted 186, as here. The error die seems to have been the one to strike the most coins. Although opinions differ, the author believes that the 1865 $10 pieces were made with a full 1865 logotype, not just 186 with the 5 added later. Per this scenario, the entire date 1865 was first punched in an inverted position. Under high-power magnification, only part of the date can be seen, this including much of the upright of the 1 (mainly obscured by the final 5), much of the top part and some of the bottom part of the 8 (the very bottom part of the 8 having been ground away on the die), and just part of the 6 (seemingly mostly ground away and also obscured by the 8.) No traces of the inverted 5 are seen, but we attribute this to such traces having been removed from the die.

Key to collecting: Very scarce, but more available than the "perfect date" 1865-S.

Market News and Commentary

In December 1960 New Netherlands Coin Co.'s 55th sale, Collection Cicero, included lot 1108: "1865-S over inverted 186 [*sic*]. Date first begun rotated 180° from its normal position, then corrected. Strictly Very Fine. Discovered by R.J. Salisbury. The only one yet reported. Estimates of value would be idle guesswork." It sold for $225.

This was the initial appearance of this variety. As the error is so obvious it is amazing that it was not published earlier. John J. Ford later related to the author that this variety was discovered by him and Walter Breen, not by Mr. Salisbury, in spring 1960, while reviewing an auction consignment from a friend of Mrs. Emery May Holden Norweb.[23]

The May 1999 Bowers and Merena Galleries' sale of "Treasures from the SS *Brother Jonathan*" included lot 49, far and away the finest known: "1865-S over inverted date. MS-64 PCGS." It sold for $115,000. The purchaser at auction was Ronald J. Gillio, who placed it on exhibit at the Treasures of Mandalay Bay Museum in Las Vegas. This was an extensive exhibition featuring many rare coins. Visitors could hear a narrative recorded by James Earl Jones from a script by the present author.

VF-20	EF-40	AU-50	AU-55	AU-58	MS-60
$7,500	$15,000	$21,000	$27,500	$35,000	$45,000

1866-S, No Motto

Circulation-Strike Mintage: 8,500

Notes regarding mintages: The mintage number is estimated—the *Annual Report of the Director of the Mint* gave a total figure for the year without regard to the motto.

All examples were struck in February 1866 using dies shipped from Philadelphia in November 1865. These eagles circulated at par in the West at a time when gold coins were not seen in circulation in the East or Midwest (until after December 17, 1878).

Estimated population (Mint State): *1–2.* None were seen before 1980 by the author or David W. Akers.

Estimated population (circulated grades): *50–65.*

Submissions certified at highest grades (as of March 2017): *PCGS:* AU-50 (2), AU-53 (1), AU-55 (2), AU-58 (1). *NGC:* AU-50 (2), AU-53 (4), AU-55 (4), AU-58 (4), MS-60 (1).

Die data: Three obverse dies were shipped to San Francisco in November 1865, these going the usual way by steamer to Panama, across the Isthmus via the Panama Railroad, and continuing in the Pacific on another steamer. It is probable that only one obverse die was used to strike the 1866-S, No Motto, coinage. Perfectly serviceable, the other dies were used to make 1866-S, With Motto, coins.

Although the reverse motif was slightly modified in 1859 (most evident on the new version by the eagle having shorter and more delicate claws), the San Francisco Mint used reverse dies remaining from earlier years, and thus all are of the earlier style, including the 1866-S, No Motto.

Key to collecting: VF and EF are usual grades. Very scarce. Exceedingly popular due to its isolation as the only 1866-dated $10 of the No Motto type. In the late 1980s and 1990s a handful of these came on the market from eastern European banking sources, changing the availability. Many if not most are very extensively bagmarked—a situation which, curiously, is characteristic of 1866-S, No Motto, $5 and $20 as well, but less so for other coins of this era.

MARKET NEWS AND COMMENTARY

In March 1911, in his sale of the William H. Woodin Collection, Thomas L. Elder offered lot 1304: "1866-S Without motto. About Fine, the S is large. Rare." It sold for $13.

In October 1962, in the Samuel W. Wolfson Collection, Stack's offered lot 690:

> 1866-S Without Motto. Extremely Fine. This coin is seldom offered for sale. We do not have an accurate mint record of the number struck of this variety. 20,000 struck of both varieties, but, according to available records of frequency of appearance, this type appears once for every ten of the variety with motto. [Sold for $160]

In October 1999, in the Harry W. Bass Jr. Collection, Part II, Bowers and Merena Galleries offered lot 1502: "1866-S No Motto. AU-53 (PCGS Population: 1; 1 finer (AU-55). From Lester Merkin's sale of March 1969, Lot 445." It sold for $9,775.

In its January 2006 FUN sale Heritage included lot 3534: "1866-S No Motto. AU-55 NGC. A single Mint State representative has been certified, an NGC MS-60. Census: 4 in 55, 3 finer (11/05)." It sold for $11,500.

In the August 2016 ANA World's Fair of Money sale Stack's Bowers Galleries offered lot 3349: "1866-S No Motto. VF-30 PCGS." It sold for $9,106.25. In the September 2016 Long Beach sale Heritage offered lot 5701: "1866-S No Motto. EF-45 PCGS." It sold for $15,287.93.

VF-20	EF-40	AU-50	AU-55	AU-58	MS-60
$3,000	$4,000	$12,000	$20,000	$27,500	$55,000

LIBERTY HEAD,
WITH MOTTO (1866–1907)

Designer: *Christian Gobrecht.* **Weight:** *16.718 grams.* **Composition:** *.900 gold, .100 copper (net weight: .48375 oz. pure gold).* **Diameter:** *27 mm.* **Edge:** *Reeded.* **Mints:** *Philadelphia, Carson City, Denver, New Orleans, and San Francisco.*

Motto Added

In 1866, Chief Engraver James B. Longacre modified Gobrecht's $10 design by adding IN GOD WE TRUST on a ribbon above the head of the eagle on the reverse, creating another design type. A similar modification with ribbon was done for the $5, while the $20 had the motto added within an ellipse of stars, and the $2.50 was not modified at all. The Liberty Head $10 with motto on the reverse was minted continuously through 1907.

Throughout the Liberty Head series of the With Motto years from 1866 to 1907, mintages were again continuous at the Philadelphia Mint. For most years from 1866 through 1878 mintages were small, followed by a tremendous surge in 1879—the first year that $10 gold coins circulated in the East and Midwest since the early days of the Civil War. During the span, mintage was extensive at San Francisco. The New Orleans Mint struck eagles intermittently from 1879 to 1906, the Carson City Mint for many of the years 1870 to 1893, and the Denver Mint in 1906 and 1907.

For the With Motto eagles the mintage of circulation strikes totaled over 37,000,000, while Proofs were made to the extent of over 2,000 pieces.

Production

From late December 1861 to December 1878, gold coins did not circulate in the East or Midwest. They were obtainable only by paying a premium for them in Legal Tender Notes. Accordingly, the production of eagles at the Philadelphia Mint was modest during that period. Today, most are quite rare.

The floodgates of $10 issuance opened on December 17, 1878, when for the first time since December 1861 gold coins were exchangeable at par with both silver coins and, most important, paper money. Mintages of eagles escalated upward as the denomination—new to the present generation of most Americans—was received with enthusiasm. It proved, however, that while $10 coins circulated to a limited extent domestically, in their main intended venue—the export trade—the $20 remained the gold coin of choice, with eagles occupying a distant second place. Nevertheless, many millions of eagles were sent overseas—especially after the Free Silver Movement of the late 1870s. These foreign holdings became the major source for Mint State coins in later decades. Circulation strikes for the With Motto type totaled 37,391,767, the most generous production taking place after 1879. Today, 1879 marks the year of demarcation from early dates, most of which are rarely seen in Mint State, and later dates, a number of varieties of which range from scarce to very common in Mint State.

Collecting Commentary

As a class, all eagles of this type are scarce. It is interesting, indeed ironic, that certain varieties of the *rare* early 1795 to 1804 eagles are actually more plentiful in AU and Mint State than in certain higher-mintage issues of the early Liberty Head years. The reason for this is that bullion and specie dealers were alerted to watch for eagles dated 1795 to 1804 as they were turned in by the public from the 1850s onward, while no attention whatsoever was paid to rescuing Liberty Head eagles of the late 1830s through the 1850s. Many coins that could have been obtained easily for face value were lost forever.

Many years later in the early 1900s, when collecting eagles became *slightly* popular, lists of certain pieces were circulated to bank tellers by Thomas L. Elder and possibly others, and a few low-mintage issues were fished out of deposits and bank holdings, this probably accounting for many if not most of the scarce, low-mintage 1841-O (2,500 struck) and Philadelphia Mint circulation-strike eagles from the 1860s and 1870s eagles known to exist today. In terms of availability, this created some interesting situations. For example, it seems that the higher-mintage 1844 Philadelphia eagles (6,361) were not searched for, and thus today the 1844 is rarer than the 1841-O.

No one has ever assembled a set of Uncirculated Liberty Head $10 pieces, and no one ever will, for numerous early varieties are virtually impossible to find in this preservation. In fact, no one has ever assembled a set in *AU* grade!

Among $10 gold coins of the 1838 to 1866 years, there are a number of scarce and rare issues. The 1838 is in perennial demand as the first year of its type, and while not a rarity in worn grades, is scarcely ever seen in Mint State. The 1839 type of 1840 is several times rarer than the 1839 type of 1838 and is another key issue. Over a long period of time the most famous of the Philadelphia Mint eagles has been the 1858, due to its low mintage. The fascinating story of this issue is told later. The Philadelphia eagles of the early 1860s are very rare, but as Proofs were struck of these, the demand for high-grade coins has been filled by the Proofs—although they are major rarities as well. Mint State coins of the early 1860s through the mid-1870s are virtually unknown.

After 1854 (the year that the San Francisco Mint opened for business) mintages of gold coins declined at New Orleans as, earlier, much California gold had been sent there for coinage. Accordingly, $10 coins from 1855 through the last year of New Orleans mintage of the type, 1860, are all scarce, and in Mint State they are incredibly rare.

All San Francisco $10 coins of this type are scarce, with those after 1857 being generally unavailable in grades above VF, although there are a few exceptions. The curious 1865-S over inverted date is quite scarce and stands high in the esteem of collectors, this being the only such inverted date in the entire $10 series.

Proofs are known of most of the early dates from 1838 to 1858, but are so rare that often a generation of collectors will miss the opportunity to acquire certain dates, and not even the Mint Collection (now in the Smithsonian Institution) has a complete date run. Proofs of 1859 through the 1870s are all very rare, and those of later Liberty Head dates are elusive as well, but more available overall. Collecting a full run of Proofs is a virtual impossibility, and among modern numismatists, only the late Ed Trompeter ever accomplished the task—with 20 years of effort and an unlimited coin-buying budget.

Collecting Liberty Head eagles by date and Mint is a fascinating challenge—more so than is generally realized. Of all Liberty Head gold series from $1 to $20, it seems that the $10 coins have received the least attention and, as a class, are the most difficult to find. Remarkably, the majority of dates and mintmarks can be collected in VF or finer grade for earlier years and AU or finer for later years for only a modest advance over the melt-down or bullion value!

In the early years the value of a pure ounce of gold at the Mint was $20.67. On January 31, 1934, it was raised to $35. An eagle contains about a half ounce of pure gold plus 10 percent alloy. The values of common-date eagles changed accordingly.

If you are contemplating this specialty, the Optimum Collecting Grades (OCG) are VF and EF, until, say, the 1880s, then EF and AU. From the 1890s through 1907 AU and, for many, Mint State into MS-63 are worthwhile options. You will be in good historical company, for most great old-time collections had eagles in these grade ranges.

Collection Considerations

If you are seeking a single coin to add to a type set, several issues of the 1890s and early 1900s are plentiful in high grades and in the context of eagles are inexpensive. There is no particular reason to settle for a circulated coin.

The numismatist seeking to form a sequence of date and mintmark varieties will have some very interesting, but not insurmountable, challenges. Most Philadelphia Mint eagles of the late 1860s and the 1870s range from scarce to very rare, reflective of generally low mintages. The year 1875 is a case study in itself. The Philadelphia Mint struck eagles continuously from 1866 to 1906.

The Carson City Mint opened in 1870 and struck coins intermittently until 1893. With the exception of 1891-CC, hundreds of which exist in Mint State, Carson City eagles range from scarce to very rare. The dates of the 1870s are particularly elusive and in some instances Mint State specimens are not known to exist. The 1870-CC is a fame all of its own, and the appearance of an example at auction is always a cause for excitement. Detailed information is given under each variety heading.

The New Orleans Mint, closed in 1861, reopened in 1879 and struck $10 coins intermittently during this later era, beginning with 1879-O, a date for which only a paltry 1,500 were made. Mintages were low for 1880-O (9,200), 1881-O (8,359), 1882-O (10,820), and 1883-O—which takes the prize for any and all New Orleans gold coins, with only 800. It would be interesting to know the circumstances of the latter coinage. The last eagles struck there were the 1906-O issues.

San Francisco Mint eagles are generally rare through and including 1878, with Mint State pieces being exceedingly rare in nearly every instance. From 1879 through 1907, San Francisco Mint production was generous for most years, although 1883-S, with only 38,000, is on the low side. The high water mark was reached in 1881 when 3,887,220 were struck, followed in 1901, when 2,182,750 1901-S $10 coins were made, both issues mainly for export. Today tens of thousands of 1901-S eagles exist in Mint State.

The Denver Mint opened for business in 1906, utilizing the rich Cripple Creek Gold District as a prime source for yellow metal. Eagles of the With Motto type were made there in 1906 and 1907, in sufficient numbers that they are easily enough obtained today.

At the Philadelphia Mint Proofs were made of all years from 1866 to 1907 and have mirrorlike fields. Beginning in 1902, and continuing for several years afterward, Proof dies were polished in the portrait, this being particularly obvious with the year 1903. Thus, these have a slightly different appearance.

Die Varieties

Although there are some significant variations in the placement of dates and mintmarks, eagles of the With Motto type are generally quite uniform—with relatively little available in the way of dramatic date repunchings and blunders. As is the case with the earlier type, most working dies were impressed with a four-digit date logotype, but in some instances a three-digit logotype was employed, with the final number added separately.

For detailed information on many die varieties, see the Bowers and Merena Galleries auction catalogs for the Harry W. Bass Jr. Collection, accessible on the Newman Numismatic Portal on the Internet. Douglas Winter's books on Carson City and New Orleans gold coins contain valuable information on the issues from those two facilities as well.

Grading Standards

Grading standards are the same as for Liberty Head, No Motto, coins. See pages 117 and 118 for details.

1866, With Motto

Circulation-Strike Mintage: 3,750
Proof Mintage: 30

Notes regarding mintages: The trend of low mintages at Philadelphia is continued, this being the era in which gold coins did not circulate in the East or Midwest.

All circulation-strike mintage was delivered on February 1. This and the Proof delivery date indicate that the motto IN GOD WE TRUST was adopted very early in the year.

Proofs were delivered on January 15, followed by 5 more on June 8. This would seem to indicate that the first run of 25 had been distributed in its entirety. This also indicates that the motto IN GOD WE TRUST was adopted very early in the year (the enabling act was passed the year before, on March 3, 1865). These have a *perfect date*, unlike the circulation strikes which are *all* of the repunched date variety.

Estimated population (Mint State): *4–6*. David W. Akers noted in his 1980 study, "I have seen one Choice Uncirculated piece but this particular coin has never appeared on the numismatic market. It is the variety with the date double punched." Following suit with other low-mintage Philadelphia eagles of the decade, examples are rare or, in the present case, virtually impossible to find as numismatists were not interested in circulation strikes at the time. Those few collectors who collected eagles by date bought Proofs.

Estimated population (circulated grades): *70–90*.

Estimated population (Proofs): *9–11*. Exceedingly rare.

Submissions certified at highest grades (as of March 2017): *PCGS:* AU-55 (5), AU-58 (5). *NGC:* AU-55 (11), AU-58 (1). MS-60 (2), MS-61 (3), MS-64 (1). We have the same puzzlement mentioned earlier—for coins that were considered to be great rarities or even unknown in Mint State earlier, modern interpretations have opened the gates so that many are now collectible in MS–60 to 62 certified holders.

Die data: All known circulation strikes have the date sharply doubled (Breen-6952). The date was first punched slightly to the right, then deeply overpunched in the final position. Trades of all under digits are visible.

Characteristics of striking and die notes: Some trivial lightness is usually seen at the highest hair points.

Key to collecting: Among extant specimens of the 1866, With Motto, VF and EF grades are the order of the day. AU coins are available but scarce. A handful of Mint State coins are either repatriations or graduates from the AU level.

MARKET NEWS AND COMMENTARY

In August 1942 the ANA Convention sale held by Numismatic Gallery included lot 185: "$10 Gold. 1866. Very Good. Scarce." It sold for $21. In March 1945 the William A. Knapp Collection, sold by B. Max Mehl, included lot 1058: "1866 Variety with motto. First year of this type. Extremely Fine with mint luster; just a shade from Uncirculated. Catalogs at $60 in Uncirculated." It sold for $32.50.

The January 1986 Stack's sale of the James Walter Carter and Margaret Woolfolk Carter Collections included lot 249: "1866 Motto. About Uncirculated, considerable blazing luster. Only eight appearances at auction." It sold for $2,970.

In November 2000, in the Harry W. Bass Jr. Collection, Part IV, Bowers and Merena Galleries offered lot 690: "1866 Motto. AU-58 PCGS. None have been certified in Mint State by either PCGS or NGC. Doubled Date (as are all of this issue.) Die repunched sharply east and mostly effaced. Purchased from Stanley Kesselman on November 15, 1968." It sold for $9,775.

The Stack's Bowers Galleries' March 2011 Baltimore Auction included lot 6717: "1866 With Motto, MS-60 NGC." It sold for $39,100. In its January 2015 Long Beach sale Heritage included lot 3295: "1866 MS-61+ NGC. Second finest certified." It sold for $32,900. In the August 2016 ANA World's Fair of Money sale Stack's Bowers Galleries offered lot 3348: "1866 AU-58 PCGS." It sold for $22,235.

VF-20	EF-40	AU-50	AU-55	AU-58	MS-60	PF-63	PF-64	PF-65
$1,500	$2,000	$5,000	$8,000	$17,500	$30,000	$32,500	$50,000	$85,000

1866-S, With Motto

Circulation-Strike Mintage: 11,500

Notes regarding mintages: The mintage number is estimated—the *Annual Report of the Director of the Mint* gave a total figure for the year without regard to the motto.

The new reverse dies with IN GOD WE TRUST were received on April 14. *If* all pieces struck after that date were of the With Motto type, the production would consist of 5,500 delivered in April plus 6,000 in June. However, it is by no means certain that the mottoless reverse dies were discarded after April 14, although they may have been. The precision that numismatists would like to believe, did not always happen.

These eagles circulated at par in the West at a time when gold coins were not seen in circulation in the East or Midwest (until after December 17, 1878).

Estimated population (Mint State): *None.*

Estimated population (circulated grades): *175–250.*

Submissions certified at highest grades (as of March 2017): *PCGS:* AU-50 (7), AU-53 (10), AU-55 (2), AU-58 (2). *NGC:* AU-50 (50), AU-53 (11), AU-55 (7), AU-58 (2).

Die data: Three obverse dies had been shipped from Philadelphia in November 1865. At least one of these was used to strike the 1866-S, Without Motto, coinage. The others were on hand when six new dies with IN GOD WE TRUST were received on April 15, 1866, having been sent from the Philadelphia Mint on March 26. This shipping date is an interesting reflection that the Mint was not particularly concerned that the With Motto dies be used quickly, for With Motto dies had been used in Philadelphia in January. It also probably indicates that the Without Motto dies might not have been retired immediately when the With Motto dies were received—as, again, there was no urgency.

At least two reverse dies were used: the "medium" S mintmark and the "microscopic" (or "small") S mintmark, the latter being the smallest seen up to this point. See the B.W. Smith sale citation, May 1915. Walter Breen (*Encyclopedia*, 1988) lists just one mintmark size, "minute."

Key to collecting: Once usually seen only in VF and EF grades, AU coins are now seen with frequency. Overall the 1866-S remains a scarce issue.

MARKET NEWS AND COMMENTARY

In March 1911, in his sale of the William H. Woodin Collection, Thomas L. Elder offered lot 1303: "1866-S With motto 'In God We Trust', very small S. Fine; rare." It sold for $12.50. In October 1947, in the H.R. Lee Collection (Eliasberg duplicates), Stack's offered lot 1641: "1866-S With motto, strictly Fine and sharp." It sold for $35. In October 1962, in the Samuel W. Wolfson Collection, Stack's offered lot 692: "1866-S With Motto. Very small mint-mark, which is characteristic of this variety. Sharp Very Fine and choice. Seldom offered for sale, but appears with more frequency than the variety without motto." It sold for $290.

Thirty years later in May 1992, in their sale of the H.C. ("Heck") Dodson Collection, Mid-American Rare Coin Auctions included lot 373: "1866-S With Motto. AU-50." It sold for $7,700. In October 1998, in the John J. Pittman Collection sale, Part II, David Akers offered lot 1947: "1866-S, With Motto. Extremely Fine. Purchased from Lester Merkin's sale, 6/12/68, Lot 498, for $250." It sold for $6,050.

In June 2000, in the Harry W. Bass Jr. Collection, Part III, Bowers and Merena Galleries included lot 660: "1866-S Motto. AU-55 PCGS. PCGS Population: 1; 1 finer (AU-58). Very tiny S mintmark, the smallest seen in the series to date (often called "microscopic" or "minute" mintmark). From Stack's sale of the Miles Collection, October 1968, lot 677." It sold for $10,350.

VF-20	EF-40	AU-50	AU-55	AU-58
$1,500	$3,500	$7,250	$10,000	$17,500

1867

Circulation-Strike Mintage: 3,090
Proof Mintage: 50

Notes regarding mintages: They were all delivered on January 11. At this time, continuing until after December 17, 1878, gold coins did not circulate in the East or Midwest.

There were 25 Proofs delivered on March 5 and 25 more on July 2. This would seem to indicate that the first 25 had been sold, and that others were needed. How many were sold from the second delivery is not known.

Estimated population (Mint State): *4–6*. Exceedingly rare.

Estimated population (circulated grades): *90–130*.

Estimated population (Proofs): *9–12*. Exceedingly rare. At least two are in institutions.

Submissions certified at highest grades (as of March 2017): *PCGS:* AU-55 (8), AU-58 (4), MS-61 (2). *NGC:* AU-55 (19), AU-58 (9). MS-60 (1), MS-61 (1).

Key to collecting: EF is the grade usually seen. AU and low-range Mint State coins are mainly from modern repatriations. The 1867 is a key issue at any level of preservation.

MARKET NEWS AND COMMENTARY

June 1936, sale 366, U.S. and Foreign Gold Coins held by J.C. Morgenthau & Co. included lot 41: "1867 Extremely Fine. Scarce." It sold for $33. In October 1962, in the Samuel W. Wolfson Collection, Stack's offered lot 694: "1867 Uncirculated. Field is slightly rubbed from either cabinet friction or mishandling." It sold for $380.

The January 1986 Stack's sale of the James Walter Carter and Margaret Woolfolk Carter Collections included lot 251: "1867 About Uncirculated, superb coppery toning. A handsome example of a rare coin. A recent compilation of a 13-year period shows only five appearances in this condition." It sold for $1,485.

In March 1988 the Bowers and Merena Galleries' sale of the Norweb Collection, Part II, included lot 2192: "1867 AU-50. A rarity in any grade. The present coin is a Condition Census item and one of the top half dozen finest business strikes known. From J.C. Morgenthau on June 13, 1936." It sold for $3,300.

In its March 2016 sale Heritage included lot 5082: "1867 MS-61 PCGS. High-grade examples usually are AU, and Uncirculated coins are virtually unheard-of. The population numbers confirm this with only one other MS-61 certified at PCGS, one at NGC, and none finer at either service (2/16)." It sold for $36,425.

In the August 2016 ANA World's Fair of Money sale Stack's Bowers Galleries offered lot 3351: "1867 AU-58 PCGS." It sold for $30,550. In the Long Beach sale of September of the same year Heritage offered lot 14230: "1867 AU-53 PCGS." It sold for $10,575. In the same sale the next lot, AU-50 NGC, brought $6,462.50.

PROOF MARKET NEWS AND COMMENTARY

In October 1999, in the Harry W. Bass Jr. Collection, Part II, Bowers and Merena Galleries offered lot 1506:

> 1867 Proof-64 PCGS. The Proof mintage is reported as 50 pieces, but something happened along the distribution line, and David Akers estimates that only seven or eight survive, with Walter Breen putting the number ever so slightly higher. Of these, if institutionalized and impaired pieces are deducted we may have a net of, say, just three or four attractive pieces in private hands! PCGS Population: 2; none finer. From Stack's sale of May 1974, lot 491. [Sold for $39,100]

In January 2005, the Numismatic Rarities Kennywood Collection sale included lot 991: "1867 Proof-66 NGC." It sold for $92,000. Stack's Bowers Galleries' August 2014 Chicago ANA World's Fair of Money sale included lot 13245: "1867 Proof-65 NGC." It sold for $64,625.

VF-20	EF-40	AU-50	AU-55	AU-58	MS-60	PF-63	PF-64	PF-65
$1,500	$2,500	$4,500	$10,000	$20,000	$35,000	$32,500	$50,000	$85,000

1867-S

Circulation-Strike Mintage: 9,000

Notes regarding mintages: These eagles circulated at par in the West at a time when gold coins were not seen in circulation in the East or Midwest (until after December 17, 1878).

Estimated population (Mint State): *None.*

Estimated population (circulated grades): *60–80.*

Submissions certified at highest grades (as of March 2017): *PCGS:* AU-50 (5), AU-53 (2), AU-55 (3). *NGC:* AU-50 (6), AU-53 (7), AU-55 (4), AU-58 (4).

Key to collecting: Until recent decades VF was the usually seen grade, a few notches lower than the EF coins that are typical for the 1867 *Philadelphia* $10. The West Coast coins circulated more intensely. The 1867-S is a rarity in any and all grades. David W. Akers in his 1980 study stated that he had never seen an EF or finer coin. Later repatriations brought quite a few AU coins into the market.

MARKET NEWS AND COMMENTARY

Abe Kosoff in April 1941, seeking to increase the "number" of sales he had, assigned a new number to each *session* of a sale. In April 1941 his sales nos. 6 and 7 included lot 507: "1867-S Very Good." It sold for $17. In the December 1944 sale of the J.F. Bell Collection Stack's included lot 754: "1867-S Extremely Fine. Very scarce." It sold for $52.50.

In May 1992, in their sale of the H.C. ("Heck") Dodson Collection, Mid-American Rare Coin Auctions included lot 375: "1867-S EF-40." It sold for $4,620. In May 1993 the Bowers and Merena Galleries' sale of the Stetson University Collection included lot 2054: "1867-S EF-45 to AU-50. Probably the finest known." It sold for $14,300.

That status changed with an influx of repatriated coins. In November 2000 the Bowers and Merena Galleries' sale of the Harry W. Bass Jr. Collection, Part IV, included lot 691: "1867-S AU-55 PCGS. PCGS Population: 1; none finer. From Heritage's sale of October 1995, lot 6343." It sold for $8,625. Stack's March 2009 Entlich, White Oak, Gross & St. Andre Collections sale included lot 6011: "1867 MS-62." It sold for $6,325.

VF-20	EF-40	AU-50	AU-55	AU-58
$2,250	$5,500	$9,000	$14,500	$25,000

1868

Circulation-Strike Mintage: 10,630
Proof Mintage: 25

Notes regarding mintages: At this time, continuing until after December 17, 1878, gold coins did not circulate in the East or Midwest.

Estimated population (Mint State): *20–30.*

Estimated population (circulated grades): *100–135.*

Estimated population (Proofs): *8–12.* Exceedingly rare.

Submissions certified at highest grades (as of March 2017): *PCGS:* MS-60 (2), MS-61 (3), MS-62 (1). *NGC:* MS-60 (3), MS-61 (3).

Key to collecting: EF and AU and the occasional VF are typical grades encountered. Unknown in Mint State until modern times.

MARKET NEWS AND COMMENTARY

The June 1941 sale of the William Forrester Dunham Collection by B. Max Mehl included lot 2238: "1868 Just a shade from Uncirculated but bears considerable bright mint luster. Scarce date." It sold for $23.

In March 1988 the Norweb Collection, Part II, sale by Bowers and Merena Galleries included lot 2193: "1868 AU-55." It sold for $3,960.

In July 2005 the American Numismatic Rarities sale of the William H. LaBelle Sr. Collection included lot 308: "1868 AU-58 PCGS." It sold for $7,475. In the June 2014 Pre-Long Beach sale Ira and Larry Goldberg offered lot 1895: "1868 AU-58 PCGS." It sold for $9,106.25.

In the May 2016 Rarities Auction Stack's Bowers Galleries offered lot 106: "1868 MS-61 PCGS." It sold for $25,850. In its September 2016 Long Beach sale Heritage included lot 14150: "1868 MS-61 prooflike NGC. PCGS reports two in MS-60 and one each in MS-61 and MS-62, while NGC offers four in MS-60 and two in MS-61 plus this lone MS-61 Prooflike." It sold for $35,350.

In August 2016 the Stack's Bowers Galleries' ANA World's Fair of Money sale included lot 106: "1868 MS-61 PCGS." It sold for $25,850. Heritage, in its April 2017 sale, offered lot 15960: "1868 MS-61 NGC." It sold for $12,925.

VF-20	EF-40	AU-50	AU-55	AU-58	MS-60	PF-63	PF-64	PF-65
$850	$950	$1,700	$3,500	$6,000	$17,500	$32,500	$50,000	$85,000

1868-S

Circulation-Strike Mintage: 13,500

Notes regarding mintages: These eagles circulated at par in the West at a time when gold coins were not seen in circulation in the East or Midwest (until after December 17, 1878).

Estimated population (Mint State): *None.*

Estimated population (circulated grades): *140–180.*

Submissions certified at highest grades (as of March 2017): *PCGS:* AU-50 (4), AU-53 (11), AU-55 (6), AU-58 (4). *NGC:* AU-50 (12), AU-53 (9), AU-55 (13), AU-58 (11).

Key to collecting: Most are VF or EF, but there are more than enough AU coins to satisfy advanced specialists with generous budgets.

MARKET NEWS AND COMMENTARY

In June 1946, in the William Cutler Atwater Collection, B. Max Mehl offered lot 1566: "1868-S Very Fine. Microscopic S. Record of $65 for a similar specimen." It sold for $42.50.

In May 1993, in a vastly expanded market milieu, the Bowers and Merena Galleries' sale of the Stetson University Collection included lot 2056: "1868-S EF-45 to AU-50. Condition Census." It sold for $14,850. This was prior to a wave of repatriations.

In October 1999, in the Harry W. Bass Jr. Collection, Part II, Bowers and Merena Galleries offered lot 1511: "1868-S AU-53. PCGS Population: 7; 5 finer (AU-58 finest)." It sold for $6,900. In its sale of July 2014 Heritage offered lot 3951: "1868-S AU-58 PCGS." It sold for $18,212.50. In the May 2016 Rarities Auction Stack's Bowers Galleries offered lot 107: "1868-S AU-58 PCGS." It sold for $16,450. In the August 2016 ANA World's Fair of Money sale Stack's Bowers Galleries offered lot 3354: "1868-S AU-58 PCGS." It sold for $17,625.

VF-20	EF-40	AU-50	AU-55	AU-58
$1,250	$2,250	$4,000	$5,500	$8,500

1869

Circulation-Strike Mintage: 1,830
Proof Mintage: 25

Notes regarding mintages: All were delivered on February 1. At this time, continuing until after December 17, 1878, gold coins did not circulate in the East or Midwest.

The Proofs were all delivered on February 19. Walter Breen in his *United States Eagles* monograph suggested: "The same obverse die appears to have been used on all these; date is rather thin." *Per contra*, David W. Akers (1980) stated: "Harry Bass pointed out to me that two Proof varieties exist of this date with differences in Liberty's hair bun."

Estimated population (Mint State): *8–12.* Exceedingly rare.

Estimated population (circulated grades): *80–100.*

Estimated population (Proofs): *10–14.* Exceedingly rare.

Submissions certified at highest grades (as of March 2017): *PCGS:* MS-60 (1), MS-62 (1). *NGC:* MS-60 (1), MS-61 (1), MS-63 (1).

Key to collecting: EF and AU are the typical grades. Most AU and lower ranger Mint State coins are from repatriations.

MARKET NEWS AND COMMENTARY

In May 1915, in his sale of the B.W. Smith Collection, B. Max Mehl offered lot 55: "1869 Very Fine with some mint luster. Very rare, only 1,855 coined." It sold for $18.50. In March 1945 the William A. Knapp Collection, sold by B. Max Mehl, included lot 1059: "1869 About Uncirculated with semi-proof surface. Rare date in choice condition. Lists at $60 in Uncirculated." It sold for $78.

Stack's September 1995, John D. Sayer Collection sale, included lot 488: "1869-S MS-61 NGC." It sold for $20,900. The October 2001 sale by Stack's and Sotheby's of the Dallas Bank (Jeff Browning) Collection included lot 447: "1869 About Uncirculated." It sold for $6,612.

In its September 2008 Long Beach sale Heritage included lot 3896: "1869 MS-60 PCGS. Only three examples have been certified as Mint State by either PCGS or NGC. The other two coins are a PCGS MS-62 and an NGC MS-63, and neither have appeared at auction since 1995." It sold for $34,500.

PROOF MARKET NEWS AND COMMENTARY

In October 1999, in the Harry W. Bass Jr. Collection, Part II, Bowers and Merena Galleries offered lot 1514: "1869 Proof-65 PCGS. PCGS Population: 2; 1 finer (Proof-66). On the reverse the "white" shield stripes are quite curious and irregular, the Proof surface being interrupted many times. From Stack's sale of the DiBello Collection, May 1970, lot 1078." It sold for $46,000.

In the August 2006 ANA World's Fair of Money sale Bowers and Merena Galleries offered lot 4337: "1869 Proof-67 NGC." It sold for $132,250. Regency Auction XII, June 2015, included lot 438: "1869 Proof-66+ PCGS." It sold for $199,750.

VF-20	EF-40	AU-50	AU-55	AU-58	MS-60	PF-63	PF-64	PF-65
$1,500	$2,350	$4,750	$11,500	$10,000	$30,000	$32,500	$50,000	$80,000

1869-S

Circulation-Strike Mintage: 6,430

Notes regarding mintages: These eagles circulated at par in the West at a time when gold coins were not seen in circulation in the East or Midwest (until after December 17, 1878).

Estimated population (Mint State): *4–6.* Exceedingly rare.

Estimated population (circulated grades): *55–70.*

Submissions certified at highest grades (as of March 2017): *PCGS:* AU-55 (5), AU-58 (6). MS-60 (1), MS-61 (1). *NGC:* AU-55 (9), AU-58 (4). MS-61 (1).

Characteristics of striking and die notes: Usually well struck.

Key to collecting: VF is the usually seen grade—typical for a San Francisco Mint eagle of the era. AU and lower-range Mint State coins from modern importations are sufficient to supply the specialists who can afford them. Another rarity from the 1860s.

MARKET NEWS AND COMMENTARY

In October 1962, in the Samuel W. Wolfson Collection, Stack's offered lot 699: "1869-S Very Fine, choice. Some original mint luster around stars. Low mint record, only 6,430 struck. It is very seldom that one has the opportunity to bid on this coin at auction." It sold for $220.

Years later in May 1993 the Bowers and Merena Galleries' sale of the Stetson University Collection included lot 2058: "1869-S EF-45. Condition Census." It sold for $4,400. In November 2000, in the Harry W. Bass Jr. Collection, Part IV, Bowers and Merena Galleries offered lot 693: "1869-S MS-61 (PCGS From our sale of the Fairfield Collection, October 1977, lot 1814." It sold for $17,250.

In its January 2017 FUN Convention sale Heritage included lot 5940: "1869-S AU-58 NGC." It sold for $15,275.

VF-20	EF-40	AU-50	AU-55	AU-58	MS-60
$1,500	$2,350	$4,750	$8,500	$18,500	$30,000

1870

Circulation-Strike Mintage: 3,990
Proof Mintage: 35

Notes regarding mintages: At this time, continuing until after December 17, 1878, gold coins did not circulate in the East or Midwest.

Estimated population (Mint State): *1.*

Estimated population (circulated grades): *40–50.*

Estimated population (Proofs): *10–13.* Exceedingly rare.

Submissions certified at highest grades (as of March 2017): *PCGS:* AU-58 (2). *NGC:* AU-58 (1), MS-60 (1).

Key to collecting: A rarity at any level, one of *many* hidden rarities among Liberty Head eagles. The average non-specialist would have no clue that this coin is about ten times rarer than an 1879 Flowing Hair Stella. When seen, EF and AU are typical grades.

MARKET NEWS AND COMMENTARY

In March 1911, in his sale of the William H. Woodin Collection, Thomas L. Elder offered lot 1233: "1870. Fine. Only 2,535 pieces struck, indicating its rarity." It sold for $11.50. In November 1939 the William B. Hale Collection, sold by B. Max Mehl, included this same coin as lot 1668: "1870 Nearly Uncirculated, with considerable mint luster. From the famous Woodin sale, 1911." It sold for $21.

The January 1986 Stack's sale of the James Walter Carter and Margaret Woolfolk Carter Collections included lot 256: "1870 Brilliant Uncirculated, full frosty mint bloom. Numerous bag abrasions magnified by the faint prooflike surface. A beautiful specimen and right at the head of the Condition Census." It sold for $1,485. It seems that bidders were, as they say, clueless.

Enlightenment did happen! In its September 2015 Long Beach sale Heritage included lot 3297: "1870 MS-60 NGC. This piece ranks as the sole finest certified and as the only piece encapsulated as Mint State." It sold for $25,850.

VF-20	EF-40	AU-50	AU-55	AU-58	MS-60	PF-63	PF-64	PF-65
$950	$1,250	$2,500	$6,000	$11,000	$18,500	$32,500	$50,000	$80,000

1870-CC

Circulation-Strike Mintage: 5,908

Notes regarding mintages: Similar to the other early Carson City Mint coins, the 1870-CC eagle seems to have been distributed primarily in the region in which it was minted. Few if any were exported at or near the time of issue, and any that were shipped overseas in later years were apt to already show extensive signs of wear.

Estimated population (Mint State): *1.* It was reported years ago, and none have been seen in modern times.

Estimated population (circulated grades): *40–55.*

Submissions certified at highest grades (as of March 2017): *PCGS:* AU-50 (3), AU-53 (5), AU-55 (3). *NGC:* AU-50 (6), AU-53 (4), AU-55 (5). Likely, these figures include quite a few resubmissions.

Die data: The 2001 book *Gold Coins of the Carson City Mint* by Douglas Winter and James L. Halperin lists two die marriages for the 1870-CC eagle, both of which share the same obverse. The date on this die is placed somewhat low in the field with the digits slanting down slightly from left to right. The reverse of the Winter 1-B die pairing has a small, round, high-set CC mintmark with the first C over the right side of the letter E in TEN and the second C over the left edge of the letter N in TEN. The first C is noticeably higher than the second.

Characteristics of striking and die notes: The 1870-CC eagle is the most consistently well struck of the three first-year gold issues from the Carson City Mint. Even so, this is an extremely challenging issue to obtain with sharp definition and strong eye appeal.

Key to collecting: The 1870-CC $10 challenges the super-famous 1870-CC double eagle in rarity. Among those who are knowledgeable, the 1870-CC is the most famous eagle of the With Motto type. In fact, it may be *the* most famous Liberty Head eagle, now that the status of the 1858 Philadelphia coins has changed. VF is the grade usually seen—and not very often. At the AU level the 1870-CC is a prime rarity and is a candidate for finest known.[24]

In his 1980 study David Akers noted:

> The 1870-CC is one of the two rarest Carson City Mint eagles, comparable in overall rarity to the lower mintage 1879-CC. However, if one takes condition rarity into account as well as overall rarity, then the 1870-CC would have to be rated the rarest eagle from this mint. In fact, only the double eagle of the same date surpasses the 1870-CC eagle as the rarest of all Carson City gold coins. Basically, the only specimens available (and there are really not that many) grade Fine to VF.

Since that time gradeflation plus some repatriated coins necessitate a revision of the preceding commentary. Many notable collections including the Woodin cabinet sold by Elder in 1911 did not have an 1870-CC. Years later, beginning in a significant way in the 1930s, Carson City coins began to become popular with collectors, and Thomas L. Elder, Wayte Raymond, and others took notice of them. Prior to that time catalog citations are few and far between. When interest finally did arrive in the 1930s, just about all pieces had been lost, melted, or worn extensively.

MARKET NEWS AND COMMENTARY

In view of the fame and desirability of the 1870-CC more than the usual citations are given here.

In May 1915, in his sale of the B.W. Smith Collection, B. Max Mehl offered lot 80: "1870-CC First date of the $10 gold piece of this mint. Very Good, nearly Fine. Very rare. Seldom offered." It sold for $20. In March 1938, in his sale of the Samuel H. McVitty Collection, B. Max Mehl offered lot 417: "Carson City Mint. 1870-CC About Fine. Very rare." It sold for $19.40. The passion for collecting large-denomination gold by date and mint had not caught on yet. This price was not quite much over the melt value of $16.45! In November 1939 the William B. Hale Collection, sold by B. Max Mehl, included lot 1725: "1870-CC First year of issue. Very Fine. Rare." It sold for $20.

In the 1940s the 1870-CC was still more or less asleep, but recognition of its rarity was beginning. In the December 1944 sale of the J.F. Bell Collection Stack's included lot 721: "1870-CC Very Fine. Rare." It sold for $92.50. In January 1946 the Numismatic Gallery sale of "The World's Greatest Collection" (F.C.C. Boyd) included lot 826: "1870-CC Very Fine. Scarce." It sold for $70. In June 1946, in the William Cutler Atwater Collection, B. Max Mehl offered lot 1496: "1870-CC Very Fine. Quite rare. Record over $90." It sold for $67. In October 1947, in the H.R. Lee Collection (Eliasberg duplicates), Stack's offered lot 1612: "1870-CC First year of issue, strictly Fine, can be called Very Fine, scarce." It sold for $60. In April 1949 B. Max Mehl's sale of the Dr. Charles W. Green Collection included lot 633: "1870-CC Fine, strictly so." It sold for $45.

In April 1956, in his sale of the Thomas G. Melish Collection, Abe Kosoff offered lot 2458: "1870-CC. First year of Carson City Eagles. About Very Fine, very scarce. Sold in the W.G.C. for $70 ten years ago—since then the demand for Carson City coins has increased considerably." It sold for $55. The author was at the sale, which was conducted with the Central States Numismatic Society, and did not appreciate its rarity any more than anyone else did. The popularity of Carson City coins of all denominations took a giant step forward after the discovery of several million Mint State CC Morgan dollars in Treasury vaults in 1962 and 1963. The rest is history. Today, all CC coins are on the "most active" list within a given series.

In October 1962, in the Samuel W. Wolfson Collection, Stack's offered lot 702: "1870-CC Very Fine and rather choice. First year of issue at Carson City Mint. 5,908 struck but apparently most were lost or melted. This coin appears on a number of 'Want Lists' furnished us by both dealers and collectors. Very much in demand and certainly undervalued in the reference books." It sold for $400. This was shortly before the great Treasury release of Morgan silver dollars began.

In October 1982 the Louis E. Eliasberg Collection of U.S. Gold Coins sale by Bowers and Ruddy Galleries offered lot 734: "1870-CC Very Fine-20. From the John H. Clapp Collection, 1942. Earlier from a Thomas L. Elder sale, June 1928." It sold for $3,575. The days of overlooked CC eagles were now history.

In March 1988 the Bowers and Merena Galleries' sale of the Norweb Collection, Part II, included lot 2197: "1870-CC EF-45 A sharp and very beautiful specimen of the rarest of all Carson City eagles, indeed one of the rarest of *all* coins from the Carson City Mint. From J.C. Morgenthau on December 10, 1935." It sold for $10,450.

In November 2000 the Bowers and Merena Galleries' sale of the Harry W. Bass Jr. Collection, Part IV, included lot 696: "1870-CC Net EF-45; sharpness of AU-50 with a small reverse gouge. Purchased from Joe Flynn on December 3, 1973." It sold for $19,550.

The March 2005 American Numismatic Rarities Richard C. Jewell Collection sale included lot 767: "1870-CC EF-45 PCGS." It sold for $33,350.

The July 2012 sale of the Battle Born Collection by Stack's Bowers Galleries included lot 11020: "1870-CC Winter 1-B. AU-55 PCGS. PCGS Population: only 2; and none are finer at either PCGS or NGC. Ex David Lawrence's sale of the Richmond Collection, Part I, July 2004, lot 2088; Heritage's Palm Beach, Florida Signature Sale of March 2005, lot 7033." It sold for $129,250.

The momentum was maintained, and any AU 1870-CC drew bids from all directions, such as in the January 2017 FUN sale by Heritage that included lot 5941: "1870-CC AU-50 NGC. Some lightness of strike appears on the hair curls around Liberty's brow as well as on the central portion of the eagle, as is characteristic of the issue. Census: 6 in 50, 6 finer (10/16)." It sold for $82,250.

VF-20	EF-40	AU-50	AU-55
$35,000	$55,000	$80,000	$145,000

1870-S

Circulation-Strike Mintage: 8,000

Notes regarding mintages: These eagles circulated at par in the West at a time when gold coins were not seen in circulation in the East or Midwest (until after December 17, 1878).

Estimated population (Mint State): *1–2*.

Estimated population (circulated grades): *90–125*.

Submissions certified at highest grades (as of March 2017): *PCGS:* AU-50 (8), AU-53 (5), AU-55 (6), AU-58 (2), MS-61 (1). *NGC:* AU-50 (6), AU-53 (6), AU-55 (8), AU-58 (1).

Key to collecting: In early times VF was the usually seen grade, punctuated in market appearances by an occasional EF. Anything finer was exceedingly rare. In 1980 David W. Akers commented, "The 1870-S is not often available in any grade, but when a specimen is offered for sale, it is generally only VF. A few EF specimens are known but I am unaware of any 1870-S that grades as high as AU and nothing close to Uncirculated is even rumored to exist."

This changed in later times when many AU coins were found among gold coins imported from foreign reserves.

MARKET NEWS AND COMMENTARY

In his 1907 fixed price list, Superb Collection of United States and Foreign Gold, Silver and Copper Coins, Fractional Currency, Etc., Elmer S. Sears offered lot 29: "1870

San Francisco Mint. Fine. Very rare. $15." This is among the earliest appreciations of the rarity of the 1870-S. Sears, hardly remembered today, in this era had the largest stock of high-quality American coins of any dealer. In 1912 he became partner with Wayte Raymond in the United States Coin Company. In 1907 Raymond was not affiliated and was just beginning his interest in numismatics while employed as a teller at the City National Bank in South Norwalk, Connecticut. The coin company cut a brilliant swath, although it is not well remembered today. From 1912 until the partnership dissolved in 1918 the firm conducted 42 coin auctions. Edgar H. Adams, the leading numismatic scholar of the time, helped in many ways. The company was dissolved on May 1, 1918, after which Raymond set up an office in the new building of the Anderson Studios at Park Avenue and 59th Street. Anderson evolved into the American Art Association, later into Parke-Bernet Galleries, and still later into the American division of Sotheby's, the London Art auctioneers. From 1934 to 1946 Raymond managed the coin department of the Scott Stamp & Coin Co. and became prominent in the issuance of the *Standard Catalogue of United States Coins* and in Raymond / National coin album pages. Sears faded from view in the 1920s and Raymond went on to great fame. Elmer Sears faded from view.

In June 1934 J.C. Morgenthau & Co.'s sale of coins from the Waldo C. Newcomer Collection included lot 120: "1870-S Extremely Fine. Rare." It sold for $30. In the December 1944 sale of the J.F. Bell Collection Stack's included lot 757: "1870-S Extremely Fine." It sold for $52.50. As was true of other Liberty Head eagles the 1870-S was generally ignored in the marketplace.

In October 1982, by which time Liberty Head eagles attracted quite a few specialists, the Louis E. Eliasberg Collection of U.S. Gold Coins sale by Bowers and Ruddy Galleries offered lot 735: "1870-S Choice AU-55. From the John H. Clapp Collection, 1942. Earlier from the Chapman brothers, November 1903." It sold for $4,675. In November 2000, in the Harry W. Bass Jr. Collection, Part IV, Bowers and Merena Galleries offered lot 697: "1870-S MS-61 PCGS. From our sale of the Louis E. Eliasberg Sr. Collection, October 1982, lot 735." It sold for $36,800. This is a good example why it is *completely impossible* to arrange past and present auction descriptions into any consistent listing of grades.

In its January 2014 FUN sale Heritage included lot 6891: "1870-S AU-53 NGC. The highest grade NGC has assigned to a surviving example is AU-58, to a single coin. PCGS has awarded the sole Mint State grade, an MS-61 (12/13)." It sold for $11,162.50.

VF-20	EF-40	AU-50	AU-55	AU-58	MS-60
$1,100	$2,000	$5,500	$11,000	$15,000	$27,500

1871

Circulation-Strike Mintage: 1,790
Proof Mintage: 30

Notes regarding mintages: Deliveries were made on February 6 (1,600), November 18 (40)[25], and December 21 (150).

At this time, continuing until after December 17, 1878, gold coins did not circulate in the East or Midwest. Eagles could be obtained by anyone depositing the required amount of bullion. At the time gold coins were available from banks and brokers at a sharp premium in relation to Legal Tender Notes.

Proofs were delivered on February 20.

Estimated population (Mint State): *1.* The specimen sold by Stack's in September 1994.

Estimated population (circulated grades): *100–125.*

Estimated population (Proofs): *8–11.* Incredibly rare.

Submissions certified at highest grades (as of March 2017): *PCGS:* AU-50 (12), AU-53 (7), AU-55 (10), AU-58 (2), MS-60 (1). *NGC:* AU-50 (6), AU-53 (6), AU-55 (16), AU-58 (10).

Key to collecting: EF and AU coins are typical. Modern repatriations have changed the order of rarity. Despite the increased availability of the 1871 eagle in high grades, market prices have remained strong.

MARKET NEWS AND COMMENTARY

In the December 1944 sale of the J.F. Bell Collection Stack's included lot 635: "1871 Extremely Fine. Very scarce." It sold for $100. The January 1986 Stack's sale of the James Walter Carter and Margaret Woolfolk Carter Collections included lot 258: "1871 About Uncirculated, mostly prooflike. A very rare date, only six specimens offered in this condition in the past 13 years. None are known in Uncirculated condition." It sold for $1,980.

In March 1996, in the Spring ANA sale, Heritage offered lot 6714: "1871 AU-55 PCGS. PCGS Population: 2, with none higher (1/96). NGC has graded 1 AU-55, 2 AU-58s and 1 MS-60 (1/96)." It sold for $3,740.

In the June 2014 Pre-Long Beach sale Ira and Larry Goldberg offered lot 1898: "1871 AU-58 NGC." It sold for $11,750. In the August 2016 ANA World's Fair of Money sale Stack's Bowers Galleries offered lot 3360: "1871 AU-53 PCGS." It sold for $5,405.

VF-20	EF-40	AU-50	AU-55	AU-58	MS-60	PF-63	PF-64	PF-65
$1,400	$2,400	$3,750	$8,500	$15,000	$22,500	$32,500	$50,000	$80,000

1871-CC

Circulation-Strike Mintage: 8,085

Notes regarding mintages: Deliveries were made in February (900), March (3,325), August (1,160), and November (1,800).

These eagles circulated at par in Nevada and elsewhere in the West at a time when gold coins were not seen in circulation in the East or Midwest (until after December 17, 1878).

Estimated population (Mint State): *3–5.* The Heritage, Bowers and Merena, and Lang coin sold in 2002, graded MS-62 by NGC, was for a time the only Mint State coin known to exist. However, the 2001 edition of Douglas Winter's book on Carson City coins mentioned another contender, a coin graded as AU-55 by PCGS in 1995, but by 2001 called MS-60 by NGC.

Estimated population (circulated grades): *90–110.*

Submissions certified at highest grades (as of March 2017): *PCGS:* AU-50 (11), AU-53 (3), AU-55 (7), AU-58 (3), MS-62 (1). *NGC:* AU-50 (7), AU-53 (10), AU-55 (6), AU-58 (10), MS-60 (1), MS-62 (1).

Die data: The two known die varieties of the 1871-CC Liberty eagle share the same reverse, which is a reuse of Winter's Reverse A of the first year 1870-CC issue. The mintmark is small, round, and set high in the field well to the left of the lowermost arrow feather.

Key to collecting: A rarity in the series, although not in the league of the 1870-CC or the 1872-CC. A key issue that is an object of desire for every specialist. It is worth noting that not a single coin finer than EF appeared in David W. Akers' 1980 survey of auction sales. That was then. Now is now. Since that time large quantities of eagles have been repatriated from foreign holdings. Carson City coins are a tiny fraction of these, but enough have been that AU coins, while expensive, appear with regularity on the market.

MARKET NEWS AND COMMENTARY

Read this and weep! In March 1911, in his sale of the William H. Woodin Collection, Thomas L. Elder offered a run of Carson City eagles from 1871-CC to 1893-CC, lots 339 to 352. All sold for face value except 1872 ($12.50, and for $10.50 each, 1872 to 1874 and 1877 to 1880.

In the marketplace the 1871-CC has a track record paralleling that of the 1870-CC: Passive interest years ago changing to sharp interest and focus toward the end of the 1900s.

In February 1944, in the Belden E. Roach Collection, B. Max Mehl offered lot 471: "1871-CC Very Fine. Scarce. Listed at $40." It sold for $42. In the December 1944 sale of the J.F. Bell Collection Stack's included lot 722: "1871-CC 7185 minted. About Extremely Fine. Rare." It sold for $82.50.

In January 1946 the Numismatic Gallery sale of "The World's Greatest Collection" (F.C.C. Boyd) included lot 827:

> 1871-CC Very Fine. These Carson City Mint eagles are seldom offered in any condition. We mention this fact because discriminating collectors who might normally desire one in choice condition should perhaps never get an opportunity to acquire these Carson City pieces. Most fine collections lack these dates. [Sold for $45]

These comments were well said, but cataloger Abe Kosoff's words were played to an empty audience. In June 1946, in the William Cutler Atwater Collection, B. Max Mehl offered lot 1497: "1871-CC. Strictly Very Fine; unusually bold impression. Another very scarce date with record for an equal specimen over $80." It sold for $57.50. Into the second half of the 20th century, interest in CC eagles was minimal. In April 1956 Abe Kosoff's sale of the Thomas G. Melish and Clinton W. Hester Collections included lot 2460: "1871-CC Fine, scarce. These Carson City Mint eagles are seldom offered in any condition." It sold for $32.50, or less than twice melt value.

Matters began to perk up in the 1960s. In October 1962, in the Samuel W. Wolfson Collection, Stack's offered lot 705: "1871-CC Very Fine and very choice. Very low mint record. Scarce and seldom available." The coin sold for a strong $460. Moving ahead two decades to October 1982 the Louis E. Eliasberg Collection of U.S. Gold Coins sale by Bowers and Ruddy Galleries offered lot 737: "1871-CC EF-40. Thought to be from Hans M.F. Schulman, April 1944." It sold for $2,420. By this time, and continuing to today. Carson City eagles were in strong demand. In June 2000, in the Harry W. Bass Jr. Collection, Part III, Bowers and Merena Galleries included lot 673: "1871-CC EF-45 PCGS. PCGS Population: 6; 7 finer (AU-53 finest). Purchased from Mike Brownlee, April 17, 1967." It sold for $5,290.

The March 2005 American Numismatic Rarities Richard C. Jewell Collection sale included lot 768: "1871-CC AU-58 NGC." It sold for $26,450. The July 2012 sale of the Battle Born Collection by Stack's Bowers Galleries included lot 11021: "1871-CC Winter 1-A. MS-62+ PCGS. PCGS Population: just 1 coin in all Mint State grades. Ex Heritage's Midwinter ANA Sale of March 1995, lot 5959; Bowers and Merena Galleries, to Bowers and Merena's sale of the Henry S. Lang Collection, July 2002. The present example was discovered in Europe prior to 1995." It sold for $126,500. Away we go!

In the June 2014 Pre-Long Beach sale Ira and Larry Goldberg offered lot 1899: "1871-CC AU-58 PCGS." It sold for $14,125. In its January 2017 FUN sale Heritage included lot 5942: "1871-CC AU-58 NGC. The 1871-CC ten survives today in numbers not exceeding about 100 coins, by most estimates. Census: 10 in 58, 2 finer (10/16)." It sold for $35,250.

VF-20	EF-40	AU-50	AU-55	AU-58	MS-60
$4,500	$10,000	$17,500	$27,000	$40,000	$75,000

1871-S

Circulation-Strike Mintage: 16,500

Notes regarding mintages: These eagles circulated at par in the West at a time when gold coins were not seen in circulation in the East or Midwest (until after December 17, 1878).

Estimated population (Mint State): *None.*

Estimated population (circulated grades): *110–130.*

Submissions certified at highest grades (as of March 2017): *PCGS:* AU-50 (8), AU-53 (5), AU-55 (5), AU-58 (1). *NGC:* AU-53 (9), AU-55 (12), AU-58 (4).

Key to collecting: Surprisingly scarce, but this is the rule most of the San Francisco eagles of the 1860s into the 1870s. VF and EF used to be the best grades generally available. Today, there are enough AU coins to supply dedicated specialists. Philadelphia coins of this era tend to be EF and AU in the main in two categories: those that remained stateside and those that have been repatriated. VF, a common grade for San Francisco eagles of the era, is a grade seldom seen among Philadelphia coins.

MARKET NEWS AND COMMENTARY

This is yet another rare eagle that was recognized as such in the early days. However, it was not until the late 1900s that detailed descriptions were given in auction catalogs, as merited by the increase of value by that time.

In May 1915, in his sale of the B.W. Smith Collection, B. Max Mehl offered lot 91: "1871-S Very small S over and slightly to left of N. About Fine. Scarce." It sold for $12.25. The June 1941 sale of the William Forrester Dunham Collection by B. Max Mehl included lot 2241: "1871-S Very Fine." It sold for $17.50.

In February 1944, in the Belden E. Roach Collection, B. Max Mehl offered lot 434: "1871-S Microscopic S. Extremely Fine. Scarce." It sold for $27.50. The same coin came back on the market in October 1982 in the auction of the Louis E. Eliasberg Collection of U.S. Gold Coins conducted Bowers and Ruddy Galleries and offered as lot 738: "1871-S Extremely Fine-40. One of the finest known examples of this issue. From the Belden E. Roach Collection (B. Max Mehl, February 1944)." It sold for $1,155. This price did not start a trend, for after then there were auction sales of EF coins for lower prices, such as in January 1986 in Stack's sale of the James Walter Carter and Margaret Woolfolk Carter Collections, included lot 260: "1871-S Extremely Fine. The tiny mintmark is lightly struck but still perfectly legible. A very scarce coin in this condition." It sold for $880.

Prices continued to be erratic. In May 1993, in the Bowers and Merena Galleries' sale of the Stetson University Collection, lot 2062 was described as "1871-S EF-40" and sold for $3,190. In June 2000, in the Harry W. Bass Jr. Collection, Part III, Bowers and Merena Galleries included lot 674 "1871-S EF-45. Purchased from Stanley Kesselman, June 3, 1968." It sold for $1,380.

In March 2004, in the American Numismatic Rarities Whitman Expo sale, lot 1542 described as "1871-S AU-50 (PCGS)." It sold for $5,060. Twelve years later in the August 2016 ANA World's Fair of Money sale Stack's Bowers Galleries offered lot 3362: "1871-S AU-50 PCGS." The coin sold for $3,760. As a number of 1871-S eagles came on the market in the late 1900s and early 2000s a specialist with patience could make an advantage purchase by waiting.

VF-20	EF-40	AU-50	AU-55	AU-58
$1,150	$1,850	$5,000	$7,500	$12,500

1872

Circulation-Strike Mintage: 1,620
Proof Mintage: 30

Notes regarding mintages: Delivered on January 11. At this time, continuing until after December 17, 1878, gold coins did not circulate in the East or Midwest.

Proofs were delivered on February 3.

Estimated population (Mint State): 7–9. Exceedingly rare.

Estimated population (circulated grades): *35–50*.

Estimated population (Proofs): *10–14*. Very rare.

Submissions certified at highest grades (as of March 2017): *PCGS:* AU-55 (3), AU-58 (2), MS-62 (2), MS-64 (2). *NGC:* AU-55 (7), AU-58 (1).

Key to collecting: The 1872 eagle first-class rarity in circulated grades. EF is the usually seen grade. Enough AU coins are available to supply advanced specialists, these mostly from repatriations. Apart from specialists, few people know how rare this date is. The same can be said for some other Philadelphia eagles of this era.

MARKET NEWS AND COMMENTARY

In March 1945 the William A. Knapp Collection, sold by B. Max Mehl, included lot 1060: "1872 Extremely Fine with some luster. Just very slight abrasion from being handled with other coins. Very rare date. Catalogs at $75 in Uncirculated. Seldom offered." It sold for $82.50. This was a very strong price at the time.

Decades later in May 1992, in their sale of the H.C. ("Heck") Dodson Collection, Mid-American Rare Coin Auctions included lot 386: "1872 EF-40." It sold for $5,830. Stack's, in October 1992, offered this coin in the Floyd T. Starr Collection, lot 1246:

> 1872 Brilliant Uncirculated, nearly choice. Prooflike. Among the finest known, if not a candidate for finest honors. Akers recorded our own 1976 ANA specimen as the only Uncirculated specimen then known to him. No business strike specimens were included in either the Kaufman or Norweb sales. Purchased from Henry Chapman in the 1920s.

The Starr coin sold for $35,200. Later offerings of high-grade coins, mostly AU, did well in the marketplace. In the June 2015 Pre-Long Beach sale Ira and Larry Goldberg offered lot 1921: "1872 AU-50 PCGS." It sold for $7,990. In the May 2016 Rarities Auction Stack's Bowers Galleries offered lot 108: "1872 AU-58 PCGS." It sold for $28,200.

PROOF MARKET NEWS AND COMMENTARY

Proofs appeared at auction many times over the years, sometimes punctuated by long gaps between offerings. In October 1962, in the Samuel W. Wolfson Collection, Stack's offered lot 706: "1872 Brilliant Proof. A rare date and mint. Extremely low 1,650 coined, of which 30 were in Proof. It has been many years since we have been able to offer a comparable specimen of this coin. Probably less than half of those minted exist today." It sold for $1,250.

The time for Proofs to be front row center in interest had not arrived. That changed. In October 1998 the John J. Pittman Collection, Part II, sold by David W. Akers, included lot 1950: "1872 Proof-64." It sold for $71,500. By then any Proof of this era at the 64 or 65 level brought a strong five-figure price at auction.

VF-20	EF-40	AU-50	AU-55	AU-58	MS-60	PF-63	PF-64	PF-65
$2,150	$3,500	$9,000	$12,000	$17,500	$40,000	$32,500	$50,000	$80,000

1872-CC

Circulation-Strike Mintage: 4,600

Notes regarding mintages: Deliveries were made in July (1,100), September (1,600), and December (1,900).

These eagles circulated at par in Nevada and elsewhere in the West at a time when gold coins were not seen in circulation in the East or Midwest (until after December 17, 1878).

Estimated population (Mint State): *None.*

Estimated population (circulated grades): *100–140.* A prime rarity among Carson City eagles. VF is the grade usually seen.

Submissions certified at highest grades (as of March 2017): *PCGS:* AU-50 (8), AU-53 (2), AU-55 (4), AU-58 (4). *NGC:* AU-50 (8), AU-53 (7), AU-55 (5), AU-58 (1).

Die data: There are two known reverse dies, and they were both previously used to strike 1870-CC eagles.

Characteristics of striking and die notes: Some lightness of strike at the centers is typical for 1872-CC.

Key to collecting: The 1872-CC has been a perennial favorite. Years ago the typical coin offered at auction was Very Fine, more or less. Today AU coins from modern repatriations appear regularly and bring strong prices from a corps of Carson City coin enthusiasts. These buyers are a separate set from specialists endeavoring to collect one of each date and mint of Liberty Head eagle from 1838 onward.

Market News and Commentary

The 1872-CC has been recognized as a rarity for a long time, but few people collected eagles by mintmark until the 1940s, and even then the number was fairly small. That changed later, especially with the great market expansion at the end of the 1900s.

In March 1911, in his sale of the William H. Woodin Collection, Thomas L. Elder offered lot 1340: "1872-CC Fine; rare." It sold for $12.50. There must have been strong action in June 1936 at the sale of U.S. and Foreign Gold Coins by J.C. Morgenthau & Co.'s lot 242: "1872-CC Extremely Fine. Rare." It sold for $35.50. In October 1947, in the H.R. Lee Collection (Eliasberg duplicates), Stack's offered lot 1614: "1872-CC About Extremely Fine, with some mint luster, only 5500 minted, Rare." It sold for $50. The variety was still asleep. In November 1947, in the same firm's sale of the Mason Williams Collection, there was lot 1225: "1872-CC Fine, Rare." It sold for $40, again a bargain.

The Federal Coin Exchange, in the August 1954 ANA Convention sale, offered lot 4044: "1872 Carson City. Rare. Greatly underrated. Fine-Very Fine." It sold for $62.50. This firm was operated by Michael Kolman Jr. in Cleveland. In addition to dealing in coins he handled antiquities and at one time made and sold portable oxygen units for medical purposes. In October 1962, in the Samuel W. Wolfson Collection, Stack's offered lot 708: "1872-CC Very Fine. Very scarce and desirable. Only 5,500 struck. Seldom offered." It sold for $210.

The demand for Carson City eagles changed dramatically in later years. The July 2012 sale of the Battle Born Collection by Stack's Bowers Galleries included lot 11022:

> 1872-CC AU-58 PCGS. Ex John J. Ford Jr. April 7, 1975; Bowers and Merena's sale of the Harry W. Bass Jr. Collection, Part IV, November 2000, Lot 702; Doug Winter; the Nevada Collection. Like the 1870-CC, the 1872-CC is currently unknown in Mint State. With no examples graded higher than AU-55 at NGC, a trio of AU-58s listed at PCGS are tied for the #1 ranking on the Condition Census. [Sold for $63,240]

The market remained strong, and EF and AU coins did well. Regency Auction XII, conducted by Laura Sperber in June 2015, included lot 428: "1872-CC AU-50 PCGS." It sold for $19,387.50. In its January 2017 FUN sale Heritage included lot 5943: "1872-CC EF-45 PCGS." The coin sold for $22,325.

VF-20	EF-40	AU-50	AU-55	AU-58
$7,500	$15,000	$27,500	$42,500	$62,500

1872-S

Circulation-Strike Mintage: 17,300

Notes regarding mintages: These eagles circulated at par in the West at a time when gold coins were not seen in circulation in the East or Midwest (until after December 17, 1878).

Estimated population (Mint State): *2.*

Estimated population (circulated grades): *120–140.*

Submissions certified at highest grades (as of March 2017): *PCGS:* AU-55 (14), AU-58 (8). *NGC:* AU-55 (30), AU-58 (11), MS-60 (1), MS-63 (1).

Key to collecting: The 1872-S eagle is rare overall. In keeping with other eagles, years ago the typical grade was VF more or less. Today AU coins are available and usually attract a lot of interest when sold.

MARKET NEWS AND COMMENTARY

The 1872-S has always been a rarity. The market was slow to recognize this, however.

In June 1934 J.C. Morgenthau & Co.'s sale of coins from the Waldo C. Newcomer Collection included lot 121: "1872-S Very Fine." It sold for $25. In October 1947, in the H.R. Lee Collection (Eliasberg duplicates), Stack's offered lot 1647: "1872-S About Extremely Fine, a scarce coin." It sold for $26. The market woke up and went into overdrive in later years. Today, rare Liberty Head eagles are in strong demand.

In November 2000 the Bowers and Merena Galleries' sale of the Harry W. Bass Jr. Collection, Part IV, included lot 703: "1872-S AU-55. Pleasing medium yellow and orange-gold with superb luster for the grade. Very original looking and attractive, with only a shallow scratch near Liberty's temple worthy of mention. Purchased from William Youngerman on January 6, 1973." It sold for $4,370. Regency Auction XIX, December 2016, included lot 465: "1872-S AU-55 PCGS." It sold for $9,106.25.

VF-20	EF-40	AU-50	AU-55	AU-58	MS-60
$925	$1,050	$1,500	$4,250	$8,500	$17,500

1873

Circulation-Strike Mintage: 800
Proof Mintage: 25

Notes regarding mintages: Delivered in January. At this time, continuing until after December 17, 1878, gold coins did not circulate in the East or Midwest.

Proofs were delivered in February.

Estimated population (Mint State): *1*. One has been certified as low-level Mint State.

Estimated population (circulated grades): *40–60*.

Estimated population (Proofs): *9–12*. Very rare. Over the years many of these and other Proofs have been reoffered, resulting in dozens of historical auction listings.

Submissions certified at highest grades (as of March 2017): *PCGS*: AU-50 (1), AU-53 (2), AU-55 (3), AU-58 (3) MS-60 (1). ***NGC*:** AU-50 (2), AU-53 (3), AU-55 (4), AU-58 (4).

Die data: Circulation strikes and Proofs are from the same die pair.

Characteristics of striking and die notes: All have the Close 3 date.

Key to collecting: One might think that the low mintage figure for the 1873 eagle would have acted as a beacon for a long time. It did not, and it was years before its true status was recognized—probably because "better" Proofs, themselves great rarities, have satisfied the need of the limited number of specialists of generations ago. There were exceptions in auction listings, but not many. Today in the marketplace EF and AU are the usual grades, nearly all from repatriations.

MARKET NEWS AND COMMENTARY

This is one circulation-strike eagle that was early recognized as rare. Typically, an auction offering has created a lot of attention.

In May 1915, in his sale of the B.W. Smith Collection, B. Max Mehl offered lot 56:

> 1873 About Fine. Excessively rare. Only 825 coined. The only record that I can find is the specimen sold in the Cowell Collection in 1911 and which brought $38.75. Some of the very largest collections did not have it. The Woodin sale, which contained 172 different eagles, did not have it.

This coin sold for $40. This was a very strong price for a circulated Liberty Head eagle at the time. Prices varied, sometimes widely, as in February 1921, in Thomas L. Elder's sale of the M.K. McMullin and H.C. Whipple Collections, lot 1559: "1873. Very Fine. Exceedingly rare. Only 823 pieces struck. Doubtless about all of these were worn out in circulation or else remelted." It sold for $15. In November 1939 the William B. Hale Collection, sold by B. Max Mehl, included lot 1669: "1873 Only 825 coined. Very Fine. Very rare. Cost $37.50 in 1911. Certainly should bring a great deal more today." It sold for $27.50, or far less than his Smith Collection coin in 1915.

In April 1949 B. Max Mehl's sale of the Dr. Charles W. Green Collection included lot 545: "1873 Fine. Rare. Only 825 minted." It sold for $80. This was close to the end of bargain time for a circulated 1873. The January 1986 Stack's sale of the James Walter Carter and Margaret Woolfolk Carter Collections included lot 264:

> 1873 Close 3. Strictly Extremely Fine and very close to About Uncirculated, frosty and slightly prooflike. An old scratch on the cheek, undoubtedly caused in circulation. Only 800 business strikes were made but few are extant, probably a dozen or so at best. This ranks as one of the finest in existence. [Sold for $3,960]

In May 1992, in their sale of the H.C. ("Heck") Dodson Collection, Mid-American Rare Coin Auctions included lot 389: "1872 EF-40." It sold for $11,000. In November 2000 the Bowers and Merena Galleries' sale of the Harry W. Bass Jr. Collection, Part IV, included lot 705: "1873 Close 3. AU-58 PCGS. Purchased from William Donner on October 8, 1968." It sold for $21,850.

In the May 2016 Rarities Auction Stack's Bowers Galleries offered lot 109: "1873 AU-58 PCGS." It sold for $64,625. In the August 2016 ANA World's Fair of Money sale Stack's Bowers Galleries offered lot 3366: "1873 AU-50 PCGS." It sold for $32,900. In its January 2017 FUN Convention sale Heritage included lot 5944: "1873 AU-58 NGC." It sold for $49,350.

PROOF MARKET NEWS AND COMMENTARY

In December 1890, in their sale of the Thomas Cleneay Collection, the Chapman brothers offered lot 424, a complete gold Proof set of the year 1873 ($1, $2.50, $3, $5, $10, $20). Realized for the set, $60. *Many* citations could be given for the sales of complete gold Proof sets in the 19th century. Most were broken up, the $1, $2.50, and $3 saved, sometimes the $5 as well, and the $10 and $20 spent for face value. This lack of interest in high-denomination gold Proofs extended into the 1920s. Selected examples are given later in the present text.

That changed, of course. In August 2006 the American Numismatic Rarities sale of the Old West and Franklinton Collections included lot 1547: "1873 Close 3. Proof-65 NGC." It sold for $80,500.

VF-20	EF-40	AU-50	AU-55	AU-58	MS-60	PF-63	PF-64	PF-65
$10,000	$20,000	$25,000	$47,500	$65,000	$75,000	$37,500	$55,000	$85,000

1873-CC

Circulation-Strike Mintage: 4,543

Notes regarding mintages: These eagles circulated at par in Nevada and elsewhere in the West at a time when gold coins were not seen in circulation in the East or Midwest (until after December 17, 1878).

Estimated population (Mint State): *None.*

Estimated population (circulated grades): *55–70.*

Submissions certified at highest grades (as of March 2017): *PCGS:* AU-50 (9), AU-53 (4), AU-55 (1), AU-58 (1). *NGC:* AU-50 (4), AU-53 (8), AU-55 (1), AU-58 (2).

Die data: All are of the Close 3 date style. Three obverse dies were shipped to Carson City on November 9, 1872, for the 1873-CC coinage. Sufficient usable reverses were on hand from earlier times.

Characteristics of striking and die notes: Lightly struck at the high points of the obverse. The reverse is a reuse of that which the Mint used to strike some 1870-CC and 1872-CC eagles, as well as all of those pieces dated 1871-CC. The mintmark is small, round, and set high in the field entirely to the left of the lowermost arrow feather. Both of the Cs in the mintmark are level.

Key to collecting: VF and EF were the usual grades until the late 1900s. Today, AU examples are available from repatriations. Interest in Carson City gold coins is very intense, and high-grade coins attract a lot of attention when they cross the auction block.

MARKET NEWS AND COMMENTARY

In March 1911, in his sale of the William H. Woodin Collection, Thomas L. Elder offered lot 1341: "1873-CC About Fine; scarce." It sold for $10.50. In November 1939 the William B. Hale Collection, sold by B. Max Mehl, included lot 1726: "1873-CC Very Fine. Quite rare. From the famous Woodin Sale in 1911." It sold for $21. This was the Woodin coin sold by Elder in 1911.

In January 1946 the Numismatic Gallery sale of "The World's Greatest Collection" (F.C.C. Boyd) included lot 829: "1873-CC Very Fine." It sold for $55. In April 1960, on the cusp of a bull market in coins, the month that *Coin World* was launched, New Netherlands Coin Co.'s 54th Sale, Jonathan Glogower Consignment, Etc. included lot 699:

> 1873-CC. Strictly VF. Very rare, only 4,543 struck. In terms of mintage, this is one of the four rarest Carson City eagles. This checks with how often it is missing in important collections - Memorable, Peake and Melish for instance. The Fine Dr. Green coin supposedly cost $90, a figure not really out of line now, and we obtained $67.50 for a miserable polished example in our 49th sale. The present coin should prove something of a surprise. [Sold for $140]

By October 1982 demand had increased many times over. In the Louis E. Eliasberg Collection of U.S. Gold Coins held by Bowers and Ruddy Galleries in October 1982, lot 743: "1873-CC Choice Very Fine-30," brought $1,430. In March 1988 the Bowers and Merena Galleries' sale of the Norweb Collection, Part II, included lot 2202: "1873-CC EF-45. From J.C. Morgenthau on December 10, 1935." It sold for $3,080.

In May 2000 the Bowers and Merena Galleries' sale of the Harry W. Bass Jr. Collection, Part III, included lot 681:

> 1873-CC Repunched 18. AU-53 PCGS. Close 3. A highly prized rarity, truly a fantastic coin—tied as the finest certified by PCGS. Only 4,543 were struck. Winter and Cutler wrote, "An issue which is nearly impossible to locate in any grade higher than choice Very Fine." Not only is the present piece higher than this, it is much higher! The specimen here is tied for finest certified by PCGS. As you may have guessed, the other AU-53 example of the date was Lot 1538 in our sale of Part II of

the Harry W. Bass, Jr. Collection, October 1999! No one can ever point a finger and accuse the Harry Bass Collection of a shortage of rarities or opportunities! PCGS Population: 2; none finer. This reverse die was also used for 1871-CC eagles. Purchased from Abner Kreisberg, March 1, 1968. [Sold for $12,650]

The July 2012 sale of the Battle Born Collection by Stack's Bowers Galleries included lot 11023:

1873-CC Liberty eagle. Repunched Date. Winter 2-A. Die State I. AU-58 NGC. Tied for Condition Census #1. Combined PCGS and NGC Population: just 2, both of which are listed at NGC; with none finer in Mint State. From Heritage's Long Angeles, California U.S. Coin Auction, August 2009, Lot 1301. [Sold for $92,000]

In its January 2017 FUN sale Heritage included lot 5945: "1873-CC EF-45 PCGS." It sold for $30,550.

VF-20	EF-40	AU-50	AU-55	AU-58
$12,500	$18,000	$35,000	$80,000	$100,000

1873-S

Circulation-Strike Mintage: 12,000

Notes regarding mintages: These eagles circulated at par in the West at a time when gold coins were not seen in circulation in the East or Midwest (until after December 17, 1878).

Estimated population (Mint State): *3–4.*

Estimated population (circulated grades): *95–110.*

Submissions certified at highest grades (as of March 2017): *PCGS:* AU-55 (4) MS-61 (1), MS-62 (1). *NGC:* AU-55 (10), AU-58 (8).

Key to collecting: VF and EF were the usually seen higher grades until AU coins became available in the late 1900s. Very elusive in any grade. It is truly remarkable how *rare* most Liberty Head eagles of this era and earlier are in comparison to later issues. There are *far more* 1901-S eagles in existence than the total for all dates and mintmarks from 1838 through the 1870s! This is amazing to contemplate.

MARKET NEWS AND COMMENTARY

The auction trail of the 1873-S eagle is a familiar litany: not much value recognition until the late 1900s.

In December 1908 Henry Chapman's sale of the David M. Kuntz Collection included lot 83: "1873-S." It sold for $10.10. In June 1934 J.C. Morgenthau & Co.'s sale of coins from the Waldo C. Newcomer Collection included lot 122: "1873-S Very Fine. Rare." It sold for $30. Newcomer, a Baltimore bank president, was one of the few numismatists who collected large-denomination gold coins by mintmark in the early 1900s. The June 1941 sale of the William Forrester Dunham Collection by B. Max Mehl included lot 2243: "1873-S Extremely Fine, with some luster. Scarce." It sold for

$20. In February 1944, in the Belden E. Roach Collection, B. Max Mehl offered lot 435: "1873-S Small S high. Very Fine, with some luster. Very scarce." It sold for $25.

In November 2000 the Bowers and Merena Galleries' sale of the Harry W. Bass Jr. Collection, Part IV, included lot 706: "1873-S MS-61 PCGS. A Condition Census example of the variety, quite possibly the finest available specimen. PCGS Population: 1, none finer. From Heritage's sale of October 1995, lot 6369." It sold for $19,550.

The Stack's Bowers Galleries' May 2015 Rarities sale included lot 70: "1873-S MS-62 PCGS." It sold for $47,000.

VF-20	EF-40	AU-50	AU-55	AU-58	MS-60
$1,000	$2,250	$4,250	$7,000	$12,000	$20,000

1874

Circulation-Strike Mintage: 53,140
Proof Mintage: 20

Notes regarding mintages: Most of the bullion to strike this issue was from worn gold dollars and quarter eagles that had been redeemed.

At this time, continuing until after December 17, 1878, gold coins did not circulate in the East or Midwest.

Proofs were delivered on February 14.

Estimated population (Mint State): *80–100.* The data is inconsistent. Thought to be very rare at the Mint State level years ago. In 1980 David W. Akers found only two in his survey of auction sales. Today quite a few are known from repatriations.

Estimated population (circulated grades): *500–700.*

Estimated population (Proofs): *5–7.* David W. Akers in his 1980 study of about 600 modern auction catalogs found only two listings, fewer than for any other date after 1858!

Submissions certified at highest grades (as of March 2017): *PCGS:* MS-62 (10), MS-64 (4), MS-65 (3). *NGC:* MS-62 (7), MS-63 (1), MS-64 (2), MS-65 (4).

Key to collecting: EF is the grade usually seen, but quite a few VF and AU coins exist. This is the most plentiful With Motto $10 up to this point. The estimate may be on the low side, for this date in worn grades was a common issue in overseas bank hoards years ago. Mint State coins were scarce in earlier times but are easily available today. There is not much financial incentive to certify Fine, VF, or even EF specimens of common dates, and thus population reports are of little help in figuring how many exist today. The value of lower-grade coins is tied into the current bullion price of gold.

MARKET NEWS AND COMMENTARY

The June 1941 sale of the William Forrester Dunham Collection by B. Max Mehl included lot 2244: "1874 Just a shade from Uncirculated bright mint luster. Scarce date." It sold for $19.50. This coin resurfaced in October 1947, in the H.R. Lee Collection (Eliasberg duplicates), when Stack's offered lot 1529: "1874 About Uncirculated, from the Dunham Collection." It sold for $27.50. In the December 1944 sale of the J.F. Bell Collection Stack's included lot 638: "1874 Brilliant Uncirculated." It sold for $40. This was an amazing coin at the time, but was not noticed. New Netherlands Coin Co. in its 54th sale, Jonathan Glogower Consignment, Etc., April 1960, offered lot 700: "1874. About VF. Low mintage, 53,140; another date that seems to come only VF or worse when non-Proofs are sought, as we have neither seen nor heard of any fully EF coins in late years." It sold for $28.

In the modern market, in November 2000 the Bowers and Merena Galleries' sale of the Harry W. Bass Jr. Collection, Part IV, included lot 709: "1874 MS-64 PCGS. PCGS Population: 14; 2 finer (MS-65). From Stack's sale of the Bartle Collection, October 26, 1984, lot 1121." It sold for $10,925. For Harry Bass, the more coins he could have of a given date and mintmark the better, especially if they were of slightly different varieties (evident by studying the date numerals).

Stack's March 2009, Entlich, White Oak, Gross & St. Andrew Collections sale included lot 6014: "1874 MS-62 PCGS." It sold for $4,313.

VF-20	EF-40	AU-50	AU-55	AU-58	MS-60	PF-63	PF-64	PF-65
$750	$850	$900	$925	$950	$1,500	$32,500	$55,000	$85,000

1874-CC

Circulation strike mintage: 16,767

Notes regarding mintages: These eagles circulated at par in Nevada and elsewhere in the West at a time when gold coins were not seen in circulation in the East or Midwest (until after December 17, 1878). Starting in the late 1870s during the Free Silver Movement fears many Carson City coins that had been in circulation were exported.

Estimated population (Mint State): 2. The Eliasberg and Miller-Lang coins.

Estimated population (circulated grades): *150–170.*

Submissions certified at highest grades (as of March 2017): *PCGS:* AU-50 (16), AU-53 (10), AU-55 (11), AU-58 (2), MS-63 (1). ***NGC:*** AU-50 (12), AU-53 (18), AU-55 (20), AU-58 (3).

Die data: The only known die marriage of this issue has a medium-size date evenly spaced between the base of Liberty's neck and the denticles. The reverse die is in its second appearance after being used to strike some 1873-CC eagles. The mintmark is small, round, even, and positioned below the tip of the lowermost arrow feather. A loupe reveals a very faint die scratch through the letter O in GOD.

Key to collecting: In keeping the general scenario, VF and EF coins were the rule in the early days, augmented in the late 1900s by Carson City coins found in foreign holdings. This is the first readily collectible Carson City eagle up to this point in time, although the issue is rare in relation to the strong demand for coins from this Western mint. In the early days the 1874-CC attracted little notice. Today a high-grade coin such as EF or AU coin draws bids from all directions.

Market News and Commentary

In February 1944, in the Belden E. Roach Collection, B. Max Mehl offered lot 474: "1874-CC Just a shade from Uncirculated with mint luster." It sold for $36. The December 1944 sale of the J.F. Bell Collection held by Stack's included lot 725: "1874-CC Very Fine. Very scarce." It sold for $50.

In October 1947, in the H.R. Lee Collection (Eliasberg duplicates), Stack's offered lot 1616: "1874-CC Strictly Very Fine and choice, scarce." It sold for $35. New Netherlands Coin Co.'s 46th sale, Dr. Clarence W. Peake Collection, June 1955, included lot 155: "1874-CC. Strictly Very Fine. A really desirable example of a highly popular item!" It sold for $45.

In October 1982, in the Louis E. Eliasberg Collection of U.S. Gold Coins, Bowers and Ruddy Galleries offered lot 746: "1874-CC Brilliant Uncirculated, MS-60 to Select Brilliant Uncirculated, MS-63 obverse. Brilliant Uncirculated, MS-60 reverse. From the John H. Clapp Collection, 1942. Earlier from the Chapman brothers, January 1900." It sold for $17,600.

In November 2000, in the Harry W. Bass Jr. Collection, Part IV, Bowers and Merena Galleries offered lot 712: "1874-CC MS-63 (PCGS) PCGS Population: 1, none finer. From our sale of the Louis E. Eliasberg Sr. Collection, October 1982, lot 746." It sold for $66,700. Harry Bass was one of the strongest bidders in the Eliasberg sale. He arrived in advance with his binocular microscope and was given a special area to study all of the coins 1795 to 1907 and their die characteristics. Indian Head eagles of the 1907 to 1933 years were not of particular interest to him as the dates were part of the original dies, not added later. Accordingly, there were no variations.

In its January 2017 FUN Convention sale Heritage included lot 5946: "1874-CC AU-55 PCGS." It sold for $23,552.88.

VF-20	EF-40	AU-50	AU-55	AU-58	MS-60	MS-63
$3,000	$4,500	$9,000	$17,500	$35,000	$50,000	$200,000

1874-S

Circulation-Strike Mintage: 10,000

Notes regarding mintages: These eagles circulated at par in the West at a time when gold coins were not seen in circulation in the East or Midwest (until after December 17, 1878).

Estimated population (Mint State): *None.*

Estimated population (circulated grades): *150–200.*

Submissions certified at highest grades (as of March 2017): *PCGS:* AU-50 (10), AU-53 (6), AU-55 (5), AU-58 (3). *NGC:* AU-50 (12), AU-53 (13), AU-55 (12), AU-58 (5).

Key to collecting: VF and EF are traditional grades, nicely augmented by AU coins in the late 1900s. In his 1967 *United States Eagles*, Walter Breen noted, "No specimen known to me above EF condition, and the coin is almost unobtainable above VF."

MARKET NEWS AND COMMENTARY

In February 1944, in the Belden E. Roach Collection, B. Max Mehl offered lot 436: "1874-S Extremely Fine with some luster. Very scarce." It sold for $26. The December 1944 sale of the J.F. Bell Collection held by Stack's included lot 761, seemingly similar to the Roach coin: "1874-S Extremely Fine. Only 10,000 minted." It sold for $50. In June 1946, in the William Cutler Atwater Collection, B. Max Mehl offered lot 1572, also related: "1874-S Extremely Fine. Only 10,000 minted. Brings about $50." It sold for $32. Prices did jump around!

In June 2000, in the Harry W. Bass Jr. Collection, Part III, Bowers and Merena Galleries included lot 686: "1874-S AU-58 PCGS. Reverse die also used for 1873-S eagles. From Heritage's sale of October 1996, lot 6375." It sold for $10,120. In its July 2014 sale Heritage included lot 3953: "1874-S AU-58 NGC." It sold for $12,337.50.

VF-20	EF-40	AU-50	AU-55	AU-58
$1,500	$2,500	$5,000	$8,000	$13,500

1875

Circulation-Strike Mintage: 100
Proof Mintage: 20

Notes regarding mintages: Circulation strikes and Proofs were delivered on February 13. So far as is known, no numismatic interest was evinced in circulation strikes of the 1875 $10 in its own time, and examples were routinely paid out at face value after mid-December 1878. The 1875 has the lowest published mintage of any gold coin date and mint.

Estimated population (Mint State): *None.*

Estimated population (circulated grades): *12–16.* Exceedingly rare, as the mintage indicates.

Estimated population (Proofs): *7–10.* It is considered one of the greatest of all Proof rarities after 1858. In August 1903, Augustus G. Heaton contributed an article to *The Numismatist*, "Eccentricities of Coin Valuation." Gold coins were among the items discussed:

> As gold collecting is generally the interest of the more experienced class, its branch as well as Philadelphia rarities are fully appreciated, and such pieces as the Philadelphia Mint double eagle of 1883, the eagle of 1875, the half eagle of 1887, the $3 or $1 of 1875, and the S mint quarter eagle of 1858,[26] the S mint dollar of 1870, the D mint dollars of 1855, 1856, and 1861, would raise the numismatic temperature of an auction room to fever heat.

Submissions certified at highest grades (as of March 2017): *PCGS:* AU-50 (2), AU-53 (2). *NGC:* AU-50 (2), AU-53 (1), AU-55 (1).

Die data: Date logotype is to the right of the position found on Proofs; the digit 1 in 1875, if extended upward, would pass to the right of the front of the neck. It is unusual that at least two different obverse dies would have been made for such a limited coinage.

Characteristics of striking and die notes: Generally well struck except at stars 1 and 2.

On Proof strikes, the date logotype is to the left of the position found on circulation strikes; the digit 1 in 1875, if extended upward, would pass just in front of the neck. It is unusual that at least two different obverse dies would have been made for such a limited coinage.

Key to collecting: The 1875 is *the* circulation strike of the Liberty Head eagle series. Of the 100 minted, a dozen more survive today, as indicated before. Probably, most were plucked out of bank holdings in the 1930s and by officials switching common coins for these after citizens were commanded to turn in gold. The 1875 is a very visible rarity, many of the same coins have been reoffered over the years, and a precise definition of rarity is not possible. Of the remaining examples, two are in very low grades. The others range from VF to AU. The last are probably from repatriations, for coins plucked out of bank reserves in the 1930s were apt to show extensive wear.

MARKET NEWS AND COMMENTARY

In March 1911, in his sale of the William H. Woodin Collection, Thomas L. Elder offered lot 1235: "1875. Very Good. Very rare. Only 120 coined!" It sold for $10.50. In the December 1944 sale of the J.F. Bell Collection Stack's included lot 639: "1875 Extremely Fine. Only 120 coins were struck [including 20 Proofs]. This is the second specimen of this date that we have handled in many years. Lacking in most important collections. Excessively rare." It sold for $485. This set the scene for recognition of the 1875 as a rarity worth a strong price.

In April 1949 B. Max Mehl's sale of the Dr. Charles W. Green Collection included lot 547: "1875 Strictly Very Fine with traces of semi-proof surface. Very rare in any condition as only 127 were struck. A Proof specimen has a record of $700." It sold for $235. In October 1947, in the H.R. Lee Collection (Eliasberg duplicates), Stack's offered lot 1530: "1875 Only 120 coins minted. Few specimens are known to exist. This coin while only in Extremely Fine condition is one of the best known." It sold for $500. This coin reappeared in the January 1986 Stack's sale of the James Walter Carter and Margaret Woolfolk Carter Collections as lot 270: "1875 Extremely Fine. Ex H.R. Lee Collection (Stack's), lot 1530, October 1947." It sold for $25,300.

In January 1984 Stack's sale of the Amon G. Carter Jr. Family Collection included lot 772: "1875 Very Good, evenly worn. EF is the highest grade known, and nothing AU or Uncirculated has ever been rumored to exist." It sold for $27,500. The Bowers and Merena Galleries' sale of the Boys Town Collection, March 1998, included lot 2207: "1875 AU-50 PCGS." It sold for $60,500. Boys Town in Omaha, Nebraska, had large collections of stamps and coins in its PhilaMatic Center. Most or all were sold in the late 1900s.

In October 1999, in the Harry W. Bass Jr. Collection, Part II, Bowers and Merena Galleries offered lot 1551: "1875 EF-45 PCGS. PCGS Population: 2; 3 finer (AU-53 finest). From Stack's sale of the Alto Collection, December 1970, lot 356." It sold for $42,550. The October 2001 sale by Stack's and Sotheby's of the Dallas Bank (Jeff Browning) Collection included lot 474: "1875 Extremely Fine." It sold for $36,800. In the August 2011 ANA sale Stack's Bowers Galleries offered lot 7732: "1875 AU-53+ PCGS." It sold for $345,000.

PROOF MARKET NEWS AND COMMENTARY

The June 1941 sale of the William Forrester Dunham Collection by B. Max Mehl included lot 2245:

> Perfect brilliant Proof. From the Proof set Mr. Dunham purchased in 1906. Excessively rare. I find that some of the greatest collections ever offered in this country did not possess a brilliant Proof specimen of this coin. Even such a collection as the Newcomer, which cost nearly one million dollars, only had an Extremely Fine specimen. The great Ten Eyck Collection did not have one in any condition, nor did the great Earle Sale, which realized over $50,000 in 1912, nearly thirty years ago. I consider this coin, in Proof condition, by far the rarest of all $10 gold pieces, and certainly one of the greatest of all rarities of the American gold series. Considering its rarity, I do not hesitate to state that it is well worth a price in the four-figure mark. [Sold for $250]

In January 1946 the Numismatic Gallery sale of "The World's Greatest Collection" (F.C.C. Boyd) included lot 680: "1875 Brilliant Proof." It sold for $700. In March 1976 Stack's sale of a selection of U.S. Coins from the Garrett Collection included lot 453:

> 1875 Eagle. Brilliant Proof. Deep yellow gold and simply beautiful. No record of sale in over a decade Other than our Alto Sale, December 1970, where we sold a circulated specimen, we have not sold an 1875 eagle at auction in decades. From the [Heman] Ely Collection in 1883. [Sold for $91,000]

In January 1990 the Superior Galleries' sale of the S. Chalkley and Austin Ryer Collections included lot 4818: "Proof-62 PCGS." It sold for $88,000.

In September 2003 the American Numismatic Rarities Classics sale included lot 546: "1875 Proof-64 NGC." It sold for $115,000. In July 2005 the American Numismatic Rarities sale of the William H. LaBelle Sr. Collection included lot 309: "1875 Proof-64 PCGS. From the Eliasberg Collection by Bowers and Merena Galleries, October 1982." It sold for $138,000.

VF-20	EF-40	AU-50	AU-55	PF-63	PF-64	PF-65
$150,000	$185,000	$225,000	$375,000	$165,000	$225,000	$300,000

1875-CC

Circulation-Strike Mintage: 7,715

Notes regarding mintages: These eagles circulated at par in Nevada and elsewhere in the West at a time when gold coins were not seen in circulation in the East or Midwest (until after December 17, 1878).

Estimated population (Mint State): *2.*

Estimated population (circulated grades): *80–110.*

Submissions certified at highest grades (as of March 2017): *PCGS:* AU-50 (3), AU-53 (11), AU-55 (9), AU-58 (1), MS-62 (1). *NGC:* AU-50 (8), AU-53 (6), AU-55 (5), AU-58 (1), MS-60 (1).

Characteristics of striking and die notes: Lightly struck at the obverse center.

Key to collecting: VF and EF coins from stateside circulation in the 19th century have been augmented by AU coins found in foreign holdings. The result is that today it is possible to build a higher-quality Carson City eagle collection than ever before. Such coins are not inexpensive due to the great demand for them.

MARKET NEWS AND COMMENTARY

The 1875-CC was offered in many early sales, but it was not until the late 1900s that it became valuable enough to attract wide attention—this being the usual scenario.

In the December 1944 sale of the J.F. Bell Collection Stack's included lot 726: "1875-CC Extremely Fine." It sold for $62.50. In June 1946, in the William Cutler Atwater Collection, B. Max Mehl offered lot 1318: "1875-CC Extremely Fine; tiny nick on cheek. Quite rare. Record over $100." It sold for $61.50. Also in the same sale was lot 1501: "1875-CC Extremely Fine with considerable frosty mint surface. Very scarce." It sold for $35. In April 1956 Abe Kosoff's sale of the Thomas G. Melish and Clinton W. Hester Collections included lot 2464: "1875-CC Very Fine, scarce." It sold for $32.50.

Years later in October 1982 the Louis E. Eliasberg Collection of U.S. Gold Coins sold by Bowers and Ruddy Galleries offered lot 749: "1875-CC Extremely Fine-40. Only 7,715 were minted. From the John H. Clapp Collection, 1942. Earlier from the Bradford Bank, 1895." It sold for $1,980.

Clapp made his fortune in the Pennsylvania oil fields. He was a pioneer in collecting high-denomination gold by date and mint. Regional banks supplied many of his needs, as here. The interest in CC gold was moving into the fast lane. In May 1992, in their sale of the H.C. ("Heck") Dodson Collection, Mid-American Rare Coin Auctions included lot 396: "1875-CC EF-45." It sold for $13,200.

In November 2000, in the Harry W. Bass Jr. Collection, Part IV, Bowers and Merena Galleries offered lot 716: "1875-CC AU-55 PCGS. PCGS Population: 4; none finer. Die rust at butt of arrow feather. This reverse also used on 1874-CC eagles. Purchased from Pullen and Hanks on August 28, 1978." It sold for $31,050. The July 2012 sale of the Battle Born Collection by Stack's Bowers Galleries included lot 11025: "1875-CC AU-58 PCGS. PCGS Population: just 1; with a lone MS-62 finer. The NGC Census figure is also 1/1 (MS-63 finest at that service)." It sold for $63,250.

In its January 2017 FUN sale Heritage included lot 5947:

> 1875-CC AU-55 PCGS. Population: 9 in 55, 2 finer (10/16). Ex: Harold Rothenberger Collection (Superior Galleries, 2/1994), lot 2579; Private collection; Kansas dealer; Doug Winter / Spectrum Numismatics; Nevada Collection (7/1998); Doug Winter/Lee Minshull (5/1999); the [Soluna Collection].

This coin sold for $47,000. Today in the modern market the velocity of scarce and rare coins is often at high speed, as here, in contrast to decades earlier when buyers tended to keep coins for many years. As a result, for any given coin there are more purchase opportunities than ever before.

VF-20	EF-40	AU-50	AU-55	AU-58	MS-60	MS-63
$6,000	$10,000	$15,000	$35,000	$60,000	$80,000	$150,000

1876

Circulation-Strike Mintage: 687
Proof Mintage: 45

Notes regarding mintages: At this time, continuing until after December 17, 1878, gold coins did not circulate in the East or Midwest.

As for Proof coins, 20 were delivered on February 19, plus 25 more on June 13. This would indicate that the first 20 had been sold and that more were needed. How many were distributed from the second run is not known.

Walter Breen in his *United States Eagles* monograph states: "Only one pair of dies was used [for circulation strikes as well as Proofs], the date being low, heavy, distant from truncation, the 1 nearer border than the 6."

Estimated population (Mint State): *2–3.*

Estimated population (circulated grades): *50–70.*

Estimated population (Proofs): *15–20.* Very rare, but slightly more available than most eagles of the era.

Submissions certified at highest grades (as of March 2017): *PCGS:* AU-50 (12), AU-53 (10), AU-55 (4), AU-58 (2), MS-60 (1). *NGC:* AU-50 (2), AU-53 (1), AU-55 (1), MS-61 (1).

Characteristics of striking and die notes: Walter Breen in his *United States Eagles* monograph states: "Only one pair of dies was used [for circulation strikes as well as Proofs], the date being low, heavy, distant from truncation, the 1 nearer border than the 6."

Key to collecting: Another Philadelphia Mint rarity. The story of the 1876 parallels that of the 1875. Probably most extensively circulated pieces exist by virtue of Thomas L. Elder buying them from bankers to whom he did many mailings. VF is the grade typically encountered, per Harry Bass's notes compiled from the late 1960s through the mid-1990s. Today we have AU coins from modern imports.

MARKET NEWS AND COMMENTARY

In March 1911, in his sale of the William H. Woodin Collection, Thomas L. Elder offered lot 1236: "1876. Extremely rare. Only 732 pieces coined. Fine." It sold for $16. In November 1939 the William B. Hale Collection, sold by B. Max Mehl, included lot 1670: "1876 Only 732 coined. Extremely Fine; just a shade from Uncirculated, with mint luster. From the great Wm. H. Woodin Collection, 1911." It sold for $30. In November 1945 B. Max Mehl's sale of the W.A. Philpott and Henry L. Zander Collections included lot 1651: "1876 Just a shade from Uncirculated; traces of Proof surface. Has the appearance of having been struck originally as a Proof. Rare. Only 732 minted. Catalogs at $100 in Uncirculated." It sold for $58.50.

In May 1992, in their sale of the H.C. ("Heck") Dodson Collection, Mid-American Rare Coin Auctions included lot 398: "1875-CC AU-50." It sold for $15,400. The October 2001 sale by Stack's and Sotheby's of the Dallas Bank (Jeff Browning) Collection included lot 476: "1876 About Uncirculated." It sold for $12,650. In the August

2016 ANA World's Fair of Money sale Stack's Bowers Galleries offered lot 3373: "1876 AU-50 PCGS." It sold for $17,625. In its January 2017 FUN Convention sale Heritage included lot 5949: "1876 AU-50 PCGS." It sold for $22,375.

PROOF MARKET NEWS AND COMMENTARY

In January 1946 the Numismatic Gallery sale of "The World's Greatest Collection" (F.C.C. Boyd) included lot 681: "1876 Brilliant Proof." It sold for $225. In October 1998 the John J. Pittman Collection, Part II, sold by David W. Akers, included the same coin as lot 1950: "1876 Proof-63. Ex F.C.C. Boyd and Memorable sale." It sold for $37,400.

VF-20	EF-40	AU-50	AU-55	AU-58	MS-60	PF-63	PF-64	PF-65
$5,000	$10,000	$17,500	$32,500	$50,000	$75,000	$30,000	$45,000	$75,000

1876-CC

Circulation-Strike Mintage: 4,696

Notes regarding mintages: These eagles circulated at par in Nevada and elsewhere in the West at a time when gold coins were not seen in circulation in the East or Midwest (until after December 17, 1878).

Estimated population (Mint State): *None.*

Estimated population (circulated grades): *75–100.*

Submissions certified at highest grades (as of March 2017): *PCGS:* AU-50 (11), AU-53 (6), AU-55 (1), AU-58 (3). *NGC:* AU-50 (8), AU-53 (6), AU-55 (5), AU-58 (1).

Characteristics of striking and die notes: The overall workmanship for the 1876-CC is an improvement over that seen in the 1875-CC eagle, although the centers on both issues tend to be lightly struck with a more or less blunt appearance.

Key to collecting: VF and EF were the standard grades, now augmented by many AU coins that were exported when the Free Silver Movement caused fear in the hearts of foreign bankers and merchants. Carson City eagles in bank vaults in the late 1870s and early 1880s, including many coins in the AU grades, were shipped to foreign countries.

MARKET NEWS AND COMMENTARY

This is yet another scarce Liberty Head eagle that did not come into its own media-wise until the late 1900s.

In December 1908 Henry Chapman offered the David M. Kuntz Collection with lot 86: "1876 Carson City Mint. Good." It sold for $12. B. Max Mehl's June 1946 sale of the William D. Waltman, Jack Roe, and Maurice A. Ryan Collections included lot 159: "1876-CC Extremely Fine with considerable mint luster." It sold for $66.50.

In October 1982, in the Louis E. Eliasberg Collection of U.S. Gold Coins, Bowers and Ruddy Galleries offered lot 751: "1876-CC Choice Very Fine-30. From the John H. Clapp Collection, 1942. Earlier from the Bradford Bank, December 1903." It sold for $1,540.

Clapp had tellers in several banks in the oil district of western Pennsylvania look for gold coins on his want list. In May 1993 the Bowers and Merena Galleries' sale of the Stetson University Collection included lot 2071:

> 1876-CC AU-50, prooflike. Believed to be the finest known example, in turn succeeding to the throne earlier occupied by Lot 1126 of our Miller sale coin, an EF-40 PCGS. Here is a coin for the ages, a piece the quality of which may not be equaled or exceeded in your lifetime. [Sold for $29,700]

The July 2012 sale of the Battle Born Collection by Stack's Bowers Galleries included lot 11026:

> 1876-CC AU-58 PCGS. Unknown in any Mint State grade, the finest 1876-CC eagles have been certified AU-58 by PCGS and NGC. Tied for Condition Census #1 are three coins that have been graded AU-58 by PCGS. Ex Heritage's Long Beach sale of October 1994, lot 6953; Winthrop Carner; private collection; unknown intermediaries; J.J. Teaparty, to the following; our (Bowers and Merena's) sale of the Henry S. Lang Collection, July 2002, lot 632. [Sold for $57,500]

In the August 2016 ANA World's Fair of Money sale Stack's Bowers Galleries offered lot 3374: "1876-CC AU-53 PCGS." It sold for $21,150. In its January 2017 FUN sale Heritage included lot 5948: "1876-CC AU-50 NGC." It sold for $15,275.

VF-20	EF-40	AU-50	AU-55	AU-58
$5,500	$12,500	$19,500	$35,000	$55,000

1876-S

Circulation-Strike Mintage: 5,000

Notes regarding mintages: These eagles circulated at par in the West at a time when gold coins were not seen in circulation in the East or Midwest (until after December 17, 1878).

Estimated population (Mint State): *1.* Sold by RARCOA in 1972.

Estimated population (circulated grades): *70–85.*

Submissions certified at highest grades (as of March 2017): *PCGS:* AU-50 (10), AU-53 (6), AU-55 (2). *NGC:* AU-50 (8), AU-53 (6), AU-55 (7), AU-58 (1).

Key to collecting: Grades range from VF to AU, the last mainly from repatriations. The 1876-S is rare overall, but enough exist to fill the demand from specialists.

MARKET NEWS AND COMMENTARY

The low-mintage 1876-S and other eagles of its era could be found in bank vault holdings until the early 1930s. It was not until the late 1900s that they gained sufficient market value to merit more than just a brief description in auction catalogs.

In June 1934 J.C. Morgenthau & Co.'s sale of coins from the Waldo C. Newcomer Collection included lot 123: "1876-S Very Fine. Rare." It sold for $30. In the December 1944 sale of the J.F. Bell Collection Stack's included lot 762: "1876-S Extremely

Fine. Rare." It sold for $67.50. In October 1962 in the Samuel W. Wolfson Collection Stack's offered lot 716: "1876-S Very Fine and choice. Above Average. A low mint record of only 5,000 struck." It sold for $280.

The January 1986 Stack's sale of the James Walter Carter and Margaret Woolfolk Carter Collections included lot 274: "1876-S Extremely Fine, traces of luster, coppery iridescent toning. Rare in this condition." It sold for $1,265. In March 1988 the Norweb Collection sale by Bowers and Merena Galleries included lot 2210: "1876-S EF-40. Second lowest mintage San Francisco Mint issue. From J.C. Morgenthau & Co. on December 10, 1935." It sold for $2,200.

In October 1999, in the Harry W. Bass Jr. Collection, Part II, Bowers and Merena Galleries offered lot 1555: "1876-S AU-53 PCGS. PCGS Population: 3; none finer. From RARCOA's sale of February 1972, lot 973." It sold for $5,520. In the June 2013 Whitman Baltimore Expo sale Stack's Bowers Galleries offered lot 2532: "1876-S EF-45 PCGS." It sold for $7,050.

VF-20	EF-40	AU-50	AU-55	AU-58
$1,275	$1,800	$5,500	$8,500	$20,000

1877

Circulation-Strike Mintage: 797
Proof Mintage: 20

Notes regarding mintages: At this time, continuing until after December 17, 1878, gold coins did not circulate in the East or Midwest.

Proof coin deliveries commenced with ten on February 24, followed by 10 more on May 31.

Estimated population (Mint State): *4–6*.

Estimated population (circulated grades): *70–90*.

Estimated population (Proofs): *10–12*. Exceedingly rare.

Submissions certified at highest grades (as of March 2017): *PCGS:* AU-50 (9), AU-53 (3), AU-55 (9), AU-58 (5). MS-60 (1), MS-61 (2). *NGC:* AU-50 (2), AU-53 (4), AU-55 (10), AU-58 (11).

Key to collecting: EF and AU are the usually seen grades, a *quality* slightly higher than San Francisco eagles of the era, as the latter circulated more extensively. A prime rarity in the series. Most survive from Elder's searches in the 1930s plus repatriations. The proportion of survivors to the original mintage is quite high.

MARKET NEWS AND COMMENTARY

In December 1935, sale 356, Ludger Gravel and Byron Carney Collections by J.C. Morgenthau & Co. included lot 280: "1877 Very Fine and very rare." It sold for $61. In June 1936, sale 366, U.S. and Foreign Gold Coins held by J.C. Morgenthau & Co. included lot 43: "1877 Extremely Fine. Rare." It sold for $45. In May 1939, sale 399,

Rare U.S. Gold Coins by J.C. Morgenthau & Co. included lot 367: "1877 Very Fine and very rare." It sold for $23.50. In February 1944, in the Belden E. Roach Collection, B. Max Mehl offered lot 352: "1877 Very Fine, sharp. Very rare. Only 817 minted. Catalogs at $65 to $150." It sold for $57.50. In March 1945 the William A. Knapp Collection, sold by B. Max Mehl, included lot 1062: "1877 About Uncirculated with semi-proof surface. Only 817 minted. Catalogs at $100. Very rare and valuable." It sold for $69.50.

Into the modern market, in August 1980, in Auction '80, Paramount offered lot 955:

> 1877, Uncirculated 60. This is the only known Uncirculated 1877 Eagle and it is a full ten (10) points better than the next best specimen known to us! This astonishing specimen was discovered in Europe approximately three years ago. Prior to seeing this coin, the finest business strike 1877 eagle that we knew of graded only AU-50 and that specimen still ranks as the next best we've seen. All other known 1877 eagles grade only VF or EF and so this specimen is the finest known by a wide margin. In that respect, this 1877 is similar to the 1858 and thus it also ranks as one of the most important of all U.S. $10 gold coins. No amount of money could buy a duplicate since the equal of this specimen does not exist, but realistically we expect a winning bid in the $40,000-$50,000 range.

The high expectation was not realized, and it crossed the block at less than half the low estimate, at $17,500. In July 1984 the same coin reappeared in Paramount's Auction '84 as lot 949: "1877, Uncirculated 60. Superb orange gold color and fully prooflike fields. Very sharply struck and lustrous. Ex Auction '80, Lot 955." It sold for $27,500.

In the June 2014 Pre-Long Beach sale Ira and Larry Goldberg offered lot 1903: "1877 AU-55 PCGS." It sold for $12,337.50. Stack's March 2002, Mid-Winter ANA '02 sale included lot 1157: "1877 Brilliant Uncirculated." It sold for $19,550.

VF-20	EF-40	AU-50	AU-55	AU-58	MS-60	PF-63	PF-64	PF-65
$3,500	$5,500	$10,000	$13,500	$18,500	$30,000	$32,500	$45,000	$75,000

1877-CC

Circulation-Strike Mintage: 3,332

Notes regarding mintages: These eagles circulated at par in Nevada and elsewhere in the West at a time when gold coins were not seen in circulation in the East or Midwest (until after December 17, 1878). In this era it was more convenient for the Carson City Mint to convert a given amount of gold in a deposit to double eagles than to $5 and $10 coins.

Estimated population (Mint State): *1.* Reported by David W. Akers in 1980.

Estimated population (circulated grades): *50–70.*

Submissions certified at highest grades (as of March 2017): *PCGS:* AU-50 (5), AU-53 (8), AU-55 (2), AU-58 (2). *NGC:* AU-50 (4), AU-53 (4), AU-55 (3), AU-58 (1).

Characteristics of striking and die notes: Usually lightly struck at the center of the obverse.

Key to collecting: The 1877-CC eagle is one of the great rarities in the Carson City series. The scenario is familiar: VF and EF grades were standard in old-time collections. In modern times AU imports have added to the population.

MARKET NEWS AND COMMENTARY

In December 1908 Henry Chapman offered the David M. Kuntz Collection with lot 87: "1877 Carson City Mint. Good." It sold for $12.50. In April 1937 the George M. Agurs Collection sold by B. Max Mehl offered lot 1773: "1877-CC About Fine. Rare." It sold for $36. This reflects a small contingent of specialists seeking CC gold by this time. Soon, there were more coins available than there were buyers, and prices dropped—for a while. In November 1939 the William B. Hale Collection, sold by B. Max Mehl, included lot 1728: "1877-CC Extremely Fine. Rare." It sold for $24. In February 1944 in the Belden E. Roach Collection B. Max Mehl offered lot 476: "1877-CC Extremely Fine, sharp; bright luster." It sold for $31.

In June 1957 New Netherlands' 49th Sale, Eliasberg duplicates, included lot 265: "1877-CC. Very Fine; much bolder than last, but in need of cleaning. This is one of the three rarest Carson City Eagles, with a really low 3,332 struck. The Fine Davis-Graves lot (called VF) realized $65, or almost double the insipid Guide Book valuation of $37.50." It sold for $44.

Contrary to the comment, the *Guide Book* listing was not so insipid after all. In October 1962, in the Samuel W. Wolfson Collection, Stack's offered lot 720:

> 1877-CC About Uncirculated. Only the slightest trace of wear on the obverse. Comparable specimens have been offered as Uncirculated. Lacking in a number of collections currently being assembled. Collectors are now becoming aware of how very elusive these low-mintage branch mint eagles can be. Seldom offered for sale. Whenever it does appear, it always is at a new and higher price. This choice coin should command a premium bid in excess of current quotations. [Sold for $420]

The January 1986 Stack's sale of the James Walter Carter and Margaret Woolfolk Carter Collections included lot 276: "1877-CC About Uncirculated, considerable mint luster, with prooflike surface. Ex Scanlon Collection (Stack's), lot 2502, October 1973." It sold for $2,530.

The market took giant strides by the turn of the 21st century. In June 2000, in the Harry W. Bass Jr. Collection, Part III, Bowers and Merena Galleries included lot 690: "1877-CC AU-55 PCGS. PCGS Population: 2; none finer. Purchased from Stack's, October 7, 1970." It sold for $41,400.

The July 2012 sale of the Battle Born Collection by Stack's Bowers Galleries included lot 11027:

> 1877-CC AU-53 PCGS. There are no outwardly distracting abrasions, although accuracy does compel us to mention several faint pin scratches here and there in the fields. PCGS population: just 5; with a mere three finer (AU-58 finest at both PCGS and NGC; this issue is unknown in Mint State). [Sold for $40,250]

In its September 2016 Long Beach sale Heritage included lot 14158: "1877-CC AU-53 PCGS." It sold for $49,350.

VF-20	EF-40	AU-50	AU-55	AU-58
$6,500	$12,500	$27,500	$42,500	$65,000

1877-S

Circulation-Strike Mintage: 17,000

Notes regarding mintages: These eagles circulated at par in the West at a time when gold coins were not seen in circulation in the East or Midwest (until after December 17, 1878).

Estimated population (Mint State): *3*.

Estimated population (circulated grades): *150–225*.

Submissions certified at highest grades (as of March 2017): *PCGS:* AU-50 (17), AU-53 (4), AU-55 (4), AU-58 (7). *NGC:* AU-50 (29), AU-53 (33), AU-55 (8), AU-58 (1), MS-60 (1), MS-61 (2).

Characteristics of striking and die notes: Usually well struck.

Key to collecting: VF if the grade usually encountered, followed by EF and a group of repatriated AU coins. Fairly scarce in *any* grade.

MARKET NEWS AND COMMENTARY

In November 1939 the William B. Hale Collection, sold by B. Max Mehl, included lot 1736: "1877-S Microscopic S. About Uncirculated, with mint luster." It sold for $18. In the December 1944 sale of the J.F. Bell Collection Stack's included lot 763: "1877-S Extremely Fine." It sold for $40. In October 1962, in the Samuel W. Wolfson Collection, Stack's offered lot 719: "1877-S Very Fine. Some original mint luster." It sold for $55.

In June 2000, in the Harry W. Bass Jr. Collection, Part III, Bowers and Merena Galleries included lot 691: "1877-S AU-50. Purchased from Stanley Kesselman, November 16, 1970; ex B. Max Mehl, William C. Atwater." It sold for $2,875.

VF-20	EF-40	AU-50	AU-55	AU-58	MS-60
$850	$900	$1,800	$4,500	$11,000	$25,000

1878

Circulation-Strike Mintage: 73,780
Proof Mintage: 20

Notes regarding mintages: After December 17, 1878, gold coins were available at face value (in terms of paper money and silver coins) in the East and Midwest, the first time since late December, 1861.

There were 20 Proofs delivered on February 9.

Estimated population (Mint State): *250–350.*

Estimated population (circulated grades): *500–700.* EF is about par for the typical specimen. Slightly scarce, but one of the more readily available issues of the era.

Estimated population (Proofs): *8–10.* Exceedingly rare.

Submissions certified at highest grades (as of March 2017): *PCGS:* MS-63 (7), MS-64 (9), MS-65 (1). *NGC:* MS-63 (08), MS-64 (8).

Key to collecting: This is the earliest date of the type for which the Mint State population is at a generous level (the runner-up being 1874). The population includes some at the choice level. Most came from overseas holdings in the 1990s. Before that time such pieces were rare. The late 1870s were the dawn of the era in which the Free Silver Movement caused massive exports of American gold coins (see earlier text).

MARKET NEWS AND COMMENTARY

New Netherlands Coin Co.'s 46th sale, Dr. Clarence W. Peake Collection, June 1955, included lot 156: "1878. About Uncirculated. Uncommon so choice." It sold for $24. The comment is reflective of the general non-availability of the 1878 in Mint State at that time.

That soon changed. In May 1993 the Bowers and Merena Galleries' sale of the Stetson University Collection included lot 2076: "1878 MS-62 to 63. Sharply struck and very lustrous. Possibly the finest known business strike, exceeding by a comfortable margin any others we have seen or have observed." It sold for $9,350.

The cataloger of that coin forgot about the same firm's offering of a finer specimen in the Byron Johnson Collection (January 1989). In November 2000, in the Harry W. Bass Jr. Collection, Part IV, Bowers and Merena Galleries offered lot 724: "1878 MS-64 PCGS. Purchased from Douglas Weaver on September 26, 1973." It sold for $4,830.

PROOF MARKET NEWS AND COMMENTARY

The mintage of just 20 Proofs, similar to that of recent years, reflects the lack of numismatic interest in Proof gold at the time. This is hard to imagine today.

VF-20	EF-40	AU-50	AU-55	AU-58	MS-60	MS-63	PF-63	PF-64	PF-65
$650	$675	$700	$750	$850	$1,100	$5,500	$27,500	$45,000	$75,000

1878-CC

Circulation-Strike Mintage: 3,244

Notes regarding mintages: These eagles circulated at par in the West at a time when gold coins were not seen in circulation in the East or Midwest after December 17 of this year.

Estimated population (Mint State): *1.* Reported by NGC, possibly the prooflike coin listed in Paramount's August 1974 fixed price list.

Estimated population (circulated grades): *60–90.*

Submissions certified at highest grades (as of March 2017): *PCGS:* AU-50 (5), AU-53 (6), AU-55 (7), AU-58 (1). *NGC:* AU-50 (6), AU-53 (5), AU-55 (7), AU-58 (3), MS-61 (1).

Die data: The obverse die seen has the logotype very low and several times closer to the denticles than to the neck truncation. *A raised bar is seen on the neck of Miss Liberty below the lowest curl.* On the reverse the CC letters are large, with the rightmost being directly beneath the arrow feather tip.

Characteristics of striking and die notes: Some lightness of striking at the central hair features and obverse stars is normal for 1878-CC. On the reverse some lightness is seen on the eagle's feathers at lower left and on the highest arrow feather. The reverse typically shows a clash mark from the eagle's wing to the lower beak.

Key to collecting: Yet another elusive Carson City eagle, a key issue in the series. VF and EF were the usual grades of years ago, later added to by AU repatriations.

MARKET NEWS AND COMMENTARY

In February 1944, in the Belden E. Roach Collection, B. Max Mehl offered lot 477: "1878-CC Extremely Fine. Very scarce." It sold for $28.50. In December of the same year in the sale of the J.F. Bell Collection Stack's included lot 729: "1878-CC Only 3,244 coins struck. Extremely Fine." It sold for $80.

In June 1957 New Netherlands' 49th sale, Eliasberg duplicates, included lot 268: "1878-CC. Very Fine, though marked EF. A very rare date, rarer than the 1877-CC. Exceptionally hard to find in decent shape; Henry P. Graves only had a Good to VG one, which managed to bring $65. None in the Memorable or Peake or Melish." It sold for $55.

In October 1962, in the Samuel W. Wolfson Collection, Stack's offered lot 723: "1878-CC Very Fine. Generally available only when great collections such as this are dispersed." It sold for $325. In October 1982, in the Louis E. Eliasberg Collection of U.S. Gold Coins, Bowers and Ruddy Galleries offered lot 757: "1878-CC Very Fine-20. Exceedingly elusive in all grades." It sold for $1,760.

The market headed upward, and in March 1988 the Norweb Collection, Part II, sale by Bowers and Merena Galleries included lot 2215: "1878-CC EF-45." It sold for $5,060. In May 1993 the Bowers and Merena Galleries' sale of the Stetson University Collection included lot 2077: "1878-CC EF-45. Sharply struck and very attractive. Condition Census specimen." It sold for $13,750. Accounts such as this reflect the usual VF or EF grades available at the time.

The July 2012 sale of the Battle Born Collection by Stack's Bowers Galleries included lot 11028: "1878-CC AU-58 NGC. NGC Census: just 3; with a lone MS-63 finer, and also the only Mint State 1878-CC eagle certified. The highest graded examples of this issue listed at PCGS are AU-55s. Ex Midwestern collection; and Heritage's FUN Signature Sale of January 2003, lot 8808." It sold for $80,500.

In its September 2016 Long Beach sale Heritage included lot 14159: "1878-CC AU-55 NGC." It sold for $64,625.

VF-20	EF-40	AU-50	AU-55	AU-58	MS-60
$6,500	$11,500	$23,500	$40,000	$70,000	$125,000

1878-S

Circulation-Strike Mintage: 26,100

Notes regarding mintages: These eagles circulated at par in the West at a time when gold coins were not seen in circulation in the East or Midwest after December 17 of this year.

Estimated population (Mint State): *5–7.* Very rare. Unknown in this grade until the 1990s.

Estimated population (circulated grades): *190–220.*

Submissions certified at highest grades (as of March 2017): *PCGS:* AU-55 (14), AU-58 (7), MS-60 (1). *NGC:* AU-55 (23), AU-58 (3), MS-60 (3), MS-61 (1), MS-64 (1).

Key to collecting: VF was the usually seen decades. This issue was very elusive until the late 1900s when quite a few were located in overseas bank holdings. Most were EF or so and had been shipped abroad in the eve of the Free Silver Movement.

MARKET NEWS AND COMMENTARY

In June 1934 J.C. Morgenthau & Co.'s sale of coins from the Waldo C. Newcomer Collection included lot 125: "1878-S Very Fine." It sold for $20. Newcomer had collected mintmarked high-denomination gold for many years, taking most coins from bank holdings in the early 1900s. The December 1944 sale of the J.F. Bell Collection held by Stack's included lot 764: "1878-S Extremely Fine." It sold for $67.50.

In November 1945 B. Max Mehl's sale of the W.A. Philpott and Henry L. Zander Collections included lot 1707: "1878-S Fine. Scarce." It sold for $17.25, which was less than the melt value.

New Netherlands Coin Co.'s 46th sale, Dr. Clarence W. Peake Collection, June 1955, included lot 157: "1878-S. Almost Extremely Fine. Extra nice. For the record, superior to the W.G.C. Atwater, Green (Very Good), Menjou, Davis-Graves coins, among others. Another "unimportant" item, until you need it." It sold for $27.50.

The preceding is yet another reflection of the market of long ago when VF and EF were the grades in leading collections. The author attended the Peake sale, an exciting event with a room filled with bidders and spectators. The January 1986 Stack's sale of the James Walter Carter and Margaret Woolfolk Carter Collections included lot 281: "1879 About Uncirculated, frosty mint luster." It sold for $352. In March 1988 the Norweb Collection, Part II, sale by Bowers and Merena Galleries included lot 2216: "1878-S EF-45." It sold for $1,540. In March 2004 American Numismatic Rarities Whitman Expo sale included lot 1555: "1878-S AU-58 NGC." It sold for $2,350.

VF-20	EF-40	AU-50	AU-55	AU-58	MS-60	MS-63
$850	$950	$1,750	$2,000	$3,500	$10,500	$25,000

1879

Circulation-Strike Mintage: 384,670
Proof Mintage: 30

Notes regarding mintages: The following Proofs were delivered as part of full gold Proof sets. These figures come directly from original Mint records as studied by R.W. Julian:[27] Second quarter: 7; Third quarter: 4; Fourth quarter: 10.

Deliveries (per Walter Breen): 20 were delivered on January 25 and 10 more on November 22. It may be the case that only a few of the second shipment were ever distributed.

Proofs with date logotype low, the 1 in 1879 is about twice as close to the denticles as to the neck.

Estimated population (Mint State): 600. While some of these were imported in the 1980s and 1990s, the 1879 is one date that was fairly available in Mint State before that time. In his 1980 study David W. Akers located 20 auction appearances, a generous number for a $10 coin up to this point. The floodgates opened wide as the Free Silver Movement continued to result in massive quantities of high-denomination gold coins being shipped abroad. Repatriation of these began large scale in the 1950s and has continued to modern times. In compiling this book I realized that my estimated population of 1879 and certain eagles made decades ago had to be multiplied several times over!

Estimated population (circulated grades): 3,000+.

Estimated population (Proofs): 8–10. Exceedingly rare, one of the most elusive Proofs from a decade in which all Proofs are great rarities.

Submissions certified at highest grades (as of March 2017): *PCGS:* MS-64 (12), MS-65 (1), MS-66 (2). *NGC:* MS-64 (10), MS-65 (1), MS-67 (1). Large numbers of coins have been certified in lower Mint State grades.

Die data: "1879, 9 Over 8," the so-called overdate (Breen-6993), is simply a repunched date in the view of the author and consultants.

Key to collecting: Plentiful in the context of the $10 series. AU and Mint State coins are in good supply, far more than enough to fill the demand. From about this year onward, the market value of eagles with large mintage quantities is partially dependent on the price of gold bullion, rather than on numismatic demand. In view of repatriations yielding many high-grade coins modern auction listings are not extensively cited.

MARKET NEWS AND COMMENTARY

In June 1936, sale 366, U.S. and Foreign Gold Coins held by J.C. Morgenthau & Co. included lot 44: "1879 Extremely Fine." It sold for $18.50. In November 1939 the William B. Hale Collection, sold by B. Max Mehl, included lot 1671: "1879 Uncirculated; frosty mint surface." It sold for $18.50. An early offering of a Mint State coin.

In October 1982, in the Louis E. Eliasberg Collection of U.S. Gold Coins sale, Bowers and Ruddy Galleries offered lot 759: "1879 AU-50 obverse, AU-55." It sold for $770.

In October 1999, in the Harry W. Bass Jr. Collection, Part II, Bowers and Merena Galleries offered lot 1570: "1879/8 Breen-6993. Overdate. MS-61. This variety, which may simply be a *repunching*, rather than an overdate, is what Walter Breen called the 1879/8. Breen notes the issue is extremely rare. From N.K.S. May 25, 1971." It sold for $6,325.

At the time many buyers compiled want lists based on Breen's 1988 Encyclopedia. Later, this "overdate" was dismissed by specialists.

The Stack's Bowers Galleries' March 2014 Whitman Baltimore Expo included lot 6273: "1879 MS-64 PCGS." It sold for $5,875.

VF-20	EF-40	AU-50	AU-55	AU-58	MS-60	MS-63	PF-63	PF-64	PF-65
$650	$675	$700	$775	$850	$1,000	$4,000	$25,000	$37,500	$65,000

1879-CC

Circulation-Strike Mintage: 1,762

Estimated population (Mint State): 2. The Bell Collection coin (1944) and an example (perhaps the same as the Bell coin?) offered by Paramount in 1973 seem to be the only possibilities.

Estimated population (circulated grades): *50–60*.

Submissions certified at highest grades (as of March 2017): *PCGS:* AU-50 (6), AU-53 (4), AU-55 (3), AU-58 (1). *NGC:* AU-53 (5), AU-55 (2), AU-58 (5), MS-62 (1).

Die data: The date logotype is slightly high; the 1 in 1879 is closer to the neck than to the denticles.

Characteristics of striking and die notes: Usually weakly struck at borders and at the obverse center, but there are exceptions.

Key to collecting: VF was the typical grade seen before the return of coins from overseas holdings. The 1879-CC is a rarity of formidable proportions, in about the same league as the more famous 1870-CC of significantly higher mintage. Key to the eagle series, even more than a coin with this population might have—due to the additional popularity of collecting Carson City coins.

MARKET NEWS AND COMMENTARY

The absolute rarity of the 1879-CC precluded it from being in many early auctions. When it hit its stride market-wise in the late 1900s it was typical for some auction descriptions to run into hundreds of words. Sesquipedalianism ran rampant. Of course, a lot of this provided interesting readers for catalog holders.[28]

In May 1939 in sale 399, Rare U.S. Gold Coins, J.C. Morgenthau & Co. included lot 371: "1879-CC Very Fine." It sold for $26. In the December 1944 sale of the J.F. Bell Collection Stack's included lot 730: "1879-CC Only 1,762 coins struck. Uncirculated. Rare." It sold for $100. This is the highest-grade auction citation located up to this point in time. Wonder where this gem is today?

In January 1946 the Numismatic Gallery sale of "The World's Greatest Collection" (F.C.C. Boyd) included lot 835: "1879-CC Very Fine." It sold for $40. In June 1946, in the William Cutler Atwater Collection, B. Max Mehl offered lot 1322: "1879-CC Extremely Fine, near Uncirculated with considerable luster. Record of $125 for a coin that was cataloged as Extremely Fine." It sold for $125.

In April 1956 Abe Kosoff's sale of the Thomas G. Melish and Clinton W. Hester Collections included lot 2475: "1879-CC Very Fine, scarce." It sold for $55. In June 1957 New Netherlands' 49th sale, Eliasberg duplicates, included lot 272: "1879-CC. About Very Fine. Weakly struck, especially about the borders. Technically, the rarest Carson City Mint [gold coin], in terms of number made." It sold for $70.

In October 1962, in the Samuel W. Wolfson Collection, Stack's offered lot 726: "1879-CC Extremely Fine. Many of the great collections offered in the last decade did not have this date and mint. It may be many years before another opportunity presents itself to acquire this rare coin." It sold for $1,300.

In October 1982 the Louis E. Eliasberg Collection of U.S. Gold Coins, sold by Bowers and Ruddy Galleries, offered lot 760: "1879-CC Choice Very Fine-30. From the John H. Clapp Collection, 1942. Earlier from the Bradford Bank, 1903." It sold for $3,575. In November 2000, in the Harry W. Bass Jr. Collection, Part IV, Bowers and Merena Galleries offered lot 729: "1879-CC AU-55 PCGS. PCGS Population: 2; none finer. Struck from same reverse die as Lot 725, an 1878-CC eagle. From our sale of the Fairfield Collection, October 1977, lot 1823." It sold for $28,750.

The July 2012 sale of the Battle Born Collection by Stack's Bowers Galleries included lot 11029: "1879-CC. AU-58 NGC. NGC Census: just 5; with a lone MS-62 finer (this is the only Mint State 1879-CC Liberty eagle known to both PCGS and NGC." It sold for $41,687.50.

In its January 2017 FUN sale Heritage included lot 5951: "1879-CC AU-58 NGC. Census: 5 in 58, 1 finer (10/16)." It sold for $56,400.

VF-20	EF-40	AU-50	AU-55	AU-58
$20,000	$25,000	$40,000	$55,000	$95,000

1879-O

Circulation-Strike Mintage: 1,500

Notes regarding mintages: The New Orleans facility, idle since early 1861, was refurbished in 1878 and reopened for the coining business in 1879, at which time its principal activity was making Morgan silver dollars. In addition, small quantities of $10 and $20 pieces were struck.

Estimated population (Mint State): *3–4.*

Estimated population (circulated grades): *90–110.*

Submissions certified at highest grades (as of March 2017): *PCGS:* AU-55 (5), AU-58 (7), MS-61 (1). *NGC:* AU-55 (7), AU-58 (1), MS-60 (1), MS-61 (1).

Key to collecting: VF and EF are the grades usually seen in old-time listings, later augmented by imported coins graded at the AU and Mint State levels. A key issue.

MARKET NEWS AND COMMENTARY

In March 1911, in his sale of the William H. Woodin Collection, Thomas L. Elder offered lot 1281: "1879-O Fine. Coinage only 1,500!" It sold for $21.

In June 1946, in the William Cutler Atwater Collection, B. Max Mehl offered lot 1536: "1879-O. Extremely Fine with traces of semi-proof surface. Only 1500 minted. Rare. Not in the Bell Collection. Catalogs up to $75. Another "sleeper." A much underrated coin. While it catalogs for only $75, collectors who know, value it at $200 to $250."

"Collectors who know" must have been sleeping as the coin sold for just $87.50. In October 1947, in the H.R. Lee Collection (Eliasberg duplicates), Stack's offered lot 1596: "1879-O Extremely Fine." It sold for $100.

In June 1957 New Netherlands' 49th Sale, Eliasberg duplicates, included lot 270:

> 1879-O. Extremely Fine. Unusually clean and a beautifully struck piece; a sharp impression from new dies retaining polish. This is one of the major rarities in the series. First of all, only 1,500 were coined when the New Orleans Mint reopened (after an eighteen year lapse in business occasioned by the Civil War), making it one of the seven rarest Liberty Heads. Second, such important offerings as Bell, Memorable, Peake and Melish lacked this mint mark in any condition. Third, we have been unable to locate a better specimen in any auction sale since the 1890s. The best one found, possibly this very lot, brought $87.50 in the Atwater sale, 1946. Davis-Graves had a nicked-up VF coin, which was bid up to $150. Dealer Jim Kelly was right, when he said in the 1956 Chi-ANA catalog, in describing an esthetically inferior impression, "worth double its catalog value of $100." [Sold for $165]

Again, here is a description reflective of the grade rarity of Extremely Fine at the time, without a clue that a couple of generations later there would be AU coins available. Cataloger Walter Breen had studied only a tiny percentage of auction sales since the 1890 and for early years had concentrated only on "name" sales. Fewer than 10 percent of the catalogs of Thomas L. Elder, New York City's most prominent coin auctioneer in the first three decades of the 20th century, had been consulted, for example.

In October 1962, in the Samuel W. Wolfson Collection, Stack's offered lot 727:

> 1879-O Extremely Fine. Sight even wear over entire coin. Above average. Here, we think, is a "sleeper", especially in this choice condition. A number of the large collections that have been offered at auction in recent years did not include this very rare date and mintmark. The value of the coin has more than doubled in the last few years. While the number of serious collectors tripled, the supply dwindled to just about nil. We honestly doubt if 50 pieces are in collectors' hands today. [Sold for $520]

Emery May Holden Norweb was the buyer of the Wolfson coin. In March 1988 the Norweb Collection, Part II, sale by Bowers and Merena Galleries included lot 2219: "1879-O AU-50. Possibly the second or third finest known example of this issue, for just one Uncirculated coin is known and apparently only one other AU example can be traced. From New Netherlands' sale of June 1957, lot 270." It sold for $7,425.

In May 1992, in their sale of the H.C. ("Heck") Dodson Collection, Mid-American Rare Coin Auctions included lot 408: "1879-O AU-55." It sold for $14,850. In October 1998 the John J. Pittman Collection, Part II, sold by David W. Akers, included lot 1953: "1879-O EF-40. Ex Adolphe Menjou Collection, 1950." It sold for $7,700.

In October 1999, in the Harry W. Bass Jr. Collection, Part II, Bowers and Merena Galleries offered lot 1574: "1879-O AU-55 PCGS. PCGS Population: 6; 1 finer (AU-58). From Stack's sale of the Delp Collection, November 1972, lot 812." It sold for $10,350. This coin was earlier in the Winner F. Delp Collection, Stack's, November 1971, as lot 812.

In July 2005 the American Numismatic Rarities sale of the William H. LaBelle Sr. Collection included lot 310: "1879-O AU-58 PCGS. From the Heritage sale of the Galveston Collection." It sold for $19,550. Stack's January 2007 Americana sale included lot 5251: "1879-O MS-61 NGC." It sold for $52,900. In its January 2017 FUN Convention sale Heritage included lot 5952: "1879-O AU-58 NGC." It sold for $49,350.

VF-20	EF-40	AU-50	AU-55	AU-58	MS-60
$9,500	$17,500	$25,000	$35,000	$55,000	$75,000

1879-S

Circulation-Strike Mintage: 224,000

Estimated population (Mint State): 200–300. Grades are mostly MS-60 to MS-62. Most turned up in the late 1900s from overseas hoards.

Estimated population (circulated grades): 1,300–1,500.

Submissions certified at highest grades (as of March 2017): PCGS: MS-63 (26), MS-63 (5), MS-65 (1). **NGC:** MS-63 (3), MS-64 (1).

Key to collecting: EF and AU grades are regularly seen, and Mint State coins are not hard to find.

MARKET NEWS AND COMMENTARY

In March 1907 the David S. Wilson Collection, sold by S. Hudson Chapman, offered lot 35: "1879-S Uncirculated. Mint luster." It sold for $12. In May 1939, sale 399, Rare U.S. Gold Coins by J.C. Morgenthau & Co. included lot 373: "1879-S Very Fine." It sold for $16.50.

In November 1939 the William B. Hale Collection, sold by B. Max Mehl, included lot 1737: "1879-S Extremely Fine." It sold for $18.

In October 1982, in the Louis E. Eliasberg Collection of U.S. Gold Coins, Bowers and Ruddy Galleries, offered lot 762: "1879-S Select Brilliant Uncirculated, MS-63." It sold for $1,760. In June 2000, in the Harry W. Bass Jr. Collection, Part III, Bowers and Merena Galleries included lot 700: "1879-S MS-63. From Stack's sale of the Miles Collection, October 1968, lot 711." It sold for $4,255.

The Stack's Bowers Galleries' October 2015 Rarities Auction included lot 76: "1879-S MS-63 PCGS." It sold for $4,700.

VF-20	EF-40	AU-50	AU-55	AU-58	MS-60	MS-63
$650	$675	$700	$800	$850	$1,150	$6,000

1880

Circulation-Strike Mintage: 1,644,840
Proof Mintage: 36

Notes regarding mintages: The following Proofs were delivered as part of full gold Proof sets. These figures come directly from original Mint records as studied by R.W. Julian:[29] First quarter: 17; Third quarter: 5; Fourth quarter: 10.

Deliveries (per Walter Breen): February 14: 20 and September 16: 16.

Estimated population (Mint State): 2,000+. The first really *plentiful* Mint State eagle. Most are from overseas hoards in the late 1900s. Typical grades are MS-60 to MS-63. Higher-grade coins are rare. Again, this is one of the many issues from the late 1870s onward that were exported when foreign banks and treasuries feared that Americans would try to pay their debts in silver dollars.

Estimated population (circulated grades): 12,500+.

Estimated population (Proofs): 10–14. Extremely rare.

Submissions certified at highest grades (as of March 2017): PCGS: MS-62 (328), MS-63 (71), MS-64 (20). **NGC:** MS-62 (439), MS-63 (41), MS-64 (12), MS-65 (2).

Key to collecting: Common in any grade desired, through lower Mint State levels. In view of repatriations yielding many high-grade coins modern auction listings are not extensively cited. In lower grades the value of this and other high-mintage eagles is tied into the bullion price of gold.

MARKET NEWS AND COMMENTARY

In July 1937, sale 379, Walter P. Innes Jr. Collection conducted by J.C. Morgenthau & Co. included lot 65: "1880 Fine." It sold for $16.25. Melt value was $16.45. New Netherlands Coin Co.'s 46th sale, Dr. Clarence W. Peake Collection, June 1955, included lot 160: "1880. Almost Uncirculated." It sold for $21.

In November 1955 Stack's sale of the Farish-Baldenhofer Collection included lot 1464: "1880 Very Fine." It sold for $19.

In October 1982, in the Louis E. Eliasberg Collection of U.S. Gold Coins, Bowers and Ruddy Galleries offered lot 763: "1880 Choice Brilliant Uncirculated, MS-65." It sold for $3,300. This coin later appeared in various sales. In August 2013 the Stack's Bowers Galleries' ANA World's Fair of Money sale included lot 4517: "1880 MS-65 NGC." It sold for $19,975. In the August 2016 ANA World's Fair of Money sale Stack's Bowers Galleries offered lot 3471: "1880 MS-64+ PCGS." It sold for $6,178.75.

VF-20	EF-40	AU-50	AU-55	AU-58	MS-60	MS-63	PF-63	PF-64	PF-65
$650	$675	$725	$800	$825	$950	$1,800	$22,500	$35,000	$60,000

1880-CC

Circulation-Strike Mintage: 11,190

Estimated population (Mint State): *20–26.*

Estimated population (circulated grades): *250–350.*

Submissions certified at highest grades (as of March 2017): *PCGS:* MS-60 (2), MS-61 (1). *NGC:* MS-60 (6), MS-61 (1), MS-62 (2).

Die data: A single obverse die was combined with three reverse dies for this issue (per Doug Winter).

Key to collecting: VF is the grade typically seen from old-time holdings (such as pieces found by Thomas L. Elder in the 1930s); those in imports from overseas holdings in the late 1900s tend to be a notch or two higher in grade. The 1880-CC is one of the few relatively available Carson City eagles up to this date.

MARKET NEWS AND COMMENTARY

In November 1945 B. Max Mehl's sale of the W.A. Philpott and Henry L. Zander Collections included lot 1725: "1880-CC Extremely Fine with considerable mint luster. Listed at $35 in Very Fine." It sold for $25.

In October 1982, in the Louis E. Eliasberg Collection of U.S. Gold Coins, Bowers and Ruddy Galleries offered lot 764: "1880-CC EF-40." It sold for $990. The January 1986 Stack's sale of the James Walter Carter and Margaret Woolfolk Carter Collections included lot 287: "1880-CC Brilliant Uncirculated, full luster, with prooflike surface. Ex 1976 ANA Convention Sale (Stack's), lot 2510, October 1973." It sold for $1,650.

In May 1993 the Bowers and Merena Galleries' sale of the Stetson University Collection included lot 2083:

> 1880-CC AU-58. An outstanding example of an issue which is typically seen in significantly lower grades. We point to the EF-40 Miller Sale coin and the similar Eliasberg specimen as examples. New to the market, and previously unrecorded in any literature, this 1880-CC will undoubtedly solicit enthusiastic bidding competition. When all is said and done the owner will, as is the case with so many of the pieces here, have a numismatic treasure—a coin of which few comparable examples exist. At this point it may be appropriate to give a word concerning catalogue listings. The *Guide Book of United States Coins* casually lists MS-60 as being worth $2,750, which is very misleading, as it indicates that such pieces exist. More factual is the designation in a recent PCGS Population Report that the highest specimen graded by PCGS is AU-53 (and only one was found at that level), with no Mint State coins at all accounted for. Moreover, in David Akers' study he noted that when seen, the typical coin is apt to VF or EF, and that when the study was conducted, 1980, he had seen two coins described as Mint State, "Neither of which was especially choice." [Sold for $10,450]

Matters changed dramatically in later years when large quantities of eagles were repatriated from foreign holdings. The market held strong, however, as Carson City gold coins increased in popularity. In the March 2010 Whitman Expo sale Stack's Bowers Galleries offered lot 7625: "1880-CC AU-50 PCGS. Ex Stack's June 2013 sale, earlier Stack's Wayman Collection sale 1981." It sold for $3,450.

The July 2012 sale of the Battle Born Collection by Stack's Bowers Galleries included lot 11030: "1880-CC. Winter 1-B. MS-61 NGC. Ex Ira and Larry Goldberg's California sale, October 2000, lot 1045; Doug Winter and Lee Minshull; and the Nevada Collection." It sold for $16,100. In its September 2016 Long Beach sale Heritage included lot 14161: "1880-CC MS-60 NGC. NGC and PCGS combined record 14 submissions, none finer than MS-62 (7/16)." It sold for $42,300.

VF-20	EF-40	AU-50	AU-55	AU-58	MS-60
$1,650	$2,000	$2,750	$5,500	$10,000	$20,000

1880-O

Circulation-Strike Mintage: 9,200

Estimated population (Mint State): 20–26. The number of known Mint State coins, while still small, has multiplied several times in recent decades due to repatriations.

Estimated population (circulated grades): *225–275.*

Submissions certified at highest grades (as of March 2017): *PCGS:* MS-61 (2), MS-62 (1), MS-64 (1). *NGC:* MS-61 (4), MS-62 (2), MS-64 (1).

Key to collecting: VF and EF were typical grades years ago. In his 1967 *United States Eagles* Walter Breen noted, "I have not lately seen one in fully Unc. grade, though EFs are known."

MARKET NEWS AND COMMENTARY

In March 1911, in his sale of the William H. Woodin Collection, Thomas L. Elder offered lot 1282: "1880-O Fine." It sold for $10.50. In November 1939 the William B. Hale Collection, sold by B. Max Mehl, included the same coin as lot 1717: "1880-O Small O high. Extremely Fine. From the Woodin Sale, in 1911." It sold for $27.50. The December 1944 sale of the J.F. Bell Collection Stack's included lot 706: "1880-O About Uncirculated. Scarce." It sold for $75.

In November 1945 B. Max Mehl's sale of the W.A. Philpott and Henry L. Zander Collections included lot 1692: "1880-O Very Fine." It sold for $23. In June 1957 New Netherlands' 49th sale, Eliasberg duplicates, included lot 274: "1880-O. Extremely Fine. The Very Fine one of H.P. Graves sold for $60 over three years ago. None in any grade in the 1948 Memorable sale." It sold for $26.

Years later in the June 1995 Stack's sale of the Vander Zanden Collection and the Yale University Consignment included lot 821: "1880-O Choice About Uncirculated, very close to full Mint State." It sold for $2,200.

In October 1998, in the John J. Pittman Collection sale, Part II, David Akers offered lot 1956: "1880-O, Extremely Fine. Purchased from James Kelly for $42.50, date of purchase unknown." It sold for $1,320. In its 1999 ANA Convention sale Heritage offered lot 8132: "1880-O MS-62 PCGS. The 1880-O is the most available of the trio of scarce New Orleans eagles struck between 1880 and 1882. We believe that from an original mintage of 9,200 pieces around 200-250 examples are extant." It sold for $27,600.

In June 2000, in the Harry W. Bass Jr. Collection, Part III, Bowers and Merena Galleries included lot 705: "1880-O AU-58. Purchased from Bob Roth through Stack's, October 11, 1967." It sold for $2,875.

In the November 2016 Whitman Expo sale Stack's Bowers Galleries offered lot 2156: "1880-O MS-60 NGC." It sold for $17,625.

VF-20	EF-40	AU-50	AU-55	AU-58	MS-60
$1,050	$1,250	$2,000	$3,000	$4,500	$10,000

1880-S

Circulation-Strike Mintage: 506,250

Estimated population (Mint State): 1,250+. Most have been brought back from overseas in recent decades, but there were quite a few around years ago as well.

Estimated population (circulated grades): 4,000+.

Submissions certified at highest grades (as of March 2017): *PCGS:* MS-62 (173), MS-63 (61), MS-64 (7). *NGC:* MS-62 (249), MS-63 (42), MS-64 (3), MS-66 (1).

Key to collecting: EF coins are usually seen, but there are many AU and Mint State coins around. Easy to find. In lower grades the value of this and other high-mintage eagles is tied into the bullion price of gold.

MARKET NEWS AND COMMENTARY

In March 1907 the David S. Wilson Collection, sold by S. Hudson Chapman, offered lot 36: "1880-S Uncirculated. Mint luster." It sold for $13. In the December 1944 sale of the J.F. Bell Collection Stack's included lot 766: "1880-S Uncirculated." It sold for $31.

In January 1946 the Numismatic Gallery sale of "The World's Greatest Collection" (F.C.C. Boyd) included lot 790: "1880-S Uncirculated." It sold for $40. In April 1956, in his sale of the Thomas G. Melish Collection, Abe Kosoff offered lot 2482: "1880-S. Small S. About Uncirculated." It sold for $21. Also lot 2483: "1880-S. Minute S over right side of N. Date centered. Extremely Fine." It sold for $21. Also lot 2484: "1880-S. Similar but date is low. Very Fine." It sold for $21. Also lot 2485: "1880-S. Minute S farther right. Very Fine, lustrous." It sold for $21.

VF-20	EF-40	AU-50	AU-55	AU-58	MS-60	MS-63
$650	$675	$725	$775	$825	$900	$2,250

1881

Circulation-Strike Mintage: 3,877,220
Proof Mintage: 40

Estimated population (Mint State):
15,000+. Discovered in quantity overseas
in the late 1900s, and thus common today.
Most pieces are in lower-grade ranges, MS-60 to MS-62, and are often extensively bag-marked. However, there are many around at the MS-63 level as well, but fewer higher.

Estimated population (circulated grades): *25,000+.*

Estimated population (Proofs): *12–16.* Very rare.

Submissions certified at highest grades (as of March 2017): *PCGS:* MS-61 (2,575), MS-62 (2,209), MS-63 (400), MS-64 (36); MS-65 (1). **NGC:** MS-61 (6,291), MS-62 (3,872), MS-63 (699), MS-64 (34), MS-65 (2). An expanded listing of grades is given here to illustrate that among typical repatriated coins, the vast majority are bagmarked and in lower Mint State levels, due to being frequently counted and jostled in foreign banks and treasuries.

Key to collecting: Common due to overseas hoards. Most are AU and Mint State. Common in any grade desired, through lower Mint State levels. In view of repatriations yielding many high-grade coins modern auction listings are not extensively cited. In lower grades the value of this and other high-mintage eagles is tied into the bullion price of gold.

MARKET NEWS AND COMMENTARY

In July 1937, sale 379, the Walter P. Innes Jr. Collection conducted by J.C. Morgenthau & Co. included lot 67: "1881 Fine." It sold for $16.25. New Netherlands Coin Co.'s 46th sale, Dr. Clarence W. Peake Collection, June 1955, included lot 163: "1881. Not quite Extremely Fine. Difficult to find perfect." It sold for $20. In April 1956, in his sale of the Thomas G. Melish Collection, Abe Kosoff offered lot 2486: "1881. Date centered, a bit left. Extremely Fine." It sold for $21. Also lot 2487: "1881. Similar. Breaks wing to S, F to wing, AMERICA, TEN D. About Uncirculated." It sold for $23. Also lot 2488: "1881. Similar. No break to S. Very Fine." It sold for $21. Also lot 2489: "1881. Date low. Very Fine." It sold for $21. Also lot 2490: "1881. Similar. Breaks at NI, ERICA, and TEN D. Very Fine." It sold for $21. Also lot 2491: "1881. Similar. Breaks at AMERICA, TEN D. Very Fine." It sold for $21. Also lot 2492: "1881. Date low, a bit left. Very Fine." It sold for $21. Also lot 2493: "1881. Date high. Very Fine." It sold for $21. Also lot 2494: "1881. Similar. Breaks at ICA, U. TEN D. Very Fine." It sold for $21.

VF-20	EF-40	AU-50	AU-55	AU-58	MS-60	MS-63	MS-65	PF-63	PF-64	PF-65
$650	$675	$725	$775	$800	$850	$1,200	$10,000	$22,500	$32,500	$55,000

1881-CC

Circulation-Strike Mintage: 24,015

Estimated population (Mint State): *80–110.* Typically encountered grades are low Mint State, MS-60 to MS-62, often extensively bagmarked. Most of these were imported in the 1980s and 1990s. Earlier, the 1881-CC was quite rare in Mint State. Today this is the earliest-dated Carson City eagle that in Mint State appears on the market frequently.

Estimated population (circulated grades): *500–700.*

Submissions certified at highest grades (as of March 2017): *PCGS:* MS-60 (2), MS-61 (12), MS-62 (10). *NGC:* MS-60 (12), MS-61 (22), MS-62 (11), MS-64 (1).

Die data: All were struck from a single die pair.

Characteristics of striking and die notes: On later die states a fairly bold die crack bisects the base of the date and extends toward the border after the final digit 1.

Key to collecting: VF and EF are the grades generally reported in old-time collections. Today many AU and lower-range Mint State coins are available from imports. This is a Carson City eagle for just about anyone—quite plentiful in a relative sense.

Market News and Commentary

In November 1939 the William B. Hale Collection, sold by B. Max Mehl, included lot 1729: "1881-CC Just a shade from Uncirculated, with Proof surface. Very scarce." It sold for $25. In June 1946, in the William Cutler Atwater Collection, B. Max Mehl offered lot 1507: "1881-CC Extremely Fine with frosty mint surface; in fact this coin is practically Uncirculated, and as such, very scarce." It sold for $33.

In October 1982, in the Louis E. Eliasberg Collection of U.S. Gold Coins, Bowers and Ruddy Galleries offered lot 768: "1881-CC Select Brilliant Uncirculated, MS-63. From the John H. Clapp Collection, 1942. Earlier from the Bradford Bank, 1895." It sold for $3,850. The coin then went through unknown intermediaries to J.J. Teaparty; to the Bowers and Merena Galleries' sale of the Henry S. Lang Collection, July 2002, lot 637; Doug Winter; Orange County collection; Pinnacle Rarities, to the American Numismatic Rarities sale of the Old West Collection, August 2006, lot 1352, to Rusty Goe, who formed an incredible collection of Carson City coins for a Nevada collector. It later appeared in the July 2012 sale of the Battle Born Collection by Stack's Bowers Galleries as lot 11031: "1881-CC MS-64 NGC. The single finest certified." It sold for $97,750.

VF-20	EF-40	AU-50	AU-55	AU-58	MS-60
$1,350	$1,850	$2,500	$3,500	$5,000	$8,500

1881-O

Circulation-Strike Mintage: 8,350

Estimated population (Mint State):
15–20. Low levels.

Estimated population (circulated grades):
250–325.

Submissions certified at highest grades (as of March 2017): *PCGS:* MS-60 (3), MS-61 (1). *NGC:* MS-60 (8), MS-61 (5).

Key to collecting: VF and EF are about par. This was one of the eagles on Thomas L. Elder's "watch for" list distributed to bankers and other financial officials in the 1930s. Available in AU and lower Mint State ranges due to modern repatriations.

MARKET NEWS AND COMMENTARY

In March 1911, in his sale of the William H. Woodin Collection, Thomas L. Elder offered lot 1283: "1881-O Very Fine; coinage 8,350 pcs." It sold for $10.50. In November 1939 the William B. Hale Collection, sold by B. Max Mehl, included the same coin as lot 1718: "1881-O Nearly Uncirculated. From the Woodin Collection." It sold for $27.50. Note the difference in grading interpretations even in the early 1900s. Because of such situations—which are numerous—it is impossible to ascertain with precision the population of certain coins in specific grades. In June 1957 New Netherlands' 49th sale, Eliasberg duplicates, included lot 278: "1881-O. Better than VF, closer to Ex Fine. Only 8,350 minted. Slightly finer than the W.G.C. coin at $35 in 1946, or half a dozen others we could name, among them the Davis-Graves lot at $55." It sold for $47.50.

In October 1982, in the Louis E. Eliasberg Collection of U.S. Gold Coins, Bowers and Ruddy Galleries offered lot 769: "1881-O AU-50." It sold for $1,100. In June 2000, in the Harry W. Bass Jr. Collection, Part III, Bowers and Merena Galleries included lot 709: "1881-O AU-58. Purchased from Paramount, April 30, 1967." It sold for $2,070. In the January 2014 Pre-Long Beach sale Ira and Larry Goldberg offered a lot consisting of: "1881-O AU-55 PCGS." It sold for $3,525.

VF-20	EF-40	AU-50	AU-55	AU-58	MS-60
$950	$1,250	$1,650	$3,000	$6,500	$12,500

1881-S

Circulation-Strike Mintage: 970,000

Estimated population (Mint State):
3,000+.

Estimated population (circulated grades):
7,000+.

Submissions certified at highest grades (as of March 2017): *PCGS:* MS-61 (500), MS-62 (494), MS-63 (59). *NGC:* MS-61 (1,390), MS-62 (615), MS-63 (46), MS-64 (1), MS-65 (1).

Key to collecting: Very plentiful. MS-60 to MS-62, extensively bagmarked, is the typical range of condition. In lower grades the value of this and other high-mintage eagles is tied into the bullion price of gold.

MARKET NEWS AND COMMENTARY

In March 1907 the David S. Wilson Collection, sold by S. Hudson Chapman, offered lot 37: "1881-S Uncirculated. Mint luster." It sold for $12. In May 1939, sale 399, Rare U.S. Gold Coins by J.C. Morgenthau & Co. included lot 379: "1881-S Uncirculated." It sold for $16.50. Melt value was $16.45. In June 1957 New Netherlands' 49th sale, Eliasberg duplicates, included lot 279: "1881-S. Marked 'Ex Fine,' this is a trifle under our rigorous standard for that grade. With considerable luster, and far better than the Green, Menjou examples." It sold for $19.50.

In this era the New Netherlands grading was, indeed, stricter than that of most other dealers. The grading was done by John J. Ford Jr. He was very conservative—with the result that if a coin was purchased without the buyer examining it first, it nearly always turned out to be as nice as or better than described. The main cataloger, Walter Breen, was not a skilled grader although he was a genius when it came to literature, art, music, and history.

VF-20	EF-40	AU-50	AU-55	AU-58	MS-60	MS-63
$650	$675	$700	$750	$800	$850	$3,000

1882

Circulation-Strike Mintage: 2,324,440
Proof Mintage: 44

Notes regarding mintages: 25 Proofs were delivered in the first quarter of the year, followed by 2 in the second quarter, 16 in the third quarter, and 1 in the fourth quarter. This total differs slightly from the 40 usually published.

Estimated population (Mint State): *25,000+.* Extremely plentiful from overseas sources in the late 1900s. Typical grades are MS-60 to MS-63, bagmarked, very occasionally, gem pieces are encountered.

Estimated population (circulated grades): *20,000+.*

Estimated population (Proofs): *12–16.* Very rare.

Submissions certified at highest grades (as of March 2017): *PCGS:* MS-62 (2,694), MS-63 (478), MS-64 (49), MS-66 (1). *NGC:* MS-62 (4,578), MS-63 (888), MS-64 (49), MS-65 (1). Another illustration of large numbers of Mint State coins being concentrated at lower levels. MS–60 and 61 populations, not cited here, included thousands of additional coins.

Key to collecting: Common. From this era forward there are *circulated* coins in approximately the same numbers, give or take, as lower-range Mint State coins for many varieties, as coins shipped overseas during the Free Silver Movement era were mostly or nearly all Mint State. Many later eagles are more plentiful in Mint State than in circulated grades. In view of repatriations yielding many high-grade coins modern auction listings are not cited beyond a selected samples.

MARKET NEWS AND COMMENTARY

In February 1944, in the Belden E. Roach Collection, B. Max Mehl offered lot 357: "1882 Uncirculated with bright full mint luster. Catalogs at $35." It sold for $25. In May 1945 Stack's sale of the George H. Hall Collection included lot 2174: "1882 Brilliant Uncirculated." It sold for $26.

Well into the 21st century, the August 2016 ANA World's Fair of Money sale by Stack's Bowers Galleries offered lot 3472: "1882 MS-66 PCGS. From the Bull Run Collection. Finest certified by either service." It sold for $64,625. This is a poster example of *condition rarity*.

PROOF MARKET NEWS AND COMMENTARY

In January 1884 W. Elliot Woodward's sale of the Honorable Heman Ely Collection included lot 957: "1882 Splendid [gold] Proof set. 6 pieces." It sold for $45 for the set. The face value of the $1, $2.50, $3, $5, $10, and $20 in the set added up to $41.50. The buyer was a Mr. Bell, probably Charles H. Bell, who earlier served as governor of New Hampshire and who was a very active numismatist.[30]

VF-20	EF-40	AU-50	AU-55	AU-58	MS-60	MS-63	PF-63	PF-64	PF-65
$650	$675	$700	$750	$800	$850	$1,200	$20,000	$32,500	$55,000

1882-CC

Circulation-Strike Mintage: 6,764

Estimated population (Mint State): *10–15.* Data inconsistent, but in any event, Mint State coins are very rare.

Estimated population (circulated grades): *250–350.*

Submissions certified at highest grades (as of March 2017): *PCGS:* MS-60 (1), MS-61 (1), MS-63 (1). *NGC:* MS-60 MS-61 (1), MS-62 (2).

Die data: Two obverse dies and one reverse die were used for this coinage. Winter 2-A is a misplaced date variety with faint remnants of two 8s in the denticles below and slightly to the right of the primary 8s in the date.

Characteristics of striking and die notes: Usually lightly struck on the high points of Miss Liberty's hair.

Key to collecting: VF to AU grades are typical. AU coins are found easily enough, but Mint State coins are seldom seen.

Market News and Commentary

In June 1946, in the William Cutler Atwater Collection, B. Max Mehl offered lot 1323: "1882-CC Nearly Uncirculated. Limited coinage. Very scarce. Record $100." It sold for $82.50.

In October 1982, in the Louis E. Eliasberg Collection of U.S. Gold Coins, Bowers and Ruddy Galleries offered lot 772: "1882-CC AU-55." It sold for $3,090. In June 2000, in the Harry W. Bass Jr. Collection, Part III, Bowers and Merena Galleries included lot 712: "1882-CC AU-55 PCGS. PCGS Population: 12; 4 finer (AU-58 finest). From Abe Kosoff's sale of the Shuford Collection, May 1968, lot 2312." It sold for $6,325.

The July 2012 sale of the Battle Born Collection by Stack's Bowers Galleries included lot 11023:

> 1882-CC Winter 2-A. Misplaced Date. MS-61 PCGS. Ex Charley Tuppen Collection; J.J. Teaparty, to the following via private treaty; Bowers and Merena's sale of the Henry S. Lang Collection, July 2002, lot 638; Doug Winter; Orange County collection; Pinnacle Rarities, to the American Numismatic Rarities sale of the Old West Collection, August 2006, lot 1353. [Sold for $92,000]

VF-20	EF-40	AU-50	AU-55	AU-58	MS-60
$1,650	$2,750	$4,000	$9,500	$18,500	$25,000

1882-O

Circulation-Strike Mintage: 10,820

Estimated population (Mint State): *30–45.* In low Mint State grades. Very rare.

Estimated population (circulated grades): *250–325.*

Submissions certified at highest grades (as of March 2017): *PCGS:* MS-60 (8), MS-61 (9), MS-63 (2). *NGC:* MS-60 (10), MS-61 (8), MS-62 (1).

Characteristics of striking and die notes: Usually well struck and with some prooflike surface.

Key to collecting: EF and AU coins are about par. Mint State coins are scarce and expensive, but there are enough around to satisfy specialists. The population of these swelled in later years due to repatriations.

Market News and Commentary

In June 1946, in the William Cutler Atwater Collection, B. Max Mehl offered lot 1539: "1882-O Practically Uncirculated with mint luster. Limited coinage. Record up to $50." It sold for $30.

In November 2000, in the Harry W. Bass Jr. Collection, Part IV, Bowers and Merena Galleries offered lot 743: "1882-O MS-63 PCGS. Purchased from A-Mark on April 20, 1976." It sold for $13,800.

The Stack's Bowers Galleries' August 2015 Chicago ANA World's Fair of Money included lot 1315: "1882-O MS-61 PCGS." It sold for $10,012. In its January 2017 FUN Convention sale Heritage included lot 6928: "1882-O MS-60 PCGS." It sold for $8,225.

VF-20	EF-40	AU-50	AU-55	AU-58	MS-60	MS-63
$1,150	$1,250	$1,650	$2,650	$4,000	$7,500	$45,000

1882-S

Circulation-Strike Mintage: 132,000

Estimated population (Mint State): 500–750+. Mostly modern imports. Typical grades are MS-60 to MS-62, extensively bagmarked, although there are some rare exceptions.

Estimated population (circulated grades): *800–1,250.*

Submissions certified at highest grades (as of March 2017): *PCGS:* MS-62 (108), MS-63 (17), MS-64 (1), MS-65 (1). ***NGC:*** MS-62 (89), MS-63 (22), MS-64 (2), MS-65 (1).

Characteristics of striking and die notes: A letter from Charles E. Barber, chief engraver, at the Philadelphia Mint, November 1, 1883, addressed to the Honorable A. Louden Snowden, Superintendent of the Mint, reveals that there must have been some curious varieties made of 1882-S $5 and $10 pieces. Whether peculiarities are on the reverse, obverse, or both is not stated. Perhaps examination of some pieces today would show some interesting differences. As we go to press we know nothing about such pieces—but it seems that we should all start looking!

> I respectfully call your attention to the fact that some person at the U.S. Mint at San Francisco has been tampering with dies sent there for coinage. I have discovered this upon examination of those dies returned from last year's orders. To what extent this may have been carried I am unable to say, but it is very apparent on both eagle and half eagle dies. This not only causes a loss of these dies, but as you well understand it destroys all uniformity of coinage if irresponsible persons are allowed to make such changes in the engraving as to them seems necessary.
>
> It feels that I need hardly say that as the dies sent to the Mint at San Francisco are from the same hubs as those used by this Mint and all the other mints there can be no necessity for them to [make] any of their improvements, and further, if the dies sent to them are not satisfactory, they have their proper remedy in making a complaint.

Key to collecting: EF and AU are typical grades although Mint State coins are common. In view of repatriations yielding many high-grade coins modern auction listings are not extensively cited.

MARKET NEWS AND COMMENTARY

In the December 1944 sale of the J.F. Bell Collection Stack's included lot 768: "1882-S Uncirculated." It sold for $34. In August 1990, in Auction '90, David W. Akers offered lot 1923: "1882-S MS-65." It sold for $8,250. In the August 2016 ANA World's Fair of Money sale Stack's Bowers Galleries offered lot 3397: "1882-S MS-63 PCGS." It sold for $1,645.

VF-20	EF-40	AU-50	AU-55	AU-58	MS-60	MS-63
$650	$675	$700	$750	$800	$850	$3,000

1883

Circulation-Strike Mintage: 208,700
Proof Mintage: 49

Notes regarding Proof mintages: There were 40 delivered on February 10 as part of full gold Proof sets, 1 stray Proof was delivered in March, 5 more in June, and a final 3 in September. The total of 49 differs from that usually published.

Estimated population (Mint State): *2,000+.* Common. Mostly in grades from MS-60 to MS-62 with bagmarks, scarce to rare at higher levels. Most were imported in the 1980s and 1990s.

Estimated population (circulated grades): *2,500+.*

Estimated population (Proofs): *12–15.* Very rare.

Submissions certified at highest grades (as of March 2017): *PCGS:* MS-62 (407), MS-63 (107), MS-64 (3). *NGC:* MS-62 (468), MS-63 (157), MS-64 (3).

Characteristics of striking and die notes: Usually sharply struck.

Key to collecting: EF and AU are the grades usually seen and Mint State coins are common. In lower grades the value of this and other high-mintage eagles is tied into the bullion price of gold.

MARKET NEWS AND COMMENTARY

In March 1911, in his sale of the William H. Woodin Collection, Thomas L. Elder offered lot 1244: "1883. Date closer to bust [than on the Proof of this year]. Uncirculated." It sold for $10 (face value).

   In October 1982, in the Louis E. Eliasberg Collection of U.S. Gold Coins, Bowers and Ruddy Galleries offered lot 775: "1883 AU-50." It sold for $440. This is typical of a common coin with a value based partially on its bullion content. From the late 1870s onward common eagles in grades from AU through MS-64 and sometimes higher appeared in quantity in auctions. Prices often moved more in relation to bullion values than to numismatic demand. For that reason, modern auction listings are minimized here.

PROOF MARKET NEWS AND COMMENTARY

In March 1911, in his sale of the William H. Woodin Collection, Thomas L. Elder offered lot 1243: "1883. Date away from bust. Brilliant Proof. Very rare." It sold for $15.

In May 1939, sale 399, Rare U.S. Gold Coins by J.C. Morgenthau & Co. included lot 381: "1883 Brilliant Proof." It sold for $31. In October 1993 the same coin was offered by Stack's in the Floyd T. Starr Collection as lot 1248: "1883 Choice Brilliant Proof." Fewer than 15 Proofs are believed to survive. Breen listed seven, the Starr coin being his number five and was unfairly called 'impaired.' Breen inaccurately listed one in the Eliasberg Collection.[31] It is missing in Proof format from the Norweb and Eliasberg sales. In J.C. Morgenthau's May 3, 1939, sale, lot 381, it sold for $19,800. In November 2004 Numismatic Rarities' Frog Run Farm Collection sale included lot 1881: "1883 Proof-64 PCGS." It sold for $27,600.

VF-20	EF-40	AU-50	AU-55	AU-58	MS-60	MS-63	PF-63	PF-64	PF-65
$650	$675	$700	$750	$800	$850	$1,500	$20,000	$32,500	$55,000

1883-CC

Circulation-Strike Mintage: 12,000

Estimated population (Mint State): *10–14.* At low levels, MS-60 being typical. Very rare.

Estimated population (circulated grades): *200–275.*

Submissions certified at highest grades (as of March 2017): *PCGS:* MS-60 (2), MS-61(2). *NGC:* MS-60 (3), MS-61 (2).

Die data: One obverse die and two reverse dies were used for this coinage. All known 1884-CC Liberty eagles display a curious set of raised die lines as made, slanting down from right to left on Liberty's neck. A possible explanation, offered in the Bowers and Merena Galleries sale of the Harry W. Bass Jr. Collection Part IV, lot 749, is that these raised die lines represent heavy die file lines imparted to remove clash marks that were not subsequently removed though the finer die polishing process.

Key to collecting: Most are VF or EF but there are enough AU coins available to satisfy specialists. Mint State examples are at low levels and are on the rare side.

MARKET NEWS AND COMMENTARY

In June 1946, in the William Cutler Atwater Collection, B. Max Mehl offered lot 1324: "1883-CC Uncirculated with full frosty mint luster. Rare so choice." It sold for $82. In March 1988 the Norweb Collection sale by Bowers and Merena Galleries included lot 2234: "1883-CC AU-50. A very attractive specimen which ranks among the top dozen or so finest known. From the Palace Collection of King Farouk, February 1954, lot 210." It sold for $1,320.

In the vastly expanded market of May 2000 the Harry W. Bass Jr. Collection, Part III, sold by Bowers and Merena Galleries, included lot 715: "1883-CC AU-58. Purchased from the Goliad Corporation, January 26, 1973." It sold for $4,025. Also lot 716: "1883-CC AU-53. Purchased from Stanley Kesselman, April 28, 1967." It sold for $2,760.

The July 2012 sale of the Battle Born Collection by Stack's Bowers Galleries included lot 11033: "1883-CC Winter 1-B. MS-61 NGC. Earlier from Heritage's sale of the Midwestern Collection, January 2003, lot 8822." It sold for $32,200. In the August 2016 ANA World's Fair of Money sale Stack's Bowers Galleries offered lot 3473: "1883-CC AU-58 NGC." It sold for $30,550.

VF-20	EF-40	AU-50	AU-55	AU-58	MS-60
$1,650	$2,500	$3,500	$8,250	$18,500	$37,500

1883-O

Circulation-Strike Mintage: 800

Estimated population (Mint State): 2–3. Low level MS-60 or thereabouts. Exceedingly rare.

Estimated population (circulated grades): 45–55.

Submissions certified at highest grades (as of March 2017): *PCGS:* AU-50 (3), AU-53 (8), AU-55 (2), AU-58 (4), MS-61 (1). *NGC:* AU-50 (3), AU-53 (3), AU-55 (4), AU-58 (3), MS-61 (1).

Key to collecting: VF and EF grades were typical years ago. Today many AU coins are available as well. This date and mintmark is always an attraction when one comes on the market, as the 800 mintage figure is irresistible. Once again we can thank Thomas L. Elder who had this date and mintmark on his "want list" circulated to bankers in the early 1900s, resulting in many pieces being taken from circulation.

MARKET NEWS AND COMMENTARY

As is the other case with low-mintage New Orleans eagles of this era the 1883-O has attracted a lot of attention when offered in the marketplace. It was not until the late 1900s that condition rarity entered the equation.

In December 1935, sale 356, Ludger Gravel and Byron Carney Collections by J.C. Morgenthau & Co. included lot 292: "1883-O Very Fine and of the greatest rarity." It sold for $140. This was a very strong price for the era. In May 1939, sale 399, Rare U.S. Gold Coins by J.C. Morgenthau & Co. included lot 384: "1883-O Extremely Fine and excessively rare." It sold for $81. Oh, well!

In his March 1943 Mail Bid sale Wayte Raymond included lot 10: "1883-O EF, mint luster." It sold for $62.50. In February 1944, in the Belden E. Roach Collection, B. Max Mehl offered lot 416:

> 1883-O Practically Uncirculated with semi-proof surface. Field slightly rubbed, but I believe as perfect a specimen of this great rarity as exists. Only 800 specimens struck in all. Catalogs at $300. The rarest branch mint $10 gold piece of our entire issue. Seldom offered. Certainly worth its full listed price. [Sold for $160]

In the December 1944 sale of the J.F. Bell Collection Stack's included lot 709: "1883-O The rarest of this branch mint. Only 800 struck. Very Fine and very rare." It sold for $370.

In January 1946 the Numismatic Gallery sale of "The World's Greatest Collection" (F.C.C. Boyd) included lot 752: "1883-O Extremely Fine. It has probably never seen circulation." It sold for $260. Wonder how it became worn? In March 1948 the Memorable Collection (consigned by Jacob Shapiro) was sold by Numismatic Gallery and included lot 628: "1883-O. Extremely Fine. This specimen has probably never seen circulation. Should exceed $300." It sold for $170. Same comment! In their era the New Netherlands catalogs were probably the most inaccurate, as much information was guesswork and research as to past sales was very limited, but they were by far the most entertaining to read!

In October 1962, in the Samuel W. Wolfson Collection, Stack's offered lot 741:

> 1883-O Just about Extremely Fine, with some original mint luster. We have searched all available records, and can safely state that this is "one of the finest known." We have found, on two occasions, comparable specimens, but none to excel this. This is one of the very few times we have been able to offer the 1883-O at auction. [Sold for $750]

This was before the large influx of repatriated coins that rearranged the numismatic landscape regarding the availability of eagles in high grades.

In January 1984 Stack's sale of the Amon G. Carter Jr. Family Collection included lot 779: "1883-O About Uncirculated, a magnificent example with full frosty mint bloom and some prooflike surface." It sold for $6,875. In May 1992, in their sale of the H.C. ("Heck") Dodson Collection, Mid-American Rare Coin Auctions included lot 421: "1883-O EF-45." It sold for $8,030.

The October 2001 sale by Stack's and Sotheby's of the Dallas Bank (Jeff Browning) Collection included lot 503: "1883-O About Uncirculated." It sold for $10,350. In the November 2016 Whitman Expo sale Stack's Bowers Galleries offered lot 2157: "1883-O AU-53 PCGS." It sold for $64,625.

VF-20	EF-40	AU-50	AU-55	AU-58	MS-60
$12,500	$27,500	$40,000	$72,500	$85,000	$125,000

1883-S

Circulation-Strike Mintage: 38,000

Estimated population (Mint State): 200+. A particularly notable specimen was remembered by John J. Ford Jr.:

> One of the most fantastic coins I ever found in Europe turned up in London when I was there in the 1950s, I believe. I was visiting with David Spink, and he showed me an 1883-S eagle that was as nice as the day it was made. If it could talk, the coin would have spoken to me. When I came back to New York City I looked up all I could find about it, and realized that it was one-of-a-kind. I consigned it to a New Netherlands sale and it attracted a lot of attention. I still remember this coin today.[32]

Estimated population (circulated grades): *1,000+*.

Submissions certified at highest grades (as of March 2017): *PCGS:* MS-61 (1), MS-62 (1). *NGC:* MS-61 (23), MS-62 (12), MS-63 (2).

Key to collecting: EF and AU are the usual grades seen. If this book had been written in 1970 or 1980 the comment would have been that VF and EF are the usual grades. Today, MS-60 to MS-62 grades are typical, with heavy bagmarks. The market price of well-worn coins is in step with changes in gold bullion prices.

MARKET NEWS AND COMMENTARY

In the December 1944 sale of the J.F. Bell Collection Stack's included lot 769: "1883-S Uncirculated." It sold for $37.50. An especially high-quality early auction offering.

In October 1982, in the Louis E. Eliasberg Collection of U.S. Gold Coins, Bowers and Ruddy Galleries offered lot 778: "1883-S Brilliant Uncirculated, MS-60 obverse; Select Brilliant Uncirculated, MS-63 reverse." It sold for $1,870.

In July 1984, in Auction '85, RARCOA included lot 458: "1883-S Coronet Type. With Motto. Superb Gem Brilliant Uncirculated. In a single word, WOW! Unbelievable. Possibly the finest eagle we have ever seen, regardless of date."

That coin sold for $26,400. The piece came to the market again in 2000 in the Harry W. Bass Jr. Collection, Part IV, Bowers and Merena Galleries as lot 747: "1883-S MS-66 PCGS. Population: 1; none finer. From RARCOA's session of Auction '85, lot 458." In its encore it sold for $35,300.

In August 2013 Stack's Bowers Galleries' ANA World's Fair of Money sale included lot 5270: "1884-S MS-63 PCGS." It sold for $4,759.

VF-20	EF-40	AU-50	AU-55	AU-58	MS-60	MS-63
$650	$675	$700	$750	$800	$850	$7,500

1884

Circulation-Strike Mintage: 76,860
Proof Mintage: 45

Notes regarding mintages: Proofs were delivered thusly: 30 delivered on January 19 as part of full gold Proof sets, 4 single coins on February 29, 4 on June 28, 1 struck in September and delivered on October 4, and 6 *struck* in December but delivered on January 10, 1885 (but included in the mintage total for 1884, as the pieces were dated 1884).

Estimated population (Mint State): *350+.* Repeating a familiar scenario, the 1884 was very rare in Mint State until the 1980s and 1990s when many were imported from overseas sources. Most examples are in grades from MS-60 through MS-62, extensively bagmarked, but there are exceptions in higher grades.

Estimated population (circulated grades): *750–1,000+.*

Estimated population (Proofs): *9–12.* A classic rarity. The number of *different* specimens known is very small. Certification service data represent multiple submissions of the same coin(s).

Submissions certified at highest grades (as of March 2017): *PCGS:* MS-63 (22), MS-64 (5), MS-65 (1). *NGC:* MS-63 (9), MS-64 (4).

Key to collecting: Generally available in EF and AU grades plus a smaller number of Mint State examples.

MARKET NEWS AND COMMENTARY

New Netherlands Coin Co.'s 46th sale, Dr. Clarence W. Peake Collection, June 1955, included lot 172: "1884 Close to full Uncirculated. With a noticeable reverse abrasion mark or so, but a brilliant and desirable coin. For a value comparison, the Very Fine W.G.C. specimen brought $37.50 back in 1946." It sold for $27.50.

In October 1962, in the Samuel W. Wolfson Collection, Stack's offered lot 744: "1884 Uncirculated. Original mint frost." It sold for $65. In this era Mint State coins were scarce.

In June 2000, in the Harry W. Bass Jr. Collection, Part III, Bowers and Merena Galleries included lot 718: "1884 MS-62. From Stack's sale of the Miles Collection, October 1968, lot 729." It sold for $862.50. This citation, representative of many of the era, reflects a value tied into the bullion value of gold.

VF-20	EF-40	AU-50	AU-55	AU-58	MS-60	MS-63	PF-63	PF-64	PF-65
$650	$675	$700	$750	$800	$850	$4,250	$20,000	$32,500	$55,000

1884-CC

Circulation-Strike Mintage: 9,925

Estimated population (Mint State):
8–12. Very rare in Mint State. Typical coins hover around MS-60 or so.

Estimated population (circulated grades):
225–275.

Submissions certified at highest grades (as of March 2017): *PCGS:* MS-61 (3), MS-62 (1), MS-63 (1). *NGC:* MS-60 (1).

Die data: Five pairs of dies were sent to Carson City for this coinage.

Characteristics of striking and die notes: The obverse is always seen with raised lines and marks, the result of the die being damaged. Often lightly struck.

Key to collecting: VF and EF coins are the usual, with a few higher-grade coins from modern repatriations. Very scarce overall.

MARKET NEWS AND COMMENTARY

In April 1929 Thomas L. Elder's sale of the George W. Fash, Joseph F. Atkinson, and Carrie E. Perkins Collections included lot 1669: "1884 Carson City. Fine. Rare, not in recent sales." It sold for $11.25. In October 1962, in the Samuel W. Wolfson Collection, Stack's offered lot 746: "1884-CC Extremely Fine. Faint proof-like surface around stars and legend. Low mint record. In demand." It sold for $75.

In May 1993 the Bowers and Merena Galleries' sale of the Stetson University Collection included lot 2098: "1884-CC AU-53. Lustrous and brilliant. Sharply struck. A Condition Census example of this issue." It sold for $4,620.

In November 2000, in the Harry W. Bass Jr. Collection, Part IV, Bowers and Merena Galleries offered lot 749:

> 1884-CC MS-63 (PCGS This is one of the nicest specimens of this low-mintage Carson City issue, listed as finest known in Douglas Winter's census. Very scarce in all grades and extremely rare in Mint State, this piece is of the so-called "canceled die variety," probably more prevalent than the "normal" variety. PCGS Population: 1; none finer. Heavy die lapping marks across Liberty's bust From Paramount's sale of August 1969, lot 2150. [Sold for $25,300]

The July 2012 sale of the Battle Born Collection by Stack's Bowers Galleries included lot 11034: "1884-CC . MS-61 NGC. NGC Census: 5; and none are finer at this service. The corresponding PCGS population is 3/2 (MS-63 finest for the issue). Ex Heritage's FUN Signature sale of January 2003, lot 8824." It sold for $17,625.

In its September 2016 Long Beach sale Heritage included lot 14163: "1884-CC AU-58 NGC. Heavy die lines on Liberty's portrait are as struck." It sold for $17,825. Regency Auction XX, January 2017, included lot 282: "1884-CC AU-58." It sold for $12,337.50.

VF-20	EF-40	AU-50	AU-55	AU-58	MS-60	MS-63
$1,450	$2,250	$3,250	$6,500	$13,500	$20,000	$65,000

1884-S

Circulation-Strike Mintage: 124,250

Estimated population (Mint State): 750+. Mostly in lower levels, MS-60 to MS-62, extensively bagmarked. Nearly all known Mint State coins were repatriated in the 1980s and 1990s. Earlier, Mint State examples were rarities.

Estimated population (circulated grades): *1,200+.*

Submissions certified at highest grades (as of March 2017): *PCGS:* MS-61 (120), MS-62 (117), MS-63 (14). *NGC:* MS-61 (188), MS-62 (52), MS-63 (3).

Key to collecting: EF and AU are typical grades. Here we go again: rare generations ago, common today as noted above.

MARKET NEWS AND COMMENTARY

In November 1939 the William B. Hale Collection, sold by B. Max Mehl, included lot 1741: "1884-S Very Fine." It sold for $18.

In May 1950 the Golden Jubilee sale / Jerome Kern Collection sale by B. Max Mehl included lot 569: "1884-S. Uncirculated with mint luster. Almost equal to a semiproof. Not rare, but very scarce choice. A specimen not as good brought $33.50 in the Atwater sale." It sold for $32.50.

In May 1993 the Bowers and Merena Galleries' sale of the Stetson University Collection included lot 698: "1884-S MS-60. A noted 'sleeper' in the series. Called 'A very scarce and underrated date in all grades' by David Akers, examples of this date are most frequently found in the VF to EF range. At the MS-60 level, this date emerges as a moderate rarity." It sold for $2,640.

Today the 1884-S is in abundant supply in relation to the demand for this date and mint.

VF-20	EF-40	AU-50	AU-55	AU-58	MS-60	MS-63
$650	$675	$700	$750	$800	$850	$5,500

1885

Circulation-Strike Mintage: 253,462
Proof Mintage: 67

Notes regarding mintages: There were 30 Proofs delivered on January 17 with the full gold Proof sets, 3 extra coins in March, 5 in September, and 29 in the fourth quarter of the year. This total differs slightly from the 65 usually published.

Estimated population (Mint State): *400+.* Most are in grades from MS-60 to MS-62, but others range higher.

Estimated population (circulated grades): *3,000+.*

Estimated population (Proofs): *15–20.* The mintage of this issue is higher than usual to this point in time, and the number of survivors is somewhat larger as well. However, on an absolute basis the 1885 Proof eagle is a rarity, and anyone seeking an example is apt to have a long wait.

Submissions certified at highest grades (as of March 2017): *PCGS:* MS-63 (49), MS-64 (13), MS-65 (1). *NGC:* MS-60 (3), MS-61 (4), MS-62 (2), MS-64 (1).

Key to collecting: EF and AU specimens are regularly encountered. Mint State coins are readily available as well, due to repatriations. In view of repatriations yielding many high grade coins modern auction listings are not extensively cited.

MARKET NEWS AND COMMENTARY
New Netherlands Coin Co.'s 46th sale, Dr. Clarence W. Peake Collection, June 1955, included lot 175: "1885. Uncirculated. Highly attractive, with full frosty mint surface. Worth $35 so nice." It sold for $26.

The Stack's Americana Auction in January 2006 included lot 3162: "1885 MS-65 PCGS." It sold for $20,700. In the August 2016 ANA World's Fair of Money sale Stack's Bowers Galleries offered lot 3404: "1885 MS-64 PCGS." It sold for $2,820.

VF-20	EF-40	AU-50	AU-55	AU-58	MS-60	MS-63	MS-65	PF-63	PF-64	PF-65
$650	$675	$700	$750	$800	$850	$2,750	$20,000	$20,000	$32,500	$52,500

1885-S

Circulation-Strike Mintage: 228,000

Estimated population (Mint State): 1,000+. This is another issue that was extensively imported in the late 1900s. Many if not most were sold into non-numismatic hands, with the result that examples are not plentiful on the market at any given time. Typical grades are MS-60 to MS-62, occasionally slightly higher.

Estimated population (circulated grades): 2,000+.

Submissions certified at highest grades (as of March 2017): PCGS: MS-62 (290), MS-63 (113), MS-64 (5). **NGC:** MS-62 (244), MS-63 (58), MS-64 (2).

Key to collecting: EF and AU coins are available without difficulty. Mint State coins are common. In lower grades the value of this and other high-mintage eagles is tied into the bullion price of gold.

MARKET NEWS AND COMMENTARY

In March 1948 the Memorable Collection (consigned by Jacob Shapiro) was sold by Numismatic Gallery and included lot 644: "1885-S. Uncirculated." It sold for $28. In April 1956 Abe Kosoff's sale of the Thomas G. Melish and Clinton W. Hester Collections included lot 2513: "1885-S Uncirculated." It sold for $23. In October 1982, in the Louis E. Eliasberg Collection of U.S. Gold Coins, Bowers and Ruddy Galleries offered lot 783: "1885-S Brilliant Uncirculated, MS-60." It sold for $825.

In the August 2006 ANA World's Fair of Money sale Bowers and Merena Galleries offered lot 4361: "1885-S MS-64 PCGS." It sold for $12,075. Likely, this went to a competitor on the PCGS registry set program. The October 2014 Stack's Bowers Galleries' Rarities sale included lot 10226: "1885-S MS-64 PCGS." It sold for $7,050. By this time many additional repatriated coins had come on the market.

VF-20	EF-40	AU-50	AU-55	AU-58	MS-60	MS-63
$650	$675	$700	$750	$800	$850	$1,750

1886

Circulation-Strike Mintage: 236,100
Proof Mintage: 60

Notes regarding mintages: There were 25 Proofs delivered in February as part of full gold Proof sets, 2 additional coins in March, 6 more in June, 7 in September, and 20 in the fourth quarter. It is not known if all coins in the final delivery were sold.

Estimated population (Mint State): 500+. Most were imported in the late 1900s. Typical grades are MS-60 to MS-62, only occasionally finer.

Estimated population (circulated grades): 3,000+.

Estimated population (Proofs): *15–20.* Very rare.

Submissions certified at highest grades (as of March 2017): *PCGS:* MS-62 (117), MS-63 (42), MS-64 (8). *NGC:* MS-62 (97), MS-63 (28), MS-64 (3).

Key to collecting: EF and AU are typical grades. Mint State coins are easy to find. In view of repatriations yielding many high-grade coins modern auction listings are not extensively cited.

MARKET NEWS AND COMMENTARY

In May 1939, sale 399, Rare U.S. Gold Coins by J.C. Morgenthau & Co. included lot 389: "1886 Uncirculated." It sold for $16.50. In April 1956 Abe Kosoff's sale of the Thomas G. Melish and Clinton W. Hester Collections included lot 2515: "1886 Uncirculated." It sold for $24.

Stack's March 1991 Charlotte Collection & James W. Thompson sale included lot 1320: "1886 Choice Brilliant Uncirculated." It sold for $11,550. In June 2000, in the Harry W. Bass Jr. Collection, Part III, Bowers and Merena Galleries included lot 720: "1886 MS-62. From Superior Galleries' sale of February 1973, lot 748." It sold for $2,530. This is reflection of how much the availability of repatriated coins has changed the population reports in the early 2000s. Today an MS-62 is a very common coin in relation to the demand for it.

In the June 2015 Pre-Long Beach sale Ira and Larry Goldberg offered lot 1928: "1886 MS-64 PCGS." It sold for $3,760.

VF-20	EF-40	AU-50	AU-55	AU-58	MS-60	MS-63	PF-63	PF-64	PF-65
$650	$675	$700	$750	$800	$850	$3,000	$18,500	$32,500	$52,500

1886-S

Circulation-Strike Mintage: 826,000

Estimated population (Mint State): *4,500+.* Another date imported in quantity in the late 1900s. Typical grades range from MS-60 to MS-62, not often higher.

Estimated population (circulated grades): *8,000+.*

Submissions certified at highest grades (as of March 2017): *PCGS:* MS-62 (793), MS-63 (314), MS-64 (26), MS-65 (2), MS-66 (2). *NGC:* MS-62 (1,256), MS-63 (272), MS-64 (18).

Key to collecting: EF and AU are typically seen grades. Mint State coins are very common. In lower grades the value of this and other high-mintage eagles is tied into the bullion price of gold.

MARKET NEWS AND COMMENTARY

In November 1939 the William B. Hale Collection, sold by B. Max Mehl, included lot 1742: "1886-S Brilliant Uncirculated." It sold for $20. In April 1949 B. Max Mehl's sale of the Dr. Charles W. Green Collection included lot 690: "1886-S Uncirculated. Brilliant mint luster. Scarce so choice." It sold for $25.

In the June 2015 Pre-Long Beach sale Ira and Larry Goldberg offered lot 1929: "1886-S MS-64 NGC." It sold for $2,115. In its January 2017 FUN Convention sale Heritage included lot 6930: "1886-S MS-65 PCGS." It sold for $2,056.25.

VF-20	EF-40	AU-50	AU-55	AU-58	MS-60	MS-63
$650	$675	$700	$750	$800	$850	$1,250

1887

Circulation-Strike Mintage: 53,600
Proof Mintage: 80

Notes regarding mintages: Walter Breen (*United States Eagles,* 1967) stated that this coinage "must have been executed late in the year," and that" the Mint must have been experiencing a recurrence of its old trouble in disposing of eagles, for half eagles and doubles were vastly preferred (San Francisco was of course coining most of them)."

Proof deliveries were made in March (25), June (25), and December (30).

Estimated population (Mint State): *225+.* Some were imported in the late 1900s, but the date remains fairly scarce. Most are in grades from MS-60 to MS-62.

Estimated population (circulated grades): *1,000+.*

Estimated population (Proofs): *20–30.* Rare on an absolute basis, but one of the more available of the era.

Submissions certified at highest grades (as of March 2017): *PCGS:* MS-62 (29), MS-63 (6), MS-64 (2). *NGC:* MS-62 (15), MS-63 (2), MS-64 (1).

Key to collecting: VF and EF are the usual grades encountered, although AU and Mint State coins are easy to find.

Market News and Commentary

New Netherlands Coin Co.'s 46th sale, Dr. Clarence W. Peake Collection, June 1955, included lot 179: "1887. Better than Extremely Fine. Just 53,600 regularly coined, and a date to remember." It sold for $25. In April 1960 New Netherlands' 54th sale, Jonathan Glogower Consignment, Etc., included this lot 704: "1887. Very Fine plus, lustrous but bag marked. Another sleeper; mintage in class with 1874." It sold for $27.

In May 1993 the Bowers and Merena Galleries' sale of the Stetson University Collection included lot 2104: "1887 AU-58. Brilliant and lustrous. Fairly scarce, and quite unappreciated." It sold for $2,420. True then but not applicable today. In its January 2017 FUN Convention sale Heritage included lot 8182: "1887 MS-61 NGC." It sold for $881.25, mostly reflecting the bullion price plus a modest premium. By that time the 1887 was extremely common due to repatriations. The auctions of Heritage, Stack's Bowers Galleries, and other firms included many common eagles that commanded little numismatic premium in comparison to years gone by. Such listings are therefore minimized here.

Proof Market News and Commentary

In March 1911, in his sale of the William H. Woodin Collection, Thomas L. Elder offered lot 1251: "1887. Brilliant Proof. Very rare." It sold for $16.

In May 1939, sale 399, Rare U.S. Gold Coins by J.C. Morgenthau & Co. included lot 390: "1887 Brilliant Proof." It sold for $26. In October 1992 Stack's offered the same coin in the Floyd T. Starr Collection as lot 1249: "1887 Choice Brilliant Proof. From J.C. Morgenthau's May 3, 1939 sale, lot 390, accession date recorded as May 8." It sold for $15,950.

The June 1941 sale of the William Forrester Dunham Collection by B. Max Mehl included lot 2256: "1887 Perfect brilliant Proof; partly wire edge." It sold for $30.25.

In January 1984 Stack's sale of the Amon G. Carter Jr. Family Collection included lot 783: "1887 Brilliant Proof. A most attractive and choice example in greenish yellow gold, pale cloudy toning." It sold for $18,700. In the January 2014 Pre-Long Beach sale Ira and Larry Goldberg offered lot 1832: "1887 Proof-63 PCGS." It sold for $20,562.50.

VF-20	EF-40	AU-50	AU-55	AU-58	MS-60	MS-63	PF-63	PF-64	PF-65
$650	$675	$700	$750	$800	$850	$4,500	$18,500	$32,500	$52,500

1887-S

Circulation-Strike Mintage: 817,000

Estimated population (Mint State): 4,500+. Most are in MS-60 to MS-62 grades and were found in overseas bank holdings in the late 1900s.

Estimated population (circulated grades): 8,000+.

Submissions certified at highest grades (as of March 2017): *PCGS:* MS-62 (353), MS-63 (111), MS-64 (5). *NGC:* MS-62 (654), MS-63 (71), MS-64 (11), MS-65 (1).

Key to collecting: EF and AU coins are readily available. Once rare in Mint State, these are common now except for higher levels. Mint State coins are easy to find. In lower grades the value of this and other high-mintage eagles is tied into the bullion price of gold.

Market News and Commentary

In November 1939 the William B. Hale Collection, sold by B. Max Mehl, included lot 1743: "1887-S Uncirculated, with full mint luster." It sold for $19.75. New Netherlands Coin Co.'s 46th sale, Dr. Clarence W. Peake Collection, June 1955, included lot 180: "1887-S. Extremely Fine plus. The W.G.C. coin was VF, Atwater's Fine, Green's Fine, and Davis-Graves VF." It sold for $21. This commentary reflects the rarity of high-grade coins in an earlier era. Today the situation is vastly different.

In the March 2014 Whitman Expo sale Stack's Bowers Galleries offered lot 6274: "1887-S MS-64 NGC." It sold for $3,828.75. The Stack's Bowers Galleries' February 2015 Americana sale included lot 2570: "1887-S MS-65 NGC." It sold for $25,850, probably to a registry set competitor. In its January 2017 FUN Convention sale

Heritage included lot 15974: "1887-S MS-64+ PCGS." It sold for $16,450. At the same time an MS-62 or MS-63 was worth but a tiny fraction of that price.

VF-20	EF-40	AU-50	AU-55	AU-58	MS-60	MS-63
$650	$675	$700	$750	$800	$850	$1,600

1888

Circulation-Strike Mintage: 132,921
Proof Mintage: 75

Notes regarding mintages: There were 30 Proofs delivered on February 29 with the full gold Proof sets, 12 more coins in June, 20 in September, and 10 in December.

Estimated population (Mint State): *250+*. Most are in lower grades, MS-60 to MS-62. Very scarce prior to late 1900s imports.

Estimated population (circulated grades): *2,000+*.

Estimated population (Proofs): *16–22*. Very difficult to locate.

Submissions certified at highest grades (as of March 2017): *PCGS:* MS-61 (63), MS-62 (51), MS-63 (8). *NGC:* MS-61 (138), MS-62 (46), MS-63 (4).

Key to collecting: EF and AU examples are readily obtained, and Mint State coins in lower ranges are easily found as well.

Market News and Commentary

In February 1944, in the Belden E. Roach Collection, B. Max Mehl offered lot 363: "1888 About Uncirculated with frosty mint surface." It sold for $21.75.

Years later in November 2000, in the Harry W. Bass Jr. Collection, Part IV, Bowers and Merena Galleries offered lot 752: "1888 MS-62. From Pine Tree Auction Company's sale of March 1974, lot 249." It sold for $2,990. This was before a surge of repatriated coins.

VF-20	EF-40	AU-50	AU-55	AU-58	MS-60	MS-63	PF-63	PF-64	PF-65
$650	$675	$700	$750	$800	$850	$4,500	$18,500	$32,500	$52,500

1888-O

Circulation-Strike Mintage: 21,335

Estimated population (Mint State): *800+*. This is the earliest-dated New Orleans eagle that is readily available in Mint State, rather remarkable in view of its low mintage. Most are in grades from MS-60 to MS-62. Some of these have been on the market for quite some time, dating from imports by James F. Kelly in the 1950s and augmented by later finds.

Estimated population (circulated grades): *300–500+.*

Submissions certified at highest grades (as of March 2017): *PCGS:* MS-62 (149), MS-63 (25), MS-64 (1). *NGC:* MS-62 (154), MS-63 (12).

Key to collecting: EF and AU are usually seen grades. Very popular as are all New Orleans Mint eagles. Mint State coins are easy to find.

MARKET NEWS AND COMMENTARY

Although in the contest of New Orleans eagles of this era the mintage of the 1888-O is generous, examples offered at auction have attracted a lot of attention, especially beginning in the late 1900s.

In March 1911, in his sale of the William H. Woodin Collection, Thomas L. Elder offered lot 1285: "1888-O Mint luster; scarce state." It sold for $10 (face value). In February 1944, in the Belden E. Roach Collection, B. Max Mehl offered lot 417: "1888-O Practically Uncirculated with full mint luster." It sold for $26. The December 1944 sale of the J.F. Bell Collection held by Stack's included lot 710: "1888-O Uncirculated. Rare." It sold for $70.

In October 1998, in the John J. Pittman Collection sale, Part II, David Akers offered lot 1966: "1888-O, Uncirculated examples of this quality are only moderately scarce, but in Choice Uncirculated or higher grade, this issue is very rare and almost never available. Acquired by JJP from James Kelly on 3/12/59 for $42." It sold for $963.

In August 2013 the Stack's Bowers Galleries' ANA World's Fair of Money sale included lot 4518: "1888-O MS-64 PCGS." It sold for $21,150. In its April 1916 sale Heritage included lot 5913: "1888-O MS-63 PCGS." It sold for $6,168.75.

VF-20	EF-40	AU-50	AU-55	AU-58	MS-60	MS-63
$725	$800	$850	$1,000	$1,100	$1,250	$6,000

1888-S

Circulation-Strike Mintage: 648,700

Estimated population (Mint State): 3,000+. MS-60 to MS-62 are the usually seen grades. Another issue imported in quantity in the late 1900s, although the 1888-S was plentiful before them.

Estimated population (circulated grades): *7,000+.*

Submissions certified at highest grades (as of March 2017): *PCGS:* MS-62 (560), MS-63 (180), MS-64 (5). *NGC:* MS-62 (699), MS-63 (86), MS-64 (4).

Key to collecting: Very common, as previously indicated. Mint State coins are easy to find. In lower grades the value of this and other high-mintage eagles is tied into the bullion price of gold.

MARKET NEWS AND COMMENTARY

In the December 1944 sale of the J.F. Bell Collection Stack's included lot 774: "1888-S Uncirculated." It sold for $30. In April 1956 in his sale of the Thomas G. Melish

Collection Abe Kosoff offered lot 2522: "1888-S. Date left; Extremely Fine." It sold for $21. Also lot 2523: "1888-S. Date centered. About Extremely Fine." It sold for $21.

In the June 2014 Pre-Long Beach sale Ira & Larry Goldberg offered lot 1907: "1880-S MS-64 NGC." It sold for $8,518.75. The buyer was probably a contestant in the NGC registry set competition. At the time MS-63 coins were common and sold for but a fraction of this price.

VF-20	EF-40	AU-50	AU-55	AU-58	MS-60	MS-63
$650	$675	$700	$750	$800	$850	$1,500

1889

Circulation-Strike Mintage: 4,440
Proof Mintage: 45

Notes regarding mintages: There were 35 Proofs delivered in June and 10 in the second half of the year.

Estimated population (Mint State): *100–150.* Usually seen in or around MS-60.

Estimated population (circulated grades): *300+.*

Estimated population (Proofs): *9–12.* Exceedingly rare, for reasons unknown.

Submissions certified at highest grades (as of March 2017): *PCGS:* MS-60 (14), MS-61 (30), MS-62 (7). *NGC:* MS-60 (23), MS-61 (27), MS-62 (8), MS-63 (1).

Key to collecting: EF and AU are usual grades for this low-mintage issue. Mint State coins are in lower levels within that category.

MARKET NEWS AND COMMENTARY

In September 1934 Thomas L. Elder's sale of the Robert J. Bouvier Collection included lot 1457: "1889 Very rare. Only about 4,000 struck. Extremely Fine." It sold for $18.50. In May 1993 the Bowers and Merena Galleries sale of the Stetson University Collection included lot 2109: "1889 AU-58 or slightly finer. Sharply struck, brilliant and lustrous." It sold for $3,520.

In November 2000 in the Harry W. Bass Jr. Collection Part IV Bowers and Merena Galleries offered lot 753: "1889 MS-62. Typically encountered at VF to EF, with AU and finer specimens quite scarce. From Paramount's sale of May 1966, lot 612." It sold for $1,840. In the August 2016 ANA World's Fair of Money sale Stack's Bowers Galleries offered lot 3413: "1889 AU-58 PCGS." It sold for $2,115. By that time such coins were very common.

PROOF MARKET NEWS AND COMMENTARY

In April 1956 Abe Kosoff's sale of the Thomas G. Melish and Clinton W. Hester Collections included lot 2524: "1889 Superb brilliant Proof, scarce." It sold for $180. In March 1988 the Bowers and Merena Galleries' sale of the Norweb Collection, Part II, included lot 2248: "1889 Proof-63/64. A splendid coin, and a great rarity. Abe Kosoff's sale of the Melish Collection, 1956." It sold for $14,300.

In January 1984, Stack's sale of the Amon G. Carter Jr. Family Collection included lot 785: "1889 Brilliant Proof. A choice example in deep yellow gold with pale cloudy toning." It sold for $17,600. In October 1998 the John J. Pittman Collection, Part II, sold by David W. Akers, included lot 1967: "1889 Proof-65. Ex Stephens." It sold for $71,500.

Stack's October 2003 68th Anniversary sale/Rothschild included lot 2185: "1889 Proof-65 NGC." It sold for $48,875. Stack's Bowers Galleries' August 2014 Chicago ANA World's Fair of Money sale included lot 13246: "1889 Proof-64 NGC." It sold for $23,500.

VF-20	EF-40	AU-50	AU-55	AU-58	MS-60	MS-63	PF-63	PF-64	PF-65
$875	$925	$950	$1,200	$1,350	$2,500	$10,000	$18,000	$32,500	$52,500

1889-S

Circulation-Strike Mintage: 425,400

Estimated population (Mint State): 2,500+. Most are in grades from MS-60 to MS-62. Another issue that was found in quantity in overseas holdings in the late 20th century.

Estimated population (circulated grades): 5,000+.

Submissions certified at highest grades (as of March 2017): *PCGS:* MS-63 (254), MS-64 (24), MS-65 (1). *NGC:* MS-63 (9), MS-64 (8).

Key to collecting: EF and AU grades are readily available. Mint State coins are easy to find. In lower grades the value of this and other high-mintage eagles is tied into the bullion price of gold.

MARKET NEWS AND COMMENTARY

In February 1944, in the Belden E. Roach Collection, B. Max Mehl offered lot 449: "1889-S Uncirculated, frosty mint luster." It sold for $21.75.

Well into the 21st century, in the June 2015 Pre-Long Beach sale Ira and Larry Goldberg offered lot 1934: "1889-S MS-64 PCGS." It sold for $1,997.50.

VF-20	EF-40	AU-50	AU-55	AU-58	MS-60	MS-63
$650	$675	$700	$750	$800	$850	$1,350

1890

Circulation-Strike Mintage: 57,980
Proof Mintage: 63

Notes regarding mintages: It is likely that no more than 30 Proofs were distributed. Under magnification it is revealed that the die for the portrait of Miss Liberty was touched up before striking, leaving polished areas near the ear and eye. Most of the field below the portrait also has been polished in the die, and curls behind the neck are incomplete. This characteristic is true of all authentic Proofs.

Estimated population (Mint State): *800+.* Very scarce until the late 1900s when many were found overseas. The usual grades are MS-60 to MS-63.

Estimated population (circulated grades): *600–1,000+.*

Estimated population (Proofs): *22–28.* Rare. It seems that many if not most gold Proofs of this era were handled very carelessly at the Mint—jostled around in drawers and nicked and marked—as, indeed, Walter Breen commented in his Proof coin *Encyclopedia.* Thus, by the time that the typical piece left the mint, it was probably closer to Proof-63 than to Proof-65!

Submissions certified at highest grades (as of March 2017): *PCGS:* MS-62 (102), MS-63 (16), MS-64 (1), MS-65 (1). *NGC:* MS-62 (54), MS-63 (6).

Key to collecting: VF and EF are the usually seen grades. Mint State coins are easy to find. In view of repatriations yielding many high-grade coins modern auction listings are not extensively cited.

MARKET NEWS AND COMMENTARY

In May 1993 the Bowers and Merena Galleries' sale of the Stetson University Collection included lot 2111: "1890 MS-60. Brilliant, lustrous, sharp. A definitive specimen of the date, mintmark, and grade. Definitely Condition Census." It sold for $5,060. A once-upon-a-time comment later rendered obsolete by extensive repatriations.

In June 2000, in the Harry W. Bass Jr. Collection, Part III, Bowers and Merena Galleries included lot 726: "1890 MS-62. Purchased from Stanley Kesselman, April 15, 1971." It sold for $1,035. In July 2005 the American Numismatic Rarities sale of the William H. LaBelle Sr. Collection included lot 317: "1890 MS-63 (PCGS)." It sold for $4,140. In its January 2017 FUN Convention sale Heritage included lot 6931: "1890 MS-63 NGC." It sold for $3,585. By that time MS-63 coins generated only modest interest due to their increased availability.

VF-20	EF-40	AU-50	AU-55	AU-58	MS-60	MS-63	MS-65	PF-63	PF-64	PF-65
$650	$675	$700	$750	$800	$850	$4,000	$12,500	$16,500	$25,000	$47,500

1890-CC

Circulation-Strike Mintage: 17,500

Estimated population (Mint State): *300–400.* Readily available. Grades from MS-60 to MS-62 are standard.

Estimated population (circulated grades): *500–750+.*

Die data: Only one pair of dies is known for this coinage.

Submissions certified at highest grades (as of March 2017): *PCGS:* MS-62 (50), MS-63 (1), MS-64 (1). *NGC:* MS-62 (37), MS-63 (7).

Characteristics of striking and die notes: Usually well struck.

Key to collecting: EF and AU are the grades typically seen, a far cry from the average quality of Carson City coins dated 15 to 20 years earlier. Although many examples of 1890-CC were imported in the late 1900s, this variety was plentiful enough in the 1970s. Mint State coins are easy to find.

MARKET NEWS AND COMMENTARY

In May 1945 Stack's sale of the George H. Hall Collection included lot 2188: "1890-CC Brilliant Uncirculated." It sold for $65.

In October 1982, in the Louis E. Eliasberg Collection of U.S. Gold Coins, Bowers and Ruddy Galleries offered lot 794: "1890-CC Choice VF-30." It sold for $550.

In August 2012, in the Battle Born Collection sale, Stack's Bowers Galleries offered lot 11035: "1890-CC MS-64 PCGS. Earlier ex: Heritage's Long Beach Signature Auction of June 2006, lot 3537." It sold for $55,812.50.

In August 2015 at the Chicago ANA World's Fair of Money Stack's Bowers Galleries offered lot 10264, from the Genoa Mill Collection: "1890-CC MS-62+ PCGS." It sold for $13,512.50. In the August 2016 ANA World's Fair of Money sale Stack's Bowers Galleries offered lot 3416: "1890-CC MS-62 PCGS." It sold for $9,400.

VF-20	EF-40	AU-50	AU-55	AU-58	MS-60	MS-63
$1,150	$1,350	$1,650	$2,250	$3,500	$4,500	$22,500

1891

Circulation-Strike Mintage: 91,820
Proof Mintage: 48

Estimated population (Mint State): 750+. Most are in grades from MS-60 to MS-62.

Estimated population (circulated grades): *2,000+.*

Estimated population (Proofs): *14–20.* Very rare.

Submissions certified at highest grades (as of March 2017): *PCGS:* MS-62 (155), MS-63 (54), MS-64 (4). *NGC:* MS-62 (227), MS-63 (50), MS-64 (1), MS-65 (1).

Key to collecting: EF and AU are the grades usually seen. Mint State coins are easy to find. This is one of many later eagle issues that are not common overall, but for which an ample supply exists in view of the relatively small number of specialists in collecting eagles by date and mint.

MARKET NEWS AND COMMENTARY

There are many offerings of this issue, mostly in lower Mint State grades. For just one example, in its February 2017 sale Heritage included lot 8184: "1891 MS-62 NGC." It sold for $1,175.

VF-20	EF-40	AU-50	AU-55	AU-58	MS-60	MS-63	PF-63	PF-64	PF-65
$650	$675	$700	$750	$800	$850	$2,500	$16,500	$25,000	$47,500

1891-CC

Circulation-Strike Mintage: 103,732

Estimated population (Mint State): 1,500+. Common. The most plentiful Carson City eagle in this grade. Most are in lower levels, MS-60 to MS-62, heavily bagmarked. While many were imported in the late 1900s, the issue was readily available before that time.

Estimated population (circulated grades): *1,250+.*

Submissions certified at highest grades (as of March 2017): *PCGS:* MS-62 (416), MS-63 (84), MS-64 (4). *NGC:* MS-63 (107), MS-64 (7), MS-65 (1).

Die data: Three pairs of different dies were used for this coinage.

Key to collecting: EF and AU coins abound but lower-range Mint State pieces are even more plentiful.

Market News and Commentary

In November 1939 the William B. Hale Collection, sold by B. Max Mehl, included lot 1731: "1891-CC Uncirculated, with frosty mint surface." It sold for $18. In the December 1944 sale of the J.F. Bell Collection Stack's included lot 737: "1891-CC Brilliant Uncirculated." It sold for $32.50. In May 1945 Stack's sale of the George H. Hall Collection included lot 2190: "1891-CC Brilliant Uncirculated." It sold for $37.50.

New Netherlands Coin Co.'s 46th sale, Dr. Clarence W. Peake Collection, June 1955, included lot 186: "1891-CC. Uncirculated. Worth a record price so nice." It sold for $40. Years later in March 1988 the Norweb Collection sale by Bowers and Merena Galleries included the Peake specimen as lot 2252: "1891-CC MS-63. An attractive and Uncirculated example of this later Carson City Mint issue. From New Netherlands sale of the Peake Collection, June 1955." It sold for $4,840.

In November 2000 the Bowers and Merena Galleries' sale of the Harry W. Bass Jr. Collection, Part IV, included lot 757: "1891-CC MS-62 Purchased from the Goliad Corporation, January 26, 1973." It sold for $2,990.

The July 2012 sale of the Battle Born Collection by Stack's Bowers Galleries included lot 11036:

> 1891-CC Liberty eagle. Winter 2-B. MS-65 NGC. This is the single finest certified 1891-CC eagle. It is also one of only two Carson City Mint eagles of all dates certified finer than MS-64, the other being an 1874-CC in NGC MS-65. Ex Heritage's sale of the Dr. Mani and Kay Ehteshami Collection, September 2010. [Sold for $57,500]

In its February 2017 Long Beach sale Heritage included lot 4003: "1891-CC MS-64 PCGS. This well-detailed specimen shows an arcing die crack through the stars on the left and the remnants of an undertype C are easily seen protruding from the right side of the second C in the mintmark." It sold for $10,575.

VF-20	EF-40	AU-50	AU-55	AU-58	MS-60	MS-63
$1,100	$1,250	$1,400	$1,900	$2,500	$2,750	$7,000

1892

Circulation-Strike Mintage: 797,480
Proof Mintage: 72

Estimated population (Mint State): *10,000+.* Very common. Many have been sold outside of numismatic circles, but thousands have been certified. Most are MS-60 to MS-62, but higher-grade pieces are occasionally seen.

Estimated population (circulated grades): *15,000+.* No solid figures are available, as this is considered to be a common issue, plentiful in overseas holdings, and not often certified in circulated grades. EF and AU coins are plentiful. Many were imported in the late 1900s.

Estimated population (Proofs): *22–28.* Very rare. As is the case with virtually every Proof $10, less than half of the original coinage seems to have survived.

Submissions certified at highest grades (as of March 2017): *PCGS:* MS-62 (1,810), MS-63 (296), MS-64 (22), MS-65 (5), MS-66 (1). *NGC:* MS-62 (3,356), MS-63 (704), MS-64 (30), MS-65 (6), MS-66 (2).

Key to collecting: Very common. Mint State coins are easy to find. In lower grades the value of this and other high-mintage eagles is tied into the bullion price of gold, this being the case for the *majority* of Liberty Head eagles from the 1880s onward.

MARKET NEWS AND COMMENTARY

In May 1939, sale 399, Rare U.S. Gold Coins by J.C. Morgenthau & Co. included lot 395: "1892 Extremely Fine." It sold for $16.50. In July 1952, in the ANA Convention sale, New Netherlands Coin Co. offered lot 4112: "1892. Uncirculated. A brilliant coin, but with heavy indications of 'bag handling.'" It sold for $24.

Many years later in the January 2017 Collectors Choice sale Stack's Bowers Galleries offered lot 91536: "1892 MS-64 PCGS." It sold for $1,645. By that time such a coin was common.

PROOF MARKET NEWS AND COMMENTARY

In December 1908 Henry Chapman's sale of the David M. Kuntz Collection included lot 102: "1892 Brilliant Proof. Very rare in this condition." It sold for $12.50.

In October 1998, in the John J. Pittman Collection sale, Part II, David Akers offered lot 1971: "1892, Choice Proof. In Proof, the 1892 eagle is slightly less rare than the 1891 and of virtually the same rarity as the 1890; only 20-25 specimens are thought to exist." It sold for $28,600.

VF-20	EF-40	AU-50	AU-55	AU-58	MS-60	MS-63	MS-65	PF-63	PF-64	PF-65
$650	$675	$700	$750	$800	$850	$1,200	$7,500	$16,500	$25,000	$47,500

1892-CC

Circulation-Strike Mintage: 40,000

Estimated population (Mint State): *100–150.* Very scarce in Mint State. Most are at lower levels, MS-60 to MS-62, but upon occasion MS-63 and, less often, MS-64 coins are encountered.

Estimated population (circulated grades): *1,500+.*

Submissions certified at highest grades (as of March 2017): *PCGS:* MS-62 (18), MS-63 (1), MS-64 (1). *NGC:* MS-62 (6), MS-64 (3).

Die data: Two obverse dies and a single reverse die were used for this coinage. The last is the Tripled Die Reverse with tripling which is most prominent at the letters in the words IN GOD WE on the scroll above the eagle.

Key to collecting: EF and AU specimens are seen with frequency on the numismatic market. Enough Mint State coins exist to satisfy the demand for them. All Carson City eagles, scarce to rare, have a wide following and always attract attention at auctions.

MARKET NEWS AND COMMENTARY

In his fixed price list of 1907 Elmer S. Sears, one of the most important retail sellers of U.S. coins at the time, offered lot 32: "1892 Carson City Mint. Extremely Fine and scarce. $12.50." In February 1944, in the Belden E. Roach Collection, B. Max Mehl offered lot 483: "1892-CC About Uncirculated, brilliant." It sold for $25.

In October 1982, in the Louis E. Eliasberg Collection of U.S. Gold Coins, Bowers and Ruddy Galleries offered lot 798: "1892-CC Choice Brilliant Uncirculated, MS-65 to Gem Brilliant Uncirculated, MS-67. A few tiny flecks. From the John H. Clapp Collection, 1942. Earlier from the Bradford Bank, 1895." This coin sold for $9,990. This coin had several later market appearances. The July 2012 sale of the Battle Born Collection by Stack's Bowers Galleries included lot 11037: "1892-CC Winter 2-A. MS-62 NGC. The PCGS Coin Facts website identifies a Tripled Die Reverse of the 1892-CC eagle, which is most prominent at the letters in the words IN GOD WE on the scroll above the eagle." It sold for $5,750.

VF-20	EF-40	AU-50	AU-55	AU-58	MS-60	MS-63
$1,250	$1,500	$1,850	$2,250	$3,000	$4,750	$30,000

1892-O

Circulation-Strike Mintage: 28,688

Estimated population (Mint State): *900+.* Most are MS-60 to MS-62. Any higher-graded coin is a rarity. While many were imported in the last two decades of the 20th century, quite a few were in American collections before that time.

Estimated population (circulated grades): *1,000+.* EF and AU coins are plentiful.

Submissions certified at highest grades (as of March 2017): *PCGS:* MS-61 (167), MS-62 (173), MS-63 (8). *NGC:* MS-61 (310), MS-62 (145), MS-63 (1).

Key to collecting: EF and AU coins are plentiful and Mint state coins from repatriations are easy to find. That was not always the case. In view of this modern auction listings are not extensively cited.

MARKET NEWS AND COMMENTARY

In the December 1944 sale of the J.F. Bell Collection Stack's included lot 711: "1892-O Uncirculated." It sold for $60.

In April 1956, in his sale of the Thomas G. Melish Collection, Abe Kosoff offered lot 2534: "1892-O. Break at TA to Scroll. Uncirculated, very scarce." It sold for $45. This offering inspired the following description in April 1960 in the New Netherlands Coin Co.'s 54th sale, Jonathan Glogower Consignment, Etc. as lot 706:

> 1892-O. This brilliant piece will be unhesitatingly graded Uncirculated by any dealer and most collectors other than absolute perfectionists. However, we can only call it a high caliber AU. Rare, mintage only 28,688. The current listings of $45. and $47.50 doubtless derive from the record of $45 in the Melish sale, nearly four years ago, and that is the only Mint State one we have encountered in auctions recent enough to mean anything for the current market. [Sold for $45]

In this era the New Netherlands catalogs were the only ones to have detailed descriptions with market comments, occasional slings and arrows against their competitors (all of whom were perceived as less knowledgeable), and other observations. As noted earlier, these publications were viewed as entertaining and a "good read" at the time.

The March 2005 American Numismatic Rarities Richard C. Jewell Collection sale included lot 783: "1892-O MS-62 NGC." It sold for $1,955. In November 2011 the Stack's Bowers Galleries' Baltimore Whitman Expo sale included lot 9740: "1892-O MS-63 PCGS." It sold for $9,200. In its January 2016 FUN Convention sale Heritage included lot 4537: "1892-O MS-62 NGC." It sold for $1,645. In the August 2016 ANA World's Fair of Money sale Stack's Bowers Galleries offered lot 3421: "1892-O MS-62 PCGS." It sold for $2,056.25.

VF-20	EF-40	AU-50	AU-55	AU-58	MS-60	MS-63
$725	$800	$850	$900	$975	$1,150	$8,000

1892-S

Circulation-Strike Mintage: 115,500

Estimated population (Mint State): *450+.* Most are MS-60 to MS-62, punctuated by the occasional MS-63. Any higher-graded coin is a rarity.

Estimated population (circulated grades): *1,500+.*

Submissions certified at highest grades (as of March 2017): *PCGS:* MS-63 (75), MS-64 (3), MS-65 (1). *NGC:* MS-63 (24), MS-64 (1).

Key to collecting: EF and AU specimens are usually seen. Once again there are more than enough Mint State coins to supply specialists who collect by date and mintmark.

MARKET NEWS AND COMMENTARY

In the December 1944 sale of the J.F. Bell Collection Stack's included lot 776: "1892-S About Uncirculated." It sold for $24.

In October 1982, in the Louis E. Eliasberg Collection of U.S. Gold Coins, Bowers and Ruddy Galleries offered lot 800: "1892-S Choice Brilliant Uncirculated, MS-65." It sold for $4,950.

Steve Ivy, in his May 1983 sale of the Wallace Ralston Collection, included lot 2759:

> 1892-S AU-50 Semiprooflike obverse. Pink toning at the obverse periphery; dusky green at the reverse. Light, even contact marks are more obvious on the obverse. A very scarce and underrated date; before the small hoard of baggy Uncs. turned up in 1977, this date was unknown in strict Mint State. [Sold for $330]

In its February 2017 sale Heritage included lot 5119: "1892-S MS-63 NGC." It sold for $2,585.

VF-20	EF-40	AU-50	AU-55	AU-58	MS-60	MS-63
$650	$675	$700	$750	$800	$850	$2,500

1893

Circulation-Strike Mintage: 1,840,840
Proof Mintage: 55

Notes regarding mintages: The Proof die for the figure of Liberty was polished near the ear and in the field beneath Miss Liberty, this being characteristic of all authentic specimens.

Estimated population (Mint State): *40,000+.* Very common. Many have been sold outside of numismatic circles, but thousand have been certified. Most are MS-60 to MS-62, with many MS-63 coins as well. Higher-grade examples are very rare.

Estimated population (circulated grades): *20,000+.*

Estimated population (Proofs): *15–20.* Very rare. Take away pieces in museums as well as damaged coins and it is probably the case that fewer than 10 really nice examples are in private hands.

Submissions certified at highest grades (as of March 2017): *PCGS:* MS-62 (8,584), MS-63 (2,680), MS-64 (349), MS-65 (7). *NGC:* MS-62 (14,068), MS-63 (7,240), MS-64 (773), MS-65 (25), MS-66 (1).

Die data: The 189 *three*-digit date logotype numerals are fairly widely spaced. The 18 is closest and the 89 is wider. The small ball of the 9 is close to the upper curve and may touch on some deep impressions. The 3 was added separately to working dies and varies in spacing and alignment. Varieties (all mints considered as a group) have been seen with the 93 close, with the 3 centered, with the 3 high, and with the 3 low. The 3-digit logotype plus individually added final digit was used on all dies for all mints.

Key to collecting: As this is considered to be a common issue, once plentiful in overseas holdings and now common in the United States, Mint State coins are easy to find. Except in the very highest grades this and related eagles with large surviving populations respond more in price to gold bullion value changes, not to changes in numismatic demand.

MARKET NEWS AND COMMENTARY

In February 1944, in the Belden E. Roach Collection, B. Max Mehl offered lot 366: "1893 Brilliant Uncirculated with semi-proof surface." It sold for $22.50. In May 1945 Stack's sale of the George H. Hall Collection included lot 2193: "1893 Brilliant Uncirculated." It sold for $26.

A long time afterward, July 1985 in Auction '85, Paramount offered lot 1455: "1893 Gem Uncirculated (65/65+). An abrasion on Liberty's chin but the coin is otherwise quite exceptional." It realized $2,530.

In May 2000 the Harry W. Bass Jr. Collection, Part III, sold by Bowers and Merena Galleries, included lot 732:

> 1893 MS-63. Date nicely impressed. 1 equidistant from truncation and dentils, left edge of lower serif over left edge of dentil. The reverse shows die cracks. The editor believes that $10 gold coins of the year 1893 were made with a three-digit logotype 189, with the fourth digit added separately. There seem to be some notable differences among 1893 eagles as to the spacing of the 9 and the 3. If any readers have any specific comments we would be pleased to receive them (QDB note). From Stack's sale of the Miles Collection, October 1968, lot 751. [Sold for $920]

In later years the 1893 became common, and offerings at auction in a grade such as MS-63 attracted medium interest at best.

PROOF MARKET NEWS AND COMMENTARY

In June October 1908 Thomas L. Elder's sale of the James B. Wilson Collection included lot 77: "1893 Complete [gold Proof] set. 4 pieces." It sold for $47.50 for the entire set. Face value was $37.50.

VF-20	EF-40	AU-50	AU-55	AU-58	MS-60	MS-63	MS-65	PF-63	PF-64	PF-65
$650	$675	$700	$750	$800	$850	$1,000	$5,500	$16,500	$25,000	$47,500

1893-CC

Circulation-Strike Mintage: 14,000

Estimated population (Mint State): *16–22.* Very rare in Mint State. Grades typically range from MS-60 to MS-62 with extensive bagmarks.

Estimated population (circulated grades): *150–225.*

Submissions certified at highest grades (as of March 2017): *PCGS:* MS-60 (1), MS-61 (4), MS-62 (4). *NGC:* MS-61 (1).

Die data: The 189 *three*-digit date logotype numerals are fairly widely spaced. The 18 is closest and the 89 is wider. The small ball of the 9 is close to the upper curve and may touch on some deep impressions. The 3 was added separately to working dies and varies in spacing and alignment. Varieties (all mints considered as a group) have been seen with the 93 close, with the 3 centered, with the 3 high, and with the 3 low. The 3-digit logotype plus individually added final digit was used on all dies for all mints.

Characteristics of striking and die notes: The date logotype for all known 1893-CC eagles is large, set low in the field, and slants down from left to right. Three reverse die varieties are known. Winter 1-A was described in the 2001 book, *Gold Coins of the Carson City Mint*, by Douglas Winter and James L. Halperin. A second and apparently newly discovered reverse was described under lot 11038 of the 2012 Battle Born Collection sale by Stack's Bowers Galleries.

Key to collecting: VF is the typical grade of coins found in old-time collections. EF, AU and Mint State coins are nearly all from modern repatriations.

MARKET NEWS AND COMMENTARY

In March 1911, in his sale of the William H. Woodin Collection, Thomas L. Elder offered lot 1352: "1893-CC Very Fine; rare." It sold for $10.50. The variety was recognized as rare in this era, but only a few numismatists sought high-denomination gold coins by date and mintmark varieties. Coins such as this were available for face value in banks and would be for many years to come, until 1933.

In June 1946, in the William Cutler Atwater Collection, B. Max Mehl offered lot 1331: "1893-CC. Just a shade from Uncirculated, with considerable luster. A very tiny nick on obverse. Record over $100." It sold for $88. Also lot 1514: "1893-CC Last year of issue. About Uncirculated with frosty mint surface. Scarce. Recent record $50." It sold for $48.50.

The May 1993 Stetson University Collection, sold by Bowers and Merena Galleries, included lot 2120: "1893-CC AU-55, prooflike. A superb specimen, Condition Census, of a variety seldom seen in this grade. Indeed, the Miller Sale coin was AU-50. A recent PCGS Population Report notes that that firm has attributed no examples in the Mint State category, just one in AU-58, and only three in AU-55." It sold for $4,730.

In October 1998, in the John J. Pittman Collection sale, Part II, David Akers offered lot 1975:

> 1893-CC, Extremely Fine to Almost Uncirculated. Lustrous, semi-proof surfaces and attractive medium orange gold color. Light scratch in the field by the 1st star. I have long considered this to be a very underrated issue. It is similar in overall rarity to the CC Mint eagles of the early 1880's (except the 1882-CC which is more rare), but despite its low mintage, this issue has never received much recognition as a scarce issue. However, it is very difficult to find in grades above EF and mint state examples are very rare. Purchased from James Kelly for $32, date of purchase unknown. [Sold for $3,300]

The July 2012 sale of the Battle Born Collection by Stack's Bowers Galleries included lot 11038:

> 1893-CC MS-62 PCGS. The reverse exhibits a medium size, evenly spaced mintmark with both Cs level. The first C is over the left edge of the letter N in TEN and the second C is centered over the right upright of the letter N [this being a new discovery] PCGS Population: just 3; and none are finer either of the major

certification services. Ex Bowers and Merena Galleries' sale of the Charity Collection, October 2005, lot 7602. [Sold for $32,200]

In its September 2016 Long Beach sale Heritage included lot 14167: "1893-CC MS-61 PCGS. PCGS has certified just eight Uncirculated 1893-CC tens and none finer than MS-62." It sold for $30,550.

VF-20	EF-40	AU-50	AU-55	AU-58	MS-60
$1,350	$1,650	$2,850	$5,000	$8,750	$15,000

1893-O

Circulation-Strike Mintage: 17,000

Estimated population (Mint State): 700+. Most are MS-60 to MS-62. Any higher-graded coin is a rarity. While some were imported in the 1980s and 1990s, before that time examples were plentiful.

Estimated population (circulated grades): *1,000+.*

Submissions certified at highest grades (as of March 2017): *PCGS:* MS-61 (125), MS-62 (167), MS-63 (13). *NGC:* MS-61 (157), MS-62 (79), MS-63 (10).

Die data: See information under Philadelphia listing.

Key to collecting: EF and the rare AU coin were the grades usually seen (see 1960 Glogower listing later), added in later years by repatriations of AU and Mint State coins. Mint State coins are easy to find.

In his 1967 *United States Eagles* Walter Breen stated that the AU coin in New Netherlands Coin Company's Cicero Sale, 1960, "appears to be the finest one around."

MARKET NEWS AND COMMENTARY

In the December 1944 sale of the J.F. Bell Collection Stack's included lot 712: "1893-O About Uncirculated." It sold for $62.50.

In April 1960 New Netherlands' 54th sale, Jonathan Glogower Consignment, Etc., included this lot 707:

> 1893-O. Far better than Extremely Fine, nearly full mint brilliance; lightly but extensively bag marked. Rarer than last; 17,000 struck. Significantly, we have no record of an equal example; the nearest one is the Dr. Green coin, EF, and Mehl mentioned a previous record of $60 for this mintmark in describing that lot. [Sold for $33]

Not surprisingly for New Netherlands, Stack's well-publicized sale of the J.F. Bell Collection was conveniently ignored. In October 1982, in the Louis E. Eliasberg Collection of U.S. Gold Coins, Bowers and Ruddy Galleries offered lot 803: "1893-O Brilliant Uncirculated, MS-60 to Select Brilliant Uncirculated, MS-63." It sold for $1,100.

In November 2000, in the Harry W. Bass Jr. Collection, Part IV, Bowers and Merena Galleries offered lot 763: "1893-O MS-63. This is the only specimen that Harry Bass found suitable over decades of searching. From Stack's sale of the Miles Collection, October 1968, lot 752." It sold for $2,990.

Were he alive today Harry Bass would find many coins to his liking. While the 1893-O is no longer rare, eagles from the New Orleans Mint remain very popular.

VF-20	EF-40	AU-50	AU-55	AU-58	MS-60	MS-63
$725	$800	$850	$975	$1,000	$1,200	$5,000

1893-S

Circulation-Strike Mintage: 141,350

Estimated population (Mint State): 1,000+. Most are MS-60 to MS-63, although some higher-graded pieces are seen now and then (and are scarce). In his 1980 text David W. Akers stated that a small hoard of Mint State coins had been discovered in the mid-1970s. "Since almost all of the pieces in the hoard were of very average quality, the 1893-S is still rare in choice or Gem Uncirculated condition." Beyond that there have been many repatriations since 1980.

Estimated population (circulated grades): 2,000+. EF and AU grades are typical.

Submissions certified at highest grades (as of March 2017): *PCGS:* MS-61 (117), MS-63 (210), MS-64 (1), MS-65 (1), MS-66 (1), MS-67 (1). *NGC:* MS-61 (262), MS-62 (156), MS-63 (19), MS-64 (1), MS-65 (1), MS-66 (1).

Die data: See information under Philadelphia listings.

Key to collecting: This is another issue that is plentiful in any grade desired up through lower Mint State levels.

Market News and Commentary

In February 1944, in the Belden E. Roach Collection, B. Max Mehl offered lot 451: "1893-S About Uncirculated." It sold for $27. In the December 1944 sale of the J.F. Bell Collection Stack's included lot 777: "1893-S Extremely Fine." It sold for $24.

In November 1945 B. Max Mehl's sale of the W.A. Philpott and Henry L. Zander Collections included lot 1760: "1893-S Fine." It sold for $17.50.

In October 1982, in the Louis E. Eliasberg Collection of U.S. Gold Coins, Bowers and Ruddy Galleries offered lot 804: "1893-S Gem Brilliant Uncirculated, MS-67. A truly superb, outstanding specimen of this San Francisco Mint issue. From the John H. Clapp Collection, 1942. Earlier from the San Francisco Mint, November 1893, at face value." It sold for $10,450.

In its February 2017 sale Heritage included lot 5124: "1893-S MS-63 PCGS." It sold for $1,645.

VF-20	EF-40	AU-50	AU-55	AU-58	MS-60	MS-63
$650	$675	$700	$750	$800	$850	$2,500

1894

Circulation-Strike Mintage: 2,470,735
Proof Mintage: 43

Estimated population (Mint State):
30,000+. Very common. Many have been
sold outside of numismatic circles, but thousands have been certified. Most are MS-60 to MS-64, plus a few at the MS-65 level.
Any higher-grade coin is a *rarity.*

Estimated population (circulated grades): ***50,000+.*** No solid figures available, as
this is considered to be a common issue, plentiful in overseas holdings, and not often
certified in circulated grades. EF and AU grades are commonly found.

Estimated population (Proofs): ***15–20.*** Very rare, one of the most elusive of the era.

Submissions certified at highest grades (as of March 2017): ***PCGS:*** MS-62 (8,912),
MS-63 (2,180), MS-64 (187), MS-65 (1) (a coin that would seem to be on a perilous
grade perch considered the large number of MS-64 pieces next to it and the passion for
resubmitting coins). ***NGC:*** MS-62 (15,853), MS-63 (6,155), MS-64 (436), MS-65 (16).

Key to collecting: Very common. Mint State coins are easy to find, but several generations ago such were rare. Except in the very highest grades this and related eagles
with large surviving populations respond more in price to gold bullion value changes,
not to changes in numismatic demand.

MARKET NEWS AND COMMENTARY

In June 1934 J.C. Morgenthau & Co.'s sale of coins from the Waldo C. Newcomer
Collection included lot 357: "1894 Uncirculated, brilliant." It sold for $20. New Netherlands Coin Co.'s 46th sale, Dr. Clarence W. Peake Collection, June 1955, included
lot 190: "1894. Brilliant Uncirculated. Not perfect, but the best we've handled." It sold
for $26. In April 1956, in his sale of the Thomas G. Melish Collection, Kosoff offered
lot 2541: "1894. High date. Uncirculated." It sold for $24. Also lot 2542: "1894. Low
date. About Uncirculated." It sold for $21.

In the dynamic market of November 2000, in the Harry W. Bass Jr. Collection, Part
IV, Bowers and Merena Galleries offered lot 764: "1894 MS-63. From Stack's sale of
the DiBello Collection, May 1970, lot 1126." It sold for $805. Stack's February 2008
Rich Uhrich Collection sale included lot 2235: "1894 MS-65 PCGS." It sold for $7,820.
In its January 2017 FUN Convention sale Heritage included lot 6937: "1894 MS-64+
PCGS." It sold for $3,290.

PROOF MARKET NEWS AND COMMENTARY

In March 1911, in his sale of the William H. Woodin Collection, Thomas L. Elder
offered lot 1256b: "1894. Brilliant Proof." It sold for $11. As noted several times earlier,
in the early 1900s there was little numismatic premium on high-denomination gold
coins, and many if not most $5, $10, and $10 coins were spent.

In October 1982, in the Louis E. Eliasberg Collection of U.S. Gold Coins, Bowers
and Ruddy Galleries offered lot 805: "1894 Select Brilliant Proof-63 obverse, Proof-65.
Purchased from the Philadelphia Mint." It sold for $10,450.

In October 1998, in the John J. Pittman Collection sale, Part II, David Akers offered lot 1977:

> 1894, Very Choice Proof. In Proof, the 1894 eagle is similar in rarity to the 1891 and 1893. Of the 43 Proofs struck, only an estimated 15–20 pieces have survived, no more than a handful of which are comparable in overall quality to this beautiful specimen. The date is low in the field with the 1 nearer the denticles than the bust; the 9 is closed. The reverse die appears to be the same die used to strike the 1893, but repolished. [Sold for $71,500]

VF-20	EF-40	AU-50	AU-55	AU-58	MS-60	MS-63	MS-65	PF-63	PF-64	PF-65
$650	$675	$700	$750	$800	$850	$1,000	$7,500	$16,500	$25,000	$47,500

1894-O

Circulation-Strike Mintage: 107,500

Estimated population (Mint State): 400+. Most are MS-60 to MS-62. Any higher-graded coin is very rare.

Estimated population (circulated grades): 1,500+.

Submissions certified at highest grades (as of March 2017): *PCGS:* MS-62 (57), MS-63 (13), MS-64 (1). *NGC:* MS-62 (58), MS-63 (12), MS-64 (2), MS-65 (1).

Key to collecting: EF and AU coins are plentiful, VF pieces less so. Mint State coins are nearly all from modern repatriations. Mint State coins are easy to find. The addition of a few New Orleans eagles to any auction listing always spurs interest, even if, as here, they are not rarities.

MARKET NEWS AND COMMENTARY

In the December 1944 sale of the J.F. Bell Collection Stack's included lot 713: "1894-O Brilliant Uncirculated." It sold for $27.50. In May 2000, in the Harry W. Bass Jr. Collection sale, Part III, Bowers and Merena Galleries offered lot 734: "1894-O MS-62. Purchased from Douglas Weaver, September 26, 1973." It sold for $1,955.

In September 2005 the American Numismatic Rarities sale of the C.L. Lee Collection included lot 1320: "1894-O MS-65 NGC." It sold for $21,850. Another, one graded MS-62 by NGC, in the same sale brought $1,840, a par excellence example of condition rarity.

VF-20	EF-40	AU-50	AU-55	AU-58	MS-60	MS-65
$725	$800	$850	$975	$1,000	$1,200	$5,500

1894-S

Circulation-Strike Mintage: 25,000

Estimated population (Mint State): *100–150.* Rare. Known examples are in lower-grade levels hovering around MS–60 and 61.

Estimated population (circulated grades): *400+.*

Submissions certified at highest grades (as of March 2017): *PCGS:* MS-60 (4), MS-61 (9), MS-62 (4). *NGC:* MS-60 (6), MS-61 (12), MS-62 (1).

Key to collecting: EF and AU coins were once the order of the day, although scattered Mint State pieces appeared in sales of years ago. Lower-range Mint State coins are mostly modern repatriations and are somewhat scarce. Certified MS-61 coins are elusive and those graded MS-62 are rare.

MARKET NEWS AND COMMENTARY

In March 1911, in his sale of the William H. Woodin Collection, Thomas L. Elder offered lot 1326: "1894-S Fine; scarce." It sold for $10 (face value). As has been seen multiple times among auction listings, there was little interest in circulation-strike gold coins at the time. Even by May 1939 in sale 399, Rare U.S. Gold Coins by J.C. Morgenthau & Co. lot 399, described as: "1894-S Extremely Fine," realized $16.50, or less than the $17.00 melt value, gold being $35 per ounce at the time.

In their April 1960 54th sale, Jonathan Glogower Consignment, Etc., New Netherlands Coin Co. offered lot 709: "1894-S. Extremely Fine, considerable mint luster. A real 'sleeper' this mintmark has private sale records of $75 and $82.50 VF, these representing the prices of a dealer who searched through thousands of eagles for his two specimens, neither of which was as nice as this piece." It sold for $62.50.

At this time huge quantities of double eagles in particular, but also many eagles, were imported from Switzerland and other foreign sources by bullion dealers. Those tended to be in grades higher than AU, so perhaps the consignor had access to some unknown domestic holding. Or perhaps searching through thousands was literary license. Cataloger Walter Breen often made things up, with some comments being rejected by John J. Ford Jr.—from my experience as being behind the scenes as an observer in many New Netherlands sales.

In its January 2017 FUN Convention sale Heritage included lot 6938:

> The 1894-S Liberty Head eagle is a rarity in Mint State. Although graded only MS62, this lustrous wheat-gold example is tied for the finest known. The strike is boldly executed, and both sides display only light chatter in the fields rather than distracting abrasions. The surfaces are original and truly unworn, and eye appeal is thus much stronger than expected for the grade. Population: 4 in 62, 0 finer (11/16).
> [Sold for $11,750]

VF-20	EF-40	AU-50	AU-55	AU-58	MS-60	MS-63
$750	$775	$950	$1,100	$1,800	$3,500	$14,000

1895

Circulation-Strike Mintage: 567,770

Proof Mintage: 56

Estimated population (Mint State): *20,000+.* Very common. Many have been sold outside of numismatic circles, but thousands have been certified. Most are MS-60 to MS-62, but higher-grade pieces are occasionally seen, but at the MS-65 level the 1895 is rare.

Estimated population (circulated grades): *15,000+.*

Estimated population (Proofs): *16–20.*

Submissions certified at highest grades (as of March 2017): *PCGS:* MS-62 (2,978), MS-63 (646), MS-64 (76), MS-65 (4). *NGC:* MS-62 (4,815), MS-63 (1,889), MS-64 (195), MS-65 (2), MS-66 (1), MS-67 (1).

Key to collecting: Common across the board, as noted previously. Mint State coins are easy to find.

MARKET NEWS AND COMMENTARY

As was true of circulation strikes of all Philadelphia Mint eagles during this era, numismatic interest was nil until generations later. Collectors desiring examples of a given date ordered Proofs.

Perhaps it was the demand of a consignor who provided other coins of rarity that motivated Stack's in the George A. Powers Collection, December 1959, to offer this impaired coin as a single item, lot 964: "1895 About Uncirculated but initials scratched in the field." It sold for $21.

In August 2013 the Stack's Bowers Galleries' ANA World's Fair of Money sale included lot 4519: "1895 MS-65 PCGS." It sold for $11,163.

Regency Auction XIX, December 2016, included lot 464: "1895 MS-64+ PCGS." It sold for $3,642.50. Condition rarity has led the market in modern times, and a coin that can be very common and inexpensive in a grade or two lower can sell for a record price if it is a higher grade with only a few certified.

VF-20	EF-40	AU-50	AU-55	AU-58	MS-60	MS-63	MS-65	PF-63	PF-64	PF-65
$650	$675	$700	$750	$800	$850	$1,000	$11,000	$16,000	$25,000	$47,500

1895-O

Circulation-Strike Mintage: 98,000

Estimated population (Mint State): *750+.* Most are MS-60 to MS-62. Any higher-graded coin is a rarity. Many of these were brought back from overseas in the 1970s.

Estimated population (circulated grades): *1,000+.*

Submissions certified at highest grades (as of March 2017): *PCGS:* MS-61 (155), MS-62 (109), MS-63 (25). *NGC:* MS-61 (183), MS-62 (84), MS-63 (10), MS-64 (1).

Key to collecting: High-grade EF and AU coins are plentiful and have been for a long time. Lower-range Mint State coins are common as well—more than enough to fill the demand from specialists. These are very popular in the marketplace.

MARKET NEWS AND COMMENTARY

In the December 1944 sale of the J.F. Bell Collection Stack's included lot 714: "1895-O Extremely Fine. Very scarce." It sold for $37.50. Not long afterward in May 1945 the same firm offered the George H. Hall Collection with lot 2200: "1895-O Brilliant Uncirculated." It sold for $57.50.

The August 2016 ANA World's Fair of Money sale Stack's Bowers Galleries offered lot 2396: "1895-O MS-63 NGC." It sold for $6,463. Also lot 3431: "1895-O MS-62 MS-63 PCGS." It sold for $2,585. The April 2017 sale by Heritage included lot 15976: "1895-O MS-63 PCGS." It sold for $4,937.35.

VF-20	EF-40	AU-50	AU-55	AU-58	MS-60	MS-63
$725	$775	$850	$975	$1,000	$1,200	$6,000

1895-S

Circulation-Strike Mintage: 49,000

Estimated population (Mint State): *40–55.* Extremely and surprisingly rare in Mint State. Most are MS-60 to MS-62. Until modern times, in Mint State the 1895-S was virtually unknown.

Estimated population (circulated grades): *1,000+.*

Submissions certified at highest grades (as of March 2017): *PCGS:* MS-62 (5), MS-64 (1), MS-65 (2). *NGC:* MS-62 (2), MS-64 (3).

Key to collecting: VF and EF are the usually seen grades, plus a smaller number of Mint State coins in lower ranges.

MARKET NEWS AND COMMENTARY

In February 1944, in the Belden E. Roach Collection, B. Max Mehl offered lot 453: "1895-S Extremely Fine, with semi-proof surface." It sold for $23.25. New Netherlands Coin Co., in its June 1955 46th sale, the Dr. Clarence W. Peake Collection, included lot 194: "1895-S. Extremely Fine. Just 49,000 struck, a rather limited coinage for San Francisco. Superior to the W.G.C. Green, and Davis-Graves examples." It sold for $22. This was a very exciting auction with a large gallery of bidders. The market was on a strong upswing.

In October 1982, in the Louis E. Eliasberg Collection of U.S. Gold Coins, Bowers and Ruddy Galleries offered lot 810: "1895-S Choice Brilliant Uncirculated, MS-65 obverse; Gem Brilliant Uncirculated, MS-67 reverse. From the John H. Clapp Collection, 1942. Earlier from the United States Mint, October 1895, at face value." The coin sold for $14,300. In a later offering, July 1989, David W. Akers commented, "Believed to be the finest known." The era of *condition rarities* was in full force.

In July 1987, in Auction '87, Paramount offered lot 453:

> 1895-S, Choice Uncirculated 63. An amazing example of this grossly underrated date. It is by far the finest we have ever handled and the second best we have ever seen. (Eliasberg's coin, the only known gem brought $14,300 in late 1982.) This piece is fully struck with prooflike fields, absolutely radiant luster and superb coppery gold toning. Recently discovered in the San Francisco Bay area, to the best of our knowledge this piece has never before been on the numismatic market. [Sold for $4,125]

The Heritage October 2014 Long Beach sale included lot 5027: "1895-S MS-62 PCGS." It sold for $5,875.

VF-20	EF-40	AU-50	AU-55	AU-58	MS-60	MS-63
$850	$925	$975	$900	$1,250	$2,000	$8,000

1896

Circulation-Strike Mintage: 76,270
Proof Mintage: 78

Estimated population (Mint State): 2,500+. Most are MS-60 to MS-63, with MS-64 occasionally seen, and anything higher being quite rare. Most are from repatriated coins brought back from Switzerland and elsewhere beginning in the late 1940s.

Estimated population (circulated grades): 4,000+.

Estimated population (Proofs): 25–35. Very rare.

Submissions certified at highest grades (as of March 2017): *PCGS:* MS-62 (425), MS-63 (168), MS-64 (17). *NGC:* MS-62 (623), MS-63 (242), MS-64 (25), MS-65 (1).

Key to collecting: Mint State coins are plentiful. There is no need to buy a circulated example.

MARKET NEWS AND COMMENTARY

In October 1947, in the H.R. Lee Collection (Eliasberg duplicates), Stack's offered lot 1551: "1896 Brilliant Uncirculated, with frosty mint surface." It sold for $25.

In December 1960 New Netherlands Coin Co.'s 55th sale, Collection Cicero had lot 87: "1896. Brilliant, frosty Uncirculated. A few minute bag marks away from "gem" level. Rarely seen in this quality; Melish's was inferior, and others lately offered have not even been Mint State. Mintage 76,270; scarcer than this figure would indicate." It sold for $32.

In the August 2016 World's Fair of Money sale Stack's Bowers Galleries offered lot 3433: "1896 MS-64 PCGS." It sold for $2,350.

PROOF MARKET NEWS AND COMMENTARY

Lyman H. Low's March 1900 offering of the Leopold Gans Collection included lot 47: "1896 gold Proof set, 2-1/2, 5, 10, and 20 dollars." The full set realized $37.50 (face value!).

In February 1944, in the Belden E. Roach Collection, B. Max Mehl offered lot 369:

> 1896 Perfect brilliant Proof struck in yellow gold. Rare and in great demand as are all of the Proofs. Collectors now realize the great rarity of our gold coins in Proof condition. They are only available when great collections come on the market. With the greatly increased interest in our gold series, it is only natural that collectors who begin modestly in forming a gold collection, soon realize the great advantage in owning Proof coins. I feel confident in making the statement that the present price these Proof coins are bringing will seem insignificantly low in the very near future. Even their present—what I consider low prices—are more than double the prices they sold for just a few years ago. [Sold for $52]

Once again, true words, but prices remained modest for years afterward. In the December 1944 sale of the J.F. Bell Collection Stack's included lot 660: "1896 Perfect Brilliant Proof. Gem." It sold for $75. In June 1946, in the William Cutler Atwater Collection, B. Max Mehl offered lot 1474: "1896 Struck in light-colored gold. Brilliant Proof gem. Record $75." It sold for $80.

In October 1962, in the Samuel W. Wolfson Collection, Stack's offered lot 782: "1896 Brilliant Proof." It sold for $600.

In October 1982, in the Louis E. Eliasberg Collection of U.S. Gold Coins, Bowers and Ruddy Galleries offered lot 811: "1896 Choice Brilliant Proof-65. From the John H. Clapp Collection, 1942. Earlier directly from the Philadelphia Mint." It sold for $8,800. In the August 2006 ANA World's Fair of Money sale Bowers and Merena Galleries offered lot 4371: "1896 Proof-65 PCGS." It sold for $49,450.

VF-20	EF-40	AU-50	AU-55	AU-58	MS-60	MS-63	MS-65	PF-63	PF-64	PF-65
$650	$675	$700	$750	$800	$850	$1,200	$12,000	$16,000	$25,000	$47,500

1896-S

Circulation-Strike Mintage: 123,750

Estimated population (Mint State): 150–225. Most are in grades from MS-60 to MS-63. Until the late 1900s, when examples were brought back from foreign holdings, the 1896-S was an incredible rarity in Mint State. Today, it remains scarce if not rare, but enough are around that the specialist can find one without difficulty. Still, it is one of the more elusive varieties of the late 1890s.

Estimated population (circulated grades): 3,000+.

Submissions certified at highest grades (as of March 2017): PCGS: MS-62 (25), MS-63 (29), MS-65 (1), MS-66 (1). **NGC:** MS-62 (12), MS-64 (2).

Key to collecting: Mostly from modern imports, but not in large quantities. Mint State coins are not common, but there are enough to satisfy the demand from specialists.

MARKET NEWS AND COMMENTARY

In February 1944, in the Belden E. Roach Collection, B. Max Mehl offered lot 454: "1896-S Uncirculated; brilliant luster." It sold for $25.75. This was an outstanding coin in terms of market appearances in this era. In the December 1944 sale of the J.F. Bell Collection Stack's included lot 780: "1896-S Uncirculated." It sold for $24. Another notable high-grade specimen.

In October 1982, in the Louis E. Eliasberg Collection of U.S. Gold Coins, Bowers and Ruddy Galleries offered lot 812: "1896-S Choice Brilliant Uncirculated, MS-65 to Gem Brilliant Uncirculated, MS-67 obverse; Choice Brilliant Uncirculated, MS-65 reverse. From the John H. Clapp Collection, 1942. Earlier directly from the San Francisco Mint." It sold for $10,450.

In May 1993 the Bowers and Merena Galleries' sale of the Stetson University Collection included lot 2130: "1896-S AU-58 or finer. Condition Census at the lower level of the range." It sold for $7,150. Large-scale repatriation, not envisioned at the time, was yet to come.

In September 1994 the sale by Bowers and Merena Galleries of the Richard and Jean Salisbury and Ted K. Woods Collections included lot 3311: "1896-S AU-58 PCGS. A rare and underrated date that David Akers calls 'very difficult to locate in any condition.' Deep golden surfaces display strong cartwheel luster and rich golden toning highlights." It sold for $1,980.

The Stack's September 2009 Philadelphia Americana sale included lot 5545: "1896-S MS-63 PCGS." It sold for $8,637. The Heritage December 2013 sale included lot 38711: "1896-S MS-63 NGC." It sold for $6,756.25.

VF-20	EF-40	AU-50	AU-55	AU-58	MS-60	MS-63
$725	$750	$775	$850	$900	$1,650	$8,000

1897

Circulation-Strike Mintage: 1,000,090
Proof Mintage: 69

Estimated population (Mint State): *15,000+.* Very common. Many have been sold outside of numismatic circles, but thousands have been certified. Most are MS-60 to MS-62, but higher grade pieces are occasionally seen, through MS-64 and the very occasional MS-65.

Estimated population (circulated grades): *20,000+.* No solid figures available, as this is considered to be a common issue, plentiful in overseas holdings, and not often certified in circulated grades. VF and EF are the usually seen grades, but many AU coins also exist.

Estimated population (Proofs): *20–25.* Very rare.

Submissions certified at highest grades (as of March 2017): *PCGS:* MS-63 (2,351), MS-64 (160), MS-65 (12), MS-66 (3). *NGC:* MS-63 (1,425), MS-64 (176), MS-65 (22), MS-66 (5), MS-67 (1).

Key to collecting: Common as fleas on a stray dog.

MARKET NEWS AND COMMENTARY

In July 1951 James F. Kelly in *Kelly's Coins and Chatter*, Vols. 4–7, offered: "1897 Uncirculated. $25." Kelly was the first American dealer to tap overseas holdings, mainly starting with Swiss banks, to repatriate American gold coins in quantity.

In December 2004 the American Numismatic Rarities Classics sale included lot 526: "1897 MS-66 (PCGS)." It sold for $11,500. In the June 2015 Pre-Long Beach sale Ira and Larry Goldberg offered lot 1942: "1897 MS-65 PCGS." It sold for $7,991.25.

In November 2011 the Stack's Bowers Galleries' Baltimore Whitman Expo sale included lot 9749: "1897 MS-65 NGC." It sold for $5,175. In the August 2016 ANA World's Fair of Money sale Stack's Bowers Galleries offered lot 3435: "1897 MS-65 PCGS." It sold for $2,585 MS-65 coins, once exceptional, by this time were surpassed by many coins certified in higher grades.

PROOF MARKET NEWS AND COMMENTARY

In June 1907 the Chapman brothers sale of the Major W.B. Wetmore Collection included lot 40: "1897 Brilliant Proof." It sold for $11. This is one of hundreds of listings of 19th century Proof eagles that brought little more than face value, resulting in many being spent.

The June 1995 Stack's sale of the Vander Zanden Collection and the Yale University Consignment included lot 823: "1897 Brilliant Proof. Obverse rim at top and bottom with light marks, hallmark of the Kaufman coins. Ex N.M. Kaufman Collection (RARCOA, August 4, 1978, lot 899)." It sold for $8,250. Kaufman, a bank officer in Marquette, Michigan, displayed his magnificent collection by fastening coins to a hard backing using three tacks at points around the border.

VF-20	EF-40	AU-50	AU-55	AU-58	MS-60	MS-63	MS-65	PF-63	PF-64	PF-65
$650	$675	$700	$750	$800	$850	$1,000	$6,000	$16,000	$25,000	$47,500

1897-O

Circulation-Strike Mintage: 42,500

Estimated population (Mint State): *350–450.* MS-60 to MS-62 grades are typically seen, but a few higher-grade pieces are known.

Estimated population (circulated grades): *1,000+.* EF and AU coins are plentiful.

Submissions certified at highest grades (as of March 2017): *PCGS:* MS-63 (18), MS-64 (8), MS-66 (1), MS-67 (1). *NGC:* MS-63 (7), MS-64 (3), MS-65 (1), MS-67 (1).

Key to collecting: Slightly scarce and very popular, are all New Orleans eagles. Always in strong demand.

MARKET NEWS AND COMMENTARY

In February 1944, in the Belden E. Roach Collection, B. Max Mehl offered lot 420: "1897-O Just a shade from perfect Uncirculated but with full mint luster." It sold for $23.50. In the December 1944 sale of the J.F. Bell Collection Stack's included lot 715: "1897-O Brilliant Uncirculated." It sold for $52.50. This was another unusual offering of an Uncirculated coin.

In October 1982, in the Louis E. Eliasberg Collection of U.S. Gold Coins, Bowers and Ruddy Galleries offered lot 814: "1897-O Gem Brilliant Uncirculated, MS-67, reverse." It sold for $10,450. This was bought directly from the New Orleans Mint by John M. Clapp.

In December 2005 the American Numismatic Rarities sale of the Old Colony Collection included lot 1622: "1897-O MS-63 NGC." It sold for $3,738. Stack's July 2009 "Treasures from the SS *New York*" sale included lot 1485: "1897-O MS-64 PCGS." It sold for $12,650. In August 2012 the Stack's Bowers Galleries' ANA World's Fair of Money sale included lot 12449: "1897-O MS-63 PCGS." It sold for $9,775. The Heritage January 2017 FUN Convention sale included lot 6942: "1897-O MS-63 PCGS." It sold for $8,225. Although many repatriated coins have entered the market, prices for higher-level Mint State coins have remained fairly strong.

VF-20	EF-40	AU-50	AU-55	AU-58	MS-60	MS-63	MS-65
$725	$750	$775	$900	$1,000	$1,050	$5,000	$27,500

1897-S

Circulation-Strike Mintage: 234,750

Estimated population (Mint State): 300–450. Most grade from MS-60 to MS-62. This is another of the numerous varieties among late-date Liberty Head eagles that years ago was a formidable rarity, until significant imports of the late 1900s.

Estimated population (circulated grades): 7,000+. Represented in modern imports, but not in large quantities. VF seems to be the grade usually seen among those retrieved from domestic sources, although many EF and AU coins exist as well, the last primarily from imports.

Submissions certified at highest grades (as of March 2017): *PCGS:* MS-63 (26), MS-64 (3), MS-65 (1), MS-66 (3). ***NGC:*** MS-63 (1), MS-64 (2), MS-66 (1).

Key to collecting: Slightly on the scarce side, but enough are around fill the need of specialists.

MARKET NEWS AND COMMENTARY

In February 1944, in the Belden E. Roach Collection, B. Max Mehl offered lot 455: "1897-S Practically Uncirculated with full luster." It sold for $21.75. In the December 1944 sale of the J.F. Bell Collection Stack's included lot 781: "1897-S Uncirculated. Gem." It sold for $37.50. The market was just beginning to be aware of exceptional-grade coins.

In October 1982, in the Louis E. Eliasberg Collection of U.S. Gold Coins, Bowers and Ruddy Galleries offered lot 815: "1897-S Gem Brilliant Uncirculated, MS-67. From the John H. Clapp Collection, 1942. Earlier directly from the San Francisco Mint." It sold for $8,800.

David Akers, whose comments on gold coins usually created attention after his series of books (starting with $1 in 1875) became popular, said this in Paramount's July 1983 catalog of Auction '83, lot 418:

> 1897-S, Uncirculated 60. With most known specimens in the VF–EF range, the 1897-S is really very rare in full Mint State. In our opinion, this date, along with the 1894-S, 1895-S and 1896-S eagles, is one of the most underrated issues in the entire U.S. gold series. True Uncirculated coins such as this are anything but common and probably no more than a couple dozen still exist. A real sleeper! [Sold for $742.50]

Stack's January 2008 Franklinton Collection, Part II, sale included lot 1029: "1897-S MS-66 PCGS." It sold for $47,150. The Heritage January 2017 FUN Convention sale included lot 6943: "1897-S MS-63 PCGS." It sold for $4,700. This reflects the demand for condition rarity. In Heritage's November 2016 sale lot 4626, an MS-62 PCGS coin, brought $1,116.25, and in the same firms October 2016 sale lot 8342, an MS-61 PCGS coin, fetched $881.25. Such differentials are representative of countless sales of eagles of the late 1800s and early 1900s.

VF-20	EF-40	AU-50	AU-55	AU-58	MS-60	MS-63	MS-65
$650	$675	$700	$750	$800	$850	$4,500	$25,000

1898

Circulation-Strike Mintage: 812,130
Proof Mintage: 67

Estimated population (Mint State): *7,500+.* Very common. Many have been sold outside of numismatic circles, but thousand have been certified. "Most are MS-60 to MS-62, but higher-grade pieces are occasionally seen, including MS-64 and the stray MS-65 now and then." I wrote the preceding words in the 1990s. Since then coins certified (actually *submission events*) MS-63 and higher have become common, due to repatriated coins plus gradeflation plus resubmissions.

Estimated population (circulated grades): *12,000+.* No solid figures available, as this is considered to be a common issue, plentiful in overseas holdings, and not often certified in circulated grades. EF and AU coins abound.

Estimated population (Proofs): *30–40.*

Submissions certified at highest grades (as of March 2017): *PCGS:* MS-63 (287), MS-64 (78), MS-65 (9), MS-66 (2). *NGC:* MS-63 (382), MS-64 (109), MS-65 (23), MS-66 (6), 67 (2).

Key to collecting: Very common.

MARKET NEWS AND COMMENTARY

In November 1939 the William B. Hale Collection, sold by B. Max Mehl, included lot 1684: "1898 Uncirculated; frosty mint surface." It sold for $19.80. In April 1960 New Netherlands' 54th sale, Jonathan Glogower Consignment, Etc., included this, lot 711: "1898. Brilliant Uncirculated, choice. A few bag marks away from superb." It sold for $26.

In July 1989, in Auction '89, David W. Akers offered lot 1419: "1898 Gem Uncirculated 66. The 1898 is one of the more common dates of the series but, in this condition, it is very scarce, if not rare." It sold for $11,000. It is not known how PCGS or NGC would have graded the Akers coin. By the second decade of the 21st century high-level MS coins traded frequently.

PROOF MARKET NEWS AND COMMENTARY

In October 1998, in the John J. Pittman Collection sale, Part II, David Akers offered lot 1984:

> 1898, Very Choice Proof. On Liberty's chin, there is a slight "shiny" spot "as made", something common to many Proof eagles. JJP purchased this coin from Garland Stephens, a connoisseur and specialist in U.S. Proof gold coins, at the 1961 ANA convention in Atlanta for $550. Although similar in mintage to most of the other Proof eagles of this decade, the 1898 is more common than any of the Proofs preceding it. Of the 67 Proofs minted, an estimated 30–35 specimens still exist; however, not many of them are as attractive and original as this one.

The Pittman coin sold for $60,500. In October 1999, in the Harry W. Bass Jr. Collection, Part II, Bowers and Merena Galleries offered lot 1648:

> 1898 Proof-65 PCGS. Quite a few extant Proof 1898 eagles have been scratched or damaged, and a few are held by museums. There are probably no more than a half dozen to 10 pieces that are in a class with the lovely Bass Collection gem. PCGS Population: 9; 6 finer (Proof-67 finest). From Stack's sale of the Forrest Collection, September 1972, lot 538. [Sold for $34,500]

In December 2004 the American Numismatic Rarities Classics sale included lot 525: "1898 Proof-65 (PCGS)." It sold for $29,900. In the August 2016 ANA World's Fair of Money sale Stack's Bowers Galleries offered lot 3476: "1898 Proof-66 Deep Cameo PCGS." It sold for $111,625.

VF-20	EF-40	AU-50	AU-55	AU-58	MS-60	MS-63	MS-65	PF-63	PF-64	PF-65
$650	$675	$700	$750	$800	$850	$1,200	$6,500	$16,000	$25,000	$47,500

1898-S

Circulation-Strike Mintage: 473,600

Estimated population (Mint State): 900+. Most are MS–60 to 63 and the occasional 64. Any higher-graded coin ranges from scarce to rare. These started coming on the market in quantity in the late 1970s, from foreign holdings. Earlier, Mint State 1898-S eagles were rarities.

Estimated population (circulated grades): *8,000+.* VF and EF coins are the grades usually seen in old-time collections. AU pieces are mostly from later imports. The population is rather low in comparison to the generous mintage.

Submissions certified at highest grades (as of March 2017): *PCGS:* MS-63 (45), MS-64 (8), MS-65 (2), MS-66 (1). *NGC:* MS-63 (21), MS-64 (3).

Key to collecting: Somewhat scarce.

MARKET NEWS AND COMMENTARY

In February 1944, in the Belden E. Roach Collection, B. Max Mehl offered lot 456: "1898-S Uncirculated; brilliant luster." It sold for $21.75. In October 1982, in the Louis E. Eliasberg Collection of U.S. Gold Coins, Bowers and Ruddy Galleries offered lot 817: "1898-S Choice Brilliant Uncirculated, MS-65 to Gem brilliant Uncirculated, MS-67. From the John H. Clapp Collection, 1942. Earlier directly from the San Francisco Mint." It sold for $6,050.

A few Uncirculated pieces are said to have been found in a "tiny hoard" in 1977.[33] At the time such coins were rare. Today the hoard has no lasting market significance.

The Heritage January 2017 FUN Convention sale included lot 6944: "1898-S MS-64 PCGS." It sold for $7,696.25. At the same time an MS-63 was worth about $1,100 to $1,300.

VF-20	EF-40	AU-50	AU-55	AU-58	MS-60	MS-63	MS-65
$650	$675	$700	$750	$800	$850	$2,500	$15,000

1899

Circulation-Strike Mintage: 1,262,219
Proof Mintage: 86

Estimated population (Mint State): *20,000+.* Very common now and decades ago as well, although the population swelled

in the late 1900s following imports. Many have been sold outside of numismatic circles, but thousands have been certified. Most are MS-60 to MS-65, of which there are many thousands. The price of these and related common late 1800 and early 1900 eagles is affected by the market for gold bullion.

Estimated population (circulated grades): *25,000+.* No solid figures available, as this is considered to be a common issue, plentiful in overseas holdings, and not often certified in circulated grades. EF and AU coins abound.

Estimated population (Proofs): *30–40.* Rare.

Submissions certified at highest grades (as of March 2017): *PCGS:* MS-63 (2,443), MS-64 (478), MS-65 (50), MS-66 (6). *NGC:* MS-63 (6,208), MS-64 (1,393), MS-65 (180), MS-66 (19), MS-67 (4).

Key to collecting: One of the most common eagles. Scrooge McDuck would have had no problem hoarding a bin full.

Market News and Commentary

New Netherlands Coin Co.'s 46th sale, Dr. Clarence W. Peake Collection, June 1955, included lot 200: "1899. A hair's breadth from Uncirculated. Dullish, frosty mint surface. Desirable." It sold for $21.

In September 2005, at which time the number of collectors had expanded many fold, the American Numismatic Rarities sale of the C.L. Lee Collection included lot 1322: "1899 MS-65 NGC. From our sale of the Allison Park Collection." It sold for $3,975. Stack's March 2008 Dominic Gaziano and Papyrus Way Collections sale included lot 1156: "1899 MS-63." It sold for $6,325. In November 2011 the Stack's Bowers Galleries' Baltimore Whitman Expo sale included lot 9753: "1899 MS-66 NGC." It sold for $6,613. Regency Auction XIX December 2016 included lot 467: "1899 MS-65 PCGS." It sold for $5,052.50.

Proof Market News and Commentary

In June 1907 the Chapman brothers sale of the Major W.B. Wetmore Collection included lot 42: "1899 Brilliant Proof." It sold for $11.

In June October 1908 Thomas L. Elder's sale of the James B. Wilson Collection included lot 83: "1899 Complete [gold Proof] set. 4 pieces." It sold for $38 for the entire set (face value was $37.50). The nearly complete lack of a secondary market for Proof gold coins and sets continued, as incredible as this is to contemplate today.

Stack's November 2006 Norweb Collection sale included lot 1361: "1899 Proof-64 ANACS." It sold for $15,525. Stack's October 2008 73rd Anniversary sale included lot 1072: "1899 Liberty Head, Proof-67 NGC." It sold for $94,875. Stack's Bowers Galleries' 2015 Chicago ANA World's Fair of Money sale included lot 10265: "1899 Liberty Head, Proof-67 PCGS." It sold for $88,125.

VF-20	EF-40	AU-50	AU-55	AU-58	MS-60	MS-63	MS-65	PF-63	PF-64	PF-65
$650	$675	$700	$750	$800	$850	$975	$2,750	$15,000	$23,500	$45,000

1899-O

Circulation-Strike Mintage: 37,047

Estimated population (Mint State): 300+. Fairly scarce at all levels. Most are MS-60 to MS-63. Any higher-graded coin is a rarity.

Estimated population (circulated grades): 1,000+. EF and AU specimens are available enough to supply the needs of specialists, although they are not common.

Submissions certified at highest grades (as of March 2017): PCGS: MS-62 (46), MS-63 (16), MS-64 (5). **NGC:** MS-62 (23), MS-63 (7), MS-64 (1), MS-65 (1).

Key to collecting: Fairly scarce, but the supply is sufficient to take care of demand. High-level MS coins always attract attention. New Orleans eagles are the most popular issues of this era as noted.

MARKET NEWS AND COMMENTARY

In March 1911, in his sale of the William H. Woodin Collection, Thomas L. Elder offered lot 1292: "1899-O Fine." It sold for $15.50. This was a high price for a circulated coin of relatively modern issue and is reflective that the scarcity of 1899-O was beginning to be recognized. In the December 1944 sale of the J.F. Bell Collection Stack's included lot 716: "1899-O Brilliant Uncirculated." It sold for $77.50.

In October 1982, in the Louis E. Eliasberg Collection of U.S. Gold Coins, Bowers and Ruddy Galleries offered lot 819: "1899-O Gem Brilliant Uncirculated, MS-67. From the John H. Clapp Collection, 1942. Earlier directly from the New Orleans Mint." It sold for $24,200. In the May 2015 Rarities sale Stack's Bowers Galleries offered lot 71: "1899-O MS-63 (PCGS)." It sold for $7,637.50. The Heritage August 2016 ANA World's Fair of Money sale included lot 4317: "1899-O MS-64 PCGS." It sold for $21,150.

VF-20	EF-40	AU-50	AU-55	AU-58	MS-60	MS-63
$750	$775	$800	$950	$1,000	$1,250	$7,000

1899-S

Circulation-Strike Mintage: 841,000

Estimated population (Mint State): 300+. Most are MS-60 to MS-62, plus the occasional MS-63 and still rarer higher grade.

Estimated population (circulated grades): 15,000+. No solid figures available, as this is considered to be a common issue, plentiful in overseas holdings, and not often certified in circulated grades.

Submissions certified at highest grades (as of March 2017): *PCGS:* MS-64 (15), MS-65 (2), MS-66 (1), MS-67 (1), MS-68 (1). *NGC:* MS-64 (11), MS-65 (5), MS-67 (1), MS-69 (1).

Key to collecting: Common in nearly any grade through AU and scarce but available in lower Mint State ranges.

MARKET NEWS AND COMMENTARY

In November 1939 the William B. Hale Collection, sold by B. Max Mehl, included lot 1745: "1899-S Uncirculated. Scarce so choice." It sold for $18.60. In the December 1944 sale of the J.F. Bell Collection Stack's included lot 783: "1899-S Uncirculated. Gem." It sold for $32.50. Still, the idea of paying a sharp premium for a gem coin had not caught on with most numismatists.

In October 1982, in the Louis E. Eliasberg Collection of U.S. Gold Coins, Bowers and Ruddy Galleries offered lot 820: "1899-S Gem Brilliant Uncirculated, MS-67. From the John H. Clapp Collection, 1942. Earlier directly from the San Francisco Mint." It sold for $13,200.

In March 1988 the Norweb Collection, Part II, sale by Bowers and Merena Galleries included lot 2276: "1899 S EF-40." It sold for $275. What a difference grades meant by that time! The 1988 price was figured on bullion value at the time plus a modest premium.

The Heritage January 2016 FUN Convention sale included lot 6556: "1899-S MS-65 NGC." It sold for $6,462.50, probably to a registry set competitor. The same firm's 2016 sale included lot 21205: "1899-S MS-63 PCGS." It sold for $1,292.50, reflecting the market price for an eagle of this era that is readily available at this grade level.

VF-20	EF-40	AU-50	AU-55	AU-58	MS-60	MS-63	MS-65
$650	$675	$700	$750	$800	$850	$2,000	$15,000

1900

Circulation-Strike Mintage: 293,840
Proof Mintage: 120

Estimated population (Mint State): 5,000+. Very common. Many have been sold outside of numismatic circles, but thou-sands have been certified. Most are MS-60 to MS-63, but higher-grade pieces are occasionally seen.

Estimated population (circulated grades): 9,000+. No solid figures available, as this is considered to be a common issue, plentiful in overseas holdings, and not often certi-fied in circulated grades. EF and AU coins are plentiful.

Estimated population (Proofs): 35–45. Rare.

Submissions certified at highest grades (as of March 2017): PCGS: MS-64 (248), MS-65 (27), MS-66 (4). **NGC:** MS-64 (365), MS-65 (68), MS-66 (4).

Key to collecting: Very common.

MARKET NEWS AND COMMENTARY

This is a very common issue that in modern times has been of no particular account—easy to find in Mint State. There are, however, scattered single listings for worn examples. Mint State listings run into the hundreds.

In May 2000, in the Harry W. Bass Jr. Collection, Part III, sale Bowers and Merena Galleries offered lot 741: "1900 MS-63 Purchased from Jack Klausen, June 17, 1968." It sold for $741.50. Harry Bass, unique among collectors, sought these by minute dif-ferences in dies. Most descriptions of Bass coins in the various sales have detailed die descriptions (not quoted here, but see original catalogs on the Newman Numismatic Portal or hard copies). Similarly, in November 2000, in the Harry W. Bass Jr. Collec-tion, Part IV, by the same company offered lot 772: "1900 MS-63. Date logotype nicely impressed and centrally located both horizontally and vertically. Purchased from Julian Leidman, October 28, 1971." It sold for $460.

In August 2015 Stack's Bowers Galleries' ANA World's Fair of Money sale included lot 10266: "1900 MS-66 PCGS." It sold for $20,563. In the August 2016 ANA World's Fair of Money sale Stack's Bowers Galleries offered lot 3442: "1900 MS-65 PCGS." It sold for $2,585.

PROOF MARKET NEWS AND COMMENTARY

In June 1907 the Chapman brothers sale of the Major W.B. Wetmore Collection included lot 43: "1900 Brilliant Proof." It sold for $11. In October 1908 Thomas L. Elder's sale of the James B. Wilson Collection included lot 84: "1900 Complete [gold Proof] set. 4 pieces." It sold for $38 for the entire set (face value was $37.50).

In October 1999, in the Harry W. Bass Jr. Collection, Part II, Bowers and Merena Galleries included, lot 1652: "1900 Proof-65 PCGS. PCGS Population: 5; 6 finer (Proof-67 finest). From Stack's sale of May 1974, lot 506." It sold for $36,800. In January 2005 Numismatic Rarities' Kennywood Collection sale included lot 1003: "1900 Proof-65 PCGS." It sold for $74,000.

VF-20	EF-40	AU-50	AU-55	AU-58	MS-60	MS-63	MS-65	PF-63	PF-64	PF-65
$650	$675	$700	$750	$800	$825	$950	$3,500	$15,000	$23,500	$45,000

1900-S

Circulation-Strike Mintage: 81,000

Estimated population (Mint State): 300+. Most are MS-60 to MS-63. Any higher-graded coin is a rarity, although a number of gems exist.

Estimated population (circulated grades): 3,000+. EF and AU coins are readily available, although in the context of eagle of this era, the 1900-S is scarce.

Submissions certified at highest grades (as of March 2017): PCGS: MS-62 (44), MS-63 (22), MS-64 (2), MS-67 (1). **NGC:** MS-62 (10), MS-63 (6), MS-64 (2), MS-65 (2), MS-67 (1), MS-68 (2).

Key to collecting: Common in circulated grades. Slightly scarce in lower Mint State ranges.

MARKET NEWS AND COMMENTARY

In February 1944, in the Belden E. Roach Collection, B. Max Mehl offered lot 458: "1900-S Brilliant Uncirculated, almost equal to a Proof. Scarce so choice." It sold for $30. Mehl's "almost equal to a Proof" comment was frequently used in his catalogs. The December 1944 sale of the J.F. Bell Collection held by Stack's included lot 784: "1900-S Uncirculated." It sold for $32.50.

In October 1982, in the Louis E. Eliasberg Collection of U.S. Gold Coins, Bowers and Ruddy Galleries offered lot 822: "1900-S Gem Brilliant Uncirculated, MS-67, reverse." It sold for $14,300. David W. Akers later gave it this description in July 1983, Auction '83, lot 420:

> 1900-S, Superb Gem Uncirculated 67. A simply amazing coin, obtained directly from the Mint in 1900 by numismatist John Clapp, and sold to Louis Eliasberg with the rest of the Clapp Collection in 1942. Few Liberty Head eagles of any date or mint come close to matching the overall quality of this coin. Ex Eliasberg Collection

Sale, lot 822. Today, the price should be closer to $20,000. In our opinion, this is the finest known 1900-S eagle. We like it a little better than the super coin that sold in the Bowers and Merena Central States Auction in April, its only real competitor. As a date, the 1900-S is quite rare in all grades and the typically available specimen is usually only EF or so. The lover of rare and matchless quality coins will be thrilled at again having the opportunity to bid on this specimen. [Sold for $14,850]

The same coin was offered by Ira and Larry Goldberg in February 2003 in their sale of the Benson Collection, Part III, lot 2123: "1900-S MS-67 PCGS. The United States Gold Coin Collection (Bowers and Ruddy Galleries), October 27–29, 1982, lot 822." It sold for $50,000.

VF-20	EF-40	AU-50	AU-55	AU-58	MS-60	MS-63
$650	$675	$700	$750	$800	$850	$5,500

1901

Circulation-Strike Mintage: 1,718,740
Proof Mintage: 85

Notes regarding mintages: On Proofs of this issue, the head of Miss Liberty is typically very frosty giving a nice cameo effect against the mirror fields. Some of these have been called "cameo Proofs," but all are the same. Most of these seem to have disappeared, and probably no more than 30 different pieces can be accounted for today.

Estimated population (Mint State): 20,000+. Examples range from MS-60 upward, with MS-64 and MS-65 pieces being sufficiently plentiful that just about anyone seeking a specimen can find one in short order, although most are in significantly lower grades. In the early 1990s Spectrum Numismatics handled a group of about 2,000 especially choice pieces, ranging up to superb gem quality. These were from a European source and were sold quickly into the market.[34]

Estimated population (circulated grades): 80,000+. No solid figures available, as this is considered to be a common issue, plentiful in overseas holdings, and not often certified in circulated grades. EF and AU coins are very common, but are scarcer than if in Mint State. Mostly in higher grades such as AU. Numismatically unimportant.

Estimated population (Proofs): 25–30. Most are in lower ranges, Proof-60 to about Proof-63.

Submissions certified at highest grades (as of March 2017): *PCGS:* MS-65 (342), MS-66 (37), MS-67 (1). *NGC:* MS-65 (663), MS-66 (57), MS-67 (7).

Characteristics of striking and die notes: Usually well struck. Circulation strikes as well as Proofs are sometimes seen with copper spots due to incomplete mixing of the alloy.

Key to collecting: Extremely common. Except in the very highest grades this and related eagles with large surviving populations respond more in price to gold bullion value changes, not to changes in numismatic demand.

MARKET NEWS AND COMMENTARY

In June 1959 New Netherlands Coin Co., known for its prolixity, offered this in its 53rd sale featuring the G. Straus Collection, Part II, lot 1672: "1901 Brilliant, frosty Uncirculated. Obviously in a Mint bag for a while, but still nice. Scarce so; the only Liberty Head eagle commonly seen in Mint State is the 1901 'S.' Peake's similar example brought $27.50, which was far above the usual VF-EF market of 1955." It sold for $28.

Similarly, in April 1960, in the firm's 54th sale, the Jonathan Glogower Consignment, Etc., lot 714: "1901. Brilliant Uncirculated, comparatively clean. Touches of tarnish. Lists at $35 and $37.50 (latter *Standard Catalogue*) so, but has not brought comparable prices." It sold for $26.

Although the 1901 was and is common, in January 1991 the Bowers and Merena Galleries' description of a gem coin in the Greenwich Collection reflected its rarity in a PCGS holder, lot 257: "1901 MS-65 PCGS. According to the October 1990 PCGS Population Report, only two examples had been graded as high as this. Yet another prize for the discriminating collector." It sold for $6,050.

At this time PCGS was young and only a small percentage of coins had been submitted to it. A much more important factor is that massive repatriations were still in the future.

In September 2005 the American Numismatic Rarities sale of the C.L. Lee Collection included lot 1327: "1901 MS-64 (PCGS)," that sold for $1,495. The same sale included an MS-65 by NGC and one in similar grade by PCGS that sold for $3,623 and $2,795 respectively, and an MS-66 (PCGS) that brought $5,290—all of this being a reflection of the desire to acquire coins that are common in lower grades but have relatively few certified at higher levels.

In August 2006 the American Numismatic Rarities sale of the Old West and Franklinton Collections included lot 1561: "1901 MS-67 NGC." It sold for $13,800. The same sale included MS-63 (NGC) for $920, MS-64 (PCGS) $1,495, and MS-65 (NGC) at $4,140—a nice reflection of the importance of certified grading numbers. During the next decade the number of certified high-grade 1901 eagles expanded greatly.

The Heritage April 2017 sale included lot 18661: "1901 MS-63 PCGS." It sold for $822.50, a typical price. The availability of attractive Mint State eagles for reasonable prices generated many more specialists than were active years earlier in 1980 when David W. Akers published his study on this denomination.

PROOF MARKET NEWS AND COMMENTARY

Stack's August 2007 J.A. Sherman Collection sale included lot 3332: "1901 Proof-66 NGC." It sold for $69,000. Also lot 1073: "1901 Proof-66 NGC." It sold for $60,000.

VF-20	EF-40	AU-50	AU-55	AU-58	MS-60	MS-63	MS-65	PF-63	PF-64	PF-65
$650	$675	$700	$750	$800	$825	$950	$3,000	$15,000	$23,500	$45,000

1901-O

Circulation-Strike Mintage: 72,041

Estimated population (Mint State): 500+. Most are MS-60 to MS-62 plus the occasional MS-63. Still higher-graded coins are seldom seen.

Estimated population (circulated grades): 2,000+. EF and AU coins are frequently encountered, lower grades less so. Scarce in relation to many other eagles of the era.

Submissions certified at highest grades (as of March 2017): PCGS: MS-63 (78), MS-64 (20), MS-66 (1). **NGC:** MS-63 (22), MS-64 (5), MS-65 (1), MS-66 (2).

Key to collecting: Slightly scarce compared to many other eagles of the era, but easily enough found through lower Mint State grades. Higher Mint State coins have caused a lot of excitement at auction. Popular as are all New Orleans eagles.

MARKET NEWS AND COMMENTARY

In the December 1944 sale of the J.F. Bell Collection Stack's included lot 717: "1901-O Extremely Fine. Rare." It sold for $45.

In November 1945 B. Max Mehl's sale of the W.A. Philpott and Henry L. Zander Collections included lot 1701: "1901-O Extremely Fine." It sold for $17.

In September 2005 the American Numismatic Rarities sale of the C.L. Lee Collection included lot 1328: "1901-O MS-62 PCGS." It sold for $1,265. In the August 2016 ANA World's Fair of Money sale Stack's Bowers Galleries offered lot 3445: "1901-O MS-62 PCGS." It sold for $1,175. In the February 2017 Collectors Choice sale Stack's Bowers Galleries offered lot 91726: "1901-O MS-64+ PCGS." It sold for $10,575. Also lot 91726: "1901-O MS-64 PCGS." It realized $7,050.

VF-20	EF-40	AU-50	AU-55	AU-58	MS-60	MS-63	MS-65
$750	$775	$800	$925	$975	$1,250	$3,250	$15,000

1901-S

Circulation-Strike Mintage: 2,812,750

Estimated population (Mint State): 70,000+. Very common. Many have been sold outside of numismatic circles, but thousands have been certified. Most are MS-60 to MS-65, but higher-grade pieces are found with relative ease, through MS-67.

These have been plentiful for a long time. In the early 1940s, circa 1942 to 1944, these were the most often seen $10 Mint State issue of the era (*e.g.* in sales including obscure offerings such as those of Barney Bluestone).

Estimated population (circulated grades): 150,000+. No solid figures available, as this is considered to be a common issue, plentiful in overseas holdings, and not often certified in circulated grades.

Submissions certified at highest grades (as of March 2017): *PCGS:* MS-65 (1,144), MS-66 (230), MS-67 (2). *NGC:* MS-65 (1,331), MS-66 (231), MS-67 (20). The 1901-S holds the record for the most-certified high-grade $10 gold coin.

Key to collecting: Extremely common. There are more than 10 coins available for every member of the ANA (not that it makes a difference). This is an ideal coin to add to a type set if you are seeking a high-grade coin at minimum cost. Worn examples are not generally sought and are priced at bullion value plus a modest premium.

MARKET NEWS AND COMMENTARY

In March 1911, in his sale of the William H. Woodin Collection, Thomas L. Elder offered lot 1333: "1901-S Mint bloom, rare so choice." It sold for $10.50. Wonder what Elder would say if he were alive today! In the December 1944 sale of the J.F. Bell Collection Stack's included lot 785: "1901-S Uncirculated. Gem." It sold for $32.50.

In October 1982, in the Louis E. Eliasberg Collection of U.S. Gold Coins, Bowers and Ruddy Galleries offered lot 825: "1901-S Gem Brilliant Uncirculated, MS-67, reverse." This sold for $7,150. In August 1990, in Auction '90, David W. Akers offered lot 1921: "1901-S MS-66. (PCGS)." It sold for $19,250; followed by lot 1922 with the same grade but not certified, sold for $9,250. PCGS and NGC were just catching on, and nearly everyone viewed their grading to be conservative at this early time. Hopefully, the buyers of these coins also collected colonial coins, early silver, Civil War tokens, obsolete currency, or some other series that have multiplied in value since 1990!

In June 2006 the American Numismatic Rarities sale of the Lake Michigan and Springdale Collections included lot 2618: "1901-S MS-66 NGC." It sold for $6,325. The same sale included an MS-64 (NGC) that brought $2,300. In August 2006 the American Numismatic Rarities sale of the Old West and Franklinton Collections included lot 1566: "1901-S MS-67 NGC." It sold for $13,800. The same sale included MS-64 (PCGS) that sold for $3,270. In November 2011 the Stack's Bowers Galleries' Baltimore Whitman Expo sale included lot 9760: "1901-S MS-67 NGC." It sold for $18,400.

The Stack's Bowers Galleries' February 2014 Americana sale included lot 3253: "1901-S MS-66 NGC." It sold for $7,638. In the June 2015 Pre-Long Beach sale Ira and Larry Goldberg offered lot 1954: "1901-S MS-66 PCGS." It sold for $4,935. The Stack's Bowers Galleries' February 2015 Americana sale of U.S. Coins included lot 2088: "1901-S MS-66 PCGS." It sold for $17,625. In the November 2016 Whitman Expo sale Stack's Bowers Galleries offered lot 3086: "1901-S MS-65 PCGS." It sold for $2,820. By this time MS-65 coins were common. The Heritage April 2017 sale included lot 18664: "1901-S MS-64 NGC." It sold for $1,028.13, a generic price for a common eagle in this grade.

VF-20	EF-40	AU-50	AU-55	AU-58	MS-60	MS-63	MS-65
$650	$675	$700	$750	$800	$850	$1,000	$3,000

1902

Circulation-Strike Mintage: 82,400
Proof Mintage: 113

Notes regarding mintages: Proofs are from an obverse die with polished portrait of Miss Liberty and reverse with polished eagle, in contrast to the frosted devices used earlier. The date logotype is bold in the die and is half again as close to the dentils as to the neck truncation.

Estimated population (Mint State): *2,000+.* Most are MS-60 to MS-62, plus enough MS-63 coins that the specialist will have no problem finding one. Coins at still higher grades are very elusive.

Estimated population (circulated grades): *3,000+.* Examples are plentiful in EF and AU grades in relation to the demand for them, as most market interest is directed toward Mint State coins.

Estimated population (Proofs): *50–65.* Rare.

Submissions certified at highest grades (as of March 2017): *PCGS:* MS-64 (13), MS-65 (5), MS-66 (1). *NGC:* MS-64 (15), MS-65 (5).

Key to collecting: Common.

MARKET NEWS AND COMMENTARY

The August 1942 ANA Convention sale held by Numismatic Gallery (Abe Kosoff) included lot 189: "1902. Uncirculated." It sold for $20.50. The June 1955 sale by New Netherlands of the Dr. Clarence W. Peake Collection included lot 206: "1902. Extremely Fine. Two or three obverse nicks, one at the bottom rim. A very scarce date, but 82,513 minted." It sold for $25. A year later in April 1956 Abe Kosoff's sale at the Central States Numismatic Society Convention of the Thomas G. Melish and Clinton W. Hester Collections included lot 2572: "1902 Uncirculated." It sold for $26.

PROOF MARKET NEWS AND COMMENTARY

Stack's Bowers Galleries' August 2013 Chicago ANA World's Fair of Money sale included lot 4521: "1902 Proof-65 NGC." It sold for $34,075.

VF-20	EF-40	AU-50	AU-55	AU-58	MS-60	MS-63	MS-65	PF-63	PF-64	PF-65
$650	$675	$700	$750	$800	$850	$1,750	$9,000	$15,000	$23,500	$45,000

1902-S

Circulation-Strike Mintage: 469,500

Estimated population (Mint State): *5,000+.* Very common. Many have been sold outside of numismatic circles, but thousand have been certified. Most are MS-60 to MS-63, but higher-grade pieces are occasionally seen. David W. Akers commented (1980): "With the release of a sizable hoard in the early 1970s, many gems of this date are available." Since that time, even more have been imported.

Estimated population (circulated grades): *12,000+.* No solid figures available, as this is considered to be a common issue, plentiful in overseas holdings, and not often certified in circulated grades. VF is the grade usually encountered in old-time collections. In the late 20th century large numbers were imported, including many EF and AU pieces.

Submissions certified at highest grades (as of March 2017): *PCGS:* MS-65 (107), MS-66 (7), MS-68 (1). *NGC:* MS-65 (114), MS-66 (10), MS-67 (1).

Characteristics of striking and die notes: Usually well struck and with satiny fields.

Key to collecting: Very common.

MARKET NEWS AND COMMENTARY

In the December 1944 sale of the J.F. Bell Collection Stack's included lot 786: "1902-S Uncirculated. Gem." It sold for $32.50. May 1951 was in the middle of a coin market slump, perhaps accounting for what happened to the coin in M.H. Bolender's sale of the Fox Collection, lot 1072: "1902-S Uncirculated." It sold for $11.50.

The market was certainly different in October 1982 when, in the Louis E. Eliasberg Collection of U.S. Gold Coins, Bowers and Ruddy Galleries offered lot 827: "1902-S Gem Brilliant Uncirculated, MS-67, $19,800. This was, of course, a coin of exceptional quality from the John H. Clapp Collection, 1942, earlier from the U.S. Mint." It sold for $12,190.

In March 2006 the American Numismatic Rarities sale of the New York Connoisseur's Collection included lot 1682: "1902-S MS-66 NGC." It sold for $9,775.

In the August 2016 ANA World's Fair of Money sale Stack's Bowers Galleries offered lot 3447: "1902-S MS-65 PCGS." It sold for $2,820. Regency Auction XIX, December 2016, included lot 468: "1902-S MS-66 PCGS." It sold for $7,431.25.

VF-20	EF-40	AU-50	AU-55	AU-58	MS-60	MS-63	MS-65
$650	$675	$700	$750	$800	$825	$950	$3,000

1903

Circulation-Strike Mintage: 125,830
Proof Mintage: 96

Notes regarding mintages: As was the case in 1902, the Proof dies this year must have been prepared by an apprentice, for the portrait of Miss Liberty was lightly polished in the die, in contrast to the cameo-like frosty finish of most other years.

Estimated population (Mint State): *2,500+.* Most are MS-60 to MS-63, although there will be no problem finding an MS-64 or MS-65. Anything higher is rare today.

Estimated population (circulated grades): *4,000+.* Little data is available. EF and AU coins are plentiful in relation to the demand for them, but the 1903 is by no means common.

Estimated population (Proofs): *25–35.* Rare.

Submissions certified at highest grades (as of March 2017): *PCGS:* MS-64 (48), MS-65 (7), MS-66 (1). *NGC:* MS-64 (29), MS-65 (11).

Characteristics of striking and die notes: Circulation strikes exist with a highly prooflike surface.

Key to collecting: Common.

MARKET NEWS AND COMMENTARY

In October 1947, in the H.R. Lee Collection (Eliasberg duplicates), Stack's offered lot 1558: "1903 Uncirculated, frosty surface." It sold for $23. In April 1956, in his sale of the Thomas G. Melish Collection, Abe Kosoff offered lot 2575: "1903. About Extremely Fine." It sold for $23.

In the August 2016 ANA World's Fair of Money sale Stack's Bowers Galleries offered lot 3448: "1903 MS-64 PCGS." It sold for $2,115.

VF-20	EF-40	AU-50	AU-55	AU-58	MS-60	MS-63	MS-65	PF-63	PF-64	PF-65
$650	$675	$700	$750	$800	$850	$1,250	$7,000	$15,000	$23,500	$45,000

1903-O

Circulation-Strike Mintage: 112,771

Estimated population (Mint State): 2,250+. Most are MS-60 to MS-62 plus the occasional MS-63. Any higher-graded coin is rare.

Estimated population (circulated grades): 3,000+. EF and AU coins are plentiful in relation to the demand for them, but are scarce in an absolute sense.

Submissions certified at highest grades (as of March 2017): *PCGS:* MS-63 (148), MS-64 (22), MS-66 (1). *NGC:* MS-63 (45), MS-64 (7), MS-65 (1).

Key to collecting: Common in just about any grade desired, but in strong demand in view of the popularity of New Orleans coins.

MARKET NEWS AND COMMENTARY

In March 1911, in his sale of the William H. Woodin Collection, Thomas L. Elder offered lot 1293: "1903-O Uncirculated." It sold for $10.50. In the December 1944 sale of the J.F. Bell Collection Stack's included lot 718: "1903-O Brilliant Uncirculated. Rare." It sold for $45. In October 1947, in the H.R. Lee Collection (Eliasberg duplicates), Stack's offered lot 1609: "1903-O Brilliant Uncirculated, full mint frosty surface, rare." It sold for $32.50.

In October 1982, in the Louis E. Eliasberg Collection of U.S. Gold Coins, Bowers and Ruddy Galleries offered lot 829: "1903-O Gem Brilliant Uncirculated, MS-67." It sold for $8,800.

VF-20	EF-40	AU-50	AU-55	AU-58	MS-60	MS-63	MS-65
$725	$750	$800	$925	$1,000	$1,200	$3,000	$17,500

1903-S

Circulation-Strike Mintage: 538,000

Estimated population (Mint State): 1,500+. Most are MS-60 to MS-63, although there are quite a few MS-64 coins around—hardly common at the latter grade, but available enough that the specialist can find one without difficulty. MS-66 and still higher coins come on the market now and then and are always highly desired.

Estimated population (circulated grades): 15,000+. Little data is available. High-grade circulated coins are common.

Submissions certified at highest grades (as of March 2017): *PCGS:* MS-65 (69), MS-66 (26), MS-67 (3). ***NGC:*** MS-65 (73), MS-66 (44), MS-67 (6).

Die data: The four-digit date logotype is widely spaced; 0 leans to the right.

Characteristics of striking and die notes: Usually well struck and, if in high grade, of handsome appearance.

Key to collecting: Common, although not extremely so.

MARKET NEWS AND COMMENTARY

In November 1939 the William B. Hale Collection, sold by B. Max Mehl, included lot 1747: "1903-S Uncirculated; mint luster; just the slightest marks of contacts with other coins." It sold for $17. In April 1956 Abe Kosoff's sale of the Thomas G. Melish and Clinton W. Hester Collections included lot 2578: "1903-S Uncirculated." It sold for $24.

In October 1982, in the Louis E. Eliasberg Collection of U.S. Gold Coins, Bowers and Ruddy Galleries offered lot 830: "1903-S Gem Brilliant Uncirculated, MS-67. From the John H. Clapp Collection, 1942. Earlier directly from the San Francisco Mint." It sold for $8,800. Stack's January 1990 James A. Stack Sr. Collection sale included multiple eagles, each described as Brilliant Uncirculated—lot 1311 sold for $19,800, lot 1742 brought $13,750, lot 1743 sold for $8,525, lot 1744 realized $7,150, lot 1745 realized $12,100, and lot 1747 sold for $5,770. There must have been wide differences in quality, as this in an era before many dealers used grading numbers.

Stack's Bowers Galleries' November 2012 Baltimore Auction included lot 3297: "1903-S MS-67 PCGS." It sold for $25,428. Heritage's sale of April 2014 included lot 5777: "1903-S MS-67 PCGS." It sold for $24,675. Regency Auction XV, December 2015, included lot 437: "1903-S MS-66+ PCGS." It sold for $13,512.50.

VF-20	EF-40	AU-50	AU-55	AU-58	MS-60	MS-63	MS-65
$650	$675	$700	$750	$800	$850	$1,000	$3,500

1904

Circulation-Strike Mintage: 161,930
Proof Mintage: 108

Estimated population (Mint State):
4,000+. Most are MS-60 to MS-62 and
the occasional MS-63. Any higher-graded
coin is a rarity. The 1969 ANA Convention sale included 64 Mint State coins, which
provided a supply on the market for a time (cf. David W. Akers, 1980), but later
imports were so extensive that this quantity faded into insignificance.

Estimated population (circulated grades): ***6,000+.*** Little data is available. EF and
AU coins are common.

Estimated population (Proofs): ***30–40.*** Rare.

Submissions certified at highest grades (as of March 2017): *PCGS:* MS-64 (57),
MS-65 (2), MS-66 (1), MS-67 (1). *NGC:* MS-64 (35), MS-65 (4), MS-66 (2), MS-67 (1).

Key to collecting: Common.

MARKET NEWS AND COMMENTARY

Circulation strikes of the 1904 eagle attracted little attention until *condition rarity*
became popular across all series in the second half of the 20th century, the statement
being true of all dates in the series.

In April 1956 Abe Kosoff's sale of the Thomas G. Melish and Clinton W. Hester
Collections included lot 2580: "1904 No break from right wing. About Uncirculated."
It sold for $20. In the August 2016 ANA World's Fair of Money sale Stack's Bowers
Galleries offered lot 3451: "1904 MS-63 PCGS." It sold for $1,292.50.

PROOF MARKET NEWS AND COMMENTARY

Proofs of the 1904 eagle in the marketplace fared about the same as other dates from
the 1890s onward. Through the 1920s many were spent as they had little premium
value. Beginning in the 1940s strong attention was paid to them, by which time many
were lost or impaired.

In June 1907 the Chapman brothers sale of the Major W.B. Wetmore Collection
included lot 45: "1904 Brilliant Proof." It sold for $10 (face value). A typical illustra-
tion of why many Proofs of this era were simply spent. There was little resale premium
value to them.

In January 1990 the Superior Galleries' sale of the S. Chalkley and Austin Ryer
Collections included lot 4857: "Proof-64+ PCGS." It sold for $24,200. Heritage's sale
of June 6, 2013, included lot 4814: "1904 Proof-66 Cameo. PCGS." It sold for $64,624.

VF-20	EF-40	AU-50	AU-55	AU-58	MS-60	MS-63	MS-65	PF-63	PF-64	PF-65
$650	$675	$700	$750	$800	$850	$1,500	$8,500	$15,000	$23,500	$45,000

1904-O

Circulation-Strike Mintage: 108,950

Estimated population (Mint State): *2,000+.* Most are MS-60 to MS-63. MS-64 specimens are very hard to find, and any higher-graded coin is a notable rarity.

Estimated population (circulated grades): *3,000+.* EF and AU coins are fairly scarce.

Submissions certified at highest grades (as of March 2017): *PCGS:* MS-64 (13), MS-65 (6), MS-67 (1). *NGC:* MS-64 (7), MS-65 (4), MS-68 (1).

Die data: The reverse die for the 1904-O was also used on certain 1894-O, 1895-O, 1897-O, and 1903-O eagles, per the research of Harry W. Bass Jr.

Key to collecting: Common.

MARKET NEWS AND COMMENTARY

In February 1944, in the Belden E. Roach Collection, B. Max Mehl offered lot 423: "1904-O Uncirculated with full mint luster. Scarce so choice although not a rarity." It sold for $24.50. The December 1944 sale of the J.F. Bell Collection held by Stack's included lot 719: "1904-O Brilliant Uncirculated." It sold for $42. In June 1946, in the William Cutler Atwater Collection, B. Max Mehl offered lot 1550: "1904-O Uncirculated with mint luster. Record over $40." It sold for $30. Mehl, in his May 1950 Golden Jubilee sale, included lot 567: "1904 O. Uncirculated with brilliant mint luster. Very scarce. Record $65." It sold for $36.

The Federal Coin Exchange (Michael Kolman Jr.) offered this in August 1954 in the ANA Convention sale (Federal Coin Exchange), lot 1735A: "1904-O Brilliant Uncirculated. Gem. Note: It is usually most difficult to find gold in this condition. [Estimated value] $50." It sold for $240. Some alert buyers must have been on hand! In October 1982, in the Louis E. Eliasberg Collection of U.S. Gold Coins, Bowers and Ruddy Galleries offered lot 832: "1904-O Gem Brilliant Uncirculated, MS-67. Purchased from the New Orleans Mint." It sold for $6,050.

In August 1989, in Auction '89, David W. Akers described lot 1422: "1904-O MS-68 or better. Since it was sold in Auction '88 to the present consignor, the coin has also been "slabbed" (graded MS-68 by NGC) and the envelope is included with the coin. It states "First Gold Coined 1904, W.J. Brophy, Coiner, U.S. Mint, $10 and $5." It sold for $104,500.

By August 1990 certified coins had become important in the marketplace. At that time in Auction '90 David W. Akers offered lot 1928:

> 1904-O Gem Uncirculated 65. A very scarce date in any condition and definitely rare above MS-63. (PCGS has graded only 22 pieces in Mint State including just six above MS-62. Compare this, for instance, to the commonest date of the type, the 1901-S, with nearly 1,800 pieces graded above MS-62. That's a factor of 300 difference! Do you agree that the rarer dates are undervalued in comparison to the most common ones? [Sold for $5,280]

At that time most PCGS and NGC grades, a relatively new market concept, were viewed as being quite well considered. Gradeflation was in the future as were more repatriations of gold coins stored overseas. Today as you read these words the marketplace has placed *basic numismatic rarity* in a position of importance far below *condition rarity*.

Stack's March 2009, Entlich, White Oak, Gross & St. Andre Collections sale included lot 6030: "1904-O MS-65 NGC." It sold for $16,100. Heritage's sale of April 2011 included lot 5434: "1904-O MS-65 PCGS." It sold for $23,000.

VF-20	EF-40	AU-50	AU-55	AU-58	MS-60	MS-63	MS-65
$725	$750	$800	$925	$1,000	$1,200	$3,000	$20,000

1905

Circulation-Strike Mintage: 200,992
Proof Mintage: 86

Notes regarding mintages: Portrait partially polished in the Proof die, the procedure followed beginning in 1902, but in the present instance a combination of polished and satiny surface.

Estimated population (Mint State): *4,000+.* Most are MS-60 to MS-63, although MS-66 and finer coins, while in the minority, are regularly available.

Estimated population (circulated grades): *4,000+.* Little information is available. EF and AU coins are plentiful.

Estimated population (Proofs): *25–35.* Rare.

Submissions certified at highest grades (as of March 2017): *PCGS:* MS-65 (21), MS-66 (7), MS-67 (4). *NGC:* MS-65 (10), MS-66 (7), MS-67 (7).

Key to collecting: Common.

MARKET NEWS AND COMMENTARY

In December 1908 Henry Chapman's sale of the David M. Kuntz Collection included lot 118: "1905 Uncirculated. Mint luster." It sold for $10, typical for the era. In November 1939 the William B. Hale Collection, sold by B. Max Mehl, included lot 1688: "1905 Beautiful Uncirculated specimen; just as perfect as the day it was minted." It sold for $18.50 In April 1956 Abe Kosoff's sale of the Thomas G. Melish and Clinton W. Hester Collections included lot 2585: "1905 Uncirculated." It sold for $23.

Stack's / American Numismatic Rarities' October 2006 Buckhead sale included lot 290: "1905 MS-66 NGC." It sold for $11,500. Heritage's FUN sale of January 2012 included lot 4982: "1905 MS-67 PCGS." It sold for $54,625. Stack's Bowers Galleries' November 2011 Baltimore Expo Auction included identical coin as lot 9768: "1905 MS-66 NGC." It sold for $8,625. Stack's Bowers Galleries' November 2013 Baltimore Auction included lot 2227: "1905 MS-67 PCGS." It sold for $31,725.

VF-20	EF-40	AU-50	AU-55	AU-58	MS-60	MS-63	MS-65	PF-63	PF-64	PF-65
$650	$675	$700	$750	$800	$850	$1,200	$5,500	$15,000	$23,500	$45,000

1905-S

Circulation-Strike Mintage: 369,250

Estimated population (Mint State): 600+. Most are MS-60 to MS-62. Higher-grade coins are very elusive. Until the late 1900s when many were imported, Mint State examples were exceedingly rare.

Estimated population (circulated grades): 7,000+. VF is the grade found most often in old-time auction citations (cf. David W. Akers, 1980), but modern imports have included many higher-graded pieces.

Submissions certified at highest grades (as of March 2017): *PCGS:* MS-63 (11), MS-64 (4), MS-65 (1). *NGC:* MS-63 (4).

Key to collecting: Common in circulated grades, slightly scarce in Mint State.

MARKET NEWS AND COMMENTARY

In March 1911, in his sale of the William H. Woodin Collection, Thomas L. Elder offered lot 1336: "1905-S Uncirculated, bright." It sold for $10. An unusual early offering of a Mint State coin, never mind that it only brought face value when sold. The December 1944 sale of the J.F. Bell Collection held by Stack's included lot 788: "1905-S Uncirculated." It sold for $29.

New Netherlands Coin Co.'s 46th sale, Dr. Clarence W. Peake Collection, June 1955, included lot 213: "1905-S. Abt. Extremely Fine. Unusually choice and desirable. Better than the W.G.C. Green (Fine) or Menjou pieces." It sold for $24. Today with the 1905-S in "About Extremely Fine" grade, such a coin would be of little interest to buyers and would sell largely based on its melt value. The same firm in April 1960 in its 54th sale, Jonathan Glogower Consignment, Etc., offered lot 718: "1905-S. Recut mintmark. Mostly brilliant Uncirculated, of similar quality to the 1901 'S'. For some reason, both the Peake and Melish examples were markedly inferior, and we have no other records of specimens anywhere near this one in grade! Undoubtedly rare choice!" It sold for $27.

The grade of this coin—AU? Nearly Uncirculated? Uncirculated but only partially brilliant?—would be another with no buyer interest today.

Stack's October 2008 73rd Anniversary sale included lot 1416: "1905-S MS-63 PCGS." It sold for $5,750. Heritage's ANA Convention sale of August 2010 included lot 6079: "1905-S MS-67 PCGS." It sold for $24,675. Stack's Bowers Galleries' August 2013 Chicago ANA World's Fair of Money sale included lot 4522: "1905-S MS-64 PCGS." It sold for $18,400.

VF-20	EF-40	AU-50	AU-55	AU-58	MS-60	MS-63	MS-65
$650	$675	$700	$750	$800	$850	$5,000	$30,000

1906

Circulation-Strike Mintage: 165,420
Proof Mintage: 77

Notes regarding mintages: The portrait was polished in the Proof die, following the procedure in force since 1902. Held at an angle to the light, the typical Proof reflects light in a manner to reveal that the obverse die is not *plane*, but is slightly bulged, upward toward the rim and portrait, lower in the field. The logotype is slightly high. A raised dot or "pimple" is on the right part of the 9 near its center.

Estimated population (Mint State): *2,500+*. Most are MS-60 to MS-62, with MS-63 being scarce and anything higher being especially scarce.

Estimated population (circulated grades): *2,500+*. EF and AU coins are plentiful in relation to the desire for them. However, on an absolute basis they are scarce.

Estimated population (Proofs): *25–35*.

Submissions certified at highest grades (as of March 2017): *PCGS:* MS-65 (8), MS-66 (1), MS-67 (3). *NGC:* MS-65 (5), MS-66 (2).

Key to collecting: Common.

MARKET NEWS AND COMMENTARY

In November 1939 the William B. Hale Collection, sold by B. Max Mehl, included lot 1689: "1906 Uncirculated; frosty mint surface." It sold for $18.75. Stack's October 1948 sale of the S.E. Goldsmith Collection included lot 1712: "1906 Brilliant Uncirculated." It sold for $31.50. New Netherlands Coin Co.'s 46th sale, Dr. Clarence W. Peake Collection, June 1955, included lot 214: "1906. Brilliant Uncirculated. Minor indications of contact with other coins. Full mint luster." It sold for $22.

Stack's March 1990 James A. Stack Sr. sale included lot 1317: "1906 Brilliant Uncirculated." It sold for $5,775. In November 1995 Numisma '95, conducted by three dealers, included lot 2636: "1906 Choice to Gem Uncirculated. One of only 5 certified MS-64 by PCGS as of 9/95, with one MS-65 higher. PCGS-65." It sold for $4,090.

Heritage's Long Beach sale of September 2006 included lot 3877: "1906 MS-67 PCGS." It sold for $34,500.

PROOF MARKET NEWS AND COMMENTARY

Heritage's FUN Convention sale of January 2013 included lot 5919: "1906 Proof-67 Cameo. NGC." It sold for $61,687.50. Stack's Bowers Galleries' March 2014 Baltimore Auction included lot 4101: "1906 Proof-66 NGC." It sold for $52 875.

VF-20	EF-40	AU-50	AU-55	AU-58	MS-60	MS-63	MS-65	PF-63	PF-64	PF-65
$650	$675	$700	$750	$800	$850	$1,750	$9,500	$15,000	$23,500	$45,000

1906-D

Circulation-Strike Mintage: 981,000

Notes regarding mintages: The first specimens were coined on March 12, 1906. These were the first gold coins made in Denver, with the double eagle being first struck in April and the half eagle in June. David W. Akers commented: "Reportedly, a small number (12?) of 'Proof' or presentation pieces were struck to commemorate the opening of the Denver Mint. I have not seen one so I am unable to comment on them."

Estimated population (Mint State): *8,000+.* Very common. Many have been sold outside of numismatic circles, but thousands have been certified. Most are MS-60 to MS-63, but higher-grade pieces are seen with enough frequency that there will be no problem acquiring an MS-64 or MS-65. Still higher graded coins are rare.

Estimated population (circulated grades): *10,000+.* Plentiful in high circulated grades. Repatriated in quantity in the 1980s and 1990s.

Submissions certified at highest grades (as of March 2017): *PCGS:* MS-64 (217), MS-65 (27), MS-66 (3). *NGC:* MS-64 (147), MS-65 (22), MS-66 (1), MS-67 (1).

Key to collecting: Common. Popular as the first Denver Mint issue.

MARKET NEWS AND COMMENTARY

In July 1937 in sale 379, the Walter P. Innes Jr. Collection, J.C. Morgenthau & Co. offered lot 75: "1906-D Uncirculated." It sold for $17. This was followed by lot 76: "1906-D Uncirculated." It sold for $18. In February 1944, in the Belden E. Roach Collection, B. Max Mehl offered lot 485: "1906-D Brilliant semi-Proof, almost equal to a Proof. Rare condition. Undoubtedly a very early impression of the die." It sold for $26.25.

In April 1956, in his sale of the Thomas G. Melish Collection, Abe Kosoff offered lot 2588: "1906-D. First year of operation of the Denver Mint. Low date. Mint mark nearer talon on left. Uncirculated." It sold for $26. This was followed by lot 2589: "1906-D. Low date. Mint mark nearer arrow on right. Uncirculated." It sold for $24.75. Next was lot 2590: "1906-D. High date. D closer to talon. Extremely Fine." It sold for $23. The list ended with lot 2591: "1906-D. High date, D closer to arrow. Extremely Fine." It sold for $23.

In October 1982, in the Louis E. Eliasberg Collection of U.S. Gold Coins, Bowers and Ruddy Galleries offered lot 836: "1906-D Gem Brilliant Uncirculated, MS-67." From the John H. Clapp Collection, 1942. Earlier directly from the Denver Mint." It sold for $6,800. In August 1990, in Auction '90, David W. Akers offered lot 1929: "1906-D MS-65." It sold for $4,400. Heritage's sale of April 2014 included lot 5778: "1906-D MS-66 PCGS." It sold for $14,100.

VF-20	EF-40	AU-50	AU-55	AU-58	MS-60	MS-63	MS-65
$650	$675	$700	$750	$800	$850	$1,100	$6,500

1906-O

Circulation-Strike Mintage: 86,895

Notes regarding mintages: There was no gold coinage in New Orleans in 1905. In *The Numismatist* of May of that year Farran Zerbe reported on the facility:

> A visit to the Mint at New Orleans found it, the now oldest building used for coinage purposes in this country, not operating. It has not been in operation since November 1904; those in charge expected it would resume operation July 1, 1905. Of the $32,000,000 in coin stored in its vaults, $29,000,000 is in silver dollars, and the anticipated work is the re-coinage of the stock of dollars into subsidiary coins. The building is sufficient evidence of its age, except for which, it stands practically as completed in 1838. Most of the machinery and equipment appears as antiquated as the building."[35]

Estimated population (Mint State): 700+. Most are MS-60 to MS-62, with MS-63 being scarce and anything higher being rare.

Estimated population (circulated grades): 1,500+. EF and AU coins are plentiful in relation to the specialized demand for them, but on an absolute basis they are scarce.

Submissions certified at highest grades (as of March 2017): *PCGS:* MS-64 (18), MS-65 (3), MS-66 (2). *NGC:* MS-64 (12), MS-65 (4), MS-66 (2).

Key to collecting: The 1906-O was the swan song of New Orleans Mint eagles. Although they have never been viewed as rarities, they have always been in great demand.

MARKET NEWS AND COMMENTARY

In 1918 Elmer Sears' *Choice U.S. Gold, Silver and Copper Coins* fixed price list included this: "1906-O Uncirculated specimen with Mint lustre. Very rare. $20." Also: "Another, Extremely Fine. Rare. $16." At the time there was relatively little price differential between Extremely Fine and Uncirculated examples of most gold coins.

In November 1939 the William B. Hale Collection, sold by B. Max Mehl, included lot 1724:

> 1906-O Last year of issue. Beautiful brilliant Uncirculated specimen; as perfect as the day it was minted. Mr. Hale paid $25. For this coin many years ago, and it should be worth a great deal more today especially in this wonderful condition. I'm almost tempted to call it the finest known, but I have sworn off of making such statements. I can and do say that it is the finest known: as far as I know. [Sold for $22]

In the December 1944 sale of the J.F. Bell Collection Stack's included lot 720: "1906-O Last year of issue. Brilliant Uncirculated. Very scarce." It sold for $65.

In November 1945 B. Max Mehl's sale of the W.A. Philpott and Henry L. Zander Collections included lot 1703: "1906-O Last year of issue. About Uncirculated with mint luster." It sold for $22.

New Netherlands Coin Co.'s 46th sale, Dr. Clarence W. Peake Collection, June 1955, included lot 215: "1906-O. Last year of issue. Extremely Fine; marked "About Uncirculated." Very scarce." It sold for $24. In October 1982, in the Louis E. Eliasberg Collection of U.S. Gold Coins, Bowers and Ruddy Galleries offered lot 837: "1906-O Gem Brilliant Uncirculated, MS-67. From the John H. Clapp Collection, 1942. Earlier from the Elmer S. Sears sale, 1910." It sold for $2,860.

In November 2000, in the Harry W. Bass Jr. Collection, Part IV, Bowers and Merena Galleries offered lot 780: "1906-O MS-66 PCGS. PCGS Population: 2; none finer. From Stack's sale of the DiBello Collection, May 1970, lot 1163." It sold for $11,500.

Heritage's sale of February 2009 included lot 2962: "1906-O MS-66 NGC." It sold for $25,300. In the February 2017 Collectors Choice sale Stack's Bowers Galleries offered lot 91731: "1906-O MS-64 PCGS." It sold for $9,400.

VF-20	EF-40	AU-50	AU-55	AU-58	MS-60	MS-63	MS-65
$725	$750	$800	$925	$1,000	$1,100	$4,750	$20,000

1906-S

Circulation-Strike Mintage: 457,000

Estimated population (Mint State): 700+. Scarce. Most are MS-60 to MS-62, with MS-64 being slightly scarce and anything higher being rare.

Estimated population (circulated grades): 7,000+. EF and AU coins are plentiful in relation to the demand for them, but are otherwise scarce.

Submissions certified at highest grades (as of March 2017): *PCGS:* MS-65 (1), MS-66 (3), MS-67 (1). ***NGC:*** MS-65 (2).

Key to collecting: One of the scarcer issues of the era. Well-worn coins were the order of the day until modern repatriations.

MARKET NEWS AND COMMENTARY

After the April 1906 earthquake and fire the San Francisco Mint was the only building left standing in its district. For many months it was the command center for communications and was the provisional location for several banks.

In May 1939, sale 399, Rare U.S. Gold Coins by J.C. Morgenthau & Co. included lot 413: "1906-S Very Fine." It sold for $16.50. In November 1939 the William B. Hale Collection, sold by B. Max Mehl, included lot 1749: "1906-S Extremely Fine." It sold for $18. In February 1944, in the Belden E. Roach Collection, B. Max Mehl offered lot 463: "1906-S Extremely Fine; considerable luster." It sold for $25. In the December 1944 sale of the J.F. Bell Collection Stack's included lot 789: "1906-S Uncirculated." It sold for $32.50.

In May 1945 Stack's sale of the George H. Hall Collection included lot 2219: "1906-S Brilliant Proof." It sold for $27. Hmm. Interesting. New Netherlands Coin Co.'s 46th sale, Dr. Clarence W. Peake Collection, June 1955, included lot 216: "1906-S. Not quite full Uncirculated. Brilliant and lustrous. Ahead of the W.G.C. (VF), Green (Fine), Menjou (VF) and Davis-Graves (VF) pieces." It sold for $28. This account is amazing to contemplate today. The author attended the Peake sale in person and remembers well the excitement in the gallery at the time.

Well into the 21st century, in the May 2016 Rarities Auction Stack's Bowers Galleries offered lot 110: "1906-S MS-64 PCGS." It sold for $8,812.50.

VF-20	EF-40	AU-50	AU-55	AU-58	MS-60	MS-63	MS-65
$650	$675	$700	$750	$800	$850	$4,000	$16,500

1907

Circulation-Strike Mintage: 1,203,899
Proof Mintage: 74

Notes regarding mintages: Many of these were exported, later to become available to numismatists.

Estimated population (Mint State): 20,000+. Very common. Many have been sold outside of numismatic circles, but thousand have been certified. Most are MS-60 to MS-63 or even MS-64 with some as MS-65, but higher-graded pieces are elusive.

Estimated population (circulated grades): 30,000+. High-grade pieces are common from overseas holdings.

Estimated population (Proofs): 35–45. Rare.

Submissions certified at highest grades (as of March 2017): PCGS: MS-63 (4.003), MS-64 (811), MS-65 (34). **NGC:** MS-63 (6,335), MS-64 (1,065), MS-65 (83), MS-66 (7).

Key to collecting: Extremely common.

MARKET NEWS AND COMMENTARY

In February 1936, sale 360, J.C. Lighthouse Collection by J.C. Morgenthau & Co. included lot 21: "1907 Old Head. Uncirculated." It sold for $23. In November 1939 the William B. Hale Collection, sold by B. Max Mehl, included lot 1690: "1907 Liberty head. Last year of this type. Uncirculated." It sold for $18. In May 1945 Stack's sale of the George H. Hall Collection included lot 2220: "1907 Liberty Head, Brilliant Uncirculated." It sold for $28.

Stack's June 1995 Vander Zanden & Yale University sale included lot 826: "1907 Liberty Eagle $10, Brilliant Uncirculated." It sold for $5,610. Stack's Bowers Galleries' February 2017 Collectors Choice Auction included lot 91731: "1906-O MS-64 PCGS." It sold for $9,400.

PROOF MARKET NEWS AND COMMENTARY

In May 1939, sale 399, Rare U.S. Gold Coins by J.C. Morgenthau & Co. included lot 414: "1907 Old type. Brilliant Proof." It sold for $25. In February 1944, in the Belden E. Roach Collection, B. Max Mehl offered lot 380: "1907 Last year of Liberty head type. Perfect brilliant Proof; wire edge. Scarce and in demand." It sold for $42.

In the December 1944 sale of the J.F. Bell Collection Stack's included lot 671: "1907 Liberty Head. Brilliant Proof. Gem." It sold for $55. In October 1962, in the Samuel W. Wolfson Collection, Stack's offered lot 813: "1907 Liberty Head. Brilliant Proof. Last year of issue of this design. Rare and seldom offered in this remarkable condition. Only 74 struck, probably less than half exist today." It sold for $520. In January 1984 Stack's sale of the Amon G. Carter Jr. Family Collection included lot 800: "1907 Brilliant Proof. A choice specimen in greenish yellow gold with a pale coppery tint." It sold for $14,300.

In October 1998, in the John J. Pittman Collection sale, Part II, David Akers offered lot 2004:

> 1907, Liberty Head Type, nearly in the Choice category. This is the lowest mint-age Proof Liberty Head Eagle from 1899–1907, but the survival rate of the Proofs of this year must have been slightly greater than for some other years since the 1907 is actually one of the most common of all Proof Liberty Head eagles. Approximately 35–40 Proofs are known, placing this issue in the same rarity class as the 1902, 1903 and 1904. [Sold for $37,400]

Stack's August 2010 Johnson-Blue Collection sale included lot 1203: "1907 Proof- 66 PCGS." It sold for $47,500. Stack's Bowers Galleries' June 2012 Baltimore Auction included lot 4377: "1907 Proof-66 PCGS." It sold for $48,875.

VF-20	EF-40	AU-50	AU-55	AU-58	MS-60	MS-63	MS-65	PF-63	PF-64	PF-65
$650	$675	$700	$750	$800	$850	$1,000	$5,000	$15,000	$23,500	$45,000

1907-D

Circulation-Strike Mintage: 1,030,000

Notes regarding mintages: The first day of striking was March 8, 1907.

Estimated population (Mint State): 3,000+. Most are MS-60 to MS-63, with MS-64 being scarce and anything higher being especially elusive.

Estimated population (circulated grades): 15,000+. Mostly from overseas holdings. AU coins are plentiful. Little account has been kept of such coins as they are not often certified and are ranked as common issues.

Submissions certified at highest grades (as of March 2017): *PCGS:* MS-62 (204), MS-63 (127), MS-64 (61). ***NGC:*** MS-62 (2-5), MS-63 (74), MS-64 (48), MS-65 (8).

Characteristics of striking and die notes: Usually well struck. A few have prooflike surfaces.

Key to collecting: Common.

MARKET NEWS AND COMMENTARY

In October 1939 J.C. Morgenthau & Co. offered this in sale 405, lot 708: "1907-D Old type. Uncirculated. Very scarce." It sold for $20.

The December 1944 sale of the J.F. Bell Collection held by Stack's included lot 803: "1907-D Liberty Head. Uncirculated gem with brilliant Proof surface." It sold for $42.50.

New Netherlands Coin Co.'s 46th sale, Dr. Clarence W. Peake Collection, June 1955, included lot 220: "1907-D. Second and last year for Miss Liberty. Choice Uncirculated. A brilliant first-strike, just about perfect. Listed in both books at $35. Uncirculated." It sold for $27.50. The books were the *Standard Catalogue of United States Coins*, the popularity of which had faded to a very low level, and the *Guide Book of United States Coins*, considered by just about everyone to be the standard reference.

Fast forward to the 21st century. Heritage's sale of April 2006 included lot 4083: "1907-D MS-65 NGC." It sold for $10,925.

VF-20	EF-40	AU-50	AU-55	AU-58	MS-60	MS-63	MS-65
$650	$675	$700	$750	$800	$850	$1,750	$13,500

1907-S

Circulation-Strike Mintage: 210,500

Notes regarding mintages: For many years the 1907-S was inadvertently omitted from Mint reports, an error compounded each issue when past reports were copied.

Estimated population (Mint State): *600+*. Most are MS-60 to MS-63, with MS-64 being much scarcer and any higher-graded coin being quite rare. In Mint State the 1907-S was a notable rarity until many were imported in the late 1900s.

Estimated population (circulated grades): *3,500+*. This figure is guesswork. EF and AU coins are mostly from imports. Traditionally, the grade often seen in old-time collections is VF (cf. David W. Akers, 1980).

Submissions certified at highest grades (as of March 2017): *PCGS:* MS-63 (20), MS-64 (9), MS-66 (2). *NGC:* MS-63 (15), MS-64 (5), MS-65 (1), MS-66 (1).

Key to collecting: Slightly scarce in very high grades.

MARKET NEWS AND COMMENTARY

In March 1911, in his sale of the William H. Woodin Collection, Thomas L. Elder offered lot 1338: "1907-S Mint bloom." It sold for $10. In March 1938, in his sale of the Samuel H. McVitty Collection, B. Max Mehl offered lot 420: "1907-S Old type. No record of mintage, but apparently a quantity was coined. Very Fine." It sold for $37.50.

In November 1939 the William B. Hale Collection, sold by B. Max Mehl, included lot 1750: "1907-S Practically Uncirculated, with mint luster. Some confusion with the mint records, as for a time there was no record of any eagles being coined at the San Francisco Mint in this year." It sold for $17. The June 1941 sale of the William Forrester Dunham Collection by B. Max Mehl included lot 2278: "Old type. Very Fine. No official record of any having been coined. Record up to $50, but since then several have been discovered." It sold for $18.25.

In February 1944, in the Belden E. Roach Collection, B. Max Mehl offered lot 464: "1907-S For a time there was no mint record of eagles of this year of the old type having been minted at the San Francisco Mint. Nearly Uncirculated. Scarce." It sold for $24.75. In the December 1944 sale of the J.F. Bell Collection Stack's included lot 790: "1907-S Liberty Head. Uncirculated gem." It sold for $35. New Netherlands Coin Co.'s 46th sale, Dr. Clarence W. Peake Collection, June 1955, included lot 219: "1907-S. Final year for the type. Just about brilliant Uncirculated. Not in the Atwater collection; the W.G.C. example realized $35, well over nine years ago." It sold for $24.

There have been countless sales in modern times. As an example, Heritage's sale of March 2014 included lot 10677: "1907-S MS-65 NGC." It sold for $9,987.50.

Although by 1936 mintage figures had been published in several places, still among gold coins in particular there was a great lack of basic information, including which issues were rare and which were not. The situation was poignantly demonstrated in an exchange of correspondence related by Alex. J. Rosborough in the July 1936 issue of *The Numismatist* under the title "Another S Mint Rarity":

I received quite a numismatic thrill the other day when a lonesome mystery coin came drifting in to take first place in my coin collection. It was not however, until I set about listing the piece, that the discovery was made that no record for such a coin could be found. It is a 1907 $10 gold, Liberty Head, S Mint issue. I consulted my numismatic friends about the coin and they were at a loss to recognize it. I went over to the branch mint at San Francisco, and while it was admitted there that the coin was a genuine issue from that mint, no record was on file as to any number to be turned out, or order for any such issue by this branch.

On May 3, 1936, I wrote to the Director of the U.S. Mint at Philadelphia, Pennsylvania, as follows:

"The records of the branch mint at San Francisco make no mention of the coinage of a Liberty Head $10 gold for the year 1907, although such a coin was issued (the S being very close to—almost touching—the eagle's claw). *Green's Numismatic Reference and Check Book* and other books purporting to give a record of all coins issued make no mention of this piece. The existence of this $10 coin, 'without a mint record,' has drawn the attention of collectors all over the country to it, and any information you can give us about the number issued by the San Francisco Mint will be of great interest to us all."

Under date of May 19, 1936, an answer to my letter came, which read:

"This will acknowledge receipt of your letter of May 3, 1936. For your information, the Director of the Mint's report for the year of 1907 shows no Liberty Head $10 gold coin was struck at the San Francisco Mint that year. Very truly yours, Edwin H. Dressel, Supt."

What do you think of that? There is no such coin, and yet I have it, a genuine issued coin. About that there is no doubt. Then how could it have happened? This is my conjecture: You will remember that the earthquake and fire visited San Francisco in 1906, and although the U.S. Mint was saved, owing principally to the fact that it had its own water supply, everything was in confusion for many months thereafter. It is quite likely that the die for this 1907 Liberty Head $10 gold issue was

sent by the mother mint at Philadelphia to the branch mint at San Francisco preparatory to issuing the order to coin and designating the number of pieces, and that
upon receipt of the die the San Francisco Mint struck this coin to see that the die was
O.K. and waited for instructions. The general mix-up following the fire in all prob-
ability held up gold shipments at San Francisco, and during the delay it was decided
by the department to substitute the new Indian Head pattern and abandon this issue,
thus leaving this Liberty Head S $10 the only one coined. Alex. J. Rosborough,
ANA 2933.

Later it would develop that the 1907-S Liberty Head half dollar was indeed struck
at the San Francisco Mint, to the extent of 210,500 pieces. Further, enough examples
survived that it was not only not rare, but was indeed common and worth no premium
as a variety. Apparently the records of the San Francisco Mint were incomplete. What
an interesting footnote in 20th century numismatic history.

VF-20	EF-40	AU-50	AU-55	AU-58	MS-60	MS-63	MS-65
$650	$675	$700	$750	$800	$850	$4,000	$20,000

10

Indian Head $10 Gold Coins, 1907–1933

INDIAN HEAD, NO MOTTO (1907–1908)

Designer: *Augustus Saint-Gaudens.* **Weight:** *16.718 grams.*
Composition: *.900 gold, .100 copper (net weight: .48375 oz. pure gold).*
Diameter: *27 mm.* **Edge:** *46 raised stars.* **Mints:** *Philadelphia and Denver.*

Roosevelt and Saint-Gaudens

In 1904 President Theodore Roosevelt admired ancient Greek coins on display at the Smithsonian Institution and thought that American coinage had the potential to be more attractive. In 1905 President Theodore Roosevelt admired the work that noted sculptor Augustus Saint-Gaudens did for him on his unofficial presidential inauguration medal. Chief Engraver Charles E. Barber had prepared the usual *official* inaugu-

Augustus Saint-Gaudens.

Theodore Roosevelt.

ral medal, but Roosevelt did not like it. Today to many if not most numismatic eyes both versions of the medal seem to be satisfactory.

Chief Engraver Charles E. Barber's official medal for the 1905 inauguration
of President Theodore Roosevelt. The president rejected these as
unsatisfactory and refused to distribute them. (Shown at 75%)

Roosevelt commissioned Augustus Saint-Gaudens to create
this inaugural medal, which was to his liking. (Shown at 75%)

In 1905 Roosevelt commissioned Saint-Gaudens to redesign the entire American
coinage spectrum from the cent to the double eagle. Working in his studio in Cornish,
New Hampshire (now a National Historic Site), the artist prepared many sketches. In
failing health, Saint-Gaudens was able to complete or nearly complete work for just
two denominations, the $10 and $20, both of which were first struck in 1907.

It fell to Chief Engraver Barber to finesse Saint-Gaudens's models and adapt them
for use on high-speed coining presses. During his lifetime Saint-Gaudens had been a
vital part of the American artistic community. Barber was viewed more as a workman
than an artist, and some viewed him with contempt. One famously called Barber's
coinage art "wretched."

Designing coins had long been under the purview of the Philadelphia Mint and artists hired to work with the engraving department. When Roosevelt commissioned
Saint-Gaudens to redesign the American coinage, Barber became jealous, bitter, and
distressed. This continued after the sculptor's death. A hitherto unpublished letter
from Barber to Mint Director Frank A. Leach, September 21, 1908, reflects this:

I am sending a few more medals that I think you ought to have. I have selected a variety of subjects that I think well demonstrated to anyone that we are quite competent to execute any government medals or coins if we are only given the opportunity, and certainly so far as coins are concerned it would be more satisfactory if we had the whole matter in charge, than it is to scheme and contrive all manner of ways in order to make workable a model made by some party absolutely ignorant of all that pertains to coinage.

The morning I have been testing the piling of eagle coins and find from twenty pieces furnished by Mr. Clark that the pieces are thinner on the edge of one part of the coin than on the other. This is caused by the head being all on one side rather than in the center of coin, and therefore the pile never measures twice the same, as all depends upon how the pieces come together. You will see that it is therefore impossible to establish a standard height of twenty pieces, as each time they are put together the height differs.

The many difficulties that we have had to contend with and the very unsatisfactory appearance of the coin now that it is made should convince anyone that although a sculptor may have a reputation in his own like he is a failure when taken out of it.

Saint-Gaudens's $10 design bore on the obverse a female wearing an Indian war bonnet. The headdress is inscribed LIBERTY on a band, 13 stars are in an arc above, and the date is below.

The face was taken from an earlier study of Nike, also called "Victory," and the rest is said to have been taken from the portrait of his mistress, Davida Clark, with whom he is alleged to have had a child (although biographers have never been able to confirm this).

The reverse depicts a perched eagle with UNITED STATES OF AMERICA above, the motto E PLURIBUS UNUM to the right, and the denomination expressed as TEN DOLLARS below. The eagle on the new 1907 $10 was directly copied from the motif Saint-Gaudens used on the 1905 presidential inaugural medal for Theodore Roosevelt. Later, Bela Lyon Pratt used essentially the same motif for the reverse of the new $2.50 and $5 coins of 1908. A related bird image appeared on ancient Greek coins.

Detail of Nike. (Saint-Gaudens National Historic Site)

Face of Liberty on the gold coin.

As President Roosevelt personally objected to the use of the name of the Deity on coins, the Indian Head issues of 1907 and certain issues of 1908 lack the motto IN GOD WE TRUST. Coinage of the type was affected at Philadelphia in 1907 and 1908 and also in Denver the latter year.

By late 1907 many of the Indian Head eagles were in circulation. Howland Wood contributed this to *The Numismatist*, issue of December 1907:

The New $10 Coin

At last it has come—art in our new coinage. The new eagle, the talked of $10 gold piece, has been put into circulation.

The obverse shows a grand statuesque head of Liberty crowned by an Indian war bonnet, on the band of which the word LIBERTY is inscribed. Around the edge in the upper half of the field are 13 pointed stars, below the neck the date 1907.

The placing of the head with a blank space in front is very artistic, and it is regrettable that more designers do not realize the value of blank spaces, but rather deem it necessary to make use of every available space on a coin. At first glance the feathered bonnet looks too large, but after the eye becomes reconciled to the new type no change would be wanted. The general pose of the head, its position on the coin, and the arrangement of the headdress resembles very closely several of the old Greek coins. Symbolism occupied a prominent place on these ancient Greek pieces and evidences of it are marked on this, the position of the feathers and the stars suggest in their combination the stars and stripes in our flag. The eager attentive face, full of expression and yet full of dignity and a certain amount of serenity, is a long step ahead from the almost vacant stare of the faces depicted on our previous coins.

Owing to the high relief which Saint-Gaudens prepared the model for this coin and the necessary modification of this relief to bring it down to the modern mechanical requirements the locks of the hair above the eagle are not as well worked out as might be desired. A good deal of this effect may later be overcome.

The reverse of the coin shows the typical Saint-Gaudens eagle in a standing pose with partially drooping wings. The eagle occupies the central position on the reverse and with an impressive majesty dominates this side of the coin. The reverse as a whole shows a careful working out of type and inscription with a happy avoidance of overcrowding which cannot be said of so many of our other coins.

A noticeable change from our other pieces is the treatment of the background, both on obverse and reverse. Instead of being flat there is a general hollowing in from the edge, or cup-shaped depression from the mill to the center. This treatment of the sunken parts of the piece has been done on different European coins of recent dates, especially the French.

A still greater departure from old standards is noticed on the edge. Instead of the reeding as heretofore used, the edge on the present piece is composed of 46 raised stars, signifying the states of the Union. The coin is a magnificent conception throughout, of a refined Greek character, simple in its aspect, but grand in its dignity, and will surely find a place in the front rank with the best coins of the age.

Reviewing the New $10 Design

The advent of the Indian Head $10 prompted many numismatists and others to write to popular coin-collecting periodicals such as *The Numismatist* and the *Elder Monthly*. Letters printed in the *Elder Monthly*, Volume 2, October–November, 1907:

My dear Mr. Elder—

I am enclosing a couple of rubbings of Bryan dollars, and descriptions of another one that has parodies of "In God We Trust." A search in the bar rooms will reveal a lot more parodies for at one time these places were especially rich in such mottoes. I trust that you will speak well of the new eagle. I have just sent off to Editor Heath a word of praise about the piece.[1]

In justification of the Greek type of the new $10, the placing of the head as it is and the feathers going to the edge, almost identical types can be found among many Greek coins. I can only think of a few offhand, including the Athenian pieces, and those of Thurium, Pharsalos, and Velia.

In justification of the "pants" of the eagle, a glance at our own coins of the seated liberty type will show that trousers were worn long in those days, as well as in the time of the Ptolemies, and good examples can be found on those Ptolemaic coins with one and two eagles on the reverse. I think the design of the obverse and reverse are grand conceptions, but the technical execution or die work I do not consider good.

Yours very truly,
Howland Wood, Secretary.[2]
Brookline, Massachusetts,
November 13, 1907.

My dear Mr. Elder—

I have examined the new Saint-Gaudens ten dollar gold coin which you so kindly obtained for me and will briefly give you my opinion of it.

Upon the obverse, the head and appurtenances and date are too large for the size of the piece, and the stars too small. The face of Liberty is an anomaly. The prominent nose and chin indicate determination and strength of character, but the effect of overhanging "upper jaw" and lip with open mouth is idiotic. While the face is not that of an Indian, the headgear is not.

On the reverse, we find a turkey buzzard in pantalets. The words of the legend above and value below the effigy are not sufficiently spaced, and are too close to the outer rim of the coin. There should be a marginal space between the top of these letters and the rim. "E Pluribus Unum" is added as a postscript.

The style of letters used on both obverse and reverse and the figures of date show very poor judgment viewed from a typographical standpoint.

In one respect the piece may be called a "howling success." It is entirely different from anything ever before issued by the United States Mint, and no patent is needed to protect the designer from infringements.

The coin, both obverse and reverse, is a humiliating disappointment, without one redeeming feature, and is a "foozle."

Yours very truly,
E. Gilbert[3]

My dear Mr. Elder—

It is not strange that a feeling of exultation results from one's first glimpse of the new $10 gold coin. Chagrin and dismay have long stirred within us at sight of our coins in contrast with these of other nations, and to have one now that need not be defended save from attacks of patriotic committees from Harrisburg[4] and from over-zealous religious enthusiasts, is indeed gratifying.

To the former we might say, should we be able to assume sufficient gravity in addressing them: "Look you! A great painter or sculptor is no one-eyed camera, nor does he slavishly copy every feature before him when he works from a model, in order thus to translate more readily into the medium he has chosen, his conception of beauty, or grandeur or power."

The simple beauty and dignity of design here shown on both obverse and reverse, must eventually silence all such noisy objections, and so we listen with a show of tolerance to the criticisms noted.

Formerly at the suggestion of that great American, Benjamin Franklin, some of our coins were inscribed "Mind your business," and it has been suggested that if we must have a motto, this be reinstated as being more pertinent and characteristic.

Seriously though, it is certainly true, as President Roosevelt so convincingly showed in his recent open letter, that it has come to be flagrant irreverence to use the inscription "In God We Trust" on the country's coins. Reverence for truth and beauty is most effectively in evidence in a beautifully designed and characteristic coin, certainly—and it is because we, as a nation do not appreciate the inspiring grace and power of beautiful symbols that we have so many ugly and dispiriting ones all about us.

But now that we have it before us, we appreciate the grace and beauty of the firmly modeled head, so nicely placed, and so decoratively relieved by the stiff feathers; and the eagle remarkable for its spirited yet dignified posture and for the very evident characteristics, in drawing and modeling of the American eagle. In this we have at last a truthful, dignified and conventional American eagle.

Charles J. Connick
Boston,
November 20, 1907

The Mary Cunningham Commotion

In the meantime in 1907 a story went the rounds of newspapers to the effect that the portrait on the new Saint-Gaudens $10 was of a—perish the thought—*foreigner.* The *New York Sun* printed this:

A Pennsylvania Society has protested against the act of the late Augustus Saint-Gaudens in using as the design for the new coin the profile of a young woman born out of the United States. It is interesting to reflect that the model used for long by another artist for his typical "American girl" was also an alien.[5]

The preceding arose from a commentary datelined Harrisburg, Pennsylvania, September 19, 1907:

Victor Boyer, state counselor of the Order of Independent Americans, will personally present to Secretary [of the Treasury] Cortelyou the protest of the order against placing the profile of Mary Cunningham on the United States gold coins.

Miss Cunningham was a waitress in a Cornish, Vermont,[6] eating house when discovered by the late Augustus Saint-Gaudens, the sculptor, who selected her as the model for the design he had been commissioned to execute for the government. The Independent Americans, admitting her rare beauty, object because she was born in Ireland.

In due course, this piece of fiction appeared:[7]

Windsor, Vermont, September 21.

The Saint-Gaudens family refuse to give any information whatever regarding Mary Cunningham, the pretty young Irish waitress whom the late Augustus Saint-Gaudens took as a model when designing the new issue of gold coins.

The Cunningham girl is now employed as a domestic in the family of the late sculptor, but no outsider is allowed to see her. The Saint-Gaudens villa is secluded on a spur of the Green Mountain range with numerous signs at the entrance to the grounds announcing that no strangers are admitted.

Homer Saint-Gaudens, a son, said tonight that the statement that her face is to appear in profile on the copper cent is incorrect. He asserted, instead, that she will be shown full-length on either the ten or twenty-dollar gold piece.[8] Mr. Saint-Gaudens was not sure which.

There had been many other models for coins, and he did not see why so much fuss should be made over this one, but at any rate he was not going to add to it by giving any other information.

Mary Cunningham was a figment of someone's imagination. No such person was ever involved in the coinage design and no one of this name is known to have been associated with the sculptor.

Motto Added

In 1908 Saint-Gaudens's Indian Head design was modified on the reverse by the addition of IN GOD WE TRUST in the field at the center right. The motto, disliked by President Roosevelt as he felt it was sacrilegious, was restored by a special act of Congress, and remained in effect through the end of the series in 1933. Otherwise the Indian Head obverse and perched eagle reverse motif remained unchanged. The edges of the issues between 1908 and 1911 have 46 raised stars, while those minted from 1912 onward have 48 raised stars, reflecting an increased number of states in the Union. Most collectors have ignored the star count differences, and consider all coins from 1908 to 1933 to be of the same basic design. In the modern era of collecting in which many coins are encased in plastic "slabs" or certified holders, the edge is hidden from view, and appreciation of the star count is completely lost.

Mintage was intense and continuous of the No Motto style in 1907 and early 1908, and with IN GOD WE TRUST from 1908 through 1916, although quantities were much smaller than for double eagles, the latter being popular for the export trade.

Coinage of $10 gold pieces took place at the Philadelphia, Denver, and San Francisco mints. After 1916 no eagles were made until 1920-S, followed by a gap until the 1926 Philadelphia issue, with the next following being 1930-S, then 1932 and 1933. Business-strike mintage for the type totaled 14,385,139, while 768 Proofs were made, the latter being of the Sand Blast and Satin Finish formats (see chapter 4 for more details).

The Indian Head Eagle Varieties of 1907

In autumn 1907 the Mint produced two special varieties of the new Saint-Gaudens Indian Head design. These had a round dot or period added before and after the inscriptions on the reverse. One variety had a sharp "wire" or "knife" rim, and the other had a rounded or normal rim.

While these have been popularly called patterns, an examination of the situation leaves no room for any conclusion other than that these were "special" coins produced not as patterns, but for the profit of Mint employees and favored others. A pattern is a design proposal made in very small numbers to test the motif—often involving adjustments made by the engraver, etc., before coins are struck for circulation. In the present instance, the "special" 1907 coins with periods were placed in the hands of Mint personnel who were free to keep them as souvenirs or sell them at a profit.

Struck as delicacies for the numismatic trade, these $10 coins were "filtered" out of the Mint and into the hands of receptive coin dealers, including Henry Chapman and Thomas L. Elder, both of whom had quantities on hand for years afterward.

At the Mint at the time a number of delicacies were produced by assistant engraver George T. Morgan (who seems to have been in charge of distributing most of the rare MCMVII Ultra High Relief pattern double eagles and who is known to have made special Proof strikings of silver dollars in 1921 and 1922).[9] The pieces were "given to" officials and key employees and even the director in Washington! However, the Mint never announced how the "ordinary" numismatist could obtain one. The whole affair was shrouded in secrecy.

On February 28, 1908, Henry Chapman, who *one way or another* had acquired a number of pieces for private sale to his clients, furnished Baltimore collector Robert Garrett with information concerning the 1907 gold issues:[10]

> I wish to give you some information. If you will act quickly upon it I think we will secure for you a couple of coins which are worth large sums. In fact, I have paid $150 cash for one of them myself.
>
> The director of the Mint, Mr. Frank A. Leach, at Washington, has in his possession, and is distributing at face value, to collectors or public museums, to the latter he writes me more especially than to the former, special $10 pieces of the Saint-Gaudens design, 1907.
>
> If you will write him and ask him to send you a specimen of the $10 gold piece, Saint-Gaudens design 1907, from die No. 1 *without any border*, and die No. 2, with a wire or thin edge, you might say to him that you have been informed that he has a few of these for distribution to collections which are exhibited to the public. I would tell him that your collection is on exhibition at Princeton College and that you would like to have him send you them.

Send him $20 in gold notes and 12¢ in postage stamps, and I think you will succeed. Do not mention my name or your source of information. Of the coin without the border, 500 were made, of number 2 only 50 were kept out of several thousand that were minted. The rest were melted. As he has but a few of the wire edge, which he refuses to let me have a specimen of, I would suggest that you write immediately upon receipt of this. If you can bring to bear any influence of your senator or congressman, it might be well to do so, but I think that it is possible you will get them without bringing anyone else into the matter, which might cause delay. If you succeed in getting them, you are going to get two coins worth $400.

In his autobiography, *Recollections of a Newspaperman* (1917), Leach breezily stated that these pieces "were given" to officials and others (here excerpted):

In producing the new $10 pieces, or eagles, three models of the new design were made by Saint-Gaudens. Five hundred trial pieces were struck from the first model, and 34,100 pieces were struck from the second model, but all of this [second] lot were subsequently remelted, except 42 coins, which with those of the first lot [the 500 "Wire Rim" coins] were given to museums of art and officials and others connected with the work.

It would be interesting to know how many "museums of art" actually received such coins!

As will be seen under their appropriate studies later, the 1907 "Wire Rim" and the rarer "Rolled (or Rounded) Rim" pieces soon came onto the numismatic market and were a staple in the auctions of Thomas L. Elder and other dealers. Likely, some with connections, such as George O. Walton, could obtain these as well as MCMVII double eagles as desired from Mint officials. *Mehl's Numismatic Monthly*, September 1908, included this advertisement:

Saint Gaudens Coins

The coinage of the wire-edge, high relief (1907 Roman numeral date) was 500 pieces, followed by a second issue of 4,000 of the same design but with a smooth edge. I offer fine wire-edge coins at $35, this variety being in particular demand.

Eagles. The first issue of the ten-dollar piece was of high relief, with wire edge, date 1907. Only 500 of these were coined, and they were issued only through the office of the Secretary of the Treasury, the great demand soon exhausting the issue. This at once became numbered among the rarities of recent U.S. coinage. I offer a limited number in mint condition at $50 each.

George O. Walton, Cashier of the Commercial National Bank
Washington, D.C.

Regarding the number known, for the "Wire Rim" the usual mintage figure given years ago was 550, but in recent times the number 500 has been used—probably due to a typographical error (for, so far as is known, no new information became available). As to the number of "Rolled (or Rounded) Rim" pieces, Mint Director Leach's figure of 42 is often cited as is the number 50. The *true* figure is anybody's guess, but it must have been small.

Following the coinage of two varieties of "special" pieces, with periods before and after the legends on the reverse, the periods were discontinued. Then followed quantity mintages for circulation of eagles dated 1907 and 1908 without the motto IN GOD WE TRUST.

An article by Edgar H. Adams in the *New York Sun* issue of February 20, 1910, discussed the eagle of 1907:

> There were three varieties of the 1907 $10 piece of the Saint-Gaudens design.
>
> The first was distinguished by a sharp or wire edge and on the reverse shows periods at either side of the motto E PLURIBUS UNUM. It also had a concave field. Altogether about 550 were made, a specimen in Uncirculated condition being worth from $35 upward.
>
> An endeavor was made by the die engravers to make this design suitable for commercial purposes by lowering the relief and giving the coin a narrow border. The design was the same as the first and showed the periods at either end of the motto, but was clearly to be distinguished from the wire edge variety by the border, which was much wider and smooth. So sure were the Mint authorities that a practicable design had been reached that 20,000 of these coins were minted, but the design was not approved, and only about 50 specimens are now in existence, the remainder having been consigned to the melting pot. This coin is now held in high esteem by collectors and is quoted at a high price, although it has never yet been offered at public sale.
>
> The third variety, of course, is the common 1907 issue without periods.

Roosevelt and the New Coins

The genesis and preservation of the Wire Rim varieties commanded the attention of President Theodore Roosevelt, who on July 29, 1907, wrote to Secretary of the Treasury George B. Cortelyou:

> My dear Mr. Secretary:
>
> I return the two coins herewith and also the correspondence you enclosed. How would it do to have a few thousand coins struck with the smooth finish, and then the rest struck with the sharply cut details of the old design? Of course if the eagle stands too high as compared to the rim, the proportion between the two must be made all right by either raising the rim or reducing the eagle, whichever you think necessary.
>
> As for the high relief coins, have several hundred struck and allow the collectors of the country to obtain specimens as you suggested, none to be issued until the new issue is out. They should be preserved as the work of a great American artist.[11]

Related is this letter from Secretary Cortelyou to Mint Director George Roberts on July 23, 1907 (excerpted):

> In connection with the new coinage I intend to also refer to the President's wish to have a number of coins struck from the high relief experimental dies. I find that there is no law against our doing this under your authority, but the Mint officials should be authorized in writing and the number of pieces specified.
>
> In considering the number to be authorized I would suggest that to strike only a few will be to give them a very high money value and very likely occasion criticism.

Illustrate, an 1804 silver dollar piece, of which there are said to be only four in existence, sold in Philadelphia last week for about $3,500.

It would be better, in my opinion, to strike several hundred and to at least allow the public collections of the country to obtain copies. The Superintendent of the Mint will want to be relieved of all responsibility in this distribution.

I suggest moreover, that there should be no distribution of them until after the regular new issue is out. That will relieve interest to a great extent and lessen the pressure for the experimental pieces.[12]

The 1804 dollar referred to was the Matthew A. Stickney specimen cataloged by Henry Chapman and sold in Philadelphia from June 25 to 27, 1907. The buyer for $3,600 was Colonel James W. Ellsworth, a prominent numismatist who from 1892 to 1893 had served on the board of the World's Columbian Exposition in Chicago. Years later on April 6, 1997, the coin was sold at auction as part of the Louis E Eliasberg Collection by Bowers and Merena Galleries. It crossed the block for $1,815,000, a world's record price for any coin ever sold in public competition up to that point in time. There are eight (not four) known examples of the 1804 Class I silver dollar.

Collecting Commentary

The With Periods varieties of 1907 are nearly always encountered in Mint State. The Wire Rim pieces exist to the extent of 400 or more—in other words, the majority of those originally minted and subsequently sold to collectors. The Rolled (or Rounded) Rim coins are rarities and appear infrequently due to the smaller production number.

If you are seeking an example of the types from 1907 to 1908 and from 1908 to 1933 you will have no difficulty locating one of the more plentiful dates in Extremely Fine to AU grade. The time was when Mint State coins MS-63 and higher ranged from scarce to rare for many issues. If you read David W. Akers's 1980 study of more than 369 mostly modern auction catalogs he provides many details. Later, extensive importations took place from overseas hoards. Today, many issues that were rare decades ago are easily obtainable in MS-64 and MS-65 grades, and some higher. As of press time for this book such imports continue. For updated information see the population reports on the PCGS and SBG Web sites. These include only a tiny fraction of the coins in existence, but changes give an indication of current rarity.

The 1907 Indian Head eagles with Wire Rim and Rolled Rim were released in small quantities and are rarities today. When found they are nearly always in high grades. Their market history is very interesting and is delineated under their respective listings.

For eagles of the With Motto type minted from the summer of 1908 onward, grades can vary widely. Although facts are scarce, it seems that San Francisco Mint eagles, particularly of the 1908 to 1915 years, exist today in smaller surviving quantities than do others with comparable mintages. Mint State coins are generally scarce to rare from MS-65 onward. In contrast, most Philadelphia coins and most Denver issues, except 1911-D, are very common in high Mint State levels. On a comparative basis, eagles are *much rarer* in Mint State than are double eagles, only a handful of varieties excepted.

The center details can vary. This is an artifact of the die-making process, not of striking.

Prior to the 1960s most numismatists seeking Indian Head eagles by date and mint were satisfied with a "nice" example, EF or AU, punctuated with the occasional Mint State. Old auction listings emphasize this. Today, with condition rarity leading the market, emphasis is on high-grade coins.

If you are contemplating collecting Indian Head eagles and have comfortable means, the MS-63 level may be the Optimum Collection Grade (OCG)—a meeting point between high quality and reasonable price. Often, MS-63 coins are small fractions of MS-65 prices. After 1907 the keys to the series are 1920-S, 1930-S, and 1933, and relatively few buyers can afford these.

For details and a full appreciation of the Saint-Gaudens coinage buy or borrow a copy of the masterwork by Roger W. Burdette, *Renaissance of American Coinage, 1905–1908*.

Grading Standards

MS-60 to 70 (Mint State). *Obverse:* At MS-60, some abrasion and contact marks are evident, most noticeably on the hair to the left of Miss Liberty's forehead and in the left field. Luster is present, but may be dull or lifeless, and interrupted in patches. At MS-63, contact marks are few, and abrasion is very light.

1907. Graded MS-62.

An MS-65 coin has hardly any abrasion, and contact marks are minute. Luster should be full and rich. Grades above MS-65 are defined by having fewer marks as perfection is approached. *Reverse:* Comments apply as for the obverse, except that abrasion and contact marks are most noticeable on the front of the left wing and in the left field.

AU-50, 53, 55, 58 (About Uncirculated). *Obverse:* Light wear is seen on the cheek, the hair to the right of the face, and the head-dress, more so at AU-50 coin than at AU-53 or 55. An AU-58 coin has minimal traces of wear. An AU-50 coin has luster in protected areas among the stars and in the small field

1908-D. Graded AU-58.

area to the right. At AU-58, most luster is present in the fields but is worn away on the highest parts of the Indian. *Reverse:* Comments as preceding, except that the eagle's left wing, left leg, neck, and leg show light wear. Luster ranges from perhaps 40% (at AU-50) to nearly full mint bloom (at AU-58).

EF-40, 45 (Extremely Fine). *Obverse:* More wear is evident on the hair to the right of the face, and the feather vanes lack some details, although most are present. Luster, if present at all, is minimal. *Reverse:* Wear is greater than on the preceding. The front edge of the left wing is worn and blends into the

1907. Graded EF-40.

top of the left wing. Some traces of luster may be seen, more so at EF-45 than at EF-40.

VF-20, 30 (Very Fine). *Obverse:* The Indian's forehead blends into the hair to the right. Feather-vane detail is gone except in the lower areas. *Reverse:* Wear is greater on the eagle, with only a few details remaining on the back of the left wing and the tail.

1908-S. Graded VF-25.

The Indian Head eagle is seldom collected in grades lower than VF-20.

PF-60 to 70 (Proof). *Obverse and Reverse:* At PF–60 to 63, there is light abrasion and some contact marks (the lower the grade, the higher the quantity). On Sandblast Proofs these show up as visually unappealing bright spots. At PF-64 and higher levels, marks are fewer, with magnification needed to see any

1915. Sandblast Finish. Graded PF-65.

at PF-65. At PF-66, there should be none at all.

1907, Wire Rim, Periods

Circulation-Strike Mintage: 500

Notes regarding mintages: Roger W. Burdette has found that 500 were minted at first, plus 42 later, for a total of 542, less 70 melted, giving a net figure of 472.[13]

Estimated population (Mint State): *325–375.* Most are semi-lustrous, a hybrid between matte and mint frost. This constitutes the majority of the stated original mintage. A numismatic delicacy that met with a fine reception in the beginning, after which the supply exceeded the demand and prices fell, to recover and rise sharply in the late 1900s. See the selected auction listings in the market commentary section to view this pattern. Today these are in unprecedented demand as one of the finest representations of the beautiful Saint-Gaudens design.

In his *Encyclopedia,* Walter Breen offered this tribute: "The very first of these [the wire rim issues] are the only available gold $10s showing the Saint-Gaudens conceptions in anywhere near their pristine splendor."[14]

Estimated population (circulated grades): *15–20.* As these never circulated, such coins simply represent numismatic pieces that were mishandled or spent by someone who did not realized what he or she had.

Submissions certified at highest grades (as of March 2017): *PCGS:* MS-60 (1), MS-61 (10), MS-62 (23), MS-63 (58), MS-64 (110), MS-65 (68), MS-66 (17), MS-67 (1). *NGC:* MS- MS-61 (7), MS-62 (13), MS-63 (25), MS-64 (54), MS-65 (33), MS-66 (21), MS-67 (6), MS-68 (2), MS-69 (1).

Die data: All are from the same pair of dies, which under examination exhibit a multitude of tiny swirls or die-finishing lines. The motif differs from the circulation issue in that there are raised periods before and after the reverse inscriptions, the "With Periods" variety. On this issue the rim of the coin is raised, thus "Wire Rim," earlier generally called "Wire Edge."

Characteristics of striking and die notes: All are of pleasing appearance, but from dies that are not extremely detailed on the higher areas. Some pieces show weakness in areas, but this is not obvious. *All have the same finish,* which is now generally called "Mint State," but in the past has been sometimes designated as Proof. Over the years descriptions have varied. Take your pick. There seems to be no right or wrong. However, the finish of all pieces was *in the dies;* the coins received no "sandblast" or other later treatment.

Key to collecting: Easy enough to find, but only at a strong price. Most are of excellent quality and eye appeal.

MARKET NEWS AND COMMENTARY

A *book* could be filled with citations. Those given here reflect the earlier distribution of the variety, an interesting launch with information not widely known today. It took time until this variety gained market traction. Modern listings, not given here, usually emphasize PCGS and NGC grades. The popularity of this variety started briskly, then faded for a long time, to finally gain traction in the late 1900s.

In March 1910 Henry Chapman offered the Blair, Heaton, and Develin Collections with lot 720: "1907 1st issue. Wire edge, no border or rim. With periods in motto. Uncirculated. Extremely rare. Only 500 were issued." It sold for $43.

In March 1911, in his sale of the William H. Woodin Collection, Thomas L. Elder offered lot 1259: "1907. With sharp 'wire edge'. Only 550 struck. Rare. Uncirculated." This brought $29. In May 1913 the United States Coin Co. sale of the Malcolm N. Jackson Collection included lot 18: "1907 Periods before and after words. Wire edge. Uncirculated, very rare." It sold for $15.50. The market seems to have become suffused with these coins, and the price is quite low. Elder, in his June 1914 Public sale, offered lot 402: "1907. $10. Saint-Gaudens Rare Wire Edge, With periods. Uncirculated. Very rare. These coins have been bringing in my sales, $20 to $25, and bids of $12.50, $13, $14 and even $15 on such a piece are ridiculous in view of the facts of records up to $41 at auction sale in the past."

Many auction offerings took place during this era, and prices were indeed low, Elder's comments notwithstanding. There were far more coins available than there were collectors willing to pay a significant premium for them.

In his 1918 Choice U.S. Gold, Silver and Copper Coins fixed price list, Elmer S. Sears offered this: "1907 Saint-Gaudens design. First issue with wire edge and periods after legend. Uncirculated. $18." In May 1921 B. Max Mehl's sale of the Honorable James H. Manning Collection included lot 898: "1907 Saint-Gaudens type, the rare variety with wire edge and periods. Bright Uncirculated. Very rare. Only 500 coined. And when first issued sold up to over $50 each." It sold for $17.75. In December 1921 Henry Chapman, in his week-long sale of the John Story Jenks Collection, included lot 5739: "1907. Saint-Gaudens design. Border flat with slight wire edge. Uncirculated. Only 500 coined." It sold for $17. By 1921 the variety was 14 years old and still had not gained much interest. The market value was lower than when the first pieces were marketed.

In December 1923 B. Max Mehl's sale of the Charles Wellinger Collection included lot 244: "1907 New type, Indian Head. Reverse, standing eagle. Variety with wire edge and periods after each word. Only 500 coined and sold up to $50 each when first issued. Uncirculated, as perfect as the day it was minted. Rare." It sold for $15.00. Also lot 245: "1907 Another just as last and just as perfect." It sold for $13.50. By this time there were far more specimens on the market than there were serious buyers needing them.

In April 1931, in his sale of the Morris Collection, B. Max Mehl included lot 731: "1907 The new Saint-Gaudens type. Rare variety with wire edge and periods after each word. Only 500 specimens struck. Perfect Uncirculated specimen. This variety sold up to $50 when first issued. It now retails at about $25." It sold for $20. Also lot 732: "1907 Another just as last and just as perfect." It sold for $20. Also lot 1289: "1907. The rare variety with periods after each word and wire edge. Uncirculated. Only 500 coined, and when first issued sold up to $50 each." It sold for $24.

In his November 1932 sale of the R. Taylor Collection, this being in the depth of the Depression, Mehl included lot 971: "1907 The rare variety with wire edge and periods. Only 500 coined, and at one time this particular coin sold up to $50. A specimen at the Columbus Convention sale, which was incorrectly catalogued as the variety of which but fifty specimens were struck, brought $40. This specimen is perfect Uncirculated; just as bright as the day it was minted." It sold for $25. It was quite unusual for Mehl to comment on mistakes made in another dealer's catalog. The reference seems to have been to a regular gathering of Ohio numismatists at the Neil House, Columbus, a venue where ANA Conventions were held in 1907 and, later, 1938. J.M. Henderson, usual auctioneer at such events, seems to have been confused in his descriptions—then and later—calling the "wire edge" a "milled edge" and stating that the mintage was but 50.

In July 1937, sale 379, the Walter P. Innes Jr. Collection, held by J.C. Morgenthau & Co., included lot 77: "Saint-Gaudens type with periods before and after legends. Slight wire edge. Uncirculated. Rare." It sold for $29.

In March 1938, in his sale of the Samuel H. McVitty Collection, B. Max Mehl offered lot 407: "1907 The new Saint-Gaudens type. The rare variety with wire edge and periods. Beautiful Uncirculated specimen; as perfect as the day it was minted. Only 500 coined, and at one time sold up to $100 each." It sold for $30.

In May 1939, sale 399, Rare U.S. Gold Coins by J.C. Morgenthau & Co. included a hoard of these coins, lot 418: "1907 Saint-Gaudens. Wire edge with periods. Uncirculated. Rare." It sold for $35. Also lot 419: "1907 Saint-Gaudens. Wire edge with periods. Uncirculated. Rare." It sold for $30. Also lot 420: "1907 Saint-Gaudens. Wire edge with periods. Uncirculated. Rare." It sold for $27.50. Also lot 421: "1907 Saint-Gaudens. Wire edge with periods. Uncirculated. Rare." It sold for $28.50. Also lot 422: "1907 Saint-Gaudens. Wire edge with periods. Uncirculated. Rare." It sold for $28. Also lot 423: "1907 Saint-Gaudens. Wire edge with periods. Uncirculated. Rare." It sold for $29. A remarkable hoard! Shades of Thomas L. Elder, who had these in quantity 30 years earlier. Perhaps these were consigned by Elder, who by this time was in the sunset era of his business. In October 1939 J.C. Morgenthau & Co. offered this in sale 405, lot 707: "1907 Saint-Gaudens type. Wire edge and periods. Uncirculated. Rare." It sold for $28. By 1929 the variety was 22 years old and still had not caught on widely.

In November 1939 the William B. Hale Collection, sold by B. Max Mehl, included lot 1692: "1907 The rare variety with wire edge and periods after each word. Only about 500 coined. Uncirculated. Rare. When first issued, this coin sold up to $75. It is now listed at $50." It sold for $41. Mehl's first-issued comment, usually $50, was revised to $75. The June 1941 sale of the William Forrester Dunham Collection by B. Max Mehl included lot 2279: "The new type with Indian Head. Reverse, standing eagle. The rare variety with wire edge and periods after each word. Only 500 coined. Perfect Uncirculated specimen with frosty mint luster. Rare. At one time sold up to $75." It sold for $39.50.

In New York City in June 1941, in his auction sale no. 8, Abe Kosoff offered lot 553: "1907. Saint-Gaudens. With Periods. Wire Edge Variety. Rare. Uncirculated." It sold for $27.50. In the same month Wayte Raymond's mail bid sale included lot 665: "1907 Wire edge. Periods. Mint state." It sold for $28.50. Buyer interest remained insipid.

That changed, finally, as the general coin market surged. It was wartime and consumer goods such as automobiles, appliances, and new homes were unavailable. There was a lot of cash, and much went into buying coins. Prices rose across the board.

In February 1944, in the Belden E. Roach Collection, B. Max Mehl offered lot 381: "1907 New type, Saint-Gaudens design, Indian Head. Reverse standing eagle. The rare variety with wire edge and period after each word. Uncirculated; perfect. Rare and in demand. There were more than ten bidders for a similar coin in my last sale. ($50.00)." It sold for $41.25. Now begins the market ascent, never to turn back. This was an era in which the beauty of gold coins was being discovered by many buyers.

In the December 1944 sale of the J.F. Bell Collection Stack's included lot 672: "1907 Indian Head. Saint-Gaudens, with periods. High wire edge. Matte Proof. Rare." It sold for $125. B. Max Mehl's sale of the Will W. Neil Collection, June 1947, included lot 2679: "1907 The new Saint-Gaudens type. Rare variety with wire edge and period after each word. Strictly Uncirculated with full mint luster. From my sale of the Burton Collection in 1923. Catalogs $100." It sold for $105.

In May 1950 the Golden Jubilee sale / Jerome Kern Collection sale by B. Max Mehl included lot 540: "1907 The rare variety with periods before and after each word. Wire edge. Beautiful perfect Uncirculated specimen. Just as perfect as the moment it dropped from the die. Only 500 minted. A specimen in my last sale brought $125. This specimen is certainly worthy of its highest record." It sold for $105. From this point sale records ranged from the low to the high hundreds of dollars. The market slack was taken up, and the demand was strong.

In February 1957 Stack's offered the J.W. Schmandt Collection with lot 490: "1907 Wire Edge with periods. Uncirculated. Choice rare." It sold for $135. In May 1959 Stack's Robert H. Pelletreau Collection sale included lot 412: "1907 Wire edge with Periods. Brilliant Uncirculated. Choice. Usually brings in excess of $200. Rare." It sold for $220. I remember this era well, and hardly any clients ever asked for a 1907, Wire Rim, eagle.

In January 1984 Stack's sale of the Amon G. Carter Jr. Family Collection included lot 802: "1907 Indian Head. The very rare variety with wire edge and periods before and after each word on the reverse. This specimen is brilliant Uncirculated with a surface that closely resembles the 'Roman Finish' Proofs. A choice example with pale toning." It sold for $14,300.

In May 1998 the Dr. Thaine B. Price Collection offered by David W. Akers included lot 40: "1907 Wire Rim. Gem Uncirculated." It sold for $176,000.

In October 1998 in the John J. Pittman Collection sale, Part II, David Akers offered lot 2008: "1907, Indian Head or Saint-Gaudens Type. Wire Edge, Periods. Choice Uncirculated. Typical strike for the issue, i.e. weak at the rims, obverse stars and below the date. JJP purchased this coin from the New Netherlands 26th sale, 11/48, Lot 19, for $82.50." It sold for $40,700.

In July 2004 the American Numismatic Rarities Oliver Jung Collection sale included lot 102: "1907 Indian Head. Wire Rim. MS-66. PCGS." It sold for $120,750. In July 2009 in the "Treasures from the SS *New York*" sale Stack's offered lot 1487: "1907 Indian Head. No Periods. Wire Rim. MS-66 PCGS." It sold for $109,250. In the January 2014 Pre-Long Beach sale Ira and Larry Goldberg offered lot 1845: "1907 Indian Head. With Periods. Wire Rim. MS-65 PCGS." It sold for $99,875. In the August 2016 ANA World's Fair of Money sale Stack's Bowers Galleries offered lot 3478: "1907 Indian Head. With Periods. Wire Rim. MS-65 PCGS." It sold for $82,250.

EF-40	AU-50	AU-55	MS-60	MS-62	MS-63	MS-65
$25,000	$27,500	$29,500	$35,000	$37,500	$45,000	$75,000

1907, Rounded Rim, Periods

Circulation-Strike Mintage: 50

Notes regarding mintages: Roger W. Burdette has found that 32,500 were minted at first, less 32,450 melted, giving a net figure of only 50 available for distribution. Of the 50 saved from melting by Frank Leach, Congressman William Ashbrook acquired 12 specimens during the 1908 Assay Commission meeting. According to Ashbrook's diary, Leach offered one of the rare pieces to each of the members, but only Ashbrook wanted them, so he bought them all at face value from the other commissioners.[15]

The first specimen seems to have been struck on September 13, 1907, or one month and 10 days after Saint-Gaudens died, meaning that the artist never saw a coined specimen of his design.

No logical reason has ever been given why *any* of the 32,500 were melted. Specimens in existence today exhibit no problems that would have prevented their effective circulation.

Estimated population (Mint State): *35–40.* Nearly all are of choice or gem quality.

Estimated population (circulated grades): *1–2.* These were carelessly handled examples. See 1950 Menjou Collection citation for more information.

Submissions certified at highest grades (as of March 2017): *PCGS:* MS-62 (2), this is the lowest Mint State certified by PCGS, MS-63 (2), MS-64 (10), MS-65 (17), MS-66 (15), MS-67 (3). *NGC:* MS-61 (1), MS-62 (1), MS-63 (1), MS-64 (4), MS-65 (11), MS-66 (4), MS-67 (3).

Die data: Rim with "rolled" or rounded aspect, in contrast with the "wire" rim of the earlier issues.

Characteristics of striking and die notes: All are from the same dies, which show prominent swirl or die-finishing lines. The surfaces are lustrous and slightly matte, a very pleasing effect. All coins were intended for general circulation.

The rim has been called *round, rounded, rolled, flat,* and other designations over the years—to distinguish it from the Wire Rim variety.

Key to collecting: A classic rarity, but one that appears on the market with regularity. Nearly all have excellent eye appeal.

MARKET NEWS AND COMMENTARY

From the outset auction listing of this variety have emphasized its rarity. Cited are some early offerings. Similar to the situation for its Wire Rim sister, prices for the Rolled or Rounded Rim lagged for many years.

In his March 1910 sale of the Harmer, Blair, Heaton, and Develin Collections Henry Chapman included lot 721: "1907 2nd issue. High broad edge on border. With periods in motto. Uncirculated. Of excessive rarity. I have heard it stated that about twelve were known. These are regular issues, not patterns, and as such should greatly advance in price in the future." It sold for $140.

Then the price sagged. In March 1911, in his sale of the William H. Woodin Collection, Thomas L. Elder offered lot 1258: "1907 Saint-Gaudens design with periods before and after 'E. Pluribus Unum' and 'Ten Dollars.' Extremely rare. Only 50 struck! Uncirculated." It sold for $80. In May 1915, in his sale of the B.W. Smith Collection, B. Max Mehl offered lot 65: "1907 The new Saint-Gaudens type with Indian Head L.; standing eagle on reverse. The excessively rare variety with rolled edge and periods after each word. Only 50 specimens struck. This variety sold at $150. The specimen in my sale of the Conover Collection brought $96. Very Fine. Excessively rare." It sold for $40.

In January 1918, in his sale of the Robert Hewitt and B.C. Bartlett Collections, Thomas L. Elder included lot 1424: "1907. Beautiful Indian Head to left. Stars, date. Rev. date. Rev. Eagle strutting to left. Periods before and after inscriptions. The very rare variety with raised border. It is stated only 50 were struck. Uncirculated. Gem. Piece, with a record close to $150. The finest I have offered. Resold by owner from a former sale of mine." It sold for $22.50. In June 1921 Thomas L. Elder ,in his sale of the Lynch, Walker, and Tilden Collections, included lot 1553: "1907. Indian maiden to left, stars date. Rx. Roosevelt eagle to left. Period before and after each. Raised borders. Said only around 50 struck. Mint State. Cost $75. First record at auction I think around $150." It sold for $66.

In March 1938, in his sale of the Samuel H. McVitty Collection, B. Max Mehl offered lot 408: "1907 The rarest variety of this date; beveled edge and periods. Only 50 specimens said to have been struck, and when first issued sold up to $150, and I know of one specimen which sold for $300. It is still very rare and in point of rarity, should bring into the three-figure mark." It sold for $50. May 1939, sale 399, Rare U.S. Gold Coins by J.C. Morgenthau & Co. included lot 416: "1907 Saint-Gaudens. High rolled edge with periods. Very Fine. Extremely rare as only 42 were struck." It sold for $56. Also lot 417: "1907 Saint-Gaudens. A duplicate of preceding lot in same condition. Extremely rare." It sold for $60. In June 1941, in auction sale no. 8, Abe Kosoff offered lot 552: "1907. Saint-Gaudens. Rolled edge with Periods. A Rare Coin. Uncirculated." It sold for $60.

Similar to the Wire Rim 1907 eagle, the Rolled Rim, while rare, was available in sufficient numbers to supply the demand. That changed with the across-the-board rise of coin prices during World War II. In February 1944, in the Belden E. Roach Collection, B. Max Mehl offered lot 382: "1907 The very variety with periods and with broad or beveled edge, of which only fifty specimens are said to have been struck. Brilliant Uncirculated. Very rare and valuable. Listed at $125 and certainly worth it." It sold for $92.50. In the December 1944 sale of the J.F. Bell Collection Stack's included lot 673: "1907 Saint-Gaudens, with Periods. The rolled edge variety. Matte Proof. Very rare." It sold for $235. The Rolled Rim eagle was solidly worth in the hundreds of dollars.

In January 1946 the Numismatic Gallery sale of "The World's Greatest Collection" (F.C.C. Boyd) included lot 714: "1907 With Periods and Rolled Edge. Much more rare than generally supposed. Uncirculated." It sold for $375.

In June 1946, in the William Cutler Atwater Collection, B. Max Mehl offered lot 1487:

1907. The extremely rare variety with rolled or wider edges. With periods. Only fifty specimens said to have been struck. Beautiful perfect Uncirculated specimen with full mint luster. Although this coin has a recent record of $375.00, I believe that this record is in its "infancy." I am informed by a prominent New York collector that he has a copy of an original letter of the Director of the U.S. Mint, at that date, 1907, which tells how President Theodore Roosevelt gave a "few" of these coins to friends and that the Director of the Mint gave a few more to his friends, all totaling 42 pieces and then, as Director, ordered the remainder to be re-melted. [Sold for $445, a strong price for the time]

In April 1949 B. Max Mehl's sale of the Dr. Charles W. Green Collection included lot 582: "1907 The extremely rare variety with periods and with rolled or wide edges. Just as perfect as the moment it dropped from the dies." It sold for $525. In May 1950 the Golden Jubilee sale / Jerome Kern Collection sale by B. Max Mehl included lot 541: "1907 Variety with rolled or beveled edge and periods after each word. A beautiful perfect Uncirculated specimen." It sold for $525.

The June 1950 Numismatic Gallery sale of the Adolphe Menjou Collection included lot 1651: "1907 The rare variety with periods and rolled edge. Only 42 of these were minted and the original letter from which this information was taken is in the hands of a prominent Beverly Hills collector [R.E. Naftzger Jr.]. This coin has not been well-handled and is not quite Extremely Fine." It sold for $26. A very rare instance of a worn coin being offered, perhaps one kept as a pocket piece?

In August 1954, in the ANA Convention sale, Federal Coin Exchange offered lot 4051: "1907 Indian Head. With rolled edge and periods before and after legend. Br. Uncirculated. Gem. Much rare than catalogue indicates." It sold for $520. Similar to the market situation for the Wire Rim, the far rarer Rounded Rim did not gain much attention.

In January 1984 Stack's sale of the Amon G. Carter Jr. Family Collection included lot 801: "1907 Indian Head. The extremely rare variety with rolled edge and periods before and after each word on the reverse. This specimen is brilliant Uncirculated with a surface that closely resembles the 'Roman Finish' Proofs. Of the 42 coined we doubt if more than 15 specimens are extant." It sold for $44,000.

In May 1998 the Dr. Thaine B. Price Collection offered by David W. Akers included lot 41: "1907 Rolled Rim. Gem Uncirculated." It sold for $121,000 (which was less than the Wire Rim coin in the same grade that brought $176,000). In July 2004 the American Numismatic Rarities Oliver Jung Collection sale included lot 103: "1907 Indian Head. Rolled Rim. MS-66. (PCGS)." It sold for $299,000. In the FUN sale in January 2011 Heritage sold a coin described as Satin Proof-67 (NGC) for $2,185,000— the highest price ever recorded for an Indian Head eagle and the second highest for any eagle (exceeded only by the Pogue Collection 1795 sold in September 2015 for $2,585,000). Stack's Bowers Galleries, in the August 2013 Chicago ANA World's Fair of Money sale, included lot 4524: "1907 Indian, Rolled Edge, Periods, MS-67, PCGS." It sold for $470,000.

EF-40	AU-50	AU-55	MS-60	MS-62	MS-63	MS-65
$60,000	$65,000	$75,000	$85,000	$100,000	$165,000	$300,000

1907, No Periods

Circulation-Strike Mintage: 239,406
Proof Mintage: Unknown

Notes regarding mintages: This Proof is listed as the "1907, Sandblast Finish Proof," in the *Guide Book*.

Estimated population (Mint State): *10,000+*. Very plentiful in Mint State, sufficiently so that no serious collector will have difficulty obtaining one. Most pieces are in lower ranges from MS-60 to MS-63, but with the combination of repatriated coins and gradeflation, coins on the long side of MS-65 are readily available—in contrast to the situation of several decades ago. Over the years most important collections have included Mint State examples. While enough pieces were saved as souvenirs of the new design in 1907, most Mint State coins known today were repatriated from foreign banks in the last several decades of the 20th century.

Estimated population (circulated grades): *25,000+*. Mostly EF and AU. As Mint State coins are so readily available, most specialists have included them in their cabinets. However, on an absolute basis, far more circulated pieces exist. In his day, Virgil M. Brand must have taken a fancy to 1907 eagles, for his estate included multiple pieces in the AU category (as well as Mint State pieces).

Estimated population (Proofs): *2–3*.

Submissions certified at highest grades (as of March 2017): *PCGS:* MS-63 (1,478), MS-64 (772), MS-65 (249), MS-66 (143), MS-67 (11), MS-68 (1). *NGC:* MS-63 (1,317), MS-64 (827), MS-65 (327), MS-66 (171), MS-67 (30), MS-68 (3).

Die data: The periods after the reverse legends were discontinued, and on the present variety, the first made in very large quantities and circulated, there are no periods.

Characteristics of striking and die notes: Usually very lustrous, with surfaces often described in the literature as "satiny" or "silky," altogether a very appealing appearance.

Key to collecting: Extremely common, but always in demand. The 1907 is popular as an addition to type sets.

MARKET NEWS AND COMMENTARY

These had little premium value until the late 1900s. Modern listings mainly emphasize populations of PCGS and NGC coins.

In March 1911, in his sale of the William H. Woodin Collection, Thomas L. Elder offered lot 1257: "1907. New Saint-Gaudens type with Indian Head to left, stars overhead, date beneath. Rev. An eagle walking, 'United States of America,' 'Ten Dollars', beneath, 'E. Pluribus Unum' in right field. Type with border, without periods before and after Ten Dollars. As new." It sold for $10.50. In his April 1931 sale of the Morris Collection B. Max Mehl included lot 734: "1907 Saint-Gaudens type. The common variety with beveled edge and without periods. But a most beautiful perfectly Uncirculated specimen. As perfect as the day it was minted." It sold for $11.

In June 1936, sale 366, U.S. and Foreign Gold Coins, held by J.C. Morgenthau & Co., included lot 45: "1907 Saint-Gaudens. Uncirculated." It sold for $18.50. In March 1938, in his sale of the Samuel H. McVitty Collection, B. Max Mehl offered lot 409: "1907 Saint-Gaudens type, Indian Head. Variety with beveled edge, but no periods. Uncirculated." It sold for $17.25. By this time the price of gold was $35 per ounce. This was not much above the melt value $16.997.

In the December 1944 sale of the J.F. Bell Collection Stack's included lot 674: "1907 Saint-Gaudens regular issue. Uncirculated gem." It sold for $32.50. In November 1945 B. Max Mehl's sale of the W.A. Philpott and Henry L. Zander Collections included lot 1673: "1907 Indian Head type. Beveled edge, no periods. Brilliant Uncirculated. The least rare variety of this new type, but scarce so choice." It sold for $25.50. New Netherlands Coin Co.'s 46th sale, the Dr. Clarence W. Peake Collection, June 1955, included lot 221: "1907. The new Saint-Gaudens design with Indian Head. Regular issue; without periods. Choice Uncirculated, having full mint bloom." It sold for $27.

In May 1998 the Dr. Thaine B. Price Collection, offered by David W. Akers, included lot 42: "1907 No Motto. Gem Uncirculated." It sold for $35,750. This was an incredible price.

In September 2005 the American Numismatic Rarities sale of the C.L. Lee Collection included lot 1331: "1907 Indian Head. MS-65 NGC. From our sale of the Allison Park Collection." It sold for $6,095. In July 2004 the American Numismatic Rarities Oliver Jung Collection sale included lot 104: "1907 Indian Head. MS-66. PCGS." It sold for $12,600.

In August 2006 the American Numismatic Rarities sale of the Old West and Franklinton Collections included lot 1570: "1907 Indian Head. No periods. MS-67 NGC." It sold for $32,200, a coin that probably sold to a buyer who was willing to pay a high figure to have the finest known. Today, as shown above, there are quite a few NGC-certified MS-67 coins. The same sale also included MS-64 (NGC) for $3,680, MS-65 (NGC) $8,825, and another MS-65 by the same service $8,050. Started in 2003 by Christine Karstedt and associates, by 2006 ANR was the world's second largest rare coin auction firm.

In the November 2016 Collectors Choice sale Stack's Bowers Galleries offered lot 90530: "1907 Indian Head. No periods. MS-64 PCGS." It sold for $3,642.50.

Regency Auction XV, December 2015, included lot 439: "1907 Indian Head. No Periods. MS-66 PCGS." It sold for $10,868.75. Regency Auction XVIII, September 2016, included lot 490: "1907 Indian Head. No Periods. MS-65 PCGS." It sold for $9,400.

PROOF MARKET NEWS AND COMMENTARY

Proofs of the regular (without periods at reverse legends) 1907 eagle are not listed in the *Mint Report*, nor has any other official notice been found of them. For what one opinion is worth, these may have been made as a private venture by George T. Morgan, assistant engraver at the Mint, and sold through Philadelphia dealer Henry Chapman, who was the outlet for many if not most of the MCMVII Ultra High Relief patterns of the same year.

In a note in the Thomas G. Melish sale (April 1956) under lot 2601, described as "the regular issue without periods, in Matte Proof condition," Abe Kosoff noted:

"Apparently a few Proofs were made of the [regular design] $10 and $20 Saint-Gaudens pieces of 1907, for I have had two specimens of the $20 piece. One sold in the Menjou sale for $825." Kosoff went on to say concerning the 1907 Matte Proof $10: "An extreme rarity; I can recall but one other." However, in his 1980 work on $10 coins, David W. Akers noted matter-of-factly: "The Melish coin was not really a Proof." As Akers was a teacher in the West at the time of the Melish sale and was not into professional numismatics, he must have been shown the coin at a later time.

The Gaston DiBello Collection sale (Stack's, May 1970) offered two Proofs, one a Satin or Roman Finish piece with especially sharp details, and the other a Matte or Sand Blast Proof with lower relief.[16]

Quite possibly these pieces were made to experiment with different Proof finishes that could be used with the new design. These two Proofs remain the only ones verified today.

VF-20	EF-40	AU-50	AU-55	MS-60	MS-62	MS-63	MS-65
$750	$800	$850	$900	$1,150	$1,850	$3,000	$8,500

1908 , No Motto

Circulation-Strike Mintage: 33,500

Estimated population (Mint State): 1,500+. Most were imported in the late 1900s. Prior to that time, examples were very difficult to find. Most auction citations are for low-level Mint State pieces—punctuated by only a few choice and gem specimens.

Estimated population (circulated grades): 1,000+. Mostly EF and AU. Very scarce.

Submissions certified at highest grades (as of March 2017): *PCGS*: MS-63 (181), MS-64 (70), MS-65 (28), MS-66 (12), MS-67 (5). ***NGC:*** MS-63 (80), MS-64 (56), MS-65 (28), MS-66 (13), MS-67 (4), MS-68 (1).

Key to collecting: Slightly scarce in the context of Indian Head eagles.

MARKET NEWS AND COMMENTARY

In January 1921 Henry Chapman's sale of the John Story Jenks Collection included lot 5741: "1908. Uncirculated. Mint luster." It sold for $10. The coin brought face value. In May 1929 Henry Chapman's sale of the Frederick G. McKean Collection included 367: "1908 Same type as last. Without IN GOD WE TRUST. Uncirculated." It sold for $21. In June 1936, sale 366, U.S. and Foreign Gold Coins, held by J.C. Morgenthau & Co., included lot 46: "1908 Without motto. Uncirculated." It sold for $19.50. In the December 1944 sale of the J.F. Bell Collection Stack's included lot 675: "1908 Without Motto. Brilliant Uncirculated." It sold for $40.

In January 1984 Stack's sale of the Amon G. Carter Jr. Family Collection included lot 805: "1908 No Motto. Brilliant Uncirculated, frosty mint bloom." It sold for $2,970. In May 1998 the Dr. Thaine B. Price Collection offered by David W. Akers included lot 43: "1908 No Motto. Gem Uncirculated." It sold for $28,600.

In June 2000, in the Harry W. Bass Jr. Collection, Part III, Bowers and Merena Galleries included lot 748: "1908 No Motto. MS-64 PCGS. From Stack's sale of the Delp Collection, November 1972, lot 841." It sold for $3,910. In September 2005 the American Numismatic Rarities sale of the C.L. Lee Collection included lot 1334: "1908 No Motto. MS-64 NGC. From our sale of the Allison Park Collection." It sold for $2,760.

In December 2005 the American Numismatic Rarities sale of the Old Colony Collection included lot 1632: "1908 No Motto. MS-65 NGC." It sold for $12,650. In the same sale an MS-64 (NGC) brought $7,188 and an MS-61 (NGC) sold for $1,035. Stack's Bowers Galleries, in the August 2013 ANA World's Fair of Money auction, included lot 4528: "1908 Indian $10, no motto, MS-67, PCGS." It sold for $105,750. The same sale included lot 4529: "1908 Indian $10, no motto, MS-66, NGC." It sold for $19,975. What a difference a single grading number can make!

VF-20	EF-40	AU-50	AU-55	MS-60	MS-62	MS-63	MS-65
$800	$850	$875	$925	$1,500	$2,750	$5,500	$17,500

1908-D, No Motto

Circulation-Strike Mintage: 210,000

Notes regarding mintages: The first day of striking was June 12, 1908.

Estimated population (Mint State): *800+.* Most are MS-60 to MS-63. This issue has always been slightly scarce.

Estimated population (circulated grades): *4,500+.* Mostly EF and AU.

Submissions certified at highest grades (as of March 2017): *PCGS:* MS-63 (119), MS-64 (57), MS-65 (2), MS-66 (5). *NGC:* MS-63 (38), MS-64 (32), MS-65 (10), MS-66 (5), MS-67 (3).

Die data: One could easily call the 1908-D, No Motto, the 'Errant Mintmark' variety, for the D mintmark is way out in left field (literally), beyond the branch—in a location completely different from that used on any other mintmark in the series! This characteristic, which is found on all known specimens of the 1908-D, No Motto (but not on those with motto), is not widely known or appreciated and seems to us to lend quite a bit of interest.

Key to collecting: Common in high-level circulated grades. Slightly scarce in Mint State, a change from years ago when examples were elusive.

MARKET NEWS AND COMMENTARY

In November 1939 the William B. Hale Collection, sold by B. Max Mehl, included lot 1759: "1908-D Variety without motto. Uncirculated. Very scarce." It sold for $18.50. In February 1944, in the Belden E. Roach Collection, B. Max Mehl offered lot 487: "1908-D New type, Saint-Gaudens, Indian Head. Reverse, eagle. First issue, without motto. About Uncirculated." It sold for $26. In the December 1944 sale of the J.F. Bell Collection Stack's included lot 804: "1908-D Without Motto. Uncirculated gem." It sold for $47.50.

Forward to the late 1900s, in May 1998 the Dr. Thaine B. Price Collection offered by David W. Akers included lot 44: "1908-D No Motto. Gem Uncirculated." It sold for $99,000. In August 2006 the American Numismatic Rarities sale of the Old West and Franklinton Collections included lot 1576: "1908-D No Motto. MS-65 NGC." It sold for $29,900. The same sale included an MS-64 (NGC) that sold for $13,800. Regency Auction XIX December 2016 included lot 471: "1908-D No Motto. MS-64 PCGS." It sold for $19,975. Heritage's sale of April 2017 included lot 1253: "1908-D No Motto. MS-64 PCGS." It sold for $11,162.50.

VF-20	EF-40	AU-50	AU-55	MS-60	MS-62	MS-63	MS-65
$750	$825	$850	$875	$1,275	$2,800	$7,500	$35,000

INDIAN HEAD, WITH MOTTO (1908–1933)

Designer: *Augustus Saint-Gaudens.* **Weight:** *16.718 grams.*
Composition: *.900 gold, .100 copper (net weight: .48375 oz. pure gold).*
Diameter: *27 mm.* **Edge:** *1908–1911—46 raised stars; 1912–1933—48 raised stars.*
Mints: *Philadelphia, Denver, and San Francisco.*

Motto Added

In 1908 Saint-Gaudens's Indian Head design was modified on the reverse by the addition of IN GOD WE TRUST in the field at the center right. The motto, restored by a special act of Congress, remained in effect through the end of the series in 1933. Otherwise the Indian Head obverse and perched eagle reverse motif remained unchanged.

The edges of issues from 1908 to 1911 have 46 raised stars, while those minted from 1912 onward have 48 raised stars, reflecting an increased number of states in the Union with the addition of Arizona and New Mexico.

Mintage was intense and continuous from 1908 through 1916, after which no examples were made until 1920-S, followed by a gap until the 1926 Philadelphia issue, with the next following being 1930-S, then 1932 and 1933. The total production for the type was more than 14 million coins, with 1932 establishing the all-time high record for *any* $10 coin, an amazing 4,463,000 pieces.

Grading Standards

Grading standards are the same as for Indian Head, No Motto, coins. See pages 338 and 339 for details.

1908, With Motto

Circulation-Strike Mintage: 341,370
Proof Mintage: 116

Notes regarding mintages: Although it seems likely that most circulated coins were retained in the United States, perhaps as backing for Gold Certificates, quite a few were exported as well.

116 Proof coins were reported to have been minted, and although this is the first year of the With Motto style, it seems that no more than half of the Proof coins found buyers. The standard finish was of the "sand blast" type, but at least one Satin Finish Proof is known (see Stack's August 1976 ANA sale citation). Among the Sand Blast Proofs the color varies from light to dark.

Estimated population (Mint State): 10,000+. While most are MS-60 to MS-63, there are quite a few MS-64 and MS-65 coins in existence. These are especially prized.

Estimated population (circulated grades): 10,000+. Mostly EF and AU.

Estimated population (Proofs): 35–45. The most available Proof of the 1908 to 1915 Indian Head series.

Submissions certified at highest grades (as of March 2017): PCGS: MS-63 (933), MS-64 (278), MS-65 (82), MS-66 (38), MS-67 (6), MS-68 (4). **NGC:** MS-63 (487), MS-64 (196), MS-65 (66), MS-66 (33), MS-67 (3), MS-68 (4).

Key to collecting: Very common.

MARKET NEWS AND COMMENTARY

The Numismatist, August 1908, carried news to the effect that IN GOD WE TRUST would appear on the $10 and $20 coins that would be struck after the resumption of coinage operations at the mints on August 1.

In May 1911 S. Hudson Chapman's sale of the Julius L. Brown Collection included lot 676: "1908 Rev. with IN GOD WE TRUST. Unc." It sold for $10. In June 1934 J.C. Morgenthau & Co.'s sale of coins from the Waldo C. Newcomer Collection included lot 360: "1908 With motto. Mint state." It sold for $20. In November 1939 the William B. Hale Collection, sold by B. Max Mehl, included lot 1693: "1908 With motto. Bright Uncirculated." It sold for $16.50.

In March 1945 the William A. Knapp Collection, sold by B. Max Mehl, had lot 1064: "1908 With motto. Uncirculated, full mint luster; as perfect as the day it was minted. Catalogs $30 and retails for more." It sold for $33. In May 1945 Stack's sale of the George H. Hall Collection included lot 2218: "1908 Brilliant Proof." It sold for $72.50. In November 1945 B. Max Mehl's sale of the W.A. Philpott and Henry L. Zander Collections included lot 1674: "1908 Variety with motto. Uncirculated. Scarce so choice." It sold for $24.

In April 1956 Abe Kosoff's sale of the Thomas G. Melish and Clinton W. Hester Collections included lot 2608: "1908 With motto. Uncirculated." It sold for $24. Years later this and other gold coins gained strong traction in the marketplace. In May 1998 the Dr. Thaine B. Price Collection offered by David W. Akers included lot 45: "1908 With Motto. Very Choice Uncirculated." It sold for $11,000. In January 2006 the American

Numismatic Rarities sale of the Robert Michael Prescott Collection included lot 1085: "1908 With Motto. MS-66 PCGS." It sold for $14,950.

In the August 2016 ANA World's Fair of Money sale Stack's Bowers Galleries offered lot 3480: "1908 With Motto. MS-66 PCGS." It sold for $10,575. In the November 2016 Whitman Expo sale Stack's Bowers Galleries offered lot 2160: "1908 With Motto MS-67 PCGS." It sold for $26,000. Heritage's sale of April 2017 included lot 1253: "1908 Motto. MS-66+ PCGS." It sold for $18,800.

Proof Market News and Commentary

In 1918 the Choice U.S. Gold, Silver and Copper Coins fixed price list issued by Elmer S. Sears included this: "1908 gold Proof set. First year of new design. It is said that but ten sets were made. Sand Blast Proof. Set $75." At this time very little had appeared in numismatic print about Proofs in this format.

In May 1939, sale 399, Rare U.S. Gold Coins by J.C. Morgenthau & Co. included lot 426: "1908 Motto. Sand Blast Proof." It sold for $33. In February 1944, in the Belden E. Roach Collection, B. Max Mehl offered lot 384: "1908 Variety with motto. Perfect sand Blast Proof; wire edge. Rare and in great demand. Cost $35 three years ago." It sold for $42. In the December 1944 sale of the J.F. Bell Collection Stack's included lot 676: "1908 With Motto. Sand Blast Proof." It sold for $50. In January 1946 the Numismatic Gallery sale of "The World's Greatest Collection" (F.C.C. Boyd) included lot 717: "1908 Sand Blast Proof." It sold for $60.

The modern market saw a vast change. In August 1990, in Auction 0, David W. Akers offered lot 1934: "1908 With Motto. Sand Blast Proof-67." It sold for $60,500. The Bowers and Merena Galleries' sale of the Boys Town Collection, March 1998, included lot 2222: "1908 Sand Blast Proof-66 NGC." It sold for $33,000. In August 2006 the American Numismatic Rarities sale of the Old West and Franklinton Collections included lot 1577: "1908 Sand Blast Proof-66 NGC." It sold for $73,250. In the November 2009 74th Anniversary sale Stack's offered lot 1934: "1908 With Motto. Sand Blast Proof-66. PCGS." It sold for $66,125.

In the August 2016 ANA World's Fair of Money sale Stack's Bowers Galleries offered lot 3479: "1908 With Motto. Sand Blast Proof-65 PCGS." It sold for $58,750. In the November 2016 Whitman Expo Sale Stack's Bowers Galleries offered lot 2159: "1908 Sand Blast Proof-66 PCGS." It sold for $79,312.50.

VF-20	EF-40	AU-50	AU-55	MS-60	MS-62	MS-63	MS-65	PF-63	PF-64	PF-65
$700	$725	$750	$775	$1,100	$1,500	$2,000	$9,500	$18,500	$30,000	$55,000

1908-D, With Motto

Circulation-Strike Mintage: 836,500

Notes regarding mintages: The first day of striking took place on August 12, 1908.

Estimated population (Mint State): *1,000+.*

MS-60 to MS-64 is the usual grade range but many higher-grade coins have been certified. A scarce issue considering the demand.

Estimated population (circulated grades): *20,000+.* Mostly EF and AU.

Submissions certified at highest grades (as of March 2017): *PCGS:* MS-63 (129), MS-64 (24), MS-65 (12), MS-66 (7), MS-67 (1), MS-68 (2). *NGC:* MS-63 (28), MS-64 (24), MS-65 (3), MS-66 (5), MS-67 (2), MS-68 (1).

Die data: Mintmark position varieties exist.

Key to collecting: Common in circulated grades, less so if Mint State.

MARKET NEWS AND COMMENTARY

In November 1939 the William B. Hale Collection, sold by B. Max Mehl, included lot 1760: "1908-D Variety with motto. Bright Uncirculated." It sold for $18.50 In May 1941, sale 430, U.S. Coin Collection by J.C. Morgenthau & Co. included lot 239: "1908-D Mint. With Motto. Very scarce." It sold for $18. This is an early commentary on the elusive character of this variety. In June 1946 in the William Cutler Atwater Collection B. Max Mehl offered lot 1604: "1908-D Beautiful Uncirculated specimen. As perfect as the day it was minted. Variety with motto." It sold for $38.50.

The February 1992 Ed Trompeter Collection, Part I, by Superior Galleries included: "1908-D With Motto. MS-64 PCGS." It sold for $18,700. In May 1998 the Dr. Thaine B. Price Collection offered by David W. Akers included lot 46: "1908-D With Motto. MS-67." It sold for $82,500.

In October 1998, in the John J. Pittman Collection sale, Part II, David Akers offered lot 2013:

> 1908-D With Motto. Gem Uncirculated. This issue is one of the many condition rarities in the popular Indian Head eagle series. Although minimal quality Uncirculated examples are not especially difficult to find, at the Choice Uncirculated level the 1908-D With Motto Eagle is very scarce, if not rare, and, in Gem condition, it is one of the rarest and most desirable issues in the entire series. The mintage of the 1908-D With Motto eagle was not particularly low, 836,500 pieces, but most of the issue must have gone directly into circulation with few high quality Mint State examples saved. This specimen is distinctly surpassed only by the Louis Eliasberg specimen and the Dr. Thaine B. Price specimen. [Sold for $24,200]

Since that time there have been many repatriated coins, but the 1908-D, With Motto, remains a very popular key issue in strong demand. Stack's Bowers Galleries, in the August 2013 ANA World's Fair of Money auction, listed lot 4535: "1908-D Indian $10, motto, MS-67, NGC." It sold for $70,500, probably to a registry set competitor. Heritage's sale of April 2017 included lot 1254: "1908-D Motto. MS-66 PCGS." It sold for $39,950.

VF-20	EF-40	AU-50	AU-55	MS-60	MS-62	MS-63	MS-65
$700	$725	$750	$775	$1,150	$2,750	$6,500	$26,000

1908-S, With Motto

Circulation-Strike Mintage: 59,850

Notes regarding mintages: Probably, most of these were kept in the states and circulated in the West, although some were exported.

Estimated population (Mint State): *350+.* Traditionally a scarce and highly prized issue due to the low mintage. While most are in the MS-60 to MS-63 range, there are dozens higher, including a few marvelous specimens on the long side of MS-65. The latter create a sensation when offered—as is evidenced by several of the auction listings quoted here.

Estimated population (circulated grades): *1,500+.* Most are EF or AU.

Submissions certified at highest grades (as of March 2017): *PCGS:* MS-63 (46), MS-64 (39), MS-65 (12), MS-66 (13), MS-67 (8), MS-68 (3). *NGC:* MS-63 (20), MS-64 (18), MS-65 (12), MS-66 (4), MS-67 (2), MS-68 (2), MS-69 (1).

Key to collecting: Scarce in high-level circulated grades and elusive in Mint State. Highly regarded as a key issue and always in demand.

MARKET NEWS AND COMMENTARY

A hoard of "at least 20" is said to have been found in the 1940s and a smaller hoard in the 1970s, the latter from Europe.[17] Since that time even more have been repatriated. Most have had considerable bagmarks.

In February 1944, in the Belden E. Roach Collection, B. Max Mehl offered lot 465: "1908-S New type, Indian Head. Variety with motto, as all are of this Mint. Just a shade from Uncirculated." It sold for $28.50. The December 1944 sale of the J.F. Bell Collection held by Stack's included lot 791: "1908-S With Motto. Uncirculated gem." It sold for $65.

In later years a high-grade 1908-S has always been front row center in an auction sale. The February 1992 Ed Trompeter Collection, Part I, by Superior Galleries included lot 189: "1908-S. MS-65 PCGS." It sold for $22,000. In May 1998 the Dr. Thaine B. Price Collection offered by David W. Akers included lot 47: "1908-S MS-67." It sold for $82,500. The August 2002 ANA Convention sale by Superior Galleries included lot 2105: "1908-S MS-66 PCGS." It sold for $18,400. In November 2004 Numismatic Rarities Frog Run Farm Collection sale included lot 1901: "1908-S MS-65 PCGS." It sold for $17,825.

Stack's January 2004 public auction sale included lot 3008: "1908-S Indian $10, motto, MS-66, PCGS." It sold for $21,850.

VF-20	EF-40	AU-50	AU-55	MS-60	MS-62	MS-63	MS-65
$975	$1,100	$1,200	$1,500	$4,000	$7,500	$13,500	$25,000

1909

Circulation-Strike Mintage: 184,789
Proof Mintage: 74

Notes regarding mintages: It is likely that more than half of the Satin Finish Proof mintage remained unsold.

Estimated population (Mint State): *4,000+.* Most are MS-60 to MS-63, but there are many others than range up to MS-65 or even higher.

Estimated population (circulated grades): *4,000+.* Mostly EF and AU.

Estimated population (Proofs): *20–30.* Proofs of this year have the attractive bright yellow "Roman Finish" or "Satin Finish" surface (used in 1909 and 1910 only).

Submissions certified at highest grades (as of March 2017): *PCGS:* MS-63 (327), MS-64 (94), MS-65 (18), MS-66 (10), MS-67 (2). *NGC:* MS-63 (146), MS-64 (53), MS-65 (24), MS-66 (4), MS-67 (3).

Key to collecting: Common.

Market News and Commentary

J.C. Morgenthau & Co.'s May 1939 sale 399, Rare U.S. Gold Coins, had lot 427: "1909 Uncirculated," sold for $17.50. New Netherlands Coin Co.'s 46th sale, the Dr. Clarence W. Peake Collection, June 1955, had lot 227: "1909. Uncirculated. Full, frosty mint surface. A real beauty, just beginning to acquire iridescent tarnish. Superior to the VF Green example, as well as the Extremely Fine one in the Menjou sale (at $25)." It sold for $45.

By the late 20th century the market had changed dramatically. In May 1998 the Dr. Thaine B. Price Collection offered by David W. Akers included lot 48:

> 1909 Gem Uncirculated. The 1909 Indian Head eagle is moderately scarce in all grades, although if one is willing to settle for a coin in choice Uncirculated or lower condition, the issue is available with considerable regularity. However, this is another issue whose availability drops dramatically as the grade increases and very choice Uncirculated specimens are very scarce, if not rare; gems are very rare and seldom available except when great collections like the Dr. Thaine B. Price Collection are sold. Among all the Philadelphia issues of this series, only the 1907 Rolled Edge and 1933 are more rare, with only the 1933 being more rare in gem condition. [Sold for $12,100]

Heritage's August 2016 ANA World's Fair of Money sale included lot 4340: "1915-S MS-64 PCGS." It sold for $28,200.

Proof Market News and Commentary

For the Satin Finish Proofs, in November 1939 the William B. Hale Collection, sold by B. Max Mehl, included lot 1694: "1909 The new style Proof. Wire edge. Very scarce." It sold for $31. In February 1944, in the Belden E. Roach Collection, the same dealer offered lot 385: "1909 New style Proof, between Sand Blast and brilliant. Wire edge. Rare. Listed at $40 and now retails at that price and more." It sold for $40.

In the December 1944 sale of the J.F. Bell Collection Stack's included lot 677: "1909 Brilliant Proof." It sold for $45. In October 1980, in the Garrett Collection, Part III, sale, Bowers and Ruddy Galleries offered lot 1686: "Roman Finish Proof. Choice. Obtained by Robert Garrett from Henry Chapman on January 23, 1913." This coin sold for $28,000. In October 1982, in the Louis E. Eliasberg Collection of U.S. Gold Coins, Bowers and Ruddy Galleries offered lot 850: "Gem Matte Proof-67." It sold for $19,250. In March 1988 the Norweb Collection, Part II, sale by Bowers and Merena Galleries included lot 2306: "1909 Satin Proof-64 to 65." It sold for $37,400. In the November 2009 74th Anniversary sale Stack's offered lot 1936: "1909 Satin Proof-67 NGC." It sold for $69,000. Heritage's sale of November 2016 included lot 1241: "1909 Proof-66 NGC." It sold for $64,625.

One Sand Blast Proof is known and was offered by Stack's in July 1981 in Auction '81 as lot 1868:

1909 Matte Proof. Well struck, with the Matte Proof finish found on the 1908, and 1911 through 1915 issues. The 1909 and 1910 are known only in the more brilliant Roman finish (actually a hybrid between a matte and brilliant or mirror-like surface.) This is the first example of this date in the dull Matte Proof finish we have encountered or could find record of. Ex DiBello, lot 1004. This coin is unique. [Sold for $17,000]

VF-20	EF-40	AU-50	AU-55	MS-60	MS-62	MS-63	MS-65	PF-63	PF-64	PF-65
$700	$725	$750	$775	$1,100	$1,500	$2,000	$9,500	$18,500	$30,000	$55,000

1909-D

Circulation-Strike Mintage: 121,540

Notes regarding mintages: The first day of striking was January 12, 1909.

Estimated population (Mint State): 2,000+. Mostly MS-60 to MS-63. Available, but quite scarce in higher grades. The supply of Mint State pieces was greatly augmented by imports from the 1970s onward.

Estimated population (circulated grades): *4,000+.* Mostly EF and AU.

Submissions certified at highest grades (as of March 2017): *PCGS:* MS-63 (167), MS-64 (34), MS-65 (4), MS-66 (4), MS-67 (2). *NGC:* MS-63 (51), MS-64 (23), MS-65 (5), MS-66 (3), MS-67 (1).

Die data: Mintmark position varieties exist.

Key to collecting: Common.

MARKET NEWS AND COMMENTARY

In November 1939 the William B. Hale Collection, sold by B. Max Mehl, included lot 1761: "1909-D Uncirculated; full mint luster." It sold for $18. February 1944, in the Belden E. Roach Collection, B. Max Mehl offered lot 489: "1909-D Uncirculated, full mint luster." It sold for $28.50. In the December 1944 sale of the J.F. Bell Collection Stack's included lot 806: "1909-D Uncirculated gem. Scarce." It sold for $52.50. The May 1945 Stack's sale of the George H. Hall Collection included lot 2228: "1909-D Brilliant Uncirculated." It sold for $36.50.

In May 1998 the Dr. Thaine B. Price Collection offered by David W. Akers included lot 49: "1909-D MS-66." It sold for $71,500. Stack's January 2004 sale included lot 3010: "1909-D Indian $10, motto, MS-66, PCGS." It sold for $43,125. In the June 2015 Pre-Long Beach sale Ira and Larry Goldberg offered lot 1977: "1909-D MS-63 PCGS." It sold for $3,760. This was and is a nice "collector grade," but not a registry set winner. Heritage's ANA World's Fair of Money sale, August 2016, included lot 1238: "1909-D MS-65 PCGS." It sold for $25,850. Kagin's March 2017 ANA Auction included lot 1431: "1909-D MS-64 PCGS. PCGS Population: 33; 10 finer (MS-67 finest.)." It sold for $10,868.75. Heritage's sale of April 2017 included lot 1253: "1909-D MS-66 PCGS." It sold for $44,650.

VF-20	EF-40	AU-50	AU-55	MS-60	MS-62	MS-63	MS-65
$800	$850	$925	$975	$1,500	$2,750	$4,500	$32,500

1909-S

Circulation-Strike Mintage: 292,350

Notes regarding mintages: Probably most were retained in the United States and circulated on the West Coast, although many thousands were exported.

Estimated population (Mint State): *900+*. Usually seen MS-60 to MS-65, quite rare higher. The supply of Mint State pieces was augmented by imports from the 1970s onward as true of most Saint-Gaudens eagles of this era. Prior to that time the 1909-S was a *rarity*.

Estimated population (circulated grades): *6,000+*. The 1909-S (as part of all San Francisco Mint $10 1909-S to 1914-S) is very peculiar among Saint-Gaudens eagles of this era in that most circulated pieces in old-time collections average VF in grade, rather than EF or AU. This is probably because most circulated in the West, and many were obtained domestically from that area.

Submissions certified at highest grades (as of March 2017): *PCGS:* MS-63 (70), MS-64 (54), MS-65 (25), MS-66 (5), MS-67 (2). ***NGC:*** MS-63 (40), MS-64 (14), MS-66 (3), MS-67 (1), MS-68 (1).

Die data: Mintmark position varieties exist.

Key to collecting: Common in high-level circulated grades. Slightly scarce in Mint State.

Market News and Commentary

A hoard of "about 70 to 90 in all?" was reportedly found in South America about 1977.[18]

In 1976 about 100 Mint State 1909-S eagles turned up in Europe through Marc Emory. About 25 to 30 were purchased by John Dannreuther.[19] In an interview, Ronald J. Gillio recalled buying a related special group of 1909-S eagles:[20]

> I was doing a lot of business in Switzerland in the 1970s, going there quite often. It was sometime after 1975 that I purchased 49 original 1909-S eagles from a coin dealer in Zurich. At the time he told me he got them out of South America. I asked him if there were any more—found out that there weren't—and inquired about their history. I learned that they came from the owner of a money exchange in Argentina. The group originally included 50 coins, but the Argentinean kept one for himself. The 49 coins were just amazing—each one perfect.
>
> I came back from Switzerland and, as I usually did in the 1970s, I cleared customs at Boston, which I found to be a convenient port of entry. At the time, Jim Halperin ran the New England Rare Coin Galleries, and I would often stop to see him and sell some of my new purchases. On this trip I sold him some of the 1909-S tens. I kept the others until February 1978, when I took them to the ANA Midwinter Convention held in Colorado Springs on the floor of the ice rink at the Broadmoor Hotel. This was the memorable show in which everyone was looking for warm boots to wear, because the floor was simply sheets of wood put over the ice, and if

you had your feet on the floor for any length of time, your toes froze. So, that's the story of my involvement with the 1909-S eagles.

Since the 1970s many more have been repatriated. As is nearly always the case with gold coins returned from abroad, they filtered into the market without publicity.

Stack's Bowers Galleries, in the August 2013 ANA World's Fair of Money auction, listed lot 4541: "1909-S Indian $10, motto, MS-67, PCGS." It sold for $64,625. The same sale included lot 4542: "1909-S Indian $10, motto, MS-66, PCGS." It sold for $55,813.

In February 1944, in the Belden E. Roach Collection, B. Max Mehl offered lot 466: "1909-S Uncirculated; full mint luster." It sold for $27. In the December 1944 sale of the J.F. Bell Collection Stack's included lot 792: "1909-S Uncirculated gem." It sold for $37.50. In October 1947, in the H.R. Lee Collection (Eliasberg duplicates), Stack's offered lot 1680: "1909-S Brilliant Uncirculated." It sold for $29.

In May 1998, in a much more mature market, the Dr. Thaine B. Price Collection offered by David W. Akers listed lot 50: "1909-S Gem Uncirculated." It sold for $82,500.

VF-20	EF-40	AU-50	AU-55	MS-60	MS-62	MS-63	MS-65
$700	$725	$750	$775	$1,250	$3,500	$7,000	$16,500

1910

Circulation-Strike Mintage: 318,500
Proof Mintage: 204

Notes regarding mintages: The Proof mintage figures for all four gold denominations ($2.50, $5, $10, and $20) seem far out of line with reality in regard to actual Proof sales or distribution.

Estimated population (Mint State): *10,000+*. Very common, but mostly in grades from MS-60 through MS-63. Scarce higher, and rare at the MS-65 or finer level. The supply was greatly augmented by imports from foreign banks from the 1970s onward, this being an especially popular date.

Estimated population (circulated grades): *10,000+*. Mostly EF and AU.

Estimated population (Proofs): *15–20*. The 1910 Proof is remarkable for its rarity, especially in relation to its generous mintage, which was nearly twice that of the next-highest production (1908 With Motto, 116 coins). Proofs of this year have the attractive bright yellow "Roman Finish" or "Satin Finish" surface (used in 1909 and 1910 only).

Submissions certified at highest grades (as of March 2017): *PCGS:* MS-63 (1,284), MS-64 (340), MS-65 (70), MS-66 (26), MS-67 (3). *NGC:* MS-63 (1,216), MS-64 (363), MS-65 (103), MS-66 (20), MS-67 (13), MS-68 (1).

Key to collecting: Common.

Market News and Commentary

In December 1923 B. Max Mehl's sale of the Charles Wellinger Collection included lot 247: "1910 Type as last but without periods. New style Proof, not brilliant. Scarce." It sold for $11.50.

In June 1936, sale 366, U.S. and Foreign Gold Coins, held by J.C. Morgenthau & Co., included lot 47: "1910 Uncirculated." It sold for $18.50. The May 1945 Stack's sale of the George H. Hall Collection included lot 2229: "1910 Brilliant Uncirculated." It sold for $27.

New Netherlands Coin Co.'s 46th sale, the Dr. Clarence W. Peake Collection, June 1955, included lot 230: "1910. Uncirculated. With a dull, frosty mint surface, although not particularly bold. Valued at $35 in the *Guide Book*." It sold for $20. In May 1998 the Dr. Thaine B. Price Collection offered by David W. Akers included lot 51: "1910 MS-66." It sold for $46,750. In July 2004 the American Numismatic Rarities sale of the Oliver Jung Collection included lot 103: "1907 1910. MS-66 PCGS." It sold for $13,800.

In July 2005 the American Numismatic Rarities sale of the William H. LaBelle Sr. Collection included lot 335: "1910 MS-68 NGC." It sold for $34,500. In the same sale another 1910, MS-65 (PCGS), lot 336, sold for $5,060—a prime example of condition rarity, in this case MS-68, selling for much more.

Stack's Bowers Galleries, in the August 2014 ANA auction, included lot 13250: "1910 MS-65, PCGS." It sold for $10,577. In July 2016 Scotsman's Midwest Summer sale offered lot 833: "1910 MS-65 PCGS." It sold for $5,750. Heritage's April 2017 sale included lot 15989: "1910 MS-65 PCGS." It sold for $5,170.

PROOF MARKET NEWS AND COMMENTARY

In November 1939 the William B. Hale Collection, sold by B. Max Mehl, included lot 1695: "1910 Proof, the new style, between a Sand Blast and a brilliant Proof; wire edge. Very scarce in Proof." It sold for $27.50.

In February 1944, in the Belden E. Roach Collection, B. Max Mehl offered lot 386: "1910 Perfect Proof. Of the new style. Sharp wire edge on the reverse. Rare in Proof," selling for $37.50. In June 1946, in the William Cutler Atwater Collection, B. Max Mehl offered lot 1490: "1910 Proof, perfect in every respect. Very scarce in Proof," selling for $41.

In August 2006 the American Numismatic Rarities sale of the Old West and Franklinton Collections included lot 1581: "1910 Satin Finish Proof-67 NGC." It sold for $80,500. In the November 2009 74th Anniversary sale Stack's offered lot 1937: "1910 Satin Proof-66 NGC." It sold for $60,375. In the August 2016 ANA World's Fair of Money sale Stack's Bowers Galleries offered lot 3481: "1910 Satin Proof-65 PCGS." It sold for $70,500.

VF-20	EF-40	AU-50	AU-55	MS-60	MS-62	MS-63	MS-65	PF-63	PF-64	PF-65
$700	$725	$750	$775	$1,100	$1,500	$2,000	$9,500	$18,500	$30,000	$55,000

1910-D

Circulation-Strike Mintage: 2,356,640

Notes regarding mintages: The first day of striking was January 25, 1910. It is likely that a large percentage of this mintage was exported to Europe.

Estimated population (Mint State): *25,000+.* Common in all grades through MS-63, and with many known in MS-64 and MS-65 as well. In the highest-grade levels this is the most available Indian Head eagle. Large numbers were imported in the late 1900s. Earlier, the 1910-D was considered to be very scarce, if not rare, in Mint State.

Estimated population (circulated grades): *30,000+.* Mostly EF and AU.

Submissions certified at highest grades (as of March 2017): *PCGS:* MS-63 (2,693), MS-64 (748), MS-65 (101), MS-66 (45), MS-67 (3). *NGC:* MS-63 (2,270), MS-64 (865), MS-65 (188), MS-66 (45), MS-67 (6).

Die data: Mintmark position varieties exist.

Key to collecting: Very common. As is true of other Indian Head eagles that are very common except in higher Mint State grades, the value of such coins is largely dependent upon the price of gold bullion plus a modest premium.

MARKET NEWS AND COMMENTARY

In February 1944, in the Belden E. Roach Collection, B. Max Mehl offered lot 490: "1910-D Uncirculated, frosty mint surface." It sold for $28.50. In October 1947, in the H.R. Lee Collection (Eliasberg duplicates), Stack's offered lot 1692: "1910-D Brilliant Uncirculated, with luster." It sold for $25.

In April 1960 New Netherlands' 54th sale, Jonathan Glogower Consignment, Etc., included this lot 724: "1910-D. Brilliant Unc. For some reason, we have not been able to locate any other records of specimens in this condition." It sold for $30. This is a strange comment as by that time there had been *many* auction listings!

In May 1998 the Dr. Thaine B. Price Collection offered by David W. Akers included lot 52: "1910-D Gem Uncirculated." It sold for $19,800. The March 2005 American Numismatic Rarities Richard C. Jewell Collection sale included lot 800: "1910-D MS-65 PCGS." It sold for $4,600. Stack's November 2010 75th Anniversary sale, included lot 7149: "1910-D MS-66, NGC." It sold for $12,650.

VF-20	EF-40	AU-50	AU-55	MS-60	MS-62	MS-63	MS-65
$700	$725	$750	$775	$850	$900	$1,250	$7,500

1910-S

Circulation-Strike Mintage: 811,000

Estimated population (Mint State): *2,500+.* Most probably circulated or were stored in the United States, although many were exported as well. Usually seen in grades from MS-60 to MS-64. It is scarce in finer grades. In fact, the 1910-S is fairly scarce at *any* Mint State level.

Estimated population (circulated grades): *15,000+.* The 1910-S (as part of all San Francisco Mint $10 1909-S to 1914-S) is very peculiar among Saint-Gaudens eagles of this era in that most circulated pieces in old-time collections average VF in grade, rather than EF or AU. This is probably because most circulated in the West, and many were obtained domestically from that area.

Submissions certified at highest grades (as of March 2017): *PCGS:* MS-63 (117), MS-64 (35), MS-65 (2), MS-66 (2). *NGC:* MS-63 (22), MS-64 (10), MS-65 (3), MS-66 (3).

Die data: Mintmark position varieties exist.

Key to collecting: Common.

MARKET NEWS AND COMMENTARY

In May 1939, sale 399, Rare U.S. Gold Coins by J.C. Morgenthau & Co. included lot 430: "1910-S Extremely Fine." It sold for $16.50. In November 1939 the William B. Hale Collection, sold by B. Max Mehl, included lot 1752: "1910-S Uncirculated; full mint luster." It sold for $19. In the December 1944 sale of the J.F. Bell Collection Stack's included lot 793: "1910-S Uncirculated gem." It sold for $27.50. In October 1947, in the H.R. Lee Collection (Eliasberg duplicates), Stack's offered lot 1681: "1910-S Brilliant Uncirculated." It sold for $34.

In May 1998 the Dr. Thaine B. Price Collection, offered by David W. Akers, included lot 53: "1910-S Very Choice Uncirculated." It sold for $26,400. By this time there were at least hundreds, perhaps even thousands of collectors endeavoring to get one each of the collectible dates and mints. In March 2006 the American Numismatic Rarities sale of the New York Connoisseur's Collection included lot 1688: "1910-S MS-64 PCGS." It sold for $57,500. Possibly, the winning bidder's desire for a high-grade coin was filled by this coin, and he or she was not in competition for the next. In August 2006 the American Numismatic Rarities sale of the Old West and Franklinton Collections included lot 1582: "1910-S MS-65 PCGS." It sold for $52,900.

Stack's January 2004 sale included lot 3014: "1910-S Indian $10, MS-66, PCGS." It sold for $83,375. Heritage's January 2017 FUN Convention sale included lot 6985: "1910-S MS-64 NGC." It sold for $8,225.

VF-20	EF-40	AU-50	AU-55	MS-60	MS-62	MS-63	MS-65
$700	$725	$750	$775	$1,000	$2,750	$8,500	$50,000

1911

Circulation-Strike Mintage: 505,500
Proof Mintage: 95

Estimated population (Mint State): *12,000+.* Mostly MS-60 to MS-63, but seen with some frequency in higher grades as well. The supply of Mint State pieces was greatly augmented by imports from the 1970s onward.

Estimated population (circulated grades): *12,000+.* Mostly EF and AU. Certain later dates seem to be more plentiful in Mint State than in circulated grades, as repatriated coins are nearly all Mint State.

Estimated population (Proofs): *12–16.* It is likely that most Proofs were never sold.

Submissions certified at highest grades (as of March 2017): *PCGS:* MS-63 (1,908), MS-64 (658), MS-65 (95), MS-66 (27), MS-67 (12). *NGC:* MS-63 (1,863), MS-64 (914), MS-65 (156), MS-66 (42), MS-67 (9), MS-68 (4).

Key to collecting: Very common.

MARKET NEWS AND COMMENTARY

In February 1944, in the Belden E. Roach Collection, B. Max Mehl offered lot 388: "1911 Brilliant Uncirculated, with brilliant luster." It sold for $18.25. In May 1945 Stack's sale of the George H. Hall Collection included lot 2232: "1911 Brilliant Uncirculated." It sold for $26. In October 1947, in the H.R. Lee Collection (Eliasberg duplicates), Stack's offered lot 1568: "1911 Uncirculated, with frosty surface." It sold for $24. In May 1950 the Golden Jubilee sale / Jerome Kern Collection sale by B. Max Mehl included lot 547: "1911 Brilliant Uncirculated." It sold for $28.50. In July 1951 *Kelly's Coins and Chatter*, Vols. 4–7, offered this: "1911 Uncirculated. $27.50." At this time Kelly was several years into his large-scale importations of gold from Europe.

In the expanded marketplace of May 1998 the Dr. Thaine B. Price Collection offered by David W. Akers included lot 54: "1911 Gem Uncirculated." It sold for $20,900. The August 2002 ANA Convention sale by Superior Galleries included lot 2110: "1911 MS-65 PCGS." It sold for $6,325; the next lot with identical information sold for $7,475.

Regency Auction XIX, December 2016, included lot 473: "1911 MS-65 PCGS." It sold for $4,700. In the January 2017 Collectors Choice sale Stack's Bowers Galleries offered lot 91539: "1911 MS-65 NGC." It sold for $3,995. Stack's Bowers Galleries, in the August 2013 Chicago World's Fair of Money sale, included lot 4547: "1911 Indian $10, MS-68, NGC." It sold for $94,000. In the February 2017 Pre-Long Beach sale Ira and Larry Goldberg offered lot 1323: "1911 MS-65 PCGS." It sold for $7,050. Heritage's April 1917 sale included lot 5654: "1911 MS-65 PCGS." It sold for $7,637.50.

PROOF MARKET NEWS AND COMMENTARY

In June 1946, in the William Cutler Atwater Collection, B. Max Mehl offered lot 1491: "1911 Sand Blast Proof. Perfect. Just as perfect as the day it was struck. Very scarce and in much demand. Retails up to $75." It sold for $62.50. In April 1956 Abe Kosoff's sale of the Thomas G. Melish and Clinton W. Hester Collections included lot 2620: "1911 Matte Proof, scarce." It sold for $110.

The market had changed dramatically by January 2016 when Heritage's FUN Convention sale offered lot 5637: "1911 Proof-65 PCGS." It sold for $49,350. In May 2016 the Rarities Auction held by Stack's Bowers Galleries offered lot 113: "1911 Sand Blast Proof-66 PCGS." It sold for $64,625.

VF-20	EF-40	AU-50	AU-55	MS-60	MS-62	MS-63	MS-65	PF-63	PF-64	PF-65
$700	$725	$750	$775	$1,100	$1,500	$2,000	$9,500	$18,500	$30,000	$55,000

1911-D

Circulation-Strike Mintage: 30,100

Notes regarding mintages: The first day of striking was April 26, 1911.

Estimated population (Mint State): 500. Very scarce in relation to the great demand for it. Most are MS-60 to MS-62 plus the occasional MS-63. At the MS-64 level the 1911-D is a *rarity*.

Estimated population (circulated grades): *1,000+.* Mostly EF and AU. A key issue.

Submissions certified at highest grades (as of March 2017): *PCGS:* MS-63 (40), MS-64 (15), MS-65 (3). *NGC:* MS-63 (14), MS-64 (11).

Key to collecting: Common in high-level circulated grades, but scarce in Mint State. A key issue in never-ending demand.

MARKET NEWS AND COMMENTARY

B. Max Mehl, in his sale of the Honorable James H. Manning Collection, May 1921, included lot 903: "1911-D Uncirculated. Very scarce." It sold for $12. In November 1939 the William B. Hale Collection, sold by B. Max Mehl, included lot 1763: "1911-D Uncirculated. Rare." It sold for $21. In November 1945 B. Max Mehl's sale of the W.A. Philpott and Henry L. Zander Collections included lot 1734: "1911-D About Uncirculated with almost full mint luster." It sold for $26. Also lot 1766: "1911-D Very Fine." It sold for $22.50. In January 1946 the Numismatic Gallery sale of "The World's Greatest Collection" (F.C.C. Boyd) included lot 851: "1911-D Uncirculated." It sold for $35.

In March 1988 the Norweb Collection, Part II, sale by Bowers and Merena Galleries included lot 2313: "1911-D MS-65. A gem specimen of the lowest mintage issue of the Indian Head eagle series of the 1908 to 1933 With Motto style. Relatively few Uncirculated pieces are known, and of those that are known, few can match this. From B. Max Mehl on January 30, 1954." It sold for $132,000.

In May 1998 the Dr. Thaine B. Price Collection offered by David W. Akers included lot 55: "1911-D MS-64." It sold for $49,500.

In December 2004 the American Numismatic Rarities Classics sale included lot 537: "1911-D MS-64 (PCGS)." It sold for $31,050. In June 2006 the American Numismatic Rarities sale of the Lake Michigan and Springdale Collections included lot 3637: "1911-D MS-62 NGC." It sold for $11,500. In August 2006 the American Numismatic Rarities sale of the Old West and Franklinton Collections included lot 1584: "1911-D MS-64 NGC." It sold for $36,800.

In its 2008 ANA Convention sale Heritage offered lot 2034: "1911-D MS-64 NGC." It sold for $43,125. In the January 2017 Collectors Choice sale Stack's Bowers Galleries offered lot 91540: "1911-D MS-63 PCGS." It sold for $22,325. Heritage's January 2017 FUN Convention sale included lot 5967: "1911-D MS-63+ PCGS." It sold for $30,550. The same firm's April 2017 sale included lot 4300: "1911-D MS-64 PCGS." It sold for $70,500. In any Mint State grade the 1911-D attracts attention from all directions.

VF-20	EF-40	AU-50	AU-55	MS-60	MS-62	MS-63	MS-65
$1,250	$1,500	$2,200	$3,500	$12,500	$17,500	$35,000	$175,000

1911-S

Circulation-Strike Mintage: 51,000

Notes regarding mintages: Most were probably circulated on the West Coast, although thousands must have been exported.

Estimated population (Mint State): *450+.* (See hoard information.) Most are MS-60 to MS-62. Very scarce in comparison to the great demand.

Estimated population (circulated grades): *1,000+.* The 1911-S (as part of all San Francisco Mint $10 1909-S to 1914-S) is very peculiar among Saint-Gaudens eagles of this era in that most circulated pieces in old-time collections average VF in grade, rather than EF or AU. This is probably because most circulated in the West, and many were obtained domestically from that area.

Submissions certified at highest grades (as of March 2017): *PCGS:* MS-63 (26), MS-64 (28), MS-65 (23), MS-66 (10). *NGC:* MS-63 (7), MS-64 (9), MS-65 (9), MS-66 (2).

Key to collecting: Slightly scarce. As a general rule the San Francisco Mint Indian Head eagles are key issues in higher grade and are always in strong demand.

MARKET NEWS AND COMMENTARY

A hoard of 60 was found in the Philippine Islands circa 1976, transshipped to Spain, and then to New England Rare Coin Galleries, this per Walter Breen.[21] On several occasions, David W. Akers mentioned a hoard of 30 to 40 coins (1980 book) or 40 to 50 coins (1998 offering of the Price Collection). John Dannreuther recalls the group coming to market between 1977 and 1978, consisting of about 100 Mint State coins, probably from Europe, although the Breen story connected them through the Philippines. Dannreuther purchased some from Ron Gillio and others through New England Rare Coin Company.[22]

The story was fleshed out by Ron Gillio, who recalled the details, differing in some instances from the preceding:[23]

> The first 1911-S eagles that turned up were in a Glendining auction in London, sometime from 1975 to 1977. I do not remember precisely how many there were, but I think it was somewhere between 30 and 50 coins. Some were sold singly and others in lots. In Glendining sales at the time, Mr. French would stand on a podium, and below him would be a table going around the podium in a horseshoe arrangement. I was sitting on one side of the horseshoe, and on the other was Marc Emory, who at the time was working for Jim Halperin of New England Rare Coin Galleries. When the 1911-S tens came up, we were the only two bidders on the coins. I bought about 80% of them and Marc bought the remaining 20%. Andre de Clermont, who worked with Spink's in London, was at the sale and congratulated me. He suggested that I stop by at Spink's later that day or the next morning.
>
> I went there and he proceeded to tell me that they were the consignors of these coins to the auction. He asked if I would like to buy more, because he had additional pieces. I bought another 10, 12, or perhaps 15 coins from him. I wanted to know his source, and he said that they came from a good customer of Spink's who was from Spain. There were more in Spain, and he would try to get them. The next time Andre de Clermont and I met was at a coin show in Zurich the following October. His customer was there, and we both talked with him. He was from the Basque district of Spain near the Pyrenees Mountains. Marc Emory was hot on the trail of the deal also. As he spoke Spanish, he had an edge, and, although I never bought any more 1911-S eagles, I think that Marc Emory did. In total, I handled about 50 or 60 coins, including the Glendining pieces, and I think that the whole group amounted to about a hundred,

with the others going to Marc Emory. These were all very beautiful, really fantastic quality coins. Where they are today, I don't know. It is amazing that when such groups are sold, the people who buy them hide them away, and they soon become rare.

Others have been found, but the 1911-S remains scarce in high Mint State grades.

B. Max Mehl, in his sale of the Honorable James H. Manning Collection, May 1921, included lot 904: "1911-S Uncirculated." It sold for $10.60.

In November 1939 the William B. Hale Collection, sold by B. Max Mehl, included lot 1753: "1911-S Uncirculated; with considerable wire edge on obverse." It sold for $18.25. In the December 1944 sale of the J.F. Bell Collection the same firm included lot 794: "1911-S Uncirculated gem." It sold for $47.50.

In May 1998 the Dr. Thaine B. Price Collection, offered by David W. Akers, included lot 56: "1911-S Gem Uncirculated." It sold for $13,200.

In January 1990 Superior Galleries' sale of the Thomas S. Chalkley and Austin Ryer Collections told this in the description of lot 4901: "1911-S. PCGS graded MS-65. According to the October 1989 PCGS Population Report, only 6 pieces have been so graded, with none higher. That 'none higher' gives prospective bidders a clear indication how rare 1911-S is in Gem condition." It sold for $19,800.

Heritage, in its Baltimore sale, July 2003, offered lot 10534: "1911-S MS-66 PCGS. In the series of ten dollar Indians, the 1911-S is considered one of the premier rarities. Even after the appearance of a small hoard of 40-50 pieces in the late 1970s, this did not materially affect the availability of high grade examples. This is one of only 8 pieces to have been so graded by PCGS with none finer at either service." It sold for $14,375.

In August 2006 the American Numismatic Rarities sale of the Old West and Franklinton Collections included lot 1565: "1911-S MS-65 PCGS." It sold for $13,900. Stack's Bowers Galleries, in the August 2013 ANA World's Fair of Money auction, included lot 4549: "1911-S Indian $10, MS-66, PCGS." It sold for $44,063.

VF-20	EF-40	AU-50	AU-55	MS-60	MS-62	MS-63	MS-65
$800	$850	$925	$975	$2,000	$7,000	$11,000	$25,000

1912

Circulation-Strike Mintage: 405,000
Proof Mintage: 83

Estimated population (Mint State): 10,000+. Most are in grades from MS-60 to MS-63. The supply of Mint State pieces was greatly augmented by imports from the 1970s onward.

Estimated population (circulated grades): 10,000+. Mostly EF and AU.

Estimated population (Proofs): 8–12. The 1912 and 1913 Matte Proofs are of about equal rarity and are tied for the rarest Matte Proofs in the Indian Head $10 series.

Submissions certified at highest grades (as of March 2017): PCGS: MS-63 (1,141), MS-64 (303), MS-65 (40), MS-66 (11), MS-67 (2). **NGC:** MS-63 (1,043), MS-64 (290), MS-65 (58), MS-66 (12), MS-67 (1).

Key to collecting: Very common.

MARKET NEWS AND COMMENTARY

In November 1945 B. Max Mehl's sale of the W.A. Philpott and Henry L. Zander Collections included lot 1767: "1912 Philadelphia mint. About fine." It sold for $22.50. In May 1950 the Golden Jubilee sale / Jerome Kern Collection sale by B. Max Mehl included lot 549: "1912 Brilliant Uncirculated, full mint luster. Catalogs $30." It sold for $22.85. New Netherlands Coin Co.'s 46th sale, the Dr. Clarence W. Peake Collection, June 1955, included lot 236: "1912. Uncirculated. Just about a perfect 'gem.' A $40 coin, considering the very few found this way." It sold for $26.

Fast forward to May 1998 when the Dr. Thaine B. Price Collection, offered by David W. Akers, included lot 57:

> 1912 Gem Uncirculated. In terms of its overall population rarity, i.e. the total number of specimens known, the 1912 eagle ranks as one of the more common issues of the series. In choice Uncirculated and all lower grades, it is readily available. However, very choice Uncirculated specimens are quite scarce and gem specimens are actually surprisingly rare. In fact, in recent years it has become apparent that a gem 1912 eagle is more rare than a gem 1908 with motto, 1910, 1911, 1913, or 1915, although, inexplicably, the 1912 is still lumped with those issues price-wise in most of the standard pricing guides. Among the Philadelphia Mint issues of the series, only the 1909 and 1914 and, of course, the 1907 Rolled Edge and 1933, are more rare in gem condition than the 1912. [Sold for $15,400]

In their day David Akers' market comments were always very insightful. Perhaps his background as a university professor early in his career helped.

Stack's Bowers Galleries, in the August 2013 ANA World's Fair of Money sale, included lot 4550: "1912 MS-66, PCGS." It sold for $23,500. Regency Auction XVII, May 2016, included lot 428: "1912 MS-64 PCGS." It sold for $2,232.50; another, lot 429: "MS-65+ PCGS," sold for $13,512.50. A dramatic example of a tiny difference in grade making a large difference in price. Heritage's August 2016 ANA World's Fair of Money sale included lot 5962: "1912 MS-65 PCGS." It sold for $7,050.

PROOF MARKET NEWS AND COMMENTARY

As is the case with all Proofs, pedigree citations are few and far between, especially among early listings, and there is no way to trace their movement from one collection to another. However, over a period of several generations it is not unusual for a given coin to be included in a handful of different collections. In modern times the velocity of transactions has multiplied, and today Proofs of this ere are offered at regular intervals, often being the same coin passing from one owner to another.

In April 1939 in sale 399, Rare U.S. Gold Coins, J.C. Morgenthau & Co. included lot 432: "1912 Sand Blast Proof." It sold for $26. B. Max Mehl, in his sale of the Honorable James H. Manning Collection, May 1921, included lot 905: "1912 Sand Blast Proof, sharp. Rare." It sold for $11. In June 1946, in the William Cutler Atwater Collection, B. Max Mehl offered lot 1492: "1912 Sand Blast Proof, but not quite as dark as last. A perfect specimen in every respect with partly wire edge on reverse. Very scarce date. Record $60 but retails for more." It sold for $62.50. In May 1950 the Golden Jubilee sale / Jerome Kern Collection sale by B. Max Mehl included lot 548:

"1912 Perfect Sand Blast Proof. Very scarce. Only 83 proofs struck. Atwater specimen brought $62.50 four years ago." It sold for $60.

In January 2005 Numismatic Rarities Kennywood Collection sale included lot 1008: "1912 Sand Blast Proof-66 PCGS." It sold for $50,600, reflective of the modern market and strong demand.

VF-20	EF-40	AU-50	AU-55	MS-60	MS-62	MS-63	MS-65	PF-63	PF-64	PF-65
$700	$725	$750	$775	$875	$1,000	$1,300	$8,500	$18,500	$28,000	$55,000

1912-S

Circulation-Strike Mintage: 300,000

Notes regarding mintages: Most probably circulated on the West Coast or were stored there (later to be melted in the 1930s), although thousands were exported.

Estimated population (Mint State): 900+. Very scarce. Most are in grades from MS-60 to MS-64. Very rare in higher grades. The supply of Mint State pieces was significantly increased by imports from the 1970s onward—removing this from the "seldom seen" category.

Estimated population (circulated grades): 7,000+. The 1912-S is very peculiar among Saint-Gaudens eagles of this era in that most circulated pieces in old-time collections averaged VF in grade, rather than EF or AU. This is probably because most circulated in the West, and many were obtained domestically from that area.

Submissions certified at highest grades (as of March 2017): *PCGS:* MS-63 (85), MS-64 (80), MS-65 (14), MS-66 (1). *NGC:* MS-63 (37), MS-64 (039), MS-65 (9), MS-66 (2).

Die data: Mintmark position varieties exist.

Characteristics of striking and die notes: Usually lightly struck below the headband.

Key to collecting: Common in high-level view of repatriations yielding many high-grade coins modern auction listings are not extensively cited.

MARKET NEWS AND COMMENTARY

B. Max Mehl, in his sale of the Honorable James H. Manning Collection, May 1921, included lot 906: "1912-S Uncirculated." It sold for $10.60. In February 1944, in the Belden E. Roach Collection, B. Max Mehl offered lot 468: "1912-S Uncirculated." It sold for $26.75. In the December 1944 sale of the J.F. Bell Collection Stack's included lot 795: "1912-S Uncirculated gem." It sold for $26. New Netherlands Coin Co.'s 46th sale, the Dr. Clarence W. Peake Collection, June 1955, included lot 237: "1912-S. Uncirculated. Almost perfect; few infinitesimal signs of handling." It sold for $28. In October 1959, in the sale of the Wilson-Reuter Collections, Stack's included lot 1184: "1912-S About Uncirculated. A 'sleeper' coin, lacking in many collections." It sold for $43.

In May 1998 the Dr. Thaine B. Price Collection, offered by David W. Akers, included lot 58: "1912-S Very Choice Uncirculated." It sold for $41,250.

In 2001 in the FUN sale Heritage offered lot 8328:

> 1912-S MS-65 NGC. The typical 1912-S eagle is among the least attractive coins in the entire Indian Head ten dollar series. While the 1911-S and 1913-S issues display bold impressions throughout, poor definition on the hair around Liberty's face and the eagle should plague many extant pieces of this delivery. In addition, numerous abrasions and poor luster combine to make finding a strictly graded Gem 1912-S eagle in today's numismatic marketplace anywhere from difficult to impossible. Even a small hoard that emerged in the 1980s failed to produce a single specimen that graded finer than MS-63. Population: 3 in 65, 1 finer (11/00). [Sold for $17,250]

Stack's Bowers Galleries, in the August 2013 ANA World's Fair of Money sale, included lot 4551: "1912-S MS-65, PCGS." It sold for $64,625. Regency Auction XIX, December 2016, included lot 475: "1912-S MS-64+ PCGS." It sold for $13,337.50. Kagin's March 2017 ANA Auction included lot 1430: "1909 MS-65 PCGS. PCGS Population: 19; 11 finer (MS-67 finest)." It sold for $15,275.

VF-20	EF-40	AU-50	AU-55	MS-60	MS-62	MS-63	MS-65
$725	$750	$775	$825	$1,250	$5,000	$7,500	$45,000

1913

Circulation-Strike Mintage: 442,000
Proof Mintage: 71

Estimated population (Mint State): 12,000+. The supply of Mint State pieces was greatly augmented by imports from the 1970s onward. MS-60 to MS-62 or even MS-63 coins are plentiful. Somewhat scarce at levels beyond that.

Estimated population (circulated grades): 10,000+. Mostly EF and AU.

Estimated population (Proofs): 8–12. The 1912 and 1913 Matte Proofs are of about equal rarity and are tied for the rarest Matte Proofs in the Indian Head $10 series.

Submissions certified at highest grades (as of March 2017): *PCGS:* MS-63 (900), MS-64 (330), MS-65 (69), MS-66 (17), MS-67 (1). *NGC:* MS-63 (781), MS-64 (313), MS-65 (88), MS-66 (16).

Key to collecting: Very common including in low Mint State levels. In higher grades for this and other Indian Head eagles the demand and prices are both strong. These beautiful coins are very popular with many people.

MARKET NEWS AND COMMENTARY

In December 1935, sale 356, Ludger Gravel and Byron Carney Collections by J.C. Morgenthau & Co. included lot 304: "1913 Uncirculated." It sold for $21. In April 1937 the George M. Agurs Collection, sold by B. Max Mehl, offered lot 1783: "1913 Uncirculated." It sold for $19. In November 1945 B. Max Mehl's sale of the W.A. Philpott and Henry L. Zander Collections included lot 1679: "1913 Bright Uncirculated." It sold for $25. In October 1947 in the H.R. Lee Collection (Eliasberg duplicates) Stack's offered lot 1570: "1913 Brilliant Uncirculated, frosty surface." It sold for $26.

In May 1950 the Golden Jubilee sale / Jerome Kern Collection sale by B. Max Mehl included lot 551: "1913 Uncirculated." New Netherlands Coin Co.'s 46th sale, the Dr. Clarence W. Peake Collection, June 1955, included lot 238: "1913. Fully brilliant. Tiny obverse abrasion mark." It sold for $26. In November 1959 M.H. Bolender, in his 196th auction sale, the J. Ambrose Long and Oscar J. Butterfield Collections, included lot 32: "1913 Uncirculated, mint luster. Cat. $35." It sold for $26. Bolender, a schoolteacher by profession, dealt in coins part time by mail order. Over a long period of time he conducted many mail bid sales. He was a quiet man in person and was not often seen at conventions.

In January 1984 Stack's sale of the Amon G. Carter Jr. Family Collection included lot 822: "1913 Brilliant Uncirculated with golden russet toning." It sold for $4,400. Most of the Indian Head tens in the Carter Collection were in circulated grades.

In May 1998 the Dr. Thaine B. Price Collection, offered by David W. Akers, included lot 59: "1913 Very Choice Uncirculated." It sold for $3,300. In August 2006 the American Numismatic Rarities sale of the Old West and Franklinton Collections included lot 1587: "1913 MS-64 PCGS." It sold for $2,760. The sale had an NGC coin in the same grade that sold for $2,990, and an MS-63 (PCGS) that brought $1,610. Stack's Bowers Galleries, in the August 2013 Chicago ANA World's Fair of Money sale, included lot 4553: "1913 MS-66, NGC." It sold for $14,100. Regency Auction XV, December 2015, included lot 443: "1913 MS-65+ PCGS." It sold for $14,100. In the February 2017 Pre-Long Beach sale Ira and Larry Goldberg offered lot 1327: "1913 MS-63 PCGS." It sold for $1,028.

PROOF MARKET NEWS AND COMMENTARY

In May 1939, sale 399, Rare U.S. Gold Coins by J.C. Morgenthau & Co. included lot 434: "1913 Sand Blast Proof." It sold for $26. In November 1939 the William B. Hale Collection, sold by B. Max Mehl, included lot 1698: "1913 Sand Blast proof; sharp wire edge." It sold for $28.50. In February 1944, in the Belden E. Roach Collection, B. Max Mehl offered lot 390: "1913 Sand Blast Proof, wire edge. These bring full and more than catalog price of $40." It sold for $42. In the December 1944 sale of the J.F. Bell Collection Stack's included lot 681: "1913 Sand Blast Proof." It sold for $47.50.

Years later in October 1980, in the Garrett Collection, Part III, sale, Bowers and Ruddy Galleries offered lot 1690: "Choice Matte Proof. Obtained by Robert Garrett from Henry Chapman on January 23, 1913. Chapman obtained it directly from the Philadelphia Mint at the time of issue." It sold for $22,000.

VF-20	EF-40	AU-50	AU-55	MS-60	MS-62	MS-63	MS-65	PF-63	PF-64	PF-65
$700	$725	$750	$775	$875	$1,100	$1,500	$7,500	$18,500	$28,000	$55,000

1913-S

Circulation-Strike Mintage: 66,000

Notes regarding mintages: Most were probably circulated on the West Coast, although thousands were exported.

Estimated population (Mint State): *400+.* A key issue in the series, a highly prized variety. Most are in lower grades, MS-60 to MS-63.

Estimated population (circulated grades): *1,700+.* The 1913-S (as part of all San Francisco Mint $10 1909-S to 1914-S) is very peculiar among Saint-Gaudens eagles of this era in that most circulated pieces in old-time collections average VF in grade, rather than EF or AU. This is probably because most circulated in the West, and many were obtained domestically from that area.

Submissions certified at highest grades (as of March 2017): *PCGS:* MS-63 (27), MS-64 (13), MS-65 (3), MS-66 (1). *NGC:* MS-63 (5), MS-64 (10), MS-65 (1), MS-67 (2).

Key to collecting: Scarce all around.

Market News and Commentary

In November 1939 the William B. Hale Collection, sold by B. Max Mehl, included lot 1754: "1913-S Uncirculated; full mint luster." It sold for $19. In the December 1944 sale of the J.F. Bell Collection Stack's included lot 796: "1913-S Uncirculated gem." It sold for $47.50. In October 1959 the Wilson-Reuter Collections by Stack's included lot 1186: "1913-S Extremely Fine. Scarce." It sold for $46.

In March 1988 the Norweb Collection sale by Bowers and Merena Galleries included lot 2318: "1913-S AU-58 to MS-60. A very attractive and lustrous example of this very elusive variety. From Abner Kreisberg on September 15, 1961." It sold for $4,840. In November 1997 the Pennsylvania Cabinet & The English Collection offered by Bowers and Merena Galleries included lot 1272: "1913-S MS-64 NGC. Well known gold expert David W. Akers, in his reference: *A Handbook of 20th-Century United States Gold Coins*, ranks this issue as number 1 in rarity among all Indian Head gold eagles in Mint State preservation." It sold for $38,500. In May 1998 the Dr. Thaine B. Price Collection offered by David W. Akers included lot 60: "1913-S MS-63." It sold for $30,800.

In November 2000, in the Harry W. Bass Jr. Collection, Part IV, Bowers and Merena Galleries offered lot 786:

> 1913-S MS-66 PCGS. Gold authority David Akers is familiar with this coin, and states: "'Harry Bass' specimen, bought across the counter by a Dallas dealer in the early 1970s, is superb (MS-67 or better!) and fully lustrous and is probably the finest known." He further stated that there are no more than half a dozen known examples in MS-64 or better. While Harry W. Bass Jr. did not specialize in $10 pieces—that is, he didn't acquire them in quantity and study them in detail, simply because the date logotypes are not different from year to year—the pieces he did acquire were certainly memorable! Purchased from Mike Follett, November 21, 1974. [Sold for $71,300]

Stack's Bowers Galleries, in the August 2013 ANA World's Fair of Money sale, included lot 4554: "1913-S MS-64, NGC." It sold for $44,063. In the June 2014 Pre-Long Beach sale Ira and Larry Goldberg offered lot 1950: "1913-S MS-62 NGC." It sold for $15,862.50. In its August 2016 ANA World's Fair of Money sale Heritage included lot 4336: "1913-S MS-63 PCGS." It sold for $15,275. In the January 2017

Collectors Choice sale Stack's Bowers Galleries offered lot 91541: "1913-S MS-63 PCGS." It sold for $18,800.

VF-20	EF-40	AU-50	AU-55	MS-60	MS-62	MS-63	MS-65
$1,000	$1,100	$1,200	$2,250	$10,000	$14,000	$30,000	$100,000

1914

Circulation-Strike Mintage: 151,000
Proof Mintage: 50

Notes regarding mintages: A great rarity. It is likely that less than half the Proof mintage found buyers. Sand Blast Proofs of the 1914 to 1915 years have an especially coarse "sandpaper-like" finish.

Estimated population (Mint State): *5,000+.* Most are in grades from MS-60 to MS-63. Another variety for which the supply of Mint State pieces was greatly enhanced by imports from the 1970s onward.

Estimated population (circulated grades): *5,000+.* Mostly EF and AU.

Estimated population (Proofs): *10–14.*

Submissions certified at highest grades (as of March 2017): *PCGS:* MS-63 (469), MS-64 (179), MS-65 (38), MS-66 (11), MS-67 (3). *NGC:* MS-63 (240), MS-64 (148), MS-65 (46), MS-66 (10), MS-67 (1).

Key to collecting: Common.

MARKET NEWS AND COMMENTARY

In October 1947, in the H.R. Lee Collection (Eliasberg duplicates) Stack's offered lot 1571: "1914 Uncirculated, frosty surface." It sold for $26. In May 1950 the Golden Jubilee sale / Jerome Kern Collection sale by B. Max Mehl included lot 552-A: "1914 Brilliant Uncirculated, full mint luster. Record $32." It sold for $26. In September 1958 in his 194th auction sale M.H. Bolender included additional Items from the R. Thomas and J. Ambrose Long Collections as lot 2508: "1914 Indian Head Unc. Only 151,050 minted!" Sold for $31.

In the market of years later in August 1990, in Auction '90, David W. Akers offered lot 1939: "1914 MS-65." It sold for $3,520. In May 1998 the Dr. Thaine B. Price Collection, offered by David W. Akers, included lot 61: "1914 Very Choice Uncirculated." It sold for $14,300.

In August 2006 the American Numismatic Rarities sale of the Old West and Franklinton Collections included lot 1590: "1914 MS-65 PCGS." It sold for $8,050. The sale had another in the same grade, but by NGC, that sold for exactly the same price. Stack's Bowers Galleries, in the August 2013 ANA World's Fair of Money auction, included lot 4556: "1914 MS-67, NGC." It sold for $35,250. In the January 2017 Collectors Choice sale Stack's Bowers Galleries offered lot 91542: "1914 MS-65 NGC." It sold for $5,287.50.

PROOF MARKET NEWS AND COMMENTARY

In February 1921, in his sale of the Dr. G.F.E. Wilharm Collection, B. Max Mehl included lot 347: "1914 Sand Blast Proof. Rare." It sold for $12.40. In May 1950 the Golden Jubilee sale / Jerome Kern Collection sale by B. Max Mehl included lot 552: "1914 Perfect Sand Blast Proof. Quite rare. Only 50 proofs struck. Not in the Dr. Green Collection. Catalogs $60." It sold for $57.50.

In February 1958, in the sale of the Crosby, Mayfield, and MacMurray Collections, Stack's included lot 389: "1914 Matte Proof. Perfect flawless gem. Only 50 pieces struck. Really very rare. Worth $300." It sold for $250.

In the vastly expanded market of October 1980, in the Garrett Collection, Part III, Sale, Bowers and Ruddy Galleries offered lot 1691: "1914 Choice Matte Proof Obtained by Robert Garrett from Henry Chapman on September 30, 1914. Chapman obtained it directly from the Philadelphia Mint at the time of issue." It sold for $36,000. In January 2005 Numismatic Rarities Kennywood Collection sale included lot 1010: "1914 Sand Blast Proof-66 PCGS." It sold for $44,275.

VF-20	EF-40	AU-50	AU-55	MS-60	MS-62	MS-63	MS-65	PF-63	PF-64	PF-65
$700	$725	$750	$775	$875	$975	$2,250	$11,000	$18,500	$28,000	$55,000

1914-D

Circulation-Strike Mintage: 343,500

Notes regarding mintages: The 1914-D $10 was one of 16 earlier-dated gold coins available in Uncirculated condition for face value (plus mailing charge) from the Treasury Department in the summer of 1932. This is significant as it indicates that these were being held in quantity in storage at this time. Unsold pieces were melted several years later.[24]

Estimated population (Mint State): 5,000+. Most are in grades from MS-60 through MS-63. The supply of Mint State pieces was greatly augmented by imports from the 1970s onward.

Estimated population (circulated grades): 6,000+. Mostly EF and AU.

Submissions certified at highest grades (as of March 2017): PCGS: MS-63 (480), MS-64 (253), MS-65 (27), MS-66 (6), MS-67 (4). **NGC:** MS-63 (219), MS-64 (155), MS-65 (43), MS-66 (13), MS-67 (7).

Die data: Mintmark position varieties exist.

Key to collecting: Very common.

MARKET NEWS AND COMMENTARY

In November 1939 the William B. Hale Collection, sold by B. Max Mehl, included lot 1764: "1914-D Last year of [Denver Mint] issue, none coined in 1912 and 1913. Uncirculated. Scarce so choice." It sold for $18.50. In September 1958 in his 194th auction sale, additional Items from the R. Thomas and J. Ambrose Long Collections, M.H. Bolender included lot 2509: "1914-D mint. Unc." It sold for $30.

In his watershed dale, May 1998, sale of the Dr. Thaine B. Price Collection David W. Akers included lot 62:

> 1914-D Gem Uncirculated. A superb specimen, one of the finest examples of this issue that I have ever seen. With the sole exception of the 1910-D, the 1914-D is the most common branch mint Indian Head eagle. It is readily obtainable in Mint State grades of Choice Uncirculated and lower, and even very choice Uncirculated examples are only scarce and not rare. However, this is another example of a condition rarity issue since, in gem condition, the 1914-D is actually very rare, much more so than any of the Philadelphia Mint issues from 1908-1915 except the 1909, and roughly comparable in rarity to such more highly rated issues as the 1908-S and 1916-S. [Sold for $58,850]

After that time the combination of more repatriated coins plus gradeflation plus resubmissions altered the availability of Mint State coins that have been certified. Still, high-grade coins bring strong prices.

In September 2005 the American Numismatic Rarities sale of the C.L. Lee Collection included lot 1337: "1914-D MS-64 PCGS." It sold for $2,645. In December 2005 the American Numismatic Rarities sale of the Old Colony Collection included lot 1670: "1914-D MS-64 (NGC)" brought $6,613; another in the same grade by the same service sold for $2,990. Probably, the buyer of the first coin thought it was a good candidate for an upgrade.

Stack's Bowers Galleries, in the August 2013 ANA World's Fair of Money auction, included lot 4557: "1914-D MS-67, NGC." It sold for $30,550. Heritage's January 2017 FUN Convention sale included lot 5958: "1914-D MS-67 NGC." It sold for $30,550.

VF-20	EF-40	AU-50	AU-55	MS-60	MS-62	MS-63	MS-65
$700	$725	$750	$775	$875	$975	$2,400	$15,000

1914-S

Circulation-Strike Mintage: 208,000

Notes regarding mintages: It is likely that while thousands were exported, the bulk of this issue remained stateside and was melted in the 1930s.

Estimated population (Mint State): *900+.* Most are MS-60 through MS-63. Very scarce in Mint State.

Estimated population (circulated grades): *4,500+.* The 1914-S (as part of all San Francisco Mint $10 1909-S to 1914-S) is very peculiar among Saint-Gaudens eagles of this era in that most circulated pieces in old-time collections average VF in grade, rather than EF or AU. This is probably because most circulated in the West, and many were obtained domestically from that area.

Submissions certified at highest grades (as of March 2017): *PCGS:* MS-63 (147), MS-64 (69), MS-65 (12), MS-66 (1). *NGC:* MS-63 (57), MS-64 (30), MS-65 (11), MS-66 (3), MS-67 (1).

Die data: Mintmark position varieties exist.

Characteristics of striking and die notes: Usually with some lightness of strike at the center obverse and the highest area of the eagle's wing.

Key to collecting: Slightly scarce in high-level circulated grades. Scarcer in Mint State.

MARKET NEWS AND COMMENTARY

A 1914-S eagles were available at face value plus postage from the Treasury Department per notice received by the ANA on April 23, 1932. This means that quantities were stored in the Treasury Building in Washington, D.C. at the time.

In November 1939 the William B. Hale Collection, sold by B. Max Mehl, included lot 1755: "1914-S Uncirculated." It sold for $17.50. In the December 1944 sale of the J.F. Bell Collection Stack's included lot 797: "1914-S Uncirculated gem." It sold for $45. In June 1946, in the William Cutler Atwater Collection, B. Max Mehl offered lot 1601: "1914-S Uncirculated, full mint luster. Very scarce so choice. Record $45 made two years ago." It sold for $35.

In January 1984, by which time there were many collectors of Indian Head eagles, Stack's sale of the Amon G. Carter Jr. Family Collection included lot 825: "1914-S Brilliant Uncirculated. A bagmark is on the eagle." It sold for $1,210. In May 1998 the Dr. Thaine B. Price Collection, offered by David W. Akers, included lot 63: "1914-S Choice Uncirculated." It sold for $3,500. Unless the same coins are seen today it is impossible to correlate the Akers adjectival descriptions with present-day grading numbers. Judging by the prices, sometimes a coin described as Choice Uncirculated in 1988 might be equal to MS-63 plus or minus in today's terms. Other coins with the same description many have been MS-65 or finer.

In September 2005 the American Numismatic Rarities sale of the C.L. Lee Collection included lot 1338: "1914-S MS-63 PCGS." It sold for $5,175. In June 2006 the American Numismatic Rarities sale of the Lake Michigan and Springdale Collections included lot 2641: "1914-S MS-66 (PCGS)." It sold for $253,000. In August 2006 the American Numismatic Rarities sale of the Old West and Franklinton Collections included lot 1596: "1914-S MS-65 NGC." It sold for $19,950. The same sale had an MS-64 (PCGS) that brought $11,500.

Stack's Bowers Galleries, in the August 2013 ANA World's Fair of Money sale, included lot 4559: "1914-S MS-65 PCGS." It sold for $30,550.

VF-20	EF-40	AU-50	AU-55	MS-60	MS-62	MS-63	MS-65
$700	$725	$750	$825	$1,650	$3,750	$7,500	$30,000

1915

Circulation-Strike Mintage: 351,000
Proof Mintage: 75

Notes regarding mintages: The low population indicates that probably no more than a third of the mintage was sold. Sand Blast Proofs of the 1914-1915 years have an especially coarse "sandpaper-like" finish.

Estimated population (Mint State): *8,000+.* Fairly plentiful in grades through MS-63 or even MS-64, but elusive higher. The supply of Mint State pieces was greatly augmented by imports from the 1970s onward.

Estimated population (circulated grades): *8,000+.* Mostly AU.

Estimated population (Proofs): *12–15.* A major rarity.

Submissions certified at highest grades (as of March 2017): *PCGS:* MS-64 (338), MS-65 (60), MS-66 (13), MS-67 (1). *NGC:* MS-64 (361), MS-65 (97), MS-66 (427), MS-67 (4).

Key to collecting: Very common.

Market News and Commentary

In May 1945 Stack's sale of the George H. Hall Collection included lot 2238: "1915 Brilliant Uncirculated." It sold for $27. In October 1947, in the H.R. Lee Collection (Eliasberg duplicates), Stack's offered lot 1572: "1915 Brilliant Uncirculated, with full luster." It sold for $32.50. In February 1957 the J.W. Schmandt Collection sold by Stack's included lot 520: "1915 Uncirculated." It sold for $35. In April 1960 New Netherlands' 54th sale, the Jonathan Glogower Consignment, Etc., included this, lot 730: "1915. Brilliant Uncirculated, the usual strike; fairly clean, but not altogether free of bag marks. This is another one hard to find records of in Mint State; neither Dr. Green's, nor Peake's, nor Melish's, nor Straus's qualified at that level, and others have been worse." It sold for $22.

Actually, by 1960 there were *many* auction records.

In May 1998 the Dr. Thaine B. Price Collection, offered by David W. Akers, included lot 64: "1915 Choice Uncirculated." It sold for $2,420. In August 1990, in Auction '90, David W. Akers offered lot 1942: "1915 MS-65." It sold for $3,960.

Into the second decade of the 21st century, Stack's Bowers Galleries, in the August 2013 Chicago ANA World's Fair of Money sale, included lot 4561: "1915 MS-67, NGC." It sold for $30,550. In October 2015 the Scotsman's Collectors Auction offered lot 808: "1914 MS-65 PCGS." It sold for $9,487.50. Regency Auction XIX, December 2016, included lot 477: "1915 MS-65+ PCGS." It sold for $16,450. In its January 2017 FUN Convention sale Heritage included lot 5969: "1915 MS-66 PCGS." It sold for $30,550.

Proof Market News and Commentary

In April 1939, sale 399, Rare U.S. Gold Coins, J.C. Morgenthau & Co. included lot 436: "1915 Sand Blast Proof." It sold for $26. The June 1941 sale of the William Forrester Dunham Collection by B. Max Mehl included lot 2288: "1915 Sand Blast Proof. Very scarce." It sold for $28.50. In February 1944, in the Belden E. Roach Collection, B. Max Mehl offered lot 392: "1915 Sand Blast Proof. Slightly brighter color than the earlier Sand Blast Proofs. Perfect. Last year of the Proofs. Very scarce." It sold for $43.50.

In October 1962 in the Samuel W. Wolfson Collection Stack's offered lot 840:

> 1915 Matte or Sandblast Proof. Very rare and seldom obtainable. It is more interesting to note that with all of the choice Brilliant Proof gold Mr. Wolfson was able to assemble in this collection, he only acquired one Matte Proof eagle. This should

give you some idea of how rare these coins actually are. Only 75 specimens were coined in this remarkable condition. This is the last year that gold coin Proofs were struck. The demand for them far exceeds the supply. [Sold for $1,650]

VF-20	EF-40	AU-50	AU-55	MS-60	MS-62	MS-63	MS-65	PF-63	PF-64	PF-65
$700	$725	$750	$775	$1,000	$1,150	$2,000	$7,500	$20,000	$30,000	$65,000

1915-S

Circulation-Strike Mintage: 59,000

Notes regarding mintages: Although some may have been exported, most seem to have remained in the United States and in the 1930s were melted.

Estimated population (Mint State): *400–600.* Very elusive in Mint State. Most examples are in ranges from MS-60 through MS-63, but occasionally a finer specimen appears on the market.

Estimated population (circulated grades): *1,000+.* Fairly scarce. Most are AU.

Submissions certified at highest grades (as of March 2017): *PCGS:* MS-63 (30), MS-64 (23), MS-65 (5), MS-66 (3), MS-67 (1). *NGC:* MS-63 (12), MS-64 (12), MS-65 (3), MS-67 (1).

Key to collecting: Somewhat scarce overall. In strong demand.

MARKET NEWS AND COMMENTARY

In the December 1944 sale of the J.F. Bell Collection Stack's included lot 798: "1915-S Uncirculated gem. Scarce." It sold for $70.

In May 1998 the Dr. Thaine B. Price Collection, offered by David W. Akers, included lot 63: "1915-S Very Choice Uncirculated." It sold for $46,200. In October 1998, in the John J. Pittman Collection, Part II, sale, David Akers offered lot 2038:

> 1915-S, Gem Uncirculated. This is an outstanding example of a 1915-S Eagle, undoubtedly one of the finest known specimens of this rare issue. JJP purchased this coin from Numismatic Gallery's famous Adolphe Menjou sale, 6/15/50, Lot 1722, for $77.50. This price was nearly double the cataloguer's $40 estimate whereas most of the other Indian Head eagles in the sale brought considerably less than estimate. In any Mint State grade, the 1915-S eagle is rare, and most of the relatively few Uncirculated examples that are known grade lower than Choice Uncirculated. At the Choice Uncirculated level, this issue is very rare, and in Very Choice or Gem Uncirculated condition, the 1915-S is extremely rare and almost never available. The number of collectors specializing in this beautiful series far exceeds the number of available specimens of this issue in high grade, and the 1915-S seems to be on the want list of nearly every serious Indian Head eagle collector. [Sold for $51,700]

In the June 2015 Pre-Long Beach sale Ira and Larry Goldberg offered lot 2010: "1915-S MS-63 NGC." It sold for $13,512.50. Stack's Bowers Galleries, during the March 2017 Baltimore auction, included lot 3128: "1915-S MS-66, PCGS." It sold for $99,875.

VF-20	EF-40	AU-50	AU-55	MS-60	MS-62	MS-63	MS-65
$900	$1,000	$1,050	$1,750	$4,750	$9,500	$22,000	$65,000

1916-S

Circulation-Strike Mintage: 138,500

Estimated population (Mint State): 1,250+. Perhaps even quite a few more. Usually seen grades are MS-60 to MS-63. The supply of Mint State pieces was augmented by imports from the 1970s onward.

Estimated population (circulated grades): 2,500+. Mostly AU.

Submissions certified at highest grades (as of March 2017): *PCGS:* MS-63 (112), MS-64 (39), MS-65 (14), MS-66 (6), MS-67 (2). *NGC:* MS-63 (34), MS-64 (24), MS-65 (7).

Die data: Mintmark position varieties exist.

Key to collecting: Slightly scarce issue readily obtainable in grades from AU to MS-64.

MARKET NEWS AND COMMENTARY

In the 1970s the author received a call from a trust officer at the Beverly Hills branch of the Bank of America on North Beverly Drive in that town. The Jahn Estate was being sold, and investigation revealed a cache of gold coins that had been hidden in a vault for decades. Upon visiting the bank I was greeted by the sight of three white cloth bags, with mint inscriptions on the outside of each, one containing 500 1916-S $10 gold pieces—considered to be a somewhat scarce date—and 500 each of 1911-S and 1916-S $20 gold coins. Each coin was brilliant and lustrous and relatively free of bagmarks, averaging MS-62 and MS-63. A deal was struck, and the coins were mine. These were subsequently advertised, and were completely sold out *within four hours* of the time our offering appeared![25]

Later, a number of numismatic catalogers who never asked about this hoard of the coins or its quality, but seemed to have remarkable ESP powers, later gave the wrong number (only 125 coins or so) and also said they were all of low grades such as MS-60! Such stuff is fun (in a way) to read.

In November 1939 the William B. Hale Collection, sold by B. Max Mehl, included lot 1756: "1916-S Uncirculated." It sold for $17.50. In the June 1941 sale of the William Forrester Dunham Collection by B. Max Mehl lot 2289 was described: "1916-S Uncirculated, with full mint luster." It sold for $18.75.

Years later in March 1988 the Norweb Collection sale by Bowers and Merena Galleries included lot 2324: "1916-S MS-65. A glittering gem specimen of this popular San Francisco issue. Although Uncirculated coins appear on the market from time to time, very few merit the designation of MS-65 by today's exacting standards. From the Palace Collection of King Farouk, February 1954, Lot 224." It sold for $28,600.

The February 1992 Ed Trompeter Collection, Part I, by Superior Galleries included lot 175: "1916-S MS-63 PCGS." It sold for $20,800; followed later in the sale by another 1916-S, lot 203, PCGS, MS-64 that sold for slightly less at $18,150.

In July 1997 David Akers and RARCOA conducted Auction '96, which included lot 463: "1916-S MS-65. Nearly all Mint State 1916-S eagles come from two small hoards that first surfaced in the mid-1970s. However, almost all of those pieces graded MS-63 or less and in MS-64 or higher grade, the 1916-S is definitely a rarity, and is probably distinctly undervalued at today's levels." It sold for $18,700.

Marvelously, without asking about or seeing the coins from the hoard, my firm (Bowers and Ruddy Galleries) handled several other auction catalogers who said they averaged MS-60!

In May 1998 the Dr. Thaine B. Price Collection, offered by David W. Akers, included lot 66: "1916-S Gem Uncirculated." It sold for $52,250. The August 2002 ANA Convention sale by Superior Galleries included lot 2119: "1916-S MS-67 PCGS." It sold for $32,200. In September 2003 the American Numismatic Rarities Classics sale included lot 559: "1916-S MS-66 NGC." It sold for $23,300.

In the August 2006 ANA World's Fair of Money sale Bowers and Merena Galleries offered lot 4391: "1916-S MS-65 PCGS." It sold for $20,125. Regency Auction XIX, December 2016, included lot 478: "1916-S MS-64+." It sold for $18,212.50.

Stack's Bowers Galleries, in the August 2013 ANA World's Fair of Money auction, included lot 4563: "1916-S MS-67, PCGS." It sold for $111,625. Its provenance is as follows: From the Bentley Shores Collection, earlier ex: King Farouk of Egypt; Sotheby's sale of the Palace Collections, February 1954, lot 224; our (Bowers and Merena's) sale of the Norweb Collection, March 1988, lot 2324; our (Bowers and Merena's) sale of the Great Lakes Collection, November 1998, lot 4036; Heritage's sale of the Bill Dailey Collection, January 2002, lot 8355; Superior's sale, August 2002, lot 2119; Heritage's sale of the Belle Glade Collection, August 2007, lot 2007; and Heritage's sale of the Jim O'Neal Collection of Saint-Gaudens Eagles, January 2009, lot 3526.

Heritage's April 2017 sale included lot 15996: "1916-S MS-64+ PCGS." It sold for $15,275.

VF-20	EF-40	AU-50	AU-55	MS-60	MS-62	MS-63	MS-65
$950	$985	$1,000	$1,050	$1,250	$2,750	$6,500	$25,000

1920-S

Circulation-Strike Mintage: 126,500

Notes regarding mintages: It is virtually a certainty that nearly all of the 126,500 pieces minted were held by the Treasury Department and melted after 1933. Relatively few must have seen actual distribution, either domestically or in international commerce. No hoards are known, not even small ones.

Estimated population (Mint State): *70–90.* The 1920-S is a prime rarity in Mint State, eclipsing such issues as the 1930-S and bringing up a slight challenge to the vaunted 1933. Unlike the 1933, which when seen is nearly always in choice Mint State, the typical 1920-S is apt to be around the MS-60 level, a point more or a point less, although choice and gem pieces occasionally come to market. Most pieces are weakly struck in one or more areas.

Estimated population (circulated grades): *40– 55.* The 1920-S is a major rarity in any and all grades. Most circulated examples are at the AU level, as this issue does not seem to have been used in commerce extensively.

Submissions certified at highest grades (as of March 2017): *PCGS:* MS-63 (8), MS-64 (7), MS-65 (2), MS-66 (1), MS-67 (1). *NGC:* MS-63 (6), MS-64 (3), MS-65 (4), MS-66 (1).

Characteristics of striking and die notes: Striking seems to have been indifferent at best, with the last two or three letters of LIBERTY on the headdress often weak, usually the TY. On the reverse the eagle's left (to observer's right) leg and claw typically show weakness. The 19 of the 1920 date is sometimes weak. These weaknesses were caused by spacing the dies slightly too far apart in the coining press. Notwithstanding the foregoing, a few sharply struck specimens exist.

Key to collecting: A famous rarity. Always in strong demand.

Market News and Commentary

In May 1939 J.C. Morgenthau & Co. offered sale 399, Rare U.S. Gold Coins, which included lot 437: "1920-S Uncirculated." It sold for $17.50. The 1920-S was not recognized as being rare, and the price was just not far above the melt-down value at the time. In the December 1944 sale of the J.F. Bell Collection Stack's included lot 800: "1920-S Uncirculated gem. Very scarce." It sold for $175. The 1920-S has come into its own as a rarity. From about that point onward a 1920-S always attracted attention when offered.

In April 1949 B. Max Mehl's sale of the Dr. Charles W. Green Collection included lot 717: "1920-S Originally purchased as Uncirculated, and I believe the coin has never been in circulation, but it has minute nicks. The second rarest $10 gold piece of this mint. Record $250 and certainly worth it. I bespeak for this coin a very bright future. Someday it will be rated and valued among our real rarities." It sold for $265.

This did happen! In October 1982, in the Louis E. Eliasberg Collection of U.S. Gold Coins, Bowers and Ruddy Galleries offered lot 869: "1920-S Choice Brilliant Uncirculated, MS-65. From the John H. Clapp Collection, 1942. Earlier from T.L. Comparette of the U.S. Mint." It sold for $40,700. This coin appeared later in Superior Galleries' description of the 1920-S in the February 1992 Ed Trompeter Collection, Part I, sale by Superior Galleries as lot 209: "1920-S MS-63 PCGS. Ex Eliasberg." It sold for $50,050.

In May 1998 the Dr. Thaine B. Price Collection, offered by David W. Akers, included lot 67: "1920-S Gem Uncirculated." It sold for $82,500. In its July 2006 sale Heritage offered lot 1591: "1920-S MS-64 PCGS. Population: 5 in 64, 4 finer (5/06)." It sold for $172,500.

In its sale of March 2007 Heritage sold an MS-67 (PCGS) coin for $1,725,000, far and away the highest price ever realized for a 1920-S. Stack's Bowers Galleries, in the August 2013 Chicago ANA World's Fair of Money sale, included lot 4565: "1920-S MS-65, NGC." It sold for $199,750.

VF-20	EF-40	AU-50	AU-55	MS-60	MS-62	MS-63	MS-65
$16,500	$20,000	$25,000	$32,500	$55,000	$75,000	$105,000	$225,000

1926

Circulation-Strike Mintage: 1,014,000

Estimated population (Mint State): 50,000+. The issue is very common in Mint State and among Indian Head $10 is second only to the 1932 in this regard. Most are in the MS-60 to MS-62 range, with MS-63 pieces being fewer in number, MS-64 fewer still, and MS-65 being relatively rare. As is also true of the 1932, the typical Mint State 1926 is apt to show multiple large nicks or marks rather than many small ones. Grading interpretations can and do vary widely, and one person's MS-62 may be another's MS-64. Luster is sometimes more satiny than frosty. Many pieces show golden or greenish toning.

Estimated population (circulated grades): 10,000+. Mostly AU. Very common, but of little *numismatic* consequence due to the widespread availability of Mint State pieces.

Submissions certified at highest grades (as of March 2017): *PCGS:* MS-63 (17,772), MS-64 (3,966), MS-65 (443), MS-66 (21). *NGC:* MS-63 (15,637), MS-64 (4,661), MS-65 (603), MS-66 (52). This issue is a veritable annuity for the third-party grading services.

Characteristics of striking and die notes: Mint State pieces often have a rather "creamy" or satiny finish, rather than the deep frost seen on earlier issues. However, as striking was accomplished via multiple die pairs and production runs, characteristics vary.

Key to collecting: Extremely common.

Market News and Commentary

Eagles of this date appeared in a number of sales in the late 1930s at which time gold was $35 per ounce. A sample is provided by Wayte Raymond's April 1939 mail bid sale, lot 828: "1926 Uncirculated." It sold for $18.50. The melt value was $17.00. These attracted little attention then or later.

In May 1998 the Dr. Thaine B. Price Collection, offered by David W. Akers, included lot 68: "1926 Very Choice Uncirculated." It sold for $3,300. In July 2005 the American Numismatic Rarities sale of the William H. LaBelle Sr. Collection included lot 342: "1926 MS-66 NGC." It sold for $6,613. In October 2015 the Scotsman's Collectors Auction offered lot 1093: "1926 MS-65 PCGS." It sold for $3,335, and the same variety and grade and service as lot 1092 sold for $3,105.

VF-20	EF-40	AU-50	AU-55	MS-60	MS-62	MS-63	MS-65
$700	$725	$750	$775	$875	$900	$950	$3,000

1926-S

Reported: In an interview in the 1950s Stephen K. Nagy told the author that he obtained a 1926-S eagle from the Philadelphia Mint. This has never been verified otherwise.

1930-S

Circulation-Strike Mintage: 96,000

Notes regarding mintages: Although 96,000 were coined, it is likely that the vast majority—probably as many as 95,000—went to the melting pot after 1933.

The 1930-S $10 was one of 16 earlier-dated gold coins available in Uncirculated condition for face value (plus mailing charge) from the Treasury Department in the summer of 1932. This is significant as it indicates that these were being held in quantity in storage at this time. Unsold pieces were melted several years later.[26] Henry Chapman was among the few dealers who laid in a small stock at the time. The Depression was ongoing, and money was scarce.

Estimated population (Mint State): *150–200.* Of those relatively few pieces that do exist, most are Mint State. And, of those Mint State coins, most are MS-63 or MS-64. Due to the high value of such pieces, most pieces coming on the market in recent times have been certified or even re-certified, thus swelling the population reports.

The 1930-S is a prime rarity among the Indian Head $10 series and joins the 1920-S and 1933 as being numismatic landmarks. When seen, and that is not often, examples are likely to be Mint State. A few other Indian Head $10 pieces are rarer in Mint State, but most of these are available in lesser grades.

Estimated population (circulated grades): *5–10.* Most are AU, although several damaged pieces are known.

Submissions certified at highest grades (as of March 2017): *PCGS:* MS-63 (13), MS-64 (42), MS-65 (18), MS-66 (5), MS-67 (1). *NGC:* MS-63 (11), MS-64 (26), MS-65 (13), MS-67 (2).

Key to collecting: One of the most famous rarities in the series. These always create attention when offered.

Market News and Commentary

In his 1980 text, David W. Akers noted this: "I know of one small hoard of this date that is currently intact but I still feel that the total number of pieces in existence is likely to be less than 100."

No other information about this hoard has been learned. Have the coins been distributed by now?

In October 1939 J.C. Morgenthau & Co. offered this in sale 405, lot 22: "1930-S. Brilliant Uncirculated. Scarce." It sold for $20. This was on the cusp of wide interest in 20th century gold coins. That changed by the time of the December 1944 sale of the J.F. Bell Collection by Stack's that included lot 801: "1930-S Brilliant Uncirculated gem. Rare." It sold for $200.

From this point there were many appearances at auction and in price lists, nearly all in Mint State. In April 1956, in his sale of the Thomas G. Melish Collection, Abe Kosoff offered lot 2637: "1930-S. Uncirculated. Even scarcer than the 1920-S (I would hazard a guess that both the 1920-S and 1930-S eagles are rarer than the 1933). Should bring close to $1,000." It sold for $1,150.

In May 1998 the Dr. Thaine B. Price Collection, offered by David W. Akers, included lot 69: "1930-S Gem Uncirculated." It sold for $34,100. In October 1998 the John J. Pittman Collection, Part II, sold by David W. Akers, included lot 2041: "1930-S MS-65." It sold for $33,000.

Superior Galleries, in its August 1990 offering of Auction '90, told of certified coins in its description of lot 1371:

> 1930-S MS-64 NGC. This is the only 1930-S eagle graded MS-64 by NGC. (They've graded two higher and PCGS, for its part, has graded two higher, though no MS-64s.) Therefore, the coin offered here is one of only five high end Uncirculated 1930-S eagles available to those who prefer slabbed and certified coins. [Sold for $33,000]

In August 1990, in Auction '90, David W. Akers offered lot 1945: "1930-S MS-62." It sold for $16,500. The February 1992 Ed Trompeter Collection, Part I, by Superior Galleries included lot 209: "1930-S MS-65 PCGS." It sold for $23,100.

In December 2005 the American Numismatic Rarities sale of the Old Colony Collection included lot 1683: "1930-S MS-64 NGC." It sold for $41,400. In the January 2014 Pre-Long Beach sale Ira and Larry Goldberg offered lot 1855: "1930-S MS-65 PCGS." It sold for $79,312.50. In its January 2017 FUN sale Heritage offered lot 5970: "1930-S MS-64 NGC. Census: in 64, 15 finer (11/16)." It sold for $61,690.

VF-20	EF-40	AU-50	AU-55	MS-60	MS-62	MS-63	MS-65
$15,000	$17,500	$22,500	$24,500	$35,000	$40,000	$55,000	$85,000

1932

Circulation-Strike Mintage: 4,463,000

Notes regarding mintages: Many were exported, but most probably remained stateside. From 1933 to 1934 when the call came for American citizens to turn in their gold coins, many did just the opposite—and acquired examples from local banks. Thus, many 1932 eagles were preserved. It is likely that most 1932 $10 pieces were melted after 1933, but it is also likely that well more than a million or two were paid out, apparently mainly for use in international trade. In recent decades most pieces have come from overseas banks.

The 1932 $10 was one of 16 earlier-dated gold coins available in Uncirculated condition for face value (plus mailing charge) from the Treasury Department in the summer of 1932. This is significant as it indicates that these were being held in quantity in storage at this time. Unsold pieces were melted several years later.[27] However, the 1932 was considered to be scarce in the 1940s.

Estimated population (Mint State): *125,000+.* Extremely common at all Mint State levels MS-60 to MS-63, with many known at higher levels as well. Although such grades as MS-64 to MS-66 are scarce in comparison to lower Mint State levels, there are still enough around that any serious buyer can find one relatively quickly. As is also true of the 1926 $10, the typical Mint State 1932 is apt to show multiple large nicks or marks rather than many small ones. Grading interpretations can and do vary widely, and one person's MS-62 may be another's MS-64. The luster on the 1932 is "creamy" or satiny, rather than deeply frosty.

This is the only readily collectible United States gold coin dated in the 1930s. Many pieces have traces of reddish or deep rich golden toning from the copper alloy.

Estimated population (circulated grades): *2,000+.* Mostly AU. Very common, but of little *numismatic* consequence due to the widespread availability of Mint State pieces.

Submissions certified at highest grades (as of March 2017): *PCGS:* MS-63 (21,180), MS-64 (10,569), MS-65 (1,562), MS-66 (130), MS-67 (1). *NGC:* MS-63 (15,637), MS-64 (12,374), MS-65 (2,433), MS-66 (156), MS-67 (9). Another mainstay variety of the third-party grading services.

Characteristics of striking and die notes: Striking varies. Some are lightly struck on the highest curls of Miss Liberty on the obverse and at the eagle's right wing on the reverse, although many others are well struck. Luster is usually very frosty.

Key to collecting: Extremely common.

MARKET NEWS AND COMMENTARY

It is said that in 1932 a sea captain living on a rocky inlet on Penobscot Bay on the coast of Maine liked gold. In that year he obtained from his bank 61 freshly minted $10 gold eagles of the same date and put them in a place for safekeeping. There they remained forgotten for many years, until a descendant came across them, showed them to a leading eastern dealer in art and antiques, who contacted a rare coin dealer. The coins proved not to be rarities, for 1932 is one of the more plentiful issues of the Saint-Gaudens Indian Head design. However, nearly all were particularly nice choice or gem Mint State examples, and when they were auctioned in 1989 there was a wild bidding scramble as collectors competed to acquire them.[28]

In June 1936 in sale 366, U.S. and Foreign Gold Coins, J.C. Morgenthau & Co. offered lot 48: "1932 Uncirculated. Scarce." It sold for $19. Similarly, a "rare" 1932 was offered by B. Max Mehl in March 1938 in the Samuel H. McVitty Collection, lot 412: "1932 Beautiful Uncirculated specimen. Rare." It sold for $41. In February 1944, in the Belden E. Roach Collection, B. Max Mehl offered lot 394: "1932 Uncirculated with full mint luster. Very scarce. Record over $40." It sold for $30. It seems that relatively few were available by that time. This suggests that huge quantities were imported later from foreign holdings.

Stack's in October 1992 offered this coin in the Floyd T. Starr Collection, lot 1278:

> 1932 Choice Brilliant Uncirculated. A pleasing specimen of nearly gem quality. Final truly collectible year of the denomination. Purchased from Bern's Antique Shop (Max A. Berenstein), New York City, on April 4, 1936. Berns was located at

435 Madison Avenue in the late 1930s and early 1940s. He was a regular advertiser in the pages of the *Coin Collectors Journal*, usually offering British Proof sets of 1887, 1937, etc. [Sold for $3,080]

In May 1998 the Dr. Thaine B. Price Collection offered by David W. Akers included lot 70: "1932 MS-66." It sold for $27,000. By that time not many had been certified at that level. This situation changed dramatically, and today more than 4,000 have been certified as MS-65 or finer by PCGS and NGC.

In July 2005 the American Numismatic Rarities sale of the William H. LaBelle Sr. Collection included lot 344: "1932 MS-65 NGC." It sold for $3,105. In December 2005 the American Numismatic Rarities sale of the Old Colony Collection included lot 1885: "1932 MS-65 PCGS." Sold for $4,600.

In March 2006 the American Numismatic Rarities sale of the New York Connoisseur's Collection included lot 1697: "1932 MS-66 PCGS." It sold for $13,800.

In August 2006 the American Numismatic Rarities sale of the Old West and Franklinton Collections included lot 1600: "1932 MS-67 NGC." It sold for $29,800. The same sale also included MS-65 (PCGS) that sold for $6,900.

Regency Auction XIX, December 2016, included lot 479: "1932 MS-65+ PCGS." It sold for $3,347.50.

VF-20	EF-40	AU-50	AU-55	MS-60	MS-62	MS-63	MS-65
$700	$725	$750	$775	$875	$900	$950	$3,000

1933

Circulation-Strike Mintage: 312,500

Notes regarding mintages: It is presumed that nearly all of the 312,500 pieces minted were melted after March 1933 when gold coins were called in. Most were probably taken from Mint or Treasury holdings by government employees.

Or, perhaps most were exchanged for common coins by Mint employees, who then sold them to coin dealers, as was done with 1933-dated double eagles. *Coin World*, November 15, 2004, printed this letter from David E. Tripp, who has done much research in the field: "On March 1, the last (not the first) known authorized release of a 1933 eagle was made, not from the treasurer, but from the cashier's window in the Philadelphia Mint. Thus, the records indicate a total of five 1933 eagles found circulation through official channels."

Among numismatists with a supply was F.C.C. Boyd, the New York City coin dealer and business executive. Abe Kosoff recalled that in the late 1930s there was a steady stream of Treasury employees coming to New York City with scarce and rare gold coins that they had exchanged for common issues—a win-win situation for all concerned. Otherwise the 1933 eagle would be a formidable rarity.

Estimated population (Mint State): *45–60.* Most show bagmarks. Only a handful are in *true* gem Mint State. As the only readily collectible United States gold coin dated 1933, and as an absolute rarity in a very popular series, a Mint State specimen has always been the subject of acclaim when offered for sale.

Estimated population (circulated grades): *0–2.* Exceedingly rare (but irrelevant). As none went into circulation, such coins, if they exist, were either mishandled by numismatists or were used as pocket pieces.

Submissions certified at highest grades (as of March 2017): *PCGS:* MS-63 (2), MS-64 (18), MS-65 (8), MS-66 (1). *NGC:* MS-63 (2), MS-64 (4), MS-65 (4), MS-66 (1).

Key to collecting: The 1933 is one of the most famous rarities. Nearly all are in medium or high Mint State levels and have nice eye appeal.

Market News and Commentary

The 1933 eagle is a landmark rarity, a prize coin in any market season, and is recognized as the highlight of the 1907 to 1933 $10 gold series. The 1907 With Periods and Rolled Edge may be rarer, but other varieties of 1907 exist, whereas there is only one variety for 1933.

"Tracker: An Introduction to Pedigree Research in the Field of Rare American Coins," by Carl W.A. Carlson, was published in 1991 in *The ANA Centennial Anthology*, and informed readers that through the study of auction catalogs, "at least 25 distinct specimens have been isolated thus far; the supplementary listing of 18 specimens may well include others. Research is continuing." Carlson had examined only a small percentage of catalogs published from the late 1930s onward.

The number of different pieces listed did not include various sales by private treaty, nor was his continuing research ever published in a follow-up article. However, the listing was the most comprehensive to appear in print up to that time.

A 2017 survey by Whitman Publishing revealed that of the top seven record auction prices for eagles, four were held by the 1933: Ira and Larry Goldberg, June 2016, MS-66 (PCGS) $881,250; Heritage, April 2015, MS-65 (NGC) $822,500; Stack's, October 2004, Uncirculated (not certified) $718,750; and Heritage, June 1915, MS-65 (PCGS) $585.500.

This early offering by B. Max Mehl in the Samuel H. McVitty Collection sale, March 1938, confirms that the 1933 was considered rare almost at the outset, lot 413: "1933 Last year of issue. Very few got out in circulation. Uncirculated, with full mint luster. Excessively rare. In point of actual rarity should bring almost as much as any $10 gold piece." It sold for $233.

Dozens of later sales down to the present day have showcased these rarities. In nearly all instances extensive narrative (not quoted here) accompanied the offerings, sometimes running many paragraphs).

February 1944, in the Belden E. Roach Collection, B. Max Mehl offered lot 395: "1933 Last year of issue, and goodness only knows when the coinage will be resumed. Never put in general circulation. Uncirculated, frosty mint luster. Extremely rare and valuable. Catalogs at $200." It sold for $175. The statement, "Never put in general circulation," may have come from his friend, F.C.C. Boyd, who handled many pieces. In January 1946 the Numismatic Gallery sale of "The World's Greatest Collection" (F.C.C. Boyd) included lot 727: "1933. Uncirculated. Very rare." It sold for $375.

In May 1950, in his Golden Jubilee sale, B. Max Mehl offered lot 557:

> 1933. The extremely rare eagle of 1933. Last year of issue. The only U.S. gold coin of this date that is available and permissible to be owned by collectors. Uncirculated with full frosty mint surface. Very rare and valuable and steadily advancing in value. In 1944 a specimen brought $235 at auction. In 1946 another specimen offered brought $235 at auction. In 1946 another specimen offered brought $375, and the last specimen offered in my sale of the Dr. Green Collection, in 1949, brought $470. This coin is certainly to become one of our rarest eagles and should exceed the $500 in the near future. Sold for $490]

That happened, and in spades. In its U.S. Gold Coins Sale, May 1986, Stack's offered lot 1545:

> 1933 Brilliant Uncirculated, nearly choice. Since 1946 or roughly the past 40 years, Stack's has sold this rarity at auction 18 times, which is more than half the number offered in that period of time by all the dealers put together. In recent history, we have had the privilege of selling the DiBello specimen in 1970, the Delp specimen in 1972, the Bareford coin in 1978, the Detmer coin in 1983, the 1984 and 1985 Bartle examples, and the Carter specimen in January of this year. Ex Dupont Sale (Sotheby), lot 222, March 1983. [Sold for $77,000]

In March 1988 the Norweb Collection, Part II, sale by Bowers and Merena Galleries included lot 2329: "1933 MS-64. From the Palace Collection of King Farouk, February 1954, lot 224." It sold for $95,700. The February 1992 Ed Trompeter Collection, Part I, by Superior Galleries included lot 209: "1933 MS-62 PCGS." It sold for $65,450.

In May 1998 the Dr. Thaine B. Price Collection, offered by David W. Akers, included lot 71: "1933 Very Choice Uncirculated." It sold for $264,000. The October 2001 sale by Stack's and Sotheby's of the Dallas Bank (Jeff Browning) Collection included lot 486: "1933 Mint State." It sold for $148,500.

Stack's October 2004 69th Anniversary sale included lot 2190: "1933 MS-66, NGC." It sold for $718,750. Stack's Bowers Galleries, in the August 2013 ANA World's Fair of Money sale, included lot 4571: "1933 MS-64, PCGS." It sold for $367,188. Its provenance includes: the Bentley Shores Collection; Heritage's sale of the New York Collection, January 1999, lot 8411; our (Stack's) sale of the Wm. Thomas Michaels Collection, January 2004, lot 3032; and Ira and Larry Goldberg's sale, September 2007, lot 3404.

MS-60	MS-62	MS-63	MS-65
$275,000	$325,000	$400,000	$650,000

APPENDIX

Mintage Totals of $10 Gold Coins

The following figures are cumulative and are from the *Annual Report of the Director of the Mint*, released in 1934, by which time U.S. gold coinage had ceased. Totals for various denominations, 1795–1933, are given.[1]

GRAND TOTALS FOR ALL U.S. GOLD DENOMINATIONS

$1 gold: $19,499,337 face value (19,499,337 coins). If commemoratives are added: $19,874,754 face value (19,874,754 coins).

$2.50 quarter eagles: $50,541,475 face value (20,216,590 coins). If commemoratives are added: $51,067,082.50 face value (20,426,833 coins).

$3 gold: $1,619,376 face value (539,792 coins).

$5 half eagles: $397,684,345 face value (79,536,869 coins).

$10 eagles: $582,619,850 face value (58,261,985 coins).

$20 double eagles: $3,473,202,120 face value (173,660,106 coins).

GOLD $10 COINAGE BY MINTS

Philadelphia Mint: 34,554,932 pieces coined, for a face value of $345,549,320.

Carson City Mint: 299,778 pieces coined, for a face value of $2,997,780.

Denver Mint: 509,280 pieces coined, for a face value of $59,092,800.

New Orleans Mint: 2,361,089 pieces coined, for a face value of $23,610,890.

San Francisco Mint: 14,558,406 pieces coined, for a face value of $145,584,060.

The above figures show that among the larger-denomination gold coins ($5, $10, and $20) fewer $10 coins were made than of the other two values.

CALENDAR YEAR $10 MINTAGE FIGURES

The following are *calendar year* mintages for $10 gold coins from the *Annual Report of the Director of the Mint* from 1795 to 1804, with modern commentary added. It should be noted that these bear only an indirect relationship to the actual quantities minted with those dates, as little attention was paid to using dies in the calendar year they were dated.

1795: 2,795.

1796: 6,034. As 1795-dated $10 coins are much more available today than are those dated 1795, it is presumed that much of the mintage reported for 1796 was from dies dated 1795.

1797: 8,323.

1798: 7,974. As 1798 $10 coins are *much rarer* today than are those dated earlier, it is presumed that at least part of the 1798 mintage figure was from earlier-dated dies.

1799: 17,183.

1800: 25,965.

1801: 29,254.

1802: 15,090. As no $10 coins are known with the 1802 date, it is presumed that the entire mintage was from earlier-dated dies. In 1859 Dr. Montroville W. Dickeson noted in *The American Numismatical Manual:* "And still another instance [Dickeson earlier mentioned the 1799 $2.50 and 1801 $5 in this regard] in which the number of pieces is given, as coined by the Mint, 15,000, and not a solitary piece is to be seen or heard of. This destruction of links in our metallic chain is anything but agreeable."

1803: 8,979.

1804: 9,979. Part of this mintage consisted of 1803-dated coins, as the reverse die used to make all circulation strike 1804-dated $10 coins was used *later* to make certain of the 1803-dated coins.

APPENDIX
B
Selected
Pricing Catalogs

Beginning with the first edition of the *Standard Catalogue of United States Coins*, many guides have been issued that give current market prices for eagles. It is curious that although numismatics became a popular hobby in the late 1850s there were no texts with such information available for many years. Anyone seeking the values of eagles or other federal coins had to consult auction prices and advertisements. Today the *Guide Book of United States Coins* is the most popular annual source for retail market information, among several other titles on the market. Check the current edition for the most accurate and up-to-date prices.

THE *STANDARD CATALOGUE*

The *Standard Catalogue* was prepared under the direction of Wayte Raymond, numismatic manager of the Scott Stamp & Coin Company in New York City. It was produced in 18 editions, the last released in 1958. Scott was located at 23 West 47th Street, but in the summer of 1935 moved to new and enlarged quarters on the third floor of 1 West 47th Street in a building that would later achieve further renown as the location of the New Netherlands Coin Company. Scott had been inactive in the coin market for nearly a quarter of a century, but had been a large factor earlier.

In 1936, Wayte Raymond opened another office under the name of Wayte Raymond, Inc. at 580 Fifth Avenue, New York City; this being at Rockefeller Center, it was a short walk from Scott Stamp & Coin Company. At first it was intended that this facility be comprised of a coin department that, per a news release, would be "specializing exclusively in ancient and foreign coins and numismatic books, under the direction of Stuart Mosher. United States coins, medals, and paper money, as well as new issues of foreign coins, would continue to be handled by Raymond in the coin department he operated in connection with the Scott Stamp & Coin Company." Soon thereafter, Leonard Kusterer was the prime person tending the new office, while working occasionally at the old office with Scott Stamp & Coin. Later, Kusterer went back to spend most of his time with Scott. In any event, both Kusterer and Mosher switched back and forth between Raymond's two locations, as required.

1947: Title page of the 1947 edition of the *Standard Catalogue of United States Coins,* copyright 1946. This book, issued at intervals, had been the main source of market information since the first edition was published in 1934.

1947: Page 104, the first page of the $10 gold eagle section. The two reverse varieties of 1795 with the usual 13 leaves on the branch and the rare style with 9 leaves were not recognized. Very Fine was the default grade used for all early eagles. The publication of mintage figures, which would have emphasized the potential rarity of certain varieties, was relegated to charts in the back of the book that gave the total face value of coins, *not* the number of coins minted. To figure out mintages required mathematical calculations.

1947: Page 105, the second page of the $10 gold eagle section. Very Fine continues as the default grade. The listing of Liberty Head eagles begins. Only a few collectors specialized in Liberty Head coins, and no study of them had ever been done. The rare 1841-O is priced as a common issue. Although the 1841-O is much rarer than the 1841 Philadelphia eagle, there were enough to go around to supply the small number of collectors desiring them.

1947: Page 106, the third page of the $10 gold eagle section. Uncirculated is added to VF as a default grade arbitrarily starting with the year 1855. Absolutely no study had been done regarding rarity, and it was assumed that Uncirculated Carson City eagles were ordinary items. With gold at $35 per ounce, each coin had a melt-down value of $17.00. Of the few specialists in the market, not many collected Proofs. Accordingly, they were relatively inexpensive.

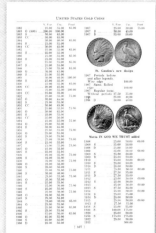

1947: Page 107, the fourth and final page of the $10 gold eagle section. The vast majority of later eagles in VF grade had very modest premium value. The listing for Indian Head eagles gave all circulation strikes a more or less generic value except for the 1920-S, 1930-S, and 1933. It was not recognized that the 1911-D and the San Francisco coins 1908 to 1916 ranged from scarce to rare in Uncirculated grade.

1947: Determining a coin's mintage involved mathematical calculations, as on this chart in the *Standard Catalogue.* Dollar totals were given for each series, such as Carson City $10 coins. To determine the number of coins struck a user had to divide that figure by 10.

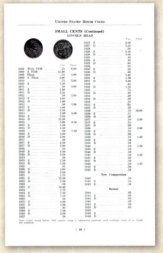

1947: The 1947 *Standard Catalogue* listing for Lincoln cents, shown here to reflect prices of the most popular American series.

1950: In *The Coin Collector's Journal* in 1950 Wayte Raymond gave the market values for Proof gold coins, including eagles. This used values from the *Standard Catalogue.*

Years later, Mosher became editor of *The Numismatist* and, later, curator of the Mint Collection. In 1946 he was the main compiler of information for the new *Guide Book of United States Coins*, published by the Whitman Publishing division of Western Printing & Lithographing Company, in Racine, Wisconsin, under the direction of R.S. Yeoman (pen name of Richard S. Yeo).

Often, Wayte and his wife Olga would journey out to their second home in Montauk at the eastern tip of Long Island. There, overlooking the Atlantic Ocean, Raymond found rest and relaxation, often curling up with a few good coin books, often in an outbuilding called the "Coin House." Through a large glass window fronting the sea their dock could be seen in the foreground and passing ships in the distance. In the 1920s Raymond bought much property in Montauk, later selling it off at a nice profit. His home was on the "best" remaining two acres.

Late in 1943 the coin department of Scott Stamp & Coin Company was turned over to the New Netherlands Coin Company, thus ending Raymond's management of it. Raymond assumed the publication of the *Standard Catalogue.* Raymond's office toward the end of his career was at 654 Madison Avenue. In 1950 he hired the young Walter Breen to do research in the National Archives (as noted in chapter 5). Later he and his wife made Montauk their permanent residence. On September 23, 1956, Raymond died at Roosevelt Hospital in New York City following a long illness. Raymond's widow Olga sold John J. Ford Jr. whatever he wanted of his rare coins and paper money, and the balance was consigned to the New Netherlands Coin Company. Ford also acquired all publication rights to Raymond's books.

Ford published the eighteenth and final edition of the *Catalogue* in 1958. He had grand ideas for completely revising the book to include additional information for specialists, but this never happened. By that time the *Guide Book,* also known as the "Red Book," had vastly eclipsed the *Standard Catalogue* in volume and market use.

The *Standard Catalogue* was arranged in a complex manner. To find information about eagles or any other specialty, a user had to look in several different places. Selections from several editions are given here.

Scott's Complete Catalogue and Encyclopedia of U.S. Coins

After the expiration of the *Standard Catalogue* John J. Ford Jr. tapped one of his two protégés, Donald A. Taxay, to work with his other protégé, Walter Breen, to create a new book of coin prices to appeal to specialists. It was to have much technical and historical information not available in the Whitman *Guide Book.* Ford enlisted the Scott Publishing Company, prominent issuer of guides to stamps, to produce and issue it. A number of prominent numismatists were enlisted and asked to give testimonials based on the advance publicity. There were high expectations when it was announced; however, the finished book fell short of expectations, embarrassing some who had acclaimed the book without seeing the printed version.

Circulation-strike coins were listed in one section, Proofs in another. Photographs were interspersed among pages and had their own page numbering sys-

1971: Cover of the first edition of *Scott's Complete Catalogue and Encyclopedia of U.S. Coins.*

tem. The illustrations were of low quality. On the positive side, it broke new ground for omitting prices for dates and mintmarks for which no Uncirculated coins had been confirmed. This is the first time such information was available in a reference book.

The book laid an egg in the marketplace. In 1976 a second edition was published, but it was not widely distributed.

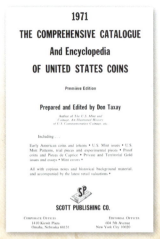

1971: Title page of the new Scott book.

1971: Page 146 of the Scott book listing circulation-strike eagles from 1866 to 1880-CC. Rarity ratings such as R7 for 1875 are on the Sheldon Scale. Helpful comments concerning Uncirculated coins are given—a very useful innovation at the time!

1971: Page 148 with information on eagles from 1901-S to 1933. The With Periods issues of 1907 are referred to as being under *Mint Patterns,* but in that section they were inadvertently omitted.

1971: Page 271 in the back of the book had information about Proof eagles (called Cabinet Coins).

1971: Illustrations were on pages numbered separately and inserted among regular numbers starting after page 137. Shown is illustration page 43, the second of two pages illustrating eagles. The illustrations had numbers but no key to what the numbers meant.

A GUIDE BOOK OF UNITED STATES COINS

Following the success of the Whitman *Handbook of United States Coins*, a guide to the prices paid by dealers, R.S. Yeoman decided to launch a book with retail listings. He enlisted Stuart Mosher to build on the framework of the *Handbook* to create an expanded guide with current market values.

Years before, in 1915, Yeoman was a newsboy for the *Daily Wisconsin* in Milwaukee. At the age of 11 he sold his first paper, receiving an Indian Head cent in payment. He took it home, cut a cent-size hole in a piece of cardboard, and may have inadvertently created the first coin holder! He cherished this, and years later it was still displayed on his desk. In 1932 he joined the staff of Whitman Publishing Company, a subsidiary of Western Printing & Lithographing Company in Racine. In 1934 J.K. Post of Neenah, Wisconsin, conceived the "penny board," a cardboard sheet with openings for coins. Western produced these on contract for Post for two years. Meanwhile, employees enjoyed filling in the spaces—a nice hobby not much different from doing a crossword puzzle. Seeing a wider opportunity Whitman purchased the rights from Post, and Yeoman expanded the line to include additional denominations.

In 1940 the board or sheet format was changed to blue folders, all under his aegis. The Whitman folders plus the notebook-style albums sold by Wayte Raymond changed the face of numismatics. Collecting by dates and mintmarks became standard, and scarce varieties that might be found in pocket change were eagerly sought. A new generation of collectors was formed by those who filled in Whitman folders.

In 1941 Yeoman supervised the production of the *Handbook of United States Coins With Premium List*, which gave the prices dealers would pay. The first and second editions were published in 1942. Next came *A Guide Book of United States Coins* in 1946. Stuart Mosher had been signed a few years earlier to develop a guide to retail prices on the same matrix as the *Handbook*. Paper rationing during World War II postponed the launch. In the meantime, leading numismatists contributed to the pricing. The red-covered volume was finally released in November 1946. Realizing that in one month a 1946 cover date would make the book appear to be out of date, Yeoman used the year 1947 on the cover. From its inception through 1965 sales totaled 6,758,482 copies, earning the "Red Book" (as it came to be known) fifth place in non-fiction nationwide book sales.[1]

In autumn 1959 Kenneth E. Bressett, a long-time collector and numismatic scholar from Keene, New Hampshire, joined the Whitman staff. He had been a consultant since 1957. From 1964 to 1968 he edited *The Whitman Numismatic Journal*, a research-oriented magazine that was highly esteemed. Bressett remained in Racine for 21 years, after which he worked with Arthur M. Kagin and the Kagin Numismatic Investment Company for two years. He then moved to the American Numismatic Association in Colorado Springs, where he directed the ANA Certification Service and their education programs. In time he retired from everyday office work, but remained active in the ANA, running for elected office and eventually becoming president. By that time he had been editor of the *Guide Book* for many years, and since then he has continued to write and serve as senior editor for many of Whitman's numismatic publications.

Throughout his career Bressett has worked as an author, editor, and publisher of books and products for coin collectors. He has also taught the subject to hundreds

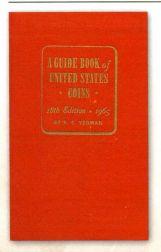
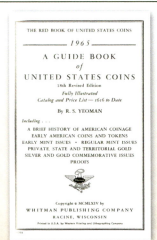

1964: Pages from the 1965 edition of *A Guide Book of United States Coins* published in 1964. The section on eagles reflected the state of knowledge at the time: it was not known what dates and mintmarks existed in Mint State. The availability of certain issues was not appreciated until into the second decade of the 21st century.

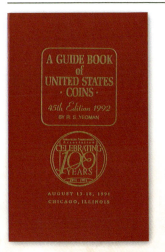

1991: Pages from the 1992 edition of *A Guide Book of United States Coins* published in 1991.

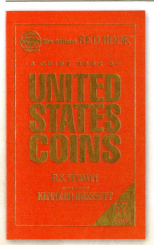

2003: Pages from the 2004 edition of *A Guide Book of United States Coins* published in 2003.

of students through courses at Colorado College and other places. Bressett was appointed to the U.S. Assay Commission in 1966 by President Lyndon Johnson, and in 1996 was made a member of the Citizens Commemorative Coin Advisory Committee. He has received numerous awards in recognition of his service and dedication to numismatics, including election to the National Numismatic Hall of Fame, the American Numismatic Society's Distinguished Service Award, the American Numismatic Association Medal of Merit, and the ANA Farran Zerbe Memorial award.

Whitman Publishing, part of Western Publishing, was headquartered in Racine, Wisconsin, for many years, as noted. Its parent company, Western Printing & Lithographing, went through several changes of ownership and relocating of headquarters starting in 1979. Eventually the firm's publishing group for non-children's books—which included Whitman Coin Products—was sold to St. Martin's Press in New York City. The *Guide Book* continued to be published throughout the years, with Kenneth Bressett coordinating editorial work for this and other publications from his home in Colorado Springs.

In 2003 St. Martin's Press sold Whitman Coin Products to H.E. Harris & Co., a manufacturer of coin albums, folders, and accessories in addition to being a noted philatelic dealership. The combined company's headquarters was moved to Atlanta, Georgia, and it took the overarching name of Whitman Publishing. Since that time Whitman has continued to publish an ever-growing line of numismatic books and related items. President Mary Burleson, publisher Dennis Tucker, editorial director Diana Plattner, and numismatic director Q. David Bowers were among the team who shepherded a modern renaissance in numismatic literature with the creation of the "100 Greatest" line of books, the Bowers Series, numerous paper-money and world-coin references, *Search & Save* book albums, and a variety of other books ranging from 96-page monographs to 900-page encyclopedias. Whitman also launched many new folders, albums, maps, boxes, cases, and other storage and display products for collectors. In the line of price guides, among the most successful is the greatly expanded version of the Red Book affectionately nicknamed Mega Red, the annual edition of which weighs in at more than 1,500 pages.

APPENDIX
C
Eagles in the National Numismatic Collection

In addition to coins, the Mint Cabinet housed various mineral specimens and small items made of precious metals. In 1842 the Mint published *A Manual of Gold and Silver Coins of All Nations, Struck Within the Past Century*, compiled by Eckfeldt and DuBois. This was not a numismatic work, but illustrated coins of precious metals and described their content. In 1851 a book by the same authors, *New Varieties of Gold and Silver Coins, Counterfeit Coins, and Bullion; With Mint Values*, was published by George P. Putnam.

James Ross Snowden, who was appointed as Mint director in 1853 and served until the change of administration in 1861, had a keen interest in numismatics. Under his aegis many restrikes, unusual die combinations, and other numismatic delicacies were made, mostly in secret and for the private profit of Mint officials, though many varieties were added to the Mint Cabinet. In 1860 a book he prepared in combination with other officials, *A Description of Ancient and Modern Coins, in the Cabinet Collection at the Mint of the United States*, was published by J.B. Lippincott. Snowden had a keen interest in the tokens and medals of George Washington and expanded the Mint Cabinet

The Mint Collection, earlier referred to as the Mint Cabinet, at the turn of the 20th century.

from a handful of pieces to many dozens. On February 22, 1860, the Washington Cabinet display was opened as part of the Mint Cabinet and drew wide interest. In 1861 his well-illustrated study was published, *Medallic Memorials of Washington in the Mint of the United States*. This became a standard reference.

In ensuing years under various directors and curators the Mint Cabinet, later called the Mint Collection, expanded many times over. In the early 1920s there were security problems at the Denver and San Francisco mints, so the current administration decided to concentrate on the main business at hand—designing and making dies and striking coins—as accommodating large numbers of visitors was considered to be a nuisance. An arrangement was made in 1923 to transfer the Mint Collection on loan to the Smithsonian. The Mint coins remain there today. Selections were put on view with the Smithsonian's own collection in the "Castle" building on the Mall.

After 1923 there was an undistinguished period of 33 years. Coins and other items were in view in glass-fronted cases, but there was no continuing interface with the numismatic community. That ended with the arrival of Vladimir and Elvira Clain-Stefanelli in 1956. The stewardship of this husband and wife team marked a Golden Age for the National Numismatic Collection with strong outreach to the numismatic community and active promotion of numismatic scholarship. The fabulous Josiah K. Lilly Collection of American (and foreign) gold was accessed in 1968. This had been formed by Lilly, a pharmaceutical executive, working exclusively with Stack's in New York City. After his passing the estate gifted it to the Smithsonian under a special act of Congress.

With regard to $10 gold coins, the Smithsonian had relatively little of importance until the arrival in 1923 of the Mint Collection coins. These included eagles of 1795 to 1804, plus a collection by date (not mintmark) from 1838 onward. For many early years and for all years after the late 1850s these were Proofs as part of full sets. The Lilly Collection furnished nearly all of the branch-mint coins and also filled in some earlier gaps.

**The opening ceremony at the Value of Money
exhibit at the Smithsonian Institution, July 15, 2015.**

This listing, compiled by Jeff Garrett, lists $10 gold coins from 1795 to 1933 in the National Numismatic Collection, the finest example of each. In many instances there are duplicates. Certain of these are on view at the Value of Money exhibit on the main floor of the Museum of American History. Scholars and others can view further coins by arrangement with the curator, Dr. Ellen Feingold, and her staff. The Smithsonian collection and staff have contributed much to numismatic research over the years and continue to do so.

Capped Bust to Right, Small Eagle Reverse, 1795–1797

1795, 13 Leaves on branch, MS-62; 1796, MS-61; 1797, Small Eagle, MS-60.

Capped Bust to Right, Large Eagle Reverse, 1797–1804

1797, Large Eagle, MS-63; 1798, 8 Over 7, 9x4 Stars, MS-62; 1798, 8 Over 7, 7x6 Stars, MS-63; 1799, Large obverse stars, AU-58; 1799, Small obverse stars, MS-64.

1800, MS-61; 1801, AU-58; 1801, MS-61; 1803, Small stars on reverse, MS-65; 1804, Crosslet 4, MS-63.

Liberty Head, Without Motto, 1838–1866

1838, Proof-63; 1839, Type 1838, Proof-66; 1839, Type 1840, AU-55.

1840, Proof-64; 1841, AU-58; 1841, Proof-65; 1841-O, EF-45; 1842, Large Date, AU-50; 1842, Proof-65; 1842-O, AU-58; 1843, Proof-65; 1843-O, AU-55; 1844, Proof-64; 1844-O, AU-58; 1845, Proof-66; 1845-O, Repunched date, AU-50; 1846, Proof-64; 1846-O, EF-40; 1847, AU-55; 1847, Proof-65; 1847-O, MS-63; 1848, Proof-64; 1848-O, AU-58; 1849, AU-58; 1849-O, EF-45.

1850, Large Date, AU-58; 1850-O, AU-50; 1851, AU-58; 1851-O, AU-55; 1852, AU-58; 1852-O, AU-58; 1853, MS-61; 1853-O, AU-58; 1854, MS-61; 1854-O, MS-61; 1854-S, AU-55; 1855, MS-62; 1855-O, MS-62; 1855-S, AU-55; 1856, AU-50; 1856-O, AU-50; 1856-S, AU-58; 1857, MS-63; 1857-O, AU-50; 1857-S, EF-40; 1858, Proof-64; 1858-O, AU-50; 1858-S, EF-45; 1859, Proof-64; 1859-O, AU-50; 1859-S, EF-45.

1860, Proof-64; 1860-S, EF-45; 1861, Proof-63; 1861-S, EF-45; 1862, Proof-64; 1862-S, EF-45; 1863, Proof-64; 1863-S, EF-45; 1864, Proof-64; 1864-S, EF-45; 1865, Proof-64; 1865-S, Over inverted date, EF-45; 1866-S, Without Motto, EF-40.

Liberty Head, With Motto, 1866–1907

1866, With Motto, Proof-63; 1866-S, With Motto, EF-45; 1867, Proof-65; 1867-S, EF-45; 1868, Proof-64; 1868-S, VF-30; 1869, Proof-64; 1869-S, AU-50.

1870, Proof-64; 1870-CC, EF-40; 1870-S, EF-45; 1871, EF-45; 1871, Proof-64; 1871-CC, EF-45; 1871-S, VF-30; 1872, Proof-65; 1872-CC, AU-50; 1872-S, EF-40; 1873, Close 3, Proof-64; 1873-CC, EF-45; 1873-S, EF-45; 1874, Proof-64; 1874-CC,

EF-45; 1874-S, EF-45; 1875, Proof-63; 1875-CC, VF-30; 1876, Proof-64; 1876-CC, EF-40; 1876-S, AU-50; 1877, Proof-64; 1877-CC, EF-45; 1877-S, AU-50; 1878, Proof-64; 1878-CC, EF-40; 1878-S, AU-50; 1879, Proof-64; 1879-CC, VF-25; 1879-O, AU-55; 1879-S, MS-61.

1880, Proof-63; 1880-CC, EF-45; 1880-O, MS-62; 1880-S, AU-58; 1881, Proof-64; 1881-CC, AU-50; 1881-O, AU-58; 1881-S, MS-61; 1882, Proof-64; 1882-CC, EF-45; 1882-O, EF-40; 1882-S, MS-61; 1883, Proof-63; 1883-CC, AU-55; 1883-O, EF-40; 1883-S, EF-40; 1884, Proof-64; 1884-CC, EF-40; 1884-S, MS-60; 1885, Proof-64; 1885-S, EF-45; 1886, Proof-64; 1886-S, AU-58; 1886-S, EF-45; 1887, Proof-64; 1887-S, EF-45; 1888, Proof-63; 1888, Proof-64; 1888-O, AU-55; 1888-S, AU-55; 1889, Proof-64; 1889-S, AU-55.

1890, Proof-64; 1890-CC, AU-50 1891, Proof-64; 1891, Proof-64; 1891-CC, MS-60; 1892, AU-50; 1892, Proof-64; 1892-CC, AU-58; 1892-O, AU-50; 1892-S, AU-55; 1893, Proof-64; 1893-CC, AU-50; 1893-O, MS-61; 1893-S, EF-45; 1893-S, VF-30; 1894, MS Circulated; 1894, Proof-64; 1894-O, MS-62; 1894-S, MS-61; 1895, Proof-64; 1895-O, MS-61; 1895-S, EF-45; 1896, Proof-64; 1896-S, AU-58; 1897, Proof-64; 1897-O, MS-62; 1897-S, MS-67; 1898, Proof-64; 1898-S, MS-61; 1899, Proof-64; 1899-O, MS-63; 1899-S, MS-62.

1900, Proof-65; 1900-S, MS-63; 1901, Proof-64; 1901-O, AU-58; 1901-S, MS-66; 1902, Proof-64; 1902-S, MS-64; 1903, Proof-64; 1903-O, MS-62; 1903-S, AU-58; 1904, Proof-64; 1904-O, MS-60; 1905, Proof-64; 1905-S, MS-63; 1906, Proof-64; 1906-D, MS-63; 1906-S, AU-58; 1907, Liberty Head, Proof-64; 1907-D, Liberty Head, MS-62; 1907-S, Liberty Head, MS-60.

Indian Head, Without Motto, 1907–1908
1907, Wire Edge, MS-66; 1907, Rolled Edge, MS-67.

1908, MS-67.

Indian Head, With Motto, 1908–1933
1908, Sand Blast, Proof-66; 1908-D, MS-60; 1908-S, AU-50 (Cleaned); 1908-S, EF-45; 1909, Satin Finish, Proof-65; 1909-D, AU; 1909-S, AU-58.

1910, Satin Finish, Proof-66; 1910-D, MS-62; 1910-S, MS-60; 1911, Sand Blast, Proof-67; 1911-D, MS-62; 1911-S, EF-45; 1912, Sand Blast, Proof-66; 1912-S, EF-45; 1913, Sand Blast, Proof-65; 1913-S, AU-58; 1914, Sand Blast, Proof-66; 1914-D, AU-58; 1914-S, AU-58; 1915, Sand Blast, Proof-65; 1915-S, MS-64; 1916-S, MS-67.

1920-S, MS-66; 1926, MS-65.

1930-S, MS-67; 1932, MS-65; 1933, MS-65.

APPENDIX
D
$10 Gold Coins from Treasure Finds

Buried treasure! Pirate gold! Treasures have always been a fascinating part of American lore and history. Over a long period of time thousands of ships have been lost in American waters (more than 6,000 on the Great Lakes alone) and many more in the oceans. While the typical vessel carried iron ore, passengers, coal, or even ice, nearly all had some money aboard. Some, such as those related to the California Gold Rush, carried substantial amounts of gold coins and ingots. The SS *Central America*, lost at sea in 1857, carried the greatest Gold Rush fortune to the bottom of the sea.

Starting in the 1950s the author kept a file on treasures. This information has been used in several books, most recently, *Lost and Found Coin Hoards and Treasures: Illustrated Stories of the Greatest American Troves and Their Discoveries*, published by Whitman. Most treasures of gold coins consisted mainly of double eagles, the largest circulating denominations. Many also had from a few to a large number of eagles. Selected finds are given here.

GOLD HIDDEN IN A BALTIMORE CELLAR

On August 31, 1934, two young boys, described as poor and underprivileged, were playing in the cellar of a house at 132 South Eden Street, East Baltimore, owned by sisters Elizabeth H. French and Mary P.B. Findlay and rented by the mother of one of the boys.[1] Henry Grob, age 15, and his companion, Theodore Sines, 14, came upon a cache of gold coins. After a brief discussion as to what should be done, the lads took the treasure to the local police station and turned the find over to the authorities. Later that evening, the boys said that they had "held out" some of the pieces, and these were subsequently added to the first group. One *Baltimore Evening Sun* article put the amount as 3,556 coins with $11,424 face value. All were dated before 1857. Meanwhile, at the police station some of the patrolmen "tried their hand at cleaning them with coal oil [kerosene] and vinegar," a procedure definitely not recommended by numismatists!

How had the coins been hidden and by whom? One story had it that they were secreted by a sea captain of a ship in the coffee trade between Brazil and the port of Baltimore, who lived in the house with his two sisters. Another story suggested that "the coins may have been buried in April 1861 by a resident who was frightened by the passing of federal [*sic*] troops through the city; the house is located close to the depot at which the troops landed in Baltimore."[2] Later research revealed that the coins were hidden by a Confederate sympathizer who lived in the city and was a member of the Knights of the Golden Circle.

Multiple claims were filed for ownership. For the rest of 1934 and into May 1935 the matter was in the courts. Meanwhile, although the gold coins were to have remained undisturbed pending the outcome, the family of one of the finders sold $185 worth for face value. Judge Eugene O'Dunne of the Second Circuit Court of Baltimore eventually awarded proceeds from the entire find to the two teenagers, negating an offer by the two ladies who owned the house to give the boys 50 percent. During the litigation, all parties agreed that the coins could be sold at auction.[3] The sale was held on May 2, 1935, at the Lord Baltimore Hotel downtown, with Perry W. Fuller serving as auctioneer. About 100 attended, including a few out-of-town dealers and many local curiosity seekers. The major buyer was Thomas L. Elder, who came from New York City. Grouped into 438 lots and casually described (most pieces were simply called "very fine") in a printed catalog, the hoard realized $19,746.15.

Leonard Augsburger, author of *Treasure in the Cellar*, a book about the find, created an inventory that included these $10 gold coins:

> 1839 (2); 1840; 1841; 1842 (2); 1842-O; 1844-O; 1845; 1845-O; 1846-O; 1847 (13); 1847-O (7); 1848 (5); 1848-O (2); 1849 (10); 1849-O; 1850 (6); 1850-O (2); 1851; 1851-O (3); 1852; 1853 (4); 1853-O (3); 1854; 1854-S; 1855 (7); 1856 (3).

THE BAIN FARM HOARD

In 1947 Jack Glasgow, a tenant farmer on acreage owned by A.I. Bain 12 miles south of Keran, Texas, and his employees, Clifton Glasgow, Henry Crook, Fred Burton, Wilmer Ely, and Fred Rhynes, plowed up a cache of 166 gold coins with a face value of $1,775. Included were these eagles:

> 1842; 1843 (2); 1847 (3); 1847-O (4); 1849 (2); 1850; 1852; 1852-O; 1853; 1854-S; 1856; 1857.

THE MERKERS KAISERODA MINE TREASURE

During World War II, under orders from Nazi leadership (primarily Hermann Goering and Heinrich Himmler), conquered people and nations were systematically stripped of art, gold, and other valuables.[4] On April 4, 1945, the Third Army, 90th Infantry Division, took the village of Merkers a few miles inside the border in Thuringia. On the morning of the sixth, Pfc. Clyde Harmon and Pfc. Anthony Kline, U.S. military policemen, stopped two women on a road outside Merkers. Since both were French displaced persons and one was pregnant, the MPs decided rather than to arrest them to escort them back into the town. On the way, as they passed the entrance to the Kaiseroda salt mine in Merkers, the women talked about gold that the Germans had stored in the mine—so much gold, they said, that unloading it had taken local civilians and displaced persons who were used as labor seventy-two hours.[5]

When American soldiers entered the Kaiseroda mine they discovered a room 75-feet wide and 150-feet deep. The floor was covered more than 7,000 numbered bags, and each bag contained gold bars or gold coins. The gold amounted to nearly 250 tons. Paper money was in bales and amounted to 98 million French francs and 2.7 billion Reichsmarks. Suitcases contained jewelry, dental fillings, and other valuables sto-

Gold in the Kaiseroda mine in Merkers, Germany.

len from individuals. In other mine passages were 400 tons of fine art works stolen from museums and individuals throughout Europe.

Analysis of the inventory committee records and reports by Roger W. Burdette revealed that U.S. gold coins were contained in 738 bags. This amounted to 1,022,919.67 Troy ounces of fine gold, or 1,136,577.41 Troy ounces of standard 0.900 fine coin gold, representing approximately $21,145,630 at face value. Further analysis broke down the U.S. gold coins by denomination and showed that most of the coins were double eagles. No determination of dates or mintmarks was possible since this information was not recorded during inventory.

The quantities of U.S. gold coins in the hoard: $1: 1,000; $2.50: 12,714; $5: 136,141; $10: 301,534; $20: 870,840.

Based upon my experience with gold coins available in Continental Europe after World War II the above figures percentage wise are not representative of what was in hoards across the continent. There were *many more* double eagles than eagles.

It is likely that most of the gold coins in the Kaiseroda mine hoard were retained in their original condition following restitution. All of the post-war governments were in need of cash, and selling a double eagle for $48 on the open market was a much better deal than melting it and getting only $33.86 for the same gold. There is no way to tell how much of the present stock of U.S. gold coins came from the Merkers treasure and how much came from bank vaults in neutral Switzerland, or South and Central America.

This stolen gold was taken from poor souls and unfortunate institutions in France, Poland, Belgium, Holland, and other countries overrun by the Nazis beginning in 1939.

A SOCIETY LADY'S SECURITY

In early 1933 the U.S. government placed stringent restrictions on the ownership of American gold coins.[6] Hearing rumors to this effect, a prominent eastern lady, possibly with the cooperation of her mother, decided to acquire and set aside some pieces for the comfort and financial security they seemed to represent in that troubled economic time.

Years later her heirs enlisted numismatist David Enders Tripp to assist with their sale into the numismatic market. The group was found to contain the following pieces, a valuable informational find for scholars, as it shows typical gold coins that could be acquired at banks in early 1933. The earlier-dated coins were for the most part worn, while some of the later pieces were gem Mint State. The following eagles were included:

$10: 1840; 1842-O (2); 1844-O; 1845-O; 1847 (3); 1847-O (3); 1849 (4); 1850 (3); 1852 (2); 1853; 1854-S (2); 1856-S; 1857; 1879-S (2); 1880 (7); 1880-S (4); 1881 (9); 1881-S (7); 1882 (11); 1882-S; 1883; 1884-S; 1885 (2); 1885-S; 1886-S (2); 1887-S (6); 1889-S (2); 1890; 1892 (3); 1893 (3); 1893-S; 1894 (2); 1894-O; 1894-S; 1895-O; 1896-S; 1897 (12); 1897-S (5); 1898 (3); 1898-S; 1899 (6); 1899-S (5); 1900-S; 1901 (11); 1901-S (10); 1902; 1902-S (2); 1903; 1903-S (2); 1905 (2); 1905-S (5); 1906; 1906-D (15); 1906-S (3); 1907 Liberty Head (4); 1907-D Liberty Head; 1907-S Liberty Head (2); 1907 Indian Head (29); 1908 (7); 1908-D (2); 1909 (2); 1909-D; 1909-S (2); 1910 (2); 1910-D (3); 1910-S (5); 1911 (5); 1912 (6); 1912-S (2); 1913 (4); 1914; 1914-D (2); 1915 (4).

THE SS NEW YORK

Constructed in 1837 at the yard of William H. Brown on the East River in New York City, the SS *New York* was a side-wheel steamship with auxiliary sails, a class of vessel generally known as a steam packet. An October 13, 1843, registration document noted that the ship had two auxiliary masts and displaced 365 tons. She was 160.5-feet long, had a 22.5-foot beam, and a 10.5-foot depth of hold. There was one main deck with a cabin section in the center, with decks fore and aft. The fore deck had a canvas cover. Above the aft or promenade deck was an open-air deck, essentially a platform, where passengers could relax if the passage was smooth, under the sun and in the open air, cooled by the breeze of forward motion.

The *New York* made her first voyage on June 15, 1837, going into service carrying passengers, cargo, and mail on the coastwise route connecting New York City to Charleston, South Carolina. In January 1846 the *New York* was sold to Captain John D. Phillips and went to the Gulf of Mexico. By that time the maritime business in the Gulf was very competitive. On April 29, 1846, early in the War with Mexico, the venerable ship was chartered by the government to transport troops to the new U.S. Army depot at Brazos St. Jago, the lease payment totaling $2,196. From then through the summer she was chartered several more times, resulting in protests from travelers and shippers of merchandise who resented the interruption of regular service.[7]

The SS *New York*.

On Saturday, September 5, 1846, the SS *New York* departed Galveston at four-thirty in the afternoon carrying 30 passengers and a crew of 23. At the helm was the owner of the ship, Captain John D. Phillips, a seasoned commander. The load was far short of capacity, foretelling a pleasant voyage with more than usual attention from the crew. Fare was $15 for cabin passage, less for steerage. Money in the estimated amount of $30,000 to $40,000 was aboard, although no authoritative figures were ever published. This consisted of gold and silver coins and, it is likely, many bank notes. We know that among the cargo was a woodworking machine. Probably there were barrels and crates of other goods as well, normal for the route, although one later account stated the hold was empty.

The voyage was expected to take two days, including overnight, with arrival on Sunday evening. The exact time of reaching New Orleans often varied, as the schedules of pilot ships to guide vessels to port were sometimes erratic, and the weather could be a factor. Some trips took three days, including two overnights. All was set for a routine transit. The weather had been foggy and rainy for nearly three weeks, and at departure time a light haze covered the harbor. The ship steamed out of Galveston Bay and headed to the open sea, with no indication of anything unusual. This changed, the seas became rough and the ship cast anchor. There was a lull the next morning, and on Sunday at 10 o'clock the anchor was weighed and the ship continued its course. Onward to New Orleans, never mind the slight delay. Throughout Sunday the storm worsened, and the ship was tossed about even more violently. The passengers huddled and tried to cheer each other. Surely the winds would subside and the sea would become quiet. Then on to New Orleans, as planned. This did not happen. The worst was yet to come. At about midnight or within an hour afterward, a cable snapped, and part of the structure gave way on the starboard side. Water rushed into the hold, the boiler fires were extinguished, and for the first time, passengers seriously feared for their lives.

Into the night men manned pumps, but to no avail. Early the next morning the ship sank, while some deck parts and the wheelhouse floated away. Survivors included 19 passengers and 18 crew, including the captain. Lost were 11 passengers and 8 crewmembers.

One of the survivors, John Todd, published a detailed account of the tragedy. In time the ship was forgotten. Years later, Avery Munson of New Iberia, Louisiana, who loved scuba diving and exploring the sea, wondered whether there might be any historical accounts of lost ships with treasure aboard in the Gulf of Mexico within each reach of this port. For several years he combed old newspapers and other accounts. Lightning struck! He found the telltale comment in the *Daily Picayune* of September 10, 1846. With this as a beginning, he enlisted several friends, forming a group of four styling themselves as the Gentlemen of Fortune, including Craig DeRouen and the husband and wife team of Gary and Renée Hebert.

The team studied newspaper articles, survivor accounts, charts, and underwater data. The Gulf of Mexico is a center for offshore oil rigs, and much mapping had been done. They consulted shrimp fishermen and others familiar with the Gulf to seek clues and ideas. The group took measurements and made estimates, and in time success was theirs. Finally, in early 2005 they had their "eureka!" moment: The ship's bell was found. In due course their ownership was successfully registered in a federal court, no other claims arose, and recovery commenced. In time my book, *The Treasure Ship SS New York: Her*

Life and Loss, 1837–1847, was published and drew nice reviews. The most important coins were auctioned by Stack's. The following eagles were included with grades given by NGC:

> 1842, Small Date: MS-61; 1842, Large Date: AU-58, MS-60; 1842-O, Large Date: AU-55, AU-58 (2); 1843: AU-58, MS-60; 1843-O: AU details, AU-58; 1844-O: AU details, MS-61 (3), MS-62, MS-63 (2); 1845-O: AU details, AU-58 (3), Unc. details, MS-61 (3), MS-62.

GOLD RUSH TREASURE: SS CENTRAL AMERICA

In the annals of undersea treasure hunting for U.S. coins the saga of the SS *Central America* is an adventure to end all adventures. Its final chapters are still being written in our own time. The author's book, *A California Gold Rush history: Featuring the treasure from the* SS *Central America: a source book for the Gold Rush historian and numismatist,* is a definitive study of the ship and the treasure and is recommended to anyone interested in the adventure and saga. Accordingly, only a synopsis is given here.

In San Francisco on August 20, 1857, more than 400 people who had booked passage on the Pacific Mail Steamship Line's SS *Sonora* hastened aboard the vessel. The destination was Panama to be followed by a train trip across the Isthmus, then a connecting passage on another ship at Aspinwall (today known as Colón) for the Atlantic run. Accompanying the passengers were more than 100 bags of mail and a cargo of gold registered at more than $1.2 million consigned by nine major shippers including Wells, Fargo & Co. The ultimate destination of the travelers and cargo was New York City. In addition to more than $1.2 million in gold listed on the manifest, many passengers had their own treasures variously estimated to average from about $1,000 to $5,000 per person, and when added to the commercial cargo, the total came to more than $2 million. The gold was in various forms including rectangular ingots and bars

Final moments of the SS *Central America*.

from various assayers, recently struck $20 pieces from the San Francisco Mint, and an assortment of other coins ranging from British sovereigns to American issues struck in California by assayers and private minters. Some of the larger coins were $50 "slugs" of octagonal shape made by the U.S. Assay Office of Gold. The coins and bullion were destined for New York clearing houses and bankers, the New York Sub-Treasury, and the Philadelphia Mint, with a lesser value to be transshipped to the London market.

With a brief stop at Manzanillo on the Mexican coast, and an overnight respite at Acapulco to take on coal for the boilers, the *Sonora* arrived at the Gulf of Panama on the evening of September 2. The trip had been uneventful, and all aboard had seemingly savored the experience. Early the next morning the passengers were transferred to shore by small boats, after which they would ride the Panama Railroad across nearly 48 miles of land. This took from three and a quarter hours for those who departed early, to nearly six hours for the last in line. Several transits were required to accommodate all of the travelers and cargo from the *Sonora*.

After arrival on the Atlantic side of the Isthmus at Aspinwall the travelers boarded at several hotels. Ahead was the final leg of the trip to New York City, about 2,000 miles, taking less time than the Pacific part of the journey. On Thursday afternoon, September 3, 1857, passengers continuing from California plus others picked up at Panama were greeted at the dock at Aspinwall by Captain William Lewis Herndon as they boarded the SS Central America for the passage to New York.

Once comfortably settled in their cabins and berths, the nearly 600 passengers and crew members aboard the *Central America* looked forward to their voyage, traveling at slightly more than 12 miles per hour, with a scheduled stop in Havana.

The 278-foot, 2,141-ton SS *Central America*, owned by the U.S. Mail Steamship Company and recently renamed from the SS *George Law*, was a veteran on the Atlantic coast-wise route, having traversed it 43 times since her first departure from New York City to Aspinwall on October 20, 1853, and having carried one-third or more of the total value of California gold shipped to Eastern banks and government agencies during that period.[8] With many amenities for passenger comfort, entertainment, and food, and with a light breeze caused by the ship's forward motion, the trip in mild September weather was surely considered by many passengers to be the height of luxury in a tropical cruise. Many on board had taken this route before as had their families. Indeed, travel from California to Panama and onward to New York City had become routine. The "adventurous" days were over. There seemed to be no real need for life preservers or safety drills.

On Monday afternoon, September 7, 1857, the *Central America* arrived at the port of Havana. Coal was taken on and a few passengers ventured on shore, but not as many as usual, for yellow fever was rampant there. At 9:25 a.m. on Tuesday, September 8, the fully loaded

The SS *George Law* before it was renamed the ***Central America*** as depicted in an early photograph.

Central America hoisted anchor in Havana and headed toward New York City via the Straits of Florida. The weather was pleasant and as usual was made even more so by a light breeze from the ship's forward motion. Everything was set for the continuation of a quite enjoyable voyage.

At 5:30 a.m. on Wednesday, September 9, the ship's second officer noted that the ship had gone 286 nautical miles in the preceding 26 and one-half hours, and that there was a fresh breeze kicking up swells. Perhaps a storm was coming. In any event, there was no alarm. This was a large ship, well equipped, and with an experienced crew capable of handling any storm. Meanwhile, the ship plowed onward toward New York. This intensified into a strong gale and mountainous waves. By Friday the lower part of the ship was flooded, some of the structure had been damaged, and the ship was help- less in the stormy sea. By mid-afternoon, the lower deck and many cabins were unin- habitable, food service had been suspended, and passengers scavenged to eat crackers and drink water or wine. A small spanker sail was rigged in an attempt to keep the ship headed into the wind, for if it was broadside to the waves it risked being swamped. However, it and all other canvas sails were soon ripped to shreds. Early in the evening the small auxiliary pump failed.

After a tumultuous wind and wave–whipped night, the powerless *Central America* wallowed helplessly in a raging sea on Saturday morning. Decks were awash. This was disaster experienced first-hand, not an ordinary tropical storm, and passengers and crew alike feared for their lives. Captain Herndon ordered the American flag to be flown upside-down as a distress signal. The Atlantic coastal route was well-traveled, and surely it would be a short time until other ships came along.

Before 8:00 a.m. the ship had listed sharply on its side, and many broken portholes were now under water. Captain Herndon once again announced that if the ship could be kept afloat for a few more hours, surely help would come from other ships plying the same route. Good news finally arrived. By 10:00 a.m. the hurricane showed signs of abating. The worst was over. However, bad news took precedence—seemingly, too much damage had already been done to save the ship.

At about 1:00 p.m. on Saturday afternoon, the sail of the brig *Marine* was seen on the horizon. This storm-damaged vessel, under the command of Captain Hiram Burt and 10 crew members, drew closer. Aboard the sinking *Central America* Captain Hern- don ordered women and children on deck, preparatory to boarding lifeboats. Women left behind unnecessary baggage. Some, "as if to illustrate how little value was the gold, brought out bags of coins and scattered them on the floor, asking all who wanted money to help themselves."[9]

In the coming hours the storm-damaged brig *Marine* took dozens aboard. Finally, men were allowed into the lifeboats, and a few went over to the *Marine* including some of the crew of the *Central America*, an action that caused many unfavorable comments in later investigations, as passengers expected that crew members would remain in the res- cue boats to shuttle regular passengers to safety. They were wrong. Meanwhile, many incidents continued aboard the stricken steamer, including threats and fights among the remaining passengers, drunkenness of several, and numerous injuries from falling or being hit with storm-tossed wreckage. In nine shuttle trips 109 passengers were saved. The *Marine* eventually drifted several miles away and could no longer render aid.

The *Central America* continued to fill with water. By now, all bailing efforts had ceased, and most of the ship was inundated. Pounding waves broke up cabin walls and floors and tore away sails, spars, and equipment. Some of the men ripped planks and railings off the ship to make crude rafts, while others found single boards. At about 7:50 in the evening, Captain Herndon ordered rockets to be fired downward to signal that the ship was sinking, meanwhile bravely trying to reassure the 438 men remaining on board that other rescue vessels were bound to come along. A few minutes past 8:00 a tremendous wave hit the SS *Central America*. She shuddered, timbers broke, and with hundreds of men huddled at the front of the ship and Captain Herndon on the starboard paddlebox, she slipped at a sharp angle beneath the waves.

Fast forward to the 20th century. In the 1980s Thomas ("Tommy") G. Thompson of the Battelle Memorial Institute in Columbus, Ohio, was a student of shipwrecks, and in 1980 he began directing his efforts toward trying to find the long-forgotten *Central America*. In 1985 a group of entrepreneurs and investors headed by Thompson and two associates, Robert Evans and Barry Schatz, formed Recovery Limited Partnership to finance the search for the *Central America*. After listening to Tommy Thompson's projections, many leading citizens in and around Columbus, Ohio, stepped up to help with financing. Early fundraising was done in several stages. Eventually $12.7 million was raised even though investors were aware of the risks involved.

The exploration was done by the Columbus-America Discovery Group and involved several years of search and recovery. Finally, the ship was found on the ocean floor 7,200-feet below the surface, off of the coast of South Carolina. When gold was brought ashore, excitement prevailed! One television anchor said the treasure was worth a billion dollars. In actuality, recovery was still underway and no inventory had been published. The news attracted dozens of claimants who held that they were owed money as they had connections to the insurance companies that paid for the loss, or that in one way or another they had aided the treasure finders. The matter went to court for about a decade and cost many millions of dollars in legal fees. Meanwhile, Christie's auction house had put up funds to pay expenses as had investors in Ohio.

The complex matter was finally solved in 1999 when an agreement was held and the court awarded the finders 92.4 percent of the treasure and the claimants the remaining part. Dwight N. Manley and his California Gold Marketing Group wrote a check to pay off the Christie's loan and other obligations and to settle all claims, then began a marketing program that lasted several years. The "Ship of Gold" display featuring a replica of the side of the ship was a sensation at several conventions. *Coin World* in 2000 called it the Story of the Year. It was not long before all coins and ingots were sold. The vast inventory of coins included these eagles:

> 1841; 1843 (2); 1843-O (2); 1844-O (2); 1845-O (3); 1846-O (3); 1847 (7); 1847-O (6); 1848; 1848-O (2); 1849 (6); 1850 (2); 1851-O (2); 1852 (2); 1852-O (2); 1853; 1853-O; 1854; 1854-O (2); 1854-S (13); 1855 (2); 1855-S (6); 1856-S (27 to the California Gold Marketing Group, 1 to the insurers; and 1857-S (9 to CGMG 3 to the insurers).

Only a small part of the wreck had been explored by the time the Columbus-America Discovery Group left the site in 1991—likely the safe room or purser's room—but much more remained untouched. Rumors swirled, including that there might have been an unregistered shipment of "Army-guarded gold" elsewhere in the hull. Tommy Thompson hoped that another series of explorations would be made on the site. This did not work out as planned. By 2013, Tommy Thompson had disappeared and investors still had not received any money from the project. There was also a list of creditors who had not been paid, including the investors in Ohio. The Common Pleas Court of Franklin County, Ohio, appointed Ira Owen Kane, a prominent attorney and businessman, as the official receiver for Recovery Limited Partnership (RLP) and Columbus Exploration, LLC, with James Henson also on the team.

Under the direction of the court to maximize the assets for the benefit of the investors and creditors, Kane began plans to revisit the SS *Central America* to resume recovery operations. The U.S. District Court of the Eastern District of Virginia confirmed RLP as the salvor in possession of the SS *Central America* in 2014. This was done under contract with Odyssey Marine Exploration, and more coins and ingots were found, a smaller quantity than on the first recovery. These eagles were included:

> 1840; 1841; 1842 (2); 1843-O (2); 1844-O; 1846-O (2); 1847 (4); 1847-O (3); 1848; 1849 (10); 1850 (2); 1851 (2); 1851-O (4); 1852 (2); 1852-O; 1853 (2); 1854; 1854-S (13); 1855 (2); 1855-S (2); 1856-S (7); 1857-S (4).

THE SS *BROTHER JONATHAN* TREASURE

The story of the SS *Brother Jonathan*, lost at sea off of Crescent City, California, on July 30, 1865, is another treasure saga. The ship was found in 1996 by Deep Sea Research, and more than 1,000 coins were recovered. Only a few were eagles:

> 1847, F-15; 1849, not graded; 1856-S, not graded; 1861-S, EF-40; 1865-S, MS-64.

THE SS *REPUBLIC* TREASURE

The ship later known as the SS *Republic* was built in Baltimore by John A. Robb, and on August 31, 1853, was launched as the SS *Tennessee*. The two-deck ship was 210-feet long, 33-feet and 11-inches at the beam, and displaced 1,149 tons. She was fitted with a vertical beam engine whose massive single piston was steam-powered by a pair of double return flue boilers and drove two 28-foot-diameter iron side wheels. The vessel could accommodate 100 passengers and about 5,000 barrels of cargo or the equivalent. The ship later sailed under different owners.

In September 1864 the Navy renamed her USS *Mobile*. The next month she was caught in a gale near the mouth of the Rio Grande River and sustained severe damage to her hull. The ship was put up for auction, sold to merchant Russell Sturgis for $25,000, repaired, and christened the SS *Republic*.

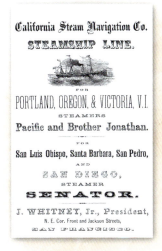

Advertisement for the
SS *Brother Jonathan*.

Her last voyage began on October 18, 1865. The *Republic* left New York bound for New Orleans with a reported $400,000 in gold coins. This was in a very uncertain financial era, with gold and silver coins of all denominations being hoarded by the public, as they had been for several years. Federal bills in circulation such as Legal Tender and National Bank Notes traded at a sharp discount to gold and silver. Specie brokers, exchange houses, and banks were well stocked with gold and silver coins and did a lively trade dealing in them. Traders and others expecting to do business in New Orleans necessarily bought such coins to take with them.

On October 22 the *Republic* passed Cape Hatteras, well known as a graveyard for passing ships. The following morning she was off the coast of Georgia when an east-northeasterly gale blew in. By evening, the storm had become a raging hurricane. The scenario was all too familiar to ship captains of the era, and in the vast majority of instances the successful challenge was to maintain forward speed and control until the storm was over.

On October 24 matters worsened, and the ship's paddlewheels stalled and couldn't carry the engine past dead center. Without power, the *Republic* was adrift and at the mercy of the elements. Steam was raised on the donkey boiler to run the pumps, but the next morning at 9:00 a.m. the donkey boiler failed and water began to pour into the hold. With little time left to spare, the crew began preparing the four lifeboats. They also built a makeshift raft from the ship's spars and boards. By 1:30, the water was above the engine room floor. All hands were called to help launch the safety vessels.

At 4:00 in the afternoon of October 25, after two days of valiant struggle to keep the vessel afloat, the *Republic* went down. Most of the passengers and crew were stowed safely on the four boats and the makeshift raft. The remaining survivors then jumped into the sea. Swimming for their lives, some found safety aboard debris and passing craft. Two are believed to have drowned while swimming through the ship's floating debris.

In July 2003 Odyssey Marine Exploration, Inc. found the wreck off the coast of Georgia in about 1,700 feet of water.[10] Strewn on the sea floor was an array of gold coins along with bottles and other artifacts. Recovery with the ROV *Zeus* began in November 2003, and by early December more than 750 eagles and double eagles, but

The SS *Republic*.

no other gold denominations, had been brought to the surface. More than 900 Liberty Seated half dollars had been found as well. This was estimated to be just a small part of the treasure. The coins were sent to Numismatic Conservation Services (NCS) to be cared for and conserved.

A news release issued by Odyssey, January 27, 2004, included this update: "To date, more than 17,000 coins, with a total face value of $54,500 (approximately 14,230 silver and 2,950 gold coins) and over 750 other artifacts have been recovered."

Eagles were found of all dates from 1838 onward, this being from the inception of the Liberty Head design in that year. By 1865, the largest quantity made of any date and mint of $10 gold coin was the 1847, of which 862,258 were struck. Not surprisingly, coins of this variety were the most numerous recovered from the SS *Republic*, with 221 conserved by NCS and graded by NGC by September 2004. In contrast, also logically, just one 1841-O eagle was found, a rarity of which just 2,500 were made.

Certain of these combine great rarity with remarkable condition. One of the most storied rarities in the eagle series is the 1858, of which just 2,521 were struck. The SS Republic coin

One of two 1859-O eagles recovered from the wreck of the SS *Republic*.

was certified as AU-58, one of the finest known, with most of its original mint frost still remaining. The solitary 1865-S is of the curious variety with regular date over *inverted* date. The date was first punched into the die upside down, and then corrected. These eagles were recovered:

> 1838 (4); 1839 (9); 1840 (11); 1841 (20); 1841-O; 1842 (17); 1842-O (17)1843 (20); 1843-O (35); 1844-O (32); 1845 (2); 1845-O (19); 1846 (6); 1846/5-O (13); 1846-O; 1847 (221); 1847-O (123) 1848 (39); 1848-O (9); 1849 (167); 1849-O (8); 1850 (72); 1850-O (16); 1851 (33); 1851-O (99); 1852 (59); 1852-O (3); 1853/2 (6); 1853 (59); 1853-O (13); 1854 (22); 1854-O (17); 1854-S (41); 1855 (44); 1855-O (7); 1856 (22); 1856-O (5); 1856-S (27); 1857 (9); 1857-O (3); 1857-S (11); 1858; 1858-O (4); 1858-S (4); 1859 (9); 1859-O (2); 1860 (9); 1860-O (4); 1860-S (4); 1861 (60); 1861-S (2); 1862 (9); 1862-S; 1863; 1863-S (3); 1864 (2); 1865; 1865-S.[11]

APPENDIX

E

$10 Gold Coins in the King Farouk Collection

THE PALACE COLLECTIONS

As a source of rare $10 gold coins the Farouk auction must be mentioned. In February and March 1954, the coins of ousted and exiled King Farouk I were auctioned in Cairo by Sotheby's under the title of "The Palace Collections of Egypt." The typical lot consisted of rare and common coins mixed together in bulk lots with very little description.

The story goes back to at least 1938. In that year former Crown Prince Farouk, born in 1920, then king since 1936, was a student in England. He had developed an interest in numismatics and purchased coins from dealers in London and, among other places, from the old-time firm of Jacques Schulman in Amsterdam, where young Hans M.F. Schulman was learning the coin trade under the guidance of his father. In that year Schulman moved to New York City to immerse himself in the nuances of the coin business in America. He kept up correspondence with Farouk and acted as his American agent.

King Farouk I of Egypt in 1939.

World War II erupted, and Hans decided to stay in New York. His family members in Holland were lost to the Nazis. Back home in Egypt, now as King Farouk I, the former prince continued to add to his collection. Hans Schulman and other American dealers were his prime source, as most numismatic offices in Continental Europe were suspended, although some of the Swiss banks had rare coin departments. Stack's in New York City sold vast quantities of rare coins to the king, including gold coins from the Colonel E.H.R. Green estate; a transaction was arranged through the Egyptian

Embassy in Washington, D.C. Abe Kosoff's Numismatic Gallery was a supplier as well, as was Robert Friedberg. In Fort Worth, Texas, B. Max Mehl also sold him many things. Most of the Farouk $10 coins came from the Green estate through Stack's.

In its issue of January 1943 *Hobbies* magazine reported:

> The Tatham Stamp & Coin Co. Springfield, Mass. opened a letter from Egypt lately. A private secretary to His Majesty, 22-year-old King Farouk, placed an order for a collection of American coins for the king's collection. The coins were delivered to Lawrence Steinhardt, United States ambassador to Turkey, who took them by clipper plane and delivered them personally to the king on a recent trip.

Although Farouk never visited America, he was mentioned now again in print and was well-known as a collector, although the extent of his holdings was not publicized. In 1943 the American Numismatic Association awarded him an honorary membership. In May 1944 *The Numismatist* included a communication from the king's private secretary:

> Deeply appreciating the kind thought that dictated the decision taken at your last Annual Convention regarding His Majesty's membership, the King has commanded me to convey to you and to your honourable colleagues His Majesty's most sincere thanks and best wishes for the constant progress of the Association.

Many items and collections were sent to Egypt in the 1940s, as the King paid just about any price asked. Although he was not an expert, Farouk was an advanced collector and could "talk coins" about many different world series.

The Numismatic Gallery sold sections of several major collections including patterns from F.C.C. Boyd to Farouk. In other instances, special strikings of medals (1946 United Nations gold "pattern") and contrived rarities (*e.g.* 1884-dated Hawaiian fantasy coins) were made up for him. He was probably the most important customer of American dealers in the 1940s.

Remittances to American dealers were made by the Egyptian treasury, always in drafts of $9,999 or less, for payments of $10,000 or more in American dollars were subject to outside approval. Thus a $20,000, $50,000, or other large transaction would be billed in multiple invoices for lower amounts.[1]

In 1951 Hans M.F. Shulman visited the king. A letter posted from his hotel address in Cairo was published in *The Numismatist* in January 1952:

Visiting King Farouk

On the evening of December 5, I had the pleasant experience of being received by the King of Egypt and, as readers of *The Numismatist* may be interested in his collecting activities I am sending you this account of my visit.

It was a great honor to be received by His Majesty King Farouk the First of Egypt, in the office of Pully Bey, with Mr. G. Garro present. His Majesty, with his cordial way of greeting, made me feel immediately at ease and I had the feeling that I was talking to a personal friend rather than to a king.

The first part of the conversation was devoted mainly to the hobby of coins and to the service we give to the palace, during which it was most interesting to remark that His Majesty handles the entire collection himself, that he opens his mail and enjoys particularly when such mail includes the remark: 'Dear Mr. Secretary, please mention to His Majesty.'

It was thus clear to me that when His Majesty receives our shipments, he is the only one who opens them, assorts and selects from them. In the course of discussing the offers we have made to the palace, His Majesty asked me if I played poker and when I said no, he said that it wasn't necessary since I was a good poker player with my prices.

The collection of His Majesty seems today to outrank any other collection of the same period in the world. The collection most generally starts at 1800 and covers all countries in all metals. Very few people have seen the collection and I will be permitted to see it shortly. One of the first times that the collection will partly be visible to the public will be in 1953 when the next numismatic exhibition will be held in Cairo and for which the international section will be under my personal care.

His Majesty felt that I should not be jealous of the beautiful flowers he had sent to Mrs. Schulman and for that reason I was given a beautiful cigarette case with gold Arabic lettering and a crown superimposed.

His Majesty seemed unhappy that a certain section in the U.S. is always out to publish unfriendly articles and I felt greatly flattered that I was given the permission to counteract such publicity with the real truth whenever or wherever I can. If I go on television, His Majesty expressed the wish that it would not be after the 'Dagmar' program.

His Majesty looked handsome in a blue suit with white stripes, tall and broadly built and quite different from the pictures American journalists tried to make of him. He is an unfatigable [*sic*] worker, personally interested in a million things of which he takes care of himself very early in the morning and often working till the late hours of the night. He seems to have a willing yearn for the little things which are so important in life.

Koubbeh Palace in Cairo as it was at the turn of the 20th century. From the 1930s to the early 1950s King Farouk kept his collections there. (*Harper's Weekly*, February 5, 1898)

I showed His Majesty three coins, one of which I mentioned as being unique; however His Majesty believed that he had this unique coin in his collection. It was a coin of the Prince of Monaco and the fact that the prince did not have this coin was no reason that it would not be in His Majesty's collection. There may be a next meeting at a later date as a guest of His Majesty at the Sporting Club.

Separately to friends after he returned home Schulman reported Farouk also collected jewelry, watches, stamps, paperweights, antiques, art objects, and pornography, all kept in Koubbeh Palace (the king's summer palace) in a special study. His collection of erotica, described as "cheap and dirty" by Schulman, was kept in separate rooms on a high floor in the palace; this was a great attraction for the ever-curious newspaper people and gave the king a lot of bad press. Schulman said that Farouk's "coin time" was usually from about 10 p.m. to 1 a.m. each day.

Schulman did not mention that the king liked to have all of his coins be brilliant. He used silver polish to brighten all of his copper and silver coins, severely reducing their value. Most gold coins were untouched.

There was trouble in Farouk's Egyptian paradise, and on July 23, 1952, he was deposed by a military junta. On July 26 he had an interview with the junta, and it was agreed that he would abdicate in favor of his son Fuad.[2] He left Egypt on the yacht *Mahroussa*, and was followed by his wife Narriman, who held the baby king Fuad. On June 18, 1953, the baby king was deposed as well, and the Revolutionary Council proclaimed the country to be a republic. Farouk's properties were confiscated, and Sotheby's of London was hired to dispose of the collectibles and art objects.

In *The Numismatist*, Spink & Son, Ltd., the London dealers, stated the following in a full-page advertisement:

A Most Important Forthcoming Auction Sale

Many of our customers will by now be aware that the Egyptian government is planning to sell by auction in Cairo the famous coin collection of the ex-king of Egypt. Progress on the cataloguing of the Farouk Coin Collection indicates the sale will take place, as previously anticipated, at the end of February and the beginning of March 1954.

The major portion of the collection comprises over 8,000 coins and medals, the majority in gold or platinum, dated from 1800 onwards. All countries are strongly represented, and include many patterns in different metals, with many patterns and Proofs never before recorded. This will be, therefore, a unique opportunity for collectors to obtain many rare coins for which they have long been looking. There is a superb and almost complete series of American coins, and in addition there are some very fine and rare classical coins.

In December in *The Numismatist*, A.H. Baldwin & Sons, Ltd. of London announced that the firm had been named to prepare the catalog of the Palace Collections of Egypt and that the event would be held at the Koubbeh Palace, Cairo, from February 24 through March 6, 1954. Spink & Son, Ltd. continued to run full-page advertisements of the same event, soliciting commissions from interested buyers.

In February 1954 *The Numismatist* reported:

The catalog of the Palace Collections of Egypt, to be auctioned February 24 through March 7, at Koubbeh Palace, Cairo, Egypt, is expertly arranged and well-illustrated with 72 plates. Its contents of 2,798 lots are listed on 306 pages. About 8,500 coins in platinum, gold, silver and copper are to be sold. Paper currency of many countries also appears. Apart from a small number of items, the sale includes only issues of the 19th and 20th centuries. Regular coinage, patterns and Proofs are represented, a number of which never before appeared at public auction.

According to the cataloguer, 'Much care was exercised in building up the collection and particular attention was given to ensure that date sequence struck at various mints were complete throughout the range of issue. To separate and sell piecemeal these series would have been to undermine the work of many years (and in some cases more than one generation) of collecting.

Many of these very desirable sets, especially in the United States section, are being offered *en bloc*; thus buyers will be able to bid for series which, if the coins were bought individually, would take very many years to complete.' Famous collections are represented. Much of the very complete United States series once belonged to W.H. Woodin, H.B. Earle, or Col. Green. French material, in large measure, comes down from the cabinet of Count Ferrari. The catalogue, prepared by Sotheby and Company of London, is a worthy record of a great numismatic event.

The auction was attended by a coterie of prominent American numismatists including Abe Kosoff, Sol Kaplan, Ambassador and Mrs. R. Henry Norweb, Hans M.F. Schulman, John J. Pittman, James P. Randall, Robert Schermerhorn, Paul Wittlin, George J. Bauer, Gaston DiBello, and Maurice Storck. The auctioneer was Lee Levy, a.k.a. Mr. Lee, (a "British subject probably of Levantine origin," who spoke a half dozen languages fluently).[3] Abe Kosoff recalled:

There were people marching down the streets with guns and swords, but he wouldn't leave without buying the coins he had come for. Two detectives watched both hands while he looked at the coins. On the last day of the sale, everyone had been so nice to the American dealers they threw a party on the lawn for the guards, finance department men, detectives, etc. which amounted to a big "drunk."[4]

In April in *The Numismatist* Abe Kosoff's report on the sale included this:

The Palace Collections Sale

'Many are the rarities and many the gems' were my thoughts as I approached the rooms where the coins were in large display cases, each one locked and sealed. At each case one man was in charge. He and his two assistants breathed down your neck as you examined a lot. Each lot was carefully checked as you returned it. No matter that you examined only one or two coins in a lot of 187 pieces, the entire lot had to be counted!

Having sold many of the coins that went into this famous collection, I was quite familiar with many sections. They were old friends, and as we sorrow to see an old friend grow ill and feeble, so did I ache when these many friends which had blossomed when I saw them last now had been made-up to fool me. I do not mean to infer that this condition prevailed throughout, but I will assert that the value of some of the coins has been diminished by no less than 30% because of mishandling.

When I recall the bloom of beauty of the 1827 quarter when it came out of my 'World's Greatest Collection of U.S. Silver Coins' and look at it now, it seems that in the nine years it has aged 80 years. Marred by a blotch caused by some acid, it bravely smiles its Proof lustre here and there. I recall it as one of the finest known specimens in 1945.

And the 1913 nickel was the second best of the five. Now it is probably the worst. I recall the rare $20 piece of British Columbia. How it has aged! It doesn't look the same. And the counterfeits! Many an American collector will be disappointed because his representative could not recognize the false pieces. He should have known better than to send his bids abroad. The examination of the coins by a competent expert was a prime requisite in this auction. Where does the blame lie? Perhaps with the Egyptian government for insisting on the sale of all the collections at one time. I might add, however, that the government was very cooperative in all matters pertaining to the sale.

Shulman had a large unpaid balance owed by the king. By special arrangement with the Egyptian authorities he had buyers of coins in the sale pay him. To entice their participation he offered them a discount! The method worked well for all involved. At the 1954 auction in Cairo, many coins were purchased by Sol Kaplan and were marketed by Kaplan and Kosoff during the next several years. The author had the good fortune to be given first opportunity to buy many of these treasures, including all or nearly all of the patterns. In addition, Sol Kaplan had quite a few remainders from the William H. Woodin estate in his stock. What a good time I had!

In exile in the late 1950s Farouk lived in a modest apartment in Rome where he had "a male secretary, a maid, two bodyguards, a chauffeur, a cook, and Irma, the rather heavy-set girl who was cheering up the king's lonely hours," Schulman remembered. For a time he hoped that his young son Fuad (also spelled Fouad) would be installed as king and military dictator Nasser would be overthrown, but that did not happen. Farouk became very corpulent and could hardly move. In his final years he was addicted to gambling and spent many hours in that pursuit.

Farouk died on March 18, 1965. His son Fuad resided in Switzerland and was gainfully employed. Rumors circulated that King Farouk had stashed large amounts of money in Switzerland while he was on the throne of Egypt, but facts were scarce. In New York City in November 1971 Schulman sold additional items that once belonged to the king.

$10 Eagles in the Palace Collection Sale

Lot 186: "First type 1795 brilliant but light scratches, 1796 Very Fine, 1797 four stars Very Fine; second type 1797-Six stars, Extremely Fine, 1798-7 four stars, Extremely Fine, 1798-7-Six stars, nearly Extremely Fine; a nice lot in a fitted case. 6 pieces."

Lot 187: "1799 two varieties, 1800, 1801, 1803, 1804. All Extremely Fine except one 1799 and 1804 which are Very Fine; a nice lot in a fitted case. 6 pieces."

Lot 188: "1838 brilliant Proof, 1839 Extremely Fine, 1839 different die, 1840; last two fine. 4 pieces."

Lot 189: "1841, 1841-O, 1842 (2) large and small date, 1842-O. Mostly Very Fine. 5 pieces."

Lot 190: "1843, 1843-O, 1844 Extremely Fine, 1844-O, the others fine. 4 pieces."

Lot 191: "1845, 1845-O, 1846, 1846-O. All fine. 4 pieces."

Lot 192: "1847, 1847-O, 1848, 1848-O. Very Fine. 4 pieces."

Lot 193: "1849, 1849-O, 1850, 1850-O. Fine or better. 4 pieces."

Lot 194: "1851, 1851-O, 1852, 1852-O. Some Very Fine. 4 pieces."

Lot 195: "1853, 1853-O, 1859-O, 1859-S, 1859. The last Extremely Fine, others fine. 5 pieces."

Lot 196: "1854, 1854-O, 1854-S, 1855, 1855-O, 1855-S. Mostly Very Fine. 6 pieces."

Lot 197: "1856, 1856-O, 1856-S, 1857, 1857-O, 1857-S. Mostly Very Fine. 6 pieces."

Lot 198: "1858, 1858-O, 1858-S, 1862-S, 1862. The last a brilliant Proof, others fine. 5 pieces."

Lot 199: "1860, 1860-S, 1860-O, 1861, 1861-S. The first a brilliant Proof, others mostly Very Fine. 5 pieces."

Lot 200: "1863-S, 1864-S, both fine; 1863, 1864, both brilliant Proofs. 4 pieces."

Lot 201: "1865, 1865-S, 1866, 1866-S Large S, 1866-S Small S. Some Very Fine. 5 pieces."

Lot 202: "1867, 1867-S, 1868, 1868-S, 1869, 1869-S. 1869 a brilliant Proof, others fine or better. 6 pieces."

Lot 203: "1870, 1870-S, 1870-CC, 1871, 1871-S, 1871-CC, Mostly fine. 6 pieces."

Lot 204: "1872 brilliant Proof, 1872-S, 1872-CC, 1873 brilliant Proof, 1873-S, 1873-CC, others fine. 6 pieces."

Lot 205: "1874 brilliant Proof, 1874-S, 1874-CC, 1875 Proof, others fine. 4 pieces."

Lot 206: "1875-CC, 1876 brilliant Proof, 1876-S, 1876-CC, others fine. 4 pieces."

Lot 207: "1877, 1877-S, 1877-CC, 1878, 1878-CC. Two Very Fine. 5 pieces."

Lot 208: "1878-S, 1879-O, 1879-S, 1879-CC, 1880, 1880-O, 1880-S, 1880-CC Mostly Very Fine. 8 pieces."

Lot 209: "1881, 1881-O, 1881-S, 1881-CC, 1882, 1882-O, 1882-S, 1882-CC Mostly Very Fine. 7 pieces."

Lot 210: "1883, 1883-O, 1883-S, 1883-CC, 1848 brilliant Proof, 1884-S, 1884-CC, others fine. 7 pieces."

Lot 211: "1885 brilliant Proof, 1885-S, 1886 brilliant Proof, 1886-S, 1887 brilliant Proof, 1887-S, others Very Fine. 6 pieces."

Lot 212: "1880 brilliant Proof, 1880-O, 1888-S, 1889 brilliant Proof, 1889-S, others fine. 5 pieces."

Lot 213: "1890 brilliant Proof, 1890-CC, 1891 brilliant Proof, Proof, 1891-CC, 1892 brilliant Proof, 1892-O, 1892-S, 1892-CC, others Very Fine. 8 pieces."

Lot 214: "1893 brilliant Proof, 1893-O, 1893-S, 1893-CC, 1894 brilliant Proof, 1894-O, 1894-S, others mostly Very Fine. 7 pieces."

Lot 215: "1895 brilliant Proof, 1895-O, 1895-S, 1896 brilliant Proof, 1896-S, others fine. 5 pieces."

Lot 216: "1897 brilliant Proof, 1897-O, 1897-S, 1898 brilliant Proof, 1898-S, 1899-S, others Very Fine. 6 pieces."

Lot 217: "1900 brilliant Proof, 1900-S, 1901 brilliant Proof, 1901-O, 1901-S, 1902 brilliant Proof, 1902-S, others mostly Very Fine. 7 pieces."

Lot 218: "1903 brilliant Proof, 1903-O, 1903-S, 1904 brilliant Proof, 1904-O, 1905 brilliant Proof, 1905-S, others Very Fine. 7 pieces."

Lot 219: "1906-O, 1906-S, 1906-D, 1907 brilliant Proof, 1907-S, 1907-D, others Very Fine or better. 6 pieces."

Lot 220: "Indian head 1907 three varieties, 1908 matte Proof and ordinary, 1908-S, 1908-D (2), others mostly Extremely Fine. 8 pieces."

Lot 221: "1909, 1909-S, 1909-D, 1910, 1910-S, 1910-D, mostly Extremely Fine. 6 pieces."

Lot 222: "1911 matte Proof, 1911-S, 1911-D, 1912 matte Proof, 1912-S, others Very Fine. 5 pieces."

Lot 223: "1913 matte Proof, 1913-S, 1914 matte Proof, 1914-S, 1914-D, 1915 matte Proof, 1915-S, others Extremely Fine. 7 pieces."

Lot 224: "1916-S, 1920-S, 1926, 1930-S. 1932, 1933. Mostly Extremely Fine. 6 pieces."

Notes

Chapter 2

1. Certain information about the mints is adapted from *United States $3 Gold Pieces* by Q. David Bowers with Douglas Winter (2005).
2. The source for the estimated total production of gold is the chart prepared by Louis A. Garnett, a San Francisco mining technician, quoted by Herbert M. Bergen in, "California Gold and the Civil War," The Numismatist, February 1962. This seems to be the best of several tables of estimates studied. The actual price of gold varied depending upon the purchaser, the location at which it was bought, its fineness, etc. In 1859 the San Francisco Mint was paying $18.60 per ounce for fine gold (nearly pure), while at the Philadelphia Mint and the New York City Assay Office the value for an ounce of absolutely pure gold was $20.67. However, gold could not be refined to this purity. Other figures, seemingly less accurate, but more widely quoted in popular texts, include these numbers used by Hubert Howe Bancroft in his, History of California, Vol. VI. 1848–1859, p. 423; and L. Stebbins's, Progress of the United States, 1870, p. 73 The figures were calculated at $20 per ounce: 1848: $10,000,000. 1849: $40,000,000. 1850: $50,000,000. 1851: $60,000,000. 1852: $60,000,000. 1853: $65,000,000. 1854: $60,000,000. 1855: $55,000,000. 1856: $56,000,000. 1857: $55,000,000. 1858: $50,000,000. 1859: $50,000,000. 1860: $45,000,000. 1861: $40,000,000. 1862: $34,700,000. 1863: $30,000,000. 1864: $26,000,000.1865: $28,500,000. Figures for California gold used at the various mints are precise (not estimates) and are from various issues of the *Annual Report of the Director of the Mint*.
3. Senate; 41st Congress, 2nd Session; Ex. Doc. No. 55.
4. *Annual Report of the Director of the Mint*, 1881.
5. R.W. Julian, "The Original 'S' Mint."
6. *Annual Report of the Director of the Mint*, 1875.
7. Thompson and West's History of Nevada, 1881, p. 557.
8. During much of the second half of the 19th century the government, industries, and private citizens were at the mercy of the railroads, who could and did charge unfair rates when they had a monopolistic situation, or charged some customers high rates and others discounted tariffs. All of this was in spite of massive government aid to railroads to encourage their expansion. Frank Norris' novel, *The Octopus*, set in California, tells much of the railroad trusts.
9. Actually, the New Orleans Mint did not strike any double eagles after 1879, and the comparison is with silver dollars alone, considered to be in the same "class of coinage," as both denominations could be struck only on the largest presses at each mint.
10. *Annual Report of the Director of the Mint*, 1906, p. 6; other sources.
11. Jacob G. Willson, "Denver Mints," *Numismatic Scrapbook*, June 1940.

Chapter 3

1. The full text is reproduced in the present work under the listing for the 1886 Proof gold $1.

2. April 1908 commentary discussing Proofs of the preceding year.

3. This fine gentleman, with whom the author had a number of conversations, was in the scrap metal business and after World War II received a contract to cut apart and sell aircraft for scrap. At Davis-Monthan Army Airfield in Arizona he was about to destroy a B-29 Superfortress when he noticed it was labeled *Enola Gay*. The historic plane, which had dropped the first atomic bomb on Japan, was called to the attention of authorities, who saved it and later facilitated its transfer to the Smithsonian, where it can be seen today.

4. Cf. Saul Teichman, from the Brand archives preserved by the American Numismatic Society. Walter Breen's pedigree information for this coin is incorrect.

5. William H. Woodin, "The Commercial Element in Numismatics," *The Numismatist*, May 1911.

Chapter 4

1. Certain information regarding the Silver Question is adapted from the author's 2013 book, *Liberty Head Double Eagles 1849–1907*.

2. The five 1933 $10 information is from research done by David E. Tripp.

Chapter 5

1. Heaton's comments were more theoretical than practical, as he had never met a collector of eagles by mintmarks. Therefore, errors were several; there was no 1861-O coinage. The 1870-CC, the rarest Carson City eagle is not mentioned for this characteristic, etc

Chapter 8

1. *Walter Breen's Complete Encyclopedia of U.S. and Colonial Coins*, 1988.

2. Mark Borckardt's description of the Long Beach Connoisseur Collection specimen, 1999, lot 418 (other aspects of which are cited elsewhere).

3. After Boyd passed in 1958, most of his holdings were purchased from his widow Helen by John J. Ford Jr., much to the consternation of Eric P. Newman, who had hoped to acquire some choice rarities in the colonial paper money series. These were on loan to Newman at the time, and Ford demanded their return. Thus began deep enmity between the two men.

4. Expanding on this, Mark Borckardt commented: "Many years ago I carefully examined and compared Heraldic Eagle dies for half dollars and eagles, and found that there are no existing dies used for both denominations. So the only possibility would be if a new die variety is discovered with a previously unknown reverse die. And then, that new die would still have to match a die of the other denomination. Not impossible, but very unlikely." (Communication, March 27, 2017).

5. His huge collection of rare paper money was mostly stored in cellulose nitrate sleeves and deteriorated to crumble into tiny pieces. His mother was the famous Hetty Green, nicknamed "The Witch of Wall Street." A book could be written about him and his activities.

6. Perhaps Dickeson was confusing this with a certain 1798 half eagle variety.

7. The term Proof was used to describe every gold coin in this early sale; at the time there were no grading standards. Probably, this would be equivalent to AU or MS today. Thus, it is classified here with circulation strikes.

8. "That's one of those things that no fellow can find out," was stated by Horace Greeley of the *New York Tribune* in the 1870s. It quickly became a widely used catchphrase.

9. For more details see the cited David Stone and John Dale Beety article in *Coin World*, November 2014. Extensive basic information can be found in *The Rare Silver Dollars Dated 1804 and the Exciting Adventures of Edmund Roberts*, by Q. David Bowers, 1999.

10. Breen and Carlson often added assumptions and guesses to their works, not identifying them as such. On balance both contributed much of value to numismatics.

Chapter 9

1. National Archives, Record Group 104, Treasury, No. 176, 1837–38 "Letters Mint and Branches." Transcribed by R.W. Julian.

2. *Walter Breen's Complete Encyclopedia of U.S. and Colonial Coins*, 1988, p. 210, quoting Alexandre Vattemare, 1861.

3. *Walter Breen's Complete Encyclopedia of U.S. and Colonial Coins*, 1988, p. 550, No. 6882. The differences are so minor that they have not been noticed in auction catalogs or other texts.

4. Each troy ounce contained 480 grains; an eagle had a statutory weight of 270 grains of metal of which 247.5 grains were pure gold.

5. The study and comparison of date logotypes on gold coins is a comparatively new endeavor, with little to draw upon in the literature, save for certain scattered comments by Walter Breen in his 1988 Encyclopedia and earlier monographs. Once the present text is published, it is likely that new discoveries will be made, and it may be that certain thoughts and theories will have to be revised.

6. This situation is discussed later in the chapter.

7. For one die crack to cross another is an unusual situation in numismatics.

8. Adapted from a commentary by Mark Borckardt, with additions by Q. David Bowers, in the *Rare Coin Review*, 1999; reprinted under lot 1360 in the Bass Collection Part II catalog. J.N. a Virginia numismatist, prompted the original study.

9. Difference described in Walter Breen's *Encyclopedia*, 1988, p. 550.

10. Difference described in Walter Breen's *Encyclopedia*, 1988, p. 550.

11. The diary is preserved in the National Archives. Citations are from an article by Rick Snow in the magazine *Longacre's Ledger*, June 2001.

12. Breen, *Encyclopedia*, 1988, p. 551.

13. This represents a change of opinion from earlier times, when the author followed the Breen and *Guide Book* listings. Detailed examination has led to the revised opinion given above.

14. The cataloger could have found additional early listings for such pieces.

15. Probably in terms of Legal Tender Notes; as common date gold coins were bringing substantially over face value; rare ones even more.

16. First identified by Beth Piper, Bowers and Merena Galleries, November 4, 1999, when examining a specimen from the Bass Collection.

17. On deeply impressed dies the 85 and 58 appear to be about the same distance apart; the extra width between 5 and 8 is not as noticeable.
18. Communication, April 11, 2017.
19. On deeply impressed dies the 85 and 58 appear to be about the same distance apart; the extra width between 5 and 8 is not as noticeable.
20. Two British Museum specimens were first reported in America by David W. Akers, 1980; earlier listed in the British Museum catalog, but not identified as to method of manufacture (circulation strike or Proof). One of the two Proofs was later sold. Today the British Museum has one.
21. A moose?
22. In his description of a Proof 1863 $5 in his June 1883 sale of the William J. Jenks Collection, lot 400, John W. Haseltine commented: "I am informed that in this year but 30 quarter eagles, and about the same number of half eagles and three dollar gold pieces were struck. Hence they must be of exceeding rarity." This is a very poignant comment, for it seems to indicate that Haseltine, whose ties with the Mint were closer than any other dealer of the time, was informed that not all Proof gold coins this year were made in the same quantity. By inference it is logical to assume that more Proof gold dollars were made (for more exist today) and fewer $10 and $20 pieces.
23. Information courtesy of John J. Ford Jr. 1998. This information differs from that published by Walter Breen.
24. Certain text is adapted from the author's cataloging of the Battle Born Collection (assembled by Rusty Goe) and sold at auction by Stack's Bowers Galleries in 2012.
25. R.W. Julian's research located this delivery, but not whether they were circulation strikes or whether they were Proofs. They are entered here as circulation strikes. If they were Proofs, which seems unlikely, the Proof mintage figure should be increased by 40 and the circulation strike total should be reduced by the same amount.
26. The 1858-S $2.50 did not exist, but Heaton was unaware of this.
27. R.W. Julian, letter, March 29, 2000. Also, Julian, "Notes on U.S. Proof Coinage II: Gold," Numismatic Scrapbook Magazine, February 1967.
28. The record may be 712 words from the July 2012 Rarities sale offering of an AU coin by Bowers and Merena Galleries.
29. R.W. Julian, letter, March 29, 2000. Also, Julian, "Notes on U.S. Proof Coinage II: Gold," Numismatic Scrapbook Magazine, February 1967.
30. Corresponding member of the Boston Numismatic Society (elected on December 5, 1867), member of the New England Numismatic and Archaeological Society (elected November 19, 1868), contributor in 1873 to Sylvester S. Crosby's impending Early Coins of America, etc.
31. Prior to writing his Proof coin Encyclopedia (1977) and complete Encyclopedia (1988) Walter Breen lost all of his research notes (he stated that they had been stolen from him), and thus many descriptions were reconstructed—often with inaccuracies and omissions—from his genius-level mind and memory.
32. Interview with John J. Ford Jr. March 11, 2000.
33. Breen, *Encyclopedia*, 1988, p. 557.

34. Greg Roberts (president of Spectrum), conversation with the author, December 9, 1999; on this day Spectrum announced its merger into Greg Manning, Inc. a publicly traded firm.

35. In 1929 these long-stored silver dollars were transferred to the Philadelphia Mint, where they were essentially forgotten until autumn 1962, when the reserve was tapped to provide coins for the holiday season demand. Exceedingly rare 1903-O Morgan dollars (*Guide Book* value $1,500—considered at the time to be the most valuable Morgan dollar) and rarities dated 1898-O and 1904-O were released at face value, igniting a frenzied scramble—the "great Treasury release"—which by March 1964 depleted all Treasury reserves in all Federal Reserve Banks and elsewhere of the hundreds of millions of Morgan and Peace dollars that had been stored there.

Chapter 10

1. Dr. George F. Heath, editor of *The Numismatist*.

2. Corresponding secretary of the American Numismatic Association, a post to which he was elected the preceding September.

3. Ebenezer Gilbert, of New York City, a close friend of Elder's, a frequent consignor to his auctions, and, years later in 1916, the author of *The United States Half Cents: From the First Year of Issue, in 1793, to the Year When Discontinued*, 1857, published by Elder. Gilbert was born in 1835.

4. Where the "Mary Cunningham" controversy reached a head; discussed later in the present text.

5. This was from the pen of numismatist Edgar H. Adams. At the time, "The American Girl" was all the rages, and depictions of the ideal American lass were drawn and painted by Charles Dana Gibson, Harrison Fisher, Philip Boileau, and others. No attention was paid by these artists as to the country of birth of their models.

6. Across the Connecticut River from Cornish, New Hampshire—the latter place being where Saint-Gaudens had his studio. The sculptor's address was often given as Windsor, Vermont, as mail was delivered there more expediently, the Post Office being larger than at Cornish.

7. *The Elder Monthly*, Vol. 2, Nos. 6–7, reprinting a newspaper account.

8. The full-length figure was used on the $20 gold coin and was taken from the Sherman Victory statue installed in New York City several years earlier in 1903; by September 1907, Homer Saint-Gaudens, the sculptor's only son, was fully aware of the designs of the $10 and $20, which had been nearly completed by that time.

9. As evidenced by documented Proof dollars sold with the Norweb Collection; also described and illustrated in *The American Numismatic Association Centennial Anthology*, 1991, in a feature by Andrew W. Pollock III.

10. As quoted in *The History of United States Coins as Illustrated by the Garrett Collection*. Original correspondence preserved by The Johns Hopkins University. Robert Garrett, a son of the late T. Harrison Garrett, inherited his father's collection and in a dilatory manner added specimens here and there including that under discussion here.

11. From Roger W. Burdette, *Renaissance of American Coinage: 1905–1908*, 2006. Cortelyou was secretary of the Treasury from March 4, 1907, to March 7, 1909.

12. Ibid.
13. Burdette communication to the author, May 6, 2007, including much other information about the 1907 coinage.
14. Breen spells the artist's name as St. Gaudens as did Elder most of the time; other variations in print range from S. Gaudens, St.-Gaudens, etc.; citations have been edited to reflect the way that both the artist and President Roosevelt spelled it in correspondence.
15. Burdette communication to the author, May 6, 2007, including much other information about the 1907 coinage.
16. DiBello of Buffalo, New York, was a genial presence at Empire State Numismatic Association shows and other conventions. An entrepreneur, he made a fortune by selling used automobiles in the 1940s when new models were not yet widely available.
17. Breen, *Encyclopedia*, 1988, p. 560.
18. Breen, *Encyclopedia*, 1988, pp. 560-561.
19. John Dannreuther, conversation with the author, January 6, 2000.
20. Interview with the author, December 29, 1999.
21. Breen, *Encyclopedia*, 1988, p. 561.
22. John Dannreuther, conversation with the author, January 6, 2000.
23. Interview with the author, December 29, 1999.
24. As printed in *The Numismatist*, August 1932. At the time the Treasury Department gladly furnished such pieces to interested numismatists. The full list: 1907-D $5, 1909-D $5, 1929 $5, 1914-D $10, 1930-S $10, 1932 $10, 1925-D $20, 1925-S $20, 1926-D $20, 1926-S $20, 1927-D $20, 1927-S $20, 1930-S $20, 1931 $20, 1931-D $20, 1932 $20. A number of these issues were later recognized as prime numismatic rarities.
25. Recollection of the author in *American Coin Treasures and Hoards*.
26. As printed in *The Numismatist*, August 1932. At the time the Treasury Department gladly furnished such pieces to interested numismatists. The full list: 1907-D $5, 1909-D $5, 1929 $5, 1914-D $10, 1930-S $10, 1932 $10, 1925-D $20, 1925-S $20, 1926-D $20, 1926-S $20, 1927-D $20, 1927-S $20, 1930-S $20, 1931 $20, 1931-D $20, 1932 $20. A number of these issues were later recognized as prime numismatic rarities.
27. As printed in *The Numismatist*, August 1932. At the time the Treasury Department gladly furnished such pieces to interested numismatists. The full list: 1907-D $5, 1909-D $5, 1929 $5, 1914-D $10, 1930-S $10, 1932 $10, 1925-D $20, 1925-S $20, 1926-D $20, 1926-S $20, 1927-D $20, 1927-S $20, 1930-S $20, 1931 $20, 1931-D $20, 1932 $20. A number of these issues were later recognized as prime numismatic rarities.
28. Sold in the catalog of the auctions by Bowers and Merena Galleries sale of the Kissel and Victoria Collections, September 1989, lots 556–606.

Appendix A

1. The totals in the 1934 *Report* do not necessarily agree with other figures and totals in the same issue of the *Report*. Moreover, there may be instances in which coins reserved for the Assay Commission were not counted (although for most years they

were), that special presentation strikings may not be included for years prior to 1860 and for some later years as well, etc. Thus, these figures, while they appear to be precise, must be regarded as approximate.

Appendix B

1. Much information is from "The World's Number One Coin Collector," by Admiral O.H. Dodson, *The Numismatist*, January 1970, reprinted from *COINage* magazine. Dick Yeoman died on November 9, 1988, and was widely mourned.

Appendix D

1. On October 24, 2014, Leonard Augsburger reviewed this section and made extensive changes based upon his research and his book, *Treasure in the Cellar*, 2008.
2. *The Numismatist*, October 1934, page 677, "A Large Quantity of Gold U.S. Coins Unearthed." Actually, Baltimore was allied with the Union, and federal troops were not an uncommon sight.
3. *The Numismatist*, April 1935, page 237, "Baltimore Hoard of Gold Coins to Be Sold at Auction."
4. Adapted from Roger W. Burdette, "U.S. Mint & Nazi Gold, Merkers Kaiseroda Salt Mine Treasure," *Journal of Numismatic Research*, Summer, 2013, Issue 3. pp. 53–61.
5. Ziemke, Earl F., *The U.S. Army in the Occupation of Germany 1944–1946.* Center of Military History, United States Army, Washington D.C., 1990, pp. 228–231. The term "salt mine" refers to potassium, sodium, magnesium and other chemical salts, not just ordinary table salt.
6. Information furnished by David E. Tripp, letter, August 1996; he appraised the coins and assisted in their sale.
7. James P. Baughman, *Charles Morgan and the Development of Southern Transportation*, p. 45.
8. Law, an important member of the firm earlier in the decade, had since departed, and it was desired several years earlier to rename the ship. However, there were regulations against this, and the renaming did not occur until 1857, after the law was changed. This was her second voyage under the SS *Central America* flag. Changing the name of a ship was bad luck, some said.
9. Account in *Frank Leslie's Illustrated Newspaper*, October 3, 1857.
10. Sources include discussion with Greg Stemm, January 8, 2004; "Another Atlantic Shipwreck Gives Up Treasure Coins," William T. Gibbs, *Coin World*, January 5, 2004; "NCS Conserves Treasure," *Numismatic News*, January 6, 2004; other media releases by Odyssey.
11. Information from Ellen Gerth and Odyssey Marine Exploration.

Appendix E

1. Reminiscence of Abe Kosoff to the author.
2. *Abe Kosoff Remembers*, Chapter 49 (January 11, 1978).
3. *Abe Kosoff Remembers*, Chapter 49 (January 11, 1978).
4. From an interview with Maurice A. Storck, *Numismatic News*, April 30, 1996, "Who's Who," by Kimberly Pichler.

SELECTED BIBLIOGRAPHY

Abbott, Waldo. "Making Money: The Mint at Philadelphia." *Harper's New Monthly Magazine*, December 1861.

Adams, Edgar H. and William H. Woodin. *U.S. Pattern, Trial and Experimental Pieces.* New York, NY: American Numismatic Society, 1913.

——. "Early United States Gold Coins: Eagles," *The Coin Collector's Journal*, July 1934.

Adams, John Weston. *United States Numismatic Literature. Volume I. Nineteenth Century Auction Catalogs.* Mission Viejo, CA: George Frederick Kolbe Publications, 1982.

——. *United States Numismatic Literature. Volume II. Twentieth Century Auction Catalogs.* Crestline, CA: George Frederick Kolbe Publications, 1990.

Akers, David W. *United States Gold Patterns.* Englewood, OH: Paramount International Coin Corporation, 1975.

United States Gold Coins: An Analysis of Auction Records, $10 Gold Eagles. Englewood, OH: Paramount International Coin Corporation, 1980.

American Journal of Numismatics. American Numismatic and Archaeological Society, later the American Numismatic Society. New York, NY, and Boston, MA: Various issues 1866 to 1912.

Attinelli, Emmanuel J. *Numisgraphics, or a List of Catalogues in Which Occur Coins or Medals, Which Have Been Sold by Auction in the United States.* New York, NY: 1876.

Baxter, Barbara A. "Coins and Medals." Chapter in *Augustus Saint-Gaudens 1848–1907.* Toulouse, France: Musée des Augustins, 1999.

Bolles, Albert S. *The Financial History of the United States from 1774 to 1885.* Three volumes. New York, 1879–1894.

Bowers, Q. David, *United States Gold Coins: An Illustrated History.* Los Angeles, CA: Bowers and Ruddy Galleries, 1982; later printings by Bowers and Merena Galleries, Inc. Wolfeboro, NH.

——. *The History of United States Coinage.* Los Angeles, CA: Bowers and Ruddy Galleries, Inc. 1979; later printings: Wolfeboro, NH: Bowers and Merena Galleries, Inc.

——. *Abe Kosoff: Dean of Numismatics.* Wolfeboro, NH: Bowers and Merena Galleries, Inc. 1985.

——. "Collecting United States Gold Coins: A Numismatic History." Chapter in *America's Gold Coinage*, the proceedings of the Coinage of the Americas Conference, American Numismatic Society, November 4–5, 1989. New York, NY: American Numismatic Society, 1990.

——. *The Rare Silver Dollars Dated 1804 and the Exciting Adventures of Edmund Roberts.* Wolfeboro, NH: Bowers and Merena Galleries, Inc., 1999.

Bowers, Q. David with Mark Borckardt. *Harry W. Bass Jr. Museum Sylloge.* Wolfeboro, NH: Bowers and Merena Galleries, 2002.

Breen, Walter. *United States Eagles.* Chicago, IL: Hewitt Brothers, 1967.

——. *Walter Breen's Encyclopedia of U.S. and Colonial Proof Coins, 1792–1977.* Albertson, NY: FCI Press, 1977. Updated edition, 1987.

——. *Walter Breen's Complete Encyclopedia of U.S. and Colonial Coins.* Garden City, NY: Doubleday, 1988.

Bressett, Kenneth E. and A. Kosoff; introduction by Q. David Bowers. *The Official American Numismatic Association Grading Standards for United States Coins.* 5th edition. Whitman Publishing, LLC.

Bullock, Charles J. *Essays on the Monetary History of the United States.* London: Macmillan and Company, Ltd. 1900. Includes information on the gold and silver situation in America in the late 1800s, the resumption of specie payments, and the political implications thereof.

Burdette, Roger W. *Renaissance of American Coinage, 1905–1908.* Manuscript of work in progress. Copy consulted in 2003 during research for the first edition of this book; later published with some changes in 2008.

Burdette, Roger W. and Jeff Reichenberger, "Congressman's Diary Reveals Original Owners of Saint-Gaudens Gold Eagles." Information from the diary of Congressman William A. Ashbrook. Manuscript furnished to the author in 2007.

Carothers, Neil. *Fractional Money.* New York, NY: John Wiley & Sons, 1930.

Coin World. Sidney, OH: Amos Press, *et al.* 1960 to date.

Coin World Almanac. Third edition. Sidney, OH: Amos Press, Sixth edition, 1990.

Coinage Laws of the United States 1792–1894. Modern foreword to reprint by David L. Ganz. Wolfeboro, NH: Bowers and Merena Galleries, Inc. 1991.

Cooper, Denis R. *The Art and Craft of Coinmaking: A History of Minting Technology.* London: Spink & Son, Ltd. 1988.

Dannreuther, John W. *United States Proof Coins Volume IV: Gold.* Memphis, TN: John W. Dannreuther Publishing, 2017.

Dickeson, Montroville Wilson. *The American Numismatical Manual.* Philadelphia, PA: J.B. Lippincott & Co. 1859. (1860 and 1865 editions were slightly retitled as *The American Numismatic Manual.*)

Doty, Richard G. *America's Money, America's Story.* Iola, WI: Krause Publications, 1998. Overview of federal and other coins and banknotes.

Dryfhout, John H. *The Work of Augustus Saint-Gaudens.* Hanover, NH: The University Press of New England, 1982.

Eckfeldt, Jacob Reese, and William Ewing DuBois. *A Manual of Gold and Silver Coins of All Nations, Struck Within the Past Century.* Philadelphia, PA: Assay Office of the Mint, 1842.

——. *New Varieties of Gold and Silver Coins, Counterfeit Coins, and Bullion; With Mint Values.* New York, NY: George P. Putnam, 1851.

Evans, George G. *Illustrated History of the United States Mint.* Philadelphia, PA: published by the author, editions of 1883, 1885, 1889, 1893.

Goe, Rusty. *The Mint on Carson Street, A Tribute to the Carson City Mint & A Guide to a Complete Set of "CC" Coins.* NV, Reno: Southgate Coins and Collectibles, 2003.

Heaton, Augustus G. *A Treatise on the Coinage of the United States Branch Mints.* Washington, D.C.: published by the author, 1893.

Hickson, Howard. *Mint Mark CC: The Story of the United States Mint at Carson City, Nevada.* Carson City, NV: The Nevada State Museum, 1972 and 1990.

Hodder, Michael and Q. David Bowers. *The Norweb Collection: An American Legacy.* Wolfeboro, NH: Bowers and Merena Galleries, Inc. 1987.

Judd, Dr. J. Hewitt. *United States Pattern, Experimental and Trial Pieces.* Racine, WI: Whitman Division of Western Publishing Company, 1959 and later editions (through the 7th edition); Atlanta, GA: Whitman Publishing, LLC, 9th edition, 2005, edited by Q. David Bowers.

Julian, R.W. "United States Proof Coinage." Manuscript created in 1980 for *Coins* magazine and published sequentially between September 1980 and December 1982.

NGC Census Report. Sarasota, FL: Numismatic Guaranty Corporation of America, various issues 1980s to date.

Numismatic News. Krause Publications, Iola, WI: Various issues 1950s to date.

Numismatic Scrapbook Magazine. Lee F. Hewitt, Chicago, IL; Amos Press; Sidney, OH. Various issues 1935 to 1976.

Numismatist, The. Dr. Geo. F. Heath, Farran Zerbe, American Numismatic Association, 1888 to date. Currently published in Colorado Springs, CO.

PCGS Auction Prices, Internet site. Newport Beach, CA: Professional Coin Grading Service, Inc.

PCGS Population Report, The. Newport Beach, CA: Professional Coin Grading Service, Inc. Various issues, 1980s to date.

Pollock, Andrew W. *United States Pattern Coins and Related Pieces.* Wolfeboro, NH: Bowers and Merena Galleries, 1994.

Raymond, Wayte. *Standard Catalogue of United States Coins and Paper Money* (titles vary). New York, NY: Scott Stamp & Coin Co. (and others), 18 editions 1934 to 1957 editions.

Saint-Gaudens, Homer (edited by). *The Reminiscences of Augustus Saint-Gaudens.* New York, NY: Century Company, 1913.

Smith, A.M. *Illustrated History of the U.S. Mint.* Philadelphia, PA: A.M. Smith, 1881.

——. *Coins and Coinage: The United States Mint, Philadelphia, History, Biography, Statistics, Work, Machinery, Products, Officials.* Also issued as *Visitor's Guide and History.* Philadelphia, PA: A.M. Smith, 1885.

Snowden, James Ross. *The Medallic Memorials of Washington in the Mint of the United States.* Philadelphia, PA: 1861.

——. (prepared and arranged under the direction of). *A Description of Ancient and Modern Coins, in the Cabinet Collection at the Mint of the United States.* Philadelphia, PA: J.B. Lippincott, 1860.

United States Mint, Bureau of the Mint, *et al. Annual Report of the Director of the Mint.* Philadelphia, PA; Washington, D.C., c. 1790s to 1930s.

Vermeule, Cornelius. *Numismatic Art in America.* 2nd edition. Atlanta, GA: Whitman Publishing LLC, 2007.

Winter, Douglas. *New Orleans Mint Gold Coins, 1839–1909, a Numismatic History and Analysis.* Wolfeboro, NH: Bowers and Merena Galleries, Inc. 1992.

Winter, Douglas and Lawrence E. Cutler, M.D. *Gold Coins of the Old West, the Carson City Mint, 1870-1893.* Wolfeboro, NH: Bowers and Merena Galleries, Inc. 1994.

Yeoman, R.S. *A Guide Book of United States Coins.* Kenneth, E. Bressett, editor. Whitman Publishing Company (and Western Publishing Company, Inc.), Racine, WI: various editions 1946 to date, current publisher, Whitman Publishing, LLC, Pelham, AL.

ACKNOWLEDGEMENTS

The following includes the names of people and institutions who have helped with the author's research files over a long period of years dating back to the 1950s.

Jeff Ambio helped with price research. The **American Numismatic Association** provided much information. The **American Numismatic Society** provided much information. **Leonard Augsburger** guided the author through research in the Newman Numismatic Portal and answered many questions.

Harry W. Bass Jr. shared much research over a long period of years from the late 1960s to the late 1990s, and provided much technical and numismatic information. **Anne Bentley**, curator at the Massachusetts Historical Society, provided images. **Kenneth E. Bressett** helped with research. **Mark Borckardt** reviewed the manuscript and made many valuable additions and edits. **Michael Brownlee** provided information about the rarity and grades of eagles of the 1795 to 1804 years.

David Calhoun helped with information from the Harry W. Bass Jr. archives and papers. **John Dannreuther** read the manuscript and was key for much information, including early Proof eagles. **Bob Evans** provided much information about the SS *Central America*. **Jeff Garrett** furnished the inventory of $10 gold coins in the National Numismatic Collection at the Smithsonian Institution. **Ellen Gerth** and Odyssey Marine Exploration furnished inventories of coins from the wreck of the SS *Republic* and the second exploration of the SS *Central America*. **Heritage Auctions** furnished images and information. **R.W. Julian** helped with research.

Christine Karstedt assisted in many ways. **John Kraljevich's** extensive research and descriptions for eagles in the D. Brent Pogue Collection Sale II were essential. **H. Joseph Levine** provided images. **Dwight N. Manley** was the key source of information regarding coins recovered from the SS *Central America*. **Jennifer Meers** helped with information in the Stack's Bowers Galleries research library. **Larissa Mulkern** helped with information in the Stack's Bowers Galleries research library. **Tom Mulvaney** photographed eagles in the National Numismatic Collection and elsewhere.

D. Brent Pogue and the Pogue family provided much information and were essential in the study of 1795 to 1804 eagles. **P. Scott Rubin** helped with provenances and auction prices. **Harvey Stack** and **Larry Stack** shared their expertise over a long period of years. **Stack's Bowers Galleries** and its antecedents furnished images and information. **David Stone** contributed information and an overview on the 1804 restrike eagle (see his essay under that listing).

Saul Teichman helped with provenances. **David E. and Susan Tripp** helped with the Garrett Collection coins. **Douglas Winter** wrote the Foreword and helped in other ways.

ABOUT THE AUTHOR

Q. David Bowers has been in the rare-coin business since he was a teenager, starting in 1953. He is a founder of Stack's Bowers Galleries and is numismatic director of Whitman Publishing. He is a recipient of the Pennsylvania State University College of Business Administration's Alumni Achievement Award (1976); he has served as president of the American Numismatic Association (1983–1985) and president of the Professional Numismatists Guild (1977–1979); he is a recipient of the highest honor bestowed by the ANA (the Farran Zerbe Award); he was the first ANA member to be named Numismatist of the Year (1995); and he has been inducted into the ANA Numismatic Hall of Fame maintained at ANA headquarters. He has also won the highest honors given by the Professional Numismatists Guild. In July 1999, in a poll published in *COINage*, "Numismatists of the Century," Dave was recognized as one of six living people in this list of just 18 names. He is the author of more than 50 books, hundreds of auction and other catalogs, and several thousand articles, including columns in *Coin World* (now the longest-running by any author in numismatic history), *The Numismatist*, and other publications. His books have earned more "Book of the Year Award" honors bestowed by the Numismatic Literary Guild than have those of any other author. He and his firms have presented the majority of the most valuable coin collections ever sold at auction. Dave is a trustee of the New Hampshire Historical Society and a fellow of the American Antiquarian Society, the American Numismatic Society, and the Massachusetts Historical Society. He has been a consultant for the Smithsonian Institution, the Treasury Department, and the U.S. Mint, and is research editor of *A Guide Book of United States Coins*. For many years he was a guest lecturer at Harvard University. This is a short list of his honors and accomplishments. In Wolfeboro, New Hampshire, he is on the Board of Selectmen and is the town historian.

INDEX